REBELS, RUBYFRUIT, AND RHINESTONES

Rebels, Rubyfruit, and Rhinestones

QUEERING SPACE
IN THE
STONEWALL SOUTH

JAMES T. SEARS

RUTGERS UNIVERSITY PRESS
New Brunswick, New Jersey, and London

Library of Congress Cataloging-in-Publication Data

Sears, James T. (James Thomas), 1951–
    Rebels, rubyfruit, and rhinestones : queering space in the Stonewall South / by
James T. Sears.
        p.   cm.
    Includes bibliographical references and index.
    ISBN 0-8135-2964-6 (alk. paper)
    1. Lesbians—Southern States—History—20th century.   2. Gay men—Southern
States—History—20th century.   I. Title.
HQ 75.6.U52 S689 2001
305.9'0664'0975—dc21

                                                                                    00-068348

British Cataloging-in-Publication data for this book is available from the British Library.

Manufactured in the United States of America

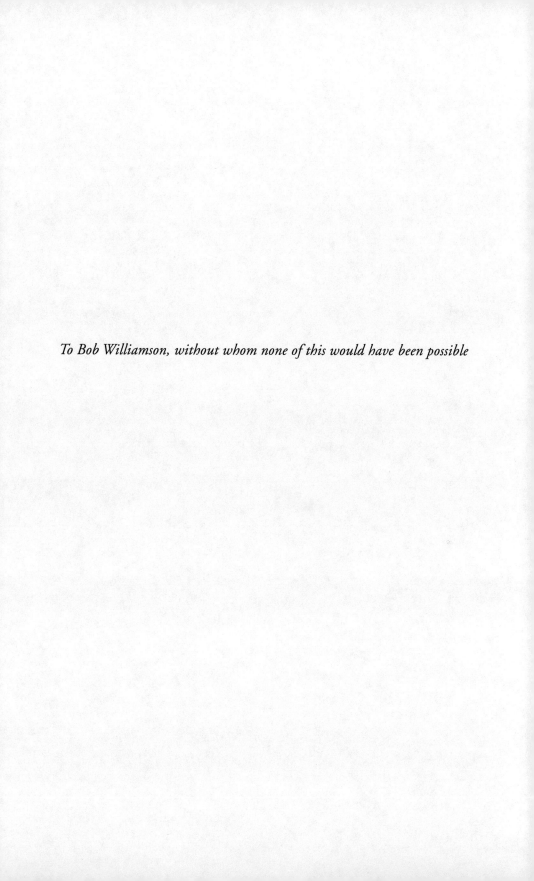

To Bob Williamson, without whom none of this would have been possible

CONTENTS

FOREWORD

Although there were some precursors many years earlier, the modern American gay movement commenced, with continuity, in 1951 in Los Angeles. For almost twenty years it remained a tiny movement, in which everyone involved knew everyone else involved. In keeping with the profoundly, often punitively repressive climate of the times on sex in general and homosexuality in particular, it was usually bland, apologetic, unassertive, and defensive. Instead of recognizing that we gays are *the* authorities on ourselves and our homosexuality, they relied upon "experts"—psychiatrists and psychoanalysts, lawyers, theologians, and so forth—who spoke about us, to us, and at us, but never *with* us.

The fledgling movement tried hard to become a grassroots movement, but never quite succeeded over its first two decades. When I first began my active involvement in what was then called the Homophile Movement, in 1961, there were only five or six homophile organizations in the country, all on either the East Coast or the West Coast, with nothing that I knew of in between (except for one chapter of the Mattachine Society in Denver, although there had been a few which had come and gone, including one in Chicago). We referred to the remainder of the country as a "vast desert," and correctly so. As the 1960s progressed, the middle began to fill in, first with the formation of a revived active group in Chicago, and then one in Kansas City, and gradually elsewhere, and then, seemingly, almost everywhere, with fifty or sixty by 1969. But, to our perceptions, the South remained a "desert" for long thereafter, with the only exceptions, perhaps, being Richard Inman's short-lived, one-man group in Florida and the Circle of Friends in Dallas, both in the mid-1960s.

We began to change the temper of the movement here in Washington, D.C., by taking an activist and militant approach toward the forces arrayed against us, at a time when those words "activist" and "militant" were still dirty words inside the movement. In 1965, at a time when picketing was still *the* extreme expression of dissent, par excellence, we picketed at the White House, at other government agencies, and, commencing annually, on July 4 at Independence Hall in Philadelphia. Active efforts were initiated to ameliorate institutionalized forms of homophobia such as the ban on federal civil service employment of gay people, the ban on gays in the military, the denial of security clearances to gay people, the categorization of homosexuality as pathological by the American Psychiatric Association, anti-sodomy laws, police harassment, and on and on. Our picketing demonstrations laid the groundwork for Stonewall by creating a previously unthinkable mindset that allowed for actual, public demonstrations by openly gay people on their own behalf.

As seen in retrospect, one final step needed to be taken in order to lay the foundations for Stonewall and the ensuing activism of the 1970s. Throughout the eons, gays had been subjected to a relentless, unremitting, absolutely unrelieved negative assault upon us as gay people, and upon our homosexuality. We were sick; we were sinners; we were perverts and degenerates; we were criminals; we were unreliable, untrustworthy, and unstable. Nothing positive or supportive was ever heard. That took its toll not only by diminishing and eroding the self-confidence and self-esteem of individual gay people, but also by sapping the initiative for political organization and action. African Americans had run into substantially the same problem in a culture in which *black* is universally equated with everything bad, undesirable, dirty, ugly, and otherwise negative in every way. They had responded with the slogan "Black Is Beautiful." In 1968, in conscious imitation of that, I coined the slogan "Gay Is Good." It was adopted by the Homophile Movement of the time, and began to be widely publicized as an affirmative, "in your face" response to the psychological and ideological assaults brought against us. In the tumult of the times "Gay Is Good" was quickly transmuted into and then joined up with "Gay Pride." Between the two, we then had the psychological underpinnings, the weapons, and the armor with which to take on the world. And in 1969 we started to do so with Stonewall. The Homophile Movement became the Gay Movement or the Gay Rights Movement, and it finally became genuinely grassroots everywhere in the country including the South. And how it became so in the South is what this book is all about.

In the past, as a northerner, being born and brought up in New York City, having lived in Cambridge, Massachusetts, for a sizable portion of my early adult life, and living since 1956 in Washington, D.C., at the very edge of the South but not really in it, I tended, along with others of similar geographical background, almost reflexively and not through conscious, calculated decision, to view southerners as a kind of mythical, exotic people, different from the rest of us Americans in manners, speech, culture, and history, in countless ways that set them apart. Of course experience and fact, numerous visits to various southern cities for lectures, demonstrations, and conferences, plus the inexorable march of time and progress, have significantly modified (or at least softened) those impressions on my part, while, simultaneously, time and progress have very much modified the South itself.

Although, of course, my impressions and reactions are subjective and idiosyncratic, and quite possibly inaccurate, and are certainly not necessarily shared by others, for myself and, I believe, for many other non-southerners, one of our impressions was of a southern gay scene in which "drag" and effeminate mannerisms on the part of males played a much more significant role—in fact a dominant one—than in the gay scene in the remainder of the country. Of course, drag has always been a highly visible element in the urban gay culture generally but, rightly or wrongly, the perception was that it was much more so in the South.

All of this represents broad, depersonalized views of the gay South from the outside, from the past, and from afar. From close up and very much from the inside, James T. Sears, in *Rebels, Rubyfruit, and Rhinestones,* presents us with a fascinating, marvelously detailed, meticulously and extensively researched and compiled, highly structured, wonderfully personalized picture of the early post-Stonewall, southern gay scene as the ferment spreading from Greenwich Village starting in 1969 engulfed the South.

Now turn the page and read about it.

Franklin E. Kameny
Long-time activist, Gay and Lesbian Civil Rights Movement,
and coiner of the slogan "Gay Is Good"

ACKNOWLEDGMENTS

All of the individuals who graciously consented to be interviewed and gladly gave of their time to review draft chapters based on those interviews.

Bob Swisher, David Williams, Roger Nelson, Vincent Astor, Roberts Batson, and Patrick Cather, local gay historians who have helped to preserve queer history in their southern communities and who kindly provided of their knowledge and expertise.

To the archivists and librarians who assisted me in accessing their collections, particularly those at: Duke University, Kentucky Gay Archives, International Gay and Lesbian Archives, Lesbian Herstory Archives, MCC-Resurrection Don Botts Collection, and the Stonewall Archives.

I would also like to thank the following individuals for providing useful background information, who kindly read excerpts from the book based on their knowledge of particular events, or who provided photographs for use in this project: Pokey Anderson, Steve Ault, Bob Basker, Jim Baxter, John Boddie, Perry Brass, Paul D. Cain, Jeffrey Day, Sister Missionary Delight, Lorraine Fontana, Sam Hunter, Elizabeth Knowlton, Ron Lambe, Marcelina Martin, Audrey May, Cecilia Mitchell, Jay Mohr, Jesse Monteagudo, Merril Mushroom, John O'Brien, Ian Palmquist, Julia Penelope, Milo Pyne, Gil Robison, Peter Taylor, Johnny Townsend, Robin Tyler, Rita Wanstrom, Bill Watson, Paul Wegman, Linda West, and Brandon Wolf. Particular gratitude goes to Jack Nichols and Frank Kameny.

Finally, to my editor, Leslie Mitchner, whose vision and support has made this book possible; as well as to Gordon Massman, my agent; the production editor of this book, Marilyn Campbell; Bobbe Needham for the fine line-editing; and my publicist, Wayne Smalley.

REBELS, RUBYFRUIT, AND RHINESTONES

INTRODUCTION

Toward a Community
of Memory

In the best-selling book *Habits of the Heart,* Robert Bellah and his colleagues detail the importance of community and commitment in everyday life. A critical element of any community is its history, or "community of memory."

> [S]tories that make up a tradition contain conceptions of character of what a good person is like, and of the virtues that define such character. But the stories are not all exemplary, not all about successes and achievements. A genuine community of memory will also tell painful stories of shared suffering that sometimes creates deeper identities than success. . . . And if the community is completely honest, it will remember stories not only of suffering received but of suffering inflicted—dangerous memories.[1]

Rebels, Rubyfruit, and Rhinestones is the second volume of a multivolume work telling the stories of queer southern life through characters who shaped and were shaped by the events following the tsunami of Stonewall. In the decade following the 1969 clashes with police at this Greenwich Village bar, the emergence of communities among southern lesbians, bisexuals, gay men, and transgender persons acquired new vibrancy. Where isolation and accommodation characterized homosexual southern life after World War II, the seventies were marked by networks and activism, immediacy and confrontation, openness and revelry. This book bridges the generation of lonely hunters who surreptitiously frequented mixed hotel bars, silently read newspaper headlines about perverts, participated in secretive social

1

clubs, and viewed with unease the quixotic efforts of a handful of homophile activists to a rubyfruit generation that danced wildly inside megadiscos, produced rebellious publications like *Pointblank Times,* organized lesbian and gay conferences, and marched in daylight to the Washington Monument by the tens of thousands.

Here, I continue the stories of Merril Mushroom, Jack Nichols, Julia Stanley Penelope, and Lige Clarke from my first book, *Lonely Hunters.* Others characters who crossed the Stonewall divide from the homophile movement to gay rights are also introduced: Rita Wanstrom, Miss P, Ray Hill, and Bob Basker. From the cascading events of the sixties—the Vietnam War, the countercultural movement, civil rights, feminism—come stories of organizing from Margo George, Elizabeth Knowlton, and Lorraine Fontana of the Atlanta Feminist Lesbian Alliance, Bob Bland of the Triangle Gay Alliance, Peter Lee of the Lambda Alliance, Pokey Anderson of the Lesberadas, Jesse Monteagudo of the Latinos por Derechos, and Mel Boozer of the Gay Activist Alliance.

Written as a spiral of individual narratives of characters whose lives variously intersect, *Rebels, Rubyfruit, and Rhinestones* uses an oral tradition, creating what June Arnold once described as "experience weaving in upon itself, commenting on itself, inclusive, not ending in final victory/defeat but ending with the sense that the community continues."[2] These interwoven stories tell of particular events through the eyes of individuals who travel through an era of change. From the Tumblebugs of Houston and Gay Freedom Movement in Norfolk, from *Trash* in Louisville to the *Front Page* of Raleigh, from Miss Gay Florida pageants to the faerie gatherings at Running Water, from gay motorcycle clubs to MCC churches, from out lesbian softball teams to gay political coalitions, communities emerged that had not been apparent during the era of Lonely Hunters. But rebel activists like Phyllis Randolph Frye and Milo Pyne unknowingly stood on the shoulders of homophile leaders such as Phyllis Lyon, Frank Kameny, Del Martin, Tony Segura, Barbara Gittings, and Richard Inman. Rhinestone revolutionaries like Logan Carter and Sam Hunter followed the stage exits of Ray Bourbon and Tony Midnite, while rubyfruit lesbians as different as Mab Segrest, Bobbi Weinstock, and Vicki Gabriner acknowledged a debt of gratitude to earlier generations of lesbians working in the South that included Lillian Smith, Laura Towne, Barbara Deming, and Laura Bragg.

Faggot revolutionaries and blue-denim reformers are the bookends of the seventies South. Beginning with the countercultural, antiwar, women's rights, and civil rights movements, *Rebels, Rubyfruit and Rhinestones* explores the queering of southern space and the emergence of queer communities. From Birmingham to Gainesville, from Austin to Charlotte, as news of Stonewall moved from the inside pages of the *New York Times* to the front pages of newly formed gay newspapers, the homophile generation marked by gradualism, civility, and accommodation gave way to the rubyfruit generation characterized by immediacy, confrontation, and resoluteness. In the span of a generation we went from long lines to view *Boys in the Band* to picket lines for those viewing *Cruising,* from lonely voices seeking political support to powerful voices wielding political clout, from women's auxiliaries in gay male organizations to the radicalesbians of the Furies, *Feminary,* and *Sinister Wisdom.*

During this era, the South was also changing, and southerners were changing history. In light of the industrial collapse of the steel and automobile industries of the "rust belt" and the demise of New Deal liberalism, the South rose again—fueled by Sun Belt economies of aerospace, oil, and technology. From the ashes of the radical sixties slowly arose the phoenix of conservatism that shadowed the remainder of the century. Led by religious conservatives buoyed by their success in defeating the gay rights ordinance in Dade County, the self-proclaimed "moral majority" decried abortion-on-demand, defeated the Equal Rights Amendment, and elected thousands to local and state offices. The Fighting South led the counter-revolutionary charge that would eventually redefine the American political landscape.[3]

As the once Democratic South turned solidly Republican, the New Frontier and the Great Society of the sixties waned. With the "fall" of Saigon and the "sell-out" of SALT II, America held hostage by Iran and OPEC, and an economy corroded by double-digit inflation and recessions, this generation of homosexual southerners witnessed the southernization of American politics and culture as they sought social and political recognition for the "love that dared not speak its name." By the decade's end, mostly white gay men—blue-denim politicos—transformed gay power into gay rights. From the battlefield to the voting booth, southern activists such as Leonard Matlovich and Gary Van Ooteghem pressed for admission into the corridors of heterosexual power and privilege.

The second American Stonewall occurred on a June day eight years after the first riots at the seedy Greenwich Village bar. The Dade County referendum, repealing gay rights in Miami, lit the fuse for mainstream political activism in the South and the country. However, had it not been for these honeycombed pre-Stonewall communities on the ball field, the stage, and the bar, as well as unheralded efforts among gay liberationist rebels, rhinestone drag queens, and rubyfruit lesbian-feminists, there would have been little infrastructure within communities to harness this energy unleashed by singer Anita Bryant and her Save Our Children crusade. This was a turning point in the modern gay movement, which became evident to all two years later when tens of thousands gathered on a chilly Sunday morning in October 1979 to march on Washington.

Southern history is never simple and seldom straight. *Rebels, Rubyfruit, and Rhinestones* tells stories of several dozen women and men who struggled—sometimes with one another—against great odds to develop communities of desire and of the heart, culminating in the March on Washington. The March, however, belied the cacophony of southern voices and experiences evidenced in queer communities separated by gender, social class, and race; in the unheard demands and unmet expectations of bisexuals and transgender persons; and in the racist and sexist practices found in some bars, pageants, and gay organizations.

In this book, you'll learn how early writings such as *The Price of Salt* and *Strange Fruit* influenced North Carolina lesbians publishing *Sinister Wisdom* and *Feminary*. Here, you'll explore how motley bands of gay liberationists in cities such as Louisville and Houston evolved into political coalitions. Here are chronicled the evolution of southern drag from the hills of South Carolina to the Fontainebleau Hotel, intimidation by FBI agents and grand juries, an unsolved murder in Mexico and a tragic fire in New Orleans. *Rebels, Rubyfruit, and Rhinestones* follows the softball lesbians in the summer of 1974, gay prisoners in Ramsey Unit II, and those who challenged the military's homophobia. In these pages you will get to know southern lesbian poets, writers, singers, and publishers who shaped the emerging lesbian consciousness of this generation. Here, too, you will learn of the emergence of the gay spirit among southerners who founded churches and synagogues as well as others who celebrated the solstices and equinoxes. These stories are our "communities of memory" that not only connect us to the past but "turn us toward the future as communities of hope."[4]

ONE

A Psychedelic Wedding

Unmoving, infinite, standing alone, never changing,
it is everywhere and it is inexhaustible.
It is the mother of all.
I do not know its name.
If I must name it,
I call it Tao.

As Baba Ram Dass reads from the *Tao Te Ching*, Francis Lee, a photo-animator who had earned an Academy Award for *Black Fox*, films a flaxen-haired matron. Clothed in a cotton gown and with flowers in her hair, Merril Mushroom strolls barefoot through a running brook.

Nothing in the world is weaker
or more yielding than water
yet nothing is its equal
in wearing away the hard from the strong.
Thus the weak can overpower the strong,
flexible can overcome the rigid.

Lee's camera scans New Jersey meadowlands and olive-hued forests, centering on birds, flowers, leaves, and insects. A scarlet rose unfolds to

Merril and John wed. Photo courtesy of Merril Mushroom.

5

the cadence of syncopated drums, a solo flute, and an Indian sitar. Wedding celebrants, simply garbed, walk singly toward a man in a lotus position. Bliss, oneness, love.

Merril kisses John, and they exchange rings. A hundred tribal companions of their beat-turned-hippie generation peer beyond the couple's gaze.

> From the still ground within the rings of desire
> comes the power that rules in peace.
> The yin and yang are drawn together
> to create new forms,
> which God speaks.

Bearded men and beaded women encircle the couple, embracing one another and swaying to the sitar, now mixed with the music of the Rolling Stones.

> Thought divides us from truth,
> the mind inhibits our feeling,
> representation disguises the real.
> It is only in love that love can be experienced. . . .
> In silence, truth enters.

Celebrating the jewel in the heart of the lotus, youthful bodies roll in the grass and frolic in the woods. Caresses and kisses between women and men, women and women, men and men commemorate the festivity. John, a gay man, and Merril, a lesbian, are wed.

> If you understand love's laws
> you will dance through your days in the wind of the spirit.

————

"Since I first laid eyes on him in the gay section of the student union, I had always felt a bond with John," reminisces Merril. During that fall semester of 1959, she was recovering from her college experience with Charley Johns. This Joe McCarthy–like senator and his "pork-chop gang" of politicians brought terror to Florida homosexuals during the late fifties and early sixties. Lives were ruined: student expulsions and faculty dismissals, divorce and suicide.[1]

During that year of Bobby Darin and Sandra Dee, John was "in the process of coming out and meeting a lot of gay people." With a false ID, he sometimes ventured into the Miami gay bars with Merril and "her dyke friends." Some of Merril's favorite bars were the Googies, the Onyx Room, the Coral Bar, and the Hi Room. It was at the Onyx Room, which sometimes featured female impersonators Charles Pierce and Jackie Jackson, that Merril and her lesbian friends Connie and Penny had performed male drag as the Tongueston Trio, a scene Merril describes:

> I was still living at home and underage. I had to sneak out for rehearsals, posing as a typical fifties teenager going out to do homework and listen to records with a girlfriend. . . . We fancied up our usual duck's ass hairdos with pompadours, and we wore black pants, white shirts, black neckties, white socks, black loafers and sunglasses. . . . The curtain parted and hot red and blue lights moved over us as we trotted onstage in perfect step, waving and smiling. Three separate spotlights came on each of us, merging into one big spot. All the girls in the room screamed—faggots, too! . . . The lights went down, all throats hushed, and out over the speakers came the opening instrumental notes of our first number, "Bad Boy," by the Jive Bombers.[2]

In 1961, Merril escaped family scrutiny and the Sunshine State by eloping with Jack—a friend of John's who was also gay. She joined Jack in Gadsden, Alabama. In this small southern town nearly devoid of organized homosexuality except for "one notorious local fairy," she taught school and worked as a salesclerk. This was the first time she witnessed the evil of Jim Crow. Expected to drink at "White Only" drinking fountains, deferred to by "Negro" men with eyes turned downward, and watching *Ben Hur* in the town's segregated movie theater, she remembers, "my eyes got real big. This is really real!"

Sometimes she and Jack drove their VW beetle down Highway 11 to Birmingham with its handful of gay-friendly taverns like Theos and the Twentieth Century Lounge, or the bars in the Bankhead and Redmont Hotels that catered to the limp wristed. During their first visit, Merril recalls, "We didn't have much to go on except hearsay. We went to the Red Room of the Redmont Hotel where we met a couple of drag queens, Lonnie Dare and Billie Bell."

On future visits, the couple stayed overnight at the men's home. "But it was not the same as having a girlfriend." Merril sighs. "It was a *very* long year. I really missed lesbians." On one occasion, Lonnie and Billie fixed Merril up with a "skinny hooker with bleached, teased hair and pasty, pale skin. She chased me around the house because I didn't want to hurt her feelings."

In 1962 the couple moved to New York City. Merril taught in a two-story brick elementary school in Harlem while Jack worked for the Social Security Administration. "Some of the kids had really good families, but it was still the inner city: they were poor; junkies were on the streets and in the doorways," she remembers. Like Sylvia Barrett in *Up the Down Staircase*, Merril confronted the realities of the chalkboard jungle.

She learned that "life was not a white middle-class paradise everywhere. There was a nine-year-old who had to steal in order to feed his younger siblings because he was in charge of the family. . . . There were teachers who really hated the kids and called them names. They were terribly racist but they had contracts and the union."

For five years she taught in her "classroom box with not enough desks, not enough books, and not enough chairs." She spent her money on materials and crafted visuals for the classroom. Working with thirty-six children and observing other teachers, Merril "began to understand how insidious and hurtful racism really could be—besides the obvious discrimination. It was the beginning of my political awareness."

While Merril was living with Jack in a middle-class Italian neighborhood in Queens, John was living on Fifty-seventh Street with another gay man and two women. Soon, Merril moved in with one of the "girls" to a West Greenwich Village flat, keeping most of her belongings in Queens.

Merril enjoyed lesbian couplehood, playing softball and riding bikes and taking her schoolchildren to Central Park, as well as frequenting the bars on weekend nights, particularly the Sea Colony and occasionally Washington Square or Page Three.

> The bars themselves weren't that much different from those that Penny and I hung out at in Florida. Washington Square could have been Googies, the Sea Colony the Coral Bar, and Page Three the Red Carpet. The Sea Colony was your typical working-class Mafia two-room plushish bar with a dance floor and tables where the bouncer and managers—all tough hoods—treated us fine.
>
> Since Charley Johns's investigation was still going strong, it was terribly dangerous to frequent Florida bars. But when the New York bars were raided, all that happened was the cops told us to leave—nobody got arrested or harassed!

In 1964 Merril broke up with her girlfriend and moved back to Queens with Jack—who continued to party with John. John had just been turned on to marijuana by a fellow social worker. Euphoric, he told Jack. Merril telephoned John later: "Jack just said you had a wonderful experience with marijuana! He's terribly worried about you. I want you to know that I smoke; Jack doesn't know. We should get together!"

One day Merril told John of Timothy Leary's psychedelic experiences and experiments. Leary, a Brooks Brothers–clad Harvard psychologist, had begun research with his fellow faculty member, Richard Alpert (who, already tuned in, would soon drop out, becoming Baba Ram Dass), into the effects of a synthetic drug secretly being tested by the CIA:

lysergic acid diethylamide. At the Center for Personality Research, the Harvard professors hosted experimental drug sessions with undergraduates and celebrities, using LSD (legal until 1965) and psilocybin in a laboratory with an aroma of incense laced with Indian music, decorated with Buddha posters, and lined with mattresses.

Merril and John began attending lectures sponsored by the International Foundation for Internal Freedom. There, Leary, the Billy Sunday of acid, preached weekly use of LSD and daily litanies of marijuana. Like the counterculture homosexual pied pipers Allen Ginsberg and Ken Kesey, Leary celebrated the "holiness" of mind-expanding drugs, opening the League of Spiritual Discovery (LSD) in a Greenwich Village basement ashram. Writing in the *East Village Other,* Leary observed:

> The "turned on" person realizes that SHe is not an isolated, separate social ego, but rather one transient energy process hooked up with the energy dance around hir. . . . "Tune in" means arrange your environment so that it reflects your state of consciousness, to harness your internal energy to the flow around you. . . . When this person "turns on," SHe sees at once the horror of hir surroundings. If SHe "tunes in," SHe begins to change hir movements and hir surroundings so that they become more in harmony with hir internal beauty. . . . Do not "drop out" until you have "tuned in." Do not "turn on" unless you know how to "tune in," or you will get "hung up!" Every "bad trip" is caused by the failure to "tune in."[3]

Inspired, Merril set up John's first acid session: "When you do LSD with someone, it's not just dropping it and going out and partying," she explains, "it's taking it as a sacrament with a religious structure around it—a transcendental experience. We spent three days together setting up for it, doing it, and processing it. We got *real* close."

For John:

> It changed my whole life! LSD helped me to recognize that there were all these other ways of being. It made me realize that I had become a horse with blinders. At the age of twenty-three this had become what was real—everything else disappeared!
>
> I was sitting on the bed with this orange in my hand. Suddenly, the side I was looking at began to bubble and become ugly. I got really nervous and turned the orange around to the part that was smooth. I realized that the orange was me: I had this ugly side and this good side. As I was thinking about the "good side," the orange started to bubble. Then I couldn't find a good side to the orange. I cried: "What's going on? Am I really rotten through and through?"

As "psychedelic gay hippies," Merril and John participated in LSD studies at Princeton. "The researchers would come to our parties and we would do acid while they talked to us and took notes." That research, described in the anthology *Psychedelics,* found that "our group—the only mainly gay one—evidenced the most profound changes!"[4]

While all LSD trips taken by the two were not equally good, each yielded lessons. Taking acid one night without anyone's guidance, John found himself in a maze of logical patterns. Coming to his rescue, Merril guided John. At that point, John says, "I realized how indispensable she was to me and how she was a really important part of my life."

The next day John sent her an unconventional Valentine—a card of hearts laced with LSD. Later, while Merril was "in a state of fantasy," John offered: "If you and Jack ever get a divorce, I'd really like to get married." Unbridled by either a marriage of convenience or conventional beliefs about family life, Merril responded in a heartfelt manner: "That's really nice, John. I'll go home and ask Jack for a divorce!"

Following their karmic marriage during that "summer of love," the couple separated from New York's gay life. "We weren't really into the gay or feminist scenes," Merril confesses. "We were more involved with the antiwar movement. We weren't even aware of Stonewall." The couple stepped to the lyrics of Pete Seeger and chanted, "Hey, Hey, LBJ! How many kids did you kill today?" in the first peace march through Manhattan. They dropped acid at the first Easter "Be-In" at Central Park. They abandoned their car on a hopelessly jammed New York highway and themselves to the sanguine balladeers of a Woodstock Nation one weekend on a rain-drenched farm.

Back in the city, the unconventional newlyweds opened Paranoia—a four-room head shop in the East Village. Here they sold psychedelic crafts handmade by local artists, fed street people, and counseled runaways. Stepping into Paranoia, customers fancied the "pressed-metal-plate ceiling which we painted different colors like a stained-glass window." In the next room, Merril goes on,

> we had a kitchen with free food for all the street kids. Then we had our "carousel room" with the wooden horses that was all done in day-glow with a black light which showed the day-glow merchandise. We started the back room as a clothing give-away room, but soon a friend turned it into the "rain forest room" with cattails, jungle plants, and a parrot.

Merril and John also hawked crafts on the Long Island circuit. They camped out for five days at the Forest Hills Country Club for the First International Psychedelic Exposition. After the exhibition closed for the night, the couple enjoyed communal dinners and drugs with other hippie entrepreneurs. Merril thinks back to those conversations, which centered on the peril of city life and the promise of intentional communities: "We didn't like all of the waste, all of the dirt, all of the consumerism. We wanted to live in a simpler fashion doing our little part in making the world a better place. We talked in great detail about adopting children who needed homes and doing community education."

As the sixties burned themselves out in Icarus-like fashion with Altamonte, the Manson family, and Belfast, Merril and John rented a house in upstate New York with other friends. The couple made weekend pilgrimages to learn organic farming and experience collective living. Over time they amassed some money and a bit more knowledge about communal life.

Merril's marriage to John was one of neither convenience nor necessity. Each cared for the other, and they shared a homestead dream of raising a tribe of "hard to place" children. In February 1970 the couple contacted Human Services. Was there a child under the age of six with mild or moderate disabilities in need of a loving couple? After their application form was completed, a petite and pleasant social worker paid a two-hour home visit. Sporting dark hair cut in a short fifties style, she efficiently went through her questions, as Merril recalls:

> Of course, she wanted to know about our family life, religion, and growing up experiences. Since we didn't say, "Hey! We're a queer couple and we want to adopt," there was absolutely no discussion about our sexuality.
>
> Three months later, as college campuses erupted in protest against the Cambodian invasion and the student massacres at Kent and Jackson State Universities, Human Services telephoned.
>
> "Will you consider a foundling?"
>
> "What's a foundling?" asked Merril.
>
> "An abandoned baby. Of course, we can't provide you any of his medical history."

They felt little hesitancy about accepting the child. "We've always felt that whoever we're offered is the one we're supposed to have," Merril affirms. The couple, though, was caught off-guard by the pace of events.

Merril and John visited Social Services the very next week to see the child and meet again with the butch-appearing social worker. As she rolled the ten-week-old out in his crib, they knew immediately that this baby with oval brown eyes was to become part of their family.

"We really love this baby!" Merril excitedly told the social worker. "How long will it take? A few days? A couple of weeks? Will we have to come back and visit him some more?"

"No," she replied. "I'll get his things."

They were stunned. "We didn't have a bottle, a diaper, or a crib!" Merril muses. Picking up the necessities of parenthood on their way home, Merril carried J'aime upstairs only to realize, "I didn't even know how often babies ate!"

The following spring John and Merril—with one-year-old J'aime and their street dog, Found—loaded their possessions and hopes into a pink schoolbus with an outrageous red stripe painted down its middle. With their last paychecks cashed, they drove it across the Verrazano Bridge.

And so this is how a boy and his gay parents and his dog began a year-long search for "hippie pie-in-the-sky"—a journey that would take them across the country, into Canada and Mexico, and ultimately, back to their southern roots.

TWO

The Queen Bee

In a land where the Kingfish once ruled and crawfish is a staple of Cajun cuisine, the ghost still haunted him. A pair of giant hands unsteadily lit a cigarette while holding a martini. His blue eyes scanned the room. Conversations flickered from gourmet dining to Mardi Gras krewes. As he gracefully moved among the party guests, whispered rumors shadowed him: assassination, conspiracy, and cover-up. No wonder he now described his life in Kafkaesque fashion, no longer feeling that the Prague novelist had overstated his case, as he told an interviewer: "Now, come on, all right, so K. can't communicate with the Castle and man and God are incommensurate, but do you have to go on at such tiresome lengths? Boy, have I changed, what a fellow feeling I have for K. now!"[1]

As the evening moved toward its climax, the crop-haired, six-foot-four Shaw talked theater and played charades with the other mostly youthful gay men sporting bell-bottom pants. "He was such great fun," remembers one of the players, Roberts Batson. "Once he leaned over to me and said, 'As a friend of mine says, that gives me a roaring soft-on.' We laughed."

Clay Shaw at a press conference holding up a newspaper announcing his acquittal on a charge of conspiring to kill John F. Kennedy, New Orleans, March 1, 1969. AP/Wide World Photos.

13

Well beyond the party's peak, those remaining sat with the poised, silver-haired don on a twisting, sixties-style sectional couch. He "spoke with a combination of wisdom and wonderment and a sort of Somerset Maugham knack for storytelling."[2] The talk turned to politics and the 1972 elections. "One of the fellows really tried to push Clay to say nasty things about Jim Garrison," Batson recollects. "But he wouldn't; he was a true southern gentleman."

Shaw had entered Kafka's castle on the afternoon of 1 March 1967, when District Attorney Jim Garrison claimed that Shaw, masquerading as Clay Bertrand (the "queen bee of New Orleans's homosexual underworld"), had conspired to murder the president of the United States.

Later portrayed by Tommy Lee Jones in Oliver Stone's fictional *JFK*, Clay Shaw was certainly "a known homosexual." Dr. Martin Palmer, another gay man and Shaw's personal physician, remembers him "cruising in a big Cadillac" and preferring "skinny young men." However, whether cruising around the railroad station or sipping a few drinks at Lafitte's or the Galley House, Clay carried a certain dignity about him—and never disguised his identity.

Martin Palmer first met Shaw "in the course of the way we would meet one another in the Quarter." It was during the midfifties "when gay life was very lively, when Miss Dixie's was really fun, when Tony Bianco's had Candy Lee's outrageous drag show," and when magazines of barely clad men, like the locally published *Art and Physique,* were passed around. Palmer along with his lover, Bobby, became a frequent party guest of Clay and his long-time companion, Jeff Biddeson, whom Shaw had first spotted at the original Lafitte's, wearing cowboy boots and hat, silhouetted against the outside light. Palmer remembers that among gay friends, Clay "was very informal and funny. I can still see him sitting on his leather couch, holding a cigarette, and laughing spontaneously. But gay life then had a veneer that you sort of kept up outside our group. When Clay was arrested, we were all shocked. Some of his friends, fearing exposure, dropped him."

Nine days before Shaw's preliminary hearing, Garrison met with James Phelan, a *Saturday Evening Post* reporter. What followed was a ten-hour "wildly convoluted" conversation with Garrison, whose

> version of the Kennedy assassination made it out to be the result of a homosexual conspiracy masterminded by Dave Ferrie. "You can understand his motivation," Garrison said. "Kennedy was a virile, handsome, successful man—everything Ferrie was not. In addition, there was the thrill of staging the perfect crime. Remember the [homosexuals] Loeb and Leopold case in Chicago? . . . He claimed that Oswald and Ruby were both homosexuals and were both involved in the plot. He implied that

Ruby—"his homosexual nickname was Pinkie"—executed Oswald to prevent him from telling all.[3]

Meanwhile, *Time* had reported that Garrison's assistants, "like small boys overturning a rock in a muddy field, have uncovered all manner of seamy, unsavory creatures. . . . Their haunts ranged from 'gay' coffee shops and bars in New Orleans' French Quarter to shadowy back streets."[4] The sleuths searched Shaw's two-story Dauphine Street carriage house. Walking through the red door, they tramped over the red carpeting as they headed up the angular stairway. Journalists played up the seizure of a novel, *A Holiday for Murder,* two pieces of leather, a black hood and cape, five whips, and a chain—among the hundreds of more ordinary items carted away.

Sixties' New Orleans, emphasizes Palmer, "would sacrifice anything to appearance, pride, and frivolity." The city's southern gentility overlaid with French forbearance masked the ugliness of oligarchy and the nastiness of homophobia. In New Orleans, "if you were known to be gay—no matter what your position, with some outstanding exceptions—you didn't get into the Boston Club." But these barriers vanished in New Orleans's steamy darkness, as Garden District men who married for convenience or family honor frequented the hustlers at Wanda's Bar.

It was in this society that Clay Shaw and Jim Garrison rose to prominence. And it was in this context that a battle ensued between Shaw, the only person brought to trial for conspiring to assassinate the thirty-fifth president, and Garrison, a man with presidential ambitions himself who "never lets the responsibilities of being a prosecutor interfere with being a politician."[5]

Both Clay Shaw and Jim Garrison were willful, brilliant, successful, and imposing figures. They, too, frequented the steam room at the New Orleans Athletic Club and—among those peering "through the looking glass" within the closeted French Quarter—there were rumors that the two shared a penchant for men, if not for a single man or one another.[6]

Shaw and Garrison, though, chose different paths. Shaw, decorated with the Legion of Merit and the Bronze Star, had risen from army private to major. Afterward, he returned to New Orleans and served as managing director of the International Trade Mart for nearly twenty years. A supporter of the arts, he was a leading figure in preserving the Quarter's rich architectural heritage.

The towering six-foot-six Earling Carothers Garrison—who relished good bourbon, bawdy jokes, Brooks Brothers clothing, and Ayn Rand—was relieved in 1952 from National Guard duty because of a psychological disability.[7] Earning a law degree at Tulane, he changed his name to

James (preferring "Big Jim") and was elected district attorney of New Orleans Parish in 1961 on an anticorruption platform that targeted notorious Bourbon Street.

Garrison "cleaned up" the French Quarter's more lurid strippers and hoarse-voiced B-girls, corner pimps and street-wise prostitutes, nelly queens and teenage hustlers. Charges of "being a homosexual in an establishment with a liquor license" also produced a useful band of gay informants.[8]

One of those who escaped Big Jim's reach was the hustler-turned-writer John Rechy. Rechy's *City of Night* portrayed the Quarter's enigmatic figures and gothic landscapes on Mardi Gras eve:

> A man is painting inside on an enormous canvas: color-smeared, savagely red, yellow; swatches of blank, inkily smeared at the edges, creating tentacles from a solidly dark body—a hungry giant insect groveling on a violent vortex of colors. . . . Now walking along that punctured area of old New Orleans, I see those famous hints of a world that disappeared long ago: depicted, sheltered like a precious memory, in books; a world that left merely the remnants of what may have been; a city scarred by memories of an elegance and gentility which may never have existed. A ghost city. . . . An almost Biblical feeling of Doom—of the city about to be destroyed, razed, toppled—assaults you. . . . The invitation to dissipate is everywhere. And you wonder how this city has withstood so long the ravenous vermin. . . . And you wonder how one single match or cigarette has failed to create that holocaust which will consume it to its very gutters.[9]

Harboring transparent aspirations for the governor's office (and higher), Garrison looked over this "City That Care Forgot." He thought about the recent Gallup Poll reporting that only 36 percent of Americans believed the Warren Commission report and scanned the current best-selling book, *Rush to Judgment,* that challenged the lone-assassin theory. These facts, combined with southerners' anti-Washington prejudice and guileless homophobia, thickened the southern mist out of which Garrison conjured the ghost of Clay Bertrand, the D.A.'s investigative phantom.

In mid-February 1967, Garrison lunched at the Shell Oil Building with a set of conservative, wealthy businessmen. Returning to the courthouse, he strolled down the corridor, where he was expectantly ambushed by reporters who had learned of his special investigation. "Any word on the assassination?" shouted a boy from the press. The brazen D.A. cocked his head, declaring that he had "positively solved the assassination of John F. Kennedy. . . . The only way they are going to get away from us is to kill themselves. . . . The key to the whole case is through the looking glass. Black is white; white is black."[10] Garrison then announced that fifty wealthy supporters—dubbed "Truth and Consequences"—would bankroll the investigation, avoiding the need for public funding (and accountability).

During the next two years Garrison directed a frenzied media through conspiratorial labyrinths as a bewildered but stoic Shaw wandered through a maze of preliminary hearings and grand jury indictments. Selectively leaked investigative reports tried Shaw's indomitable spirit, as legal fees eroded his retirement savings. "That was one of Garrison's main weapons: to try to drain him, and he did—financially," Palmer said. However, he continued, "It never seemed to wear him down physically, as terrible as it was." Throughout the ordeal, Shaw maintained his "serenity and equanimity," occasionally seeking solitude at a Gulfshore monastery.

In the early spring of 1969 Shaw finally received his day in court. The trial, corresponding with Mardi Gras, took on a carnival atmosphere with a not so hidden homosexual subtext. Prosecution witnesses, "like characters out of Bob Dylan's Desolation Row," included convicted perjurers, psychiatric clients, narcotic users, assorted felons, and homosexuals.[11]

This "gumbo of hypnotism and drugs, spiced with a soupcon of homosexual entanglement," produced questionable testimony.[12] There was the "young insurance salesman whose impeccable clothing concealed a mind in considerable disarray and whose memory had to be jogged by means of hypnosis" and sodium Pentothal injected by the prosecution's physician.[13] Then there was the prosecutorial dead man's tale of David Ferrie. A former commercial aviator and one-time seminarian, Ferrie was said to have piloted Oswald out of the country on that fateful Dallas day. However, the unstylish Ferrie, who sported a pasted-on mohair rug hairpiece and penciled eyebrows, only became the D.A.'s star witness following what Garrison called an "apparent suicide" (the coroner pronounced it a cerebral hemorrhage brought about by stress). Later Garrison admitted, "Yeah, we helped kill the son of a bitch."[14]

More colorful were the accusations of a pudgy, Blues Brothers–clad Dean Andrews—another former patient of Dr. Palmer, who later characterized Andrews as a "petty crook, shyster lawyer." In a quintessential Irish Channel accent, Andrews repeated in open court his earlier claims to the Warren Commission, that a Clay or Clem Bertrand once telephoned his law office to secure bond "in behalf of gay kids" accompanied by Lee Harvey Oswald: "The three gay kids he [Oswald] was with, they were ostentatious. They were what we call swishers. You can just look at them. All they had to do was open their mouth. That was it. Walk, they can swing better than Sammy Kaye!"[15] Andrews also claimed the same man called him following the assassination, requesting representation for Oswald. Much later, according to Palmer, Andrews confessed to him that "he made up the name and the story that started all of this when he was in the hospital and broke."

The trial was also marked by the wanton dismissal of two potential jurors:

> Now for the first time, we saw the state and the defense work together as two obvious homosexuals in succession came up for questioning. Wide grins and a few chuckles were being suppressed in the press section. . . . Once their proclivities had made themselves known, Irvin Dymond [the lead defense attorney, who had lost to Garrison in the 1962 race for district attorney] would swing around in his chair, glance at James Alcock [the assistant district attorney], who would nod, then in consort they would manage to excuse the prospect at the next slightest opportunity.[16]

Following five weeks of trial foolishness, Garrison returned to the courtroom and delivered his closing statement. Railing against the Warren Commission's purportedly flawed findings, he mentioned the accused only briefly. Despite the lateness of the hour, the jurors entered into deliberation. Forty-five minutes later, they reached a verdict.

"NOT GUILTY!" screamed the afternoon headlines of the *States-Item*. Editorialists, silent for two years, rose in customary New Orleans self-righteous criticism: "Mr. Garrison stands revealed for what he is: a man without principle who would pervert the legal process to his own ends."[17]

While Big Jim handily won his reelection bid and later ran for a seat on the state's supreme court, Clay lectured at college campuses on the "l'affaire Shaw," while defending his reputation and fending off Garrison's accusation of perjury.

Never despairing, Shaw resolved to "become the Horace Walpole of New Orleans"—a reference to the eighteenth-century erudite but discreet homosexual writer of pointed letters about Europe's upper echelons. Like Walpole, who penned gothic romances from his restored villa "set in enameled meadows with filigree hedges," Shaw lived modestly in an apartment on Burgundy Street, seeking comfort through another restoration project on St. Peter Street. And, like Walpole, who found that "every drop of ink in my pen ran cold," Shaw labored "somewhat dispiritedly on my book," based on a diary he kept during his time of troubles.[18]

In 1974, his money and health depleted, Shaw died of lung cancer. Remembered by his friends as a man who "lived his life with the utmost grace," Clay L. Shaw is reviled by strangers who know him only through labyrinthine conspiracy books or fanciful Hollywood scripts and largely forgotten by New Orleans homosexuals.

The lesson of the Shaw-Garrison affair is not lost upon Shaw's long-time friend and physician. According to Martin Palmer, Shaw was seen by Garrison as "vulnerable and prominent," a "pansy" who would quickly collapse under the weight of investigation and scandal.

Shaw, like the hero of Kafka's *Trial,* was confronted by authorities with a crime of which he knew nothing and from which he found no justice. However, unlike Kafka's bland bank assessor Joseph K, who led a joyless life, the good-humored Shaw refused to relinquish his dignity.

Stonewall occurred a few months following the Shaw trial, rendering a verdict from New York homosexuals that the era of homosexual hiding was over. In the City That Care Forgot, however, most homosexuals—riddled with self-doubt, chilled by official intimidation, and silenced by innuendo—failed to learn the real lesson of l'affaire Shaw from the gentleman who never came out, but never caved in.

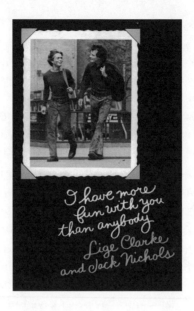

I have more
fun with you
than anybody
Lige Clarke
and Jack Nichols

THREE

Gay Is Good

New friendships come and go like flame
Or shifting shadows on a lawn,
But you were here before the dawn
And you remain when they are gone.

—Lige

The smell of fresh flowers floated above nearby Tompkins Square Park, where flower children smoked weed and parentless children played on the grass. On that spring day in 1971, two southerners—Jack Nichols and Lige Clarke—sat in their East Village kitchen, puffing on an occasional joint, choosing stories to share. Jack drifted to his wooden writing table to type, as Lige reviewed earlier revisions. It had not been quite a year since a New York publisher advised the couple to "write a book about your life together . . . it should also be a memoir of the times." Lige prevailed over Jack; there would be *no* procrastination.

Lige looked up from the manuscript with an impish expression. "What do you think happens after death?"

I Have More Fun with You Than Anybody. Photo courtesy of Jack Nichols.

Jack, whose Scottish grandfather instilled within him a love for language, quoted Epicurus, the Greek philosopher who championed pleasure as the chief good: "When I am, death is not. When death is, I am not."

Lige shrugged. "When I die it will be exciting. I'm not afraid." In his Kentucky drawl he asked, "Do you understand?"[1]

Jack nodded, disguising his bewilderment.

As the duo worked on their project in early 1971, they along with fellow members of the Gay Activist Alliance came down on two chartered southbound buses to campaign for the country's first openly gay candidate, Franklin E. Kameny. An early victim of Joe McCarthy's homosexual purge of federal agencies, Kameny was a World War II veteran and an old soldier of gay activism. He was also the movement father to Lige, Jack, and a generation of activists. He was running for the District of Columbia's nonvoting delegate to Congress; his anticipated defeat was far from a loss. Editors of Washington's *Daily News* commented: "The Harvard-educated astronomer and avowed homosexual may not have succeeded in convincing the city that 'Gay is Good' but his straightforward advocacy of the 'right to be different,' his thoughtful examination of other important issues, his generosity in praise of his opponents, must have impressed many who met him along the way that 'Gay' is not all that bad."[2]

Staring over his Royal typewriter and through the window at the bustling New York street, images whirled in Jack's head of his first encounter with a lanky twenty-two-year-old spouting "hillbilly wisdom." It was 1964 and a typical sultry D.C. summer evening. A window air conditioner at the Hideaway, a gay bar located opposite FBI headquarters, was humming as Leslie Gore scattered "rainbows, lollypops, and moonbeams" from the jukebox. Jack spotted a shapely army man wearing "a blue shirt that showed his absolute definition. His face had classic symmetry, his cheekbones high, his jaw strong, his eyes hazel with lips full. He was blonde, his hair styled in a civilian mode, a handsome wave directly above his forehead. I'd never seen anyone like him. The description penned by Old Walt in his *Leaves* came to mind: 'Dress does not hide him / The strong sweet quality he has strikes through.'"

After stumbling unwittingly into the bar the night before escorted by two army buddies, on that evening Lige was motivated by more than curiosity. "I was a little nervous, but before I could even order a beer, a guy came over to me and invited me to join him and some friends for a drink. . . . I said, 'Sure!' Later he asked me to dance, so we did and I loved it. Everything seemed so simple, so natural."[3]

Over the next decade Lige and Jack threw their lot in with a hearty band of East Coast leaders of the two major homophile organizations in the country, the Daughters of Bilitis (DOB) and the Mattachine Society.[4] Led by the hard-nosed tactician Frank Kameny, the gentlemanly New York activist Dick Leitsch, and the tireless New York DOB president Barbara Gittings, Lige found himself captivated by the movement's vision and energy: "The day after I met Jack I was in the Mattachine basement mimeographing newsletters. I knew this was something my heart would follow, something that I believed in."[5]

In the East Village apartment that spring day in 1971, Lige walked from the kitchen to the wooden writing table and began to read chapter 7 over Jack's shoulder:

> Mart Crowley, author of *The Boys in the Band,* had a most peculiar notion of what goes on at gay parties. The creeps he crowded into his play may very well have been real people, but it was a flight of fancy for him to suppose that such drearies would be likely to tolerate each other's company for more than a few minutes. Had we been invited we'd have split long before the cruel games began. If Crowley's gay friends actually behave as he depicted them, he's in need of nicer friends. Then, of course, he'd have nicer parties![6]

A Mississippi boy–turned–New York cynic, Crowley created *The Birthday Party* out of the depths of despair and rage.[7] The soon retitled two-act tragedy was set in a Manhattan apartment. Michael—Crowley's fictional alter ego—is hosting a party for his friend Harold. Prior to his arrival, Alan, an uninvited guest, appears. Michael's old heterosexual school chum interacts with the assorted characters while Michael casts sexual innuendo and homosexual suspicion.

The Boys in the Band ran for a thousand-plus-one performances following its Easter 1968 off-Broadway opening at Theatre Four. Laced with witty remarks ("A bit effeminate? He's like a butterfly in heat"), the play is remembered (and pilloried) for its brutal monologues and devilish parlor games. Toward the end of act 2, the "ugly, pockmarked, Jew fairy," Harold, clinically dissects a self-absorbed Michael: "You are a sad and pathetic man. You're a homosexual and you don't want to be. But there is nothing you can do to change it. Not all of your prayers to your God, not all the analysis you can buy in all the years you've got left to live." With Harold's departure and the stage curtain certain to fall, Michael laments: "If we . . . if we could just . . . not hate ourselves so much. That's it, you know. If we could just learn not to hate ourselves quite so very much."[8]

Created at the brink of gay militancy, *Boys in the Band* quickly became a relic of urban homosexual lives past.[9] In the space of eighteen months, the homosexual was transformed from meek and self-deprecating to confrontational and proud, as a generation of new activists proclaimed, "Gay Is Good!"[10]

As performances continued on West Fifty-fifth Street, Jack—the "sharer of my roving life," to quote Lige quoting Whitman—had moved to Manhattan with his lover. Driving up from Florida after visiting Jack's mother, Mary, the couple had stopped along the way to see Lige's family in a Kentucky town connected to the outside world by Routes 160 and 80.

About a hundred families lived in Hindman and its surrounding hills and hollows. Kin dotted the countryside like dandelions in springtime. Lige's great-great-grandfather brought into the wilderness fifty-two children with the help of various native women, creating an entanglement of relationships. Lige's father, an avid Cab Calloway fan, operated the town's general store and chaired the county Republican Party. Uncle John was postmaster.

With a black cat, Samantha, purring at his feet, Daddy Clarke welcomed Lige and Jack as the family had always done since their first visit in 1965.[11] During their weekend stay, the two companions, like Whitman's brothers-in-arms, hiked up the mountain for a picnic lunch at a cemetery with moss-covered tombstones that preserved the community of memory.

Standing by her grave, Lige recollected his mama's warning: "Don't cling to your mother's apron strings, precious. Your mother and father won't always be here." Staring out over the horizon to the roads and houses below, the memory of her singing ("You'll Never Walk Alone") resurrected more memories.

In this land of Methodists and Baptists (Lige didn't meet a Catholic until the age of eighteen), a central place in his home was reserved for the family Bible, with a stained-glass window showering light upon it. On Sundays, the Methodist church, founded by Lige's grandfather, rang chimes that echoed for miles throughout the valley and across the hills.

In 1964, Lige had fallen into bed with Jack after meeting him at the Hideaway. During the next seven years, between separations and reunions, they tumbled into love. Their most profound separation occurred in mid-1967, when an exasperated Lige walked out on the "first and only man I've ever loved," due to Jack's deepening political focus on "saving the world" instead of savoring the relationship they shared.[12]

Following a cross-country trip, a jaundiced Lige returned to Hindman. From Halloween through Christmas he recovered from hepatitis,
cared for by his aging father and an odd assortment of aunts and cousins.
Every Monday morning, Lige visited the hospital on its acres of rolling
hills, where doctors and nurses sang hymns and patients sneaked forbidden
smokes.

Following four years of service to Uncle Sam and three more years living in Washington as a homophile activist, Lige was sequestered in a dry
county. The weekly newspaper balanced Bible quotes and farm reports
with sports photos of high school heroes who piled into hot rods for some
"crowsin'" after the game.

Lige was an unsympathetic narrator for his *Our Town* life. "I'd love
to give the whole town of Hindman just one good acid trip!" he wrote
to Jack. His letter continued, "I'd start with the ministers and spinsters.
I'm sure most of them think I'm sick because of the 'wicked' life I've led
in the big city."[13]

"Turning a little more yellow each day" from the liver infection, Lige
wrote to Jack in his every-other-day letter addressed to Miss Mary Southwick (Jack's mother).[14] The otherwise disguised relationship with her son
evidenced Lige's ability to live comfortably in two worlds. As a twenty-
something lad he served both the army of Secretary of Defense McNamara
and the homophile legion of Frank Kameny, lettering signs for gay rights
protests at the Pentagon while decoding sensitive documents with twelve
top-secret clearances. Though he was no longer part of President Lyndon
Johnson's war machine, his Kentucky family held him hostage to the closet.

Lige's fear of disclosure to his aging father mirrored the realities of southern life: "For a person living in a small community, values of yourself are
often distorted by the pressures that come in on you." One of those keenly
felt pressures was carrying on the family name. As the only "single"
male among his high school classmates, Lige was teased by some of the
old-timers: "How come you're not fat? How come you're not married?"
Lige's joking response soon became, "I can never have children, and the
doctors don't know whether it's Mary's fault or mine."[15]

On occasion he walked the streets of Hindman. From Daddy's grocery and Uncle John's post office he hiked to the county square, marveling
at the "shabby strings" of Christmas lights. He sauntered to Young's
Department Store and over to Joe's for lunch. The trip generally took the
better part of a day, since he was often stopped for conversation. On his
walking tour, Lige sensed "deep scars of frustration etched on the faces
of boyhood friends." When Hindman boys reached twenty, "life was almost

over." He observed, "They did it without waiting or thinking, and before they knew it their wives had cooked them into obesity. They got bogged down with bills and payments and only a short time elapsed before they passed from bloom to gloom and, finally, to doom." He witnessed a similar fate for Hindman women. "One of my classmates . . . is going to have her fourth baby soon. I couldn't believe it, she looks about forty years of age. She looked bitter and hard. Her mouth was twisted and sour."[16]

As Lige recovered from his illness, he picked up the almost daily letters from "Miss Southwick" at the post office. One day, Uncle John's wife asked: "Where is Miss Southwick from?" Lige smiled, "Heaven." Later he wrote Jack: "I don't know what I'm going to do about Mary Southwick when I leave Hindman. She's almost a legend here now. People will be asking whatever happened to her for years to come."[17]

About a week passed before tales of another secret circulated around town, as Lige later revealed to Jack: "A sweet little old lady called me aside and said, 'Lige, are you with the Secret Service?' She whispered it just loud enough for several people to hear. I smiled very slyly and said, 'You never know, do you?' So the seed has been planted, let her take it from there." It took about a week for Aunt Hassie to learn of Lige's "CIA connections" and to tell Aunt Dula Rhae. She told Lige, in no uncertain terms, "she wasn't convinced I'm not."[18]

"Joy to the World," Billboard's number-one song for six weeks, played over an Emerson radio sitting on the windowsill. Mistyping a "Q," Jack looked up as Lige arose from a lotus position on their colorful mat. Cushions and pillows were laid about in Moroccan style. In this one-and-a-half room apartment the two slept and, with a candle burning against the sweet smell of incense, made love. "Don't anticipate," Lige often counseled, "and don't assume. . . . The kiss is not a step toward sex; it *is* sex." One evening after sexual intimacy Jack remembers shouting "exultantly in the dark: 'I have more fun with you than anybody!'" Lige laughed, "What you just said would make a good book title."

As Jack continued to tap the typewriter keys in the apartment near Tompkins Square, Lige headed down the street to pick up a fresh loaf of Russian black bread and some vegetables. Fried food, meat, sugar—staples of his southern heritage—had long been disowned. Though resistant at first, Jack had accommodated to the house menu—particularly since Lige declared that no lips that touched meat would touch his.

The lyrics of "Autumn in New York" danced in Lige's head. Events had unfolded quickly during that first year in Manhattan for the gay couple who was soon to become the "most celebrated and recognizable" in

America.[19] Jack secured a job at Countrywide Publications, where he helped to edit magazines like *Strange Unknown* and *Companion;* Lige occasionally modeled and wrote for Countrywide. At this mad production house, the two became friends with Al Goldstein, an editor who dreamed of creating a magazine that capitalized on the sexual revolution and liberalized pornography laws.

In November 1968, *Screw* hit the newsstands. Amidst the photos of female cleavage and assorted methods for achieving orgasm was a column, "The Homosexual Citizen," featuring "two lively males who have spent some very exciting years living and grooving together."[20]

Capturing the spirit of the age, Lige and Jack wrote: "To the homosexual the sex revolution means much more than greater freedom for sex relations. It means that we'll be able to build positive lives in our culture. . . . We need more of a sexual culture of our own. It does not need to be based on outworn heterosexual ethics, for these, indeed are crumbling fast."[21]

Jack, today in his early sixties, remembers their late-sixties message of sexual liberation: "Such calls hardly seemed outrageous or radical when, in fact, the counterculture had already greeted same-sex impulses with open arms. . . . [Men] in the counterculture were eager to show affection and tenderness—as part of the hippie ideology with its commitment to love-making on a planetary scale."

Writing to what was a mostly straight, albeit largely supportive, audience, in their column Jack and Lige "broke societal barriers just as the Gay Liberation Movement did."[22] They challenged the traditional male role. Lige and Jack observed that a major impact of the "hippie ethic" was "its exposure and its attempted destruction of outworn 'masculinism,'" arguing that "a truly complete person is neither extremely masculine nor extremely feminine."[23]

The duo quickly became a fixture in the New York gay cultural scene. Just as quickly, the homophile activists–turned–gay liberationists distanced themselves ideologically from the older generation of homosexual leaders. "In our discussion of the military," Jack explains, "we took the counterculture's position, namely that any chewing gum we could put into its machinery was gum well placed." This stance was in opposition to that of Frank Kameny and others who were committed to integrating lesbians and gay men into the military. Another significant difference between youthful activists such as Lige and Jack and many of their homophile elders was the belief that homosexuals did not form a minority culture and that homosexuality itself was "a socially-inculcated taboo." Jack continues: "Everyone, we began to say, would be capable of homosexual responses if only their abilities to relate to their own sex were not blocked by strict conditioning and abetted by the deliberate inculcation of fierce prejudice."

(Homo)sexual liberation, though, was slow in coming. Like the Texan Candide, Joe Buck of *Midnight Cowboy* fame, when Lige arrived in New York City he discovered that "the curse of John Calvin was nailed to almost every door." At first naïve to urban ways, Lige "assumed that it was only the hills I'd escaped that were out of step." As the doors of perception cracked, he realized city folks "were sad victims of the puritan heritage to even greater degrees. In the mountains, at least, we had learned to fuck *wildly*—at an early age, both heterosexually and homosexually. We were in touch with our bodies."

The joys of boyhood for Lige had been plentiful. "All my life," Lige revealed, "I've enjoyed sexual abundance." He was particularly partial to Sunday evening church revivals. "While adults praised the Lord inside the church," he laughed, "we young'uns, more practical by far, enjoyed automobile orgies in the parking lot out back. At an early age, you know, mountaineers often do a great deal of exploring. . . . There weren't much else to do up in them hollers. Some called it spelunking; I called it corn-holing."

By June of 1969, the couple had moved to Lower East Side four-room quarters across from Fillmore East. When bands like the Grateful Dead were not playing, lyrics from *Hair* and "Everyday People" drifted from hippie-rented apartments.

Spending the last weekend of June in the Fire Island Pines, Lige and Jack returned Sunday night. As they walked across Eighth Street, they entered the heart of Greenwich Village. On Christopher Street they spotted a few folks hanging near a partly boarded-up bar that looked like a "blackened and abandoned Tara."[24] Stapled to the plywood were flyers with fiery demands and proclamations such as "Get the Mafia and the Cops Out of Gay Bars!" and "They Invaded Our Rights." Chalked across one window was "How Can Inspector Smythe Drive a $15,000 Car on HIS Salary?" and "Support Gay Power."

Craig Rodwell, the founder of the first gay bookstore in the country, had posted these flyers. An anonymous street queen in drag described to Lige and Jack the event that defined a new generation of activism: "They had a raid, honey, and us queens, we got mad and sent those police running. Somebody pulled up a parking meter there and people threw stuff and it was one big mess, I'll tell you. There were queens doing the can-can down Christopher Street and folks chasing the pigs, yellin' 'Catch 'em, fuck 'em!'"

"Neither Rodwell nor many of the other New York Mattachine leader-ship," Jack claims, "felt disposed to support such 'revolutionary' activ-ities."[25] Dick Leitsch, a former Louisville teacher, heeding the old Mattachine philosophy, wrote the first detailed account of the Stonewall riots.[26] The result, "The Hairpin Drop Heard 'Round the World," was attached as a leaflet to the Mattachine's July newsletter.[27] The next month's edition provided detailed descriptions of the "rebellion," includ-ing Leitsch's analysis:

> Coming on the heels of the raids of the Snake Pit and the Sewer, and the closing of the Checkerboard, the Tel-Star, and other clubs, the Stonewall raid looked to many like part of an effort to close all gay bars and clubs in the Village. . . . Why the Stonewall and not the Sewer or the Snake Pit? . . . This club was more than a dance bar, more than just a gay gathering place. It catered largely to a group of people who are not welcome in, or cannot afford, other places of homosexual social gather-ing. The "drags" and the "queens" . . . formed the "regulars" at the Stonewall. To a large extent, the club was for them. Should Harry's or Julius's, for example, be closed for any reason, the middle class "respectable" customers would find another place to meet, drink, and socialize before the night was over. . . . You've got to be 18 to buy a drink in a bar and gay life revolved around bars. Where do you go if you are 17 or 16 and gay. . . . That was the one advantage to the place—for $3 admission, one could stay inside, out of the winter's cold or summer's heat, all night long. . . . The Stonewall became "home" to these kids.[28]

On 6 July, the Electric Circus invited the homosexual community to use its facilities: "If you are tired of raids, Mafia control, and checks at the front door," read the flyer, "join us for a beautiful evening." Inside, Lige and Jack found "a groovy crowd. . . . Hip moustaches, long hair, and hundreds of handsome young men. The acid-rock band blared forth a medley of fast tunes."[29]

Two years later, as Lige's and Jack's book neared completion, the Elec-tric Circus was no more. The Lower East Side, though, had changed little. In *Dancer from the Dance,* a groundbreaking novel of the search for gay love, the pseudonymous Andrew Holleran wrote that the neighborhood

> reminds some people of photographs of Berlin just after the war. And in fact along certain blocks the walls of tenement houses are thin as movie sets, whose windows disclose the rubble of collapsed buildings. . . . Poor people lived there. Artists and ghosts—Poles whose neighborhood it used to be and hippies who gathered there in the early sixties. But both of these have had their day, and St. Marks Place now belongs to hair styl-ists, pimps, and dealers in secondhand clothing. The building in which Malone took a room is a kind of history lesson of that part of town: It

once housed the Electric Circus, a discotheque that began fashionable and white, and eventually became unfashionable and black. . . . Finally they closed the place down, and music no longer throbbed out the door on winter nights, and black boys no longer stood around the stairs combing their hair, and no one came in search of spiritual insight. And it just sat there, a huge hulk of a building painted shocking blue, a tax write-off for the Mafia.[30]

Lige and Jack wrote their *Screw* column on 8 July, the fifth anniversary of their fated rendezvous at the Hideaway. Unlike Leitch, they sounded the clarion call of sexual rebellion, declaring that "last week's riots in Greenwich Village have set standards for the rest of the nation's homosexuals to follow." They cautioned, however, that the "revolution in Sheridan Square must step beyond its present boundaries. The homosexual revolution is only part of a larger revolution sweeping through all segments of society. We hope that 'Gay Power' will not become a call for separation, but for sexual integration."[31] A few columns later they added: "In the final analysis the homosexual revolution is really a revolution of love."[32]

Jack remembers the activism on the heels of Stonewall that redefined the riot on Christopher Street as a rebellion that created the long-sought turning point in the homophile movement:

> [T]he Stonewall Rebellion signaled the end of gay liberation as a homophile think tank and, because the very idea of liberation seemed literally to float on the airwaves of the era, a host of enthusiasts emerged from every quarter of New York to plan battle with the Establishment. An amorphous group held fiery meetings, calling itself The Gay Liberation Front. . . . To cement their varied ideas the Front rallied around Michael Bakunin's anarchist slogan: "Not one of us is free till all of us are free." Feminists, anti-war protestors, Marxists, anarchists, Yippies, hippies, and a variety of folk who considered themselves either moderate or apolitical met in an attempt to reach political consensus.

Not surprisingly, these meetings produced more rancor than agreement. Like others, Jack and Lige tired of these interminably lengthy gatherings characterized by ideological rhetoric and ad hominem attacks. On one Sunday night, a "crazy" disrupted the meeting, reporting that "women were being discriminated against at the Electric Circus. GLF broke up in chaos."[33] At another time, Jack, who stood at the back of the room with Lige, remembers Leo Louis Martello attempting to introduce a more moderate tone in the proceedings only to be drowned out by "cliques of organized ideologues." A conservative movement friend of Lige and Jack, Foster Gunnison Jr., "sat there stupefied—thrilled and repelled simultaneously—watching with the mixture of horror and fascination as one might observe an automobile accident."[34]

Lige and Jack soon allied themselves with others, such as Barbara Gittings, Arthur Bell, Jim Owles, Kay Tobin, and Morty Manford, who were to form a new activist group. As an alternative to GLF, Bell asked: "Why not organize a group based solely on homosexual liberation? Why not have a constitution with a preamble stating goals and purposes?"[35]

In mid-December 1969 the Gay Activist Alliance was formed. Repudiating violence, "disdaining all ideologies," and "forbearing alliances," the two-hundred-member Alliance "zapped" homophobic politicians and created the first modern gay symbol—the eleventh lower-case letter of the Greek alphabet. "In chemistry and physics the lambda symbolizes a complete exchange of energy," wrote Bell. "That moment or span of time that's witness to absolute activity."[36]

These energies—quickened by the sexual revolution, youthful rebellion, and third-world revolutionary movements—transformed Stonewall from a small-scale riot into a major political movement that attracted the attention of *Time, Newsweek, Look, Esquire,* and the *New York Times.*[37] These mainstream publications devoted feature stories to the "new homosexuals." Though far from supportive, the stories included voices of activists and researchers such as Frank Kameny, Phyllis Lyon, Dick Leitsch, and John Gagnon. Kay Tobin and her partner, Barbara Gittings, felt the time was right for a publication of these "new homosexual" voices. They urged Lige and Jack to persuade *Screw*'s publisher to match his liberal rhetoric with venture capital.

The publisher, Al Goldstein, committed $25,000 to the project, and *GAY* was launched in late 1969.[38] The cover featured Lige wearing a white fish-net tank and standing near an ocean vessel. The couple's first editorial quickly distanced these youthful veteran activists from the "homosexual as minority" approach held by the older generation of homophile activists. They wrote: "*GAY* believes that there is only one world, and that labels and categories such as homosexual and heterosexual will some day pass away leaving human beings who, like this publication, will be liked and appreciated not because of sexual orientation, but because they are themselves interesting."[39]

With Lige and Jack at the helm, "*GAY* became the newspaper of record for Gay America," with the largest circulation among any similar publications.[40] As "journalistic prophets of the post-Stonewall Era," the couple shared editorial space with feminist writers such as Leah Fritz, Mary Phillips, and Claudia Dreyfus.[41] There were regular features penned by Movement pioneers such as Virginian Lilli Vincenz, writing a general/women's interest feature, and Dick Leitsch, who wrote "History Facts Your Teacher 'Forgot' to Mention." Kay Tobin, formerly associate editor of the *Ladder,* was the paper's first news editor, and New York art critic Gregory Battcock attended museum art shows, lampooning "dorky tastes in clothes . . . mismatched colorings, frumpy lines, and ugly buttons" in his column "The Last Estate." Kathy Wakeham informed other femme fatales about Manhattan cruising, while GAA president Richard Wandel asked questions and photographed faces for "The Cruising Photographer." Diane Devlin discussed the plight of the gay teen, and Sorel David often used her wry sense of humor to tweak Marxists (her parents had been Communist Party members). Leo Martello's column, "The Gay Witch," raised scarcely an eyebrow.

GAY attracted some of the best writers in Queer America. Vito Russo was *GAY*'s film critic, and the pseudonymous Ian J. Tree wrote on the black experience. There were occasional contributions, too, by historian Donn Teal and psychologist George Weinberg.

Some of the flood of letters was published and answered by Lige under "Pen Points." The next-to-last page was reserved for personal "Wanton Ads." There were, too, an ever growing gay bar guide and a community bulletin board, as *GAY* expanded its distribution to Washington and Los Angeles. Those interested in the signs of the zodiac could refer to the paper's "Hornyscope" section, while the more studious-minded crossed over to the "Peter Puzzle."

In "The Editors Speak," Lige and Jack took issue with a variety of sacred cows, denouncing Uncle Sam as a peeping Tom, taking African American playwright Leroi Jones to task for urging blacks to avoid homosexuality as "the white man's weakness." When Troy Perry, a southern Pentecostal preacher-turned-minister to Los Angeles gays, opened his first church, a one-page picture spread read: "2,000 Years Late: A Welcome Change?" (Later, appearing on a gay radio program co-hosted with Dick Leitsch, Nichols lampooned Reverend Perry as a "country-fried parson" who "descended on Manhattan in search of converts.")[42]

Irreverent in tone and brassy in style, *GAY* mixed controversial ideals with integrationist themes, becoming the *MAD Magazine* for the New Homosexual. "Although editors of such publications are generally thought of as radicals," Lige and Jack considered themselves neither "conservative" nor "crusaders." *GAY* "was not aimed at the middle-class, uptight, furtive homosexual," they reminded their readers. "[We] want to build bridges, establish a dialogue between homosexual and heterosexual. . . [and]

keep the paper free of the defensive tone which has been typical of so many homophile publications in the past."[43]

As these two southerners began to edit a major gay newspaper and continued writing a column for the country's most provocative heterosexual magazine, one might wonder how this played with Lige's Hindman friends and relatives. In one issue of *GAY*, Lige told readers that when his sister and brother-in-law "visited us recently in New York, they let us know in many little ways that they not only *knew*, but thoroughly approved of our relationship. As for the rest of the family, we haven't bothered to explain the facts of life to them. Some of them, probably, would shit. Others would accept us (we *think*) because they're fond of us both. But sooner or later those who don't know us will figure things out and *then* they'll have to deal with us as best they can."[44]

Dealing with "us" included attending the first Gay Pride parade, held on 28 June 1970. Lige and Jack joined thousands of others to commemorate the Stonewall rioting and to mend generational and ideological splits among activists. Placards carried down Sixth Avenue read, "Homosexual is a Four-Letter Word," and "I Am a Lesbian and I Am Beautiful." Ten- and fifteen-foot banners unfurled against warm winds: "Gay Liberation" and "Christopher Street Gay Liberation Day, 1970." Amidst marchers wearing blue T-shirts with gold lambdas or the mauve halter tops of the Lavender Menace came forth cheers: "Say It Loud, Gay Is Proud!" "Hey, Hey, Whadaya Say? Try It Once the Other Way!" "Out of the Closets and into the Streets!" As marchers funneled into Central Park, Savannah-born poet Perry Brass remarked that this is "possibly the first time love had reappeared in the park on such a large scale since the first Easter Be-In three years ago."[45]

In the spring of 1971, Lige and Jack sat in their East Village kitchen recrafting their *GAY* editorial on the 1970 event for the final pages of *I Have More Fun with You Than Anybody*. They remembered it as

> a gentle day. Lovers kissed openly. Friends clasped hands. Strangers threw arms around each other's shoulders. The afternoon sun bathed the day in tender glory, casting light on the most enchanting moments in love's long stifled history.
>
> Was it more impressive, really, than the small group of ten, who had protested in front of the White House, five years before? We thought back to that long-ago spring day, when Lige had lettered the signs that Jack and nine others used to march in protest. . . . Now our eyes filled with tears as we stood together in Central Park's Sheep Meadow, hugging, cheering wildly, applauding.[46]

Six weeks before the second year's celebration, Lige turned the last page of the manuscript of their book:

> We'd always known it inwardly. But now, it seemed, an ancient fact was establishing itself outwardly. What was it? That love's wonderfully varied expressions *can* break through unreal crusts of fear and misunderstanding. That love *can* come out of the past's dark closets. Casting off the vile coating of social falsehood, men and women *can* bloom, standing proudly, as they did on that day.[47]

He looked up from the manuscript. "A lot of people think of coming out as just being 'gay' and going into the gay social world. I don't consider that really coming out."

Willing to play the straight man, Jack asked: "So, what's coming out?"

"Coming out is coming out in yourself, not in society so much. Accepting yourself and being free with yourself. Understanding yourself from your center."

"Some people might confuse what you're saying with vanity."

"There's a difference between being vain and appreciation of the finer values you have in yourself. There is nothing wrong about having a little confidence, a little arrogance, or a little unyielding pride—that's what's going to make gay liberation succeed!"

FOUR

The Pied Piper of Athena

When I started teaching in 1968 I was "in the closet," at least that's the way I thought of it. Then the women's movement began, and in 1969, Stonewall happened. And my students happened to me. —Julia Penelope Stanley

A decade before Stonewall, Julia Penelope Stanley was a "notorious short-haired bull dyke" at Florida State University.[1] But that was before Charley Johns had terrorized the Tallahassee campus, before the dean of women (a tailored-suit lesbian) stamped "homosexual" on Penny's permanent record, and before Penny's transformation from Leninist atheist to Ayn Randian objectivist.

Like Molly Bolt in *Rubyfruit Jungle,* Penny fled Florida for New York City: "Moving to New York was the thing to do! Get out of wherever you were in the South and go to New York, which is why so many southern lesbians ended up there: Bertha Harris, Rita Mae Brown, Parke Bowman, June Arnold—and, of course, Merril."

At City College, Penny Stanley, now known as Julia Penelope, was a member of (and the only woman in) the Young Conservatives Club, "much to the great dismay and horror of my South Campus friends" and Merril. Julia had brought Merril out during the heady Miami high school days

Free our Sisters. Photo © Marcelina Martin.

of duck-ass hairdos, pompadours, and penny loafers. In 1958, they had performed as the Tongueston Trio at the Onyx Room adjacent to the lesbian Coral Bar in Miami Beach. Their relationship had always been more personal than political, and when Merril came to New York with Jack, she and Julia often partied together.

Julia rode the A train alone, though, from her Washington Heights apartment to the Daughters of Bilitis meetings at a Houston Street church basement. Julia was neither a homophile activist nor a radical leftist. She refused to participate in the 1965 pickets of the White House, Pentagon, State Department, and Philadelphia's Constitution Hall because Frank Kameny required lesbians to wear dresses (and men to be seen in suits). Her writings in the *Ladder* and *ONE Magazine,* under the nom de plume Julia Seeley, were lucid and incisive analyses of the misuse of language or the absence of logic. She ridiculed a psychologist, Ernest van den Haag, who had spoken at a New York Mattachine meeting; described an imaginary interrogation by Charley Johns at Florida State; and lambasted as "odious and ludicrous" Albert Ellis's argument that homosexuality was "'wrong' based on social codes."[2]

Some of the middle-aged lesbian factory workers and "working-class dykes" encouraged Julia to go back to college. "What they saw in me was themselves. It was their desire for the freedom to be themselves—a way out." Enjoying "hanging out, drinking, and being a 'kept butch,'" she was grateful for her Blanche M. Baker scholarship from DOB that covered book expenses. However, Julia found the Daughter's meetings boring and insulting. During one of them, members discussed what they hoped to gain by demonstrating. "One butch remarked, 'I want to be able to whistle at women on the street like men!' I said, 'I won't march for that. That's not my idea of liberation for *any* of us!'"

Both Julia and her antagonist expressed anger over workplace discrimination and exclusion from traditionally male fields such as government service and the high-status professions. The last-minute inclusion of "sex" in the 1964 Civil Rights Act legitimated these issues. The publication of the President's Commission on the Status of Women's report, *American Women,* documented these discriminatory practices. And the National Organization for Women, formed in 1966 under the leadership of Betty Friedan, lobbied for government action.

The question for Julia and others was whether to reform the male-dominated system or to overthrow it. Friedan, Margaret Mead (who authored *American Women*), and Gloria Steinem assumed an assimilationist, profamily stance. Meanwhile, more Left-leaning politicos labored in male-dominated movement groups that subordinated gender to the greater liberation struggle of race (Student Nonviolent Coordinating Committee), anti-imperialism (Students for a Democratic Society), or class (Socialist Workers Party). Some of these radicals, like Jo Freeman, Shulamith Firestone, and Juliet Mitchell, departed from these liberal or politico camps and popularized feminist action and analysis.[3]

Liberals, politicos—or radicals—had little appeal for Julia Penelope. "One friend kept telling me to read *The Feminine Mystique*. I never did; it had the word 'feminine' in its title. If it had to do with feminine, I didn't want to know!"

In 1966, Julia migrated to Austin in pursuit of a doctorate in linguistics. "I was going to be a graduate student, then an assistant professor, then an associate professor, and then, someday, a *full* professor! Maybe even a dean!"[4] Within this liberal oasis situated in the parched Texan climate, there was a small antidraft student contingent, as well as a Southern Student Organizing chapter, "head shops" and coffeehouses, and students reading insurgent magazines like the local *Rag* or the *New South Student*. But there was no DOB chapter and only a couple of bars, like the Cabaret and Freddie's, which Julia seldom entered. Sometimes she drove to the local Dairy Queen on her Yamaha motorcycle, wearing jeans and a T-shirt. "Lesbians would walk up to me and we'd chat over an ice cream cone."

Barbara Grier assumed editorship of the *Ladder* the same year, 1966, under her pseudonym Gene Damon. Slowly, she moved the lesbian magazine toward a more "womanist perspective." It was a direction that many of the Daughters, including Julia, found vexing. She remembers that "all of a sudden we were talking about heterosexual women! We had this one journal, now we have to talk about *all* women?" She cancelled her subscription.

Julia was too busy to lament the changing face of the venerable magazine. She was on the academic fast track during an era when there were few female Ph.D. candidates. For one course, taught by the renowned sociolinguist Edgar Polome, Julia wrote a term paper on homosexual slang that described the linguistic devices found in the "gay" vocabulary, made up primarily of terms for male sexuality. In 1968, she completed her coursework and was on the road again.

Julia, now an assistant professor at the University of Georgia, arrived in Athens, Georgia, the summer after the summer of love. Nestled in the farmland of the northeast part of the state, the college town was largely untouched by violent student protests, political assassinations, urban riots, the Chicago Democratic Convention, and the Tet offensive that burned

1968 on our national psyche. There was only one book outlet in the town, the Campus Bookstore located in the student union, and, according to Julia, "they didn't carry real books; they didn't sell novels and books that people actually read. They just sold textbooks!"

Twenty-six-year-old Julia—her hair a bit longer but her manner no less dykey—was charged with introducing Georgia students to comparative literature, modern English grammar, and the history of the English language. Of course, the department's canon had no room for Gertrude Stein's "Miss Furr and Miss Skeene" or Virginia Woolf's *Orlando*. But she "steamed up a room" teaching Chaucer's "Pardoner's Tale." Her courses quickly filled.

Though her politics had changed little, Julia began to wear skirts sewn by her Texas lover, met on a short night train ride between New York and the Carolinas. Firm in the belief that she remained "in the closet," Penelope became the unsuspecting Pied Piper of Athenian queers. "Unknown to me, all of the lesbian and gay students were signing up for my classes!"

In between classes, Julia advised a number of campus "fringe groups," including the student women's group, which "really didn't want to know about lesbians." And, with her mother who joined her from Florida, she opened the Hobbit Habit—a pre-Borders bookstore with easy chairs and coffee that carried "real books."

Facing the hurdles of academia, Julia dedicated herself to her dissertation while isolating herself from political ferment. "When the second wave of feminism geared up in '68, I saw what was presented on television and put it on a back burner. I not only didn't have time to be political— I didn't even want to know about it!"

In June of that year, "Shulie" Firestone described the negative images of feminism in *Notes from the First Year:* "A granite-faced spinster obsessed with the vote? A George Sand in bloomers with cigar, a woman against Nature?"[5] That same month, in Florida, Gainesville Students for Democratic Society (SDS) feminists Beverly Jones and Judith Brown issued "Toward a Female Liberation Movement," soon known among activists as the "Florida Paper." Brown, who would later go on to cofound the first women's liberation organization in the South, decried *all* men as the enemy:

> Regrettably the best—radical men and their black counterparts—do not even have a political interest in female liberation. . . . While sexual and emotional alliances with men may continue to be of some benefit the peculiar domestic institution is not. Only women can define what "womanhood" might best be, and likewise men might better redefine themselves in the absence of a daily reminder of their unwarranted experience of masterdom. Theoretically, such women and men might, in the future,

liberated from this master-slave hang-up, meet and work out a new domestic institution which better serves the interest of free men and free women. . . . Some women, then, and perhaps some men will have to reject the present domestic model given us, destroy it, and build another. . . . For those in serious communes or political trenches, a continued fear of homosexuality may be the one last strand by which the male order can pull us back into tow. . . . It will be in these communes, or their less rigorous counterparts in female rediscovery, that we may learn to design new living arrangements which will make our co-existence with men in the future all the more equal and all the more humane.[6]

These writings, and publications such as *Voices from Women's Liberation,* coupled with gatherings in Maryland, Illinois, and New York (which included participation by the Daughters of Bilitis), spawned an independent women's network opposed to male supremacy. By 1969 a host of radical women's groups—far from united—had emerged, including: the prosexual, bedroom confrontational, consciousness-raising Redstockings; the karate-skilled, celibate-practicing, khaki-dressed Cell 16 feminist-separatists; and the Marxist-grounded, psychology-oriented Feminists, led by Louisiana-bred Ti-Grace Atkinson.[7]

As the seventies dawned, Julia Penelope was still laboring on her dissertation with little time to read the current best-sellers by radical feminists: *Sexual Politics, The Dialectic of Sex,* and *Sisterhood Is Powerful.* Although their authors—Kate Millet, Shulamith Firestone, and Robin Morgan—linked feminism with liberation from enforced heterosexuality, few feminists endorsed lesbianism, dismissed by Friedan as the "lavender menace" and ridiculed by the Redstockings as a "lavender herring." Liberals and politicos feared it would bring a dilution of women's energies, the loss of women's political credibility, and an affirmation of gender-based (butch-femme) roles.[8] But southern lesbians like Rita Mae Brown could not be silenced.

Like Julia and Merril, Brown was prey to Charley Johns. Attending the University of Florida, she was, in the words of her *Rubyfruit Jungle* heroine Molly Bolt, living in: "the bedpan of the South. . . . Scrub pines, Spanish moss, and blood clots of brick institutional buildings. . . . With its dull agricultural majors, grim business majors, and all the girls running around in trench coats with art history books tucked under their left armpits."[9]

As another expatriate southerner, in early 1970 Rita Mae walked out of the New York NOW office in protest of the leadership's homophobia. "Lesbian is the one word that can cause the Executive Committee a collective heart attack," she observed.[10]

On May Day, the first evening session of the second Congress to Unite Women was about to begin. The school auditorium went black. From the darkness the overflow crowd of three hundred women heard Amazonian yells, bewitched laughter, and the rustling of runners. As light vanquished the darkness, eyes refocused on stage center: two dozen brazen women modeled pink T-shirts reading "Lavender Menace." One lesbian declared, "We are being oppressed outside the movement and inside the movement by a sexist attitude."[11] Copies of the groundbreaking paper "The Woman-Identified Woman," coauthored by Brown, were passed around; clusters of women shared their bitterness late into the night.

This manifesto spread like wildfire within feminist and lesbian communities of the heart. Considered by many to be the definitive statement on lesbian-feminism, in part it read:

> As long as the label "dyke" can be used to frighten women into a less militant stand, keep her separate from her sisters, keep her from giving primacy to anything other than men and family—then to that extent she is controlled by the male culture. Until women see in each other the possibility of a primal commitment which includes sexual love, they will be denying themselves the love and value they readily accord to men.[12]

As President Richard Nixon promised an anxious electorate that "peace is at hand," Julia was dutifully completing her dissertation for her all-male committee. She also began to see lesbianism and women's issues in a new light. Chats among Left-leaning women students became intense "rambling conversations during a time that I still identified myself as a conservative" and still wore dresses and pantyhose. At her two-bedroom rented suburban house on Best Drive, these students "radicalized me!"

Discussing feminist books such as Germaine Greer's *The Female Eunuch* and Robin Morgan's *Sisterhood Is Powerful,* Julia resonated to Ti-Grace Atkinson's remark, delivered in a speech before the New York DOB Chapter: "Feminism is the theory; lesbianism is the practice." Atkinson—like the new *Ladder*—viewed feminism and lesbianism as intricately connected. Lesbians were to become the "shock troops" of women's struggle against men. Heterosexuals who experienced all but sexual intimacy with women were championed as "political lesbians," while those sexually involved with men were rebuked as "collaborators with the enemy."[13]

About this time a hippie-painted school bus rounded the suburban corners. As John (now known as Gabby) negotiated the turns and cul-de-sacs leading to Best Drive, Merril held J'aime on her lap. Her thoughts jumped from singing with Penny (now known as Julia) at the Onyx Room to wild New York weekends. Intertwined were images of campus purges in Florida and civil rights protests in Alabama.

Spending a week with Julia in Athens, Merril and Gabby experienced the South again for the first time since they had fled it nearly a decade before. "The South was completely crossed off my list of possibilities. Gabby and I had adopted a black baby; we knew that we didn't want to be *there* with all of that oppression." Merril continued, "Julia told us 'things are different here now.'"

Perhaps the times were changing. After all, it was in New York that three dozen people died from an air-and-ground assault by law enforcement officers at Attica and it was New York City's WNBC that banned "One Toke over the Line." Meanwhile, new-wave moderates such as Governor Jimmy Carter and Senator Ernest Hollings once again proclaimed a "New South." Yet, in Lamar, South Carolina, hundreds of whites mobbed a school bus carrying black students; in Mississippi, educational TV banned Sesame Street; and in Dade County, Jim Morrison was found guilty of indecent exposure following the Lizard King's near riotous rock concert, while God-fearing Floridians attended the "Concert for Decency" led by singer Anita Bryant.

Inspired by the relentless march of the movement, their minds expanded by LSD, Merril, Julia, and Gabby shared their dreams and doubts. The trio rapped until the early morning hours about the importance of returning to "the land." Here visions of intentional communities with experimental living arrangements would, like water in the Tao philosophy, wear down the power, patriarchy, and privilege of the System.

Julia recollects of this time: "I thought if they were going to do the back-to-the land thing that it would be easier in the South because of the climate and the cheap land—if they could stand the people; they weren't sure. Julia, elaborated Merril, "knew a bunch of students and a few women who had a collective house in Knoxville; Gabby figured through the lesbians he'd be able to meet the gay men."

But in Athens, with morning light, Julia had begun working on her first professional paper, and Merril had piloted the red-striped school bus toward New Mexico.

FIVE

Bobby's Story

It was 1969 and the whole world was at change. Old ideas and values were questioned. What was once important was no longer valid. Tradition was finally being broken. Guilt released, individuality praised. —Bobby

A streetwise youth–turned–*Harper's Bazaar* model continued scribbling in his spiral-bound journal: "The streets symbolized freedom. . . . There one could make a quick buck and meet almost anyone. After a long night's work usually ending around six in the morning the ladies and gentlemen of the night would meet at various clubs open till all hours of the morning. My favorite was the Down Under. Here decadence ran rampant."[1]

At this West Hollywood bar in 1969, the music played loud, as drag queens, drug dealers, and pimps mixed freely. "Back in those days to make money and party was enough for me. . . . Like most runaways my childhood was one of misunderstandings, unhappiness, rebellion, and the lack of love. Later I was to learn that love was there all the time—only I just couldn't seem to see or feel it."

Bobby was born Robert Logan Finney in 1954 in Daytona. His dancer mother, Shirley, ended her life three months later, and her mother, Bess,

The teenage Logan. Photo courtesy of Jack Nichols.

41

took custody of Bobby and his older brother, Frankie. A short time later, Bess's second husband (seeking "more out of life" than raising two grandchildren) walked out.

With little education, forty-five-year-old Bess completed beauty school. The boys, along with her older daughters from a prior marriage, lived briefly in a Tampa housing project. Between caring for the children and working in a local beauty parlor, Bess tried her luck on the dating scene. One longtime boyfriend, Vernon, an alcoholic, terrorized her family. Howard, another beau, was more of a family man.

Bobby remembers one late night when a jealous Vernon walked up their driveway: "He spotted Bess and Howard together parked in his Cadillac. Vernon was drunk as usual. He pulled out his gun. Howard shot him dead on the spot. When all was said and done, everyone knew Howard had done the right thing."

The tough-minded Howard married Bess and adopted the two boys. "Frankie was delighted, myself suspicious," Bobby details. "By this time I was bed-wetting, stuttering, and waking up each night with yellow and orange nightmares."

Despite a more stable home setting, school life remained difficult. Bobby repeated grades and was barely able to write by the fifth grade. At age eleven, he was "electrified" when a goddess appeared on the family's Sylvania black-and-white TV. Less impressed, his teacher "sent unforgivable notes home to my parents saying, 'This child won't study his history. This child won't study his arithmetic. This child is in love with Marilyn Monroe!'"

Bobby latched his dreams to a Hollywood star. In the seventh grade, "dancing away homework, skipping classes, and being gay," his goals were simple: "leave Tampa, become famous (exactly in that order). But how?"

Convincing and conniving, Bobby talked a friend into "borrowing" his grandmother's car—along with her rainy-day money, credit cards, and a dress. Before leaving, the barely teenage runaways first set out to "prove ourselves." They dropped into a local nightspot in full drag, lip-syncing to the Supremes.

As dawn's light glimmered over Tampa Bay, the pair headed West, crossing Louisiana and rambling through the Texas lowlands. Hollywood bound, the gay yearling had yet to learn that his search for love would exact a heavy price: "I knew I would have no trouble at all. I would simply check out the town, find the local chicken bars and a tall, dark, handsome, rich man—perhaps even a movie star. I didn't care just as long as he would take me in his arms and his bank and sing 'Our Love Is Here to Stay.'"

Ron was one of those men:

> He took me home to his moderate apartment. . . . He was a simple sort of man, nice, warm, and gentle. We made love that first night. I hadn't experienced the gentleness he expressed. That same night I moved in.
>
> Time passed quickly. We were out at the bars every night, socializing with everyone. I was his new-found joy in life and he mine. I was very happy for about six months. Then, suddenly, we were up and living in Burbank!

For a "newlywed runaway destined for the bright lights of Hollywood," this was a tragic turn of events. Fortunately, Halloween—Bobby's favorite holiday—had nearly arrived. Meeting Virginia, Ron's friend, Bobby entered his first drag ball. As he eyed the fifty-year-old dyeing her hair to match her gowns, memories of "weekends on end playing with a doll my great-grandmother gave to me" surfaced. "I loved the dresses she would hand-make for the doll. How I would hold this doll on my legs and watch it dance. I hated Sunday evenings saying goodbye to Granny and my secret dolls."

Bobby began spending long weekends at Virginia's duplex. The curious and attentive understudy watched her "dress in wild fashions, brightly colored costumes of yellow, purple, and orange. Feathers were draped around her neck. Rhinestone earrings, painted nails."

On All Hallow's Eve, Bobby was "escorted into a large walk-in closet containing more hats, wigs, gowns, and costume jewelry than even Zsa Zsa Gabor herself would have been pleased to own." He chose a black evening sequined dress with an overlaid cape trimmed in black ostrich feathers. "I can still feel the sensation as Virginia applied my make-up, lashes, and a platinum blonde wig."

Cinderella-like, he entered the ball eyeing the more seasoned contestants. "There was every kind of costume imaginable. Every color and design under the rainbow, each one hoping to be crowned Miss Gino's." At the end of the show, the contestants lined up as audience applause determined the winner. The loudest roar went to Bobby, who walked off the stage holding a plastic pumpkin stuffed with fifty one-dollar bills.

After a few more months of overspending Ron's credit cards, Bobby tired of "quiet evenings at home with TV dinners." With only "the clothes on my back and my finger out," he returned to Hollywood. Fifteen-year-old Bobby Carter sauntered from Sunset Boulevard to "the corner." "Hollywood and Vine . . . had tarnished into the likes of hustlers, pimps, and—yes—drag queens. Having no money and no housing for young runaways left two options: call home or hustle. I chose the latter."

He happened upon a cheap hotel whose lobby betrayed its former grandeur, despite peeling paint and trash. Bobby soon settled into a room with a small bed and an antique birdless birdcage.

> A red light hung from the ceiling. The walls were covered with posters of black-and-white gods and goddesses of movies: Brigitte Bardot clad in black leather; Marlon Brando riding a motorcycle; and, oh yes, Marilyn Monroe from *River of No Return.* Many nights I would lay in this room, my legs spread high toward the ceiling allowing whomever entering my body without a care of who they were. By now it had become routine; the sooner it was over the quicker they'd get out.

Meanwhile, Bobby kept his eye out for a more permanent living arrangement. "From experience, I knew looking as innocent as possible was a sure 'in' for a crash pad." Walking past Grauman's Chinese Theater and the Wax Museum one evening, Bobby spotted an out-of-the-way coffee shop with flashing neon lights. "As it turned out it was the infamous Gold Cup—a well-known pick-up spot."

As he hung around outside, "it wasn't long before my meal ticket came along." Bobby remembers him as "a man of about forty, short, very thin. He wore a funny, checkered hat. I was soon to learn this was the notorious Eddie the Hat."

Eddie's penchant was boys aged sixteen and under. After giving them a place to stay and handing them a few bucks, he discarded them at whim. Bobby lived with him for two months.

> His house was old, dusty, and dark. He slept in the back bedroom. The front bedroom was already occupied by another young boy. I was given a closet that had been converted so a small mattress could lie on the floor. I felt safe from the outside—that is until the Hat would come home most always drunk and insist on climbing on top of me. I remember the smell of whiskey, the pawing, and the insistence. All I could think of was please let this man pass out or get it over as soon as possible.

Soon Bobby became a "pass-around" from friend to friend—"all of whom expected a quick fuck or blow job." On one late weekend night, the Hat drove him to Beverly Hills to a mansion. Bobby remained sitting, staring out the window.

"Get out," Eddie mumbled.

"I opened the car door, stepped out, and with a quick goodbye he was off. As I made my way up the steps to the grand house I wondered what was to be expected of me this time. How had I come to this point?" An overweight fiftyish-looking gentleman answered the door. "Welcome, I'm so glad you came." He beamed. "We're going to have lots of fun."

Entering the house the uneasiness I felt was only increased by the crooked smile on his face. I was led past the orgy of about five young men all willing to provide service for a hope that maybe they would be able to leave with a little cash in hand. I was taken through a large room down stairs into a billiard room. Satin drapes were drawn to reveal a large velvet painting of a stylized Playboy bunny with beautiful blonde hair, large breasts, and a penis the size of a rolling pin.

As the gentleman grinned broadly, Bobby felt "as if I was about to be attacked by the Great Cheshire Cat."

"Why do you think you're here?" the crooked-smile man asked. Before Bobby could respond, he bellowed: "You're just a fuck! If you don't, I'll call Eddie the Hat. You'll be back on the street."

Angry to the point of tears, Bobby erupted. "Leave me the fuck alone! I am a minor and I'll call the police."

Quickly hustled back to Eddie's house, Bobby gazed into the emptiness of his bedroom closet, reflecting on "the danger of living on the streets and selling what little identity I had." With no exit, he returned to life on the Strip, its unending one-night stands, meaningless words of affection, and fleeting refuge at nameless houses with warm water and soon-to-be soiled beds.

There were two avenues open. One was Salma Street, which was mostly patronized by young seemingly macho studs, the other, Hollywood Boulevard. The latter was the more colorful of the two. Here, young men dressed in brightly colored skirts, high heels, wigs, and make-up applied so expertly that even Max Factor would have been proud. These young men seemed to know exactly what they wanted and took on an attitude of "Don't fuck with me unless you've got the cash."

Fascinated, Bobby hung around these working girls. He was taken in by Diana, who lived two blocks off Hollywood Boulevard with an older, happy-go-lucky man. "I would sit for hours watching while Diana would carefully apply her makeup, then her dress, brushing her hair out; slowly she took on another personality."

One night Marilyn Monroe appeared to Bobby. In his dream, "she said, 'Little boy, would you like to be a star like me?' And I answered, 'Yes, Monroe, desperately.'" A few days later, Diana announced that Bobby was ready for his debut. "She carefully chose a simple beige backless mini-dress, open-toed pumps. Diana instructed me to wear as little makeup as possible in order to keep the young Cover Girl look."

One last check in the mirror and Bobby went out for his first night's work in drag:

All along Hollywood Boulevard cars cruised around and around, slowly pulling up to the curb to choose just the right high-heeled man. My Cover Girl look was the hit of the boulevard!

"Hi! My name is Bobby and I'm a man. You're not with the vice, are you?"

"Of course not," they'd say. After these formalities I'd hop in the car, turn to face the driver and with my sexiest voice ask, "What can I offer you? Wha'dja got in mind?"

"Blow jobs? Twenty. A fuck will cost you fifty."

Young, old, fat, thin—it didn't matter to me, just as long as my money was paid up front. Over the next few months I learned to work the streets as if I owned them. . . . Money was easy come, easy go.

Sometimes Bobby spent a night off at one of the many Santa Monica Boulevard bars, which he remembers as

a fairly small bar with pool tables in the back. All along the sides were railings for leaning against and for cruising and drinking beer. I was dressed in my studded jeans, T-shirt, and black cowboy boots. From across the room I saw the most beautiful woman I'd ever seen. She was wearing a black mid-calf skirt, black lace-up corset top, a long red scarf wrapped around her neck. She had skin like a porcelain china doll, coal black hair that reminded me of Hedy Lamarr. The beauty of this woman was irresistible to me; she knew it. Everyone in the bar knew it. As she walked slowly over to where I was standing, my heart began to pound. What do I say? How do I act?

She lowered her dark sunglasses and, with a smile, said: "I'm an actress, but don't tell anyone. My name's Sonya. Would you like to take a drive in my Maserati? Maybe come up to my apartment in Laurel Canyon?"

"Let's go!"

As they wound their way through the canyon, Bobby pondered his heterosexual inexperience. Sonya's one-room apartment was sensual: "Soft candles were lit and pastel chiffon scarves were draped over the large satin-covered bed. She offered me a drink and excused herself."

Bobby waited nervously on her bed until the door opened. She stood there in a black and gold kimono, smiled and walked over to the turntable to play the Stones' newest album, *Brown Sugar.*

She stepped catlike toward him. Bobby laid his drink on the bedside table. Her kimono dropped to the floor.

Lying by my side she slowly undressed me. We embraced each other gently, slowly, exploring each other's bodies. As we made love, all inhibitions faded. I felt nothing existed except us. . . . Before the night was over we had fallen in love without speaking as much as a word. "Wild

Horses" played in the background, "Sister Marlene," and her favorite, Leonard Cohen's "Susanne." In the morning we sipped herbal tea and talked about her career as an actress.

Bobby told her he was a gay sixteen-year-old. "I had never made love to a woman, yet it seemed the most natural communion I'd ever experienced." Bobby moved in the next week.

The couple was inseparable. Sonya insisted that Bobby attend Hollywood High while she worked at the Twentieth Century Fox sound stages. Sometimes he'd join her at the studio sets for *Hogan's Heroes, The Brady Bunch,* or *The Love Boat.*

As days passed into weeks Bobby's interest in Sonya and school dampened. Cutting classes one afternoon, he was "shooting the breeze" with other kids at a fast-food restaurant across the street. "What I really wanted was to meet a man. My relationship with Sonya had been fulfilling, but something was missing."

As Bobby sat at one of the outside tables, "a beautiful man, tall with long brown hair and blue eyes appeared." Looking squarely at the youthful teen, he asked: "Is school over?"

"No. I'm skipping classes and haven't got anything to do. How about you?"

"Same here. How about taking a ride up to my place?"

Two years had now passed since Bobby's Hollywood arrival. "I was living on Easy Street on the wrong side of the tracks." Although the tricks kept coming (and going), Bobby's outlook had shifted since making his first twenty dollars: "Selling my body simply wasn't enough. Gone were the days of laying back and watching the wristwatch tick ten, twenty, thirty minutes. Time's up! "Goodbye, it was nice," or "You were wonderful. Hope to see you again." What was once easy money had turned into a no-way-out situation.

But one night in 1971 his situation changed. Booked on prostitution charges, Bobby fled to Tampa the next day, where "I resumed the only profession I knew. The main area of town for this line of work was centered downtown at the Federal Building. Cars would drive 'round and 'round until all hours of the night, each driver hoping for the best pickup on the block."

While on the streets, Bobby learned about an underage juice bar that featured weekend drag shows, the Horny Bull.

On a late summer night in 1971 Bobby Carter walked off the street and into drag legend.

SIX

Prometheus and the Tumblebugs

Until we are portrayed in all the media as we truly are and elevate ourselves, as the black man has out of the step 'n fetch class into the Sidney Poitier class, we will have accomplished nothing!

—*Rita, 1969 NACHO Conference*

Tape measures and pencils crowd her pockets. Tools hang over her left shoulder. Rita Wanstrom trudges upstairs. It had been one of Houston's insufferable summer days when even the hardiest workers found themselves frequenting the five-gallon bucket of ice and lemons. But the gang of RW Construction Company had hung in—including Peaches, wearing his purple rhinestone-studded hardhat, Tara with her short-cropped hair, and Loupy with his fluffed hair and overlong fingernails.

Inside the apartment, Rita kicks off her boots and rests for a spell. Rita's story wasn't that different from those of other Lone Star lesbians: a little girl with curls reading by candlelight in a medical book about unnatural romances; Tillman Bond, the "town queer," walking down the street in his neatly pressed slacks, jacket, and shirt; making teen love with her childhood sweetheart, Millie; Ricci performing at the Ace of Clubs; Texas troopers busting Rita and twelve others on "suspicion of being a homosexual."

Ricci and Rita at the Roaring Sixties. Photo courtesy of Rita Wanstrom.

Rita awakens as Ricci gently removes her pocket tools. "It's okay, Poppa Bear. Just go back to sleep. I'll set up for tonight's crowd."

Rita had been setting up and serving drinks at the Roaring Sixties for three years. It had become a "family" operation. Peaches, who was known for his flawless interpretation of "My Way," choreographed the drag queens. Leo, who could rise from alto to soprano in a single refrain, bartended. And Ricci, who flawlessly stripped and held court while Rita greeted guests beneath her oil portrait.

Known as the homosexual playground of the South, Houston was already home to a dozen gay bars and clubs when the Roaring Sixties opened on 23 June 1967. Unlike Mafia-controlled bars of many northern cities, gay clubs in "Space City" were often owned by straight women. There was Effie's Pink Elephant (which had been around since the forties), catering to older gay men; Verlon's Surf Lounge; the Round Table on Westheimer, owned by Dorothy; Rocky's, a hole-in-the-wall working-class club on West Dallas; and the Desert Room, whose famed Sunday afternoon tea dances were guarded by Hazel with a watchful eye for the police and an agile thumb set to flicker the lights.

With its checkered tablecloths, crimson drapes, and ruby walls, the Roaring Sixties was a place that a lot of folks called home. The mostly lesbian regulars quickly pass the billiard table (the site of many a pool tournament) and walk up a pair of steps to the twenty-two-foot L-shaped bar. Chatting with Leo, they perch themselves on metal barstools overlooking a huge dance floor with a sunken bandstand area off to the side. At the bar, Ricci Cortez hosts in a style reminiscent of the legendary New Orleans matron Dixie Fasnacht. On the stage, she performs in the tradition of her mentors, Gypsy Rose Lee and Sally Rand. In her signature act, "Sleepy Time Gal," Ricci holds a candle, wears a nightcap, and dons a robe—briefly. She works the crowd as a live band plays "Harlem Nocturne" and "So Rare."

Rita's long-term relationship with Ricci was a welcome follow-up to her four failed marriages. A 1942 elopement with Henry on the heels of Rita's one-night affair with Millie quickly ended in an annulment. Much of Rita's five years with her Italian husband, Chris, was spent in their New York eighteen-room home or the family's summer compound in New Jersey, overseen by her mother-in-law, Ulina. Her third marriage, to Al, began with a sunrise wedding and resulted in the birth of her only child, Stephan. Fourteen months later it ended in a bitter divorce. Rita soon hitched up with Maurice, eighteen years her senior, who "thought I'd hung the moon and the whole nine yards." Six months later he hired a detective to trail her. "I wrote his ass off. I would not be around anybody who doesn't trust me."

Amidst the romance and angst of heterosexual life, Rita sensed something missing. "I had fought being gay," she confessed. "I knew I was gay in junior high school but I thought that was something that all little girls did." Finally, "after four marriages and one or two affairs, I found out that I was a woman and that it was another woman who made me love."

It was a summer weekend night in 1951 when this femme blond of twenty-six was escorted "like a queen" to Dallas's Ace of Clubs. When "the floor show began a beautiful woman came out with a blue-sequin, fish-tail dress"—Ricci. After she finished dancing, Ricci sauntered over to the couple's table. Later she introduced her "close friend," Marion, a bleached platinum blond in a white tuxedo. Since Marion was returning to Houston and Rita's boyfriend was going out of town, Rita and Ricci agreed to shop the next day. "I was scared shitless. But when we were done she didn't even invite me in for a cup of coffee!"

In between flawed marriages and fleeting affairs, Rita had journeyed through various occupational incarnations. She operated Dallas's first private club with wide-open gambling, which was packed by aircraft workers after their early morning shift. For a year Rita had taught dancing at Fred McQurne Studios—drawing on a talent she had discovered with her father at the weekly Slavonic Benevolent Association's socials.

When not struggling with marital life, Rita lived near her parents' Bell County, Texas, ranch. Her mother's father had come to Texas about 1910 with ninety cents in his pocket and six children in a wagon. Soon he owned the first electric cotton gin in the state.

The morning of 9 July 1957 was much like any other. Rita was tending bar as her parents began the 230-mile drive from their Bell County home to Lake Travis with fast-talking Billy Boy, the family parakeet, in the back seat: "I was putting money in the register and this guy walks in. Never seen him before. He sits at the bar. I give him a beer and his change. As I turn around he says: 'I just saw a horrible wreck.' I said, 'Really?' Just making conversation. 'Yeah, two people were killed at least.' I glanced at the clock. It came over me that my mother and father had enough time to drive their car to that location."

Her intuition was confirmed. As Rita's father had headed down Highway 81, a cloud of dust from a grading truck blinded him. His car crossed over the center line, and his headlight caught that of an eastbound car full of Chicago travelers returning from a long July Fourth vacation.

Following her parents' deaths, Rita moved to Houston and took a job at Baylor University's College of Medicine. Heart research was the "only thing that saved my sanity. I was in a state of shock for two years. I believe to this day that my mother sent this guy to tell me."

The year 1957 was also an eventful one for seventeen-year-old Ray Hill, who would eventually join with Rita in forming Houston's first homophile organization. "My ancestors came here as fugitives from the law," cackles Ray, "just like Jim Bowie and Davy Crockett." By the turn of the century, however, grandfather Orsamus Hill was an East Texas politician who frequently resolved family or business quarrels and was active in the Grange. Ray's maternal grandfather, William Taylor, shared a shack (and Ray suspects a bed) with a black man, John Campbell. While the two share-cropped together, they each raised a family, with William siring twenty-one children.

Houston, Ray observes, "is a convergence of the Trinity and Brazos Rivers. People, ideas, and money all come from the same place as the water." Starved off the farm during the Great Depression, Ray's family migrated to the industrial part of Harris County. His father, Raymond, started as a janitor for oil baron Jessie Jones and worked his way up to building superintendent of the Gulf Building. Later he helped organize the community's water and sewage system and sat on the local board. Frankie, Ray's mother, was a Roosevelt Democrat. During the war she was a blacksmith at Fort Houston Iron Works, producing shell casings. Later Frankie organized nurses for the Teamsters.

The biggest influence on Ray's sexual identity, though, was the Galena High School librarian: "Miss Agnew was a club-footed old maid. One day I came in. She had wrapped a book in a brown paper sack with a rubber band around it. 'Raymond, I want you to read this. I got this especially for you.' It was a collection of Walt Whitman's more suggestive poems. When I got home, I realized I needed it. Of course, not another word was ever said."

When not roaming the neighborhood with his German Shepherd, Queen, the tow-headed teenager would go with other guys—one at a time—to the Market Street Drive-in Theater. "We would roll up all the windows. Soon you couldn't see in at all!" Two years later, Ray came out to his parents.

Frankie remembers that spring day in 1957 when she sat with her son at the kitchen table. Her "immediate reaction was relief, because I had noticed how he tended to wear coats and ties and dress as to appear to be wealthier than we were. I thought that meant he was going to grow up to be a Republican!"

After some discussion, Ray's parents decided that he should visit a psychiatrist. In their rusty red Studebaker pick-up, the family drove to the Medical Center. Ray remembers walking into the book-lined office of Lovell B. Crain. The distinguished doctor stared up from his notes:

"You're a nice-looking man. What's your problem?"
"I'm a homosexual."
"Well, the way you answer it, it doesn't seem to bother you a lot."
"It don't bother me at all, sir. But my parents are worried about it."
"I don't have time to waste my energy on people who don't have problems. Send in your parents. They're the one with the problem."

During the next few years Ray experienced life. The naïveté of an East Texas boy turned into the sanguine skepticism of a student radical. While living in New Orleans, for example, he learned the hidden history of homosexuals from two Tulane professors, William S. Woods and Haley Thomas, who had been lovers since World War I. In the midsixties Hill traveled to New York and hung around Columbia University, soaking up socialism from lecturers like Salvador Allende and C. Wright Mills. As antiwar efforts increased, Ray became more militant, staffing a table of homosexual material at a student antiwar conference.

Meanwhile, in 1966 Rita, celebrating her third year with Ricci, opened the Roaring Sixties. "A lot of club owners back then said women couldn't come in if they didn't turn their pants around" or wear dresses, remembers Rita. Two months after her club's opening, Houston's vice squad came to visit. The officers entered around ten in the evening. Separating out the more butch-looking patrons, an Irish sergeant barked out commands. "You get over here. You get over there." Twenty-five lesbians were hauled to jail for wearing clothing of the opposite sex.[1] "The enforcement of the ordinance, of course, was directed only at those people perceived to be gay," underscores Rita. Used for police harassment and extortion, it was also a convenient excuse for some bar owners to restrict lesbians. "Everyone got mad," remembers Rita. "But what could you do?" Rita paid all of the twenty-five-dollar fines and hired an all-girl band, led by "little butch" Sandra, to "pump our business back up."

A month later there was another raid. As in Stonewall, something snapped. "I don't think the other bar owners could see what was happening," swears Rita. However, she "saw the need for someone to speak out on behalf of this community." It was an unjust law that "deprived me of my right to do business."

Wanstrom sought the help of Percy Foreman, whose legal fee matched his status as the preeminent lawyer of the Southwest. Foreman was willing to represent Rita when another raid befell her club. As Rita headed down to the Roaring Sixties that evening to rally folks, "I happened to see a little tumblebug. Now, a little tumblebug will just lay there until somebody turns it over and helps it back on its feet." And so, as the summer of 1967 receded into history, the Tumblebugs were born.

Selling sweatshirts, hosting benefits, and sponsoring drag shows, the dozen or so women who made up the Tumblebugs raised Foreman's $2,500 fee. Skip Arnold, from the Jewell Box Revue in Kansas City, performed as Miss Magnolia Calhoun with his trademark big floppy hat. Mr. Cleo, who performed throughout the South, did his celebrated "Dances that Differ," and Peaches sang her rendition of "My Way."

In challenging the city ordinance, Rita hoped to get "people to think for themselves about what was happening to us and what *we* needed to do to take the heat off." However, Houston had precious little of what might be called a "gay community."[2] Aside from the mostly straight-owned gay bars and the hundred or so "A-list" gay men who hosted the Diana Awards, a parody of the Oscars, there were mostly homosexual closeted individuals, some of whom displayed the southern fondness for eccentricity.

One Diana member operated the Four Seasons on Market Square. "He had a beautiful house on Choclafile Road with a swimming pool on the second floor and live peacocks running on all of these acres of land," discloses Rita. Four bungalows surrounded the house. Here, Rock Hudson and other closeted celebrities would come to party and bring their tricks. Another Houston character was "Bluebeard," who lived in a huge house on Westheimer. "He used to order his wine by the case—gallon jugs of $1.99 white wine," Rita recalls. "He would pour with this gorgeous, tall, green-tinted carafe." As an artist of Styrofoam, "he used to do all the window decorations and all of the backdrops for shows." Bluebeard also had the most extensive pornography collection in the Southwest, which he rented out to other people in the know. "When they raided him and confiscated his collection," Rita laughs, "he was so frightened that he moved to San Francisco!"

Few Houston homosexuals harbored any expectation of organized political activity. Wanstrom declares, "If we'd have had a parade down Westheimer in 1967, we would have been stoned." And many gay men, according to Hill, "saw other people in the community almost as enemies. There was a phenomenon called 'dropping a nickel on a sister.' You'd call someone's employer and tell that he was gay. He'd get fired and you'd make application for the job. We didn't like ourselves. We didn't like one another."

"We were," Rita says, "a lost people who needed to come together."

Two nights before New Year's Eve, fate intervened. Sergeant McMenney and his men of the vice squad rushed into the Sixties and found women "dressed in men's pants, men's shirts, and men's shoes."[3] Rita reminisces:

> They lined people up and started questioning. One woman who was asked her occupation said: "I'm a weenie peeler." That just broke everyone up. More cops came in and they made her repeat it: "What do you do?" It turned out that she worked in a meat factory and when the weenies came through she would peel one to make sure it was stuffed right. So they put all of the butches in the paddy wagon.

This time, though, things were different. There was a bevy of "not guilty" pleas. A shocked magistrate stared down at the Tumblebugs as their celebrated attorney asserted: "This will not be a test of the law. . . . It will be a test of the vice squad's concept of the law."[4]

At this time Ray Hill was managing the Plantation Club, a renovated chicken restaurant on West Gray frequented by mostly white men. He also ran a private after-hours club, the Upstairs. After midnight Ray hustled everyone out and reopened with a two-dollar cover that included free soft drinks, coffee, and popcorn. A "better mix" of men and women crowded the dance floor as the corner jukebox played bluesy tunes. Spontaneous jam sessions with local musicians, including Johnny Winters and Janis Joplin, added to the club's popularity.

One February night a film crew parked across West Gray, photographing people coming into and out of the bar. Ray learned that Channel 13 was preparing a film documentary entitled "Houston-Galveston: Sodom and Gomorrah." The next day Ray contacted an "old curmudgeon," Ray Miller, who hosted a late-night talk show on a competing television station. Before Channel 13's exposé was ready to air, "The Last Word" featured a discussion about homosexuality. Debating a Baptist minister, a psychiatrist, and an officer from the Juvenile Department, Hill ably challenged selected biblical readings, psychoanalytic dogma, and other "old chestnuts" like molestation and recruitment.

Rita Wanstrom saw the midnight show. She thought: "Here is somebody that has his mind in the right direction!" David Patterson, a youngster just arrived from Kansas, also caught the TV spectacle. Patterson had traveled throughout the country and was familiar with other bar scenes and nascent homophile groups, including Kansas City's all-male Phoenix Society for Individual Freedom. Organizationally minded, David thought: "Why not a gay organization in Houston?"

At Rita's invitation, Ray and David, who had visited Rita's bar earlier, met her at the Roaring Sixties. Combining their talents, they founded the

Promethean Society, christened after the god Prometheus, who brought fire and light to mortals. While David tailored the society's bylaws from his college fraternity's constitution, Rita worked within the judicial system, and Ray worked behind the scenes. Meanwhile, Foreman reminded the media of the ordinance's silliness, musing that he hoped "the trial would be held during the Houston Livestock Show and Rodeo."[5]

In 1968, Mayor Louie Welch frequented George Howgar's bar, the Red Room on Webster Street, with his political cronies, "before queer hours." Following some discussion, Ray was summoned to "come through the back door of City Hall and walk up three flights of stairs to the mayor's office." At the appointed hour, Ray remembers, he climbed the stairs, entered through the fire exit, and met with the mayor's assistant, Larry McKaskle, in a converted maid's closet. Ray wrenched from McKaskle a promise that City Hall would indeed "check into" the lesbian bar raids.

Wearing dresses and makeup, Rita and her "girls" appeared before Judge Raymond Judice. The cases against the eleven were dismissed due to the failure of the vice officers to appear. The sergeant announced that he "definitely intended" to refile charges and to continue to enforce the ordinance.[6] Inexplicably, however, he was transferred to the Narcotics Division. Rita affirms, "They never bothered us again!"

The Promethean Society, however, was less successful than the Tumblebugs in getting "ordinary gay people involved" for its less tangible and more long-term goals. The organizers, as David Patterson recollects, were met with indifference ("I can't come tonight, *Gunsmoke* is on"), and Hill admits there was an absence of continuity and planning among the leaders.

Neither the Tumblebugs nor the Promethean Society was the first gay Texas organization. In 1965, Phil Johnson had invited four friends to his Dallas single-story home for New Year's Eve. For years Phil had been following the progress of the fledgling homophile movement: "I kept praying, 'Dear God, send us a leader in Texas,' Well. I waited and I waited. After twelve years I said, 'Well, Lord. Here I am!'" With "the doors locked and the blinds drawn," the Circle of Friends became "a place for gay people to meet gay people other than a smoke-filled, noisy gay bar. We intended to enlarge this circle by bringing in friends—but *only* friends."

Like Houston, Dallas had a long queer history. There were well-established cruise areas, most notably the corner of Akard and Commerce Streets. A revolving Pegasus (known by locals as the "flying red horse") atop the twenty-nine-story Magnolia Petroleum Building guarded "Maggie's Corner." There was a gay boarding house—the never vacant "Lavender Single" house in the Oak Cliff area—as well as the downtown YMCA and bars like Tiffany's and Club Reno. The area also had its share of bar raids, police arrests, hustler murderers, and gay parties.[7]

Phil Johnson, the son of a mechanic who had aspired to Broadway, wanted the Circle of Friends to "give depth to the gay movement."[8] Unlike the politically oriented Promethean Society, the Circle's emphasis, however, was social. Activities in 1968, for example, included a Valentine Dinner and a July celebrity bash featuring Tallulah and Salome impersonators. There were also private parties where pictures of physique models were passed around.[9]

Although Rita was familiar with the Circle of Friends, "We didn't have that much contact. I was busy, running my business, organizing." More critically, Ray observes: "We were trying, without knowing how, to do a grass-roots organization. Whereas Dallas's approach was a private club effort."

Both organizations, however, were members of the North American Conference of Homophile Organizations (NACHO)—a loose confederation of mostly East/West Coast associations such as the Mattachine and Daughters of Bilitis groups that had formed in urban pockets since the midfifties. Representing the Circle of Friends, Phil had attended the 1967 New York conference. In August of 1968 Rita, along with Ray Hill, David Patterson, and others, traveled to Chicago to attend the fourth annual conference.

Wearing a conservative suit, high heels, earrings, and "the whole bit," Rita walked into the Trip Restaurant, which served as the conference site. One of the first people she spotted was Barbara Gittings sitting at a long table speaking with others. "She pulls out a pipe and starts smoking. This is something I had never seen!"

The Houston group met activists from throughout the country. Among the seventy-five delegates representing forty organizations were cigar-smoking Foster Gunnison, Jr.; the former government astronomer, Frank Kameny; Shirley Willer, a nurse who once called Chicago home; and the leader of the Student Homophile League at Columbia University, Bob Martin (a k a Stephen Donaldson). "It was a very worthwhile experience," remembers Rita, who was one of only a half-dozen women delegates among the 268 attending. The first thing Ray noticed "was that there was a hostile distrust between East Coast and West Coast," with only a smattering of delegates from the South, including "Ted Brownsword" from the Tidewater Homophile League of Norfolk.

One of the big issues at the five-day conference, chaired by Robert Cromey (the vicar of St. Aiden's Episcopal Church in San Francisco), was whether to adopt Kameny's resolution, "Gay Is Good."[10] Ray recollects the debating "that lasted for hours." The acrimony and factionalism that characterized these annual conferences were, in Ray's view, "a reflection of something really basic. Gay people didn't like themselves and didn't like or trust one another. Nobody fights more aggressively or with greater vengeance than little churches and small powerless organizations. After they get some semblance of power and some kind of organization that can influence policy then that work is too important to squabble over. But if you can't influence jack shit you spend your time screaming at one another."[11]

The Houston group also came with an agenda: moving the fifth conference to the Space City. "We thought it would be a real feather in our cap," Rita says. "We were going to show the people what we had, what was going on here, and what could be done." To attract delegate votes, she brought a sack full of pins labeled " '69 in Houston" and hosted cocktail parties at her hotel suite. "It was politics, honey!"

Ray, too, was wholeheartedly lobbying for the Houston site: "We needed something going on at home that had a national sound. You bring important people from out of town and the real profit is that it inspires local people. Having all those people coming would have made the Promethean Society seem much more important in the minds of Houstonians. Our growth and organizational development would have moved at a rapid pace." The Houston delegation's enthusiasm was contagious. When it came time to choose the next conference site, Houston was the uncontested choice, with Kansas City selected as a backup.

At the height of their conference success, Rita and Ray received a long-distance telephone call. The vice-president of Promethean had been picked up in the men's room of the Auditorium Hotel! Ray explains: "Where did you find tricks in those days? Toilets in the hotels and in the department stores—and Houston had two very notorious hotels on Texas Avenue: the Milby and the Auditorium. The Auditorium had a dime coin slot on the outside of the main door. It took some time fumbling to get inside. As a result you could hear people coming. You could get into some pretty compromising positions and still have time to recover."

While the arrest did not bother Ray, Rita was white-hot angry. When they returned to Houston, she recalls, "things went to pot." Although Promethean's vice-president resigned, differences between Wanstrom and Hill intensified. Ray remembers being "constantly in a power struggle," while Rita points toward Ray's pushy, blunt, and outspoken style.

In June 1969 Ray responded to an IRS audit. When he was supplying the checkbook requested by an agent to verify the sources for his income, a warehouse receipt fell onto the desk. Later FBI agents secured a search warrant and soon were cataloguing stolen property at his Memphis "hideaway."

It turned out that Ray Hill was funding antiwar and gay activities through a series of commercial jewel, antique, and art thefts. The self-described Robin Hood "stole primarily for the Glorious Cause, inasmuch as Scarlett O'Hara tossed her wedding ring into the basket of gold to keep the Yankees out of Atlanta."[12] As agents traced more stolen goods to Hill, one arrest led to the next and one bail bond followed another. Rita's patience waned, she says: "I did not want that stigma on the organization." She disassociated herself from the group, refusing to provide any more money. Struggling with his mounting legal problems, Ray also "disengaged" from the society. David Patterson recalls that "by that time the split had become so great that it just collapsed."

Given these tumultuous events, Marc Jeffers, NACHO's Midwest regional chairperson, diplomatically informed members that the 1969 conference had undergone "a sudden eleventh-hour change in plans" due to "difficulties encountered in getting things squared away" and would be moved from Houston to Kansas City.[13] Meanwhile, an exasperated Rita formed the state's first chartered homosexual organization, the Texas Homophile Educational Movement, hoping to contribute to "the education of the homosexual to live in the society that we live in." Within a year, though, the mostly female THEM had become "low-keyed, if it existed at all." Meanwhile, a cluster of gay, Republican-oriented Presbyterians who sought to mainstream the gay movement organized as Integrity.

Despite such setbacks, a new militancy was migrating South. Gay liberation fronts soon popped up in cities from Auburn to Austin, New Orleans to Louisville, Columbia to Richmond, Gainesville to Tallahassee. As NACHO pronounced that "1970 is the year of NEW MILITANCY and NEW ORGANIZATIONS in the movement,"[14] Ray Hill was sentenced to twenty-eight-year concurrent sentences.[15] As a chastened Robin Hood walked into the Diagnostic Unit for the Texas prisons on 2 November 1970, the four-square-mile area near downtown Houston—bounded by the Southwest Freeway, Allen Parkway, and Shepherd and Main Streets—had become "the Westheimer Colony," as police continued their policy of benign neglect.[16] And, as queer southern space expanded, lonely hunters like Rita Wanstrom would be upstaged by rubyfruit rebels.

Stonewall was coming South.

SEVEN

Sunflowers and Trash

We can no longer allow ourselves to be characterized as sordid, perverted freaks.
—Louisville Gay Liberation Front

In 1970, three days after the Fourth of July, twenty-five-year-old Tracy Knight walked into the Jefferson County Clerk's Office with thirty-nine-year-old Marjorie Ruth Jones, a lesbian mother of three. Although Kentucky's marriage statute did not specify the gender of the marriage partners, James Hallahan refused to issue the two women a license. Fearing that such an act would "lead to a breakdown in the sanctity of government," he warned that "it could spread all over the world!"[1] The county attorney upheld his decision. There could be nothing of value in a relationship between two women, said attorney Bruce Miller, who denounced it as "simply the pure pursuit of hedonistic and sexual pleasure."[2]

Two days later four lesbians and thirteen gay men crammed into a small pink-and-blue parlor in a three-room South Fourth Street apartment. Among those attending with Knight and Jones were two hairdressers, a shoe salesperson, a public accountant, and several students. As two young

Sunflower, vol. 2, no. 1. Photo courtesy of Roger Nelson.

men held each other timidly, most only gave first names. Someone offered the title "First Ladies of Gay Liberation" to Tracy and Marjorie. Although they declined the honor, they agreed to take their case to court, and the Gay Liberation Front of Louisville was formed.[3]

Although some River City homosexuals were familiar with the gay lib movement, most were simply angry at the "indignities" they suffered, the necessity to hide, or the lack of equality before the law. Later, this group welcomed Jim Fouratt and his band of GLF freedom riders from New York's 17th Street Collective. "It wasn't about one supergroup in New York leading everybody else," Fouratt pointed out later, "it was about forming a network together, dealing with the needs of the local communities."[4]

Of course New York GLFers failed to practice this art of networking, as was evident in their internal ideological disagreement and internecine quarrels with the Gay Activist Alliance.[5] Nevertheless, the principle of building on local needs and networking would be crucial for the gay freedom movement to succeed in Dixie. Local GLF groups in the South were the first of these post-Stonewall organizing efforts that would stretch well into the mideighties.

Louisville is a unique southern community. Its history of pro-Union sentiment, a sizeable Catholic presence from early German and Irish immigrants, and a liberal newspaper distinguish it as part of the Upper South. Yet expectations regarding social propriety, commitment to tradition, and allegiance to family have existed for nearly as long as the Ohio River has separated the Bluegrass State from its Yankee neighbors. Homosexuals who adhered to these social standards had been tolerated if not ignored for generations. Aside from the raucousness of Derby week or Halloween Eve, most led comfortably closeted lives. Ever since cruising in Cherokee Park was popularized in the teens and the first "mixed" bar, the Beau Brummel, opened during the Depression, homosexual harassment was rare and notoriety infrequent.[6]

Not surprisingly, then, the July marriage application and the publicity about a "front" for gay liberation shocked many old-time lesbians, who generally disdained "the L word." The generation preceding Tracy and Marjorie's had learned to conform to social mores and subordinate their well-being to men—straight or gay. During the fifties and early sixties they sometimes attended mixed parties like those held at an old Victorian home on Sixth Street, where late-night festivities climaxed with a drag show. Others preferred lavish parties hosted by a Glendale lesbian on River Road, where one could drink comfortably near the pool after checking one's clothes at the door.

The more athletic types met on the ball fields, while others preferred the bar scene. Favorite lesbian watering holes during this era were Jimmy's, across from Seagram's Distillery, and Aunt Nora's Tavern, located in a remote area of Jefferson County on Cane Run Road. Straight men drank in the front part of that tavern. On a "good night," though, several dozen lesbians were in the rear—behind a partition. As the juke-box played Johnny Mathis or Dinah Washington, they slow danced on the pinewood floor or held hands under the table. Sometimes a would-be beau roamed around. Such occasions just as often ended in a fight as an unwelcome dance.[7]

Like the rest of the South, Louisville was changing as the seventies began, with *All in the Family* on Channel 4 and the birth of the city's Gay Liberation Front. Most homosexuals, however, contented themselves with attending private parties or cruising Fourth Street between Oak and Park, with playing softball at Cherokee Park, and with frequenting the old Downtowner on Chestnut Street or the Falls City Businessmen's Association, a seedy hangout on Finzer between Shelby and Logan whose name disguised its true design.

Unwelcome notoriety continued throughout the summer and into the fall. GLF members protested a gay bar's antidrag policy and the visit of Vice President Spiro Agnew. Meanwhile Stuart Lyon, Tracy and Marjorie's attorney, prepared for trial, and gay libbers Lynn Pfuhl and Mike Randall initiated a gay studies course at the University of Louisville. As part of the Free University, this class of thirty-five students produced more publicity and an outcry among state legislators. With this controversy still simmering, anti-Agnew gay protestors unfurled a banner that read "Freaking Fag Revolutionaries Against Agnew." Some among the mostly heterosexual demonstrators marched to the chants of "Gay Power!"[8]

In frustration, plans were afoot to organize a homosexual group to counter GLF radicalism; no coterie of conservative activists, however, materialized. Nevertheless, a columnist for the *Cardinal,* the University of Louisville paper, captured the sentiments of many: "The current Gay Liberation movement has taken on a rather unfortunate tendency toward obnoxious loudness; their obstreperous protests grow tiresome, and are ultimately self-defeating."[9]

On 10 November, one of the first cases in the country to challenge the heterosexual marriage laws went to trial.[10] Circuit Judge Landon Schmid first objected to the beige silk pantsuit worn by Ms. Knight. Finding it "offensive to the court," he dictated: "She is a woman and she will dress as a woman in this court."

Despite the occasional catcalls from the dozen GLF members in the gallery, the two-hour trial proceeded when Ms. Knight returned, wearing a green dress. County attorney Miller feigned confusion as he questioned which of the two women was the "wife" or the "husband." He then argued that legislators had no intention of sanctioning same-sex marriages, stressing the potential harm that such unions would have on the children.

Stuart Lyon, representing the plaintiffs, claimed the clerk's action violated his clients' freedom to associate as guaranteed in the First Amendment. He called a local anthropology professor to testify on various African traditions of female marriage. Unimpressed, Judge Schmid summarily declared his court was only interested in "this culture." Tracy then testified that a state-sanctioned marriage would provide her "security." And Marjorie, citing the importance of two adults caring for her three children, proudly proclaimed, "I'm a lesbian and I'm very much in love with Tracy."[11]

As the couple awaited the court's ruling, a New York activists' paper, *Gay Power,* exhorted, "The Gay Lib movement does not need these kinds of tactics."[12] Regarding a front for gay liberation as a southern paradox, the article admonished readers: "[W]hen we start imitating meaningless, bad habits of our oppressors. . . . That isn't *our* liberation. That *isn't* the equality we want. And that *ain't* revolutionary."[13]

Judge Landon Schmid agreed. His judgment on 20 February 1971 declared: "We see no reason why we should condone and abet a spirit of what is accepted as perverted lust any more than we should condone and abet a spirit of thievery or chicanery."[14] In early March the couple announced their intention to pursue the case in the Kentucky Court of Appeals.

Meanwhile, as David Bowie toured America adorned with dresses, glitter, and orange hair, and as *All in the Family* premiered on the CBS network, the Gay Lib House opened on Louisville's East Side. The two-story rental, located in the Highlands neighborhood, served as a community center. Despite dealing with the "fanatic" landlady "who sent us religious tracts" and living in a place that was "crumbling slowly under our noses," the half dozen or so residents sought to reach into the community by operating a telephone "rap line" and providing a "crash pad" for those needing a night's shelter.[15]

By that fall, however, these activists were downplaying their radical image in their irregularly published newsletter, *Trash:* "Hello, Gay Lib again. Remember us? Listen just for a minute. Forget the label 'Gay Lib.' . . . Alright you might not agree with a lot that we're into. Fine. . . . Gay Lib is not fighting against *you.* We're fighting the man who fires us from our job because we're gay. . . . The man who says 'no' when we want to get married."[16]

Articulating a more conservative message, a lone lesbian among the GLF group appealed for involvement from the butch crowd: "I'll bet you women thought that role playing, seeing yourself as butch or femme wasn't accepted in Gay Liberation. And after seeing most of the women connected with the movement, all with their long (though sometimes beautiful) straight hair, I really can't blame you. . . . However, the idea behind Gay Lib isn't long hair and look alike. It's being yourself, whatever identity you affirm."[17]

These conciliatory overtures did not extend to "Lucy Law." From its inception, the gay house on Bonnycastle Avenue was close to the "warm and tender hearts of the Louisville Division of Police and all their invisible little helpers."[18] On 17 October there was a party that included alcohol and marijuana. Gin, a twenty-nine-year-old GLFer, arrived near midnight. She watched helplessly from her parked car a half block away as one of the city's largest drug busts went down. Like a scene in *Casablanca,* nearly a dozen uninvited police rushed in, "shocked" to find drugs in the house. Twenty-five partyers were charged with various misdemeanors and five booked on felony narcotic charges.

In the aftermath, a teen informant was hustled away to a Tennessee boarding school and, against the din of "wild shrieks" from the church lady, the Gay Lib House closed on 12 November.[19] Later those arrested found their charges reduced or sentences suspended, as Judge Neville Tucker determined that "it's a greater deterrent to have a suspended sentence hanging over your head."[20]

With their plans "fragmented," one leader admitted, "We failed to reach a majority of Louisville's homosexual community." Too, there had been "disagreements from within. Personality conflicts. Disputes over basic ideology. Problems of organization."[21] Yet despite the "fact that gay people are still afraid of one another," the Louisville GLF savored small victories: "There was a soldier who we helped obtain [an honorable] discharge because he was gay. There was a young boy from Elizabethtown who was scared and lonely in the middle of the night. . . . We brought people together and people became friends. A few of us aren't as lonely and isolated as once not too long ago."[22] The group promised its supporters and detractors: "We're regrouping behind the bushes, in dark alleys, in the trees. We are going to come back!"[23]

As scores of southern activists from Louisville to New Orleans organized, marched, and sometimes "regrouped," a Gay Liberation National

Conference was held in Austin. On 25 March 1971 more than two hundred (mostly) men attended the opening session at the First Unitarian Church.[24] Aside from endorsing the coming May Day protest in Washington and an unfulfilled pledge to set up a "national communications center," little organizational work was accomplished that weekend.

Nevertheless, by accident or design, the Gay Liberation Front avoided the error of early Mattachine leaders, who had demanded dues and deference from local chapters. GLF's anarchical structure allowed for home-grown fronts that varied ideologically and tactically. Some of these (Houston and New Orleans) articulated Marxist-Leninist rhetoric and engaged in revolutionary practice, while others (Atlanta and Charlotte) espoused a social liberalism, seeking to work within the system. As some campus chapters (Austin and Lexington) invested substantial energy in securing university recognition, others (Columbia and Auburn) never went much beyond loosely organized rap groups. Despite differences, these youthful, free-wheeling bands of southerners generally found themselves as much at odds with the older homosexual generation or divided by gender and ideology as troubled by police or rejected by college authorities.

In April 1970, two male lovers active in the Student Mobilization Committee distributed leaflets on the University of Texas campus announcing a gay lib meeting at the YMCA.[25] Given the absence of police harassment and the reasonably open bar scene, their major project was recognition as a college organization. After all, most of its twenty to fifty members were students, but they had been refused access to campus meeting space.

In a scene repeated across the nation's campuses, the process of recognition met with intolerance and ultimately litigation.[26] The university's president, perhaps mindful of the legislators' scorn following recognition of the short-lived Texas Student League for Responsible Sexual Freedom five years earlier, wrote that "the University is not lacking in concern for the plight of homosexuals, it provides psychiatric services."[27]

In contrast, University of Houston radicals "employed the tactics of orderly confrontation politics." Formed in early 1970, the chapter adopted an agenda that included dismantling the judicial system in favor of a "people's court," abolishing the nuclear family, and repudiating organized religion for its "genocide" on gays. Meeting every Tuesday night, the group hosted a Gay Pride Conference on a mid-June weekend in 1971.[28] State representatives promptly demanded an investigation of the use of state funds on "political activities."

Other chapters focused on providing services to fellow students with less emphasis on official university recognition or hosting university-based conferences. In February 1971, Julius Johnson circulated flyers around the University of Florida—the site of one of Charley Johns's homosexual purges fifteen years earlier. UF-GLF met every Wednesday evening at the Episcopal Student Center. Members participated in two radio talk shows, picketed an "astonished" police station in protest against a black man's beating, started a coffeehouse, and hosted consciousness-raising groups. By the next February, however, only the coffeehouse had survived fatigue, departures, and in-fighting.[29]

Louisvillian GLFers Ginny Shelton and Bruce Kraus moved to Lexington in the summer of 1971. On the University of Kentucky campus Kraus passed out matchbook invitations for a gay lib meeting. One of the people he met was Edwin Hackney, who had started an informal social group a year earlier. Hackney, a veteran civil rights and antiwar activist, attended the first meeting in a Student Union room sponsored by the Student Mobilization Coalition. Beginning with a handful of Lexington hippies, a few feminists, and several drag queens carrying switchblades, "We polarized quickly," remembers one of its first presidents. "There was always a lot of friction between the lesbians and the men."[30]

Nevertheless, during the group's four-year struggle for university recognition through the labyrinthine process of appeals and lawsuits, this group of "misfits and nerds,"[31] dopers and intellectuals, published a newsletter, *Gay Times,* sponsored potluck dinners and dances, and provided gay counseling services. But like most fledgling campus groups, time was not on the students' side and it finally collapsed, following a series of unsuccessful legal appeals and the refusal of its president to testify before a grand jury.

Other southern campuses, such as those in Columbia, Auburn, and Richmond, experienced less intense gay lib activity. However, there, too, were themes of police informants and recalcitrant administrators, gender and ideological splits, and disregard for less radical local lesbians and gay men.

In the mid-Carolina town of Columbia an "informal group of women and men" organized in 1970. Writing in the *Carolina Plain Dealer,* they were only "beginning to see our homosexuality in a radical context, attacking those who tell us we are wrong (or perverse, evil, sinful, queer, misguided, sick, psychotic) because we can love someone of our own sex."[32] The group, however, never went beyond informal meetings and soon disbanded after learning that "a close friend in the Movement here has been a State Law Enforcement Division agent for a year, assigned to do undercover work on dope and politics in the community and infiltrate 'the homosexual ring' at the University."[33]

University of Alabama students formed the Auburn Gay Liberation Front the following year. "No longer will we hide our identity and restrict ourselves to a 'ghetto' environment," the Front informed readers of the local underground newspaper, *Praxis*.[34] Instead, these low-key activists hung out at Peeps, a straight bar that catered to countercultural types.

Also in 1971, Richmond activists met regularly at an apartment in the 1100 block of Grove Street.[35] GLF "was more a movement . . . than an organization,"[36] recalled one of its founders, Ken Pedersen. The twenty-four-year-old Pedersen, sporting disheveled long hair and beard, was also a member of the Young Socialist Alliance. At his Fan District apartment, they rapped about sexual oppression and organized two successful dances. A key question, though, was unresolved: "Will lesbians and gay men work together?"[37]

Longtime Richmond resident "Alex T," who, in the "shadows of society" during the fifties and sixties, had cruised the local movie theaters and the YMCA and attended after-hour parties in some of the old row house apartments on Cary Street, remembers that these youngsters "created all kinds of new lifestyles that Richmond was not used to." Richmond, like most southern towns, was difficult to organize when even those frequenting bars such as Eton's "might tell you their first name, but no one would tell you their last name—except after months and months, then *maybe* you'd tell them your real name and where you really lived."[38]

As the "King of Camp Rock" released *The Rise and Fall of Ziggy Stardust*, 1972 ended with most GLF chapters in the South demoralized by agent provocateurs or informants, abandoned by chimerical activists, fractured by tactical disagreements, shunned by local homosexuals, or deserted by lesbian feminists. Despite their failings, they sparked a Stonewall awareness and generated the first positive local media coverage about homosexuality.[39]

In larger cities, notably Dallas, Atlanta, Houston, and Miami, off-campus groups had formed. The Sugar Plum Fairies challenged the coverage of the underground paper the *Dallas News,* decrying its Gay Pride issue as "misleading and actually detrimental to the cause of gay liberation."[40] While the Fairies mounted an assault on the underground press, some Dallas lesbians celebrated that Fourth of July in the usual manner with pool at the Highland Lounge and then off to the King of Clubs for a night's dancing. One older lesbian, affectionately known as "Devil," who had been in the city since the early fifties, expressed ambivalence about these changing times: "From no place to go, except jail, to too many places has caused the Dallas gay group to split into cliques and splinter groups. We no longer share that feeling of "togetherness" we had years ago."[41]

But small social cliques meeting covertly and united through fear, invisibility, and harassment were precisely what these new gay militants sought to change. And Atlanta became the first southern city to march out of the darkness and into the streets.[42] The 1971 event was sponsored by the newly *incorporated* Georgia Gay Liberation Front, founded by Bill Smith, an accountant for the Model Cities Program. On the morning of the twenty-fourth of June, a Sunday, a small group gathered in Atlanta's Midtown. As a few stepped off the corner, more joined with bongos, bells, war paint. A lavender "Gay Power" banner rose in the light breeze next to a placard, "Jimmy Carter Uses Hairspray." With no parade permit, the organizers were stopped by the police; the group continued once the authorities departed. As they entered Piedmont Park the hundred or so chanted with tambourines playing in the background. Guerilla theater actors propagandized—a soldier shoots a Vietnamese to prove his "straightMAN-hood"; homosexuals collapse hearing shouts of "queer" and "dyke," only to be resurrected as gay slogans overcome homophobic jeers.[43]

Although some chapters, like Louisville's, formed from women's struggles or, like New Orleans's, emerged from the canopy of feminist organizing, these early organizations were dominated by gays socialized as southern men. Internal conflict, however, defined the Georgia GLF. Women formed their own "cell," and Smith, running meetings by *Roberts Rules,* clashed with "Severin," who was particularly fond of a certain "black and white, high-necked whirled pattern" and attended meetings in "cosmic drag." The Severin faction left GLF and after a less than exciting 1973 march, GLF folded.[44] GLFers in the South also failed to reach out to homosexuals reticent to cross the rubyfruit threshold, to exchange rhinestones for placards, or to forsake the dance floor or softball diamond.

New Orleans, like Louisville, is a creature of the river. The Crescent City boasts a general tolerance for homosexuality within its famed French Quarter. Among the most notable establishments before Stonewall were Café Lafitte, forced to move from the Blacksmith Shop in 1953 (thus becoming Lafitte in Exile), the legendary Dixie's Bar of Music (operated by the "no nonsense *doyenne,*" Miss Dixie Fasnacht, and her sister Miss Irma, whose Dixieland band played their signature tune, "Miss Otis Regrets"), the Tiger Lounge on Tchoupitoulas Street (operated by Jo-Jo, a former nun), Regent's Row (with chandeliers and carpet), the Galley House (owned by Mary Collins, who occasionally swam across the Mississippi), and the Original Brady's (with an all-women's band, A.B.'s Children). At the Original

Brady's, no touching or same-sex dancing was allowed, and the short and tough Alice Brady "would put us out of the bar at 5:00 if we didn't have skirts on."[45] There was also the Goldenrod Inn—whose front area for straight men served as a cover for a back-room lesbian bar—where one Saturday night in 1953 forty-three women were booked for disturbing the peace and being "loud and boisterous."[46]

In addition to bar life there were long-established social clubs such as the secretive, all-male Steamboat Club, replete with poetry readings, and the Gourmet Club, organized by several lesbian couples hosting monthly dinners. There, too, were the exclusive social groups of Mardi Gras (the krewes). Members of gay krewes like Petronius, Apollo, and Armenius busied themselves throughout the year with fundraising and costume-making that climaxed in private balls and carnival fun.[47]

In the year of Stonewall and the Shaw trial, 167 arrests were made for "homosexual crimes," most of which were "crimes against nature"—a felony punishable with five years in the Angola state prison. Most Crescent City barflies were unaware of the emergence of gay liberation in New York. Late that year, though, the *Quarterite,* a short-lived independent monthly "magazine of the Neutral ground," included a "homosexual column." The "Queen's Tattler," authored by "Anon," reflected a Boys in the Band consciousness: "First and I think most important of all we want a fighting chance to prove that a homosexual is not, for the most part, a perverted sexual deviate or psychopath."[48]

Meanwhile, women like Mary Capps, Barbara Scott, Sandy Carp, Lynn Miller, and Suzanne Pharr were building the political foundations for a New Orleans lesbian-feminist community. Thirty-year-old Suzanne Pharr, a native of Northeast Georgia, returned in 1969 from two years in New Zealand to attend Tulane. She had taught about the first wave of feminism at a Virginia college during the midsixties. But she had "no real awareness of there being an organized women's movement since I had left right before things broke open."

Suzanne walked off her plane into the sultry air that settles around New Orleans's dog-days season and "basically stepped into the women's movement." As the decade's last summer ended, Pharr remembers, "everything was hopping. It was an incredibly exciting time. We were doing antiwar protests on campus. We were creating these beginning institutions around women. We were reading Ti-Grace Atkinson."

Just as inevitably as Mississippi waters flow into the Gulf, so the arrival of the women's movement was carried by a current of lesbianism. The National Organization for Women was starting a chapter, and

Suzanne joined. Along with Celeste Newboro and Gold Meier, Pharr moved into various leadership roles through the women's movement. Participating in an eight-member consciousness-raising group, she and others "were exploring our lives." They spent many sessions discussing life-altering experiences: entering puberty, competing against boys, understanding gender roles. "We addressed out of our own lives certain questions we made up. We had the fervent belief in the radical notion that we were the authority on our own lives."

By the second session Suzanne recognized that "I could not talk about my life unless I talked about *my* life." She shared her story of a "hot-shot basketball player" in a rural high school in love with a cheerleader while dating the captain of the football team without "any words or people to even make sense of being a lesbian." Pharr remembers, "I had absolute stark terror at the thought of saying out loud: 'I am a lesbian.' I had such terror about not being able to be in the classroom and be connected with my family and farming community. It was the most liberating moment in my life." As each member shared her life experience, "it changed people's lives." And the consciousness-raising cluster evolved into "mostly a lesbian group." Members connected the personal with the political, and they moved into community action. "We were flying by the seat of our pants. Just sort of creating things out of our own hands and not in a very organized manner." Suzanne explains, "You would pick up some underground newspaper and there would be an article about a women's collective in New York City. So I'd said, 'Wow! We should do that here.' The first thing you'd know six of us are living together."

Political groups blossomed in this sweltering climate for southern women. The Tulane Graduate Student Union was formed and, in the Quarter, Jan Kohler and Sandy Carp founded the Amazon Tribe. Suzanne Pharr edited *Distaff*, a literary magazine created by Barbara Scott, who had opened a women's bar. Feminist and lesbian programming appeared at the public library. There also was the Southern Female Rights Union, which mobilized female domestic help under the leadership of Roxanne Dunbar, and the Women's Marxist Studies Group, which brought together women from disparate ideologies. Feminists were in front of the convention hall doing Guerilla Theater.

This flurry of organizing on campus and in town "was very much linked," according to Pharr. Some of these groups coalesced with the long-standing local chapter of the Women's International League for Peace and Freedom. The Women's Liberation Coalition published a newsletter, *In Her Own Rite*. There was also great networking among groups at the

Women's Center. The Jackson Street center had a telephone hotline and sponsored various forums on issues ranging from violence to sexuality.

"There wasn't any difference between lesbian feminism and feminism. We were it!" asserts Suzanne. "The real analysis and work was us." This, though, was not a philosophy shared by Betty Friedan and the NOW national leadership, who fomented or encouraged lesbian purges in local chapters, including New Orleans.

Frustrated with her heterosexual sisters, Lynn Miller formed the nucleus of the New Orleans Gay Liberation Front in the fall of 1970. The group raised money with Sunday buffet dinners and dancing, in addition to issuing a newsletter. Soon they were speaking at college classes and giving workshops on lesbianism at the local YWCA.

Realizing there was no place for apologies or self-deprecation, Lynn branded the use of terms like "fairy," "queer," "dyke," and "fag" as "degrading." The twenty-six-year-old prophetically observed, "We will get over our 'guilt' feeling long before society accepts our innocence."[49]

Miller was joined in her efforts by two other coordinators: Dianne Kiesling and David Solomon, a Holiness Pentecostal minister. GLF-New Orleans sought to repeal the state's sodomy statute and to expose "personal incidents of injustice" against lesbians and gay men, often perpetuated by the sixteen-member vice squad. "Society itself is sick," Miller lectured a newspaper reporter, "when it's against the law to have sexual relationships with a living body but legal to screw a corpse or dead animal!"[50]

The Front also produced Louisiana's first gay publication. The premier issue of *Sunflower* followed a series of mid-January arrests in Cabrini Park, located on Barracks Street in the French Quarter. One of those arrested described his twilight park experience:

> It was a foggy night. . . . As the fog swirled, it revealed two men who seemed to be standing talking. Thinking that a twosome could become a threesome, I walked over towards them. I joined them near the back of the park. . . .
>
> I knew one of the men vaguely—I had met him quite a while ago. His name was John, he's an actor. The other man, who I found sort of attractive, turned out to be a cop. Neither John nor I knew that at the time, of course. It seems that he had been trying to talk John into a sex scene in the park, but John had been really unresponsive. . . .
>
> Now the cop was trying to arrange a scene between John and I. He walked off, saying that he would "stand as a lookout" for us. Far out! We hardly needed a lookout. I was trying to think how I would tell John that I wasn't attracted to him—didn't find him appealing. Finally, after I still hadn't said a word, I walked off. As I left the park, I passed by the cop,

who flashed his badge and put me under arrest. Then he went back in
and found John. . . .

Electric! The park was filled with scurrying cops. . . . All this time,
the cop radio has been crackling out directions from headquarters, but
the men weren't paying any attention. They didn't really know what they
were doing. When they arrest someone they become like mad dogs, particularly on evenings like this when their masculinity is to be proved.

Booked on a "crime against nature," this unfortunate man's fate was similar to that of the dozen others arrested that night who faced a $1,000 bond
and prison time.

GLF leaders mobilized. They announced a picket of City Hall with
typical hyperbole: "Over the years, we have watched as our brothers and
sisters were carted off to jail, beaten, and tortured. We have watched as
judges, politicians, and police extorted millions of dollars from fearful,
innocent Gay people. We have watched as agents of the Vice Squad broke
all the laws they were supposedly out to enforce. We have watched
silently. Now, we have had enough."[51]

Ten days after the arrests, the first gay rights demonstration in
Louisiana was held on a warm Saturday morning in 1971. Carefully
monitored by vice officers, some of the seventy-five protesters carried placards: "We're Not Freaks, We're Human," "Lesbians Are Lovable," and "We
Are Homosexuals and Proud." Front-page stories in the two daily papers
began with provocative leads: "Gay Liberation arrived today in New
Orleans," and "The Gay Liberation Front moved east from California and
south from New York Saturday."[52]

Following four days of noontime picketing, Lynn Miller and others
met with police chief Giarrusso. Demanding an immediate end to police
entrapment and harassment as well as an independent investigative panel
on police methods, the group received only vague promises to "check it
out." Later city officials told reporters that they did "not put much
stock in GLF complaints."[53]

At one of their regular Sunday afternoon Decatur Street meetings in
the Sphinx Coffee House, GLFers decided to bring a class action federal
suit against the city. Finding individuals willing to provide statements,
even with the assurance of privacy, proved difficult. In part, this was a
reflection of the timidity of homosexuals who for years had been Gar-
risoned by Big Jim's city attorneys. It also reflected a reluctance of professional or affluent homosexuals, like Clay Shaw and his friends, to
associate with "radicals."[54] Roger Nelson had moved to New Orleans with
his life partner, Jack, two years earlier from Rockford, Illinois, where the

two had operated a gay rooming house. Nelson remembers: "The folks in GLF were antagonists. They were stirring the shit. This has always been a very genteel city and suddenly here were these insurrectionists!"

The suit was later dropped due to the unwillingness of anyone to pursue litigation. This reluctance to expose themselves politically brought disappointment to GLF organizers and furthered a growing split between lesbians and gay activists. The final issue of *Sunflower* announced that future GLF meetings would be held separately for women and men: "This is not an attempt to be mutually exclusive but a chance to work out problems that are unique to each. When friendship and self-reliance are achieved among each group then integrated meetings will take place to share what we have learned. Then we can all move forward."[55]

As the last issue of *Sunflower* went to press and the newest gay krewe, Olympus, held its first ball at the St. Bernard Auditorium, the ghost relationships of homosexuals were less invisible in a city scarred by memories. As the sixties receded into a mist of myth and nostalgia so, too, did this apparition of activism, as an emerging gay "Me generation" heralded disco, drag, and drugs as the anthems of sexual liberation.

EIGHT

The Horny Bull

Now my dears, you can gossip in the lobby, but don't go out on the sidewalk.
The police are watching this joint!

—Ray Bourbon at intermission, Carnegie Hall

Bobby Carter found the block around Tampa's Federal Building no kinder than the "cold and hard" strip of Hollywood Boulevard. Although the star-signed sidewalk in front of Grauman's had lost none of its magic, he writes, "my destiny had once again brought me back to the town I had sought to escape so many years earlier. Time and time again I'd vowed secretly to leave behind the warm sunsets, cool evening breezes, and the tall palm trees. In my youth I would sit under the palms wondering all along at their contentment—simply being part of the universal flow of nature."[1]

Strutting to the ebb and flow of late-night cars driven by desire, Bobby's thoughts turned to the Horny Bull—an underage gay juice bar on Florida Avenue. The "block" promised no future. "My goal in 1971 was simple: to be seen in the local Florida gay rag—to be noticed." The following Thursday he marched into the bar and through a double-door

Logan Carter. Photo courtesy of Jack Nichols.

archway leading into the theater—and into drag stardom. He auditioned for the "Hot Tuna Review" along with another newcomer, Kim Ross.

On a mid-July Saturday night Bobby Carter came out from behind three mandarin red curtains as Roxanne Russell, a hurricane of feminine energy. Roxanne's hips swiveled and her hair tossed as she sang "My Heart Belongs to Daddy." "Oh! I loved working at the Horny Bull," Bobby reminisces. "It was the come and get it of Dragsville. It was as if I was at Twentieth Century Fox commissioned as a contract player."

Roxanne possessed a Dietrich-like presence that stunned audiences. Unpredictable on stage, she pranced on tables and sat on onlookers' laps while lip-syncing "Falling in Love Again" or "Diamonds Are a Girl's Best Friend." Sometimes she would even escort a member of the audience onto the stage to dance.

Another rising illusionist was captivated by Bobby's talent. Paul Wegman had learned the lore and lingerie of classic female impersonation from a Tampa trailer-park queen. In his judgment, Bobby would someday fall into an exclusive class of female illusionists that included Ray Bourbon, Charles Pierce, Gene Lamarr, and T. C. Jones: "He was one of those classic artists who took on a personality. A consummate lip-sync artist. He was a man who came to work as a man and put a woman on and then took it off and went home as a man. He belonged right in that company."

The nine adolescent Tuna Review performers were family—a dirt-poor southern family—with Paul as its twenty-four-year-old matriarch. "I was the mother hen to all the little chicks. But, I wasn't a Grand Dame—yet." Most, like Gilda Golden, Lady Gail, Kim Ross, Sandy Cher, and Eve Starr, stayed with Paul in a mammoth house near Hyde Park, an old neighborhood near Hillsboro Bay. "We were poor, poor children," Bobby remembers. "We thought, 'Put on new heels and that will make you a goddess.' So, there we were flaming and looking gorgeous but at home no electricity, no gas, nothing but a big pot of cold collard greens."

Most performed to Top 40 songs, paying homage to contemporary divas. Kim Ross lip-synced Diana Ross. Eve Star stood in for Melissa Manchester. Sandy Cher chose her name because she looked like the famed TV star and singer. Lady Gail, a "redneck boy" from Georgia, danced to country and western numbers.

Paul and Bobby were different. Paul admits, "I didn't fit in at all." Relying on Broadway shows to provide his concept numbers, he emulated singers "nobody ever heard of, like Barbara McNair doing 'I Love You More Today Than Yesterday' and 'I Capricorn'—a very mysterious song. I was doing Stephen Sondheim drag in the early seventies!" Meanwhile, Bobby was perfecting his Marilyn illusion while Roxanne pulsated to high-voltage audience response. "Most southern performers of the era," Paul recalls, "picked one or two stars to impersonate and then dressed and acted like them. Bobby more carefully studied every gesture and mannerism of his screen goddess."

Marilyn Monroe was Bobby's favorite character. "She had a luminous quality about her on the screen, and it's fun to portray that on the stage. I give that excitement that she created." Reflecting back on his Tampa boyhood, he adds: "It's the idea of the illusion. As a child I always watched movies and famous women. The idea of being able to escape whatever realities I wanted to escape could be done through female impersonation."

The Horny Bull had been open for little more than a year before Paul gathered this ensemble of would-be drag divas. "But," Paul offers, "they found out if they put on a show, people showed up!" Paul, like Bobby, modeled excellence. He fostered among his young performers "the mind-set that even if we're only going to do it on Friday and Saturday, and even if we're only going to get fifteen dollars, we are going to do the damn best we possibly can!"

Paul Wegman, soon to be known by admirers as "Miss P," had arrived from New York via the carnival. During the winter of 1965 he bought his first wig and paid a visit to Dick's 43 Club—a downtown Rochester "gay spot." He remembers, "Somebody recognized me and called my mom and dad to say they had seen me dressed as a woman. *She* took it in stride."

Paul and a transvestite friend, Chuckie, soon ran away to join the circus. He worked in the show's cafeteria while Chuckie, disguised as a woman, danced in the girls' show. "The nice thing about carnival life," Paul remembers fondly, "was that the people didn't care about your past. They accepted you if you could work and get along."

As the road show wound its way down the East Coast, Paul bunked with Bill, an older homosexual with an independent wagon teamed to the carnival. After playing their last week in Valdosta, Georgia, they headed to Gibsonton, Florida—a wintering ground for carnies just south of Tampa. Crossing the Hillsboro River on the Kennedy Boulevard Bridge, Bill turned to eighteen-year-old Paul: "You're a really nice kid and it's probably best now you call home, because I'm going back to my lover."

Wanting to leave his northern troubles behind but with just a buffalo nickel in his pocket, the lad with strawberry blond hair toted his suitcase to the Desoto Trailer Park. Put up by other carnies, Paul eventually got a job at a paint factory across town and rented his own trailer.

At Gibsonton Paul met Mr. Cleo, a petite man in his late fifties. Cleo had worked with some of the legendary female impersonators during the forties and fifties. Over drinks he regaled Paul with tales of drag queens—characterized by the Pop Factory's guru, Andy Warhol, as the "ambulatory archives of ideal movie-star womanhood."[2]

Under Cleo's tutelage, Paul learned the history as well as the art of the female illusionist: the traditional Kabuki dance; the famed diplomat and social celebrity Chavalier d'Eon; the turn-of-the-century acts of Karyl Norman (billed as the "Creole fashion plate," who sang southern songs, with his mother serving as his dresser) and Julian Eltinge, who earned upwards of $4,000 a week; minstrel show acts in which one of the two men, like "Honey Boy" Evans, was the "wench"; and, the most famous vaudeville variety team of the twenties, Savoy and Brennan.

Cleo also shared amusing southern anecdotes with this neophyte performer. There was the time, in 1925, when the legendary Francis Renault, who had performed at the Majestic Theater the night before, was arrested on a Dallas street for wearing female clothing on his way to Well's, where he was exhibiting his wardrobe in the department store's window. And there was Johnny Mangum, who, like Paul, began his career in the circus. Tired of sawdust and tent life, the fifteen-year-old Mangum had abandoned the road show past midnight in Union, South Carolina. Main Street was still soaked with the late evening rain when he was picked up by the police. Johnny spent the night in jail. Waking up to church bells the next morning, he began singing church hymns in his soprano voice. At first startled and then impressed, the sergeant on duty tossed a dollar bill in his hat and passed it around. Soon young Mangum had enough train money to leave the Palmetto State and begin his drag career.

And, of course, there were Cleo's seemingly endless digressions into the theatrical origins of the word "drag," ranging from a Shakespearean-era acronym ("DRess As Girl") to the petticoats worn by nineteenth-century male actors playing female roles. More important, Paul learned the lineage of female impressionism. "Cleo knew lots of people, including Tige Jones and Ray Bourbon, and had made clothes for them. She gave me that whole sense of history, like the Jewell Box and Club My-O-My."

Female impersonation, Paul discovered, ran the gamut from glamour drag to skag drag, from those who created characters to those who paid homage to divas, from those who used their own vocal chords to those who flawlessly mimed the voices of others, and those who displayed other talents ranging from strip-tease to ballet and interpretive dance.[3] Many of these were southerners or entertainers who routinely toured the South.

Francis David began his career in Dallas, toured Texas cities and then the Windy City in the late twenties. After returning to Dallas, he opened a costume shop (with the help of his mother) and designed costumes for the "society set." In Texas clubs and at the state fair, he performed authentic East Indian, Hawaiian, and Javanese dances in female attire, but he was best known for his "Dance of Salome."

T. C. Jones, who studied for the ministry in West Virginia, debuted on Leonard Silman's album *New Faces of 1956.* Noted for musical productions like "That Was No Lady," Tige had his wardrobe and his impressive wig collection overseen by his wife. He impersonated Tallulah Bankhead for mainstream audiences at the country's top night spots, such as New York's Le Cupidon and the Blue Angel, the Black Orchid in Chicago, and Miami's Jewell Box.

Among the few African American impersonators to gain notoriety were Elton Paris and Phil Black. Paris, a six-foot-four New Orleans native, began by playing USO shows. Celebrated for his falsetto voice, swing tunes, and dead-faced expressions, he performed at San Francisco's Beige Room and later Finochio's for years. Black began as a female illusionist in a show called "Shufflin' Sam," went in semidrag when he hosted Phil Black's Harlem Ball, and later performed at D.C. clubs in self-made gowns that accented his two-hundred-pound frame. There was also a scattering of Latinos, such as Pepper Cortez, billed as the "Mexican Spit Fire with the million dollar legs," and Lynn Lopez, "the blond bombshell of dance," who also worked the carnival girl shows.

Then there was Charles Pierce, who preferred to be called a "male actress." Discovering that audiences preferred impersonators who overacted, he interspersed witty repartee with campy portrayals of screen goddesses from the thirties and forties. Pierce played venues throughout the world and also toured the South, appearing in places like Dallas's Majestic Theater and Miami Beach's Onyx Room. Best known for a comic pastiche of famous women, Pierce affectionately lampooned Mae West, Bette Davis, Gloria Swanson, Katharine Hepburn, and Eleanor Roosevelt with infamous one-liners. As Hepburn in *The African Queen* he picked leeches off Bogart's body, murmuring: "He loves me, he loves me not, he loves me, he loves me not." He sometimes finished the show with a Gloria Swanson impersonation from *Sunset Boulevard,* in which Pierce mimed her famous line as the washed-up movie queen, Norma Desmond: "I'm ready for my close-up, Mr. DeMille." Abruptly the house lights would darken, followed by a lone spotlight aimed between Pierce's legs. Other times he ended his performance with a line from the play *Home:* "If a person can't be what they are, what's the point of being anyone at all?"

Paul saw a bit of himself in this male actress: "Charles Pierce couldn't have possibly lasted as long as he did if there hadn't been some sort of intellectual challenge along with what he was doing. He challenged you to see and hear the person he was emulating and to understand the jokes he was making about those people."

But the grande dame of female impersonators was Texas-born Ray Bourbon. His career spanned five decades and included performances for the queen of England and with Mae West. Yet, as Roxanne was walking through the mandarin red curtains and into drag legend, Bourbon made his final curtain call in a Brownwood, Texas, jail.

Once tried in Beverly Hills for impersonating a woman and later arrested in Miami Beach for impersonating a man, Bourbon performed comic drag with songs on his seven albums, including *Queen of the YMCA*. His humor laced with sexual innuendo, though, had gone out of fashion with the sixties sexual revolution and Stonewall activism. His luck, too, ran out—on a Texas highway traveling south to Ciudad Juarez for a desperately needed booking. Pulling a trailer with his seventy-one dogs and cats along with a pair of skunks, his car caught fire. The pets were saved only by the heroics of a brawny trucker hauling tree-spray.

Bourbon boarded them at a kennel for fifty dollars a day, and when he finally raised enough money to redeem his animals, he learned that they had already been destroyed. Through a macabre chain of events, Ray was arrested for being an accessory to the kennel owner's murder. Tried by a prosecutor who assailed Bourbon's career, and convicted by a jury not of his peers, the (de)famed impersonator was sentenced to ninety-nine years in prison. Two years later he died of leukemia complicated by a heart ailment.

Paul remembers listening to the Bourbon albums: "I kept hearing all of this gay resonance to what he was saying. It was so firmly planted in gay images. He was using it brilliantly. He sounded like a screaming queen—that ostentatious, showy queen who was not afraid of anybody."

Another great female impersonator, Tony Midnite, like Bourbon a native Texan, left his family's East Texas farm for nearby Houston at the age of fifteen.[4] Although there had been nightly female impersonation shows in the city during the thirties, when he arrived, "there was hardly any place for gay people to go."[5] Working at shipyards and munitions plants for the war effort during the day, Tony enjoyed the nearly all-lesbian defense plant softball teams, which played nights, and he often popped into the "mixed" Capitol Bar across from the post office, where "you could usually find a few gay people." Before moving to San Francisco and seeing his first show of female impersonators, Tony attended the gala opening of Houston's first strictly gay bar, the Pink Elephant, a converted store-front located on Prairie Street.

In 1946, the eighteen-year-old returned to Texas from California. In Galveston, Tony enjoyed cruising the boardwalk along the Tenth Street beach and listening to after-hours jam sessions at the Pirates Cave, a nearby gay bar behind the Buccaneer Hotel. He soon debuted as "Tony Midnite" at the infamous Granada Club, owned by one of the infamous Post Office Street madames, Mary Russell. With the band playing, Tony walked on the stage that overlooked the dance floor, singing an Alice Faye tune, "You'll Never Know Just How Much I Love You." He wore a long, black, accordion-pleated evening dress with broad padded shoulders. Tony had picked it up at a secondhand store, trimmed it with sequins, and hiked it up in front with little pleats, allowing it to fall in a drape over his hipline. Swiftly, he went into his second number, singing: "Kiss me once, and kiss me twice, and kiss me once again, it's been a long, long time," to the cheers and tips of the mostly merchant marine and serviceman audience.

Although he was an immediate sensation, Tony was more interested in costume design, and he thought female impersonation "would give me a chance to design the fabulous gowns I had in mind."[6] While this would eventually happen, he was busted in the meantime by Texas Rangers:

> At the time I broke into drag, Galveston was very corrupt. Fred Ford was the police chief. Sam Maceo was the head mob boss. He had the penthouse at the Buccaneer Hotel. If you could pay off, you could get by with just about anything. Usually they left Galveston alone.
>
> Well, there must have been state pressure from the political scene because the Texas Rangers came down and closed everything. The whorehouses, the clubs, and even gambling run by Fred Ford's son. They made a big scene of closing our club. They didn't arrest us but took us down. I had on this big long cape and threw it over my shoulder. This one ranger was standing by the door. "Well, open a door for a lady," I said—and he did! We were let go as long as we would leave Galveston within twenty-four hours—and we did.

During the late forties and early fifties, Tony traveled the club circuit, booked for twelve-week stints. In his flashy gowns and coifed hair, he went from Long Beach's Blue Turban to San Antonio's Club 55 and from Miami's Jewell Box Revue to the 82 Club in New York City, before settling in Chicago. The South, this veteran female impersonator and costume designer of fifty years recalls, was the least hospitable: "You were lucky if you'd stay for a few months. They would have an election year and the clubs would be closed down. In the South you had no protection. In the North it was usually a club with mob ties; in the South it was at the whim of sheriffs. It was rough."

Pre-Stonewall middle-class gay life generally consisted of dinner or cocktail parties among friends. The homosexual elite, such as the social "brunch" group of Atlanta's Apollo Club, the hundred members of Houston's Diana Foundation, the secretive Steamboat Club of New Orleans, or the porno-buying Pensacola circle known as the Emma Jones Society, kept mostly to themselves.[7]

Only a handful of bars, among them Houston's Red Devil Lounge and the Terminal Bar in Miami, catered to African Americans or Latinos. Some middle-class Atlanta black lesbians and gay men traveled to different cities as a club, allowing them the freedom to be different. The less affluent frequented illegal liquor houses known as "nip" or "juke" joints scattered in the Negro sections of Virginia and the Carolinas or hosted rent parties.

Cruising spots flourished on southern boardwalks and piers, in parks and bus stations, along riverfronts and beaches, at college and courthouse T-rooms, on the ball fields and in the gyms. The few exclusively gay bars were generally found in major cities like Miami, Washington, D.C., Atlanta, Houston, and New Orleans. And, even here, police harassment or raids and local ordinances banning same-sex dancing or wearing clothes of the other gender were common. In smaller cities, gay men, and particularly lesbians, had more limited choices. Some frequented "mixed" downtown hotel bars like Louisville's Beaux Arts bar at the street entry level in the Henry Clay Hotel (which eventually staged the city's first drag shows in the back), the Gar Hole in Little Rock's Marion Hotel, or the Thomas Jefferson Hotel bar, known fondly among Birmingham homosexuals as the Snake Pit. Others drove to highway hideaway dance bars like the Aristocrat in Tipton County, Tennessee, or the Halfway Inn, seven miles south of Fort Pierce, Florida. Sometimes they caught a bite to eat at restaurants such as Norfolk's Jolly Roger, the Pad in Huntington, West Virginia, or the more elegant Candlelight in Coconut Grove. And, on occasion, a few homosexual whites visited black clubs, shot houses, and nip joints like Tee's Club on Birmingham's west side or LuLu's in Richmond's Church Hill.[8]

Given this uneven social terrain, professional impressionists generally performed to largely straight audiences in southern supper clubs. From the forties to the early seventies, New Orleans's famed Club My-O-My featured three shows nightly. The tight clique of performers hustled drinks and tips (and occasional tricks) from the largely tourist crowd, who sat at tables draped with floor-length linen in the two-tiered balconies. The program listed male names beneath female photographs. "Mr. Gene Lamarr," for example, sung arias. Performing as a female soprano, he sometimes stopped in the middle of "Ritorna vincitor" from *Aida* to tell the audience in his rugged voice: "Don't worry, I'll make it!"[9]

In South Florida there was the Ha Ha Ha Club. This Hollywood club featured famous impersonators like "the boy soprano," Nicki Gallucci; Lester La Monte, billed as "the paper fashion star"; and the Dixie balladeer of "Come Along My Mandy," Johnny Mangum. These and other well-known stars, such as Chuckie Fontaine (the "sophisticated Aly with a Southern Flair"), performed at the club's famous Babe Baker's Revue.

But the most famous was Doc Benner and Danny Brown's Jewel Box Revue, where the Las Vegas–type show was emceed by a drag king, Mickey Mercer. Performing at the Revue were many southerners. The "Dixie Belle," Jackie Jackson, wearing feathers and beads, performed to packed crowds (including one at the annual Policeman's Ball) seated at tables with small red lamps and white fringe below the club's sixteen-hundred-pound chandelier.[10] Other impersonators included Arkansas-born Harvey Lee, who performed as Jean Harlow accompanied by his Russian wolfhound, Nikki; Florida native Ricky Renee, who danced and impersonated Ginger Rogers and Josephine Baker; the "unpredictable" T. C. Jones; and Tony Midnite, who has told of performing there and for the off-season road show in 1949 and 1950: "The wardrobe was created by one of the top designers in the business, Stanley Rogers, who had done the wardrobe for the various Schubert Theaters in New York. It was fabulous! Danny Brown had gone to Paris to get the feathers and rhinestone jewelry! Nothing was spared to make this the top show of its kind."[11]

By the mid- to late sixties, however, there was a burgeoning of talented regional female impersonators performing at a growing number of gay clubs. Atlanta's Diamond Lil sang in her own voice to tunes like "Smooth Operator" at the Piccolo Lounge and later at My House. Billy Jones, known as Atlanta's "Still Living Legend," launched the Phyllis Killer Oscars in 1968 as a high-camp tribute to those working behind the show scenes. Born in nearby Griffin, Billy "was raised on Myrna Loy," the glamorous comedic movie star of the thirties who portrayed Nora Lee in the *Thin Man* detective film series.[12] Joining the navy in World War II ("I had been very much influenced by Ginger Rogers and Fred Astaire in *The Fleet's In*"), Jones returned to Atlanta to "make Peachtree beautiful" as a decorator. In the midsixties, Jones approached Frank Powell, who had just opened the Joy Lounge, about a female impersonation show. Although it was against the law, "Phyllis Killer and Her Darling Daughters" began performing on a makeshift stage, charging a fifty-cent cover. "We had a guard at the door to watch for the police because they gave us about an hourly check," Billy recalls. "The bartender would come and holler back, 'All's clear,' and we would go back into show biz."[13] Atlanta drag was born.

During this era there were also drag clubs in other southern cities. At Dallas's Villa Fontana, Florida-born Billy McAllister performed as Madame Fertilizer. McAllister began his career working medicine and minstrel shows during the Depression and settled in Dallas after being the mistress of ceremony at the Cotton Club Review of the 1964 Texas State Fair. Drag shows were also held at the Fire Pit in Birmingham, the Centaur Club in Dallas, the mostly African American Desert Room Lounge in Houston, and Biloxi's Mardi Gras Lounge.

One of the longtime Tampa homosexual hangouts was Jimmy White's La Concha Bar (known simply as Cucujo's for Jo, the "bull-dyke" lesbian who ran it). As "mean and as rough as lumberjacks," a local newspaper derisively informed its readers, lesbians in the Tampa crowd were said to run the bars "with a firm hand, often concealing switchblade knives in the pockets of their trousers."[14]

Paul often stopped by Cucujo's after his shift at the paint factory. Dropping a handful of coins in the jukebox, he'd play his favorite tune, "I Got Love" from the Broadway show *Purlie*. As the song played again and again, he'd dance his cares away.

Soon the siren call of the carnival again caught Paul's ear. Cleo found him a job touring small East Coast towns as a red-headed stripper. "Flame Fury" warmed up the burlesque crowd wearing an expansive emerald green satin cape that dropped to the floor to reveal a full-length evening gown. That, too, was discarded, as unsuspecting ticket holders eyed Flame's lace bra and pink chiffon panty. Then "I would get down in their faces" and reveal a minuscule g-string. So authentic was the performance that midway through the tour Paul became the featured stripper— the true girls performed as opening go-go dancers.

Tiring of life on the road and fearing retribution should an outraged spectator's groping uncover his secret, Paul returned to Tampa by bus in 1967. On the weekends, he bartended at the Kikiki, "a tiny hellhole" located across from the cruisy downtown bus station. Owned by Caesar and Rene Rodriguez, the bar itself took up three-quarters of the rectangular room. Here Paul cut up with the customers. His crazed antics and offbeat personality birthed Miss P.

One weekend Paul and his friends drove up Interstate 4 for a show at Orlando's Palace Club. A former warehouse converted into a "private bottle club," it opened late at night and attracted huge weekend crowds. They entered to the voice of Chita Rivera and "there on stage was this queen, Miss Honey, doing 'Spanish Rose' from *Bye Bye Birdie*. Of course, I knew every word of it!" One of Paul's friends turned to him: "You'd like to do that, wouldn't you?" "You're damn right," Paul replied. "Well, let's see if we can book you here!" A month later, the Palace Club presented the Lady Pauline. With her face made up to look like a bird, she lip-synced Streisand's "What Are You Going to Do, Shoot?"

Paul quit his day job and joined the weekend cast at Cucujo's. Pauline did the first show in glamour drag and the second in its opposite, skag drag. One night the sound system failed. Jo canceled the show. All dressed up but with nowhere to perform, Paul and his friend Sandy trotted over to Kikiki's on Morgan Street: "Of course we had to sit at the two barstools that were right inside the doorway. The door was left open that night. A police car pulled up. The officers saw us sitting there. They came in and arrested us. They thought we were women. We thought, 'How foolish—arresting us as women for prostitution in a gay bar!'" Bailed out by Jo (Sandy was forsaken), Paul soon left Cucujo's to perform at the Horny Bull, where he formed the Hot Tuna Review.

Six years had passed since the boy with strawberry blond hair had first arrived in Tampa. "Things now *seemed* more open," says Paul. The investigative tentacles of Charley Johns had withered and Tampa police no longer penciled down license plate numbers of bar patrons. The state's university system—the site of faculty dismissals and student expulsions for homosexuality during the late fifties—was now under siege by youthful bands of gay liberationists.

While police harassment, bar raids, and payoffs to vice officers were far from over in the Stonewall South, openly gay bars mushroomed during the early seventies.[15] Grand show bars and dance clubs appeared in mid-size cities: Lexington's Living Room and Louisville's Badlands, Chapel Hill's Electric Company and Charlotte's Oleens, the Gizmo and the Outer Focus in Birmingham, as well as the Carousel Club of Knoxville. In the nation's capital, where "a few years earlier, even the word, homosexual, was rarely uttered in public," as a Washington *Post* reporter observed, and where as late as 1969, the newspaper judged the "the prospect of open gay activity . . . as 'unthinkable' . . . a greater freedom exists."[16]

Southern drag exploded in the South, and 1972 marked the birth of two of the most venerable female impersonation pageants.[17] Miss Gay

America was originated by Nashville bar owner Jerry Peak, who had planned a regional event. Contestants, however, came from every region of the country. On June 25, Hot Springs, Arkansas's Norma Kristie was crowned the first Miss Gay America at the Glass Menagerie. She was followed by Lady Baronessa and then Shawn Luis—both of whom performed at the Sweet Gum Head in Atlanta.

Another bar owner, Keith Landon, produced the first Miss Florida pageant. The title awarded that spring honored Atlanta's Tricia Marie. The next few years witnessed memorable performances from the great divas of southern drag: Tiny Tina, dressed as the Statue of Liberty, fiery torch in hand, singing "God Bless America" to the voice of Kate Smith; Hot Chocolate, surrounded by leopard-loined boy savages, leaping out of a gorilla costume to become Queen of the Disco; Noly Greer, changing from a glamorous woman to a beefcake model in a leather bikini riding a motorcycle while singing "The Party's Over." These rhinestone celebrities were the first ladies of the Stonewall South. As gay libbers marshaled a small retinue of supporters, drag divas attracted legions of followers.

Bobby Carter hoped to become one of these icons of gender liberation as he entered the Miss Gay Tampa contest in July 1972. Backstage at the Horny Bull he sat in front of the dressing-room mirror rimmed with makeup lights. Scrawled in lipstick was "ROXANNE" with a heart-shaped *O*.

Someone gave Roxanne the up-next call. "Who's next?" Bobby remembers dithering. "Me? Oh, shit! Help me, girl. I don't even have my lipstick on." Within minutes, Roxanne walked on the stage pantomiming to Liza Minelli's "Mein Heir" from *Cabaret*. Like Jim Bailey, famed for his impersonations of Judy Garland and Barbra Streisand, Bobby had studied Liza's every movement and gesture. "He had an immediate audience identification," lauds Paul. "He was way, way before his time."

Next Pauline, wearing a three-foot-high headdress covered with angel hair in the shape of curls, performed the "I Capricorn" number. Emerging from a cloud of dry ice, she glittered with zodiac signs strategically placed in her hair. This Las Vegas showgirl performance dazzled the audience—and the judges. "This was no Diana Ross singing 'I Capricorn' and wearing astrological signs," declares Paul. "*I* was the one."

Bobby still relishes the outcome. "Miss P, my sister, deserved to win. But as she was announced the winner, the audience began to scream: 'Roxanne! Roxanne!' I felt the title was mine." After the contest, a grand party was held. Bobby, who placed second, goes on: "Quaaludes, grass, and LSD were passed out freely. Partake or you're not one of the gang! Grass to me was one of the sociable mind-altering drugs of the time. As I smoked I felt more creative. One after another, people felt it necessary to tell me I should leave Tampa, get out, do bigger and greater things."

The merrymakers also wished Paul well in the upcoming finals for the Miss Orlando pageant. He had just won the Fourth of July semifinals, doing Shirley Bassey's "Goldfinger," in which his gold-painted body slowly spun out of a flaxen cape to reveal a golden g-string. For the Labor Day finals Paul appeared in a white face with a curly blond wig dancing to his ballet version of *Coco* from the Katharine Hepburn Broadway show. "My concept was that it was this older woman who went back into her mind to when she was a little girl. She was trying to explain to someone why she was the way she was: Her father didn't show up when he was supposed to. At that time, she was crushed. Some time after that she learned to be independent. But wait! This was not just Coco's story, it was mine."

The Lady Pauline was crowned Miss Gay Orlando 1972. Bill Miller, the producer of the pageant and "the man" in the city's bar scene, praised Paul. "*You* are to be watched out for," he observed. "There is something very special about you and somebody needs to learn to let it happen." He invited Paul to move his act to the Palace Club.

Meanwhile, another queen-maker, Rene Rodriguez, zeroed in on Bobby. Rodriguez, a diminutive Cuban whose former drag persona still occasionally flared, had opened Rene's. Occupying a city block, this was *the* Tampa nightclub. Flaming torches, highlighting the bamboo plants, greeted hundreds of weekend partiers.

"If I get you a new hat and some new clothes," propositioned Rene, "you may dance upon my stage. Perhaps I can make you a star."

In flare, Roxanne replied: "I'm ready for my close-up, Mr. DeMille."

NINE

Brigadistas and Barricades

I went to the Isle of Youth to pick lemons, hoping to come back and fulfill the worst nightmares of Mississippi senator Eastland and the House Internal Security Subcommittee.
—Clint Pyne

A steady Atlantic breeze crossed the starboard side of the Cuban-bound freighter *Conrado Benitez* during the last week of August 1970. Aboard were 405 revolutionaries in training who expected to return from Cuba and "kick the props out from under the plastic monster." Among these firebrands were five Gay Liberation Front activists and Clint Pyne, who "wasn't actually out at the time" but had heard about gay liberation from "a brother" in his North Carolina circle of friends, Bob Bland.

As a first-year student at the University of North Carolina, Clint had participated in the students' "counter-orientation." Soon he was organizing student support of the mostly black female food workers, chairing meetings of the Chapel Hill Revolutionary Movement, and writing for the *Protean Radish*, a statewide alternative paper founded by a chapter of the Southern Student Organizing Committee (SSOC). On campus, he had met an organizer for the third Venceremos Brigade—formed by a coalition of New

On board the *Conrado Benitez.* Photo by Tina Green, courtesy of Milo Pyne.

Left organizations that chose Che Guevara's popular slogan, "We Will Win," as its name.

Named to honor his father and his father's father, George Clinton Pyne came from a matriarchal line of southern progressives. His father's mother was a follower of women's rights advocate Margaret Sanger. His mother's mother was the first female judge in North Carolina. And his "mannish-looking" great-aunt Ethel, known as "Bucky," worked as a school principal and lived for years with "her friend," Miss Mabelle, a social worker.

As a high school student, Clint had often walked up Chapel Hill Street to the Durham House of SSOC, which he characterizes as a "southern SDS and a white SNCC."[1] (Its symbol was black and white hands shaking over a Confederate battle flag.) There he would "hang out," rap with members, and read the *New South Student*. "That's where I learned a lot about the radical parts of southern history."

His introduction to radical politics, though, began even earlier. Clint participated in a loose discussion group with other junior high school students "who listened to Joan Baez and talked nuclear war and civil rights." These episodic ventures into radicalism resulted in "people calling me 'queer' before I knew what sex was!"

On the week-long trip aboard the *Conrado Benitez,* bound for the first socialist country in the Americas, the Cubans asked the seditious passengers to organize cultural presentations. There were caucuses for women, Puerto Ricans, southerners, and blacks. GLF members, who viewed themselves as similar to other revolutionaries fighting against oppression and in solidarity with other leftist groups, formed their own caucus.

Clint was excited "to meet the gay people in our brigade." At the time, he saw himself as "an ally of the gay movement." Few of his fellow travelers shared this attitude. "The Gay Caucus got a lot of hassle from other Norteamericanos who did not want to concede the relevance of gayness or gay people to the revolution."

While the male revolutionaries had little to do with GLF members, women were somewhat more open. Elaine was the lone female who came out during the women's discussion group on the ship's deck. Her lesbianism spawned multiple dialogues: "As soon as people would find out, they'd come over and have questions, and we'd start another group. . . . The last night on the ship I was pretty freaked out. . . . It seemed like a curious contradiction: the fact that I could love a woman completely separated me from the other women. So, I just cried most of that night."[2]

Arriving in Havana's harbor to a thunderous welcome of singing and dancing, the brigadistas were soon working alongside youth contingents from North Korea, Bolivia, North Vietnam, China, and Laos. Picking and packing fruit eight hours a day, Clint found that four weeks of "collective living, working, and studying" made a lasting impression on him—and his government. Following his return, the Charlotte FBI office recommended that Clint be placed on the Security Index.[3]

As the antiwar movement reached a crescendo during that 1969–70 school year, Clint's campus activism mirrored that of thousands of other students. His generation, schooled in the democratic ideals of the post-war era, was radicalized by the trial of the Chicago Seven, disappointed by May Day demonstrations, and shocked by the shooting of protesters at Kent and Jackson State. "Events overwhelmed everybody," Clint recollects. "The energy was totally out of control."

However, in a region where zealotry for the Alabama Crimson and Red was second only to antipathy for those in solidarity with the red tide, southern vigilance followed revolutionary inclination. Like the naïve southern lawyer George Hanson in *Easy Rider,* Clint found that talk of rebellion and hippie tribes didn't sit well with folks fond of grits, God, and glory. While Hanson's fate came by a shotgun blast from a speeding pickup truck, Clint's destiny would be more tangled—politically and sexually—as a beefy guy, dressed in khaki clothing and sporting dark glasses, snapped photos of Clint Pyne.

The Venceremos experience also made an impression on Earl Galvin, one of the five GLF brigadistas. He had mistakenly assumed that solidarity extended across sexual borders: "I would go to sleep at night and people would be hollering: 'Oh, there's homosexuals trying to get into my bed!' One time after work, I came in and this guy was sitting on his bed and he said, 'I need some homosexual repellent.'"[4]

During this American brigade's Cuban stay, the Communist Party's Central Committee condemned the "social pathological character of homosexual deviations." Of course, this position was little different from that taken by North American politicians, psychiatrists, police officers, and ministers. And the homophobia found in Cuba's revolutionary newspaper, *Granma,* was easily matched by U.S. Marxist weeklies like the *Guardian,* as well as by mainstream dailies.

During the year following Stonewall, coverage of gay issues or activities was meager. The few southern gay publications were fleeting leftist mimeos like *Sunflower* and *Trash;* chit-chat, gossipy bar guides like *Skipper's Newsletter* and *Nuntius;* and *Circle of Friends* and a few other scattered newsletters. Underground southern newspapers such as the *Great Speckled Bird, Protean Radish,* and *Daily Texan* were awash with stories on the Vietnam

War and national liberation movements but carried little about the war against heterosexual oppression or gay liberation fronts. Generous amounts of copy were also given to local dope busts and national boycotts, folk heroes like Angela Davis and Timothy Leary, and the cultivation of marijuana and "survival foods." Free verse and biting political cartoons competed for space with announcements about rock concerts and head shop ads. If one was progressive, queer, and living in the South, however, there was little information about the gay movement, details regarding queer organizing, or critiques of the "straight male caste" or "straight-defined homosexuality."

However, the same month that Clint departed for Cuba, the *Carolina Plain Dealer* brought a broader political and geographical coverage to the Carolinas, declaring: "We want Carolinians in their self-imposed exiles to come home again and help liberate their land."[5] This paper routinely carried articles, cartoons, and information about gay liberation.

In 1971, other underground southern papers, most notably the *Great Speckled Bird,* began to devote more space to gay issues, following criticism for its lack of coverage of that as well as women's issues.[6] Later that year, Atlantans, contemplating the formation of a GLF chapter, queried *Bird* readers: "What is Gay Liberation? Is such an organization needed in Atlanta?"[7] By 1972, the *Bird* devoted a centerfold spread to gay liberation for the pride events but, in 1973, many of the straight staff walked out when an entire issue on gay rights was planned.[8]

Clint Pyne wrote for the *Plain Dealer* but he did not involve himself in gay politics, unlike fellow revolutionary Bob Bland. A self-described "country boy from rural eastern North Carolina," Bob was "putting it in a political context." Joining Clint in a little radical "affinity group," Bland began to share his budding Stonewall consciousness. Bob recalls: "When I found out about gay liberation, it was more an attractive idea than that I was specifically attracted to men sexually. Gay liberation offered better explanations for human sexual choices and behavior than I had ever been offered."

Soon Bob confronted a fundamental question: "Are you a gay radical who works for other people's causes or are you a gay radical who works for gay liberation?" This was resolved when he, Clint, and others journeyed to Winston-Salem for a Black Panther Party rally. "Everything was faggot this and that," Clint Pyne recalls. "We were trying to be white radicals who were supportive of the Black Panthers. But the whole thing was preposterous. It blew Bob's mind. That was the watershed for him." Clint continues: "While I was involved with a lot of straight people, Bland was becoming a militant gay separatist."

As Clint prepared to travel south that summer of 1970, Bob Bland trekked north. Arriving toward the end of June, Bland looked in the Yellow Pages for "Gay Liberation." Not finding a telephone listing, he walked to the offices of the Liberation News Service, which dispatched weekly packets of articles and camera-ready photos to some of the nation's eight hundred underground newspapers. That night he enjoyed his first sexual experience as a "revolutionary faggot."

The next afternoon, Bob marched in the Christopher Street Parade along with new friends Jim Fouratt and Allen Young. Soon the 17th Street Collective coalesced around Bob. This intense male commune on the city's West Side published a shrill leftist weekly, *Gay Flames,* connecting Marxist-Leninist politics to gay liberation. Bob also formed the Gay Revolutionary Party and published its house organ, *Ecstasy.* The party's manifesto prophesied: "Gay revolution will see the overthrow of the straight male caste. . . . Gay revolution will not lead to freedom of association for gay people in a predominantly straight world, nor will it lead to straight-defined homosexuality with marriages and exclusive monogamy."[9]

As Bob was drafting this manifesto, Clint arrived in Canada from Cuba's Isle of Youth. "Just sort of drifting and checking things out," Clint traveled to New York late that fall and connected with Bob's urban gay collective. "Still confused and insecure about my sexual identity," Clint remembers "people coming out of the woodwork," including the charismatic Jim Fouratt. Two weeks later, Clint hitched a ride to North Carolina with Jim and some female impersonators. Dropping Clint off in North Carolina, Fouratt and company went back on the road to preach gay liberation in Louisville and other towns on their way to the GLF conference in Austin.

As Clint arrived in Durham, twenty-six-year-old Brad Keistler returned to Charlotte from a summer of staying in cheap hotels and hostels in Europe. Unwilling to return to corporate work, he opened the Asterisk*, a head shop on Sixth Street. Selling black lights, posters, butterfly dresses, tie-dyed T-shirts, and smoking paraphernalia, he made "only enough profit to barely stay in business."[10] Luckily, he soon moved into a downtown commune, Red Worms, where sixty dollars covered his rent, utilities, and food. Soon the Sixth Street storefront across from the public library was a "gathering place" for some of Charlotte's cultural malcontents, high school hippies, budding revolutionaries, and closeted types.

Nightlife, like gay political activism, was negligible in 1970 Charlotte. Except for the ubiquitous presence of gay men cruising the "block" on Trade Street or closeted lesbians laboring at the NOW chapter office, a couple of bars offered the only homosexual refuge. Sandwiched between a "colored nightclub" and a bus station was "the only bar in town with chandeliers over the pool tables," attracting four to five hundred lesbians and gay men over a weekend. The straight owner, who, according to the local paper, had paid off his house and bought two new cars, confided to the reporter: "These people might be weird, crazy, or sick. . . . But if they are willing to respect me and give me their business, then I'll stick up for them. I feel like they're mine."[11]

Meanwhile, despite the social and political life in Gotham's Sodom, Bob Bland yearned to "go back to North Carolina and try to bring gay liberation to the state." When the 17th Street Collective disbanded, he came home "*not* with the idea of trying to find gay people within the radical movement but finding them within the gay community."

Later described by the *Charlotte Observer* as a "bushy-haired, uneffeminate" activist, Bob chose for his first evangelistic sojourn the "notorious" Queen Bee.[12] This Victorian-decorated bar near Raleigh's bus station was wary of gay crusaders. He found a more receptive audience at Chapel Hill's popular Pegasus, the city's first all-gay, gay-owned club, on West Franklin. "The people who ran the bar were supportive. . . . The Triangle area had heard that there was a gay liberation movement. So I came down as something of an apostle bringing the good news from Jerusalem."

Identifying a core group of local gay activists, Bob set his mind to forming a collective household while he worked at the Raleigh library. As fate would have it, a recently divorced man was stuck with a two-story house at 412 Kinsey Avenue. Bob rented it.

To announce the first meeting of the Triangle Gay Alliance, Bob distributed flyers describing this "beautiful house where gay brothers get together to love, talk, and help each other out." About thirty people attended the November 1971 meeting, mostly men: "There was practically no press coverage," Bob remembers. "So for average gay people their knowledge of the movement came by word of mouth. Some wanted to know 'What are you trying to do and why are you making waves?' Others were just interested in what could be done and looking for an alternative to the bars."

A sundry tribe of rebels, rubyfruits, and rhinestones joined Bland in his four-bedroom collective. There was the black female impersonator, Jimmi Dee, a town native who by decade's end would become Miss Gay South and Miss Gay America. Two lesbians also took up quarters there, "Bobby, who didn't look like a woman and whose driver's license identified her as male, and Lynne, a woman who came from a prominent family but who was committed to radical lesbian/gay politics."[13] The diversity of its residents, as Bob recalls, "brought in a lot of different people who would have never participated in the gay movement in New York City: from Glenn who drove a Continental, had four poodles, and a house full of bric-a-brac to a cook . . . who billed himself as Cleopatra and was the grandson of *my* grandmother's cook."

Of course, there had long been hidden cliques of homosexuals but to assemble publicly, proclaiming "Gay Is Good," was Bob's vision. Formal gatherings occurred on Sunday midafternoons and at a dinner on Friday nights. There were less programmed encounters after the midnight Saturday closing of bars. "People wanted something to do and we were mainly looking for new people," Bob explains. "So we opened the house and the place would be packed. There were caravans running from Chapel Hill!" Soon the Alliance mushroomed to 155 members.

Bob Bland, though, was not the lone North Carolinian trying to organize Tar Heel homosexuals in the early seventies. One summer afternoon Asterisk* owner Brad Keistler ambled over to the Crazy Horse Bookstore adjacent to his head shop. Among the "radical books" of poetry and politics, he spotted a little orange pamphlet from GLF-New York. Reading it, he recognized: "This is me!" A few days later he came across a flyer announcing the "May Day Gathering of Tribes."[14]

Instantly, Brad "knew I had to go to it." As a "gay brother," he later wrote about his experience in the *Plain Dealer:* "Gay people gave the Energy to the Conference. While 'straight' people talked and discussed and planned ('The Empire is crumbling.' 'Even though the Empire is crumbling, we must still work for the Revolution.'), we sang and danced, kissed and touched, celebrated our lives, and laid waste to the 'straight' myth that homosexuality is homo-SEX-uality. . . . Revolutionary love. . . . When I left, I left a country. I left Woodstock Nation. I left the Revolution."[15]

Eventually, Brad came out to members of his Red Worms commune at one of their weekly meetings. The women and men responded positively, sharing stories of past same-sex experiences. And Brad slept with several of the "straight" southern men who "were open to experimenting because they were 'liberated.'" More significantly, one female member introduced Brad to another gay man, Charles Shoe, who lived with Greg, his black companion, just up the street.

In October 1971, the three men started GLF-Charlotte. Gay Liberation Front was chosen as the group's name since it was mistakenly believed to be "less radical and more organized" than the rival Gay Activist Alliance. These Charlotte activists distributed flyers in the mostly straight-owned gay bars: "We don't need to hide anymore! The bars are fine for entertainment, but don't you want to be able to walk down the street holding hands?"

Despite the considerable "hippie" presence in Charlotte, and a new regional university campus, North Carolina's largest city lacked the critical mass needed to organize. Unlike the Raleigh effort, only a dozen or so people, mostly young, male, and white, attended any given GLF-Charlotte meeting. Weekly consciousness-raising sessions were held in a dimly lit living room of the Myrtle Avenue collective or at Charles and Greg's place, where individuals shared coming out stories, planned activities, and helped one another feel "a little less like freaks and rejects."[16] During Charlotte-GLF's eighteen-month existence, members openly showed affection at antiwar demonstrations, coffeehouses, and countercultural gatherings. There also were two panel discussions at UNC-Charlotte, same-sex dancing at a straight nightclub (where they were promptly wrestled out the backdoor!), and two gay dances. "We thought we didn't have to do a lot being gay activists," Brad admits. "Just by being ourselves, we were already changing society."

In Raleigh, the Triangle Gay Alliance continued growing. A "hotline" telephone number was published in local papers. Besides organizing Kinsey House social events, the group mailed questionnaires to 140 political candidates running in the May primary and supported Clint Pyne's write-in campaign for agriculture commissioner. Most memorable, however, was a drag show fundraiser. Bob recalls:

> Jimmi Dee and David, a drag person from Chapel Hill who also was the bartender at the Pegasus, along with some people from Greensboro decided that this would be a good way for them to show off their talents and to raise money for the group. So the question was where to hold it. Someone said, "Why don't we call the Municipal Auditorium and see if we could hold it there," somewhat as a joke. The next day we called them and they said: "Surely. Here is the date we have available."

The 1971 event attracted nearly two hundred people. "Being such a public place," notes Bland, "hardly any of the people from Raleigh came. They were terrified!" The fundraiser left something to be desired. As political theater, however, it marked the state's first major public gay event.[17]

During this early era of activism in Raleigh and Charlotte, Clint Pyne lived at Tick Creek, a commune near Pittsboro. His move to a rural setting had been a political decision: "The Cuban Revolution had its greatest impact on the lives of the people in the country. It is very illuminating for people who have grown up in an urban environment to become aware of the possibilities for socialist transformation in rural areas. . . . For some people, living in the country means a retreat from the struggle, but the movement to re-inhabit the land stems from the need to find our roots and lose the colonial settler mentality."

When Clint had first driven his old blue Buick down the long winding road to Tick Creek in rural Chatham County, he had found a disillusioned band living on eighty acres with a pond. Within a few months, other May Day demonstrators joined the Tick Creek Tribe. Its character as well as composition changed. "There was a turnover in the sexual politics. The women were not as willing to be subservient and people were more open about their sexuality. Anyone who was homophobic either had to shut up or leave."

At the commune, Clint enjoyed relationships with both women and men, including Loomis, an old black bee keeper who lived in a shotgun shack down the creek on a dead-end road. Tick Creek also attracted human strays, including gay men. "People would just turn up when we had articles about gay liberation," Clint recalls. One of those was Brad Keistler.

Clint and several others had visited the Red Worms commune in late 1971. Brad says he was attracted to Clint, this "cute little activist with long, straight raven hair almost down to his butt." Affairs of the heart merged with political activism. During his Tick Creek visits, Brad did paste-ups for the *Plain Dealer*. "As we networked more with gay activists," Clint remembers, "the content of the paper also changed."

In its December issue, pink centerfold pages highlighted information, photos, and cartoons about gay liberation in North Carolina. In announcing the first two gay groups formed in the state, one writer boasted: "Gays are already far ahead of straights in the work of creating a non-paranoid loving world. . . . Gay men don't have to worry too much about confusing guns with cocks."[18]

In the next issue, Bob Bland wrote:

"Gay Is Good"—I know you all mean well as you go around chanting these worn out words, but I can't quite relate to being good, and I am most definitely Gay. . . . After more than five years of "cruising," "the Gay bar scene," "the trucks in New York," "the rest areas of Salisbury, NC," "the fuck movies," "the orgies," "the loneliness," and the insanity that accompanies it all; being good seems to be a misplaced adjective. Granted it can be fun at times, it's exciting no doubt, but it is not good. If we have to be good to gain your acceptance, then you can hang it up. If we are really into creating a new world, if we are sincere about our culture, then this "Gay Is Good" stigma has to go. We are sick of being "good" for you.[19]

Meanwhile, Clint was still being cruised and photographed by J. Edgar Hoover's G-men. The FBI maintained surveillance on the Tick Creek Tribe that, according to one report, was "working to nourish the seed of a revolutionary society." Clint, a "known subversive," was targeted for an "interview" in an "attempt to establish him as an informant." But, as with Paul Newman's character in *Cool Hand Luke*, there was a failure to communicate. By the time Hoover died—leaving his Tenleytown house to his longtime companion, the deputy director of the FBI, Clyde Tolson—the Bureau eventually had given up on "turning" Clint, although it continued to monitor his "revolutionary activities."[20]

Communication problems also existed at the Kinsey Street house. Despite the success of the drag show benefit, tempers flared over unpaid phone bills and the purchase of drag clothes with house funds. "It was an unstable situation that got more unstable," as Bob explains: "The group wasn't deep enough without the few people who were actually doing the work. More than anything else, it really lacked roots in the community. The people who were in it were the real flamboyant, overtly gay people or the politically aware people who were not going to be long in the area."

Bob Bland foresaw a bleak future ahead of him as a local librarian and held out little hope for a future with his boyfriend, whose mother was an FBI agent. Burned-out and love-starved, Bob departed for Atlanta in the summer of 1972. A few months later, Brad Keistler, steadily losing money at the Asterisk*, moved to Los Angeles with his boyfriend. GLF-Charlotte cofounders Charles and Greg moved to San Francisco.

Brad, like Bob, became politically inactive. "When we saw that there was going to be no major revolution happening," he relates, "we started working on our inward growth, focusing more attention on local involvement and working within the establishment." Later, both participated in organized sports, helping to enlarge gay culture beyond the bar scene.

In mid-January 1973 the Tick Creek farmhouse burnt to the ground. "A whole phase of our lives ended at that point," laments Clint. "We made it through that winter in makeshift housing."

Pooling their resources, the tribe began a search for cheap land. Two women friends visited acquaintances in Nashville and spotted a newspaper advertisement. "It was exactly our fantasy: remote, inexpensive, forested," Clint recollects. In June 1973, Pyne and a convoy of VW vans and pickup trucks drove across the Smoky Mountains to their two-hundred-acre farm in remote Cannon County, Tennessee. Not far behind were Hoover's boys and queer history.

TEN

Fire and Decadence

United we stand, divided we fall.
                                        —Brotherhood of Man

At 2110 Barracks Street in New Orleans on Labor Day weekend 1972, a diverse and bored set of college friends were sweating out their last weekend of summer. "We all felt like outcasts either because of political views or sexual orientation or because of race," Frederick Wright, a rotund African American, recollects. "Although New Orleans was as liberal as they came," that Labor Day weekend "the impulse to head back [to the house] to party was that *we* really didn't belong in the streets. In the early seventies there were places where blacks wouldn't have been welcomed in the Quarter."[1]

Most New Orleans gay and lesbian bars attracted a unique and loyal body of customers—generally segregated by race and gender. Gigi's on the North Rampart bar strip, the Safari House, and Lafitte's were the only ones to genuinely welcome men of color. Charlene's (which routinely had a Mardi Gras sign hanging from its Elysian Fields door that announced "If You Ain't Gay, You Can't Stay") served women. Lesbians also hung out at the rougher Quarter Horse or played pool at Vicki's on nearby Decatur.[2]

With the defeat of the discredited Big Jim Garrison by Harry Connick Sr. in the district attorney race, there was a trend toward more opulent gay bars that catered to a white clientele. Decorated with stalactites and stalagmites, the Caverns (across from Pete's discothèque) had a

Bill Larson in the Up Stairs Lounge window as Fire Chief McCrossen investigates the scene. Photo by and courtesy of Ronald LeBoeuf.

sunken dance floor. At Lafitte's in Exile, wall-to-wall bodies and an eternal torch greeted patrons particularly partial to Bloody Mary's. Soon the bar would expand to the second floor, and the Caverns would be transformed into the upscale Bourbon Pub.

There were, of course, gay bars off Bourbon Street. The Galley House catered to an older clientele (a glittery sign in one corner read, "I Remember It Well"). The red-flocked-wallpapered Up Stairs Lounge was a watering hole for those who enjoyed quiet conversation and piano playing (walking up the wooden stairs, one spotted Queen Victoria's portrait with the caption, "Even a Queen Can Get the Clap"). A block down, in the wilderness of Iberville Street, was the notorious Wanda's, with more than its share of fights, knifings, and Mardi Gras nude dancers.

So this motley crew of outcasts sought asylum at their Barracks Street complex: a two-story former slave quarters with squeaking wooden doors and sloping pine floors tucked behind a dilapidated house. In this make-shift household, there was a communal spirit with "a bathroom painted silver that was quite large and a tub—no shower. You had to plan your bath, but there was a couch. So I would go in there and read things like *Streetcar Named Desire* when the other person was in the tub," remembers Ed Seale, one of the outcasts, who painted a tarantula on the front porch sign and labeled it "Tarantula Arms." On the other side was printed "Belle Rêve"—named after Blanche DuBois's mythical plantation.

As the odor of jasmine floated amidst tropical plants and fig trees between the two houses, Maureen sat in the kitchen of the former slave quarters, which overlooked the backyard. She had just moved from Manhattan to join her friends. "I was bitching about nothing to do in this town. It was hot! I had to start graduate school, so they gave me something to do by having this party." Officially, the party was to say farewell to a Belle Rêve resident. The other goal, whimsically recalled a friend, was to "shut her up. . . . We named it a Southern Decadence party: come as your favorite southern decadent."

The party began late that Sunday afternoon (with the expectation that Labor Day would allow for recovery). Fifty people drank, smoked, and carried on near the big fig tree. Frederick Wright rates it as "a good party, better than most, but nothing out of the ordinary."

Even though Maureen still complained about the humidity, the group decided to repeat the Southern Decadence party and inaugurate a parade the following year. At that second party, revelers began at Johnny Matassa's grocery, parading back to Belle Rêve as decadent luminaries: Tallulah Bankhead, Belle Watling, Mary Ann Mobley. Along the way, they stopped at Esplanade and Rampart Street bars as well as some in the Tremé district.

For their third party in 1974, Frederick Wright was named parade marshall. To insure the safety of the raucous and inebriated group, he established traditions still associated with what has become a multimillion-dollar festivity. "Once I got the invitation in the mail, I *knew:* I got a whistle!" Frederick reminisces. Dressing a "little wacky, but not enough to draw police attention to yourself," he planned a route with frequent bar stops between Matassa's and the Golden Lantern. "You cannot drink uncontrollably in this heat and still walk a mile and a half and get to the party—in heels!"

Carrying a baton and dressed as the "All-American Boy," Frederick led off the parade. More folks joined the celebratory wandering, including Ruthie the Duck Woman and the Bus Lady. As the rag-tag group turned onto Rampart Street, Frederick crossed paths with four black women returning from Sunday afternoon services "and picking up their fried chicken dinners. I led the procession past their car; I could smell the chicken! I reached in and took a couple of pieces. But she begged me not to take her breasts! But, I got a wing—and a leg! 'What's the occasion?' they said to me. 'Southern Decadence.' They pretended that they knew what it was all about: 'Oh, yes, yes.'"

Within a few years Southern Decadence mushroomed from a Belle Rêve party to a Labor Day weekend tradition, attracting 150,000—mostly lesbians and gay men—and generating $60 million in tourist revenue. This revelry and debauchery that characterized Southern Decadence in particular, and the New Orleans social scene in general, had been momentarily silenced, however, with a tragic event during the city's 1973 gay pride weekend.

William P. Richardson is a wisp of a figure. Born in 1909 to a plantation belle and a business-minded father in Lexington, Kentucky, he received his calling to the ministry at the age of fourteen. After attending the University of the South, he entered the Union Theological Seminary in Manhattan. Finally, tiring of the "dreary, cold climate" of the North, he moved to New Orleans with his wife and their two children in 1953, and to St. George's, a distinguished Episcopal church that had come into disrepair and neglect, with more funerals than confirmations to its credit. "Father Bill" rebuilt the church and its congregation, attracting other assistant ministers (some of whom were homosexual) by his gentle yet activist pastoral style. As the church grew, so did its outreach services, as well as late-night phone calls for help. Father Bill recounts the story of one of them, that began when the phone rang at about two o'clock in the morning.

"Hello," Bill mumbled in a dreamlike state.

"Bill Larson has been burned to death in a fire," exclaimed the voice at the other end of the line.

Father Bill had met the fifty-five-year-old, "clean cut" Larson two years earlier when he asked to use St. George's for Sunday afternoon services for the newly formed Metropolitan Community Church, of which he was minister. Father Bill had then just returned from a summer seminar sponsored by Union Theological Seminary entitled, "Homosexuality, Women's Liberation, and Communal Living." As he explains, he "didn't know about any of these things, so I went to find out." The Gay Liberation Front of New Orleans had collapsed that spring, and Father Bill had come back from the seminar determined "to do everything within my power to help gays and lesbians accept themselves" and to foster acceptance of them. Soon the minister's "stunned" conservative parish heard that homosexuality was "not a choice," and St. George's opened an alternative bookstore, stocking feminist and gay liberation works. Bill also counseled those struggling with their sexuality.

Now Father Bill hung up the phone, shocked and distressed. He prayed. Unable to sleep, he brewed some coffee and sat down. As he listened to the chimes of the clock, he remembered this man whom he had come to love as a friend. Sharing a history of heterosexual marriages and service to God, he and Bill Larson had enjoyed frequent dinners together at St. George's parish house. During their long conversations, they explored liturgical styles. MCC's liturgy, Father Bill thought, "was quite scrambled." Nevertheless, he had supported the church's six-month use of St. George's side chapel for Sunday afternoon services—although he had been warned by an elderly parishioner that it would need to be "exorcised of evil spirits."

It was nearly midnight on the West Coast when Rev. Troy Perry, the founder of the Metropolitan Community Church, returned to his Los Angeles home after celebrating gay pride. A message waiting for him was marked urgent. As he read the note, the phone rang. Rev. John Gill, Southeast District coordinator, ministering at the Metropolitan Community Church in Atlanta, asked:

"I guess you know what has happened?"

"I don't know. I just walked in. What is it?"

"You haven't heard anything?"

"No, I haven't. What's wrong?"

"It's a very bad fire in New Orleans and they say a lot of people have been burnt to death."

"Were any of our members hurt?"

"Yes, apparently a lot have been burnt in the fire. I think Bill Larson, the pastor, was one."

Meeting John Gill at the New Orleans airport the next afternoon, Troy Perry picked up the local papers and immediately assumed the role of gay spokesman for the New Orleans community.[3] Newspapers reported "bodies stacked like pancakes" and a "charred, cooked-out pile of human flesh." Local talk-radio jockeys joked, "What will we bury the ashes of queers in? Answer: Fruit jars." Cabbies wisecracked that "the fire burned their dresses off." The *States-Item* quoted Major Morris, chief of detectives: "We don't even know if these papers [found on the bodies of the victims] belong to the people we found them on. Some thieves hung out there and you know this was a queer bar."[4]

At a Monday afternoon press conference, Perry challenged Morris's remarks: "In a fire where rings had been melted down and there was nothing left . . . what does he expect?" He then chastised the media:

> The time in history for calling people niggers—and kikes—and queers is over in the United States of America. And it's high time that you people in New Orleans, Louisiana, got the message and joined the rest of the Union!
>
> Incidentally, I know some of you in front of me are gay. If you think you're fooling anyone by sniping at your own community, you're wrong. So listen to Reverend Perry's advice and get your act together—even if you aren't yet ready to come out of the closet. Too many people are now being hurt and suffering from your complacency![5]

On Tuesday, media coverage became more compassionate, and the police refrained from further comment—although the department never issued an outright apology.

The Up Stairs Lounge was a second-floor, three-room complex between Wanda's and the Greek bars on Decatur Street, an area frequented by hustlers. That past Sunday, the five-to-seven o'clock dollar beer bust had ended, but twenty-three-year-old David Gary was still playing ragtime tunes on the white baby grand sitting on the corner platform. Patrons Lindy Quinton, Stewart Butler, and others joined in the festive singing. Buddy Rasmussen, a Houston native and military veteran who managed the bar, was spending an idle moment with his partner of five years, Adam Fontenot. Mike Scarborough had come in around a quarter before five. He was still drinking draft beer at one of the backroom tables with his navy buddy and lover, Glen Green, on his way to Burgundy House.

On Sunday afternoons, the Up Stairs attracted a crowd in a city where neighborhood bars are more like family parlors than pick-up joints. Regulars brought their favorite records for the jukebox, couples celebrated anniversaries, "Jocko," the bar hound owned by Stewart, sometimes sat on a stool lapping up vodka and milk, and a cross-section of actors, professionals, and street people indulged in conversation and drink. The place had been that way since Phillip Esteve had opened it on Halloween night, 1970.

Joslyn Fosberg, a bar regular voted "honorary lady faggot of the year," has nostalgic memories of

> bursting in during the "Happy Hour"—best drinks in town, fifty cents. Everybody there. Buddy cracking jokes. Somebody plays the jukebox. . . . All of us up there at the Up Stairs were friends. That's the way Phil (big, handsome, bearded Phil) planned it when he took over the bar . . . Phil made it a place to have fun in—a place to relate to, a place to go. There were no more literate conversations than those to be had at the Up Stairs, no better place to go. A place to go if you wanted to have fun . . . a place to find friends if you were in need. . . . A place, perhaps, to find love.[6]

Many of the sixty or so patrons remaining that muggy evening had been there since the beer bust started. Members of the MCC, which only recently had moved its services to Larson's apartment, were there to thank a bar patron for donating an air conditioner. Courtney Craighead, a deacon at the MCC, had arrived at five o'clock. The temporary assistant pastor, George "Mitch" Mitchell, dropped his two children off at a Disney film and arrived with his lover, Louis "Horace" Broussard, a few minutes later. Troy Perry remembers Mitch as "a talkative person who dressed like an unmade bed, interrupted everybody's conversations, and was still impossible not to like."[7] Despite occasional flare-ups, Mitch was devoted to the younger Horace, who worked at Chap's Barber Shop.

Among others enjoying the evening were Jimmy Warren and his younger brother, Eddie. The two gay sons were taking their Alabama-reared mother, Inez, out for the evening. Members of the Up Stairs Players were meeting in the back room to plan the crippled children benefit show scheduled that next Saturday. Leon Maples, "the kind of guy that if he only had three dollars left, he'd buy you a beer,"[8] was having his usual at the twenty-eight-foot bar, while another regular, Perry Waters, a Metairie dentist who provided free care to those in need, was enjoying drinks with a heavy-set friend. Stewart Butler was there with his younger lover, Alfred, who had just migrated from San Francisco. Talking with Horace, Stewart made plans for a haircut that next week.

A bit after seven, a sometime hustler and petty thief, twenty-six-year-old Rodger Dale Ñunez, started "agitating and smart-talking" an Up Stairs regular, Mike Scarborough. Mike punched him in the jaw. One of the bartenders, Hugh, picked up Ñunez, drug him down the thirteen steps, and tossed him out into the street. According to Scarborough, the long-haired youth promised to "burn you all out."[9]

Around 7:45, Alfred tugged at Stewart. It was time to head to their down-home bar, Wanda's. As the two trudged down the stairwell draped with fabric, David's piano music trailed them onto the street.

Five minutes later, the downstairs buzzer used by taxi drivers began to ring relentlessly, as the crowd was ending the beer bust with their singing of "United We Stand"—an anthem of the bar and of the time. Since no one had called a cab, Buddy asked Luther Boggs to send the cabbie along. He headed to the rear storeroom. As Luther opened the steel fire door, an orange fireball surged up the stairwell, knocking him to the floor.

"Fire!" exclaimed another customer.

Black smoke darkened the room. There appeared to be no exit as flames covered the doorway and raced through the drop-ceiling. The electricity failed. Panic erupted. Piano bar patrons swarmed across the dance floor.

Those thin enough to do so, like Lindy, slid through windows barred from the inside. Two men jumped from the second-story window, clothes blazing, to the street below. Some who had successfully escaped the inferno now lay lifeless on the pavement; blood ran into the gutter. Lindy slid down a drainage pipe, suffering only minor cuts.

In the fire and smoke, Buddy yelled, "Follow me!" He ran to the end of the bar near the piano, tapping and grabbing people as he passed. About twenty, including Mitch and Courtney, followed in an orderly procession. The group stumbled through the archway separating the first two rooms and then scurried twenty-five feet across the rectangular room and over the stage where "nellydrama" cabaret productions for charities were held. Moving some costumes, Buddy, in his pink tie-dyed jump suit, led the group through an exit door that he unlocked. Pulling patrons out onto the Ship Ahoy building roof, he went back into the theater area, calling out for others. Hearing no response, he closed and latched the fire door, joining others on the roof. They rushed through an apartment and scurried down the stairs.

Safe on Iberville Street, Mitch looked around. Louis was nowhere to be seen. Pushing aside firemen, Mitch returned to the flaming lounge. Inside, people were crowded near the windows shrieking for help. Lindy spotted Bill Larson at one. "He had one arm out and I heard him scream, 'Oh, God, no!'"[10]

Peering from the street below, Buddy witnessed a giant "flash over." Inside, liquor bottles exploded, Fourth of July decorations and leftover Mardi Gras streamers flashed yellow, red-flocked velvet wallpaper crumpled into ash, windows cracked, Burt Reynolds posters and the Queen Elizabeth portrait blistered; water from the corner fountains vaporized, barstools hurled across the room, the piano crumbled, rings on fingers melted. Patrons crawling over one another to the iron-barred windows were engulfed in the firestorm.

Fire department superintendent William McCrossen, who oversaw the eighty-seven fire fighters and thirteen engines that battled the sixteen-minute blaze, entered the building about quarter past eight. Expecting to find five or six persons, he was "flabbergasted." The veteran chief found bodies fused together or burnt to the bone.

Mitch's arm lay over his lover's body. David Gary guarded his smoldering white baby grand. On the platform behind the piano was Inez, covered by one of her sons. Still sitting on a nearby barstool was Adam Fontenoit.

Gawkers filtered through Iberville Street past midnight, staring at the window display of manikin-like creatures. Bill Larson's hairless head pressed against the bars. His right arm, partly covered by a ripped, soot-covered, green shirtsleeve, caressed the windowsill. The curious and morbid-minded visited for three days. Mourners brought bouquets and lilies while a crusty shrimper, who sometimes got help from Up Stairs patrons when his money ran short, stood sentinel.

Some, like Joslyn, the bar's "honorary faggot," expressed the loss of this Up Stairs community in written testimonials. Joslyn described Adam, Buddy's partner of five years, as

> small and delicate, a lock of heavy chestnut hair continually fell across his forehead, his whole face seemed chiseled out of irony. He had a couple or three master's degrees, spoke six languages fluently, and was an expert in musicology. Too intelligent, too sensitive, there seemed no place for him in the world until he met Buddy. . . . Tall, handsome, capable, brilliant, and yet tender. . . . And, after five years together, the radiance that lit their faces when they were together was unmistakably love. . . . "I remember him as the King in our last children's show. He was my favorite," said my friend Tracy, age five. The children knew him, loved him.[11]

Twenty-eight men and one woman—some gay, some not—died that night; fifteen were hospitalized. Three died within weeks, including Luther

Boggs—terminated from his teaching job while fighting for life with third-degree burns over 50 percent of his body. Larson's family refused to claim the minister's body, telling MCC members to cremate him and keep the ashes. Three other unclaimed persons were buried in paupers' graves.

Those who survived physical injuries confronted additional trauma. Newspapers printed their names as patrons of the "homosexual hangout."[12] Those not inside also suffered. Stewart Butler, who was at Wanda's when the fire trucks roared by at 7:56 P.M., remembers, "The most difficult thing for me was the fact that I had to go to work the next day and I had to shield the grief because I wasn't out of the closet."

In this "City That Care Forgot," the team of outside activists also faced a hesitant if not hostile group of New Orleans homosexuals. At an early meeting with some of the gay bar owners, Perry recalls someone asking, "Why are you carpetbaggers making trouble for us queers here?" He responded, "Well, we 'queers' here—some of us—are southerners. Somebody has to speak up and speak out! We can't be frightened of this or it will only be worse next time." Then one of the local drag queens stood up: "Reverend Perry is absolutely right! Either we stand up or we die."

Meanwhile, in Father Bill Richardson's quiet manner, arrangements had already been made for Reverend Perry to hold a memorial service that Monday evening at St. George's, "providing that you keep it low-keyed." Richardson's demeanor reflected his early life experience and southern ways of respectful discretion and gracious indirection: "Growing up in Kentucky, I had often wondered what it would be like to have sex with a man. But, I didn't even know how in those days. . . . There was no discussion of homosexuality. About half of my uncles, though, never married. . . . There was one relative who stayed very much to himself in a little holler. They called him very 'queer' and a 'strange' person."

About fifty souls, who learned of the service by word of mouth, attended that evening. Perry officiated. Bill Richardson and David Solomon, a former member of the local GLF and founder of the MCC chapter, assisted. Perry spoke directly to the congregation, which had lost one-third of its members: "Someone said it was just a bunch of faggots. But we knew them as people, as brothers and sisters."[13]

News of the service appeared in the next day's morning paper. The telephone rang early. Father Bill recalls the halting conversation.

"Bill, this is the bishop!"

"Good morning, Bishop."

"Have you read the morning newspaper?"

"Yes, I have, Bishop."

"Is it true that this service was at St. George's *Episcopal* Church?"

"Yes, Bishop, it is true."

"Well, what am I going to say when people start calling my office?"

"Bishop, you can say anything you want as far as I am concerned. But do you think that Jesus would have kept these people out of His church?"

There was a long pause.

Bishop Noland was not satisfied, however, with Father Bill's response and demanded to know why the service was not held at the MCC. Although Bill explained that the small congregation's meeting place was too small for the crowd, the bishop's anger was not allayed. Later he called back, informing Father Bill that he had received more than one hundred angry calls from local Episcopalians. Father Bill's mailbox was full of hate letters, and members of his congregation asked, "What kind of Christian are you to allow a thing like this to go on in our church?"

A more ecumenical memorial service in the Vieux Carré was planned for that Sunday, 1 July. Perry remembers that he called Bishop Noland: "I never got to him but his number two person told me that they would not be interested. I called the Catholic bishop and was told only Catholics could use their churches. I tried to call a Baptist church; they hung up on me."

Perry reports that he then contacted the Vieux Carré Commission. Its president, "a wonderful, southern gentleman," responded supportively. Clay Shaw and the commission approved holding the service outside the Up Stairs Lounge if no church in the Quarter was found.

St. Mark's Methodist volunteered its facility. In preparation, Perry stopped by the wooden church located on Rampart Street. He came across an older woman who was a member of the board of directors:

"I got to ask you a question, Reverend Perry. Is your mother's name Edith?"

Seldom startled, he paused. "Who are you?"

"I was Bucky Harold's wife."

In a world where people are connected by six degrees of separation, the distance in the South is measured fractionally. Mrs. Harold was Troy's mother's best friend when his family lived in Tallahassee.

Three thousand flyers were distributed announcing the memorial service. By two o'clock, 250 people, who had refused to stay in their little closets of sorrow, filled the church's pews, crowded its balcony, and lined the aisles. Charlene Schneider, the wiry proprietor of Charlene's, was among the mourners. Wearing a beige dress and an orange hat, she attended despite protests from her girlfriend. She "didn't want me to go because there was going to be cameras."[14]

Following prayers, hymns, and Scripture readings, Troy Perry delivered a eulogy of forgiveness and hope and announced, "Before we close the service we'll sing the song that was sung at the Up Stairs Lounge by the pianist, who always finished the beer bust every Sunday afternoon with 'United We Stand.'"

In the midst of the third stanza, Perry recollects that he received a note: "There are TV cameras set up across the street out in front." He interrupted the organist and spoke to the congregation: "I cannot control what is happening across the street. I just want to tell you that you can go out of the side door . . .[and] leave through the alley." One woman stood up: "I am not ashamed to be here. And I am walking out the front door!"[15]

Although twenty-five years have passed, Perry pauses in the story's retelling. Wiping away his tears, he declares: "As someone who has involved himself as a gay activist, I have never felt so proud in my life. This was one of the high points in the gay movement. In a city where people were *really* frightened, nobody left by the back door. We sung and held hands. People held themselves high; they walked out with their heads held high knowing that 'I have the right to the sunlight here in New Orleans.'" He sobs. "At that time, at that moment, people really started standing up in New Orleans. And it gave courage to the larger gay rights movement. It so galvanized us nationally that we said we can *never* let anything like this happen again!"

> And if our backs should ever be against the wall,
> We will be together—
> Together—you and I.

ELEVEN

Atlas Shrugged

Female homosexuality . . . as different as day from night from male homosexuality.
—*Lillian Smith*

The first time Julia "Penny" Stanley called herself "lesbian" was in 1972. Continuing to teach, she continued to learn: "I really came to the women's movement through gay liberation. The media had been a tremendous influence in spreading dissent, and the students picked up from the media. While I wasn't watching TV much, what the students were talking about made sense: feminism is one of the most encompassing analyses I have ever encountered."

That fall quarter at the University of Georgia Julia officially sponsored the student women's group. As its members were "turning lesbian like a wildfire through Athens," the group joined with the campus Committee on Gay Education and the Georgia Gay Liberation Front to organize a regional conference.

The preceding March, the Committee on Gay Education had planned a dance at the student union. The Office of Student Affairs, however, denied permission for the event. The director claimed that it would violate the state's statute by "condoning, aiding, and abetting illegal acts of sodomy." A sit-in was held on the day after the dance's cancellation, presenting the dean of student affairs with a list of demands. The committee's faculty advisor resigned under pressure.[1] But, on the weekend of 11 November, two weeks after ABC television premiered *That Certain Summer* (a sensitive

ALFA at Atlanta's Gay Pride Parade. Photo by and courtesy of Lorraine Fontana.

depiction of a gay relationship) on its *Wednesday Movie of the Week,* the student organizers held their conference. Of course, a court first issued a restraining order against the university, which had refused to provide space.

The call to arms for this Southern Convention and Association of Gay Militants had been circulated throughout the Southeast:

> A year or so ago, many gays were shouting, "Out of the closets and into the streets!" Now, it appears, the acceptance of traditional gay roles is spreading throughout the gay ghettos. . . . [E]mphasis in the movement put on "liberated" life-style counter cultures has resulted in retreat from struggle. . . . Local gay organizations are essential, but just as essential are active regional and national organizations. The South can lead in this respect. . . . We can, and must, change history.[2]

More than sixty "delegates" came from nearly "every state of the Confederacy," mostly from larger cities, including Memphis, Jackson, Knoxville, Charlotte, Lexington, Raleigh, Miami, and the District of Columbia.[3] The geographic diversity, however, belied its mostly male, white, and middle-class composition. There were just one African American and a handful of women in attendance.

The first general session on Friday set the weekend agenda—and its tone. The chairperson, wielding *Roberts Rules of Order* and "doing it all with a half macho/supercilious, half flippant/camp attitude," quickly alienated some within the ideologically diverse audience, Julia recalls. It also became clear to her and others that folks held differing goals for what would be the South's first regional coalition, as the *Lavender Wave* reported:

> Some people were interested in forming an organization primarily geared toward ensuring that socialist revolution in the US would . . . include the liberation of gay people. Others were primarily interested in a group to coordinate legal reform and educational measures. Some wanted the group to move primarily in the direction of a union with female liberation. And still others were looking for better social life and were turned off by all the politics.[4]

By mid-Saturday business was "suspended." Discussion turned to specific areas of reform (e.g., repeal of antisodomy statutes) and to tactics and strategies. Again, differences of ideology emerged as participants debated whether to organize as a "united front of gay people . . . or a united front of all oppressed people."[5] There was, however, a consensus to form "interest groups" that would avoid "conflicting with those who differed from us but who shared the goal of gay liberation."[6]

For the conference, organizers had enlisted the help of WomanSong Theater and the Atlanta Lesbian Feminist Alliance. ALFA was the first lesbian-feminist organization in Georgia.[7] The group had formed that past June from a cadre of women holding various movement credentials and an anonymous $3,000 donation. Some, like Vicki Gabriner, had been active in Atlanta Women's Liberation, were veterans of earlier struggles for civil rights and against the Vietnam War, and had participated in the Venceremos Brigade. Others, like Lorraine Fontana, were veterans of the early gay pride marches and interracial community work.

Lorraine attended the weekend conference as a writer for the *Great Speckled Bird*. The daughter of a Queens working-class Italian American family, she had first come to Atlanta as a VISTA volunteer in 1968. She helped poor whites and blacks, who lived in shotgun row houses and one-story housing complexes, organize food-buying clubs. Lorraine started writing for the *Bird* two years later, after she dropped out of graduate school at Emory University. During the next couple of years, she met other women in political work, including those in Atlanta Women's Liberation and the Georgia GLF. There were also women who participated in the Anti-Imperialist Coalition, organized antiwar activities, or had just returned from Cuba with one of the Venceremos Brigades. "Through a mixing of these groups, a bunch of women were becoming feminists," Lorraine recalls. "We started living in houses together and coming out."

Not far from the Emory campus, right off Moreland Avenue, Lorraine remembers an "old, rundown neighborhood with lots of houses broken down into apartments." Women migrating into this area known as Little Five Points sometimes assigned names to their collective households. "Upstairs/Downstairs" begot other collective residences, such as Lavender Coven, Ruby Fruit, Butterfly Bottoms, Edge of Night, and Libra Rising.

One of the women who eventually found her way into this neighborhood was Vicki Gabriner. As a member of the second Venceremos Brigade, she had participated in the ten-million-ton sugar harvest. Vicki, a self-described "femme from the word go," in the 1950s had watched her "politically savvy" mother lead the PTA in struggles for a new elementary school and traffic lights, at the height of the McCarthy era. In the tradition of her politically progressive parents, themselves children of Eastern European Jewish immigrant families, Vicki became politically active in the southern civil rights movements during her undergraduate college years. During the midsixties, she did civil rights work in West Tennessee, as well as antiwar work at the University of Wisconsin. Near the decade's end, she joined the Weathermen, a group of antiwar activists that emerged from the Students for Democratic Society. In the spring of 1970, laboring in the Cuban sugar cane fields, she worked alongside sisters and brothers from Atlanta. Afterward, she joined them in the New South.

Like Lorraine, Vicki became a writer for the *Bird*.[8] She participated in the paper's female caucus and helped assemble the women's liberation issue that fall—activities that gave rise to Atlanta Women's Liberation. Later, as ALFA members, Lorraine and Vicki shared stories of the group's beginning and its collective structure with those attending the Athens conference. "We didn't have the name at first," Lorraine told a few of the interested women. "The big discussion was lesbian-feminist alliance. Should this be for *all* lesbians, and therefore not just lesbian-feminist? Does lesbian-feminist alliance mean lesbians *and* straight feminists allied together? That was the biggest question. After all of this discussion, it was agreed that this was going to be a *lesbian* group but that there isn't a litmus test—you don't have to pull out your lesbian ID card!"

Since its founding five months before the conference, ALFA had grown to several dozen members. Despite differences in ideology, temperament, and tactics, they were united in their commitment to fight against sexism and heterosexism. Atlanta Women's Liberation "was too straight and the Gay Liberation Front was too male," Vicki explained.[9] "We need to organize ourselves; we need *not* to have to fight with these notions of sexism," proclaimed Lorraine. "We want a women's-only space—a *place* where women who come from other neighborhoods or outside of Atlanta, where they can come to just be with other lesbians."

The three-story wood frame structure on Mansfield Avenue in Little Five Points was such a place. Concrete steps led from the street past the wild garden to the front porch of this twenties-style house. Lorraine and the other women living in the Edge of Night collective agreed that the downstairs would become the ALFA meeting house. The space allowed for small groups to gather and to focus energy on a variety of activities. During the next few years these would range from theater and softball to newsletter publishing and political outreach. However, on this fall weekend, they were alongside members of WomanSong Theater troupe.

Julia Stanley was among the audience for WomanSong's Saturday-evening performance. Calling herself "gay," she still held to a philosophy of radical individualism. Like the archetypal figure John Galt in *Atlas Shrugged*, Julia disdained the collectivist ideals of "secondhanders" who unknowingly need but treat society's "prime movers" viciously. Like the doer-thinker in the Ayn Rand novel, Julia "never lived for the sake of another"[10] until that Saturday-night performance at the student union, which she describes: "The stage faced the center of the lounge, where the audience sat in easy chairs and couches or, according to taste, on the floor.

It was a small (not more than seventy) but noisy and appreciative crowd, eager to hear and applaud the more radical message brought to Athens from our sisters to the west in Atlanta. They kept me in stitches—and they radicalized me." Most vividly, Julia remembers, "One of the women did a skit in which she appeared in male drag, carrying a whip, and lip-syncing to the Rolling Stones' 'Under My Thumb.' She was good! I probably wouldn't have thought anything of that song's lyrics had I not seen her lip-sync it." By the end of the evening, Julia was applauding loudly: "My thinking had changed."

The next day, she recalls, some of her "gay students" invited their professor to the organizing session of the Southeastern Gay Coalition: "I didn't get there until the very end of the meeting. One of my students nominated me as a co-coordinator. I was on the spot: Put up or shut up. I didn't withdraw my name because I didn't think anyone would vote for me! Talk about a miscalculation!"

That Monday Julia was "out" on campus, courtesy of a story in the student newspaper, the *Red and Black*. "Someone told me that one of my colleagues in the coffee room quipped, 'Well, everyone knew but did she have to have it on the front page?'" Soon the female faculty in the department were coming up "at the rate of one a day to announce that they were heterosexual." She remembers one female colleague who called Julia into her office:

> "You know, Julia. I'm different from you."
> "Oh, really? How?"
> "Well, I'm more *conventional*."
> Julia feigned ignorance. "I'm sorry, I don't understand what you mean."
> "Well, I'm more *conservative*."
> "I still don't understand," Julia pressed. "Perhaps you could give me an example of the kind of distinctions you're making."
> Hesitating, Julia's colleague answered: "I don't teach in blue jeans."
> "Neither do I."
> The colleague stammered, "Well, I'm married."
> "That's true."
> "And," she went on, "I have a child . . . and . . . I'm hetero."
> Julia paused before responding. "Well, you know, you needn't suffer anymore. There are doctors who can cure that now!"

During that November weekend, Julia had encountered other lesbian and gay activist collectives. Those from Knoxville published a mimeographed newsletter, *Mother Jones*. Julia found them "very radical and very vocal." There were also Lexington activists as well as those from Atlanta and Raleigh—all of whom were prime movers in the conference.

Out of the conference, Julia explains, emerged a "skeletal structure of a regional organization" that evidenced the divisions in ideology and interest. A steering committee had representation from caucuses and interest groups, including Feminist, Transient Workers, Marxist, Reform—and Flame.

The Feminist Caucus reconvened in January 1973, with the lesbians quickly splitting from the heterosexual women and gay men. The next month these lesbians met in Athens to develop a position paper to carry back to the Southeastern Gay Coalition. Among the North Carolina participants who drove down from the Triangle Area was twenty-eight-year-old Elizabeth Knowlton.

Four and a half years before, Knowlton had arrived in Chapel Hill to pursue a Ph.D. in English literature with her husband—who soon left her. Although familiar with *The Feminine Mystique* and *The Second Sex,* she recalls finding "no one to talk to about these ideas." Then, in early 1969, Elizabeth overheard a radical visiting film maker chatting in the cafeteria: "I had always perceived left-wing groups like that as places for women just to serve men—as in other places. And I said a few sentences to that effect." The man turned to her and said, "Well, you'd be interested in Women's Liberation." Elizabeth was stunned. "I had never heard those two words linked before."

The next week she attended her first women's meeting. "My life changed," she reports. Most of the women were socialists who, though "sick of men in the left wing," expected to "go back working with men." Knowlton, a self-described "crazy lady . . . hated men and was angry and mad at what men had done to us! I was angry at the whole system. Men ran everything; they determined everything." One of the first essays Elizabeth read was "The Florida Paper," produced by the Florida feminists in Gainesville. Before, she didn't use four-letter words, "but as soon as it was connected with my anger, then it was normal."

Elizabeth helped produce the *Triangle Women's Liberation Newsletter.*[11] Gradually, the socialist women realized that this "wasn't just a cell developed out of their antiwar or civil rights group," Knowlton recalls, and she became more politicized. "When we started we didn't have any idea about gays or anything." Some of the women involved in the newsletter were married, and sometimes their husbands worked on alternative papers like the *Protean Radish.* Others, like Elizabeth, dated men. "You were just expected to have a boyfriend." However, when the women gathered, there "would be such completeness, such oneness, that I used to think how strange it was that we would all go off to our boyfriends or husbands."

Every once in a while a woman would move, and "word would come back that she had come out. I would think, 'Why don't they ever do it here?'"

An enormous influence on Elizabeth was *off our backs*. She and her roommate, Linda, read every issue of this feminist newspaper.[12] And, in 1971, they became a couple. "At first, we didn't say anything," remembers Knowlton. Then her roommate-turned-lover told a member of her women's group who was considering joining the two in a living collective. The woman laughed. It turned out she also had a female lover. "Bit by bit, we came out."

But it was difficult to find others. Hearing about the lesbian caucus meeting in Georgia at a very late date, Elizabeth had canceled her planned weekend activities, including a Friday-night women's basketball game, a Saturday evening of folk dancing, and a Sunday meeting to help plan a fine arts festival. As she, Linda, and another woman from Raleigh made the eight-hour drive Friday night, Knowlton's thoughts went back to the South Atlantic Modern Language Association meeting the previous November in Jacksonville. She remembered that "there was this woman, and I thought, 'She's a lesbian.' I kept sliding up to and following her around, but she didn't pay the slightest bit of attention to me."

When the North Carolina car finally turned the corner onto Best Drive at one o'clock in the morning, Elizabeth walked up the sidewalk and rang the doorbell at the address they had been given for the caucus meeting. A figure in a nightshirt appeared. Elizabeth looked at her and exclaimed: "You're in English!"

Smacking her forehead, Julia muttered: "Is it written here?"

It was the same woman Elizabeth had followed around at the Jacksonville conference! "Athens," Elizabeth remembers, "was the most notorious place in Georgia, and Julia Stanley was the most notorious person in Athens." Knowlton adds: "She did what she wanted; she looked like a diesel dyke. There was no hiding! Women would migrate over to Atlanta after they finished at the University of Georgia and talk about her in awe. Gays in that era could walk around campus holding hands at a time when nowhere else was that going on. It was because of her; she provided a nucleus for that atmosphere."

During that February weekend, Elizabeth introduced Julia to writings of the Furies and Radicalesbians, including "The Woman-Identified Woman," which proclaimed: "As long as we cling to the idea of 'being a woman,' we will sense some conflict with that incipient self, that sense of I, that sense of a whole person. It is very difficult to realize and accept that being 'feminine' and being a whole person are irreconcilable. Only

women can give each other a new sense of self."[13] After reading their statements, Julia recollects, she found "they had spoken for me!"

While echoing the profeminist sentiments of "The Woman-Identified
Woman," the Lesbian Caucus's position paper, written in Athens in
February 1973, also challenged the emerging gay male culture:

> Too often, gay men define freedom as the right to continue to define them-
> selves and other men as sexual objects. . . . Freedom is not a sexist, gay
> male publication that includes advertising about baths and places to cruise.
> . . . In addition, there are gay men who parody women in their speech
> as well as in their portrayal of their concept of womanhood, thus main-
> taining the stereotypes of women and perpetuating the sex roles we
> detest as women. . . . We are equally oppressed by gay men who are so
> ashamed of their own gayness that they are insulted if anyone calls
> them effeminate.[14]

Proposing that each caucus "function as a separate entity" and that the
Coalition become a "communication center," the Lesbian Caucus concluded they had "deep reservations about working within the Southeastern
Gay Coalition because of the way men relate to us. Men are sexist; gay
men are sexist."[15]

As the only woman of the five-member coordinating committee
(which included Bob Bland from Raleigh and others from Knoxville,
Atlanta, Miami, and D.C.), Julia hoped to engage the various factions
in dialogue. The committee of five gathered for long weekend meetings
in Knoxville, Athens, and Raleigh. A second conference was set for the
weekend of 16 March 1973. There the divergent interest groups presented position papers.

The all-male Reform Caucus, led by Atlanta's Bill Smith, met only once
during the interim from November to March. However, they supported
the Lesbian Caucus proposal that the Coalition's primary role should be
facilitating communication. Another band of males—the WarmeBruder
Caucus (named for the German idea of "warm brothers")—was less
sympathetic, arguing that "all people are included in the term mankind."
However, they agreed with the Lesbian Caucus that "continuing in these
parodies we are hurting ourselves; we are keeping ourselves from being
what we feel inside." They turned Marx on his head, though, declaring
that "the destruction of the fundamental sex role structure will inevitably
include the liberation from class."[16]

Following these presentations, the lesbian position paper was adopted.
The Lexington GLF group reprinted excerpts in its *Gay Times*.[17] Later
it published a different perspective written by a woman involved in "les-

bian feminist politics" for about a year. Her essay voiced displeasure with the growing lesbian-separatist movement: "It may be advisable and even necessary to withdraw from the mainstream of society in order to effectively reorganize the perspectives of the individuals involved. But then we became increasingly involved in discussing stale and pointless rhetoric, and being 'more-separatist-than-thou.' . . . If a revolution is to be effective, it must be for everybody, not only for white middle-class Anglo-Saxon separatist Lesbians."[18]

At the time of this March meeting the Coalition's *Lavender Wave* was already into its second issue. As Bob Bland edited the newsletter, Julia traveled to organize in other southern communities. "Mostly what was in the South," she found during the winter of 1973, "were women's groups in some universities and a few gay men, some from socialist groups. Stonewall really hadn't had any impact."

While this was perhaps true, the rebellious chants of "Sisterhood Is Powerful," the sirens of Bilitis, and the Furies' outcry were already echoing through southern mill and mining villages, campus and coastal towns, urban centers and suburbia. In the early seventies, more than a few southern communities enjoyed feminist activity, attracting a cohort of youthful lesbian activists who would profoundly shape the Stonewall South. Their efforts, though, failed to bridge the divide between twenty-something lesbian-feminists, often unaware of the contributions of earlier generations of southern lesbians, and women from earlier decades for whom the "L word" was often as distasteful as women burning bras or wearing jeans.[19]

In Charlotte, a mostly student group had started consciousness-raising groups in the summer of 1968 among female factory workers. Within three years, Charlotte was a feminist hotbed.[20] A federation of women's groups joined to form Charlotte Women United, with its own Women's Center funded by monthly contributions. At the center a variety of counseling and consciousness-raising groups were available, as well as short-term lodging for women in need, a lending library, a newsletter, and a clothing exchange. The center, like others around the South, generally attracted twenty-something women, radicalized by feminism, civil rights, or the Vietnam War.

Richmond had been another center for feminist activity ever since the first wave of feminism. By the 1920s there was a literary circle that included novelist Ellen Glasgow and her "very warm friend," Mary Johnson, who formed the Equal Suffrage League of Virginia, led by Lila Meade Valentine.[21] There was also Helen McCormack and her Charleston lover, Laura Bragg, at the newly reorganized Valentine Museum, as well as Grace Arendts, whose philanthropy supported the first free library.[22]

Two generations later, however, there was little memory of these Virginians' efforts, and whispered rumors of lesbian or Bolshevik influences had waned. "Lesbian" was still an alien word to the tongues of older single women who ran YWCAs, served as deans of women or library directors, and organized church groups or literary events. By 1970, a new generation of Richmond women was emerging. In the fall of 1971, after she attended the Virginia Women's Political Caucus convention, Beth Marschak was a cofounder of the Organization for Women's Liberation (OWL).

Marschak was brought up in a working-class Richmond Southern Baptist family: "We were practically in church the whole day Sunday—and then there was Wednesday night. And, if there was a revival we were there every day!" Although a male-centered institution, the church provided opportunities for female leadership in gender-segregated areas. "As in all predominantly same-sex groups," Beth observes, "there were other lesbians there and some of the leaders were single women who were missionaries." From a very early age Beth assumed leadership positions and, at age twelve, began preaching. "Some of my activism does stem from this," Beth smiles.

Under Beth's leadership, OWL brought together a group of ten to twenty women. Holding informal discussions and campus programs, they involved themselves in campus politics, including an investigation of the salary differences between men and women professors that created "quite a commotion," Beth recalls. As her interest drifted from chemistry to women's history, she began to link the personal with the political.

Despite the emergence of women's centers and organizations in southern towns, there were few safe spaces for lesbian-identified women in the early seventies.[23] "Lesbians had no reason to trust straight women or men. Both had betrayed us," Julia Stanley asserts. "So, we were never really comfortable, we were always on the periphery—marginal. That's why we set out to create something for ourselves."

When Julia heard of another women's conference to be held at the University of Georgia in the fall of 1973, she was excited. That was, of course, before she learned of its orientation: middle-class, white, heterosexual. "Some of the faculty, including me, and the students were angry that this was going to be a 'proper conference for the ladies.'"

Merril Mushroom, who joined Julia for the conference, remembers that "Julia was in such a stew because the sponsor, the women's committee of the American Association of University Professors, were putting on a white academic women's conference and charging a lot of money to attend. They didn't have child care. There were no workshops about lesbians, poor women, or prisoners. But they did have a workshop on female sexuality—conducted by a man!" The disgruntled faculty and students met with the AAUP Women's Committee members to discuss these concerns, but, Merril recalls, "they didn't want to hear it."

Merril had arrived in Knoxville with Gabby, J'aime, and their street dog, "Found," only two months earlier, marking the end of their road atlas caravan. They had discovered that hog farming in the dry New Mexican climate was not to their liking, and they lacked the money for travel to the Northwest. Shrugging off their prejudices, they journeyed to the South. In Knoxville, there were jobs available, a lesbian community, and land nearby that might fulfill their dream of an intentional community.

Merril found the Knoxville lesbian community diverse but not divided:

> There were the southern ladies but there were also Knoxville dykes from families living in Oak Ridge whose fathers were scientists. There were some working-class women, students, and professors. But the professors wouldn't associate with us because they were too closeted; they were not as overwhelmed with feminism as the younger women. There, too, were the local softball lesbians, who overlapped with the physical education students.

When Julia discovered Gloria Steinem was to be the keynote speaker at the AAUP Women's Conference in Athens, she telephoned *Ms.* magazine. Steinem promptly returned her call. Calmly but forcefully, Stanley recalls, she presented her case: There was "no lesbian visibility, nothing about working-class situations, nothing on racism, just academic papers on home economics and literary analysis." Steinem agreed to speak at the alternative conference across the street without a fee.

Nearly a hundred women attended the October alternative conference, which featured free child care and topics censored by "the ladies." Held at a local church across from the university-sponsored conference, Merril reminisces, "It was phenomenal!" She adds: "Some of the women from the other conference offered to loan their badges if anyone wanted to go across the way."

The next month Julia went to New York's John Jay College for the first national conference of the Gay Academic Union (GAU), a collection of academic-oriented activists that began on a Saturday afternoon in a Manhattan apartment the previous March and quickly expanded from the original eight individuals into biweekly gatherings. At the "Universities and the Gay Experience" conference, she was a member of the "coming out" panel and attended the Lesbian Caucus.[24] "This was something

I had never experienced!" she says. "Here were all of these lesbians from the Gay Liberation Front and Gay Academic Alliance who were very articulate and aggressive with their politics (which is how we came to have the lesbian caucus because they had to fight for it within the GAU)."

At the caucus, Jean O'Leary, founder of Lesbian Feminist Liberation, spoke informally but eloquently and with precision, Julia recollects: "She held forth with her analysis of the situation at the GAU; I liked that analysis—which was lesbian-separatist. (Within months, of course, she was no longer a separatist.) But one of the points Jean made was the importance of lesbian-only space. I realized that I had *never* had that in my life— except, to some extent, in the Miami bars."

Following this epiphany, Julia Stanley thought and read more deeply. She realized that "*gay* is a pseudo-generic, like *man*. It really means *gay* men—and there's safety in that! Being part of a larger group that contains both sexes is safer for a woman than being part of a women-only group."

By December, she considered herself a separatist, "but I continued to work with gay men, like Louie Crew, in the GAU."[25] However, Julia was less tolerant of the male-centered university and had "tired of academic politics. I put a position paper to all of my male colleagues in their mailboxes telling them about what I thought."

Julia Stanley continued to teach through the winter quarter of 1974, finding solace in her conversations with other women and encouraging lesbian students to find their own space and pursue feminist scholarship. One master's degree student was working on her thesis about Edith Wharton. This was a time, Julia remembers, when "there wasn't much besides Gertrude Stein and the pulp novels of the fifties. *Rubyfruit Jungle* was really the first book that we had to talk about." During one of their frequent sessions, teacher and student discussed *Rubyfruit,* Brown's coming-of-age novel:

"It's not well-crafted in a literary sense," piously observed the student.

"I don't care, it's funny!" In an irreverent tone, Julia asked, "Isn't it about time that we had a literary vehicle for laughing about *our* lives?"

With the same vigor with which Molly Bolt, the Florida tomboy, had struggled to find herself and gain lesbian space in Brown's novel, Julia Stanley resigned and sued the university for the inequitable salaries of women in her department. She also telephoned Merril. "I want to throw in with you when you do the commune."

"Okay, come on up when you're ready," beckoned Merril.

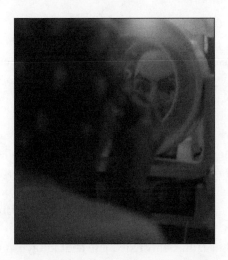

TWELVE

The Promised Land

We liberate ourselves before we liberate society. —Lige Clarke

On New Year's eve 1959, Fidel Castro arrived on the world scene. "People were running through the streets, shouting. I heard father tell mother that Fidel and his troops were about to enter Havana: 'El es dia nuevo por los pueblos de Cubano!'"

Five-year-old Jesus Gustavo Monteagudo's world was about to change. He recollects that

> after the Revolution, *I Love Lucy* was no longer shown (it had been dubbed in Spanish). Instead there were messages about the revolution. There was also a situation comedy in which the characters would volunteer to help with the sugar cane harvest or set the alarm clock for five A.M. so they could attend one of Castro's marathon speeches (all humorously, of course). The government also tried to produce homegrown comic books—they were never the same as my American favorites like *Superman*.

With little American-style television to watch or comics to read, "Jesse," as Jesus preferred being called, found himself with time on his hands. His Uncle Gustavo—who later came out as gay—was a member of the religious order that operated the elementary school that Jesse

Creating the Drag Lady of the Evening, 1976. Photo courtesy of Paul Wegman.

attended. But Castro expelled the Spanish and French clergy from Cuba; the school closed. Jesse did not attend the public school that was creating the "New Socialist Man," he relates, because "my father didn't want me to be indoctrinated."

Memories of this revolutionary experience include long lines and ration cards. Jesse recalls waiting with his family for a visa to leave the country. "There was a lot of red tape involved. You had to know people in government in order to get a visa *and* you needed an American sponsor."

In June 1962, a prosperous South Carolina Presbyterian couple—friends of Senator Strom Thurmond—sponsored Jesse's family. The couple had come to know Jesse's father, christened Jesus but known as Chucho, through the tourist trade on their frequent visits to Cuba. Jesse says, "They were staunch anticommunists and perhaps thought that sponsoring a Cuban family would mean they were doing their bit to fight godless communism!"

At the age of nine, Jesse, his younger sister, Margarita, and their parents boarded a flight that traveled ninety miles, as Jesse puts it, from "communism to democracy." Following their Miami arrival, they stopped first at the Freedom Tower on Biscayne and Sixth Street—"the Cuban version of Ellis Island." There his family, like several thousand other middle-class Cubans, waited for papers to be processed, picked up welfare checks, and accepted long bars of American cheese, processed milk, and other Army surplus food.

Journeying to the upcountry of South Carolina, Chucho worked in a Greenville textile mill while his family became "a curiosity piece. These local missionaries promised to help my father get a better job if we converted. We never did, allegedly because I threw up a ruckus at the thought—even then I rebelled against southern fundamentalists!"

For the next two years the Monteagudo family lived in a guest cottage owned by their sponsoring couple near the town of Taylor, off I-85. Though they were viewed by neighbors and friends as "embodiments of anticommunist resistance," Jesse did not have many friends. "Fortunately," he continues, "as Cubans of European descent, we never suffered from any racism that I can remember. In fact, marrying Cuban women was sort of chic within the social circle of our sponsoring couple."

Quickly learning English, Jesse grew up amidst momentous events in this capitalist paradise nestled near the mountains. He visited the region's only mall and ate his first Whopper. He read about the Birmingham Sixteenth Street Church bombing and the admission of Harvey Gant as the first African American student in nearby Clemson. And he watched with weekly delight *The Mickey Mouse Club* and *Bozo the Clown*.

In 1964, the family returned to Miami's Little Havana—an area just southwest of downtown whose main thoroughfare, Southwest Eighth Street or the Tamiami Trail, had already been rechristened Calle Ocho. Jesse vividly remembers "old men playing dominoes, coffee shops dispensing rivers of café Cubano, statues of the saints beaming from store windows and car windshields, and fiery speeches shouted from street corners or the airwaves."

Being a "fat and nerdy boy with eyeglasses and not yet accepting my sexuality," Jesse recalls that he generally was alone—reading when not strolling down Calle Ocho. Living across from his family in another "run-down" apartment, however, was an "outrageous queen," Angel, who appeared in local theater productions. "He lived with his widowed mother and maiden aunt. Angel was as skinny as Ichabod Crane and fluttered about screeching at a high decibel. He and the local hairdresser were the only gay role models I had. My parents told me to 'stay away from that *mariconé;* he will do something to you.'"

Suspecting their son might be a little Angel, Jesse's parents sent him to the YMCA to become, in his words, "more masculine and show an interest in girls." Yet, in judo class, he only learned "how to fall on the floor with my legs up in the air—a skill that I would later find useful!" Jesse soon found himself sitting in a psychiatrist's office—though he avoided the hormone shots inflicted on Little Havana's more effeminate gay boys.

When Jesse graduated from high school in 1972, his gay education continued at Miami Dade Junior College: "I used to borrow gay books in the library and practice gay sex in the men's room. I particularly enjoyed *The Gay Mystique.* Like the author, I wanted to meet 'a nice Jewish boy in leather'—I eventually did!" Other favorite books included Clarke and Nichols's *I Have More Fun with You Than Anybody* and Rechy's *City of Night*—a coming-of-age novel told in a bluesy, rock 'n roll rhythm through the eyes of a half-Mexican, half-Scottish Texas hustler—and an upbeat narrative by a southern couple.[1]

I Have More Fun with You Than Anybody contrasted with Rechy's pre-Stonewall sonnet of desperate love and despairing sexuality. Lige Clarke, the lanky Kentuckian, and Jack Nichols, the Whitmanesque Washingtonian, celebrated the coming out of their book that June with a party on Central Park West hosted by George Weinberg, author of *Society and the Healthy Homosexual.* In September 1972, Lige and Jack embarked on a two-week bicoastal book tour. "Our growing mini-fame made it impossible to go anywhere in the city's gay haunts without being recognized," Jack reminisces.[2]

As editors of *GAY* and authors of a book that soon went into its second printing, they were among the A-list gays and met celebrities like David Bowie, Andy Warhol, and Cab Calloway. Attending gala openings and premieres, they enjoyed weekends at Fire Island and danced shirtless at Pier 9 and similar clubs.

Amidst the traveling and New York hoopla, Lige dutifully answered a growing number of letters, publishing some of his responses in the "Pen Points" column. *GAY* continued to turn out provocative issues, including a two-page spread, "In Praise of Leather: An Inside Look at S&M," and an interview with a rising star at the Continental Baths, Bette Midler, who sang accompanied by her piano man, Barry Manilow.

Meanwhile, Miami Beach prepared to welcome both political parties that summer, and pressure mounted there to repeal two cross-dressing ordinances. Nearly a decade earlier a Miami cab driver, Richard Inman, had engaged in the "politics of dialectics" to abolish such laws.[3] His efforts generated few tangible results and, in 1967, the South's first state-chartered homophile organization, the Atheneum Society–turned–Mattachine-Florida, disbanded.

As Inman worked with an ACLU attorney on his Supreme Court appeal to invalidate these ordinances, Miami vice raided his Atheneum Book Shop on Southwest First Street. A reluctant judge tossed out the obscenity case on a technicality, returning 1,265 magazines, thirteen packets of photographs, and a twelve-minute film.[4]

In mid-January, the high court refused to hear his appeal, but Inman did hear from Foster Gunnison Jr. The affluent "apparatchik," who operated another one-man operation (the Institute for Social Ethics) in Connecticut, informed him that Lige had moved to Miami.[5] Like Foster, Lige and Jack had been comrades in arms with Richard during the old Mattachine Society of Florida days.

Caring for his eighty-pound Aunt Monte, Lige wrote Jack, who was living with his mother in Cocoa Beach, that Inman was "wondering why I haven't gotten in touch. . . . I'll be expecting to hear from you soon about whether I should call Richard Inman."[6] Lige's polite but curt chat did not appease Richard, who pestered Lige to join in his bookstore exploits, casting Jack as the villain.[7] "I'm hardly the type to sell pornography," Lige flatly stated.[8]

Lige and Jack soon reunited as a couple and departed for Manhattan, abandoning Richard Inman to his political machinations and pornographic hustling. As Jack drove their black 1965 Cadillac through the hills surrounding Hindman, Kentucky, Lige's hair tossed in the breeze. "When we're seventy years old," he shouted to Jack, "I'll write a book entitled *Every Day Is Spring*." Lige's eyes twinkled, "Or maybe *How to Keep a Life-time Romantic Lover*." Jack smiled.

Another homophile activist who encountered Richard Inman was Robert S. Basker. Under the alias Robert Sloane, Bob had organized Chicago Mattachine Midwest in the summer of 1965, quietly financed by bar and baths owner Chuck Renslow, who would later cofound the Mr. International Leather Contest.[9] Like Richard, Bob quickly got the reputation for "creating waves." Unlike the fiercely anticommunist Inman, Basker was a stalwart of socialist causes and civil rights activities during the sixties.

Bob Basker moved to Miami in 1966. This gregarious executive for Encyclopedia Britannica was a sharp contrast to Inman, who preferred the solitaire of political intrigue. Chastised by Richard as a "pinko of the worst kind,"[10] Bob traveled to Havana, by way of Canada, that October to live near his two children, whose new stepfather had brought them and his wife to Cuba. Teaching English and serving on the board of the Norteamericano Amigos de Cuba, Basker tried to make "as much of a contribution to the Revolution as I can."[11] Less helpful to the Cuban government, he organized support for two Cuban lesbians at the school where he worked, who faced dismissal by authorities.

During this time Jesse Monteagudo, whose family had fled Cuba four years earlier, was living in a "self-contained community," he recounted, where "supermarkets, pharmacies, and dime stores tried to outdo each other in their devotion to La Causa by displaying large Cuban flags and portraits of Cuban heroes Jose Marti and Antonio Maceo. My parents' generation then took it for granted that *el exilio* was only a temporary condition and that they would soon be able to return to *la Cuba libre*." Despite anti-Castro sentiments, Jesse's parents' generation, like Basker's revolutionary counterparts, were "planted deep in the soil of Spanish machismo and Roman Catholicism." Both shared an uncompromising view of homosexuality and were intolerant of political dissent. "The world was divided between the Cubans and the *Americanos*," Jesse observes. "Having created a replica of Old Havana in their new home, Miami's Cuban community sought to prevent the emergence of a progressive movement that it believed was responsible for the revolution."

As a patriot of the fatherland, Jesse's father refused to tolerate difference—particularly when it came to communists, civil rights agitators, and homosexuals. "My father swore that all rock singers were queer," Jesse continues. "When I turned thirteen my father sat me down and gave me a

stern lecture warning me to watch out for prowling perverts. . . . Whenever change could not be blamed on communism, it was attributed to
homosexuals."

Following a nine-month stay in Havana, Bob Basker arrived in Canada
aboard the Soviet ship *Karachaevo-Cherkessija.* He moved to Greenwich
Village, then returned to Miami in 1969. Meanwhile, Richard Inman had
departed the Sunshine State for new ventures in Southern California.[12]

As Bob sipped coffee on an August morning, his eye caught the feature
article in the *Miami Herald's Tropic Magazine.* It fleetingly mentioned
"Inman, until recently the ubiquitous spokesman for Miami homosexuals."
The story observed that the Miami gay "subculture shows few signs of the
minority group syndrome. Since the demise of the Mattachine Society of
Florida . . . Miami has had neither homosexual organizations nor militants. A politically docile, socially invisible subculture, it attracts little attention, and less support."[13]

South Florida homosexuals preferred the beaches or bars to organizing or marching. Accepting this boys-in-the-sand mentality, Bob bided
his time.[14] Unlike Inman, whose cloak-and-dagger politics were coupled
to an abrasive personality, Basker plied the politics of seduction. A tactician like Richard, Bob explains that he hoped to "neutralize and involve
politicians at the city level" by establishing personal connections in organizations that could pressure elected officials to cease police harassment,
rescind punitive laws, and eventually to support gay rights. Within two
years Basker was a board member of the Florida ACLU, a leader in
Concerned Democrats (the liberal wing of the party), and, although a lifelong Jew, a cofounder of an MCC group, becoming a church elder.

Activities in Miami began to gel as the twin national political party
conventions appeared on the city horizon. A small but determined group
advanced "tactics toward the strategy to get the law changed," according
to Basker, "setting all of the pawns in place for the grand move." And,
in the late evening of 6 November 1971, the game began in earnest.

Posing as patrons, Miami undercover agents entered the Bachelor II
Lounge on Southwest Twenty-second Street. Among other customers they
observed thirty-six-year-old Enrique Vela serving a drink to a fifty-something homosexual. A short time later police stormed into the Coral Way
bar, arresting six, four of whom were employees. A disappointed sergeant
later told a news reporter that "about fifty customers took off through
the doors. Otherwise we would have had more homosexuals."[15]

Unlike gay men arrested in other bar raids, which occurred as regularly
as the winter migration of Yankee snowbirds, those taken into custody at

the Bachelor Six did not retreat into their invisible subculture. They—like the Houston Tumblebugs—entered not-guilty pleas in municipal court. Their attorney, "Rose Levinson"—like Pearl Hart in Chicago—was a secret lesbian who had long represented gay men charged with various offenses. Levinson challenged the constitutionality of the ordinance.[16]

Two weeks before Christmas, Judge Donald Barmack tossed out the cases, declaring: "You cannot label a person a homosexual or a lesbian or a pervert and refuse to serve him or her a drink." Noting that neither Plato nor Oscar Wilde could legally visit a Miami bar, he continued: "You pass a law like this and pretty soon you can refuse to serve somebody because he's a Democrat or Republican or blue-eyed."[17] Later the city quietly repealed the ordinance, and the Florida Supreme Court struck down the state's 103-year-old "crimes against nature" law for its "vagueness and uncertainty in language."[18] A new era had begun.

Favorable press coverage began appearing in both city newspapers. The *Miami News* included articles such as "Gay Bars Misunderstood" and the less flashy *Herald* printed a Sunday feature story entitled "New Visibility of Homosexuality Merely Hints at Hidden World."[19] Citing recent political activities, as well as the formation of the MCC, the statewide publication of *David* magazine, and the formation of a Bar Owners' Association, the *Herald* article concluded with two assessments of visibility and vision within an emerging gay underground. The first, by a college professor—probably recalling the days of Charley Johns and Richard Inman—observed: "The gay community just doesn't have enough unity within itself to see a goal and attain it." In contrast, the second opinion came from a college dropout, who declared: "We've been too timid. But sure as hell I'm going to demand my right to be let alone."[20]

Capitalizing on the turning political tide, Bob Basker rallied support for New Party candidate Alan Rockway, a bisexual running for the Miami City Commission. Described as the "first overt illustration of organized gay power,"[21] the campaign generated more momentum in a movement that a few years earlier had existed only in a cabbie's dreams. On the wave of the successful legal challenges, positive media coverage, and germination of Stonewall consciousness among those of Jesse Monteagudo's generation, the Gay Activist Alliance-Miami (GAA-Miami) was born.

Tactically, GAA capitalized on concerns among city officials about potential negative media coverage and targeted Miami Beach's cross-dressing ordinances. "We knew that there were gays coming down from all over the country," remembers Bob Basker. "It was important to make sure that the police did not harass them."

Basker and others met with police chief Rocky Pomerance to under-score the ordinances' selective enforcement and ambiguity. "Does the Miami Beach Police Department intend to prevent the Eden Roc plans to book a female impersonator?" "In this age of unisexual clothing, what precisely constitutes clothing not becoming or appropriate to one's sex?"[22] The group also requested a permit for a parade in support of gay rights during the political convention. "You may parade," the Chief said, "but our officers shall enforce the city's transvestite ordinance."[23]

The ACLU attorney, Bruce Rogow, took Chief Pomerance to U.S. dis-trict court. Cross-dressing paraphernalia were placed in evidence during the two-hour hearing. Asked if an item, such as a shoulder bag, was an item of female clothing, the chief admitted that enforcement of the law "might vary from police officer to police officer." Judge William O. Mehrtens, interrupting Pomerance, noted, "If a Greek soldier walked down the street in his dress uniform," he might be jailed. The chief reminded the judge that only eleven people had been arrested since 1971, includ-ing "a male clad in a black see-through jump suit, high heels, pantyhose, and pancake makeup carrying a purse with red feathers." Decrying their "chilling effect on the parties' First Amendment rights," Judge Mehrtens promptly struck down the Miami Beach ordinances as "over-broad."[24]

Celebration followed this first-in-the-nation federal court's overturn-ing of a cross-dressing ordinance. Outside, Robert Barry, GAA-Miami presi-dent and a lighting engineer, screamed to fellow activist Charles Lamont: "Bring out the gowns!" Lamont, a former Methodist minister, turned to another friend: "You mean you're not in your drags yet, honey?"[25]

As Republican and Democratic conventioneers sunned themselves around lavish Miami Beach hotel pools, Jesse Monteagudo enjoyed the summer afternoon darkness at the cinema. Besides *Deliverance* and *The Godfather,* he saw *The Boys in the Band,* featuring the odious cast of homo-sexual misfits, an experience he describes as "very different than my earlier view of homosexuality from porno novels with gorgeous bodies and great sex where there was no gay bashing or negative characters. What I remember most, though, was the audience reaction. The mostly Cuban kids were whooping, hollering, and making jokes about the fags."

The self-hating timidity of playwright Mart Crowley's homosexuals was at odds with the demeanor of those who gathered in the thirty-six-acre Flamingo Park to organize and protest during the two political conventions.[26] The gay rights plank, included in the minority platform, was voted down in a voice vote during the predawn hours of 12 July. How-ever, this Democratic convention witnessed the first openly gay delegates addressing the assembly. Jim Foster, an officer of the San Francisco–based Society for Individual Rights, spoke for the first ten minutes, and Madeline Davis, a leader of the Buffalo Mattachine Society, followed, proclaiming: "I am a woman. I am a lesbian."[27]

More festive activities—in contrast to the 1968 Chicago convention—occurred outside. A marriage ceremony was officiated over by Troy Perry and Miami MCC minister Brad Wilson. Meanwhile, Charles Lamont celebrated the Eucharist and a kiss-in. The Miami Gay Alliance sponsored a dance that attracted an ABC News crew, while several drag queens performed in high fashion. Later that week about fifty demonstrators, including a dozen men wearing fancy hair, dresses, and spats, marched on the convention hall.

When not enjoying summer matinees at the Southside Theater or attending Miami-Dade Community College, Jesse Monteagudo spent his time parking cars at the Saxony Hotel on Miami Beach, about a mile from Flamingo Park. "Though I knew about the demonstrations, I did not take part in them, or even visit Flamingo Park," he says. Later he was in a serious car accident and spent the rest of the summer convalescing.

As voters entered polling booths to give Nixon four more years, a fully recovered Monteagudo was now working at the Southside Theater. One evening the owner made an offhand comment about the local "fag bar" around the corner. The next night Jesse strolled into the Nook, finding a "pool table, juke box, and drag queen." Arriving home drunk, he came out amidst a late-night family quarrel: "Where have you been?" "What bar did you go to?" "Who'd you go with?" "Finally, I blurted out my secret and offered to move out then and there. But my parents, for whom the family unit is paramount, wouldn't hear of it. Apparently, they found out that my reputation (and theirs) would be safer if I remained under parental supervision."

Quickly moving into the Cuban gay male scene, the once self-described "dumpy boy"–turned–"cute-looking man" frequented bars, beaches, and *posadas*—rent-by-the-hour motels on Southwest Eighth Street for would-be lovers suffering from parental imprisonment:

> I was able to enjoy many of the pleasures Little Habana's gay demimonde had to offer. From other gay Cubans I learned how to dress (bell-bottom pants and platform shoes were then the rage—I almost fell off one of those shoes!), to stay up late, to hold my liquor, to cruise, and deal with rejection (nonchalantly). I even "learned" to camp it up, adopt an effeminate pose, and to refer to myself and others as "she"—though this was something I never cared for. There were probably more drag queens per square foot in Little Habana than anywhere in South Florida!

In Central Florida drag was also heating up. On Halloween weekend 1972, Miss Pauline, Paul Wegman, debuted at the Palace Club, located in a once abandoned East Orlando warehouse on Humphries. Paul, the boy with strawberry hair who had arrived in Florida via the carnival seven years earlier, remembers his opening night:

> There was this wonderful song, "What's Out There for Me?" from the Broadway show *Jimmy*, about New York's mayor Jimmy Walker. Here the audience was drunk-up with the first show at one in the morning. I am doing a real Frank Sinatra with a suit on, a gray coat slung over my shoulder, and a fedora, walking through the bar singing the song, disappearing into the dressing room, flying around, and coming out at stage right as the curtain opened in drag.

At the Palace Club there were two divas, Paul reminisces: "Miss Honey, my competition, and Miss Cherry, a six-feet-five entertainer, who had a dressing room of their own on one side of a huge stage. All the rest of us—the cattle—had the dressing room on the other side." Joining Paul was Raleigh's Jimmi Dee, impersonating Diana Ross.

Like Tampa's, Orlando's gay scene was quiet and reserved. Unlike Miami, there were few problems with local authorities. The Diamond Head was upstairs over the blood bank in a downtown building that used to be the Orlando Opera House. "No sign whatsoever," Paul recalls. "If you didn't know where that staircase was to take you up to the club, you would never find it." Another bar was located on Orange Avenue. "But Bill Miller's places were always bigger and drew the most people," Paul continues. "He pretty much controlled Orlando from 1972 to 1980. His lover, Mike, was very personable and would be at the door and greet everyone. It was very secretive and undercover. Even the Palace Club, if you didn't know where that warehouse building was, you would have never found it. Mr. Miller was also very in with the city fathers, who said, 'Keep it clean, keep it going, keep it undercover.'"

Meanwhile, on an autumn Saturday, Bobby Carter looked into his makeup mirror, whose cord wound around the wall of his small kitchen in his Tampa apartment. Undecided about which songs to perform at Rene's that night, he listened to records, seeking the tune that fit his mood. "I'm taking on another personality," the boy who had escaped the clutches of LAPD and returned to Tampa as Roxanne offhandedly told a friend. "As I take off my shirt, apply moisturizer, and shade my eyes, my attitude and characteristics start to change." That night, Bobby, the nineteen-year-old with a "hillbilly accent" who couldn't carry a tune, transformed into Marilyn.

By May 1973, Bobby as Roxanne was ready to enter *the* pageant. "We would talk about Miss Florida all year long," Paul recalls. "So naturally a queen in Orlando or Tampa would want to be part of that—but she had to get one of the bars behind her."

Rene Rodriguez was behind Roxanne. "He was just a tyrant and needed something in his life to feel important," Paul relates, calling the former Cuban performer to mind. "Roxanne helped him do that." Participants had to raise money for the entry fee but "Rene took care of Bobby. He didn't have to spend a thing. Rene groomed him for Miss Florida. Bobby was going to be Miss Florida!"

That May mortals were captivated as reigning divas held court in the Grand Dining Room of Miami Beach's Dunes Hotel and street transvestites took the police to court following a raid on the Stonewall disco. Emory DuBois, a towering African American in his early thirties with an easy humor, won the title with a Shirley Bassey number. Up the beach, police were harassing gay men between Twenty-first and Twenty-third Streets—as they had for two decades: "Faggots have no rights!" "Animals!" "Get lost!"[28] Paddy wagons pulled up to the Stonewall club on Twenty-first Street, arresting several inside the club. Angela Keyes Douglas, also known as Douglas Czinky, refused to go gently into that night and filed suit against the Miami Beach police.

In addition to the suit, Bob Basker was also encouraging gay groups to appear at a series of statewide hearings of the Florida Commission on Human Relations, scheduled for that September. Seeking to include sexual orientation among the nondiscrimination classes covered, he wrote the GAA-Miami statement, arguing: "Known gays are virtually excluded from employment. Suspected homosexuals are told, . . . 'We hire only family men.'"[29]

Basker met with one state senator over drinks but generally met with as little progress as the suit or efforts to maintain GAA's momentum accomplished. In November, a disgruntled leadership sang the now all too familiar refrain:

> The greatest menace to freedom is an inert people. The few stalwarts who have been carrying the ball are tired. We have decided to withdraw from being stuck with carrying the whole load. We have agreed to put GAA on ice until some new condition or new happening requires its re-emergence. . . . There is much important work to be done. Our Dade County Commission keeps extending human rights to additional classes of citizens . . . but has made no move to include sexual orientation.[30]

Like Bob Basker, Bobby Carter was disappointed but not despondent on failing to achieve his immediate goal, the Miss Gay Florida title. That summer, Bobby did the Georgia club circuit with Larry Edwards (Hot Chocolate), a former fashion student who worked at Club III on Atlanta's West Peachtree. Just as Bob Basker had tipped the first set of dominos that would let loose a chain reaction from coast to coast, so would Roxanne Russell and Hot Chocolate refashion southern drag. Bob, however, found few takers for his tonic of activism and reform—South Florida homosexuals, like Jesse, preferred drinking Cuba Libres at the Nook or gin and tonic at the Stonewall. Meanwhile, Roxanne and Hot Chocolate traveled from one Peach State show bar to another.

One afternoon Bobby Carter and Larry Edwards stopped at a restaurant on the outskirts of a one-traffic-light town. As the two he/shes—one white and one black—walked to the end of the counter, Larry spotted the waitress giving them the "evil eye," as Bobby tells it. Bobby spoke under his breath: "It's these eyebrows." Shifting her two hundred pounds from hip to hip, she walked over to them and snarled: "What ya'll have?"

The two, still in eyelashes and mascara, looked at one another and broke out laughing. The evil-eyed waitress barked to the Negro in her kitchen: "Bring me that shotgun, boy! I'm going to hold these two freaks here till the police come." Bobby and Larry leapt from their stools and dashed toward the door as the locals began rising to their feet. Like characters in a Charlie Daniels song, they sped out of the parking lot and down a Georgia dirt road.

> Illusion is our game
> All we want is fame
> A dollar bill or two
> We're really just like you:
> Sissies! Sissies! Sissies![31]

THIRTEEN

The Sorority

*How is there going to be a Lesbian Nation if we don't organize
in the Waycross, Georgias, of the world?*   *—Anastasia, letter to Julia*

In March 1974, Julia Stanley, after leaving her teaching position at the University of Georgia, postponed life on the Tennessee farm to join her poet-lover, Sylvia, in New York City. Through Julia's feminist and Gay Academic Union networks, she recounts, "I became friends with most of the important lesbians of the time—writers, poets, intellectuals." Occasionally, she lunched with Rita Mae Brown and shared analyses with Phyllis Birkby and Charlotte Bunch.

Stimulated by this emotional and intellectual intensity, Julia put ideas to paper. She shared drafts of "Sexist Slang and the Gay Community."[1] One of those who read it, a former university student, wrote Julia:

> Rita Mae Brown wrote of her experiences—solution New York City. What about the rest who don't want to compromise their space in order to be themselves? . . . I guess if all lesbians want to live in New York City it can become Lesbian City. . . .
>
> I flash on this quote from your paper that arose much discussion when we were all together:
>
>> Can one be a lesbian if she says that her primary love is for other women, or does calling oneself a lesbian depend upon having had sexual experiences with another woman? We're arguing not just about labels, but the concept behind the label and its application to other women and ourselves. And, to complicate these discussions,

ALFA home movie. Photo courtesy of Marcelina Martin.

the labels aren't even ours. We didn't make them up, so that the original concept that required the label is not in our possession either.[2]

Julia's writing also influenced longtime friends. "She taught me to think
about what I was saying and what I was hearing," lauds Merril Mushroom.
"She explained how people can use language to manipulate and oppress
other people, to misinform and not take responsibility." And Merril's thinking was further challenged when Julia invited her to join a panel discussion
with Rita Mae Brown, Beth Hodges, and others at the second Gay Academic Union Conference that fall. "I hung out with Ginny Apuzzo and
Betty Powell," exclaims Merril. "In fact, we couldn't stop talking. I went
back to where I was staying with Gabby and the kids, telling them I
wouldn't be back until the next day!"

At the conference, she also chatted with Julia about the farm on which
Julia had decided to "throw in" with Merril, her husband, Gabby, and cousin
Billy. Six months earlier Billy had been skimming a two-year-old *Mother
Earth News,* a magazine that catered to back-to-the-earth readers. He spotted an ad: "Hi! We just moved to this fabulous place in Tennessee and we
would love more counter-cultural people to move to the area. If you are
looking for land, drop us a note and we can put you up for a little bit."
Gabby continues the story: "We wrote the couple a note and went up to
visit. They lived at the end of a road that went in and out of a creek. It
was really bizarre for us city folks." This group of friends settled on the
hundred acres without a mule near Dowelltown in an area known as Dry
Creek. With Julia in Manhattan and Billy traveling, Merril and Gabby drove
to the middle Tennessee farm on weekends from their Knoxville home.

Merril returned from the conference "really hot" to expand lesbian activities: "I got with the Knoxville Lesbian Feminist Alliance and we decided
to have a prom at my house. We had this huge basement decorated with
streamers and crepe paper. Around forty or fifty lesbians wore gowns and
tuxedos. There were even Lesbiana Senior High School Dance Cards that
you wrote down the name of your dance partners. It was the *real* thing!"

After the prom, some agreed to meet at the "lesbian-free" women's center, operated by two lesbians, and talk politics. Out of those meetings emerged
a consciousness-raising group and a coffeehouse. Merril found that her "own
feminism erupted in Knoxville. A lot came up in the C-R groups: being
a southerner, a southern lady, coming from a southern family. . . . Everything snowballed in Knoxville"—as it did throughout the South.

In the Triangle area of North Carolina, for example, women's groups
ranged from local NOW chapters and a Rape Crisis Center to the
women's radio collective (WDBS) and Womancraft, which operated a

handiwork store involving products made by country women.[3] The year-old Durham Women's Center, housed at the YWCA on Chapel Hill Street, was working "to educate and involve more women in the area in the struggle against women's oppression." The center offered workshops on feminist issues and gave free classes on self-defense as well as sponsored "A Women's Place" coffeehouse and a women's health cooperative. And the *Feminist Newsletter* had expanded, changing its name to *Feminary*, a title suggested from Monique Wittig's *Les Guérillères*.[4]

Five years had elapsed since Elizabeth Knowlton entered the women's movement. Now living with her lover, Linda, in a Carrboro collective with three other women, Knowlton was certain that "living your politics was not just something that you learned at a meeting."[5] The women grew organic vegetables, participated in countercultural activities, and labored with love on the *Whole Woman Carologue*.[6]

Since joining Women's Liberation, Elizabeth had sought to bring as many women into the movement as possible. She organized consciousness-raising groups and encouraged self-generating projects such as the theater, craft store, day care center, and publishing groups that grew out of them. However, there was relatively little lesbian organizing in the Durham–Raleigh–Chapel Hill area.[7] Although the *Feminist Newsletter*, for which Elizabeth wrote, had changed its name, it was still feminist— not lesbian—in orientation. "The place was too small to become divided," Elizabeth points out. While this gave the Triangle its feminist intensity, it also made it difficult for those seeking lesbian-only space.[8]

Five years of social activism also brought this granddaughter of a Richmond doctor to an understanding that she, too, had "profited from the segregation, never really thinking about political things." Effort invested in overthrowing the patriarchal system and changing men, Elizabeth Knowlton concluded, was energy drained from her and her sisters. "Perhaps, if we worked on just strengthening ourselves, the rest would fade away or transform itself." She also acknowledged an inner wisdom that another dissertation destined for a library shelf would neither change the world nor bring fulfillment.

In the spring of 1974 Elizabeth "felt the steam of the women's movement petering out." Initially believing that all women would leave men and become lesbians, "I realized that most women were just not willing to go beyond a certain point."[9] She also sensed that "the part of me, making my community more lesbian-feminist, was the stronger part—and the part that was going to survive." Elizabeth and Linda joined their lesbian sisters in Georgia.

There was a burgeoning lesbian scene in 1974 Atlanta, and the atmosphere at the Atlanta Lesbian Feminist Alliance house was electrifying.[10] Elizabeth threw herself into expanding the library. She thrived on cajoling book and magazine donations and filing newspaper clippings, fliers, correspondence, and photographs. In addition to magazines arranged on newly installed metal shelves, there were rows of novels and nonfiction works given by members. Knowlton reviewed books like Bertha Harris's *Sister Gin,* Joanna Russ's *The Female Man,* and Kate Millett's *Flying* for the *ALFA Newsletter.* She also expanded exchanges with magazines like *Quest* and *Lavender Woman* and insured that ALFA publications, such as the poetry collective's *Rewarding Amazons,* were readily available.

However, "books were a very small part" of Elizabeth's library work, she reveals. She checked in the mail received each week: "There would be these letters from every kind of place you can imagine in the Southeast: women who were lonely, women who were going to move to Atlanta, women who needed a place to live or a lover. They would just pour out their hearts to us."

Among scores of letters were those from Janice, Norah, Cisco, Libby, Dot, and Shirley:

I've been in Atlanta five years, realized I'm a lesbian four years ago and I've only known three in my life—and we weren't friends.

—*Janice, Atlanta*

Freddie's trial [for same-sex kissing in a gay bar][11] was put off again, and now everything is going wrong. . . . The woman lawyer who was going to be on the stand for us is now working for the "prosecution." The lawyer that legal aid is going to give us flunked the bar exam twice. . . . He had talked to the judge and the judge was willing to just fine Freddie $50 and drop the charge to Public Nuisance!!! Freddie said no, and we are going to still take it to court. . . . They are trying to be so *kind,* telling Freddie they won't think of her as a "sexual pervert," but only as a "public nuisance." I AM A LESBIAN. I am NOT a nuisance.

—*Norah, Birmingham*

I understand ALFA; for I understand love.

—*Cisco, Columbia, South Carolina*

Thank you for sending your newsletter. I turned in my two week notice to quit at work and told my parents that I was going to Atlanta.

—*Libby, Kingsport, Tennessee*[12]

We have lived together for four years. We are both welders in a steel plant. We both have children. We are middle aged and are lesbians. We are interested in knowing other women like us. We'd like to live in a bigger world.

—*Dot and Shirley, Chamblee, Louisiana*[13]

How the hell do you address a letter like this? Gentlewomen: sounds too much like a Victorian novel. Dear Dykes: nah, it'll never work. Fellow Fighters in the Quest Toward Liberty in Love? Jesus! You ain't giving a speech. Esteemed Members of ALFA? I give up!

—*Auburn-Opelika area*[14]

Another southern woman moving to Atlanta in 1974 was Barbara Weinstock. Bobbi had been an undergraduate at Athens in the late sixties, where she was involved with civil rights and antiwar issues. Her boyfriend at the time, a professor, had encouraged her to meet his colleague, Julia Stanley—but she never did.

Moving to Richmond in late 1970, Bobbi had dated a bisexual African American, Sonny. She had been working in the black community elsewhere and says she found its "warm acceptance" important to her as a Jewish southerner who had lived in military towns such as Warner Robins, Georgia, as a child. In Richmond, Weinstock hung out "at the nip joints or shot houses—illegal operations where they sold drinks by the glass, cooked nice meals, and if you got too drunk to drive you could always crash there." In the black gay community these were about the only places to go. "Somebody would sit around and start singing, telling jokes—it was almost like a community center." Some houses opened during the week; others served only on weekends. "Whites came in and out," remembers Bobbi, "but only if you knew someone." One of her favorites was LuLu's, a predominantly lesbian joint in Church Hill. "It was very, very clear who was butch and femme. You had *no* options." But, it "was a first step to being accepted."

Bobbi was unaware of the options in Richmond's emerging feminist and gay communities. By 1974, these included a women's center and the newly formed Gay Awareness in Perspective. GAP, begun by three Virginia Commonwealth University women, was inspired by a Rita Mae Brown lecture. This humanist-oriented group of lesbians and gay men met weekly near campus, published *Gap Rap,* and held informal counseling sessions.

Another Richmond lesbian, Beth Marschak, attended some early GAP meetings held at Pace Methodist Church. Beth, though, relates that she "was more into conscious raising but this was very encounter group oriented. . . . One time they wanted everyone to wear this name tag with the 'tree you would like to be.'" Many of the lesbians wanted "to talk about issues around sexism and racism, which GAP shied away from."

Since the formation of Organization for Women's Liberation, Marschak had become active with the Richmond Women's Political Caucus and chaired its Alternatives Committee, which dealt with lesbian and progressive issues. Some caucus members also wanted to start a women's center, as did other women in the community. This group began meeting at the Woody Guthrie Center, connected to the Workers World Party. Beth notes that, "unlike national feminist groups with more reform orientation focusing mainly on equality, we had a radical perspective. We looked at women and men's roles historically with a more analytical and systemic analysis. Issues around lesbians just obviously would come up with women interested in matriarchal societies and the whole Amazon idea."

When the Guthrie Center folded, the women's group moved to the YWCA on Fifth Street. As a women's center, they published a newsletter, *Women's Pages,* offered C-R groups, hosted potluck parties, and began an information and referral telephone service, "Women Helping Women."

Being both "very radical" and "very naïve," Beth acknowledges her naïveté about the Y's sexual politics. "Eventually, some on the board read one of our newsletters. They totally flipped out!" The issue in question, according to the board, was a "pornographic" and "vulgar" July edition that featured a lesbian love poem and a suggestive line drawing of a woman. While Center members, most of whom identified themselves as heterosexual but radical, were comfortable with lesbianism, the Y board was not. Notified of their eviction, Beth and several others met with the director.

Neither defending nor condoning the board's actions, the pant-suited, fiftyish woman told these rubyfruit renegades: "You know, the way you younger women are doing things now is not my way." Refusing to become a lipstick lesbian or for the Center to be shoved back into the closet of YWCA herstory, Marschak orchestrated a media campaign. Despite the publicity and some fund-raisers, the Center, lacking a place to meet, eventually disbanded.

For lesbian-feminists there was seldom "a room of one's own." Many southern towns lacked a critical mass of lesbian-feminists to form separate groups, let alone organized living collectives. Like Beth Marschak in Richmond, lesbians such as Merril Mushroom in Knoxville, Elizabeth Knowlton in Durham, Pokey Anderson in Houston, and Suzanne Pharr in New Orleans provided energy and leadership to women's centers whose tolerance toward lesbian activities varied. In other cities—such as Jackson and Louisville—lesbians simply abandoned these centers, forming their own groups (Jackson Women's Coalition and Lesbian Feminist Union) or formed Sexuality and Lesbianism Task Forces within NOW chapters (Memphis and Miami). ALFA House, in Atlanta's Little Five Points neighborhood, was one of the few safe spaces for women-loving women who shared progressive or radical views.

Bobbi Weinstock moved to Atlanta in 1974. She was neither a lesbian nor a feminist. As a bisexual, she lived with Sonny, who did a lot of amateur drag, and another gay man. Attending graduate school at Atlanta University, on weekends she'd go to the boy bars with her two roommates. One night she saw a notice about ALFA and decided to visit. "When I walked into ALFA House," she reminisces, "it was like this long-lost sorority. It was so comfortable." Bobbi goes on, "They had a library! It was the first time I'd ever seen a lesbian novel! Everything made so much sense to me about women's power; that you couldn't get strong if you spent a lot of your energy giving it to men. Living with two gay men I felt real depleted. ALFA was absolute heaven. I gained a lot of strength from that separatism."

Only two years old, ALFA had just moved from its Mansfield Avenue location to McLendon Avenue.[15] Women lived in the next-door apartment, and the house was open one evening a week in addition to scheduled meetings and events. Members, though, were involved in a flurry of activities. The political action committee, including Lorraine Fontana, networked out to the gay community of Atlanta for gay pride marches, anti-Klan actions, police harassment, and racism in the gay bars. "It was like we wanted to smash the patriarchy," Lorraine explains, "and whenever events called for community activism or response, we wanted to join others to demonstrate and let them know we're here. Back then we didn't have the saying, 'We're here, we're queer, get used to it.' But we had that feeling!"

One of the women who moved into the McLendon house that year was "Karla Brown," an African American. She learned about a job at an Atlanta record company from a gay friend, Clyde, whom she had first met in Charlotte after visiting the Neptune Lounge four years earlier.

It had been on a Friday night in 1970 that a gay friend and five straight women had invited Karla to go with them to a "gay bar," Karla recalls. "What's that?" she asked. "It's where queers go." Attending a mostly white women's college near Charlotte, Brown already "knew I was 'different' in that I didn't particularly care to date men." A tomboy who became a physical education major, Karla enjoyed sports and always led when dancing. Her college dates had all been "disastrous," and she spent a lot of time with her "close girl friends, although I didn't have a clue I was a lesbian."

Karla had a difficult time settling into college with the other two dozen or so black students. "I was more a flower child. I wore bell-bottoms and tie-dyed T-shirts." Unlike her best friend, Brown's political cause was the movement against the war, not the black nationalist movement. "When she found out I was into the nonviolent scene, I lost my best black friend since high school."

As they drove into Charlotte that night, the Temptations' "Psychedelic Shack" played over the radio. Karla walked into a square-shaped bar with black walls, fluorescent posters, and black lights—and into another lifestyle. The mostly white gay men at the Neptune "seemed to be having a great time. It only took me about a minute to realize this is where I should have been long ago."

It took more time, however, to discover four years later that she wasn't welcome at that Atlanta record company. During her telephone interview a few days earlier, Karla was told this meeting was just a routine formality. "It'll be just a little while longer," the receptionist offered after Karla had been sitting uncomfortably for two hours in the company's cheerless foyer. "He's on a long conference call."

On a mid-afternoon in Atlanta's midtown in the midseventies South—the much ballyhooed New South—skin color still mattered in the "City Too Busy to Hate." It was not until 4:30 that Karla was escorted into an executive office with huge windows and mahogany furniture. After a polite but brief conversation, the man informed her that there had been a "mistake"; the company wasn't hiring after all.

"It was very shocking," Karla spells out. "I ended up staying at ALFA House." Unlike the Charlotte feminists she had known, Karla found ALFA women welcoming—even though she brought a male baby from her former lover. "There weren't a whole lot of children around. But he was accepted by everyone." Karla, too, felt "they adopted me."

Her color was different, but it was her background that separated Karla from her ALFA sisters. "Most of them were middle-class white women. Most were older than me and had finished school. They had their own places to live and weren't going through the same kind of struggles."[16] Although Karla participated in the house meetings and some of the rap groups, she found that "a lot of it was simply over my head. I was struggling to try to get on my feet and become an independent woman. My interests just weren't theirs. And I was turned off by the two feminists I knew in Charlotte; I was treading very carefully."

The McLendon Avenue house was a torrent of activity in 1974. Members marched as the first open Georgia lesbian group to support the Equal Rights Amendment, and Radio Free Georgia—hosted by an ALFA member—aired the city's first weekly lesbian/gay programs. Elizabeth Knowlton was active on the library committee, Lorraine Fontana was involved with the political outreach committee, Vicki Gabriner wrote for the newsletter and cochaired Georgians for the ERA, and Bobbi Weinstock became involved with National Gay Task Force media alert. There were also groups meeting at the ALFA House, including women's self defense and DAR II, which met to discuss socialist and feminist theory every week or so. Another lesbian who became involved with ALFA in 1974, Margo George, explains: "We were just sitting around talking about what we wanted to do and believed in and kicking around names. The Daughters of the American Revolution was this very conservative organization. So we thought, 'Aha! Here we have it: Dykes for the Second American Revolution.'"

Margo George's family in the South goes back to before the American Revolution. Her grandmother's father fought for the Confederacy, her grandmother spent her entire married life in West Union, South Carolina, and her mother was a member of the Children of the American Revolution. Margo adds: "My mother, Lavinia, went to Agnes Scott College, where she got introduced to the Movement for Racial Justice and the labor movement in the early forties. She became a labor organizer for Amalgamated Clothing Workers Union and attended the interracial Highlander Center in the 1940s."

Lavinia first met her future husband, Bill, who was an economist for the War Production Board from New York's Lower East Side, at a labor picnic. Bill founded the first chapter of the American Civil Liberties Union (ACLU) in Atlanta and was investigated during the McCarthy era while working at the National Labor Relations Board for his earlier work organizing the unemployed during the Depression. Later, in a series of appellate victories, Lavinia and Bill, both lawyers, shaped workers' compensation law in Georgia through their representation of injured workers.

Not surprisingly, the political views of Margo's family differed significantly from those of her Atlanta classmates. As a fifth grader she circulated a petition to the governor for clemency for a black teenager who had received a death sentence. Two years later, in 1962, she began sitting at the back of city buses "doing my little protest." Eventually, she worked summers organizing for the ACLU and at Head Start.

In late 1971, after dropping out of U.C. Berkeley the previous year, Margo returned home with her lover, Cathy Karrass. Living in a yellow duplex on McLendon Avenue, Margo chose to enter the working-class world, becoming a waitress, a grocery cashier, a printer, and a nonunion carpenter—before entering Local 225's apprenticeship program and becoming the first woman to complete it. Margo George's commitment to the building trade was more political than financial. "I would have left a long time before except for resistance of my male co-workers and the union hierarchy." It also was directly related to the influence of her parents' efforts.

Soon after Margo and Cathy settled into their Little Five Points duplex they attended an event sponsored by Atlanta Women's Liberation. They were invited to participate in a socialist reading-discussion group composed of a dozen or so members and their mostly heterosexual lovers, who were either working at the *Great Speckled Bird* or active in women's liberation. Although the couple lived next door to Lorraine Fontana and just around the block from Vicki Gabriner, neither Margo nor Cathy involved themselves with ALFA or in the activities of the Georgia Gay Liberation Front. "I saw myself as being more a socialist-feminist rather than a lesbian-separatist," says Margo. "At that point, I was alarmed by lesbian-separatism because I thought that was divisive. I also saw the other, primarily male, part of the lesbian-gay movement as seeking acceptance rather than fundamental change in society."

Margo George's involvement with ALFA, however, changed. By 1974 the socialist reading group was unraveling as some of the women entered lesbian relationships while their male lovers were having affairs with other women. Several of these socialist women-turned-lesbians became active with ALFA, forming DAR II and bringing Margo "together with lesbians who had a similar vision of wanting to change the world. Reading lesbian-separatist theory made me feel more comfortable with it and see it as something that had a purpose."

ALFA House also afforded space for regular meetings of the Atlanta Socialist Feminist Women's Union, a chapter formed by local lesbians and nonlesbians who had attended the national organizing convention held at Antioch College. As one of the cofounders, Margo disclosed that "many of the women involved had overlapping memberships." Thus, with its move to McLendon Avenue, ALFA House was the hub for many Little Five Points women, as she explains: "Actually having a physical place in the community was important. Bringing so many different lesbians together in a place strengthened the whole community and brought about coalitions that might not have happened if we were meeting in different places."

When Margo George "made a conscious choice to join" ALFA, her goal "was to bring more women into the House and its orbit in order to get them involved in political activities." This included African American lesbians such as Karla Brown, for whom, as southern lesbians, George explains, "we brought more experience interacting with people of color because most of the white people from the North who were involved had very little experience with people of color although they never grew up with legislated Jim Crow. It was easier for us to reach out for people of color even though I think we did not do that as successfully as we could have."

Close relationships among a growing number of women from different backgrounds—as different as Bobbi, Elizabeth, Karla, Lorraine, Margo, and Vicki—energized an emerging lesbian community in Little Five Points. "There was a reason why we were friends," Lorraine says, "and it just wasn't that we had to live next to each other. We formed a family."

While Elizabeth Knowlton and Bobbi Weinstock were drawn to the intensity of a larger city, as 1974 ended, Julia Stanley elected "to work out a lesbian lifestyle at the periphery of a patriarchal society." Along with her lover, Sylvia, she departed for middle Tennessee, where she joined the Dry Creek Farm collective, comprised of Merril Mushroom, Gabby Haze, their two adopted sons, and Merril's unemployed cousin Billy. Julia felt reasonably comfortable with the decision. Generally, men's presence around the cabin and surrounding hollows, creeks, and cornfields was expected to be minimal. Gabby was to journey from Knoxville for weekend homesteading, while cousin Billy was expected only now and then.

Perhaps, in the seclusion of Dry Creek, Stanley could contemplate Anastasia's haunting question: "How is there going to be a Lesbian Nation if we don't organize in the Waycross, Georgias of the world?"

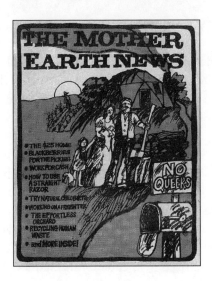

FOURTEEN

Separations

The caravan of VW vans and pickup trucks carrying Tar Heel emigrants wound around the three-mile narrow ridge overlooking steep wooded hollows. As the band approached the summit of Short Mountain, they turned off onto another gravel road leading them down into a two-hundred-acre enclave of apple trees, groundhogs, and spring waters.

On that warm day in 1973, Clint Pyne's first task was to unload the goats, which "a guy named Jimmy claimed were descendants from those at the Carl Sandburg home." As he settled the animals in the old barn, fellow travelers from the burnt-out Tick Creek Collective hauled wood stoves into the two-room log cabin, divided by a chimney with a fireplace on either side.

During the first couple of weeks these rural revolutionaries cooked meals in the barn. Clint remembers rambling discussions by kerosene lantern light: "how to find happiness, friends, and a free life . . . how to create

Mother Earth News parody in *RFD*.
Illustration by Allan Troxler, republished by permission of RFD Press.

and nurture a secure base where ideas of social change and of new (non-nuclear) families can find a home."

During the late sixties and early seventies, intentional communities dotted "Amerika," particularly in the Southwest and South, where land was cheap and neighbors distant. Most of these, such as the Skinnerian-blessed Twin Oaks Community in Virginia and Steve Gaskin's The Farm near Nashville, were heterosexual oriented.[1] Hippie homesteaders had abandoned the urban-based political assault on "the System" of unfettered capitalism and runaway consumerism. Less noticeably, lesbians and gay men—tiring of the Castro or Fire Island or burned out from lesbian-feminist or gay liberation organizing in the cities, entered rural life. And some of those retreating to such enclaves, like Pyne, abandoned their heterosexual identities. Gay, straight, or in-between, this new Aquarian Age of homesteaders embraced principles of self-sufficiency, nonviolence, vegetarianism, participatory governance, and eco-awareness.

Not everyone, of course, shared these new-society principles. Sometimes Hoover's boys would drive up from their Memphis field office. Peering out through the oak and sassafras trees, they monitored their "subject . . . with brown braided hair, a moustache, and goatee, and wearing gold earrings" living with a group of " 'hippies' . . . in a 'teepee' and an old house."[2]

Clint Pyne, though, had cast aside his given name as well as the Tick Creek political activism for the anonymity, solitude, and simplicity of Short Mountain. Visions of a swift political revolution had met an Icarus-like fate and the post-Nixon "climate was very different." Clint, now known as Milo Guthrie, explains: "Once the peace treaty was signed, the war issue had been defused as a major issue for demonstrations. People just wanted to get back to their lives and not be so intensely socially active."

Milo was hopeful when he and five others purchased the Tennessee property: "I naïvely imagined that my needs and visions were shared by all. I also naïvely assumed that these twenty or so people would continue to be able to live together and communicate with one another, and that we could continue to live and grow as a people." But, as winter approached, divisions within the Short Mountain tribe appeared, particularly between the "communalists and the nuclear family folks."

Fern, one of the six deed holders, built a yurt (a round wooden structure) on the ridge past the big barn, with his girlfriend, Laura. Although friends with both, Milo "hung out more with the communally oriented group" in the teepee. The teepee "wasn't practical for the long term," he admits. "But it symbolized people who wanted a rough-and-tumble communal experience versus those who were more traditional."

Back-to-the-land rebels were generally more into the communal lifestyle in theory than in fact. Short Mountain folks, Milo recalls, wanted "to take everyone's feelings and points of views into account." But, by mid-November, Janice (known as Daisy) was already troubled by Fern and Laura. "They're into such a different place than me," she jotted in her journal. "I'm into grubbing and living in a tipi and being real and not being a hippie; I don't see myself as a hippie farmer."[3] Participatory decision making also suffered among the realities of everyday life. While Fern and Laura would be doing "their own thing" with their baby, Milo says, "a lot of times things just happened—and that was part of the problem."

Besides the communalists and the nuclear family folks, there were the "bad girls," who were willing to "throw all conventions to the wind," and who included lesbian relationships among the possibilities for their lives. Daisy became the lover of a woman who was married to an older man. "It got very out of control," declares Milo. "But as far as the Short Mountain group was concerned that was just part of the changes people go through." Pro-feminist members like Milo also clashed with those who "didn't have much patience with all the changes people were going through around feminism and women's liberation." Meanwhile, Milo "was exploring my sexuality in various ways. I was involved with James—one of the more consistent relationships with a man" but had occasional "one-night stands" with women.

Other tenderfoot counterculturalists were also moving into middle Tennessee. Merril Mushroom and Gabby Haze, along with their cousin Billy, Julia, and her lover, Sylvia, were living on Dry Creek at the base of Short Mountain. "I was amazed of the fact that we lived in the middle of nowhere but there was this intense countercultural thing happening," recollects Gabby. "Some of it was gay, most of it was straight—all of it was drug related at some level. We wondered, Is it going on everywhere? Is there this madness happening in every little nook and cranny or are we sort of this special place?"

In addition to the Short Mountain and Dry Creek folks, there was a group known as Door Ajar near Temperance Hall. These social activists eventually published the *People's Paper*, filling the "gap between the *Smithville Review* and the *Cannon Courier*" and providing a forum for ideas. Like settlers of old, Merril continues, "People would come from sixty miles around and have barn-raisings and dances, picnics and cook-outs, pot lucks and bar games. That's how we met the hippie straight people on Short Mountain."

Members of the various collectives and extended households often gathered at the local food coop, the Good Earth. At one coop meeting, Gabby spotted a man "with long hair and kind of effeminate. I whispered to Merril, 'Do you think he's gay?' She said, 'Of course he's gay! Go and talk to him.'" As Gabby got to know Milo, "the original people at Short Mountain were beginning to drift apart." Summer visitors and hangers-on would stay for a time, but the Short Mountain collective was teetering on collapse as most of the original members departed.

Milo's midseventies memory "is littered with stories of communal groups split up, broken; land lost or vacant. I know many people who shared these reefer-dreams with me, who touched the earth with me, who have to one degree or another (apparently) given up the search for radical modes of living and accepted straight jobs, marriage, or individual city life as their lot." While some fled the back-to-the-land movement for the normalcy of straight jobs, others "living straight lives in hippie clothing"[4] moved from one collective to the next. Meanwhile, most rural gays led secretive lives invisible to their rural communities, collectivist friends, and the gay press.

After one uneventful coop meeting, Gabby chatted with Milo. "Do you know anything about this new magazine for rural gays?" he asked. "I know all about that!" Milo smiled. "Friends of mine have already sent me a copy of *RFD*!"

Milo had first heard of the publishing venture as a People's Party organizer attending the spring 1974 Midwest Gay Pride Conference. There he met Stewart Scofield, who worked at an Iowa agricultural research station. At the University of Iowa conference, Scofield spoke informally about the need to network country gay people. He met with an immediate positive response, particularly from his two best friends, Iowa farm boys Don Engstrom, a "serious art and SDS person" (then known as Don-Tevel), and his partner, Rick Graff, a carpenter.

"The original RFD'ers thought it was really important to build culture," Don emphasizes. From the politics of the street to the culture of the farm, "we would withdraw from the larger community to sort out our own stuff, build our power and understanding. But we always went back to the large community and acted. The early *RFD* was *never* about isolationism; it was about transforming culture."

By the midseventies, "gay culture" was already undergoing a transformation. Gay liberation rags like *Sunflower* were distant activist memories as gay lifestyle magazines and newspapers such as the *Advocate* crowded city newsstands and sold briskly at newly opened gay bookstores.

Like the nascent culture of urban gay narcissism, these publications were "full of the latest news of cha cha palaces in San Francisco, shows off off-Broadway, trendy fashions from West Hollywood, Gloria Gaynor's latest album, and how to make a killing in the real estate market."[5]

Stewart had returned from a two-month stay at the epicenter of gay culture, the Castro, in late 1973. Lodging with six "straight but lovable" communalists in an Iowa "windy farmhouse," he, like Milo, found himself cut off "with two feet of snow on the ground, short winter days, lots of coffee on the stove, and an empty mailbox at the end of the driveway."[6] As Scofield thumbed through an issue of the California magazine *Country Women,* he wondered why there wasn't something similar for gay men. "I just knew that I couldn't be the *only* gay man who liked rural life— though it sure seemed that way."

Stewart penned a note to *Mother Earth News,* a longtime journal with advice on rural living, and enclosed payment for a brief notice in its Position and Situation listing: "Country isolation, need to share, especially among gay people." Six months later he received from *Mother Earth* his unpublished ad and an "agonized, soul-searched" letter: "Many of our readers are not young, hip, open-minded folks, but are little old ladies in tennis shoes."[7] But, by then, Stewart had already taken action.

Stewart arrived at the 1974 Midwest gay conference envisioning a "sort of counterculture gay *National Geographic* written by the men who read it." Talking to Steve McLave, Stewart was advised to write two men living in Wolf Creek, Oregon: Carl Wittman, a longtime activist and author of the "Gay Manifesto," and his lover, Allan Troxler, a graphic artist from North Carolina.

Stewart heard back quickly from the pair. They were excited "to discover another island of thought about a rural gay men's publication."[8] Stewart and Don traveled to Oregon that July, and the foursome talked "for days" about how to network rural gay folks. Ideas ranged from a mimeographed newsletter to a chain letter. Carl, remembers Don, "was the first of us to start talking about how politics was truly about creating culture versus subverting culture."

Don and Rick connected with the Iowa City Women's Press collective. The press agreed to print the "newsletter" in an offset magazine format at a reduced rate. The men chose the solstices and equinoxes as publishing dates, and borrowed the title from the U.S. Postal Service acronym "Rural Free Delivery."[9]

RFD, echoing the need for rural outreach, premiered as "Rustic Fairy Dreams" just in time for the autumnal 1974 equinox.[10] The first cover of the twenty-four-page magazine, designed by Troxler, was filled with golden sunflowers and wheat stalks. Subsequent issues followed, like "Really Feeling Divine" with a front cover of a flock of birds and stapled on the back cover a package of "pansy seeds" to "the flowers of faggots . . . tougher than most people realize."[11]

These early quarterly issues emphasized the use of herbalism and organic gardening, natural food recipes and Chinese medicines, and explored building domes, outhouses, and the uses of "shit." Each issue also included poetry, photography, and fiction, reader letters, contact lists, and prisoner correspondence. Underlying the magazine was the belief that gays are a "special people" with their own culture and unique spiritual gifts.

"All of us recognized that queerness was a type of spiritual gift," Don emphasizes. In those early years, however, "we didn't know anything about contemporary wiccan stuff since we were all very political; spirituality and politics were never mixed." Thus, early issues conveyed little sense of this pre-Christian queer spirituality: "We didn't know how to write about it or what to do with it."

As a "nomadic child," *RFD* had "its own self-generating energy."[12] Rural faggots like Faygele ben Miriam, living at the Elwah Collective—a gay rural collective on Washington's Olympic Peninsula—and one-time GLF leader Allen Young, now living at Butterworth Farm in Massachusetts, each assembled an early issue. The Iowa and Wolf Creek collectives oversaw the overall production. Soon *RFD* expanded to forty-eight pages with a press run of two thousand.

As the magazine grew, however, so did problems. "A lot of us who were in the early *RFD* were all people who had broader concerns than our regions," Don says. "But regionalism did reemerge," as the distance between Oregon and Iowa widened. He continues: "We set ourselves up for conflict. We didn't talk to each other face-to-face, so we'd write a letter and there would be some little misunderstanding and in the letter it would seem more extreme than it actually was." Put simply, the Wolf Creek folks "felt left out of the day-to-day life of the magazine and of the decisions."[13]

However, there were genuine differences in philosophy that personal interaction could not resolve. The Oregon people, who had largely come from West Coast cities, were into "political correctness issues," remembers Don. "For us it was more important that the garden was planted than if it was correct to buy seeds from a local person or not."

Relations between *RFD* and the feminist press also became strained.[14] And, by the time the fifth issue was published ("Raving Flames Diary"),

Scofield had tired of collective heterosexual country life and the pressures of publishing.[15] On a June evening, he went out to the organic garden to pick some broccoli, as it was his turn to cook. "But I didn't know where it was planted. I stood in the garden and cried and sobbed to myself."[16] He departed Iowa and read the next issue of *RFD* at a friend's home in South Carolina.

In 1976, the RFD office moved to Wolf Creek. Like Short Mountain, this was also an area with different collective households, ranging from Allan and Carl, who lived in Golden, which had a truck and chainsaw as well as electricity, to folks like Landon and Sean from Lilac Ridge, which had neither electricity nor hot water. Nine miles away was Creekland.[17] *RFD* remained at the Creekland Collective until that group collapsed two years later. Following one issue published in San Francisco, *RFD* relocated to the South.

Meanwhile, back at Dry Creek, the strains of collective southern life and between lesbians and gay men were also surfacing. Julia Stanley and her lover had moved to the homestead (which they shared with cousin Billy) in January 1975. "Billy was straight," Julia remembers. "Jewish or not I had no reason to trust a straight man." Nevertheless, "he was fairly laid back. But, he could occupy the entire 125 acres with his voice. I could be at the very end of the hollow and hear his booming voice on the phone at the house. There was no escape from this male presence."

Julia persevered, pursuing a "hectic and crammed" writing schedule. Between baking bread and making Danish rings, Julia wrote essays whose topics ranged from the nonexistence of "generics" and the "stylistics of belief" to an "analysis of the lesbian buffer zone" and a critique of gay slang.[18]

In the latter essay, which appeared in *College English,* she warned: "One must speak of a 'gay community' with caution, since only the most fragile bonds link the lives of lesbians with those of gay men."[19] This fragility was apparent not only between her and cousin Billy but in the correspondence between Julia and another English Ph.D., Louie Crew, during her stay at Dry Creek. Although Julia considered herself a separatist, Julia and Louie collaborated in the Gay Academic Union as well as professional groups like the Modern Language Association and the National Council of Teachers of English, where they engineered resolutions and formed lesbian and gay caucuses.[20]

Crew's willingness to communicate across the gender border was unusual during an era in which lesbian separatism was often considered political betrayal by gay activists and generally viewed by social gays with indifference. Communicating proved more difficult, however, when a male lived in the same house. Personal relationships with cousin Billy deteriorated at Dry Creek. "Things are pretty awful here right now," Julia confided to Crew. We "are planning to pull out as soon as possible."[21] The end came on an April weekend. "I don't think I can continue to live here because of Billy," Julia explained to Merril. But her old friend took Billy's side and "in my book that was male identification," asserts Julia.

That fall Stanley dashed off a letter to another southern friend, Beth Hodges, who had just finished editing a special issue of *Margins* on lesbian writing and publishing. Leaving Dry Creek and separating from her lover had taken its toll. "Things here have been extremely hectic and painful," Julia wrote from Nashville. "Desperation and poverty have finally pushed me over the brink and into work."[22]

As Julia met writing deadlines and applied for college teaching positions, Merril and Gabby continued to live in Knoxville for another year in order to buy out the land shares of those who had naïvely entered into the Dry Creek venture. Merril remained friends with Julia, of course. As the two exchanged letters, however, they found themselves writing from differently lived worlds. Merril, responding to Julia's papers on separatism and feminist language, described her struggles: "It has been a hell of a winter all the way around, it seems. . . . J'aime had tonsillitis and then chickenpox. Then we went to Florida and visited. David got the chickenpox. Then we came back and J'aime got black measles. On the way back we lost our fourth gear which cost us our tax refund. And Gabby was laid off."

Meanwhile, cold weather approached and Milo was alone on Short Mountain. "My personal life was at a low ebb." Staring into the fire one night, he took pencil and paper in hand. "Flying South for the Winter?" he wrote to *RFD* readers. "Solitary faggot needs winter guests. The other (non-gay) members of our group have left me with the goats and cow, on a beautiful middle-Tennessee mountain. Come and visit if you're passin' thru."[23]

FIFTEEN

Awakenings and Departures

When you travel, it's nice to look behind you.   —Lige

Sporting an Afro, a nineteen-year-old walked up to the horseshoe-shaped bar, wearing blue hip-hugger bell-bottoms, a cut-off pink shirt ending just below his nipples, and a set of giant earrings. Blacks were on one side of the single-room club; whites stayed on the other. Queens wore beaded dresses or pantsuits; guys were in boots or leather.

The Patio Bar was the only gay bar in South Carolina's "up country"— that region of the Piedmont mountain range ravaged by carpetbaggers, outlet malls, revenuers, and soldiers for Jesus. On that summer night in 1974, Sam Hunter entered a gay bar for the first time—and was shocked: "I remember seeing impressionists doing Dolly Parton's 'Jolene,' Diana Ross's 'My Mistake Was to Love You,' and Cher's 'Halfbreed.' Now—I was used to straight-out soul music. Whoa!"

After a drag show, there was another surprise: guys dancing with guys. It was not unexpected, however, that whites danced with whites and blacks with blacks or that "they didn't want their friends to see them leav-

"Africa," Ms. Gay Charleston, 1979. Photo © Greg Day.

ing with either a white guy or a black guy." He quickly hooked up with a "red-boned" black man and was "in paradise."

Sam was one of eight Hunter boys. The family lived "deep down in the country" about a mile outside Greer in the all-black community of Odum. As a "sissy boy," Sam had comfortably integrated into his family. He sewed and played house with his niece, with whom he shared "secrets and talked about boys." "There's a total difference between the white and black communities," Sam observes. "Back then, being black and growing up gay, even a little child could 'clock you'—they could tell what you were right off the bat!"

Singing in the church choir, doing talent shows, and acting in school plays, Sam could "always make people laugh." He was just thirteen when he hosted his first talent show: "I used to take a flashlight and wrap aluminum foil around it to make a glow on the wall like a spotlight. My niece and two brothers would come out and we'd do Diana Ross and the Supremes (I'd *always* do Diana). We'd charge the neighborhood kids five cents, which covered their potato chips, cookies, and sodas." Sam also remembers doing other shows at the community center, wearing hot pants and an Afro wig. "They thought it was the ticket! That's all you'd hear for months: 'Oh, you wore that talent show out. I know those girls were mad at you because you looked better!'"

Although his father died when Sam was eleven, the clan still took turns hosting the weekly house party with two other families. Catfish and chicken were fried to southern goodness and cards were dealt into the night; dance music filled the unsoiled air. "We had to make our own entertainment during the weekend," Sam reminisced. "They'd sell bootlegged beer and shots of corn liquor. And this was also in the heyday of Boone's Farm. They'd make thunderbirds—wine mixed with orange juice and vodka." At these house parties one relative or another would always urge Sam, "Dance for me, baby!" As the family's old box record player crackled out "Chain of Fools" or "The Dock of the Bay," he swayed in ecstasy.

In these Carolina foothills, Joker Sherman ran a juke joint that looked much the same as Harpo's Place in *The Color Purple.* "On Sundays everyone would get out of church, put on their cool comfortable clothes, and go party," Sam said. On occasion, the drinking, dancing, and storytelling were interrupted by the local sheriff, tired of Joker selling homebrew or in the mood to do some policing. But mostly it was just a carefree day of carrying on without the reckoning of white folks' eyes.

At Joker's, Sam encountered his first drag queens: "There were five of them with hot pants and three-inch shing-a-ling jackets. One of them said: 'There's Larry's brother. I know he's gay. I'm going to say something to him.' It scared me so bad I ran all the way home!"

By high school, though, Sam was doing "pump shows and dances" at Joker's:

> When we'd walk in they'd say, "Oh! Here come the pumps." We were always the highlight of the night: high fashion, big wigs, wild satin outfits with hot pants, and little wedge shoes. We'd dance with our girl-friends. Sometimes the guys would just get up and dance with us. They didn't care. We used to carry on with the guys who gave us little codes so the girls wouldn't know that they were trying to go home with us.

Besides subtle eye or head movements, the boys used a form of pig Latin. "Oda ouya antwa ota uckfa ema?" Sam not infrequently asked. "That's how we used to pick up trade. The girls didn't know what we were saying!" Being the sissy, Sam was also attuned to the homosexual high school scene. In his Future Farmers of America class, "when the lights went out and the film started showing, the corn would really grow!" And, in the locker room, "all the boys would make these plays with eye contact and sneak me out to the laundry room. It was wild!"

A generation and a state line separated the experiences of Sam Hunter from those of Quinton Baker. Born on the North Carolina coastal plain, Baker had been a civil rights leader in the Triangle area with his white homosexual lover during the early sixties.[1] Like Sam, he had employed pig Latin (the "Aga" language) for hidden sexual comments and found a quiet acceptance of homosexuality ("being funny") within his segregated community. But, while Quinton was of the generation reading *Another Country* and practicing civil disobedience, Sam's generation was brought up in the era of black power, reading nationalist writers like Eldridge Cleaver. Diana Ross, not Angela Davis, however, caught Sam's interest. And Quinton was as distant from Baldwin's bisexual street hustler Rufus Scott as Sam was from the homophobic rhetoric of *Soul on Ice.*

Nevertheless, both Quinton and Sam experienced the fluid bound-aries between black and white when the sun of Jim Crow went down. These "ghost relationships" were born from incestual communities with lega-cies of cross burnings and collard greens, colored and white water foun-tains, Confederate Memorial Day and Juneteenth, black mammies and church bombings. It was another country, foreign to northern activists—civil rights or homosexual—who seldom appreciated the southern com-plexities of social life and the simplicities of rural living.

As Sam prepared to graduate from high school in the spring of 1973, an East Coast activist from the hollers of Appalachia, Lige Clarke, emp-

tied a closet in his Manhattan flat. He rummaged through a stack of letters from the *Screw* column, his *GAY* advice section, and reactions to *I
Have More Fun with You Than Anybody*. Sitting cross-legged on a rug,
Lige read through a random pile from the nearly ten thousand letters
he'd answered during the past four years.

A letter from Juan of Miami, writing about his "desire to wear
women's clothes," caught Lige's eye. This would-be *mariconé* recounted:
"I'd be afraid to go out in public and I'd almost die of embarrassment trying to buy women's clothes." The *GAY* duo had replied: "Drag queens
in the gay world . . . [are] flamboyant and garish. . . . A preoccupation with
clothes and fashions is difficult for us to grasp. . . . But if it gives you pleasure and fits your values comfortably, then we say 'Right on!'"[2]

Lige separated this and other letters into "yes," "no," and "maybe" piles
on the living room floor. A well-disposed Jack read through the maybes.
And "that's how the book *Roommates Can't Always Be Lovers* came about,"
tells Lige. "The main subject we dealt with in our letters was loneliness."

Resigning as editors of *GAY* in the summer of 1973, Jack began work
on *Men's Liberation: A New Definition of Masculinity* while Lige finished
up the *Roommates* book.[3] As winter set in, a light-footed Lige tried unsuccessfully to lure his older companion on board the cruise ship
Vistafjord. "I needed a stable (rather than a moving) environment to write,"
remembers Jack. "I told him how great it was that he'd received such a
golden opportunity."

At the New Year, Lige set sail "under a beautiful moon over snow-
covered Manhattan."[4] One of only three Americans on the crew, Lige
enjoyed long walks on A Deck, talking with the mostly elderly female passengers. Making twenty-three ports of call, the *Vistafjord* was "like the
YMCA all the time—only the people are really beautiful."[5] So taken by
the tranquility of the sea and the gaiety of foreign shores, Lige signed up
to work on other Norwegian line cruises. He corresponded with Jack during the predawn morning hours in "moments of stillness [that] seem as
long as an afternoon in the woods."[6]

As Lige cruised foreign ports, discos and show bars flourished in the
South. And Atlanta was the Hollywood of drag. My House, Onyx
Lounge, King's Kastle, and Club III offered entertainment near one of
the sundry peach-named streets. Even the popular Cove on Worchester
Drive, which had long advertised "NO DRAG SHOWS," would soon
be hosting two a night.

But the preeminent showplace in the South was the Sweet Gum
Head on Cheshire Bridge Road, owned by Frank Powell. Like Bill Miller

in Orlando, Powell wielded great influence in Atlanta's bar and drag community.[7] Powell also had an eye for talent. Rachel Wells hailed from Bard-
stown, Kentucky. Crowned Miss Gay Atlanta '72, she directed shows every
night, performing as Rita Hayworth. Madame, accompanied by Daw-
son, Georgia, native Wayland Flowers, also performed at the Sweet
Gum: "I went to Disneyland," quipped Madame. "I sat on Pinocchio's
nose and said, 'Lie, kid, lie!'"

Homosexual citizens of Atlanta, New Orleans, Houston, Miami,
and Dallas had long enjoyed such shows, as well as a menu of men's bars.
The sexual permissiveness of the midseventies South coupled with the
emergence of bar magazines like *Chanticleer, David, Cruise,* and *UpFront*
and gay newspapers such as *Contact,* the *Barb, Gaiety,* and the *Free Press*[8]
amplified the new homosexual freedoms, as megadiscos were widely
patronized in midsize cities,[9] while baths and escort services in Atlanta,[10]
Miami, and Houston operated openly. And every southern town of consequence featured at least one well-regarded show bar and drag diva.

In Memphis, George's Truck Stop and Drag Bar was located on
Madison Avenue between Idlewild and Auberndale. By the midseventies,
the original single-storefront bar had expanded and was the place to be,
with innovative and dynamic drag shows, a huge dance floor, a downstairs bar, and a patio that attracted a thousand on a weekend night.[11]
Miss Peaches—who at the age of five turned down the role of king in the
school play, insisting on being queen—was active in his church, held the
title of Miss Black Memphis for eleven consecutive years, and hosted classic Harlem-era rent party buffets.[12] From Knoxville's Carousel 2 and the
Powder Puff Lounge in Chattanooga to Mae's Cabaret in Jackson and Birmingham's Chances R Lounge, drag queens such as Cicely Manchester, Jamie
Sommers, Jamie Chambers, Jimmi Dee, Daisy Dalton, and Misty Lamour wooed huge crowds of mostly gay men. These southern farm clubs
of drag, sponsoring their most talented in pageants, were hubs for emerging gay male communities.

Local organizations also sprang up, such as the Awards Board of
Norfolk, sponsoring balls and pageants. This group, led by local star "Diana
Ross," upgraded local entertainment at the College Cue, where local
impersonators appeared along with national stars like Jimmy James and
Jim Bailey. From Mobile's We Three Lounge to the Hy Camp Lounge
in Fort Smith, a new generation of hopeful stars dreamt of becoming a
Miss Gay Somethang.

In the spring of 1974, Bobby Carter walked onto center stage of
Miami Beach's Marco Polo Hotel as Roxanne Russell to win the Miss

Florida pageant. Miss P emceed, but the night belonged to Roxanne. Roxanne first performed "My Heart Belongs to Daddy" from George Cukor's Oscar-nominated movie *Let's Make Love.* She mimed the flashy Monroe, who played opposite the sulky older character of Yves Montand. With dancers on either side, Roxanne, dressed in black, segued into "Diamonds Are a Girl's Best Friend" from *Gentlemen Prefer Blondes.* "Suddenly, overnight I was a star!"

In that certain summer of Roxanne's coronation, Evita's presidency, and Nixon's abdication, Sam Hunter passed through the looking glass into white homosexuality. As he became more feminine, Sam frequented Joker's less often. Within a year Sam was performing at the Patio Lounge. Working for twelve dollars a night, "Samantha" danced to the alto-pitched lyrics of Gladys Knight's "If I Were Your Woman." Not knowing "anything about illusions, I just did the show as Samantha." Then one day, as she was painting her face and putting on eyelashes, she said, "Wow! I can do Diana Ross—easy." Soon Samantha was singing "Ain't No Mountain High Enough" and "Reach Out, I'll Be There" live.

Sam's "gay mama," Bobby Whiteside, a local church-going boy who dressed in drag, "opened up doors for me," Sam extols, and encouraged Samantha to keep on going. "Don't let anybody try to pick on you because you're gay," Bobby advised. "If that's your choice, live it. But live it in a manner that you'll get respect." Roxanne Russell also offered advice to her drag daughters. Female impersonation is "only one expression of the self. If a man is using makeup, he must not think that he has actually become the image that the makeup creates. . . . Makeup is quick to wash off."

Doing the club circuit as Miss Gay Florida, Bobby reminisces, "these were the good old days. Nothing to be afraid of. The world was open and you could fuck with anyone and everyone if you wanted. If you got a disease, no problem; take a pill. Better yet, a shot would work even faster."

Seeking solace from the solitariness of writing, Jack Nichols drove across Highway 50 to Orlando. He cruised the Palace Club: "I'd initially despaired because its patrons appeared lifeless. Then, suddenly, an impersonator, dressed as Bette Midler, entered the barroom with appropriate fanfare." Jack's thoughts turned to a night at the Continental Baths when he and Lige had watched the original Bette perform decorated with only "fifteen cents worth of fake cherries" and a pink towel. Eyeing Bobby at the club's theater, Jack admired "the poise and energy that went into this impersonation," which "dazzled me beyond all expectation."

At the Palace Club there was no offstage announcer for performers, as was the custom. A rasping Miss P, dressed in a lime green Jean Harlow gown, interspersed their numbers with off-color one-liners reminiscent of Ray Bourbon. It had been only six months since Miss P first emceed the Palace Club: "They put that damn microphone in my hand," she remembers. "I went out there and said quickly something—it had a lot of connection with fruit: 'Squeeze an orange' or 'Peel my banana,' with a rude gesture toward my crotch. People laughed; that's all it took."

As the night wore on, Jack spotted a young man wearing jeans and a T-shirt. Dumbfounded, he gazed into the boy's hazel green eyes. "He returned my stare, his face communicating without saying a word. Instead of saying 'hello,' I placed my hand gently behind his neck and kissed him." They drove to Cocoa Beach.

In this midsummer night adventure, Bobby shared his dreams. Planning a stage and screen future, he "shied from using 'Bob,'" Jack recounts. "He worried 'it sounded too crew cut–businessman.' His middle name, Logan, I advised, had potential." As the older man whispered a verse from Whitman's *Leaves of Grass,* Bobby was born anew as Logan.

Masqueraders of gender have long bridged the sexual abyss of southern life. In a culture where belles adorn virginal pedestals, gentlemen sometimes traverse the racial boundary in airless gothic nights. Sam, as Samantha, crossed this divide, picked up white men, preferring the illusion of a woman, across from the Greenville Court House. He found it "exciting" to go home with "mostly business type" whites burdened by families and mortgages, or to sneak outside the Patio with a white date in tow. The southern façade of propriety and gentility, however, returned with the light of day.

From New Orleans mulattos to Miami *mariconés,* brown has been less a social barrier than has ebony. And it was in this time, "idealized by some as the golden age of gay sexuality," that Jesse Monteagudo ventured into the Club Miami. Nestled behind palms in Miami's southwest side, the club was particularly popular among youthful Latinos and their Anglo admirers. Like "a kid in the candy store," Monteagudo would get a locker (cheap with his youth discount), stroll through the maze of darkened cubbyholes, and "hang out by the pool, the whirlpool, or the orgy room. I'd stay all night and come home in the early morning—to my parents' outrage."

Absent memories of an earlier era when well-dressed gentlemen discreetly eyed one another across a hotel bar or treasured stolen dances at a club on the edge of town, Jesse and other sweaty twenty-somethings, inhaling amyl nitrite, danced to "Never Can Say Goodbye" and "Rock Your Baby" at the Warehouse VIII. Opened before Saturday Night Fever, the Village People, and Disco 54 would capture the fancies of the unimaginative, this spandex, lamé, and glitter crowd rarely gathered before midnight. Beyond the disco dance floor was a Levis-leather bar with an upstairs cruise area and a rooftop bar. The cavernous building was deafening, as Jesse and his friends danced to brassy music and primal tunes. "Soul Makossa" merged with human dancing machines pulsating to tribal rhythms in drug- and machine-induced mists.

As *The Parallax View* flickered on movie screens and "The Night Chicago Died" filled the radio waves, Lige arrived in New York from cruising around the world in 196 days. There was a decade of difference between the young Pentagon employee with nine security clearances lettering Mattachine signs, and the sage traveler who had "walked the most exciting streets imaginable, everything from Greek temples to African witchcraft to Indian elephants to Chinese junks."[13] He and Jack reunited at a Greenwich Village apartment that served as a springboard for their media appearances.

Promoting *Roommates Can't Always Be Lovers,* Lige told one talk show host: "People are beginning to accept it more. . . . Homosexuals are beginning to accept themselves more." Speaking to gay youth: "As long as you think that you are the only gay person in the whole world, you pretty much are." He counseled young people "growing up in small towns. . . . Try to be as happy as you can wherever you are. No matter where you are living . . . I am sure there is a gay organization nearby."[14]

Five years after Stonewall the first wave of southern Gay Liberation Front chapters with mimeographed newsletters and rap houses had disappeared. The midseventies marked another phase of building queer communities in the South. Atlanta and Dallas held gay pride parades. Small student bands of campus groups, cells of lesbian-feminists, and local sexuality and lesbian task forces were active and growing in many towns. Motorcycle clubs, softball teams, and church groups were starting or expanding. Southern homosexuals were publishing gay newspapers and bar magazines. Nevertheless, this second activist wave washed up against southern social sensibilities and a flourishing bar and bath scene, and found its energy dissipated in eddies of gender difference, racial separation, and political indifference.

In 1975, for example, the Charlotte Gay Alliance for Freedom, chaired by Barbara Bradford, and Don King's Alternative Sexual League organized, hoping to be more successful than GLF-Charlotte several years earlier. They weren't. Social life defined gay liberation in the Queen City.[15] Club Baths Charlotte operated on East Morehead Street, the French Art Cinema had opened with twenty-three new peep shows, and After Dark sold X-rated magazines and films. Oleens, the show bar, catered to drags and femmes, while the longtime Honey Brass Rail and Neptune Lounge continued to serve their regulars. For those into the dance scene, there was JB's, the only club owned and operated by gay people, and Scorpios, which had just remodeled its six-thousand-square-foot facility with 730 color lamps and strobes.

As an *Advocate* reporter concluded his story of a middle-aged bank vice president, caught in a bus station bust but bailed out by a textile heiress: "It is not surprising that any attempt to organize gay people has met with little success. After all, to organize you have to recruit; and, to recruit, you have to identify; and identification, except for the few 'New Charlotteans,' is unthinkable."[16]

Up Highway 29 two budding activists, Jim Baxter and Phillip Pendleton, formed the Guilford Gay Alliance. Baxter began writing a column, "On Being Gay," for the alternative monthly newspaper, the *Greensboro Sun.*[17] One response to his August 1974 column was from a one-time local man, Allan Troxler, living in Oregon with his companion, Carl Wittman; the two were assembling a new journal for rural gay men, *RFD.* "I go to Boston to come out, you to Greensboro," wrote Troxler. "Everybody to somewhere for liberation, it seems. Now, if we'd all stay put, couldn't that be the revolution?"[18]

Baxter echoed this sentiment in a letter penned to the *Advocate* that summer:

> You declare that "Gay Pride Is Everywhere!" a statement with which I beg exception, as much as I wish it were true. . . . In this area there is very little gay pride and very little gay consciousness. Would you like to know what Gay Pride week was like in this area? . . . Down on "the block," gays were cruising. . . . In the one bar in town, gays were joking, drinking, and cruising—as usual. Even when, on Thursday of Gay Pride Week, there was trouble over the bar's liquor license . . . was there a riot anywhere near that of the Stonewall? Hardly. Everybody simply went up to the other bar in Chapel Hill for the weekend and resigned themselves to the circumstances during the week.[19]

Baxter recalls his first experience entering the Renaissance, a bar owned by Joan McCoy in the Lawndale Shopping Center off Battleground Avenue. The first night he spent an hour outside before working up the courage to enter and pay the three-dollar cover. "I thought I'd stumbled into a lost road company of *The Boys in the Band.* I was in a time warp. Everyone was using female pronouns and carryin' on about Judy," he describes the scene. There was a staccato of queer chit-chat:

"Where *is* everybody?"

"They died. The obituaries were *full* this morning."

"Well, ain't you butch!"

"Don't worry honey, she's still a lady."

"Well, I really need to go home and get my shovel."

"For what?"

"My shovel and a wreath, honey—this place is dead."

Baxter continues: "While it could hardly be called an enlightened atmosphere (the unofficial policy is 'no dykes and no blacks allowed') it offers the only 'community' around—the only sense of continuity and history."[20] Later, echoing Nichols's *Men's Liberation,* he imagines "men evolving into non-masculine, non-feminine, non-competitive relationships. Whitmanic. The kind of relationship men's lib hasn't been able to deal with because of its avoidance of homosexuality."[21]

However, in building this Whitmanesque community, the Greensboro activist, like many others during this era, questioned the value of drag: "Why put on a dress? Why the mask? Why is it necessary? Why is it desirable? Why should it be encouraged? . . . Putting on a 'dress' is not talent; lip-syncing to a record is *not* entertainment. . . . Why do gay men want to look at a gay in a dress unless they think that's what 'gay' is—that faggots want to be women?"[22]

When asked whether the gay community was "one," Lige—on the road promoting *Roommates Can't Always Be Lovers*—replied honestly: "You really wouldn't call it a community because people don't really relate." He added: "At a particular time, in any minority group's fight for equal rights, you have to have your people identify with heroes. 'Gee! They're not afraid. They're just like me. Why should I be afraid? If they can do it, certainly I can.'"[23]

The heroes for midseventies southerners, however, were not gay liberationists with queer placards and clenched fists but heroines adorned with rouge and rhinestones. Southern drag queens did more than imitate Vivien Leigh; they stood resolute against the ravaging of their homosexual Taras. As in Stonewall, divas with attitude were the vanguard for the gay freedom movement. North Carolina's Brandy Alexander first started doing drag as a Sarasota student in 1964. Refusing to be intimidated by police bullying, she was frequently "pulled out of the bars and beaten by the cops with billy clubs." Atlanta's legendary "jailhouse Jezebel," Diamond Lil, earned her moniker following a raid of a "masquerade" party held in a Savannah "dungeon" operated by "Cousin Cora"—herself known for assembling South Georgia's best rough trade, aristocratic closet belles, and top drawer entertainers. And in Tidewater, longtime activist "Diana Ross" mounted a court challenge to her police abduction from the local Steak 'n' Egg.[24]

These "shock troops of a much-needed male-role revolution," as Nichols aptly describes them, rejected the macho Castro clone.[25] Roxanne Russell, playing at Fort Lauderdale's Copa, performed with China Black, who emulated Eartha Kitt, and Gilda Golden, who lip-synced to Barbra Streisand. In the style of the Andrews Sisters, the trio began: "Lipstick, cotton and paint/ Will make me what I ain't." China soloed: "I ain't a lady." Gilda chimed in: "I can't faint." And Roxanne completed: "I can't qualify as a saint." The trio harmonized to the finale:

Now the curtain's up
You see us as we is:
Sissies! Sissies! Sissies![26]

As a few gay white men organized handfuls of would-be political activists in a dozen or so southern communities, Roxannes in every city performed to overflowing crowds intoxicated with revelry and desire. At Rene's, the reigning Miss Gay Florida sang "Wait for Me, Marlena" and danced to the music of *City Lights*. In an elaborate production of "Sweet Transvestite," from the just released *Rocky Horror Picture Show*, Roxanne, a tireless propagandist for androgyny, appeared half male (smooth chest and biceps) and half female (garters and a painted face).

In mid-May, at the Persian Room of the Marco Polo Hotel, Roxanne (Bobby) relinquished her Miss Gay Florida crown to Noly Greer. The year 1975 also marked Bill Miller's purchase of a rundown hotel on Orange Blossom Trail. Not quite as seedy as the *Hot l Baltimore,* premiering that year on ABC, it was nevertheless "unknown territory." Transforming the drug-infested accommodation into a gay entertainment complex, Miss P remembers, "was the boldest thing that anyone had *ever* thought about doing in Orlando. Opening not a gay bar, but a gay hotel? The Parliament House was the first to have its name outside. People *wanted* to work there!"[27]

Hotel rooms overlooked a tropical swimming pool or a pond with a sandy beach, with a single going for twenty-nine dollars a night. The hotel balconies were the sexual bingo capital of the South. Guests and their friends dined at the Abbey Room restaurant, danced in the Powerhouse Disco, shopped at Michael's of Florida boutique, drank at the Levi-and-leather-clad Stable, and prettied up at Gay Blades hair styling.

The Parliament House was P's theatrical paradise. "Mr. Miller let me have that whole showroom to do whatever I wanted," he reminisces. The first of Paul's lavish production shows was *A Chorus Line,* which was playing at the Public Theater in New York to sell-out audiences. Paul credits Bobby, now known as Logan, with getting him interested in the production. "He had just gotten back from New York. Logan was a CL fanatic—able to recite lines from the monologue and the songs."

For Paul, coming from a carnival and Broadway show background, "it was just another one of the albums you bought as soon as it was released— so I knew the music." But, he continues, "Michael Bennett was very guarded about that show. Logan filled in all the rest of it for me; he just enthused me with it to the point where it became something I wanted to try."

The drag version of *A Chorus Line* appeared at Parliament House that fall: "People were just agog! They were used to the little drag show, one on, one off with me talking in between. All of sudden one night here we are, no curtain on the stage, people walking out in their dance clothes and finding a spot and warming up. The music comes up. . . . They didn't know what in the hell was that. After that, Mr. Miller asked, 'What's the next one going to be?'"

Next, P created a show entitled *Night Life.* "Looking at the seamy side of life," it was a pastiche of musical pieces with narratives weaving the songs together, she explains. "There were a lot of prostitute numbers. We did 'Cell Block Tango' from Chicago, a recording from Gypsy that has 'Alright girls, pack up your apples and back to the trees'—the Adam and Eve ballet that Gypsy did—I had these great trees and boys standing around in practically nothing, and all these drag queens running around with apples!" Paul's Playhouse Players went on to other productions, including "Christmas Fantasy," a version of Studs Terkel's *Working,* and a "big blow-out" for Centennial.[28]

In late October 1975, a friend of Jack Nichols invited him to the legendary Upper East Side bar, the Blue Angel. That Sunday evening Jack "watched in awe" as Logan performed "What Makes a Man a Man?" Though many had gathered to see his uncanny Monroe impersonation, the audience erupted in frenzied applause as Logan ended the show by sitting at a makeup table. A haunting melody sung by Charles Aznavour played. With perfect timing, Roxanne gradually removed her female attire, sat naked for a moment, and then transformed herself into the athletic Logan. The performance, Logan later explained, "teaches us the answer is in what's inside. I believe that when you peel off the clothes, women and men are essentially the same."

After the show, Jack slipped "into the hall where, in black T-shirt and jeans, Logan was leaning against a wall. His eyes opened wide as I strode toward him. But, once again, we spoke not a word as I kissed him hello."

Moving into Logan's Manhattan apartment, Jack brought a statue of Buddha and placed it on a theatrical trunk near the window. One afternoon, Jack and Logan walked in the East Village. They passed David, a florist, from whom Jack had often purchased a single rose for Lige. "David squinted at Logan and, to my embarrassment, said what I'd secretly thought: 'He looks just like a youthful Lige.'"

It had been two years since Lige and Jack had returned to winter in Florida after their book tour. Lige had begun listening to audiotaped interviews for a book on Fire Island while Jack thought through his new book for Penguin on bisexuality. Just before Christmas 1974, Lige returned to Miami to nurse his Aunt Monte. On his return, "he put increased efforts into his writing," recalls Nichols. In early February 1975, Clarke proofed the final galleys of *Men's Liberation,* which Jack had dedicated to Lige, who had "taught me that a man can learn to bend like the willow."

Three days later, Lige went on a "short jaunt" with two friends. Jack remembers that Lige "was concerned I'd react with dismay at his hurried decision to leave. I didn't fuss. I knew he'd soon return. And he loved me much for the calm manner I radiated. Before he stepped into the car, he kissed me, saying, 'Now I love you more than ever.'"

With few clothes and less money, Lige took along work for his Fire Island book. Traveling across I-10 that Friday evening in Charlie's white Ford pinto, Lige hummed to Gloria Gaynor's "Honey Bee" as he read favorite passages from *Song of the Open Road.*

Charlie was at the wheel. He had just moved from North Carolina into an apartment on the same floor Jack and Lige lived on. Quickly, he ingratiated himself with the duo, serving as a chauffeur to Lige and an errand boy for Jack. Although he worked at the Cocoa Beach post office, he took off days at a time. "His backwoods accent and his big ears created for him the likeness of a redneck," Jack recollects. Although he "surprisingly seemed to hold radical political opinions that matched mine and Lige's."

Juan was the third passenger in the Mexico-bound Pinto. He'd just returned from Bogota with money in hand and a pressing desire to visit Lige. A former member of Mattachine-Washington, the "Cuban royalist who moved in high Washington circles . . . was clever," emphasizes Jack, "and very well read. He was capable of anything." Lige, too, had his suspicions: "He lives in a Bogota highrise," wondered Lige, "and he works for the Peace Corps?"

Since the lowest of Lige's security clearances was "Top Secret," he was required to notify authorities whenever he left the country. Generally, he ignored this condition of his army discharge. Although Lige never discussed with Jack or friends the specifics of this government work, there had been whispered rumors in Hindman of CIA connections and some movement folks quietly wondered how an assistant to the Pentagon brass could have so easily pursued Mattachine work.

The trio arrived in New Orleans the Saturday before Mardi Gras. In morning light, the city was magical and mysterious. Lige and Charlie expected to sleep in Jackson Square; Juan, though, insisted on a hotel. They resolved the conflict by departing for Mexico. At the outskirts of Houston, however, Juan insisted on being shuttled to the airport for a Washington flight. The other two continued driving through the night to Brownsville, Texas.

Lige and Charlie arrived at the border crossing the morning of 9 February. "They were letting everyone through as a matter of routine," reported Charlie. But his car was searched thoroughly, and his luggage scrutinized, and "when they saw our typewriters it seemed to freak them out."[29]

After several hours of detention, the two began their trek on Mexican dirt roads, finally settling on Tampico for a Kentucky Fried Chicken dinner. Charlie studied the map. Tuxpam, near Vera Cruz, was not too distant, although it required crossing the river by ferry. Lige took the wheel, leaving Tampico around eight o'clock; Charlie went into the backseat to sleep. On the ferry, Charlie later claimed, two men kept careful watch on the pair. Whether he told Lige to look behind him is unclear, though Charlie fell back to sleep.

Lige shakes Charlie excitedly. His eyes open. The car is stalled, the motor running. There were men on either side of the car with flashlights and automatic weapons. The car windows are up. Bullets rip through the morning air. Glass shatters. "Oh my God, help us!" shouts Charlie.[30] Lige's foot falls from the clutch. The Pinto lurches forward, resting against an embankment on the other side of Federal Highway.

Lige lunges toward Charlie "as if to reach out for help or to help me." Blood gushes from his mouth and nose. With five .45 caliber bullets in his chest, Lige utters something unintelligible. He goes limp on his fellow traveler's left shoulder. Charlie writes later: "I held my breath and closed my eyes and tried to play dead. The men came over to the car and took the wallets off of us but took nothing else from the car. I heard cars pull off and hoped they were gone."[31]

Not far from El Cid Carro ranch, Charlie waved down an early-morning bus. The driver refused to look inside the car where lay the young man with long blond hair. A bloodstained volume of *Leaves of Grass* rested on the seat.

For five hours over the next two days, Charlie was interrogated by the federal police at Tuxpam Civil Hospital. "They tried to associate me with the CIA and claimed we were down there for purposes other than what we had claimed," he recounted shortly after his release. Although these "bandits" had posed a frequent problem in the area, the police report noted that nothing else of value was taken—no watches, not the typewriters, no tires or eight-track tapes.

A week after Lige's murder, Jack returned to the Kentucky hills of his lover's hometown. A light morning rain was falling. Jack joined the family of mourners at the mossy cemetery. Choking away tears, he listened to a matronly relative eulogize her love. Jack's thoughts crossed time to when he and his comrade-in-arms hiked up that mountain for a picnic lunch. Like the two boys clinging together ("Arm'd and fearless, eating, drinking, sleeping, loving"),[32] Old Walt "sang about the whispers of heavenly death. They've never sounded so loud to me," Jack later wrote his friends. "Across the valley, in the mist."

Charlie visited Cocoa Beach two months later. Jack "sat with him and listened to his impassioned account." While he had his say, Jack, who had not yet received a copy of Charlie's letter to Shelbiana, Lige's sister, had no way to explore the tale's inconsistencies. Jack adds: "There are times when I imagine him as the Angel of Death. . . . He moved rapidly after his April visit. Months later I get a postcard from Charlie showing San Francisco's Lombard Street, oddly explaining that it is 'the crookedest street in the world.'"

A year after the "accident," Charlie's last correspondence read: "Jack, I trapped a butterfly and held it in my hands. I was blinded to its beauty. Its wings struggled to expand. A ray of sun caught my eye and set the captive free. As it flew away it sprinkled its secrets upon me."

SIXTEEN

Seventy-five Lesbians

Women were being kept in line in the same way blacks were in the South.
We scared some people; we looked different.
                                                            —*Pokey Anderson*

"PUT SOMEONE ELSE'S NAME DOWN!" whispered the person next to her.

Scribbling "Pokey" on the sign-in sheet, the five-foot-three senior from Eckerd College walked into the Roaring Sixties. Wearing a pleated skirt, her brown hair trailing to her waist, Pokey Anderson stepped up to the bar and ordered a ginger ale. The bartender winced, as if to ask, "Do you know where you are?"

Identifying herself as a feminist and a lesbian, Pokey was neither a separatist nor "out" in early seventies Houston. Unlike her mother, who had been a "civil rights troublemaker" in college, according to Pokey, she was never a student activist. And, like her father, a social worker, she wanted to work "within the system." Pokey had confessed her same-sex feelings—hidden since junior high—to a college boyfriend; she had yet to reveal her secret to B.J., her straight girlfriend, whom she followed to Texas.

Rita and Millie. Photo courtesy of Rita Wanstrom.

While living in suburbia with B.J. and her parents, Pokey occasionally sneaked downtown to walk along "Peculiar Street" in the Westheimer Colony. Houston was "on the cusp of change from the bar lesbian to the lesbian-feminist," Pokey explains. The lesbianscape was a set of loosely networked communities of women who met on the ball fields, at private social gatherings, or in the bars. Most, like those frequenting the Roaring Sixties or Just Marion and Lynn's, "had lived this existence in the closet for all of these years reciting the mantra, 'If you don't rock the boat, you'll be okay.'" But a new lesbian wave, generally unaware of an earlier generation of activists like Rita Wanstrom and her Tumblebugs, was about to tip the boat of Houston heterodoxy. And Pokey Anderson would be leading that new lesbian tide.

After the dramatic demise of the Promethean Society and the low-key collapse of the Texas Homophile Education Movement, Rita Wanstrom seemed content to operate her bars and construction business. Downtown was Poppa Bears. This Old Market Square bar featured exotic dancing and drag shows. Serving the mostly straight male crowd in her black cocktail dress, Rita claims she "could put a hammerlock on a customer faster than anyone" but would "rather fight with a drunk man than a woman anytime."

Despite Rita's early political efforts, Houston's lesbian scene remained social. Not-so-closeted lesbians played fast-pitch softball at Memorial Park and relished the annual International Softball Tournament at summer's end. Meanwhile, the A-list lesbians enjoyed outings like Easter egg hunts on Lake Japhet and Halloween parties. The Diana Foundation, established in 1951, also was going strong; Rita designed costumes for its annual charity salute to the Oscars.

Pokey, who Rita first remembers as "a quiet, shy, and retiring person," was not part of the A-lesbian group. When not reading and "reveling in a whole new perspective on life [in general] and my life [in particular]," Anderson recalls, she would generally head over to Memorial Park and watch the women play softball.

Two hours up I-45, Dallas lesbians were organizing politically. In November 1972, four female members of the Circle of Friends, tired of the "sexism of that organization," formed the Dallas chapter of the Daughters of Bilitis.[1] Meeting at the Women for Change offices, the group, as one founder recalls, "began just in our minds and I don't think we were aware of how badly we needed a woman's organization until we actually began one."[2]

Christy, then president of the Circle, describes events leading up to the lesbian walk-out:

We had many meetings and conversations among our brothers. At one meeting we discussed, "Why don't we have more women in the club and why are they leaving?" We explained, explained, and had conversations. I thought there was some progress when one of the men who had been active in the organization, but was in the closet, said: "But, I don't really understand that. I don't see what the problem is. We elect the officers." But, actually, they elected the people who could do the work and [that they could] trust to do the work—and that turned out to be the women, which is frequently the way it turns out. I wasn't a feminist at that point—not until the DOB Forum.[3]

As 1973 began, Pokey was about to become a feminist. She attended the first National Women's Political Caucus convention held at the Rice Hotel. "Sissy Farenthold, Betty Friedan, Gloria Steinem were all there—right in front of *me*!" exclaims Pokey. But the caucus was "very straight, although there were people in the closet"—including Pokey—who "kept sneaking off" to a sexual orientation workshop on the top floor. There she learned about the Montrose Gaze Community Center that had officially opened three months earlier, inspired by the Dallas gay pride parade that past June.[4]

A few days later, Pokey parked her VW bug near the corner of Fairview at Whitney. After watching people march up the center's wooden steps, she hesitantly stepped out of the car and walked toward the bungalow. Inside she found a couple of dozen people, mostly men, hanging out. Funded by the bars, there was a pool table and space for rap groups and dances.

Integrity/Houston, which evolved from a small Dignity group at Holy Rosary Church three years earlier, "was probably the only general-purpose organization," according to Pokey. "But, again, it was all gay guys—mostly older, conservative, closeted men." This self-described "fellowship for homophiles" included founders Bill Buie, Mark Barron, Hugh Crell, and Keith McGee.[5] As an unaffiliated political group, it provided gay speakers, sponsored VD screening, and supported political candidates.[6] Through her contacts at the Montrose Gaze and Integrity, Anderson began appearing on a radio show as an open lesbian. Then one day a queer message was left on B.J.'s answering machine. Now seeking answers to questions about her sexuality never before asked, Pokey moved out.

Later Pokey wrote a children's fable, "Star and the 75." This is a story of Star's love for Laura, who abandoned her for a man. Star, wondering if she was "the only woman in the world who thought women were important enough to love for real," went to the center: "But there were mostly men there. So, as a joke, she would always pretend there were really seventy-five women there. Her friend John would say, 'Oh you just missed them. The seventy-five just left. . . .' And Star would always say, 'Darn, I missed them again.'"[7] Pokey explains that "back then, it was a total fantasy to find seventy-five lesbians anywhere in Houston, except for a bar."

Both lesbians and gay men were vital in building communities of queer southerners that emerged during the seventies. However, men and women set different cornerstones, attracted unequal publicity, and received disparate historical treatment. As Anderson figured out: "Men's history is institutionalized and has lots of capital letters. Women's history tends to be small letters . . . little groups that get together and read books together and play softball. . . . The strands are different . . . they connect, at times and they diverge at times."[8]

In Houston, a bevy of newspapers and radio shows, an array of groups ranging from softball teams to motorcycle clubs, and a stable political infrastructure transformed Montrose from an "amorphous cohesiveness" of individuals in 1970 to the "San Francisco of the South" a decade later.[9]

When Integrity was founded in 1970, a local printer, Floyd Goff (under the name Phil Frank), published *Nuntius,* using money produced from his "swinger's club" newspaper and bingo parlor receipts to subsidize the paper.[10] An alternative radio station (KPFT-FM) also started that year, and within a couple of years a live show with taped programs to "enlighten the straight community" had evolved into the show "Out of the Closets, Into the Streets" that aired every other Sunday afternoon.

Meanwhile, Houston women switched from fast- to slow-pitch softball, opening up ball fields at Memorial Park to scores of other lesbians. Women formed basketball and touch football teams. Some men formed or joined biker communities. In 1972, the Houston Motorcycle Club held club meetings at Mary's bar. A year earlier, the Texas Riders, Houston's oldest motorcycle club, had begun publishing a newsletter. Headquartered at the Locker on Westheimer, these men of leather held Christmas and pledge parties, conducted change-of-command ceremonies, and sponsored interclub activities with local and regional "runs." Finally, during the tragic summer of the Up Stairs fire, the Gaze Center hosted meetings for Christian gays. Eventually this study group, led by Arnold Lawson, would become MCC of the Resurrection.

Pokey moved across many of these early groups. Her "strategy was to hang out where you are useful, where you are wanted, and where things are happening," she explains. Keeping one foot at the Gaze Center and another at the Women's Center located on Milam, "I'd be in the gay movement for a while and then get fed up with the sexism and then go back to the women's movement, where I would get fed up with the heterosexism." As Anderson became more active, she realized that "we might actually have here a movement rather than just assorted people who got together and sat around."[11]

In 1973, Harla Kaplan, a relatively "new lesbian," started a local Sexuality and Lesbianism Task Force in the Houston NOW chapter. As in other localities, this proved to be a "breeding ground for lesbians," Anderson says. Kaplan, in particular, was determined to get a large crowd of lesbians at the first meeting at the Milam Street house.[12] Pokey remembers that "Harla had gone to places like the Roaring Sixties trying to recruit. Now, she was a large, Jewish woman with long fingernails! People were not taking her seriously at that bar, but she had gumption. In those days it was just this wildest dream like you're going to take a walk on the moon next week. . . . We were coming out of the closet and making lots of noise—being political! Old-timers like Marion Pantzer saw us as 'aliens.'"

In particular, Pokey recollects an older lesbian couple "who had a lovely house on Bissonnet—and they looked like lesbians: big, truck-driver types. They had their little clique of friends, mostly couples, whom they had known for years. They were 'not going to come out to anybody, anytime.' They told me, 'Pokey, you come out. And when it's safe you let us know.'"

But Pokey, Harla, and others who dared to speak the "L-word" wouldn't be deterred. Their goal was equality. "It was real simple in a world where it should be incidental that whether you are male or female you should have the same rights," argued Pokey.[13] But, from the older generation's perspective, these outspoken lesbians missed the point. "We should be equal. But they weren't willing to *work* to be equal," Rita quips.

As the lesbian-feminist movement unfolded in Houston, Rita Wanstrom worked hard to be the first among equals in the bar and construction business. Over the years, an interesting assortment of folks visited the mostly lesbian Roaring Sixties on South Shepherd. In addition to lesbian regulars like Dee Dee, who'd waltz in with slacks, cuffs turned up, hair slicked back, and tanned Mexican shoes, there was the one-armed guy who'd shoot pool with Rita for twenty dollars a ball. Rita used one of her matched pair of San Toeos; he used the end of a broomstick—and "cleared the table." Rita also had gotten used to a security tap placed on the phone because "I had beat the cops."

During the seventies, the city bar scene grew proportionately with the gay population and its increasing openness. As the *Rocky Horror Picture*

Show premiered at a London experimental theater and Mary Renault's *Persian Boy* enjoyed its twenty-third week on the *New York Times* best-seller list, a new generation of lesbians and gay southerners felt a spring-time of sexual liberation. Among the city's thirty-odd queer bars, the most notorious and oldest was the hustler-friendly, poorly lit Exile on Bell Street (billed as "Texas' Oldest Western Bar") and La Caja on Tuam, boasting a back patio rife with sexual activity. One of the biggest gay dance halls between the East and West Coasts, the Bayou Landing, opened in 1973 on Kipling. Both women and men would crowd onto the dance floor on a weekend night. It was there that Pokey learned to do the Cotton-Eyed Joe. This was an era, as David Patterson, one of the founders of the Promethean Society, remembers, when "the war on drugs was almost non-existent. It was easy to get almost any drug you wanted: tabs of acid, Quaaludes, pot, uppers."

Leaders of Integrity/Houston called on bar-goers to practice "enlight-ened self-interest," reminding them of the frequent appearances of plain-clothes vice officers. Silk-screened posters that reinforced the old Mattachine message—"What I do reflects on you. What you do reflects on me. What we do reflects on the entire gay community."—were dis-tributed to the bars. In one newspaper column, the coat-and-tie leaders of Integrity emphasized: "If you involve yourself in public drug trafficking or public sexual encounters you are exposing all around you to arrest. If you witness such activity and do not report it to the manager, you are not an innocent bystander."[14]

Meanwhile, fifty women showed up at the Milam Street house for the first meeting of the Sexuality and Lesbianism Task Force. "There was just this wild energy, to everyone's surprise," Pokey exclaims. Three coordinators were selected, including Pokey. "I remember feeling like that old Army story, 'Who wants to volunteer?' and everyone else takes a step back! And there I was. To be a leader in the gay movement during the early seventies all you had to do was *not* take one step back."

Pokey continued her involvement in gay groups, including the Hous-ton Gay Political Coalition. In May 1973, Billy Walker, Chuck Berger, and Bob Osborne stood before the Houston City Council. As leaders of this new political advocacy group formed out of the Gaze Center, the trio politely requested an end to police harassment of homosexuals, a liaison to the Police Department, and a declaration of Gay Pride Week. Mayor Welch walked out, and the infamous homophobe council member, Frank Mann, shouted: "You're abnormal! You need to see a psychiatrist instead of City Council."[15]

That fall, the Gaze Center was unable to renew its lease, as interest and funding waned. Although the center as well as the coalition fell on hard times, gay businesses—ranging from janitorial services and dry cleaners to the bars and baths—were booming. Rita's construction company was doing so well that she hired one person whose only job was to clean up around the saw.

As Rita was "out doing construction and building for our future," Ricci, the exotic dancer who was Rita's lover, hosted at the Roaring Sixties. One evening, Rita walked into the club to find Ricci sitting at a table with another woman. Pulling her aside, Rita cautioned, "Ricci, you shouldn't pay all attention to just one customer; we have a lot of customers in here."

Rita reminisces, "I kept a blind eye for a long time. But Ricci was just a little girl." Asked why Ricci—who had chosen her name because it would fit on the marquees—would ever want to leave, Rita replied: "White Horse scotch, honey! This new girl blew smoke you wouldn't believe, telling her that she was going to do all of this for her. But it was all of the money she had embezzled." Ricci, in turn, led the new girl to believe that much of the wealth of the bars, construction company, and other enterprises was hers. "They both got fooled!" exclaims Rita. "But I experienced no joy in that."

At the end of July—ten years, one month, and three days after they had begun a new life together—Rita and Ricci broke up. "I was afraid to pick up a saw," Rita reveals. "It was such a shocker." She was devastated, as were lesbians in her community. "That was the first time I had been truly, truly in love—and rebuffed. It wasn't just what she did to me, but there was fallout in the entire gay community. It affected the business. People were used to seeing us as a team, an institution. It shattered ideals between couples. Also, the butches were afraid to bring their fluffs in because I was a bachelor again."[16]

During the dog days of August 1973, after Lou Reed's "Walk on the Wild Side" had dropped out of the Top 40, Texas lesbians and gay men also had a shock. The grisly discovery of the bodies of twenty-seven young men, tortured and murdered by Dean A. Corll in his Pasadena apartment with the assistance of two teen accomplices, generated headlines across the nation.[17] Two weeks later, a "homosexual procurement ring" was uncovered in North Dallas. There police raided a second-floor apartment on Cole Street and arrested a forty-five-year-old who managed the Odyssey Foundation, linking teen "fellows" with adult "sponsors."[18]

The *Dallas Times Herald,* informing its readers that a "possible link in the two cases may emerge," reported that the word "kill" was written on tape that bound four teen photos. The story warned that this "may be homosexual terminology for no longer using those particular individuals in the Dallas operation and does not necessarily mean the persons pictured were marked for death."[19] The *Dallas Morning News* along with a local television station also linked these two stories. Channel 8 News reported on a possible torture-murder ring in Dallas, while the newspaper quoted a citizen-vigilante who declared: "You ought to string them all up," and a psychiatrist who expressed concern about homosexuals teaching "young boys."[20] Houston's police chief Herman Short (George Wallace's designee as FBI director during the 1972 presidential campaign) sought to quell fear among local gays, telling a reporter that "homosexuals need not fear police reprisals because of the murders" and adding that "many sex deviates would not resort to murder."[21] Nevertheless, bars and clubs reported increased surveillance and harassment.

Although local gay leaders in Houston and Dallas ably represented their mostly invisible constituents, one Integrity leader made an observation that would become a mantra for southern lesbian and gay activists: "The biggest problem of Houston gay organizations is apathy. The recent mass murders seem not to have any effect on this."[22] Despite this bleak assessment, when Mayor Welch chose not to run for reelection that fall, Integrity/Houston invited the three top candidates to speak at a private meeting. Only one accepted: Fred Hofheinz. His father, Judge Roy Hofheinz, a "cocksure impresario who fancied cigars and other forms of opulence," had presided over the "well-planned harassment" of gays as well as the planning of the Astrodome.[23]

Fred Hofheinz differed on many issues with the judge, and offered a poorly publicized statement supporting gays at a Montrose block party. On the evening of 28 October 1973, Integrity members entered the Travis Street office not knowing who was going to speak. The candidate walked into the closed-door session alone and engaged in an hour-plus rap session. "The initial audience mood was skeptical, but as Fred stated unequivocal positions and answered some very pointed and even hostile questions, the mood changed to one of enthusiasm."[24]

Integrity circulated flyers to twenty-five gay bars on election eve supporting Hofheinz's candidacy during his runoff election with city councilman Dick Gottlieb. Although his opponent was supported by the mayor and construction interests, Hofheinz won with a margin of about three thousand votes—allowing Houston gays to claim credit for his narrow victory.

Mayor Hofheinz brought in a new police chief, with whom representatives of the gay community met in early February 1974. Chief C. M.

Lynn gave the community "a degree of respect and confidence" toward the Houston Police Department.[25] Further, he pledged not to raid bars if no illegal activities occurred. This was particularly welcome news for Marion Pantzer—Rita's friend of twenty years—who had recently opened Just Marion and Lynn's.[26] Sometimes the diminutive Marion sat outside the old bar, generally wearing a T-shirt and walking shorts with golfer socks. Her dogs kept the "bad people out and let the good people in," baying when cops, who felt little obligation to heed the new mayor's pledge, approached. With the breakup of Rita and Ricci and the subsequent demise of the Roaring Sixties, Marion's bar on the corner of Fairview and Converse became the preferred lesbian hangout.[27] Pokey remembers that Marion "always kept everything totally under control in the bar. She knew who was in the bar and what they were up to at all times—like she had eyes in the back of her head. People who didn't belong in the bar were stopped before they got three feet inside the door."

Marion, like Rita, became an institution in Houston's lesbian community. As the fairy godmother of Montrose, Wanstrom arranged funerals as well as officiated at marriages. Rita's first of three hundred wedding ceremonies was performed in 1968 for two men, one of whom was about to be shipped overseas. As the only person performing same-sex weddings in Texas, Rita pronounced them "loving partners for life," noting it was a "commitment before witnesses."[28] When Bob, the husband of one of Rita's waiters, was killed in a car accident, Poppa Bear sponsored a series of drag shows to cover burial expenses. Rita also fixed the hair of women who died "because I knew what they looked like. I was there to help."

The social services performed by Rita, Marion, and several other bar owners—coupled with the southern penchant for discretion, a flourishing social scene, and the absence of sustained public hostility—perhaps explains why "the expression of one's sexuality remained confined to the bars and small groups of friends," with little interest shown in political activity.[29] This was true in other southern cities as well where coming out, during the midseventies, was a social, not political, decision. Lesbians and gay men joined religious groups like the St. Jude MCC of Columbia or Dignity Richmond and read the *Free Press* in Charlotte or *Gaiety* in Memphis. Lesbians played on softball teams, including the ALFA Omegas and the Houston Ducks, as well as participated in local lesbian and sexuality task forces, attended all-women's musical concerts and festivals, and enjoyed novels about southern lesbians like *Lover, Catching Saradove,* and *Nerves.* Mostly gay men danced in glitter discos of Atlanta's Back Street and Belle Whatley's in Birmingham, partied on Labor Day weekend at

Southern Decadence or with Emma Jones on the Fourth of July, frequented the baths in Charlotte, Tampa, or Knoxville, participated in drag contests from the Miss Zodiac Pageant in Virginia to Miss Gay Florida, and rode on bike runs with the Thebans of Florida or the Knights D'Orleans.

Although local homosexual political groups were no longer quixotic operations in 1974, they certainly lacked a critical mass of homosexual southerners, who generally preferred reading a just released novel, *The Front Runner,* or a *New Yorker* gay short story, quietly switching the TV channel from *Marcus Welby*'s "The Outrage" or *Police Woman*'s "Flowers of Evil," or weekend dancing to "The Hustle" or "Never Can Say Goodbye." Three years would pass before a former Miss America runner-up and an encyclopedia salesman would square off in Dade County to ignite the second Stonewall rebellion.

Not surprisingly, gay political activists began to see the value of networking beyond their towns' borders. Texas was the first Confederate state to assemble local activists and organize statewide reform efforts.[30] Under the leadership of Ken Cyr and his partner, Charles Gillis, and sponsored by the Fort Worth/Dallas Metroplex Gay Council, the first statewide gay conference was held on the weekend of 21 June 1974 with the theme of "Together We Can."[31]

Political stalwarts Franklin E. Kameny, Freda Smith, and Barbara Gittings stirred the crowd of two hundred with keynote addresses. Outside the community services building of St. Stephen's Church, police wrote down automobile license plate numbers.[32] Nevertheless, by Sunday, there was a new statewide organization to press for state reform, the Texas Gay Task Force. Abolishing laws that discriminate against gays, insuring a communication network among various local gay organizations, and developing a program of public education headed its agenda.[33]

Meetings with other Texas activists also helped to reinvigorate local activism. A month after the Fort Worth conference, Integrity founder Bill Buie wrote Kameny to request his assistance in "presenting a municipal civil rights bill to Houston. . . . As far as we can determine, we have only one city councilman who would actively work to defeat the bill. We feel the time is ripe and there is really only one way to find out.[34] While it would be well into the next decade before the city council would act on such an ordinance, the momentum, resources, and networking generated from this and subsequent state conferences were critical as Houston entered a new phase of mainstream political organizing.

As the Montrose boys organized politically, in the spring of 1975, Cy, a Lone Star lesbian returned from New York after four years away from

Houston. During the next couple of months she visited the Women's Center, talked to Pokey Anderson, attended a softball playoff, and subscribed to the *Pointblank Times*. Recalling her discovery of "what is commonly referred to as the 'lesbian community,'" she later wrote in *PBT*: "I made the decision to remain in Houston. That decision was influenced, in part, by the lesbian community which exists here." Nevertheless, it was still a community largely invisible to women who loved women. "I think it's possible to live and die in Houston and never realize a community exists." She concluded: "Houston is a collection of pockets of women and picking pockets is an area in which few of us were trained."[35]

Alison McKinney and Linda Lovell worked hard to reduce this isolation and invisibility. Alison, who a year earlier produced a gay radio show for KPFT, had begun to "agitate" among women for a creative lesbian outlet early in 1975. The pair, who both had contributed to *Mockingbird* (an early feminist newspaper published in Houston), distributed the city's first lesbian-feminist periodical in March to friends and at women's bars like the Lamp Post on Times Boulevard.

After the first issue, Alison and Linda hosted an "organizational meeting" to decide the content for future issues.[36] They explained to Pokey and the twelve other women who attended that the name *Pointblank Times* was chosen in honor of Point Blank, Texas. This rural San Jacinto County town was originally named Blanc Point by a French woman who had journeyed from Alabama.[37]

Soon the *PBT* collective was printing a monthly ten-to-twelve-page newsletter with news analysis, stories, poetry, and upcoming events at a red brick building on West Alabama—the House of Coleman—simply for the cost of the paper. Working weekends at Marion Coleman's shop, "It was a struggle to keep it going," recalls Pokey Anderson. "We had to learn from scratch how to do lay-out, half-tones, etc. But we learned." And even in Marion's own building, she steadfastly kept to the closet, as Anderson reveals: "Her printer was a Christian man and straight as a board. Marion was afraid he would find out that she was a lesbian—even though she was his boss! We had to take all of our trash with us just in case he might find something when he came in on Monday."[38]

One Friday evening, as the collective worked on its second issue of *PBT*, Rita's phone rang.

"Bunny?"

"This is Bunny."

"This is Millie!"

Rita nearly dropped the phone. She had not heard from her childhood sweetheart in thirty-three years. Married with four children, Millie had been searching for Rita since 1964.

They made arrangements to meet the next morning. Dressed in heels, dress, and lipstick, Rita answered the knock at the door, "trying to walk across the dining room floor to get to her after all of these years." Spending time over a leisurely breakfast, they agreed to meet again that evening. After spending some time with Millie's cousin, Rita invited Millie to choose where she'd like to go next. "I was prepared to take her to some straight place where we could meet dudes," Rita recollects.

"Where would you go if I was not here?" asked Millie.

Rita thought to herself, "Oh, shit! Now what do I say?" Feigning composure, she responded: "Are you serious?"

Millie nodded.

They drove to Just Marion and Lynn's. Drinking a malt scotch on the rocks at a corner table, Rita couldn't believe that "the love of my life was sitting here in *my* kind of place. I had kept her picture for all of these years! I was in la-la land."

Millie stirred Rita from her dreamlike state: "Are you going to ask me to dance or what?" As they stepped out onto the floor, "it was like we'd never stop dancing." Later the two lost lovers drove to Ursula's on West Alabama Street. "It's still not dawning on me," relays Rita. "Then she reaches across the table and kisses me. And the bell starts ringing! We spent the night together."

SEVENTEEN

Out in the Outfield

In everyone's life, there should be a summer of 1974.   —*Vicki*

"I never considered myself an athlete," Vicki Gabriner says. But during that summer, playing second base for the ALFA Omegas, "I *could* make the bat hit the ball, I *could* catch, I *could* run, I *could* throw."

In 1974, the Atlanta Lesbian Feminist Alliance was moving "from a more consciously political to a more socially and athletically oriented organization."[1] Among the mostly white members, the activity that drew the largest participation was its "out-lesbian" softball team, the Omegas.[2] "We were the daughters and sisters of Billie Jean King, Joan Joyce, Wyomia Tyrus, Babe Didrikson Zaharias, and Title IX," declares Vicki.

Although the Omegas lost their first game to the Stumps, 17–12, Vicki remembers that softball summer as "a little piece of heaven"; they won the rest of their regular games, including the tough Gulf Duffers and the undefeated Southern Bell Rams. Vicki continues: "We had some women who were incredible athletes and other people, like myself, who weren't. We played in a very supportive way with each other—and we won our games! We were in a competitive league: We played and were political."

Besides Vicki Gabriner and Karla Brown playing the infield, there was Lorraine Fontana pitching, with Elizabeth Knowlton soon cheering from the stands. As the Omegas raced onto the field, fans stood, shouting: "Two bits, four bits, six bits, a dollar. All for the queers, stand up and holler." Cheer after cheer, "it was us and the fans," reminisces Vicki,

ALFA softball, circa 1974. Photo © Marcelina Martin.

"we were one." Lorraine adds, "Other people would sort of look as if to ask, 'Who are they?'"

Word spread with each City League game the Omegas played. Lorraine continues: "In Atlanta, some women who had never been to ALFA but who were lesbian (and maybe not even out of the closet), would hear 'ALFA is that man-hating, separatist group.' As people started cheering, people would come to the game to watch. That really helped ALFA get known: 'Maybe they're not like we heard.'" Although ALFA was never completely successful in altering its image, within six months membership had more than tripled, confirming the observation of lesbian folksinger Alix Dobkin: "Softball is the single greatest organizing force in lesbian society."[3]

Being "out" in the field and applying lesbian-feminist theory to softball principles distinguished the Omegas from other city teams who may have had lesbian players. Once an umpire whispered to the opposing team about their competitor's lesbianism. "The funny thing was we knew most of the women on the other team," Gabriner chuckles, "and they were almost all lesbians."

"We tried to organize [softball] in a very political manner," stresses Lorraine. "Everybody got a chance to play, you didn't just play the 'good' people." There was no competition for positions and every team member participated. Batting rosters were collectively decided and there was a careful tally of innings each woman played. A lesbian astrologer even produced charts for the games.

Following a festive afternoon on the diamond, players with white pants turned Georgia-clay red and spectators with voices turned hoarse crowded into the Tower Lounge—an after work, blue-collar lesbian bar on Forrest Road.[4] Located under a towering radio antenna, the bar had pool tables, occasional concerts, dancing, and quarter beers on Tuesday and Thursday nights. ALFA members mixed easily with the other customers. Some of these older women remembered years earlier when the lounge had been a restaurant, serving a clientele of lesbians and working-class heterosexual men. This was the kind of woman, observes Vicki, "who had been lesbian in the 1950s and '60s, who had come up through the school of hard knocks of lesbian life. As I met this group of lesbian southerners, I was very drawn to all of them, feeling that each of them had a piece of history that helped me to understand the world I was entering."

Elizabeth Knowlton remembers well those evening and weekend summer afternoons at the Tower: "We didn't have many public places. The Tower Lounge was really important to us. What we found out very soon in the women's movement was that if you had a critical mass, you changed the space. And, at ALFA, we did everything in a mass!"

"But," as Vicki remembers, "things got more complex after that summer." As planning began for the 1975 season, scores of women signed up, creating unanticipated challenges. The Omegas, for example, wanted to retain their original members. After considerable discussion, two additional teams were formed, the ALFA Amazons and the Tower Hotshots.

Perhaps the highlight of the second season was the league game between the Amazons and the Omegas. "Many rules of competition were broken that night," Gabriner says. "It was probably the first time in City League history that two opposing teams warmed up together, sat on the same bench, cheered each other's good plays, and had the same fans root for both."

"Give me an A! Give me an L! Give me an F! Give me an A! Whaddya have? Dykes! Dykes! Dykes!" Cheering in one of the city parks' falling-down stands, Elizabeth Knowlton, as "a femme and a totally active spectator," was one of ALFA's most loyal fans. Attending every game—rain or shine—she watched her new partner, Jo, play outfield for the Hotshots and later pitch for the Amazons. "Jo loved it; she had softball in her blood." Between innings, Knowlton sometimes recalled her sports-free childhood: "Softball, like other sports, was unknown territory to me. . . . In the out-out-outfield . . . is where I used to spend my time during spring gym classes in grade school; it was peaceful out there—the grass was long and concealing, the daisies plentiful, and the sounds of distant clamor from the infield went almost unheard. Sometimes several innings would pass before I would be remembered and called in to take my turn—my three strikes—at bat."

ALFA softball teams coupled players with meager childhood sports experience and athletic ability with women whose adolescent and adult life had been defined by sports. Karla Brown was one of those women with sports in her blood. She started playing when she was six. "I was just one of the boys," she reminisces. When her father started a Little League team, Brown was the star pitcher. At twelve, however, her mother "decided that she didn't want me to play with boys anymore and started our black community's first girls' softball team." Karla also was a keen basketball player, practicing in the grade school gym several days each week. But when she transferred to an all-white junior high school, she merely warmed the bench. "They didn't want me to play, even though I made the team. I even had a different uniform. Mine was cotton, the others were made of a silk material."

Playing on the ALFA diamond was the first time Karla had played with white women "who didn't know how to play!"[5] Nicknamed Hank ("Every time I hit the ball it was out of the park!"), Karla helped to design the uniforms, played first base, and coached. In the process, her appreciation of feminism and her ALFA sisters grew, as did their admiration and understanding of her.

> A lot of the whites were seeing a black woman as a strong woman for the first time. I had a lot of admirers. When I first started admiring Lorraine, it was because of her courage; she had never really played softball on a formal team. She picked it up and learned how to pitch in a short period of time. I could tell she really loved it. So we developed a mutual interest. And that was the beginning of breaking down some barriers that I had instilled by those radical feminists in Charlotte when my lover had a boy child and we had to find another place to live because they could not accept a male being around in any form.

The Atlanta Lesbian Feminist Alliance bridged the usual split between lesbian-feminists and sports-oriented lesbians. "Somehow we played a balanced roster and won our games," marvels Vicki. "We were able to pull off this magic." The marriage of backgrounds and outlooks sometimes created tensions as well as alliances, however.[6] Some, for example, worried. A 1976 *ALFA Newsletter* article was concerned that the "women in ALFA give contradictory messages. As lesbian feminists, we aspire to transcend roles in their traditional sense, but at the same time, there is a premium on the butch. Examples are the various cheers at softball games (competence being rewarded with various dyke cheers, fumbles being met with femme calls)."[7]

Not surprisingly, women who were more competitive and skilled found it a different and, sometimes, a difficult experience. Karla remembers: "That was an adjustment for me because I never had been affiliated with any team that had this philosophy. I had learned that you always have your best starting and only substitute them if they fall on their faces."

Another talented athlete, who became player-coach for an ALFA team, later wrote: "The characteristic that separates this past season from any others is talk. I have never talked so much softball in my whole life."[8] As a fifteen-year veteran of competitive softball, she experienced a dilemma similar to Karla's: "We wanted to win, but we didn't want that to overshadow the fun we wanted to have. We wanted to learn how to play well, but we didn't want a team ruled by some ironhanded, dictatorial coach. We knew we had wide ranges of ability and experience, but we wanted everyone to be able to play equal amounts of time."[9]

At a personal level, however, feminist principles sometimes clashed with diamond realities, this veteran recalled: "I might have played a balanced roster, but that didn't prevent me from feeling like shit if we lost. One of our more experienced players really believed that ability should not determine how often a woman played, and yet she couldn't help but feel bad when taken out of a game. On the other hand, one woman playing for the first time said she felt that at times her mistakes might be costly and would prefer to be taken out of the game."[10]

Differences, she concluded, often boiled down to "whether we were a team because we wanted to play softball or whether we were primarily serving a political purpose."

For softball players like Vicki Gabriner, the ball field was political theater: "Politics is about touching lots of different aspects of people's lives. So, for me, softball was part and parcel of that whole experience. A political woman is not only of meetings and demonstrations; softball is one of the things that women bring to 'politics.'"

That was certainly true for Karla Brown, who had little initial interest in lesbian-feminism:

> Everything ALFA did, of course, was political. Everything had to go through policies and procedures. Softball ground rules weren't just developed on the field but discussed *at length* at ALFA meetings. Now, when I first moved to the ALFA house, I felt somewhat intimidated. I wasn't on the same level because of my immediate needs [eking out a living as a gas station attendant and helping her former lover and son]. The softball team really helped me identify with some of the philosophies of feminism. That was what brought it all together for me. It wasn't just something that was happening in the house, it was a way of life.

As a way of life, "ALFA was a community as well as an organization." Vicki elaborates:

> I do not mean a vague sense of community. I mean that hundreds of dykes lived within blocks of each other. We ran into each other not only at lesbian-identified events, like the women's bars, social gatherings at each other's homes, political meetings, and concerts, but at the local supermarket, health food store, inexpensive Chinese restaurant, bookstore, laundromat, karate class, feminist therapy center, or lesbian chiropractor.

But, as ALFA expanded, the civil rights and antiwar struggles were foreign to the younger women, who had become politicized through the lesbian-feminist movement. Vicki acknowledges: "I was extraordinarily frustrated by the fact that some people didn't have the kind of history to understand the connections between the lesbian-feminist movement and other social movements that had come before it and were going on at the same time."

The founding mothers of ALFA shared a herstory of activism from the Venceremos Brigades to May Day organizing, from the *Great Speckled Bird* to Sojourner Truth Press, from Marx to the Great Goddess.[11] Atlanta lesbians and feminists—struggling through a disco-driven, recession-mired decade of pet rocks, gas station lines, and primal screams—these women built on earlier generations of women's efforts to affirm female relationships and establish women's networks in the South.[12]

Atlanta was not the only community practicing lesbian-feminist principles on the ball field that summer of 1974.[13] One summer evening, members of the Houston NOW chapter's Lesbian and Sexuality Task Force approached seasoned fast-pitch player Jan Cunningham about coaching their would-be team.

Ever since grade school, Jan had been interested in sports. Her paternal grandfather was an outstanding boxer, baseball player, and roller skater. But, by the age of twelve, Jan, like Karla, could only watch as "my brothers were playing baseball with a real field, with a real fence, with real dugouts. . . . I was mad and I didn't understand."[14]

In the early sixties, she attended Wayland Baptist College with hopes of earning a position on its outstanding basketball team, the Flying Queens; but, unable to make the cut, Cunningham transferred to nearby Texas Women's University. Settling in Houston after graduation, she worked in jobs that enabled her to "satisfy my avocation of sports."

Throughout the sixties and into the seventies, Jan played fast-pitch softball at Memorial Park with seven or eight teams, including the Rebels and the Comets. "With fast pitch there were a lot of lesbians playing," she recalls, "but it was never really acknowledged."

Off the field, Jan hung out with her teammates at the Roaring Sixties. "In Houston it was a big social context with the bars and softball." Sometimes folks were regaled with softball herstories. There was one story, for instance, about a group of Brooklyn ballplayers traveling the fast-pitch circuit who were jailed in Fort Worth for "persisting" in a game at a city park that did not allow ball playing. "The bloomer aggregation became 'brassy' and was run in. . . . In the corridors and cells the girls raised a 'rough house.' They sang up-to-date 'topical' songs, roasted the jail officials and male prisoners, turned handsprings, stood on their heads, did high kicking, wide splits, and other startling performances."[15]

On a midsummer night in 1972, Jan started reading *Ms.* magazine. "Something clicked," and she finally understood her childhood anger. Visiting the NOW office on Milam Street, she soon became the local coordinator for girls and women in sports. "It was an unusual step for me to take and certainly not one that all my friends were doing—stepping away from that softball-hangout and the bar mentality."

Around this time, she goes on, "We went from our protective little fast-pitch world with pretty high-quality players and hanging together being lesbians to slow pitch with predominantly straight women." Cunningham recalls, too, that "there wasn't high-quality pitching around as much."

So, on that particular evening in 1974 when Jan was approached at the Milam Street house, "I didn't have any problem with coaching them—at that moment." Later, on the sunlit field, she questioned her judgment: "A lot had virtually no athletic ability at all. We had people who would get up to bat and shut their eyes. We had one player, Bunny, who used to spend her time in the outfield looking for a four-leaf clover! But they saw it as empowering them as women." Following practice, the players hung out at Just Marion and Lynn's. Between rounds of beer and pool, they searched for a team identity. Jan remembers: "We couldn't decide on any name. But there was a group of women in Houston called Women Who Want to Remain Women, a Phyllis Schlafly-type organization—known simply as WW2. So, we decided to name ourselves Women Who Want Women; but we just shortened it to the Ducks." Second-base player Pokey Anderson seconded the team name because "it wasn't so aggressive like the Sharks or the Bruisers."

After two months of evening and weekend practices at Woodrow Wilson School, the Ducks were ready for their first outing. Jan describes how she "lined up a game with a group of lesbian fast-pitch players," the Armadillos, at Memorial Park. The Ducks were boosted by a stand of madly cheering fans led by NOW officers standing on the baseline, shaking blue-and-white pom-poms. Losing 26–2, "we were humiliated—cheerleaders and all." Jan continues: "They were a very rag-tag group of players—even when they got better. In tournaments, the first team we came up against had uniforms. That was very intimidating. I finally convinced them that they needed some uniforms. But Pokey absolutely refused to wear matching socks!"

In Houston, where softball is nearly a year-round sport, the Ducks moved on to a new season. Playing City League teams like Shell and Pennzoil, "we got hammered unmercifully," Cunningham recollects. "We were just dykes and all that went with that. You just knew it; it was an atmosphere we played in."

Besides weekly practices and league games, Pokey Anderson and other team members attended softball tournaments. She remembers "the third-base side of the stands was more lesbian, the first-base side was more the families. Even in those days of lesbian invisibility, many of the straight people were aware of our presence."

Standing in front of Pokey in the long restroom line at one tournament was a perky woman. She chattered in a disapproving voice strained with unease. "I can't believe all of these lesbians in this ballpark!"

Wondering what she would say next, Anderson nodded.

The disapproving fan pressed her point. "There are *really* a lot of 'em here! And," in a lowered voice, she warned, "if you say anything to 'em, they'll knock you flat!"

Pokey laughed, passing up the chance to support the woman's prejudice.

Insisting they were "Ducks, not Dykes," Jan Cunningham recalls the team's struggle between feminism as theory and softball as practice: "We had all of these women who were becoming athletes and being empowered, thinking that every woman should have a say in how the team is run, what happens on the team, who plays, and everyone should play equally."

The Ducks "had a lot of initial controversy about it." Unlike ALFA's player-coaches, Cunningham was insistent that "you just can't go out there and have this democratic society running a softball team. It doesn't work!" Regrettably, as she tells it, "the conflict got worse as the team got better. I just tried to maintain that I was a coach and I had enough supporters on the team that they couldn't get rid of me. But there was always that tension between those that understood the game and *really* knew how it had to be done and the ones pushing to assert themselves as leaders."

During their first three years, the Ducks improved their on-field play while playing the political field. "It was our main political network," Pokey explains. "You had to practice at least once a week and play once a week. Twice a week is more often than you usually see people. So we were pretty close. Whenever you have people meeting at a predictable place you can say, 'Hey, we're having a poetry reading. Hey, we're having a concert. Hey, we're having a protest.'"

From these personal connections emerged an expanded lesbian community: *Pointblank Times,* poetry readings with Judy Grahn and Pat Parker, the Lesberadas and Out and Out productions, and the write-in political candidacy of Pokey Anderson.

Similarly ALFA, energized by a growing number of softball-attracted members, helped to expand Atlanta's lesbian community and further networked lesbians in the region. On Memorial Day weekend in 1975, for example, the group hosted its Great Southeast Lesbian Conference with the theme "Building a Lesbian Community."[16] Three hundred women from eighteen states attended—nearly a hundred from Atlanta, including those from Lorraine Fontana's and Elizabeth Knowlton's collective—as did Charlotte Bunch, an editor of *Quest*, Elana Nachman, author of *Riverfinger Women*, and Laurel Galana, co-editor of *Amazon Quarterly*. Twenty-six workshops ranged from FBI harassment and the spiritual community to third-world lesbians and lesbian separatism.

These groups were often challenging and, at times, according to Knowlton, "rather unsettling." She describes the lesbian-separatist workshop offered by Charlotte's Drastic Dykes: "Because we had not been clear about it on the program, no one knew that the separatists wanted to meet only with other separatists—no arguments, no explanations, just meeting. Nonseparatists could not accept this; therefore the meeting became a movement from room to room, as the separatists attempted to separate themselves."

Knowlton, finding herself "an elitist of sorts," didn't feel part of either group. Although she had been a separatist when living in North Carolina, fifteen months later, "while I continued to know myself separate from men, I did not feel separate from puzzled lesbians who wanted to discuss the issue."

In addition to the several dozen workshops, the weekend events included a standing-room-only performance by the Red Dyke Theatre group, a buffet dinner at the Tower Lounge, and a musical concert.

Five North Carolina dykes from the conference entered an all-night restaurant on Ponce de Leon Avenue, often frequented by ALFA women and gays, for an early Saturday breakfast. One of the women argued with the cashier (and then the owner) over some undelivered wheat toast. Elizabeth recalls: "In the process of arguing with him, she used language that we always used. He turned to an off-duty police officer: 'You heard her. Arrest them!' When he began trying to arrest her, not understanding that he was a policeman, she resisted, naturally. We were taught to fight back, right?"

Later, in the *ALFA Newsletter*, the "Durham Five" completed the tale:

> He was so out of control that the rest of us reacted in an effort to get him away from her, but never touched him. He finally released her throat and handcuffed her to the nearest one of us and told the rest of us to leave or we would be taken to jail, too. We asked what the charges were, but he had no answer. When the police cars arrived, he told us we were all arrested for creating turmoil and criminal trespassing. . . . A gay man who remarked to the cops, 'You shouldn't treat ladies that way,' was arrested for obstructing an officer.[17]

Money for bail was raised during intermission of the Red Dyke Theatre and at the Tower Lounge. Knowing "our appearance as a group would have an affect on the outcome"[18] of their case, the Durham dykes attended the Monday court hearing "dressed nicely," recollects Elizabeth. The trespassing arrest was tossed out. Four women were found guilty of "creating a turmoil," fined thirty-five dollars each, and slapped with a ten-day suspended sentence.

Afterward they found more poetic words to describe their Peachtree State experience:

> The breakfast was greasy
> The bill was all wrong
> The cashier was sleazy
> But thought FUCK a bit STRONG.[19]

Later that summer ALFA hosted the First Annual ALFA Invitational All Women's Softball Tournament, sanctioned by the Amateur Softball Association.[20] Inviting only female-led city teams ("no girls, no ladies"), women umpired the day's games, which began after everyone stood to sing Meg Christian's "Ode to a Gym Teacher." Following the lesbian anthem, cheers filled the air and spectators were invited to join a team.

Meanwhile, Houston's spring brought out lesbians "going ape-shit," wrote Pokey to an Atlanta friend. "People whose normal maximum output of energy at any one time is lifting a beer bottle are out running miles—or at least blocks. Sore muscles and bruises abound."[21] Midway through their 1975 softball season, however, the Ducks lost their fourth consecutive game. To raise spirits, *PBT* editors Linda Lovell and Alison McKinney wrote a fairy-tale-style dramatization of the team's history.[22] Near the story's end, a good fairy helps the team to finally score, only to learn "these women are Feminists! Let them do the rest on their own!!!" With the score nearly tied, one runner on base, two outs, and the opposing team's homerun hitter at bat:

> The Coach called a time out.
> The team came into the field for some quick C-R.
> "All my life I've felt alone," said one.
> "Me too," said another.
> "My lover left me yesterday," said a third.
> "I wish I had a job," said another.
> "I feel like a total failure."
> The Coach said, "Try playing together, for a change of pace!"[23]

And then the magic happened.

EIGHTEEN

Lexington Six

I was not born a warrior,
I was not bred for courage
But there are some things I have seen.

—*Susan Saxe*

On the evening of 27 March 1975, Vicki Gabriner tuned to the six o'clock news. Susan Saxe had been arrested with her girlfriend, walking along a Philadelphia street. Wearing blue jeans and a lavender blouse to her court hearing, Saxe later told the press, "I intend to fight on in every way as a lesbian, a feminist, and an amazon."[1]

"My heart immediately leaped out to her that first night," says Vicki, remembering Susan's "clenched-fist body, stating that she was a lesbian, an amazon. I felt a gut connection that has stayed all these years, feeling that there but for the grace of the goddess go I."

Most Americans, who got snippets of information from one of the three television networks or slick weekly newsmagazines, felt no such connection. At the decade's midpoint, *Happy Days* nostalgia and *Jaws* escapism already had dulled revelations by the Senate Intelligence Committee of

Vicki Gabriner. Photo © 1970 Marcelina Martin.

twenty-five years of CIA assassinations of world leaders, FBI burglaries over "domestic subversive targets," and National Security Agency routine monitoring of citizens' overseas cables. Instead, Americans focused on the FBI's Most Wanted list, half of whom were "domestic terrorists," including Weather Underground leaders Bernardine Dohrn, Mark Rudd, and Kathy Boudin. "They are aided," embellished *Newsweek,* "by a vast, unstructured network of kindred spirits, whose particular interests may range from grass to granola but who share a kind of us-against-them ethos and a resistance to asking or answering intrusive questions."[2]

That spring of 1975 Vicki, facing her own trial for actions as a member of the Weathermen—a faction of the Students for a Democratic Society—prepared for the Great Southeast Lesbian Conference with the theme "Building Our Community." At a Saturday workshop called "FBI Harassment of the Lesbian Community," there was extensive discussion about underground activists, FBI harassment, grand juries, and government infiltration.[3]

"Women who were not sympathetic to Susan Saxe," recalls Vicki Gabriner, "resented the flak that came down on lesbian communities." One participant, for example, pointed out that "lesbian-feminists such as Susan Saxe and Katherine Power [who] have been able to hide out from the FBI within the women's movement have given us a bad name."[4] The lesbian community, notes Vicki, was "divided over whether or not to support her."

Certainly the most vocal national leader was Jill Johnston, author of *Lesbian Nation,* who denounced Saxe as a "liability to the movement." In a scathing *Village Voice* essay, she wrote:

> The association of the "sisterhood" with the 1970 bank robberies is a telescopic deception used (by the media) to discredit a movement without credit and without responsibility for individuals who committed crimes in the context of the patriarchal contest between fathers (right) and sons (left). . . . Many sisters no longer wish to help the sons undo the fathers who in turn oppress the sisters. . . . The FBI wants fugitives who robbed banks and were accessories or agents of murder. They're not "infiltrating" any movement, there isn't anything to infiltrate, they're going about their business and harassing a lot of innocent people while they do it.[5]

Not surprisingly, in this environment Gabriner found it difficult to explain the historical context for political actions leading to the arrests of Saxe, herself, and other radical activists. "It took a lot of effort and thought to explain this to the lesbian-feminist community in Atlanta. Although the community began with women who were involved with left politics and then came out, that changed as the community expanded. It was no longer the central thread of its political identity. Younger women did not have our shared political history that stretched back to the antiwar and civil rights movements."

But the question was how to convey the sense of participatory democracy that had marked 1969's October Moratorium, when almost two million citizens marched to end the war. "Part of what made it complicated," admits Vicki, "was that I had a range of complex feelings about Weathermen, which made it very difficult for me to figure out how I was going to talk about my arrest and defense with people." She explains:

> On the one hand, I was clear about my opposition to the War in Vietnam, and passionate about my desire to turn around the racial, gender, and economic injustice that marked our society. And I understood how, driven by frustration at how long it took to effect social change, I was drawn to the idea of armed struggle. On the other hand, I had experienced a kind of cruelty and naïveté within the organization. Numbers of Weather people were deeply wounded on a psychic level as the Weather leadership attempted to rather simplistically adapt the revolutionary principles of Mao Tse-Tung to the struggle in the United States. It took me a long time to recover, and the Weathermen period remains a profound cautionary tale for me as I move through life. So how was I to pull this together in a public persona? I never doubted which side I was on, but it was difficult to express the gray areas in linear speech.

The Weathermen, a group that derived its name from a Bob Dylan lyric, formed at that fractious SDS convention in June 1969.[6] Soon the group split—some favored winning Americans' "hearts and minds;" others advocated violence against the government and industries waging war in Southeast Asia.[7] Near the end of 1969 the Weathermen leadership, known as the Weather Bureau, "determined that people with multiple arrest records from their antiwar activism might have to leave the country at a moment's notice," Gabriner details. "We were instructed to get false passports for certain people. My codefendant, who had spent eight months in a Massachusetts state prison for his antiwar work, was one of them. In order to get a fake passport you either had to create identification papers, often by obtaining the birth certificate of someone who had died, and with that, get a driver's license. Or you had to go to the passport agency with someone who had valid identification who would sign an affidavit stating the person knew you to be whatever name you were using." With no arrest record, Vicki Gabriner signed the affidavit. "I walked out of Boston's JFK Building, turned to my codefendant, and said: 'This is the stupidest thing I've ever done in my life.'"

It was a time of madness. In 1970, Nixon expanded the war into Cambodia, and protesting college students were killed at Jackson State and Kent State Universities. There were bombings of corporate businesses and university campuses. The trial of the Chicago Seven had begun, and Black Panthers had been gunned down in California. Federal legislation provided for the "preventive" detention of "dangerous" suspects, the death penalty for campus bombers, and steep prison sentences for drug trafficking. There were also accidental explosions in "safe houses" with unanticipated loss of life. One robbery of a Brighton, Massachusetts, bank resulted in a policeman's unplanned death. That fall, three men were quickly apprehended; the female "accessories," Susan Saxe and Katherine Power, disappeared underground.

Saxe and other revolutionaries challenged the "simplistic standard," that "the absence of violence—as it is usually defined—is a supreme objective." In 1970, the intellectual activist Howard Zinn further reasoned that failure to engage in these actions "may mean reconciling oneself to the status quo . . . [that] itself may include a number of evils (forms of violence, really, if we go beyond the usual definition)."[8]

Revolution, Left-leaning intellectual activists asserted, was a birthright. "The purpose of society," argued historian Staughton Lynd, "is not the protection of property but fulfillment of the needs of living human beings." Declaring that "good citizens have the right and duty . . . to overthrow incurably oppressive governments," Lynd insisted that "the language of the Declaration of Independence remains relevant as an instrument for social transformation."[9]

The revolution was stillborn—a consequence of economic and political upheavals, the New Left's apocalyptic rhetoric and ideological divisions, and government subversion and media manipulation.[10] Five years later, popular talk of revolution had abated as feel-good politicians kicked off the nation's yearlong bicentennial celebration at Boston's Old North Church. Symbolic politics and corporate sponsorships were the order of the day. In 1970, three-quarters of U.S. college students had agreed that "basic changes in the system" were required to improve American society;[11] five years later, two unelected men—an accident-prone congressman, Gerald Ford, and the grandson of an oil robber baron, Nelson Rockefeller—occupied the White House. In 1973, federal troops had kept at bay 100,000 antiwar protesters opposed to Nixon's "coronation," and a CIA-funded coup had overthrown Chile's democratically elected government. Two years later, in 1975, Saigon fell to the North Vietnamese army and there were revelations of unlawful CIA surveillance of 300,000 American citizens.

Among those thousands of citizens who were spied upon by the government were homosexual Americans. The three hundred attending the ALFA conference on Memorial Day weekend in 1975, following Susan Saxe's arrest in March, included lesbians from Kentucky. Like the emerging lesbian community in Atlanta's Little Five Points, there was a cluster of lesbians and feminists who lived at the Lexington Avenue collective near the University of Kentucky campus. Among the most radical and open was Kentucky native Jill Raymond. A committed socialist with a penchant for writing, she sent frequent letters across the desk of the student editor of the *Kentucky Kernel.*

The town, though, lacked the critical mass of lesbian-feminists found in Atlanta or Houston. Many more lesbians, like gay men, preferred Lexington's social networks, softball games, private Derby season parties, or late nights at The Bar—an East Main Street storefront that a decade earlier was called the Gilded Cage; then, slightly refurbished, it was known as the Living Room, before it was reclaimed as Montparnasse by horse-farm owner Bill Sheehan.[12]

In 1974, twenty-three-year-old Jill Raymond had welcomed into the women's community Lena Paley and May Kelley. The pair was on a cross-country trip visiting women's communities across the Lesbian Nation. Introduced to them by a bookstore owner, Jill invited Lena and May to the collective and into her socialist-feminist-lesbian group. May soon took a secretarial position, becoming active in the recently opened Rape Crisis Center. Lena began working as a bake chef at Alfalfa, a vegetarian restaurant across from the university, where Carey Junkin was also employed.

Junkin, a nineteen-year-old with long sculpted hair, lived across from Lena and May on Mill Street. He was president of the Gay Coalition. This successor to Lexington's Gay Liberation Front had been no more successful in securing university recognition than had the GLF when it was organized three years earlier.[13] Nevertheless, members tenaciously pursued their case as Junkin, a charismatic Birmingham lad and freshman senator, persuaded student government to sponsor a gay dance early that next year.

Throughout its three-year struggle, the gay student group had met at the university center under the auspices of the People's Party, a fledgling third national political party in which Jill was active. She had "circulated around the edges" of the male-led Gay Liberation Front since its founding and sometimes joined others in speaking at Psychology 201 classes.[14] Most of her energy, though, was focused on socialist and feminist issues. During that summer and fall of 1974, she also enjoyed visiting Lena at Alfalfa's, as one scholar writes. "Lena became known as a skilled and innovative cook. She was also known for her discourse on politics and food. The layout of the restaurant allowed for conversation between cook and patrons. In the same breath, Lena could criticize a male co-employee for being sexist while warning him about the dangers of eating saccharine."[15]

That fall Lena departed Lexington, following her partner May's sudden exit several weeks earlier.

In 1975, many youth in this Tom Wolfe–defined "Me Decade" were adorning themselves with mood rings, buying up Trekkie paraphernalia, or doing the hustle. Others, like the five characters in *Kennedy's Children*, a hit Broadway play written by a Texas gay man, Robert Patrick, lamented the broken dreams of the sixties in the malaise-ridden seventies.[16] But in Kentucky, those in the gay social life were in good spirits.

Around nine o'clock each evening, the second-floor disco of the Montparnasse opened. Glitter-laden men glided up the spiral staircase lured by sounds of "Never Can Say Goodbye" and "I Love to Love You, Baby." Neon lights and a mirrored bar reflected down on the "deep but narrow dance floor lined on both sides with church pews. . . . The crowd was very group-oriented or cliquish. The pews were practically reserved for the same people every weekend."[17]

Not surprisingly, "the black gay men in Lexington, the older ones in particular, didn't relate to the white gay bar scene."[18] Edwin Hackney, a self-described "rebel" and an early Lexington gay activist, noted one exception—James Herndon. Known by all as Sweet Evening Breeze, the rumored hermaphrodite lived in an antique-filled house on Prall Street. Well into his eighties, "Sweets would come out to the local bar, particularly on Halloween," where, Edwin remembers, "the queen in residence" held "court."

Observing that gay Lexington during this time was "more a network of friendships," Hackney found "it was much easier to meet new people from Lexington by going away from Lexington"—particularly in Louisville.

Unlike Lexington's bars, which closed at 1 A.M., Louisville's were open until four in the morning. Lexington queers often traveled an hour on I-64 for a weekend night on West Main Street between Brook and Second Streets.[19] The Downtowner, operating for twenty years on Chestnut Street, had been destroyed by arson the year before and just reopened in July 1975 as the New Downtowner on West Main. At the entrance was Mama Iguana's, a boutique selling poppers, rolling papers, Bob Damron bar guides, and men's magazines. When not hustling to the disco beat, blowing whistles on the checkerboard dance floor, and watching Tooti, a fluorescent-painted three-hundred-pound black go-go dancer atop the DJ booth, the weekend partiers were entertained by three nightly revues of "Those Fabulous Fakes." The host, Mr. Ethel Waters, was a hefty African American performer who sometimes performed her signature song, "Stay with Me," in a red dress covered with diamond-shaped mirrors.

The place to be, though, was Badlands Territory, a disco that opened on Derby Eve, 1973. As you walked into the Texas-style bar, there was a ticket booth with jail bars (cover was weekends only) and a nearby wall plaque reading: "No Punks, Thugs, or Pock-Marked Kids Allowed." Along the entire east wall was a bar with meat racks of muscle-toned customers. Skin-tanned men, wearing outfits from J. Rigging's, rested against the opposite wall. A set of double doors led into another room with a small dance floor. The jukebox and bar stood along either side of walls covered with saloon-red Victorian wallpaper.

David Williams first came out at Badlands a week after the grand opening. "About eleven on Saturday nights," he remembers, one of the bartenders (usually Ray) would always announce the same thing over the speaker system: "Gentlemen, the second floor is now open for your dancing and cruising pleasure." Up the wooden stairs, "the place was packed with men dancing through artificial fog" below a "high ceiling topped by wall-to-wall skylights." Aramis cologne and Jovan musk mixed with the smell of pot and poppers while the DJ mixed records, worked the gutter lights, took requests, and jostled a pencil in the turntable's center sampling K.C. and the Sunshine Band.

Meanwhile, the new school term had begun ominously at the University of Kentucky. The student senate voted to rescind its sponsorship of the gay dance—front page news in the *Kentucky Kernel*. A day earlier, a less noticed wire-service story appeared on an inside page of the student paper: "FBI Says Two Murder Suspects Lived in Lexington Last Year."[20]

Throughout those early months in 1975, the FBI terrorized leftists and lesbians within the community. Hackney remembers "plain-clothes local detectives as well as out-of-town types with white socks and shiny shoes, going around to local businesses, visiting people at night, and asking all kinds of real strange questions."[21] The "threatening and overbearing"[22] agents used electronic surveillance, intercepted personal mail, questioned "witness" relatives (including a seventy-eight-year-old grandmother) about political ideology and sexual orientation, threatened subpoenas, and contacted employers.

In early March, six homosexuals who had refused to cooperate with the FBI, including Jill Raymond and Carey Junkin, were summoned before a federal grand jury to answer questions regarding their knowledge of Susan Saxe and Katherine Power, alias Lena Paley and May Kelley. Raymond recalls:

We were claiming that once we said, "No, we didn't knowingly harbor fugitives; no, we didn't have knowledge of a felony committed," our personal lives were our personal lives. If you have the right to ask me everything about what Lena Paley said and I said, on the night of October 3, 1974, when she and I went out to the bar and drank beer for three hours, then I must surrender any privacy that would attach to that relationship. To say that the law has a right to everyone's evidence is not to say the law has the right to the sum total of their knowledge, their personal acquaintances, lifestyles, and everything else.[23]

All refused to answer questions posed by U.S. attorney Eugene Siler. Junkin walked onto the fourth floor of the Federal Building on Barr Street wearing a gray T-shirt with large black letters: "STOP FBI HARASSMENT." Cited for contempt by Judge Bernard T. Moynahan Jr., the "Lexington Six," as they became known nationally, issued a statement:

The entire procedure represents the extent of the grip that male institutions and masculine value-systems have on the lives of all of us. It is a patriarchal premise that the most effective way to relate to people is through the use of power. . . . Women who separate themselves from men, sexually and psychologically, pose a totally unique kind of affront to masculine power, and are likely to suffer the vengeance of the police and the courts in an especially severe way.[24]

While defense attorneys argued that this was a case of grand jury abuse, an *Advocate* feature story characterized the unfolding events as "a tangled story complete with conspiracy theory. . . . The FBI apparently believes there is a 'lesbian underground' that is protecting and hiding the fugitives."[25]

Edwin Hackney remembers it as an odd and sobering time among the tiny band of activists who found Lexington to be "one of the most difficult towns to organize." He continues: "One of the jokes among us was that Mark Rudd—who had gone underground after the riots at Columbia University . . . was alive and well and living on Tates Creek Pike. . . . Now there were FBI agents telling the local paper that there *was* a lesbian feminist socialist conspiracy in central Kentucky to overthrow the government. . . . This was a town that couldn't even support one bar!"[26]

Of course, "the fact that these persons are homosexuals," wrote two UK students, has meant that some "are happy to hear that 'the queers have been put away where they belong.'"[27] This was a point acknowledged by the Lexington Six: "Laws protecting us have been initiated in some cities and states, but as yet no noticeable change has come about in the majority of people's minds toward the rights of gays. Therefore, we as gay people . . . seek changes . . . to live our lives as we damn well please, without the interference from any tool of the patriarchy."[28]

The Lexington Six were handcuffed and shackled. They found themselves scattered about not-so-nearby county jails, where they would sit until they testified or the end of the grand jury's term—fourteen months.

The first of the Six, finding herself "in a cage . . . and trapped" and fed a greasy diet of fatback, potatoes, beans, gravy of lard and salt, and cornbread, testified six days after incarceration.[29] Junkin held out another two weeks until Saxe's capture and a disappointing court of appeals ruling.[30] Following his testimony before the grand jury, the history major (who earlier in the year had been thrashed by fraternity boys for his gay activism) detailed their plight: "The Madison County jail can only be described as a place sterile of all feelings towards other humans and there was a concerted effort made to break my will and humanity. . . . On several nights we were gassed by a guard with a canister of tear gas. I was beaten and thrown into solitary confinement several times for my lifestyle and politics. . . . I felt trapped, caged, and dehumanized. The boredom, loneliness, and repression just got to me."[31]

As imprisonment extended to a second month for the remaining four grand jury holdouts, a defense committee formed and protests mounted. A local gay leader remembers: "We were doing things and really flying high and all of a sudden the FBI comes down into our little group. . . . The radicals on campus, who were really not that involved in the gay issue, did get involved."[32]

During an hour-long campus rally of about seventy-five students, an evangelist paraded around with a dozen disciples, interrupting the crowd with his booming microphone: "I'm here to spread the Gospel of Jesus. I'm here to speak against homosexuality."[33] Armed with "the sword of the spirit," the street preacher rebuked those who showed "rebellion and disrespect against those in authority." One of the six who was released from jail told the crowd: "I still have four sisters in jail." The preacher yelled back: "They're prisoners of the devil. . . . You'll all burn in lust. . . . Today, women are lying with other women. . . . The flesh profits nothing; it's the spirit that counts. Come you communists, socialists, and revolutionaries, Jesus is the great liberator. . . . Everyone sing with me, God Bless America."[34] Ignoring the preacher's invitation, about thirty-five protesters marched down Harrison Avenue to Main Street and up the block to Limestone, and stopped at the Federal Building, where they chanted, passed out leaflets, and held signs.

In early May, three of the four remaining women agreed to testify. "We fought them on their own ground for as long as we could," said one.[35] Reunited with their dog, two of them picked up their apartment possessions, telling a reporter: "The six of us went into this united. We made our own individual decisions about what to do. We all had different politics. But nobody wanted to be a martyr or a hero."[36]

As the local paper was informing readers that little was learned from these women's testimony, Jill Raymond was transferred to the Franklin County jail. There she wrote: "That some of us have been coerced into jail and into testifying against Saxe and Power is no more their fault than is the fact that we live in a repressive society. . . . On that day back in September of 1970 . . . perpetrating the 'largest manhunt in New England history.' . . . They were hunting us."[37]

As the Lexington lesbians shared their story with others at the 1975 Memorial Day weekend conference hosted by ALFA, Vicki Gabriner knew firsthand about government repression. Unlike the Lexington lesbians who were singled out because they were part of a lesbian community, Vicki was arrested within a lesbian community for actions that occurred prior to her coming out. Two years had passed since that morning knock at her Little Five Points collective household on 15 May 1973, when seven FBI agents took her into custody.

Gabriner had been identified by the FBI the previous November following an application she submitted to the Radcliffe Institute to write about Susan B. Anthony.[38] Determining that Vicki, a subject with a "history of hostility toward law enforcement," was living in a "feminist commune," the Bureau directed its field office to "determine activities" at the Euclid Terrace house.[39] Three months later, however, agents were frustrated by "the fact that the subjects live in a tightly knit feminist commune and are apparently lesbians."[40] The FBI's interest in Gabriner was to determine whether the "missing non-fugitive" had had contact or given support to Weathermen fugitives. Unable to infiltrate this "commune" of lesbian-feminists, the Atlanta field office hoped to set up an "interview" with Vicki, who "adheres somewhat (degree unknown) to lesbian practices," at a time when she "can be removed from their present surroundings."[41]

Her May arrest on charges of passport fraud and conspiracy to commit passport fraud provided the pretext for such an "interview." Advised of her rights, Gabriner refused to sign the form acknowledging this advice and to answer any questions posed by the agents. What followed were continued FBI surveillance and seemingly endless pretrial motions requesting dismissal due to improper delays, bad faith prosecution, illegal wiretaps, and so forth.[42]

As Jill Raymond waited for the grand jury's term to end, Vicki Gabriner awaited her trial.

NINETEEN

Tidewater Struggles

You're not responsible for the way the world was before you're born. When you die you are responsible for making the world a better place. —*Leonard P. Matlovich*

"Gays On the March," was the *Time* cover story for the second week of September 1975. Readers were informed about "jolting evidence of the spread of unabashed homosexuality." Tales from what was once the lavender sexual underground included a "lavish ranch outside Austin" that hosted three hundred gay men who "ate barbecue, smoked pot, and paired off for lovemaking" and "an East Coast version," where like-minded men sailed out of Fort Lauderdale harbor aboard the SS *Renaissance* for a Caribbean holiday. "As police harassment has declined, the bars have proliferated," *Time* went on. "Once seedy, dark, and dangerous, many gay bars are now bright and booming."[1]

At mid-decade, national appeals for gay rights had replaced coastal battle cries of gay liberation; activism shifted from liberation fronts, gay rap sessions, pride marches, and mimeographed newsletters to task forces, consumer focus groups, pride parades, and slick publications. For a few southerners, island cruises replaced T-room cruising; for some, assembling mainstream gay men and lesbians in nonbar social settings was more suitable than interminable meetings among those on the political fringe; and for most, disco dancing and bar hopping supplanted tight-lipped after-hour gatherings and cloistered dinner parties.[2]

Indeed, the times seemed to be changing. New Mexico, California, and New Hampshire joined ten other states in repealing sodomy statutes.

Sgt. Leonard Matlovich, 1976. Photo by and courtesy of Brandon Wolf.

An icon of "the Establishment," Rev. Billy Graham, publicly endorsed the ordination of male homosexuals while a front-page story in the *Wall Street Journal* featured the *Advocate,* recently purchased by a former New York broker. *Blueboy, Mandate,* and *Drummer* magazines premiered on newsstands, Washington Redskins linebacker Dave Kopay came out, and *Consenting Adult,* a coming-of-age novel, sold briskly at bookstores. Meanwhile, in more than thirteen hundred discos, polyester dancers jived to "That's the Way (I Like It)" and "Get Down Tonight."

During this era, a new generation of gay men, such as David Goodstein of the *Advocate,* Bruce Voeller of the National Gay Task Force, Troy Perry of the Metropolitan Community Church, and Jack Campbell of the Club Baths, crossed Madison Avenue and Wall Street with the Castro and Montrose. As many grimacing Stonewall-era revolutionaries— energized by antiwar, profeminist, civil rights, and non-Establishment sentiments—looked on, these new "assimilationists" trumped club-faced Marlboro Men over diamond-candelabra Liberaces. And, as the Civil Service Commission and medical associations reversed antigay policies long the target of stalwart Frank Kameny, the new reformers joined with pre-Stonewall activists like Kameny, turning their sights to other institutions of homophobia, particularly the military.[3]

In this campaign, winning the hearts and minds of American people would be as important as selecting the appropriate test case for litigation. Wanted: a Norman Rockwell poster boy with an impeccable service record, a desire to remain in the military, and a willingness to publicly declare his homosexuality.

On 6 March 1975 a ruddy-faced, blue-eyed technical sergeant walked into his commander's office at Langley Air Force Base in Virginia and handed him a letter. "I think you ought to sit down before you read it," suggested the lanky southerner, who had three tours of Vietnam and a twelve-year military record under his belt.[4] His African American commander, Capt. Dennis Collins, gradually slumped in his swivel chair as he read: "After some years of uncertainty, I have arrived at the conclusion that my sexual preferences are homosexual as opposed to heterosexual. I have also concluded that my sexual preferences will in no way interfere with my Air Force duties."[5]

"What the hell does this mean?" asked Captain Collins.

"It means *Brown v. The Board of Education,*"[6] replied Leonard Philip Matlovich, a Bronze Star and Purple Heart recipient.

Leonard had transferred from Florida a year before this confrontation to work at the headquarters for the air force's national human and race relations program. When not visiting bases to evaluate programs, he would cross Chesapeake Bay, frequenting Norfolk's "fabulous" College Cue on the corner of Forty-sixth and Killam.

Before Tony Pritchard had christened the Tidewater area's first *big* dance bar with that name, there was the Continental, operated by two Jewish brothers on West Tazewell Street. Outside were the usual street fights among lesbians, and inside the race track–shaped bar, the usual sexually repressed pre-Stonewall ambience. Among those interested in the action was the head of the local vice squad. "Every once in a while," remembers one former sailor, "Jack," shipped here from Connecticut but discharged for his homosexuality, "you'd look toward the street and in would come a couple of lugs behind this six-feet-four man wearing a cowboy hat—Mr. Robinette. Everything would get tense. The music stopped. And there would be all sorts of shhhs." Another regular, Marge "Clearwater" Reed, who stayed in Tidewater after her seven-year stint in the navy, adds: "It was scary. My heart would race as my girlfriend and I would make our way, as quickly as possible, out the front door."[7]

Despite such harassment, Tony Pritchard remembers Norfolk's popularity. "People would fly in from all over the country."[8] In the sixties, cruising on Granby Street was as common as it was during the thirties, when a set of mixed bars clustered around the navy's YMCA on Brooke Avenue. The sailors, of course, were the major attraction. Jack reminisces: "I was right there for plucking; all you had to have was an automobile, basically good looking—the car and you—and be there on Friday and Saturday nights. There was literally a procession of cars and sailors from one end of this town to the other."[9]

As in Houston's dance bars, the Cue had a lighting system for the dance floor. When the light went on, women and men changed to opposite-sex partners. Jim Early, another former sailor and bar regular, recalls: "Up through '73 or '74, arrests were still fairly frequent. As many as five or six vice would come into the Cue with dark overcoats and position themselves throughout the club. They all looked so different from the rest of us! They just stood there for ten or twenty minutes and then took several people out. On weekends, we'd make sure that there was at least a hundred dollars in the trunk of our car and that others had keys to that trunk if bail money was needed."

Not long after opening the Cue in 1971, Tony Pritchard "decided to do something. We were sitting here and *nothing* was being done! We were being walked over, stepped on, and stomped." The Gay Freedom Movement was born. A small group, including Jim Early, wrote to local and state politicians or attended city council meetings. They also met with the police chief, although he had little effective control over Robinette's vice detail. And, as Jim witnessed firsthand, "the military were the prime victims of the harassment. They would look for people with crew cuts because they would be jeopardized as civilians *and* as military. They were in double jeopardy—and the vice squad liked that!"

By the midseventies, Norfolk's gay nightlife really opened up.[10] There was no longer an urgent need to keep money in a car trunk. However, the military remained unchanged. Not surprisingly, when a lanky gentleman with a military-style haircut, bell bottoms, and an unfamiliar face entered the Cue in mid-1974, he seemed a bit nervous. Tony Pritchard struck up a conversation with the well-mannered sergeant.

Leonard Matlovich, he quickly learned, was a "military brat." Born to a career air force man and a South Carolina belle at a Savannah military base during the early morning hours of 1943, he had traveled with his family all over the world. Leonard, however, spent most of his teen life in Charleston and "identified himself as a southerner,"[11] with a fascination for southern history and Confederate flags. Attending the Catholic high school in Charleston during the late fifties, Matlovich recalls "going through the black parts of town on the bus shouting, 'Nigger!' and yelling, 'Two, four, six, eight, we don't want to integrate. Yea, Little Rock!' "[12]

"I was the typical southern redneck," Leonard explained to Tony in his easygoing, honest manner. But gradually this bookish youngster—born two days after the Fourth of July—began to realize the true meaning of the Stars and Stripes. "The USAF assigned him to instruct enlistees on racial issues," remembers Cliff Anchor, later Leonard's lover.[13] "He thought it was amusing for a 'southern boy' to be teaching such a course." Only later would he come to terms with his identity, according to Anchor:

> Being as polite and well-mannered as he was, I can understand why Leonard felt he could champion others' civil rights and teach about racial prejudices, yet be unable to champion his own. Certain things are just "not done." And it is a *huge* break from tradition and the trappings of southern society to "come out of the closet" and publicly declare oneself as being gay. . . . In the military, particularly the air force, any hint or innuendo was sufficient to clobber a career. Leonard was constantly on his guard, but his southern upbringing and ability to conceal himself, he said, helped.

Like most southerners, Leonard had learned the fine art of deception and circumspection. At Bishop England High School, he dated girls, often praying the Rosary with them before going out. Leonard avoided any homosexual contact. But, as he made plain, "kids have a sixth sense. When

I was in grammar school, they called me a faggot. Then when I was in high school, they did the same. I was always trying to cover for it. But I was also always looking for a special friend. . . . When I was a sophomore, I had a mad crush on a guy who was a freshman. People called me a queer because of that."[14]

At age fourteen, Leonard learned the price of finding a "special friend" during Charleston's sensational candlestick murder trial.[15] Like Norfolk, Charleston was a deep-water port city awash with military studs, where cruising on King Street or along the Battery was common.[16] The bludgeoning of the stocky, thirty-year-old Jack Dobbins by an airman brandishing an ornate antique brass candlestick from the bedroom fireplace mantel telegraphed a clear message to Leonard and Charleston's furtive homosexuals who frequented the back room of Club 49.[17] It seems that the eighteen-year-old, leather-jacketed airman had met the coat-and-tie credit manager at the club. Following late-night Halloween bar-hopping at the Elbow Cocktail Lounge and the Cove, Dobbins brought the slender teen to his pink stucco Queen Street house for a whiskey "nightcap." Early the next morning the airman returned to base with a cigarette lighter, silver fingernail file, and twenty-some dollars.

The young, Catholic airman's lawyer entered a plea of not guilty by virtue of "self-defense" before an overflowing, "highly partisan" courtroom.[18] Three days later, the all-male jury of mostly navy base workers returned a not guilty verdict. The airman, dressed in his uniform, hugged his widowed mother; the courtroom erupted in applause. The assailant was championed, his victim recast as victimizer.[19] Lying alone on his bed that mid-December night, when the first snowfall since 1914 covered the ground, Leonard Matlovich whispered a prayerful question: "My God, am I one of those terrible creatures?"[20]

Sixteen years later Leonard guzzled a beer at the Cue. His thoughts turned to more recent events. During a three-year hitch at Florida's Elgin Air Force Base, he had progressively expanded discussions of race relations to include homosexuality. Well-liked and respected by his peers, he even invited an air force investigator to defend the military's antigay policies. Reading up on the subject for his class, Matlovich found an article, "Homosexuals in Uniform," published in a special issue of *Family,* a weekly magazine published by *Army/Navy/Air Force Times.* The author mentioned the work of longtime gay rights activist Frank Kameny, who had first raised the military issue in an August 1962 demonstration at the Pentagon.

A decade after the article's publication, a shy Matlovich called Kameny and told him about the course. Leonard was surprised to hear of a search for "the ideal case" to challenge the expulsion of gays from the military. Reticent about disclosing his homosexuality for fear of losing respect and friendship, Matlovich simply told Kameny he might have "someone in mind for you."[21]

A short time later ("about a million pounds must have come off my shoulders that night"), Leonard entered Robbie's Yum Yum Tree West, an upscale Pensacola gay club forty miles from Hurlburt Field.[22] Soon, he met another serviceman at the Yum Yum. Leonard later told a reporter, until that night "I had never said 'I love you' or 'I care about you' to another human being. I never touched or felt the loving touch of another person."[23]

Matlovich again phoned Kameny. "We talked further," Kameny says, "and finally he said, no, it really was him he had been talking about." He continues: "He was already in for a transfer to Langley Air Force Base down here in the Norfolk area. And I said, 'Well, fine. Wait 'till you transfer. At that point, you'll be accessible to Washington. And then contact me then, and we'll pick up on it.'"[24]

Chatting with owner Tony Pritchard at the Cue, Matlovich learned that the two shared a connection to Kameny. Pritchard had first met the D.C. activist—characterized by the *Washington Post* as a "short, lean and intense" man who speaks in "machine gun bursts"—when Frank visited the Tidewater around 1967.[25] Working through the D.C. Mattachine group, Tony had organized sit-ins in a city where it was illegal for restaurants or bars to become a gathering place or "bawdy house" for homosexuals. Although the statute was seldom enforced, Tony recollects, nevertheless it "made us feel like we were second-class citizens. We'd go into a restaurant and say, 'We are gay and we want to be served.' That took a lot of courage."

Courage was something Matlovich had learned from his father, a thirty-two-year veteran sergeant. It was a trait he felt himself lacking during the past four years. "I was telling my students to get involved in the country and make it a better place . . . and I felt like a hypocrite."[26]

Leonard made arrangements to meet with Frank Kameny in July 1974. As the two huddled in the longtime activist's northwest Washington home, they explored the possibilities of Leonard becoming the test case. "Up to now," Kameny explained, "military efforts to discharge homosexuals have arisen when a third party charges a serviceman with homosexuality or he is caught in a sexual act."[27] Frank challenged Leonard to consider the consequences should he choose this path.[28] Kameny, however, was far from neutral or noninfluential, later acknowledging: "The Matlovich case, I created."[29] Cliff Anchor underscores Frank's influence on Leonard: "Frank Kameny is one of those well-bred gentlemen to whom Leonard could relate, and he is one of the most persuasive people one could ever meet. Only when he met up with Frank Kameny did Leonard even dream of outing himself publicly."

As Matlovich returned from Washington with the letter to his commanding officer in early March 1975, Naval Investigative Service (NIS) was intercepting letters between two other homosexual southerners. Ensign Vernon E. "Copy" Berg III had just been transferred to Italy, while his Virginia lover of three months, Lawrence Gibson, a former theological student teaching English as a second language, had remained stateside.[30]

Berg had been student council president and a star athlete at Virginia Beach's Cox High School. The crew-cut teen was tagged "Copy" because of his physical and temperamental similarities to his father, Navy chaplain Commander Vernon Berg Jr. Although Copy dated girls as a teenager, "my best friend was my lover. . . . Our relationship continued all the way through high school."[31]

Entering the U.S. Naval Academy in 1969, the tenor-voiced Berg traveled around the country with the glee club. "Wherever we performed, we were met by demonstrators. They would walk up to us and ask us how many babies we'd burned." For the naïve and conservative young man who'd never fought in battle or smoked pot, it was "a surreal experience."[32]

At the Academy, Berg ran track and swam and demonstrated a proficiency in French. Graduating in 1974, he first served as a weapons specialist. The ensign, on a career fast track, was soon assigned to the USS *Little Rock* in Gaeta, Italy. Working as a public affairs officer for the Sixth Fleet flagship, Ensign Berg would become the first officer to challenge the military's antigay stand.

Meanwhile, back in the Tidewater, Matlovich's hopes of working out an accommodation with the air force were dashed. In mid-May he received a letter from his commander informing him that action was being initiated "against you with a view of effecting your [less than honorable] discharge."[33] Leonard was placed on administrative leave.

Given that the objective was to alter military policy, tactics changed. Leonard's ACLU attorney arranged a *New York Times* interview for him. On Memorial Day 1975, the story broke as front-page news.[34] A media avalanche descended on this career military man who, according to Kameny, was "not terribly sophisticated in the ways of the world."[35]

NBC News flew from New York by helicopter to cover the story, and the *Washington Post* declared Matlovich "a godsend" to homosexual activists.[36] The telephone at his red Hampton bungalow rang relentlessly. As an American flag fluttered atop an eighteen-foot pole outside his two-bedroom home, supportive calls came in from gay GIs around the country. He also "got a phone call from an *Advocate* reporter, saying, 'We'd like to interview.' Over the hum of the air conditioner, Leonard guile-lessly asked: 'What's the *Advocate*?'"[37]

As Matlovich awaited a hearing, Berg and Gibson were summoned by NIS in late July. Only a few weeks earlier Copy had received top-secret security clearance for his seventeen-hour-a-day job under Vice Admiral Frederick Turner. Navy investigators presented the two with the fruits of their six-month investigation garnered from "the shadowy network of pro-tected informants, the pernicious use of surveillance, the monitoring of personal correspondence, the unlawful search of his private residence, and the dissemination of fabricated and defamatory information."[38]

The inquisitors confronted the pair in separate rooms. Assuming good cop/bad cop roles, they posed intimate questions and played on the couple's jealousy. Copy remembers being given "a little sheet that stated our rights at the beginning of the interview, but there was a gut emotional response that if I refused to answer their questions, their assumption would be that I was guilty, that I had something to hide."[39] Gibson was swiftly terminated. Berg was reassigned to Northern Africa—with greater respon-sibilities—by a chief of staff whose desire for a two-week vacation over-rode concerns about the ensign's fitness for duty.

A month later Copy shipped out to Norfolk. As his papers were being "shuffled from desk to desk," he and Gibson were stranded in the Tide-water. During those "months of uncertainty," Berg was placed on surveillance and his phone monitored.[40] Before his case was heard there had been little publicity, "primarily because people didn't know we were here," he said. "We were each scared to death, and we were afraid to talk to people. For example, we were even afraid to come downtown and go to a place like the Cue because we felt we would further jeopardize ourselves."[41] Berg later told the local gay newspaper that he "read about Matlovich in the newspaper and went and talked to his attorneys in Newport News, which was just across the river. These were the first people who actually said, 'Your career is worth fighting for. Your reputation is good. You're going to get a dishonorable discharge if you don't fight it.'"[42] Soon Copy accepted an attorney from the newly formed Lambda Legal Defense Fund.

As Matlovich's hearing was about to begin at nearby Langley Air Force Base, Leonard heard from an anonymous caller: "I'm not trying to scare you, but a group of men met last night, and they're coming to get you. They're going to cut your tongue and your balls off and put lye in your eyes. They have surgical instruments to do it with and something to stop the bleeding, because they don't want you to die. Can't tell you who I am, because I've got a wife and two kids."[43]

The hearing began without incident in Building 58 on 16 September 1975. Among the thirteen spectators who were able to find seats was a Suffolk sergeant. He candidly told one reporter that the air force "is more upset because Matlovich is standing up for what he believes than because he is a homosexual. They can't stop his convictions."[44]

In testimony over the next two days the defense argued about the unlawful imposition of moral standards and invasion of privacy while the other side asserted that sexual morals were directly related to military fitness and organization. In one dramatic moment, Matlovich refused to sign a contract promising not to engage in homosexual acts.

A week after the *Time* cover, four days after the hearing, and following more than four hours of deliberation, the three-member Administrative Discharge Board judged that the much decorated sergeant was "not considered a candidate for rehabilitation" and recommended a less than honorable discharge.[45] Inside the cramped courtroom, a woman murmured: "Thank God! Thank God! Thank God!"[46]

Disheartened but undeterred, the chestnut-haired Sergeant Matlovich walked outside to the little porch of the clapboard structure. Leonard was all smiles amidst several dozen applauding supporters. Vowing to "cross any stream and climb any mountain" in his continued fight, he held up a bicentennial half-dollar: "It says two hundred years of freedom. Not yet—but it will be some day."[47]

Matlovich became a civilian on 22 October 1975. One of 149 women and men discharged that year for homosexuality, he was not allowed to reenlist or to receive benefits. Leonard, though, felt liberated: "I was always afraid to wear bright clothing, for fear people would think I was gay. After my trial, I went right out and bought a flowered shirt!"[48] Citizen Matlovich could now freely visit the Cue as well as another downtown gay bar, the Pantry, opened that month by Stephen Errol Brown, a stout and amiable local man.

The Pantry on West City Hall Avenue was just around the corner from two hole-in-the-wall cruise bars, Mickey's and the Ritz on Brooke Avenue. It had been a sailor bar owned by Steve Brown's parents. In the sixties, on Tuesday nights, the Tuxedo Restaurant and Lounge was "about half lesbian." Steve goes on: "It wasn't advertised or encouraged. Most of them were butch and my father told me: 'The dykes are okay, they're not troublemakers.' And he would kick out any sailor who would cause trouble with them."

Following the death of his parents and less than satisfactory management by someone else, Steve took over the bar. With a jukebox, pool tables, and a small dance floor, the Pantry soon attracted a crowd, ranging from the plaid-shirted men with leather boots from Mickey's to the college and military types frequenting the Cue.

During that fall of 1975, those who were "out" generally walked the bar circuit, cruised on Freemason Street, played softball at Lafayette and Ingleside Parks, or gathered for quiet dinner parties in the refurbished area of Ghent. Marge Reed played on the Bayside Bombers. "I was pretty femme in those days so I had to fight for my position against all the butchy women." After a game, this all-lesbian team headed out to Arthur Godfrey's, a bar on Tidewater Drive.[49] "Playing softball and shooting pool, dancing and drinking—that's what we did," muses Marge. "We didn't have a feminist or political thought in our heads."

There was some interest also among a handful of Unitarian-Universalists to communicate "across sexual orientations."[50] A couple of weeks after the verdict, Matlovich addressed a group at the church on Yarmouth Street where the Gay Freedom Movement had organized four years earlier. "He was very well spoken and an ideal person to come out and to help straight people come out from their prejudice," recalls Will Frank, a long-time church member. In fact, it was Will's wife, Mary Scripp, who had set these events in motion two years earlier.

In 1973, there was an ongoing study group at the church on human relationships.[51] Mary became involved in a subgroup on gay relationships. This flowed naturally from her commitment to civil rights, her work with homosexuals in the arts, and her thesis on the gay composer Ned Rorem. Will and Mary had come to know Linda Woods, a "quiet mover and shaker" who also happened to be a lesbian, participating in a con-sciousness-raising group.

In the summer of 1975, Mary and Will invited Linda over to gauge her interest in speaking at a Sunday service on the theme of gay and lesbian issues. Linda agreed and, two weeks before the Matlovich talk, she spoke about the "freedom to be yourself," the church newsletter reported, express-ing "her need for our real love and understanding," pointing out that "to gain this understanding we need to get together and talk," and acknowl-edging that "there are hostilities on both sides to be aired and overcome."[52]

The very positive reaction to the sermon, coupled with interest in the trial at Langley, had led Mary and Linda to invite Matlovich. Following his speech, the social hall beckoned listeners with card tables, chairs, and refreshments to sit together and talk. The idea, Frank recalls, "was to build trust across the orientation lines." However, the evening conversation proved too brief: "I didn't want to let it go. I met some people I liked and people seemed to be searching for a spiritual path. We had a lot of unfinished business; it was too superficial. Could there be some way we could carry this forward?"

The following Tuesday night fifty or so folks gathered again to talk across sexual borders. These "Freedom to Be Yourself" workshops extended from the fall into the spring of 1976 and put into practice the recommendation of the church's minister thirteen years earlier—that "our questions *may become worthy* of their consideration."

There were no "Freedom to Be Yourself" workshops in the U.S. Navy. After months languishing in Virginia's port city, Copy Berg requested a hearing. In preparing his case, a Justice Department's response to an interrogatory yielded a long-suppressed study funded by the Pentagon that undermined the military's antigay position.[53] Copy also learned of "a vendetta by two non-Academy officers who were jealous of his talents and quick ascendancy."[54] And, as for Berg, there were threats and publicity: "I was recognized almost everywhere I went. I had teenagers throwing things at me from their cars. People screamed at me on the streets, 'Get lost, faggot!' . . . I was the small-town-boy-made-bad. . . . I even got one letter that was addressed to 'The Gay Ensign, Norfolk, Virginia,' and it was delivered to my home."[55]

From 19 through 28 January 1976 administrative discharge hearings were held for Ensign Berg. The navy presented a series of condemnatory affidavits from those who had worked with Berg (not a single officer or enlisted man responded to defense requests for affidavits nor did Berg's commanding officer provide performance evaluations).[56] In one of those affidavits, a non-Academy officer grudgingly acknowledged that Copy was "honest, sober, trustworthy, and possessed a positive attitude toward the Navy." Although his testimony included no personal knowledge of Berg's sexual behavior, the lieutenant asserted: "[T]here is no doubt in my mind, however, that he possessed the standard traits attributed to . . . homosexual tendencies." These included "an over-sensitivity towards others and towards objects—much in the same way as a woman might react," as well as "an overly expressed interest in flowers and the arts."[57]

Supporting Berg was expert testimony given by John Money, an internationally known professor of medical psychology at Johns Hopkins University. He, along with former superintendent of the Naval Academy

Vice Admiral Mack, strongly urged Berg's retention. Most dramatic, however, was the testimony of Ensign Berg's father, who had just returned from Vietnam only to learn of his son's homosexuality. The board asked "my father questions that I had never had the courage to ask him about homosexuality, his attitudes toward it, homosexuality in the military, and about my own personal integrity, moral code, and life style."[58] Not only did he support his son, but the military chaplain testified that many gays were presently serving in the service, including at least one rear admiral—an embarrassing revelation.

"His father stood by him the whole time," remembers Tony Pritchard. "It cost a lot of money for him to finance Copy since he couldn't get a job." It also cost his father his career, as he was later passed over twice for promotion. Through it all, Tony helped Copy and Lawrence Gibson get through the hard times. "No person in Norfolk or beyond," Lawrence later declared, "has been as supportive as Tony Pritchard. Because of his support, we felt we had the endorsement of the gay community at large, and we knew we were doing the right thing."[59]

Berg and Matlovich challenged Tidewater gays' silence. During those fourteen months, "area newspapers and radio and television stations recounted their struggle" and elevated the consciousness of local lesbians and gay men.[60] "It was closely followed by the daily newspaper and it was much talked about." Jim Early, who had been involved with the Gay Freedom Movement in Norfolk during the early seventies, also says: "People I knew generally thought what Lenny was doing was wonderful. When he came into one of the bars, people would point him out. I was quite cheered by the courage of his stand and the desire to remain in the service. But I did not know of anything to do. There was *no* gay community. We were so fragmented and isolated that you couldn't identify a reaction."

By the spring of 1976, it was clear to some that something had to be done in the face of judicial indifference, public intolerance, and police harassment. In March, the U.S. Supreme Court "summarily ruled"[61] on a Richmond district court's decision upholding the state's eighteenth-century sodomy statute that had been challenged by two Virginia homosexuals. Supported by the National Gay Task Force, this "major defeat" left "homosexual activists thunderstruck" and further evidenced the merits of seeking avenues other than the Court.[62]

That month, too, Norfolk vice raided the Pantry, which had been doing a bustling service since opening the previous October. Twelve people were arrested on different charges ranging from kissing and holding hands to operating a "bawdy place and a house of ill repute." According to owner Steve Brown, "Things had calmed down after Robinette left. But there was a younger vice squad leader who thought the Pantry was owned and operated by the Mafia. Of course, he was wrong."

Bailed out, Steve called a meeting. "It was discussed whether to fight the charges or just plead guilty. I said, 'If it was me, and if you agree with me, we will fight. Everything will be paid by me.' Everyone voted to fight the case."

The twelve defendants dressed in coats and ties for the hearing. The town's prosecutor was surprised to see a prominent attorney representing the group; each member entered a plea of not guilty. One by one, each misdemeanor case was dismissed. But when it came down to the manager charged with running a "bawdy house," the city prosecutor argued forcefully against dismissal. The judge listened intently. Briefs, he declared, were due from both sides in sixty days. In May, a judgment of neither innocent nor guilty was rendered—provided that similar charges were not filed during the next two years.

Meanwhile, Unitarian-Universalist member Will Frank traveled to Washington on church business. While there, he arranged a meeting with an associate minister who was heading up the denomination's Gay Caucus that had formed in 1971. On his return to Norfolk, Will distributed materials to the Tuesday night group. One of the Unitarians who expressed interest in the national group was Joseph McKay, a recent Old Dominion University graduate and a member of the church for the past three years.

The cascading impact of the twin military trials and publicity, the retention of Virginia's sodomy statute, the conversations at the "Freedom to Be Yourself" workshops, and the bust at the Pantry began to weigh on local homosexuals like Marge Reed, Joseph McKay, Steve Brown, and Fred Osgood. The Matlovich and Berg cases "had a big impact" on Marge, who was "absolutely appalled that they should even think about kicking them out." Fred, a onetime mainstream Republican operative who had come to Norfolk in the late sixties, was "annoyed" and particularly unnerved by the Pantry bust, although the Cue was the bar he patronized. "I started thinking about being involved in an organization that could respond to something like that."

In June, Fred's partner, Darrel Haven, contacted Betty Fairchild, a D.C. activist in the parents of gays group. She referred them to Joseph McKay who had just returned that month from the General Assembly. Completing another year of teaching journalism at Cox High School, McKay had committed himself to the national Unitarian Universalist group.

By the early summer, attendance at the local church workshops had waned and the Tuesday-night sessions were at "low ebb." Fred and Darrel met at McKay's apartment at Hague Towers, a highrise next to the Unitarian church overlooking the Elizabeth River. The couple told Joseph of their interest in being involved in a gay group. Fred recalls: "He was charged up, having just been at the national meeting. He thought we could organize a group here with that name and under that umbrella."

During the next few weeks, they'd meet at the Cue on Saturday afternoons, playing pool and making plans for a kickoff event. Osgood recruited a handful of his friends and Joseph got approval from the UU Board for the group to gather at the church. Flyers about a spaghetti dinner circulated in the local gay bars, including a remodeled Pantry, now renamed the Nickelodeon (a title Steve lifted from a Bob Damron bar guide).

As Steve's new bar opened in July and plans for the dinner were underway, federal district court judge Gerhard A. Gesell upheld the discharges of both Matlovich and Berg, citing the four-month-old Supreme Court decision on the Virginia case. Nevertheless, he pronounced Matlovich a "distressing case" and described Berg as "in every respect a first-class, top-notch, efficient, well-trained, competent naval officer."[63] It was time, he opined, for the military to reexamine its policy.[64] As in most matters, the military took its time. It would be two and one-half years before a U.S. Court of Appeals verdict and another two years before justice was rendered.

As some gay and lesbian southerners, like the John Doe in the Virginia sodomy case, migrated north to the anonymity of New York City, Fred Osgood, Joseph McKay, Linda Woods, Tony Pritchard, Steve Brown, Marge Reed, Jayr Ellis, and others laid the groundwork for a gay organization in Norfolk. On 2 August, seventy persons attended the spaghetti dinner. Tony Pritchard, who once lost his license for staging *The Boys in the Band,* donated food to the event. Linda Woods and her friend, Andrea, recruited lesbians from the women's community.

"We were thrilled with the attendance" and, Fred Osgood stresses, "we made decisions." An organization was formed, a newsletter authorized, and meetings set for Tuesday nights. According to Fred, "a significant percentage of the gay people were in the military and wanted to remain anonymous. This was some of our motivation in organizing the Unitarian Universalist Gay Caucus as strictly a social organization. We figured that was the least threatening environment for people to come and participate in a gay group."

Six months later "the group," as it became known, was attracting about fifty persons to its Tuesday-night meetings. As committees reported on their work, weekly topics ranged from games people play in bars to same-sex marriage. During the business part of the Tuesday gatherings, Joseph could often be spotted in the circle grading papers. Following a break, the group usually reconvened for the social part of the program. Jayr Ellis, who was raised in Suffolk County by his grandmother and two maiden aunts, generally organized these with another friend, Mario. They "would help people loosen up and talk to each other," Fred recollects. "Sometimes they were entertaining, sometimes touchy-feely." Donna Motley, a hippie from California with whom the unemployed Ellis lived, says: "He had great organizational ability and was able to reach across different groups because of his grandfatherly, nonthreatening style."

The group helped people find apartments and sponsored an array of other social and fund-raising events. There were bake sales on Colley Avenue, nature walks and potluck dinners, a Halloween costume party, and a clothing drive for the Salvation Army. Ellis organized other activities, such as the receipt campaign that allowed lesbians and gay men to anonymously "reveal" their economic impact on local businesses. Once a project was completed, Jayr would collapse in exhaustion. And, as events progressed that fall, a Friday-night People's Coffee House at the church attracted another crowd. Music played in the background, as women and men gathered around candlelit tables to play cards, eat, and talk. "I made a lot of good friends during those coffeehouses," Marge reminisces.

Other activities not directly related to the UU group also emerged. Marge Reed and others began the first "dyke bowling teams," the Rubyfruit Bowlers. Jayr Ellis, understanding the need for the group to stay clear of overt politics, formed one of his many one-person organizations, Tidewater Area Gay Alliance, sending letters to stunned legislators. Jack Maurizzi, who had attended the spaghetti dinner, began going to the bar in boots, harness, leather jacket, cap, and chaps with other members of the newly formed Militia motorcycle club. And, by the spring of 1977, *Our Own Community Press* had gone from a one-page flyer to a four-page newspaper, operating out of the church's unfinished tower room by its editors, Darrel Haven and Joseph McKay.

"Gay life in Norfolk had been given a shot in the arm of energy," declared Steve Brown. This would be evident to all in the week of 6 June.

TWENTY

Time of Miracles

We are the first generation of our people that have made any claims on personhood.
—Ray Hill

On the day of Susan Saxe's arrest—27 March 1975—Ray Hill walked out of a Texas penitentiary. He had served four years, four months, and sixteen days for burglary. The cofounder of the Promethean Society in Houston and self-described Robin Hood of the gay movement had survived. However, Red Alexander, Corpus, Big Sid, and Coon would not soon fade from his memory.

As he awaited sentencing in 1970, Hill now recalls, "I thought this is no big deal because the revolution would come and my friends would drive down and release me." Hill's bravado crumbled with a judge's gavel.

One day, as Ray Hill awaited transfer from the Harris County jail, an officer yelled over to a burly man in the cell's corner.

"What's your name?"

"Same as it was the last time you goddamn suckers booked me—I'm still Red Alexander—if you're too ignorant to remember."

Hill slid over to the old thief.

"Mr. Alexander."

"They call me Red, son."

"Red, how am I going to do this time?"

"If somebody is going to kick your ass or cornhole you, boy, they're

Reverend Falls, Ray Hill, Jerry Miller, and Pokey Anderson
at news conference announcing formation of GPC.
Photo courtesy of the *Houston Chronicle,* 13 July 1975, staff photo.

going to do that anyhow," Red grumbled in a matter-of fact-tone. "Just leave a few marks on him. Put up a reasonable fight. Courage is the one thing we respect."

At two o'clock, on a cold November morning, Hill and a hundred other prisoners were loaded into the Huntsville-bound bus. "I got in the back. With convicts, blacks and whites are mixed; gays are not." Ray was linked to them in an unbroken chained circle. Icy stares matched the coldness of the metal bench. Four hours later, they arrived at the diagnostic unit.

With sleet on the ground, the prisoners hurried into the cement hallway that stretched north to south. Hill's hair was cut to the scalp with dull clippers. Hustled into a foggy room, Ray faced an elephantine black man in white trousers. Hoisting a bronze container over a muscle-toned shoulder, the man, armed with an iron hose connected to a long copper tube, ordered: "Bend over and spread your ass, boy." After delicing, after a soapless cold shower, after squeezing into a pair of overalls four sizes too small, Raymond Wayne Hill, now Inmate #213398, awaited his psychological interview in a six-by-six room: "Texas prison psychologists (known affectionately as 'Nut Doctors' by the inmates)," Ray explains, "conduct barking interviews with incoming inmates. They bark; we respond. They make notes on our responses and bark some more. When I responded to the question: 'Do you get fucked by other men?' with 'Sometimes but there is usually more to it than that,' he was a little taken aback. He was not expecting a no-guilt response. In 1970, he had never encountered an out and proud gay person."

Two weeks later, Hill was assigned to Ramsey Units, at Otey, Texas, housing 2,800 inmates. He petitioned for the "Punk Tank—the Montrose living area of prison." Ramsey II had six wings and two cellblocks to house the 900 mostly gay inmates. In Ramsey I, there were three other gay wings—black, brown, and white—holding another couple of hundred queers.

When Ray first arrived, Sidney Lanier was warden. He had known Ray's grandfather, Orasmus, an East Texas politician. "Big Sid" resolved himself to "nurturing my prison career" and "keeping the Major off of my ass." Ray became Sid's unit maintenance bookkeeper and quickly got to know "all the honchos who depended on me to do their household chores and repairs."

Most new arrivals, as Ray admits, were not so lucky: "Texas prisons are plantations. Most people start out in the fields picking cotton and seeding corn or soybeans. If you can't keep up with the big boys in the field, there's the garden squad: raising carrots, onions, radishes, and greens."

Hill quickly found that "the more campy and the more courage you had about your identity inside, the more freedom you had to express it—

and experience it." When lights went off in the prison dormitory, most of the convicts slid "under the bunk. There was also romance, gossip, and lovers' quarrels."

Some gay men had lived together for years. One couple from Snyder, Texas, kept house in a B-Wing cell: Buddy was a tall, slender blond with Scandinavian features, and Jesse had Hispanic features and was more talkative. They sat next to each other for meals, attended diagnostics together, and bantered over bridge "just like an old married couple." Twice before they had been released after serving time for sodomy. At their third arrest, the sheriff of the west central Texas county drove sixteen miles to their farm, kicked in the door, and arrested the mixed-race couple. They now served life sentences as "habitual criminals."

In some ways, it was "kind of like life in an apartment house for gay people." But, Ray cautions, "gay refers to who you were on the streets," not necessarily what you do in lockup. "If it had not been for Red Alexander—as dumb as he was—I would never have made it."

Prisons are predatory places. At Ramsey, the punks had the hardest life. In those days of building tenders (long-term, violent offenders who worked as inmate guards), each had his punk—usually a young white straight lad—who provided sexual services and assumed other wifely duties.

As Hill walked to work one morning, a human rag doll fell along his path. Ray peered up to see where the defiled young man had come from. Two smiling building tenders gazed down from the floor above.[1] "What are you going to do about this!" demanded Ray, intruding on the building major in his office. This overseer of many a gruesome beating dismissed Hill with a spiteful eye. The response would come soon enough.

Corpus had been building tender for Ray's wing for two years. A lifer convicted for armed robbery and murder, he told Ray that the new warden, J. V. "Wildcat" Anderson, had decided to take Hill "off his high horse," as Ray had begun "the unconscionable act of communicating with Texas legislators." Before long, Corpus got word that a contract was put on "Mickey"—a prison nickname Hill earned for his seventeen-jewel stainless-steel wristwatch with a silver band. Ray continues: "Normally, if the warden did this, Corpus would just go and beat the shit out of someone. The prisoner would be slid out in a cotton sack that kept blood from staining the floor. But he refused to do that: 'Mickey's not a problem to me.' But the warden wanted me taken down."

Coon, a turnkey from East Dallas, was contracted out to "whip" Ray. A guard escorted Hill out of the dormitory and into the bowels of the prison. There, Coon stood resolute, his back arched. "Mickey, you're going to get an ass whippin'," he boasted. Coon's count boy, Soda, skirted the perimeter along Hill's blind side. "Yeah," Hill acknowledged, "I know there's a contract on me." The guard walked out.

As the metal door slammed, Coon "cold cocked" Ray, who went "stumbling down. I knew I could get up and run for the back of the tank, but he'd just come and get me." Hill staggered up and eyeballed his assailant. Coon's six-foot-three frame, all two hundred and fifty pounds, came down again on the thirty-three-year-old. Face bloodied and teeth loose, Ray, in a scene lifted from *Cool Hand Luke,* rose again. Coon turned to Soda: "I ain't goin' to whip this ignorant son of a bitch. He has more nuts than sense and he's enjoyin' this shit!" Coon trudged out.

Patched up at the dispensary, Hill realized "it reaches a point when you're better off just paying attention to what is going on around you rather than trying to keep up with what's going on outside."[2] Nevertheless, one of Texas's earliest gay activists could hardly ignore events as 1973 unfolded: the Corrl-Henley mass murder case and the Dallas boy-prostitution ring; the opening of the Montrose Gaze center and the formation of the Houston Gay Political Coalition; Houston's inaugural gay radio show on KPFT and the first gay pride march in Dallas; the opening of Bayou Landing and the closing of the Roaring Sixties. Texas legislators also revised the state's penal code, first adopted in 1856. As in Illinois, the sodomy statute was deleted. But Governor Dolph Briscoe, a hardcore Baptist who had banished bourbon and branch water from the mansion, refused to sign off. Trying to do the least harm, progressive legislators, like Houston representative Craig Washington, passed Section 21.06.

Effective the first day of 1974, under Section 21.06, homosexual conduct was a Class C misdemeanor punishable with a fine of up to two hundred dollars. The state, though, had a group of gay felons imprisoned under the old sodomy statute, including five at Ramsey. In addition to the couple from Snyder, there was a diminutive, bitter, feisty man, Alvin Leon Buchanan. In 1969, he was arrested under the old Article 524 in a public restroom. Through the support of the Circle of Friends, Buchanan had challenged the sodomy conviction in court.[3] In January 1970, a three-judge federal district court in Dallas tossed out the verdict, declaring the statute "void on its face for unconstitutional overbreadth."[4] "He put up a good fight," lauds Ray Hill, "but he went to jail" on another conviction.

As a prison trustee, Ray met with the group of five, informing them of their imminent transfer to Huntsville for release the next day. They talked most of the night, with Ray supplying the cigarettes, coffee, and an occasional candy bar. When Hill returned to his bunk, he began to think "about what sorts of things I would do when I got out to advance the cause of lesbian and gay rights." Finally, he concluded: "It was not appropriate for me to get involved in the leadership role again. I obviously had some information that other people did not have from my experience sitting at William S. Woods's feet and my work in the Promethean Society. But I thought it would be more appropriate for me to background someone else—to work in the shadows of the movement."

Ray walked out of prison in the spring of 1975 and returned to Houston. To his surprise, a new leadership of reformers, not revolutionaries, had emerged: "In Stonewall there were college kids, street punks, drag queens, and hustlers. Well, in Houston, there were school teachers, bankers, ribbon clerks, retail merchants, bus drivers, and college professors who would not likely want to blow the universe up for their rights."

As in other cities, midseventies Houston gay leadership was white, middle class, and mostly male. Integrity/Houston still preached the old Mattachine message, "What you do reflects on me." Founders Bill Buie and Hugh Crell continued to lead the small group, supporting the reelection of Rep. Ron Waters, meeting with the community relations representative of the Houston Police Department, organizing protest letters on the airing of the *Marcus Welby, M.D.,* television episode "The Outrage," and approaching Mayor Hofheinz for the inclusion of gays in the city's fair housing law.

Paxton Goff still published the chatty *Nuntius* and Henry McClurg was near the end of *Contact*'s seventeen-issue run. In April, the quarterly meeting of the Texas Gay Task Force was held at St. Anne's Church under the auspices of Integrity/Houston. Plans were finalized for its second Texas Gay Conference in San Antonio the weekend of 20 June, with the theme "Loving, Living, Learning TOGETHER."[5] And, that month, Lyle Black distributed the first issue of a bar magazine, *This Week in Texas.*[6]

In Houston, as in other southern cities, gay men and lesbians seldom loved, lived, or worked together. Linda Lovell and Allison McKinney had just circulated the first issue of *Pointblank Times* and launched their KPFT gay radio show. The Milam Street NOW house bustled with women's energy as the Sexuality and Lesbianism Task Force organized consciousness-raising groups, a speakers' bureau, and a referral list of gay-friendly professionals. And lesbians continued to play softball at Memorial Park. Here, reality began to match myth. In the final scene of the softball fairy tale, the magic happened: The hitter "nailed the next pitch," the center fielder returned the ball, and each player assisted in the play before tagging the runner out. "The game was won! Sadteam was a Happyteam! They went to that certain bar and got drunk."[7] In the real world, the Houston Ducks, after losing four consecutive games, celebrated at Just Marion and Lynn's on winning their first game. As the seventies went into their sixth inning, "the team changed and became more highly competitive."[8]

One of the first political actions Ray took when he arrived home was to visit the KPFT to donate his hundred dollar prison "gate money" to the station's fund drive. Ray also knew he "needed an institution" as a base, and he became involved with the University of Houston's Gay Activist Alliance, which had recently formed.

In June, he attended the Texas gay conference held at San Antonio's HemisFair, where he "was generally shunned . . . because I had just been released from prison. I tried to strike up a conversation with Carl Hays and Hugh Crell, but they both turned and walked away. Then I ran into this old curmudgeon who was a keynote speaker. Morris Kight was also doing some workshops. I told him I wanted to help. His part was how to do the news conference; my part was how to control it."[9]

Hill explained to this Comanche County–born Texan turned Los Angeles activist that he "needed somebody to background." Kight reached into his suit pocket and pulled out a small notebook with a pencil stuck in the spiral. After fumbling around to get the pencil out, he passed the notebook to Ray. "Give me your name, address, and telephone number."

Ray scribbled the information, telling Morris: "As a group, convicts are more tolerant of my being gay than gay people are of my being a convict. I am *not* who I am in spite of being a gay ex-convict. Ray Hill is who Ray Hill is because he is an ex-convict!"

Ray handed back the notebook. Kight ripped the page out and gave it to Hill. "Get in touch with this fellow when you get back."

Ray returned to Houston and "I called a news conference."

Meeting the press with Ray would be Pokey Anderson. Only a month before, she had returned to Houston from a dramatic "Rites of Spring" campout at Paleface Park in the Texas Hill Country. More than seventy-five lesbians faced down a truckload of drunken Saturday-night Texas rednecks carrying rifles, throwing rocks, and shouting obscenities.[10]

Following the Paleface Park episode, Pokey and others found themselves ambushed by Texas good-old-boy legislators. State representative Craig Washington had buried a one-line repeal of Section 21.06 in an omnibus bill. At the end of a marathon legislative session, he had hoped it would pass unnoticed. It didn't.

At 2 A.M. on 29 May an argument ensued over the proposed repeal. During the course of the fifty-minute debate—punctuated by raucous

laughter, schoolboy snickers, and occasional catcalls—Washington persevered: "You can stand up there and demagogue 'till hell freezes over. . . .
You can verbally abuse me if you want. . . . You can persecute people because
you don't understand them. You can laugh about it, but that doesn't
make it right."[11] Thirteen other legislators supported the repeal in the face
of 117 nays.[12]

Momentum had certainly been building for Pokey that spring.
Through *Pointblank Times,* she had arranged to bring poet Judy Grahn
to Houston for a reading at Just Marion and Lynn's. And Anderson had
just returned from the Great Southeast Lesbian Conference held in
Atlanta. "The fantasy of being in a room with seventy-five lesbians was
no longer just a fantasy," she says.

Several days later, Pokey and her puppy, Mobi, hosted Hugh Crell,
Bill Buie, and Keith McGee at her Maryland Street apartment, furnished with the usual creative castoffs. "I had read an article about how
San Francisco had started a political caucus, screening candidates, and
block voting," recalls Pokey. "I thought it was perfect."[13]

That fateful evening discussion centered on how many of the city's elections were won or lost by 5 percent or less of the vote—and the number
of voters was declining. "We could sway a lot of elections. Vote together and
you don't have to come out of the closet if you don't want," Pokey asserted.
"The whole iceberg could be under water!" But the prospect that in six years
Newsweek would be able to report that "for every gay vote the GPC [Gay
Political Caucus] brings in, an additional straight vote hews to the GPC
line," was one they did not imagine.[14] "My honest vision," Anderson admits,
"was that we would eventually find a little group of twenty people. I had
no idea that we would have thirteen thousand people on our mailing list!"

As June passed, "we sort of mucked around with it."[15] Meanwhile,
Pokey, as a leader in the Texas Gay Task Force, readied herself for the conference and "tried to keep an eye on things," interjecting "a checkpoint
to white, middle-class sense of male privilege."[16]

Like Ray Hill, Pokey attended the San Antonio conference. Unlike Buie
and Crell, she did not run into Hill, because she was "networking (okay,
maybe cruising) women from other cities." Anderson rode back from the
weekend event with one of the men, "just chatting about relationships,
sex, and so forth. It was an opportunity we wouldn't have otherwise."

The culminating event of Houston's first Gay Pride Week, a news conference, was held on the following Wednesday afternoon at the MCC store-
front on Waugh Drive at Indiana. As Ray Hill remembers it: "Bob Falls,
pastor of MCC-R, and I put out the call with the help of some students

at the GAA organization. I personally delivered the copy [of the press release] to news assignment directors at the major TV stations and the two daily newspapers. We invited Integrity/Houston to join us after the news release went out. The Integrity membership cast lots to determine who would come out of the closet and appear at the news conference. Jerry Miller lost."[17]

"I'm the voice in the wilderness." Ray Hill's words boomed inside the cramped makeshift church. "During the late fifties and early sixties in gay Houston, I traveled alone as the fool who thought it was okay to be queer." Hill continued his welcoming remarks at the news conference: "Houston's gay community is a large community. . . . It now has organizations reaching out to support it and organizations reaching out to influence it."[18] Four individuals were then introduced.[19]

Minister Bob Falls spoke about the history of the MCC fellowship and the newly chartered Houston chapter. Pokey Anderson described NOW's Task Force on Sexuality and Lesbianism, noting the "uneasy middle ground between the feminist movement on the one hand, and the gay movement, on the other." Jerry Miller described Integrity/Houston's four-year record of local accomplishments.

As chair, Hill noted that if these are organizations "you've never heard before, it's because the community has not used the media as the proper input that it should. . . . From now on you're going to be hearing from us collectively and individually." He then announced that the Gay Activist Alliance would pursue a "media evaluation project."[20] Ray promised, "We'll be checking on your response to the gay community . . . [and] you'll feel our gentle tap." Hill then asked Anderson "to tell you something about the newly formed, this week, uh Houston—what is it—Gay—?"[21]

Pokey rescued Ray, responding: "The Houston Gay Political Caucus." Referencing the legislative debate over Section 21.06, she told reporters: "To be laughed at is not something that's very pleasant. So we have decided, in Houston, to form the Gay Political Caucus" to screen and support local candidates in "large meetings."[22]

The lead in a Sunday article in the *Houston Chronicle* read: "Not too long ago, most homosexuals in Houston wanted only one thing from the rest of the community: to be left alone. Suddenly, they want to be a political force."[23] Hill was prominently featured in the stories that followed and was the centerpiece of a *Houston Chronicle* photograph.[24] "I wore a rust-colored suit. Now if you're a photographer and if you got to balance a picture and there are people in light-colored suits and dark-colored suits, the rust-colored suits goes in the middle."

Given Ray's media savvy and dynamic personality, it was not surprising that some Integrity and TGTF folks "really resented me coming. I obviously stood for the breaking down of their little card castle." But, in the excitement following the successful news conference, "we forgot that I was not welcome."[25]

The first organizational meeting of the Gay Political Caucus, however, would not occur for six weeks—on the heels of Gary J. Van Ooteghem's public coming out. He had been hired as Harris County's comptroller of the treasury following a national search that brought him from Chicago. Although he organized a gay volleyball group that year, Van Ooteghem spent his time with other closeted friends. However, this year's Memorial Day avalanche of publicity over a decorated sergeant's battle with the military had captured Gary's imagination.

When the 25 June press conference was held, Van Ooteghem was in Washington, meeting with fellow veteran Leonard Matlovich. He spent five "really great" days with Leonard as well as got firsthand exposure to the lobbying efforts of the National Gay Task Force. Following the sergeant into battle, the comptroller decided to "take up the fight."[26]

In late July, the thirty-three-year-old CPA informed his boss, Hartsell Gray, the country treasurer, of his decision to speak before the Commissioners Court. Gray, fearing his budget and staff might be reduced, insisted that Van Ooteghem "confine himself to the office." Nevertheless, Van Ooteghem spoke before the Harris County Commission's 1 August meeting. Announcing "I am a homosexual," he argued for the importance of prohibiting job discrimination for all minorities rather than waiting until the federal government "pulls you screaming and kicking into the twentieth century."[27]

The commissioners refused to take such action.[28] Gray dismissed Van Ooteghem for "politickin' on county time;" Gary Van Ooteghem sued.[29] He gave up his $26,000 salary, put his house on the market, and gave away his two dogs. "But," he told a reporter, "there are certain things I believe in more than money—my right to be what I am and be honest."[30]

Other individuals spoke before Houston's elected bodies during that summer of 1975. On the day he came out to his mother, Hugh Crell argued before City Council, "which had greeted our proposal with embarrassed silence, or, in the case of Mr. Mann, by fleeing Council Chambers," that it should adopt an ordinance to end job discrimination.[31] Declaring that GPC will have "the names of five thousand qualified, registered gay voters by the November elections," Crell—whose physical demeanor belied his analytic mind and sense of justice—counseled: "We are not an exotic band of sexual libertines and social misfits clamoring for special privileges and favors. . . . We enrich a city that discounts us. Were it not for Houston's gay community, the Montrose area would still be a district of dilapidated homes . . . instead of a revitalized neighborhood whose tax base has more than trebled in seven years."[32]

The thirty-three-year-old computer programmer warned that should City Council continue to be "unresponsive to its homosexual constituency . . . the Gay Political Caucus shall do its best to secure a new council." Like Van Ooteghem's, Crell's speech fell upon deaf ears.

Neither Ray Hill nor Pokey Anderson had ever heard of Gary J. Van Ooteghem before 1 August. Hill was attending an MCC conference in Dallas. "It was at breakfast in the Adolphus Hotel that I read the news story of Gary being fired. I realized that he had nothing to lose, and that he had the training and experience to provide leadership to an organization." Independently, Anderson came to the same assessment. She telephoned Gary and soon found herself sitting in his living room: "He knew a lot of other closeted people. It was a nice match of the activists, outside banging on the doors, and the business people, who had been in the closet, working in a way only people used to power know how."

When Hill returned from Dallas, he contacted Jerry Miller of Integrity regarding Van Ooteghem. The first organizational meeting for GPC came within a week. About a dozen people, including Ray, Pokey, Hugh, and Gary, attended. Hill agreed to chair the bylaws committee "since I actually had a copy of General Roberts's fine book—and knew how to use it." At the time, Crell confided: "My only trepidation is in having so many leadership-type personalities working on an equal basis."[33]

In September the bylaws were ratified and Gary Van Ooteghem became GPC's first president. Not surprisingly, middle-class professionals like Crell and Van Ooteghem clashed with the street-wise Hill. Clearly, there was "no love lost between the Founding President and Ray Hill."[34] But, from Hill's perspective, "I don't necessarily think tension is a bad thing. If you don't have some tension—ideological tension or tension in terms of approaching style—within your organization, then your meetings start getting dull and people stop coming."

Attendance was no problem. There was "so much happening in Houston that I can't believe it's Houston. The Gay Political Caucus," wrote Crell at the time, "drew ninety-four people to its last meeting, has a treasury of nine hundred dollars, has registered fifteen hundred new gay voters, has a mailing list of over three thousand gay people, and is taking on City Hall."[35]

This same sense of "something happening" was being felt by other Texans. An editorial appearing in *Contact* apologized for the "dreadfully dull . . . endless reports of legislation, judicial decision, election campaigns." But, it crowed: "Majority America is awakening to its 200-year-old commitment to 'liberty and justice for all.' . . . Things are starting to happen for the gay community."[36] And, in a letter to the newspaper, a Dallas reader asked: "Have you noticed lately, you don't hear so much from the sillyass queens who used to scream so loudly, 'What good is the gay movement doing except rocking the boat?' . . . With each court victory, with every gay pride parade, with all the gay organizations, gay businessmen, and gay politicians coming out of the closet each day—all this proves we ARE overcoming 2000 years of oppression. Not only are we doing it, we are doing it in an amazingly short time. Let no one doubt, this is a time of miracles."[37]

By October's end, the caucus had registered more voters and endorsed incumbent mayor Fred Hofheinz, who had met with thirty community representatives at the MCC church. Unlike his visit to the Integrity group two years earlier, the incumbent now spoke as a "practical politician." Hofheinz refused to support an ordinance prohibiting discrimination in housing or employment, and, when questioned about the continued brutality and harassment of local police, weakly responded: "The attitude of the Mayor cannot control the attitude of a large number of city employees."[38] However, he agreed to establish a liaison officer for the gay community and to include human sexuality courses in the police cadet program.

Not surprisingly, this endorsement stirred controversy. Feminist strategist and PBT collective member Barbara Cigainero wrote: "The meeting with the mayor was not a 'privilege' but a right . . . [and] we do not have to be grateful when a 'practical' politician shows some meager sign of support."[39] Hugh Crell responded: "A politician who is not in office has little to offer us. . . . The alternative is for us gays to once again become political cannon fodder as Houston's most liberal mayor by far gets shot down waving the gay lib banner."[40]

Meanwhile, GPC members prepared for electoral combat. Keith McGee headed up the voter registration project. Don Hracovy, a chemical engineer, organized the mailing list on his Heath kit computer. Gay and lesbian voters were sent letters telling them *how* to vote and then telephoned to insure they *did* vote. Hill stresses: "This kind of sophistication did not exist in other political circles; it existed simply because Don had this vision. . . . If he couldn't find you through a change of address slip, he would call your ex-companions because you were in his computer identified with this guy who you lived with for six months and with this other guy who you lived with for six years. Don was absolutely obsessed!"

The November election swept Hofheinz into a second term, although the gay vote was not an important factor due to the margin of victory. Throughout the winter and spring, relations between the police department and the gay community appeared tolerable—until midsummer. In July thirty-six people were arrested when the Exile, a slender hole-in-the-wall on Bell Street behind Simpson's Diner, was raided. Hill challenged the raid as well as the "educational" outreach of the police "chicken hawk squad" in a set of acrimonious City Council meetings.

Then, five days before Christmas, Gary Wayne Stock, a bartender at the Inside/Outside, was killed. When he made an illegal left from Elgin onto Main Street, a police car followed him with red lights flashing. According to the police report, Stock turned right on Dennis and stopped four blocks down the street. An officer approached his car. Stock allegedly tried to run him down with his Cadillac, and Stock was shot.

Fred Paez, who Ray first met through the Gay Activist Alliance when he was released from prison, had his suspicions. Paez had always been attracted to police work and was a part timer at the Bates School of Law College of Prosecutors and Criminal Defense Lawyers. According to Hill, Fred had figured out that Stock was having a quarrel with a police officer's sister who lived on the same floor of Stock's apartment complex. Paez's investigation continued, as Ray details: "We looked at the Cadillac. The windshield was intact. The driver's side window was broken. We got the glass shards from the scene and started to put the pieces together. There was no indication of heat or a radial shatter as from a bullet. The window had not been shot out but broken out with the butt of a gun. Then we got the autopsy report and found that the bullet that killed Gary Wayne Stock had entered under his arm and traveled up through his body! For that to be true, he had to be lying down in the seat on his right side with his arms up over his head, not sitting behind the wheel driving a killer car. We tried to get the media or the authorities interested, but got nowhere." The attitude evidenced in these events alleged by Paez and Hill seemed to be "Why should we put up with these people giving us a hassle? They're only queers anyway."

Stock's death further activated the Houston Gay Political Caucus. The caucus established a rumor hotline, which included information about bars being raided or closed; distributed a list of rights and duties of person under arrest; and initiated Operation Documentation for antigay police harassment. By year's end its budget was thirty thousand dollars.

The year 1976 witnessed more activism and greater visibility for the gay community. Three hundred marchers, shouting "Off of the sidewalks, onto the streets," rallied at Main and Bell for Houston's first gay pride march. *The Wilde 'n' Stein Show,* cohosted by Ray Hill and Kathy Feller, began airing two hours every other Wednesday. That year, too, the Wilde 'n' Stein bookshop was opened on Richmond Avenue by Charles Gillis, who had moved from Dallas with his companion, Ken Cyr. They joined Mary Taylor, the owner of the feminist Bookstore on Bissonnet, selling movement material. And the Metropolitan Community Church of the Resurrection continued to grow under the enthusiastic leadership of Rita Wanstrom, who assumed duties as the worship coordinator with the resignation of Bob Falls. Even the *Advocate* took note:

> The Montrose Activity Center has been around for over a year and is currently preparing El Grande de Coca Cola, a musical comedy farce. . . . There are two gay churches, the MCCR and the Christ's Communion Church, a charismatic congregation. Ray Hill's gay radio show has the largest audience of any program on the local Pacifica affiliate, and a gay television program should be on the air in the near future. Baseball and volleyball leagues have been formed for some time and there is even a gay scuba club. The city supports three gay publications. . . . Within easy walking distance of the [Elgin and Main Street] intersection are two baths . . . also nearby are the city's two gay cinemas . . . as well as numerous gay clubs and countless bookstores and movie arcades.[41]

In the meantime, at the annual spring Montrose Block Party, city councilman Frank Mann labeled the area a haven for "odd-wads and homosexuals," igniting a storm of protest and reaffirming the need to oust this longtime homophobe.[42] And, with the initial success of the Gay Political Caucus, Integrity/Houston "was able to hang up its 'activist' hat and concentrate on its primary function . . . that of being a social organization."[43]

In August 1976, a *Houston Post* headline stretched across an inside page of the Sunday edition: "Homosexuals Gain Momentum in Battle to Gain Rights,"[44] and Pokey Anderson became the first openly lesbian political candidate in Houston history when the incumbent of the Montrose seat for community development neighborhood commissioner unexpectedly stepped down. Seeing a "chance to open up the channels of decision-making to the people who are most affected by the decisions," Anderson agreed to run as a write-in candidate. She argued that since "gay people helped convert Montrose from a slum to one of the most desirable neighborhoods in Houston," everyone should have a voice in the distribution of $734,000 of federal funds for the next year.[45] Although Pokey refused "to smoke stogies or kiss babies," she received an impressive 41 percent of the vote.

Looking back at the year of the Bicentennial, Jean O'Leary, codirector of the National Gay Task Force, pronounced: "We are very optimistic." Seventeen states had repealed sodomy laws, including West Virginia, and twice as many communities had passed antidiscrimination ordinances, including a first-reading approval by the first southern city of any size, Miami. *Blueboy,* too, proclaimed 1976 to be "the Year of the Gay," citing the television networks' turnaround.[46] There were male lovers on *Mary Hartman,* gay magazine publishers chatted with Tom Snyder, Ms. Dickinson's character on *Policewoman* was vindicated by a lesbian friend, a football hunk came out to *Alice,* and the *Streets of San Francisco* featured an openly gay cop.

Gay leaders, however, had yet to confront a sustained, well-financed, politically astute opposition. Ironically, it would be religious conservatives—led by a crusading orange juice diva—who would transform chants of "gay power," kindled in the fires of a Stonewall bar by drag queens and faggot revolutionaries, into demands for "gay rights," articulated by blue-denim homosexuals of the New South.

TWENTY-ONE

Saving Children

Now Bryant reads the Bible, and the Good Book says it's bad
For you and me to go to bed, it makes God God-damned mad.
— *"Ballad of Anita Bryant"*

The endless disco night ended for Jesse Monteagudo in 1975. He had tired of sexual hide-and-seek on the Warehouse VIII dance floor and the exaggerated machismo along Little Havana's Calle Ocho. "I wanted to break with my surroundings, finish college, find a place of my own, and get a lover."

Having abandoned Catholicism four years earlier, Jesse started attending Shabbat services at Etz Chaim, Miami's lesbian and gay synagogue that was meeting at the downtown YWCA: "I liked what I saw. . . . I admired the Jewish commitment to their brothers and sisters, the strong Jewish belief in social justice, and the joy and beauty of the Jewish Sabbath. . . . I also saw a strong parallel between the Jewish people, with their history of struggle and survival, and lesbians and gay men."[1] Monteagudo directed his secular energy into the fledgling South Florida gay political scene.

Bob Basker, 1977. Photo courtesy of Bob Basker.

226

By mid-decade, the Gay Activist Alliance of Miami was bereft of focus. With the last army helicopter fleeing from a Saigon rooftop and student peace activists already AWOL from the campus battlefront, gay Florida student leaders had hunkered down for campus organizing.[2] Meanwhile, an older generation of homophile activists continued to struggle as gay power morphed into gay rights.

One of those homophile activists was Robert S. Basker, who had returned to Miami during the year of Stonewall via Havana and Greenwich Village. Christened by the *Advocate* "Dade County's chief salesman for gay rights,"[3] this lean, fifty-something gentleman with bifocal glasses began organizing Chicago homosexuals in 1963. Behind his unassuming demeanor were also decades of antiwar and civil rights work.

Growing up as Solomon Basker within a staunchly religious East Harlem immigrant family, he had been a cantor at the Uptown Talmud Torah.[4] During the Great Depression, Basker, along with his brother and parents, hawked papers on the New York subway. This precocious teen soon discovered various public restrooms on the Lexington Avenue subway stations and also encountered "bushwhackers" (masturbating men in Central Park bushes) near Fifty-ninth Street and Fifth Avenue. "Camping" with other gay kids at the park, he eventually entered the sexual underground. Some of the men Bob met schooled him in the opera, ballet, literature, and classical music. Meanwhile, his African American friends escorted Basker through Harlem's gay life. There he frequented the Paradise Club on 135th Street and Seventh Avenue with its straight nightclub downstairs and an upstairs bar for men. He also became part of a clandestine social group of fairly well-to-do black lesbians and gay men known as the JUGGs ("Just Us Guys and Gals"). With them, Basker frequented black drag shows and Saturday-night house parties.

As a City College of New York night student, Basker led student peace strikes and distributed Workers' Library pamphlets. While earning his accounting degree, he also served as president of the Marxist Study Club and joined the George Washington Carver Negro Cultural Society, becoming a delegate to the National Negro Congress.

Wars of liberation, civil rights organizing, and student strikes linked Basker across the gay generational divide. That divide also separated him from many homophile leaders, particularly Richard Inman. Unlike Inman, founder of the first state-chartered gay organization in the South and former head of the Mattachine Society of Florida, Basker reached out to others. "You don't widen your influence by being sectarian," he argued. "For coalition purposes, you *always* have open arms."

During the seventies era of greater sexual freedom and elevated political consciousness, Basker found "more receptivity" in South Florida than Inman had a decade earlier. A natural salesman, Basker married individuals' interests to like-minded groups. In 1971, for example, he put his "two cents into hustling," organizing, and recruiting gay Christians for the Miami chapter of the Metropolitan Community Church. "At that time, there were a lot of people who wouldn't get involved in gay political issues but you could convince them to participate in a gay church!" And, three years later, through the support and encouragement of Keith Davis, the local MCC minister, Basker along with B. Jay Freier and his roommate, Phil Wallach, helped form the Etz Chaim—the Tree of Life—congregation.

Jesse was still discoing at the Warehouse VIII when Bob was selling the movement. At local gay bars or community meetings, Bob recalls, "I wouldn't talk about me. I'd talk about *you* and your needs." Merging Alinksy-style organizing with the positive thinking of Dale Carnegie, he strategized: "When you get somebody with a resonance that sounds empathetic, you latch on to them. *And* you use them for gathering others." Rejecting the single-issue position that was the hallmark of the New York–based Gay Activist Alliance, Basker preached "cross-pollination" in movements: "I still remember pushing memberships at gay meetings for the American Civil Liberties Union. 'If we want their help, we got to help them!' Don't limit your issues to just your own situation. Do you want people to come and support you? You're not going to get them to support you if you don't do something to help them on issues that are not contradictory to your own."

Basker practiced what he preached, laboring across sundry groups, ranging from Citizens Against the Death Penalty to migrant workers' rights. As chairperson of the legislative committee for the Florida affiliate of the ACLU and a board member of the Dade County's Concerned Democrats, Basker worked hard to prevent passage of HB2810, legislation that classified sodomy with anyone who was not a "spouse" as a misdemeanor.[5]

Despite these activities, as 1975 began, Bob seemed no closer to his goal of securing a local gay rights ordinance. He had been inspired two years earlier by another homophile leader, Frank Kameny, with whom he had become acquainted during the Mattachine-Midwest days. On 16 November 1973, Basker had entered Washington's city council chambers with Kameny, who had run for Congress two years earlier.[6] "He'd done his homework and lobbying," Basker observes. As one vote followed another in support of the District of Columbia's gay rights ordinance, Bob recalled Frederick Douglass's admonition: "Power concedes nothing without a demand."

Returning to Miami, Basker pushed for a "rebirth of activity and commitment" by South Florida homosexuals to work for passage of a similar ordinance. Echoing Douglass in the GAA-Miami newsletter, he wrote: "Find out just what people will submit to and you will find the exact amount of injustice and wrong which will be imposed on them."[7] Basker's call, however, fell on ears deaf from the din of disco.[8]

Although there was no visible progress toward an ordinance in 1975, "small groups had begun to flower" as Bob "kept everything perking." There was the Lesbian Task Force of the local NOW chapter, which published *Lesbiana Speaks,* a Bar Owners' Association, *David* (the gay bar magazine), as well as religious groups: the MCC church, Etz Chaim, a chapter of Evangelicals Concerned, a Dignity chapter, and the Center for Dialog, which offered VD screening and a place for gay Lutherans to meet. There was also the Thebans, the state's first gay motorcycle club, founded in 1974. The biker group published the *Theban,* hosted the annual run known as the Theban Sun, and was a founding member of the Southern Conference of Motorcycle Clubs.[9] Its balding leader, Marty Rubin, affectionately known as "Your Old Bike Daddy," was also a synagogue member. Initially, there was little understanding between the club and other groups, most notably lesbians, Christian gays, and "lavender limp-wrists." Rubin, self-described as "tacky, insouciant, irreverent, and iconoclastic," remembers the leather scene was "so universally ill-regarded . . . that a group of bikers could run all the fairies out of a fluff bar. . . . They would flee shrieking and twittering up into the rafters."[10] Within two years, however, this "most discriminated [-against] element within Miami's gay community . . . feared, maligned, misunderstood," would become a key group in Miami's gay political scene, and Bob Basker, "not a motorcycle person myself," would be awarded an honorary membership in the Sacred Theban Band.[11]

By mid-1975 Basker had just about "set all my little pawns in place for the grand move." He wrote to the Executive Committee of the Bar Owners' Association, which had been formed a year earlier in response to police harassment. Bob proposed an organization to "broaden the base of support" for the losing campaign of BOA president Jack Campbell.[12] He suggested a new "organizational name" that "will imply input from the entire gay community": the Dade County Coalition for Gay Rights.[13] Although BOA did not adopt the name, there was wisdom in establishing a more politically independent organization. The Alliance for Independent Rights (AIR) was formed.

Jesse Monteagudo first became involved in these community groups in early 1976, when he attended an AIR political fundraiser at Campbell's Coconut Grove home. Jesse, who had known the Ohio entrepreneur from frequenting his Club Baths on Corral Way, describes the rotund Campbell—a distant descendant of Queen Victoria—as "manor born. He had money and knew how to use it: fancy clothes, cars, men, and politics."[14] There he also met Jay Freier, "a charming individual, who resembled the actor Jack Haley," and Bob Basker, with whom he quickly became friends.

When Jesse entered this gay political community, one of his political mentors was Alexias Ramón Muniz. Alex, a dark, husky, bearded Cuban émigré, renamed himself after the hero in Mary Renault's novel *The Last of the Wine* when he became a U.S. citizen. Participating in the Stonewall riots and active in New York's GLF and GAA groups, Alex was one of those activists "latched onto" by Basker. Muniz was a cofounder of the Gay Community Services of South Florida, whose fifty members hosted fundraisers and social events, published a newsletter, provided a professional answering and referral service, and offered medical and legal referrals. Muniz moderated the Thursday-night rap sessions.

As the bicentennial year began, Bob elected to "actively push with whoever would listen" a local ordinance protecting gays from discrimination. He reached out to "different people at different meetings," from the ACLU to local religious leaders. Bob even engaged in a wide-ranging conversation with Richard Pettigrew, a former state legislator who had worked behind the scenes with Inman years earlier.[15] Sitting in the lawyer's high-rise Miami office, Basker found Pettigrew "supportive" but reticent about the political prospects for such an ordinance. Undaunted, Bob also met with each of the nine county commissioners. At one such meeting, a commissioner upbraided Basker, asserting, "I don't think the community is ready for it." He countered with "This is going on in different cities, including the capital of our country!"

True. Some form of a gay rights ordinance had been adopted by thirty-seven cities. However, only two were in the South: Austin and Chapel Hill—liberal oases in a land parched by fundamentalist intensity. And, despite its abundance of beach and sunshine, high-rise hotels and opulent yachts, Yankee retirees and multinational residents, Dade County, "like Los Angeles sprayed thinly over an ill-cleared swamp," still extolled small-town, conservative values.[16]

In February 1976, as cartoonist Garry Trudeau drew the sensitive gay character, Andy Lippincott, into his *Doonesbury* comic strip,[17] Bob Basker unveiled a proposed amendment to the Metro Code of Dade

County at the Democratic county convention.[18] Although members adopted a resolution to downgrade certain victimless crimes, the endorsement of an amended code to protect homosexuals from discrimination in employment and housing was narrowly defeated.

Immediately following the convention, Basker fired a letter off to Jack Campbell, who had lost the previous fall's election, receiving about 20 percent of the vote for city commissioner. Despite his appeal to a half-dozen AIR members attending the convention, none, he grumbled to Jack, had shown up for the critical Sunday meeting where the resolution was discussed and beaten down.[19] It was "time for some serious self-examination," Bob asserted. This was particularly important since he had picked up a "personal commitment" from county commissioner Harvey Ruvin to place the proposed amendment on the Dade County Commission's agenda when local gays were ready.

In early July, Basker prevailed upon Campbell to host an invitation-only meeting with representatives from local gay groups, "putting them to work together in a coalition." Basker had also enlisted the support of thirty-four-year-old Bob Kunst. This tailor's son and rabbi's grandson was characterized by Jesse Monteagudo as "a single-minded, hard-driven person who had nothing in his life but the Cause," and was remembered by Jack as a garrulous maverick "who once threw so much information at me I felt like my body was levitating—mesmerized." Basker first got to know Kunst, who had also worked as an encyclopedia salesman, through local People's Party politics.[20]

Sitting on sofas in Campbell's sun-drenched, cork-paneled living room on Poinciana Avenue were Jay Freier, Alex Ramón Muniz, Keith Davis, Marty Rubin, Lisa Berry (the assistant pastor at MCC), Alan Rockway, Barbara Bull of the Lesbian Task Force, Bob Kunst, and bar owner Bob Stickney. They listened as Basker declared, "It's time to get our asses into political activity to guarantee the existence of social activity!"

Although queer organizing was transgressing on southern land, and legions of southerners had come out since Stonewall, the personal had yet to become the political. southerners were social animals watering at the ever-expanding network of bars and baths, partaking in motorcycle runs and drag shows, roaming cruise parks and rest stops, migrating to churches and synagogues, and dashing around softball diamonds. Political gains and movement momentum, Basker argued, required victories small enough to win but large enough to matter.

From this meeting a loose coalition of eleven groups agreed to enter the political arena. As Jack Campbell, who joined with Kunst and Berry as cochairs,[21] later told South Florida gays: "Only by presenting a united front, will the gay community (Lesbians and Gay Men) accomplish its goals of legislative reform and liberation."[22] For the Dade County Coalition for the Humanistic Rights of Gays, an amended county nondiscrimination ordinance to include homosexuals was the first step toward these aims.

Coalition weekly meetings soon moved to Stickney's members-only Candlelight Club. Over the years Basker had stopped by this Coconut Grove landmark among the banyan trees, where he'd sometimes spot celebrities like Roy Cohn and Barry Manilow dining on rack of lamb and drinking Chateauneuf du Pape. Jesse Monteagudo's first visit, though, was at the invitation of Jay Freier. Attending one of many early Tuesday evening meetings, Jesse recalls: "While the prosperous, closeted, and politically apathetic club members ate, drank, and socialized, Coalition members discussed strategy. Most of the participants were men—a state of affairs that would continue to hold true throughout the organization's history; there were no blacks, and only a handful of Latinos like myself and Ramón."

At the 4 August meeting, members agreed to pursue legislative action, to document cases of harassment, and to screen and endorse political candidates.[23] Basker convinced the Coalition to meet with County Commission candidates and those running for other offices.

The scope and influence of South Florida gays, however, was left to politicians' imagination. "There wasn't that much of a support network. So we had to bluff our way through as best we could," Basker remembers. Nevertheless, "people began to feel that there was an influence of gay activity." And among the sixty-five candidates interviewed at the downtown YWCA were individuals "who in the past wouldn't have considered talking to a gay group."

Meanwhile, Coalition legislative efforts appeared on track. On the evening of 23 September, the Fair Housing and Employment Appeals Board unanimously recommended to the Board of County Commissioners to amend the 1975 county ordinance that forbade discrimination in housing, public accommodations, and employment. As the board met to discuss the ordinance's implications with the county attorney, the Coalition agreed to endorse forty-nine candidates and several politicians not interviewed "who may be helpful to our cause."[24]

Of course, not everyone within the gay community appreciated or supported the Coalition's political efforts. Since Warehouse VIII's Bob Stickney was on the Executive Committee, the Coalition enjoyed unlimited access to the area's largest disco. Other bar owners were more reticent about mixing politics with alcohol. For example, the owner of the Double R, a Levis-western bar, refused to allow Coalition flyers.[25] More ominous was apathy among rank-and-file lesbians and gay men. "There were very few people who were willing to be organized and who were motivated," notes Basker. The Thebans were one exception, as club brothers distributed thousands of Coalition leaflets as part of their effort to "promote our club's image" and to fulfill "our standards, our ideals, and our traditions [that] date back to the time of Agamemnon."[26]

On Election Day, thirty-five Coalition-endorsed candidates won. "We took credit for the winning, although many of them would have won anyway," admits Basker. "A lot of that was bluff. Kunst kept accenting our victory." Some South Florida activists, believing this media spin, boasted that the "politicos are impressed with our voting block. The stronger we get, it could be another S.F."[27]

Among those Coalition-endorsed winners was Ruth Shack, a housewife and liberal activist. Her husband, Richard, was a theatrical agent for a number of entertainers, including Anita Bryant, a Miss America second runner-up who had also endorsed Shack for county commissioner as someone "I want in my corner of the world."[28]

In early November, the Coalition finalized plans for Shack to introduce the amendment with a second from Commissioner Ruvin. Basker quietly worked the commissioners, bringing documentation of what was going on in different parts of the country. Two weeks later, Coalition expectations were that six of the nine commissioners would support an amended ordinance.[29] Although the group discussed "potential opposition," no one had "an inkling," according to Basker, of its eventual scope.

The Metro commissioners met on the morning of 7 December—the thirty-fifth anniversary of Pearl Harbor. In front of a handful of placid spectators, the ordinance's first reading passed unanimously once an amendment allowing landlords to evict tenants practicing "illegal acts" on their properties was approved.[30] A six-week interval and another vote were required, however, for this amendment to become law. It would be a long six weeks.

Three days later a *Miami News* editorial lambasted the commission's action as a "gross distortion of what should be the priorities" of the commissioners and reminded readers that the original ordinance was "to bury once and for all the discrimination against *real* minorities."[31] On 6 January Shirley Spellerberg, an earlier incarnation of Rush Limbaugh and leader in the "Stop ERA" movement, incited an avalanche of irate callers, inviting loyal "Speak Out Miami" listeners to the second reading, scheduled in twelve days.

Anita Bryant was listening to this radio show from her thirty-four-room Villa Verde stucco mansion overlooking Biscayne Bay.[32] Christened "the Carry Nation of the sexual counter-revolution" by *Newsweek* for her Orange Bowl "Concert for Decency," following Jim Morrison's infamous Coconut Grove appearance seven years earlier, Bryant felt "personally embarrassed" because she had made radio commercials supporting Shack's election.[33] Bryant telephoned Ruth Shack.

"I am going to have to oppose you," Bryant told her. She then pulled out her red-leather-bound Bible and quoted from Leviticus. Shocked, Shack responded: "I grew up during the Holocaust. . . . I see this as a human rights issue." Bryant countered, "There are no human rights to corrupt our children," and hung up. Bryant then wrote to each of the commissioners, arguing that the ordinance would be "discriminating against me as a citizen and a mother to teach my children . . . God's moral code."[34]

Although the majority of the letters to commissioners were pro-ordinance, Jesse learned that most phone calls to the commissioners were negative. With less than $800 in the Coalition's bank account (much of it generated from the Thebans' Christmas fundraising at Warehouse VIII), little effort was expended to counter a growing opposition. Nevertheless, Basker, fighting to "keep our votes together," counseled others, "We're home free *if* we keep these people voting the same way."

On 18 January 1977 an overwhelmingly anti-ordinance crowd gathered in Room 252 of the Flagler Street County Courthouse well before the morning gavel sounded. Jesse Monteagudo, who had just gotten off work, was stunned to see a phalanx of Baptist church buses flanking the street. Stone-faced churchgoers armed with Bibles had metastasized into antigay activists. Placards read, "God Says NO! Who Are You to be Different?" and "Don't Legitimate Immorality for Dade County." Flocking into the chambers, they stood four deep along the walls and overflowed into the hallway.

"We passed the word to our people to get there," Basker says defensively. "And *some* of our people came early." But, like Monteagudo, they found themselves outnumbered eight to one. Bob sat in the overcrowded chambers as a crowd of five hundred listened to moral platitudes and biblical prophesies. Anti-ordinance citizens prayed, wept, shouted. Anita Bryant's "voice that refreshes" choked with emotion as she lectured about the corrupting influence of homosexuals. Pastor William Chapman of the Northwest Baptist Church preached in double entendres: "The Bible teaches us that whenever a generation or an individual eats forbidden fruit, you always suffer the consequences. I think we are on the verge of eating forbidden fruit."[35] Finally, Coral Gables city commissioner Robert Brake pronounced the measure unnecessary since "homosexuals are perfectly free to go into their closets."[36]

The Bob Basker who sat through those forty-five minutes was the man who a dozen years earlier had addressed members of Mattachine-Midwest at Chicago's Midland Hotel: "A lack of rights is often taken for granted. . . . It sometimes takes centuries of dreamers, philosophers, and finally revolutionaries to shake people out of their lethargy. . . . Each generation has the responsibility to guard those rights already achieved and to advance the cause of freedom for all people."[37]

In the commission chambers, those supporting the amended ordinance addressed the commissioners. Jesse Monteagudo recalls that "jeers and prayers punctuated the less emotional presentations" by Basker, Rabbi Joseph Narot, Richard Pettigrew of the Community Relations Board, and Bob Kunst. Even former county commissioner Harry Cain spoke "up and out for those whose sexual practices are anathema to me."[38]

Ninety minutes later, Ruth Shack moved the adoption of the ordinance "with deep respect for all who have testified." The roll call vote began. Eight commissioners swiveled uncomfortably in their high-backed padded chairs. Only Ruth Shack's vote was certain.

In quick succession, "no" votes were cast by Neal Adams, an African American Baptist minister who had pledged to support the measure as a candidate, and Clare Oesterle, who collapsed in tears after the roll call. Then, hundreds—hopeful, angry, unbending, fearful eyes—looked at Bill Oliver, a forty-two-year-old, crew-cut carpenter's union chief. As a born-again Christian, he spoke against the misuse of the Bible during the civil rights movement and voted aye. Four more ayes followed in a hurried cadence.[39]

After the 5-3 vote a scornful crowd chanted: "Recall! Recall!" In the hallway Anita Bryant was "not only aflame but on fire," promising reporters a swift repeal.[40]

"It was a big victory," Monteagudo thought at the time. "But I wasn't sure it was going to affect me that much." Bob Basker concurs: "They had been adding a new category each year—sex, marital status. . . . This was just one more salami slice of freedom."

As the two competing Miami newspapers bickered on the merits of the ordinance,[41] Coalition leaders scattered: "Basker to his vacation, Campbell to his business, and Kunst to Broward County to draw support for his newly formed Broward County Coalition for the Humanistic Rights of Gays." Those few who remained, Jesse adds, did not take seriously Anita Bryant's pledge to gather the necessary ten thousand signatures within thirty days to force a recall or referendum. "We dismissed Bryant as a joke; a cracker from Oklahoma who still lived in the pre-disco age."[42]

Save Our Children volunteers circulated petitions in Greater Miami synagogues, distributed leaflets in Spanish (quoting Cuban patriot José Marti: "Children are the hope of the future"), and received the support of the Diocesan Council of Catholic Women, who stationed themselves at every county church.[43] Meanwhile, in the gay capital, San Francisco, homosexuals were organizing a boycott of orange juice, given Bryant's prominent role as the Florida industry's spokesperson. "We automatically saw it as a national battle," remembers Howard Wallace, a part-time truck driver and full-time labor activist; "Bryant was a national figure and orange juice was sold nationally." Joining with several other early gay activists, Wallace formed the Miami Gay Support Committee. There was increasing concern among Coalition leaders. Basker, who had planned on relocating to San Francisco, concluded, "This is no time to leave." A strategy meeting was held at Jack Campbell's home, at which Jesse Monteagudo "got a lesson in ego trips and petty politics."

Most at the meeting recognized the inevitability of a referendum, and Bob Kunst urged the Coalition to endorse the boycott. "Though Kunst was at his impassioned best," Jesse recalls, "his ideas were rejected outright by most of us who were present." Basker explains: "I took the position that this was an excellent idea for people *outside* of Florida. It was not strategic for us to be leaders of a local boycott. We had some heavy arguments about this subject and Kunst lost overwhelmingly." Kunst soon formed his own antireferendum organization, the Miami Victory Campaign.

The Coalition, like its allies nationwide, targeted Bryant's sponsors, who soon felt the wrath of Coalition allies. The Miami tourist bureau received scores of angry letters from loyal winter vacationers; gay bars throughout the country switched to Tang or cranberry juice; Jack Campbell initiated a withdrawal of accounts from a local bank that used Bryant commercials; and the Singer Sewing Machine Corporation canceled Bryant's contract for a "sew-and-chat" television show.

"'The black-listing of Anita Bryant has begun,' Bryant said solemnly. . . . Strain was lining out her peachy make-up."[44] Refusing Singer's offer to keep her new thirteen-hundred-dollar sewing machine, a sparkle returned to her eyes when Bryant learned that brigades of women were picketing Singer stores and some sympathetic Kentucky protesters had even burned a Singer for Jesus.[45]

On 1 March, Anita Bryant marched up the courthouse steps arm-in-arm with Bob Green, a former disc jockey who had found a more lucrative career as Anita's manager-husband after a courtship carried on mostly through correspondence.[46] Behind Bryant were Robert Brake, the architect of the repeal language, who had also tried to ban *Woodstock* from local theaters, and a thirty-seven-year-old advertising whiz, Mike Thompson, the former state chairman of Citizens for Reagan. They delivered 64,304 citizen signatures.

Suddenly, the county commissioners faced the unpleasant choice: repeal the amended ordinance or place it before the voters in a costly referendum.[47] With the *Miami Herald*'s headline declaring that "Gay Rights Is Not a $400,000 Issue,"[48] Basker found himself losing ground among the commissioners. "The pressure was on them to cover the expense of the referendum; they were ready to renege."

Going to the Coalition with this dilemma, Basker faced down those arguing that the ordinance be allowed to die, with gays championed as the taxpayers' friend.[49] Finally, he wrenched a commitment from Campbell and the Coalition to finance it "if necessary." Bob then invited Save Our Children to raise half the total cost, telling the media that "you can't equate human rights with money. . . . We're doing it for the entire community."[50] This tactical decision saved the support of teetering politicians; the referendum was approved, 6-3, in mid-March.[51]

On the last day of March, the *Miami News* reported that two-thirds of its readers supported the ordinance, with an expected turnout for the referendum in June of less than 15 percent.[52] On the second and third of April, Tom Wood, a professor at the University of Miami, conducted a more scientific poll at the Coalition's expense. He not only found that 56 percent would vote in support of the ordinance, but that nearly half felt that the county should pay for the referendum and another third believed that Save Our Children should pick up the tab.[53]

Despite these numbers, Jack Campbell was worried: "We thought we could challenge it in the courts. We didn't think it would go to an election. We didn't know for sure that it was going to an election [until the final court ruling] and then we had to find people. I knew a lot of people in San Francisco; David Goodstein came to our aid."

Characterizing Goodstein "as the godfather to the whole operation," Howard Wallace, who would spend several weeks organizing in Dade County, notes that "the people who were into direct action," like Basker, had been "really setting the pace." But then the Coalition, according to Wallace, was confronted with "this rich benefactor saying I have a prepackaged campaign for you, all you have to do is agree and take orders." Campbell's task was primarily to "keep the lid on local matters," while the Goodstein-inspired team, who "had nothing but contempt for militant activists of *any* type," handled the day-to-day operations.[54]

Arriving in Miami in early April, Ethan Getto, with his campaign assistant Michelle deMilly, "found no campaign operation geared towards winning an election at all . . . [and] tremendous fragmentation in the gay community."[55] Getto, the thirty-something special assistant to the Bronx borough president, had accepted the paid position to head the Coalition's efforts to defeat the referendum. Later, Getto explained his decision, saying, "We had a shot. . . . I thought it was important to show the nation that there were talented, skilled professionals in politics who would come in and give their services to gay people."[56]

Getto placed little faith in the gay people to whom he provided service. He was "disappointed" at the Coalition executive committee's "low level of political consciousness."[57] Calling Basker a "big yenta" because the activist consistently offered advice based on years of community organizing, Getto quickly concluded that the cherub-faced "Campbell was the man pulling the strings and that if I wanted to get anything accomplished I would have to work with him."[58] And, within four days, the Bronx operative had developed a "reconstruction plan." Changing the executive committee to a handpicked five-person campaign policy steering committee, he opted for a "rational hierarchy," not "a Gay movement structure."[59] Getto vested Campbell as president with policymaking authority outside the regular Tuesday-night meetings. Bob Basker, who bristled at Getto's Yankee bluntness, was unceremoniously deposed as executive director. Getto, however, retained Bob as community coordinator so as "not to create a revolution."[60]

One of Ethan Getto's first-line decisions was to commission a five-thousand-dollar poll from an associate of Lou Harris, Richard Dresner of the National Corporation for Telephone Research. Among the 21 percent of the five hundred Dade County citizens who expressed an "excellent" likelihood of voting, Dresner found the referendum was rejected by a single percentage point, 44 to 43 percent.[61]

Downplaying the finding that 59 percent believed the referendum was unnecessary or a waste of money and that support had already declined ten points in two weeks, Getto honed in on Dresner's finding that those who were most supportive cited human rights as their justification. Thus, in line with the pollster's recommendation, Getto crafted the campaign on the singular belief that "a lot of people, even those who found gay people repulsive, felt in the abstract that gay people were entitled to basic human rights."[62]

The problem, of course, was that the opposition, ignoring such abstract niceties and pandering to fears, exploited the homophobic bogeymen of child molestation and homosexual recruitment.[63] It produced flyers with headlines like: "Would You Want a Homosexual 'Big Brother' for Your Fatherless Boy?" Anita Bryant worried to the press about homosexual teachers showing up to work "in drag,"[64] and newspaper ads warned that homosexuals "must reproduce through recruitment." One television commercial opened with

> columns of pretty, long-legged majorettes. "The Orange Bowl Parade— Miami's gift to the nation. Wholesome entertainment," a voice intones with approval.
>
> There is a quick dissolve to a gay rights parade in San Francisco, a bizarre sight calculated to shock conservative southern sensibilities. The voice turns stony with disapproval. "But in San Francisco, when they take to the streets, it's a parade of homosexuals. Men hugging other men. Cavorting with little boys. Wearing dresses and makeup. The same people who turned San Francisco into a hotbed of homosexuality and want to do the same thing to Dade County."[65]

Basker lobbied hard for the Coalition to confront "the scoutmaster and choir leader ploy" and to mount an educational campaign "to raise consciousness" from the African American community of Liberty City to Latinos of Hialeah. "We needed to neutralize the negativity" and not just focus on the Jewish condo owners and the hip Coconut Grove set, Basker argued.[66]

"I didn't have the time to change people's minds," Getto later responded. "I thought it would just confuse things."[67] Asserting that "there's very little that you can do that can ever counter a scare tactic,"[68] he chose an aerial campaign rather than a ground assault. Relying on polling data, Getto pressed human rights: "No matter what you think about homosexuality, don't homosexuals deserve a job? A roof over his or her head? To be able to eat?"[69]

Leonard Matlovich assumed the role of spokesperson and cochair in mid-April. The only southerner in a leadership team castigated by Save Our Children as "carpetbaggers,"[70] Leonard was more skeptical than the press release that announced his appointment and trumpeted the Coalition's twelve-point lead.[71] He sensed hostility beneath a veneer of placid gentility as southerners politely listened to smooth human rights slogans and responded in a less than honest manner to pollsters. Evidence of this enmity, however, was visible on some cars whose bumper stickers read "Kill a Queer for Christ" and among marauding youths. Getto reported:

Our younger volunteers were constantly beaten up in front of the head-quarters. Cars were followed. Cars were firebombed. . . . Jim Foster [the political field director] pulled up at a red light and a car pulled up next to him. A voice in the next car said, "We're gonna blow your fucking brains out." He had a shotgun pointed at his face. The light changed and he raced off. . . . Every time we picked up the phone we'd hear, "You fuck-ing faggot, we're gonna cut your nuts off." . . . It was like an armed camp. We were under constant police guard. Jack Campbell, the most visible gay leader, always wore a bulletproof vest and was accompanied by pri-vate security guards wherever he went. You always had to look twice before walking out of a door.[72]

Basker also disagreed with these political operatives on the extent of community outreach. Getto and Foster had targeted about one hundred key precincts, including Miami Beach condo owners and Coconut Grove liberals, under the formula: "Beach + Liberals + Condos + Gays = Victory."[73]

Two months earlier, Jesse Monteagudo, with Alex Ramón Muniz, Manolo Gomez, Ovidio Heriberto Ramos, and several others, had formed Latinos pro Derechos Humanos (Latins for Human Rights). Although Monteagudo served as president, Gomez, an openly gay jour-nalist working on *Cosmopolitan*'s Spanish edition and "a public rela-tions whiz," garnered most of the publicity.[74] This small band of gay Cuban activists found little support among the eighty-six thousand registered Latino voters or among this community's closeted homosexuals. "Manolo searched for an event that he could use to break the wall of silence," Jesse recollects. On 14 March, he and several of the other Derechos members—including Ramón (with theology books in hand), Jesse, and Herb (who was, at first, fearful to give his real name)—went on WQBA, a local Spanish-speaking radio station.

In what was billed as a "debate" between the pro and con referendum forces, the Save Our Children folks actually went on first, followed by Monteagudo and his compatriots. "We were shocked at the hatred spewed by the callers, which was extreme even by Miami Spanish talk show stan-dards," remembers Jesse. Herb was "unduly upset by our radio experience."

Disappointed, members agreed on a meeting to plan their next strat-egy. Two days later Jesse was startled by a late-night phone call from Herb's landlady: "Herb has blown his brains out with a revolver!" Jesse contin-ues: "Manolo saw his death as an opportunity to launch a public relations campaign that would help our cause. Before the end of the week, 'Ovidio' Ramos became a symbol of gay oppression. We told the world he was a budding activist who was hounded to his death by uncaring parents and by bigots who called the radio station to heap abuse upon this sensitive young victim." As revised by Manolo and the Latins for Human Rights, Ovidio Ramos became a gay legend.[75] Immortalized in magazine and news-paper stories,[76] Ramos was later caricatured in the novel *Ed Dean Is Queer*.[77]

Soon after Ethan Getto's arrival, Jack Campbell directed Jesse Monteagudo to cease organizing within the Latino community.[78] In exchange, the group received a seat on the executive committee, a bargain Jesse now regrets:

> All of these politicos, like Ethan Getto, decided that they would write off the Latin community because it was too conservative. "They are going to vote against us anyway, so we better let sleeping dogs lie."
>
> Getto suggested that we would do a good service to the cause by *not* holding meetings or getting volunteers to work with the Coalition. . . . Of course, while we ignored the Latin community, the other side was encouraging the Latins to come out and vote—and they did! While most Latins would have voted against us in any case, we wouldn't have cost the Coalition any votes had we been in there fighting. We might have gotten more people to come out.

Getto and Company also differed with Bob Basker and several other Coalition members on the use of outside volunteers activated by the TV coverage from *Today, Tonight,* and *Tomorrow.* Howard Wallace, supported by organized labor, arrived in Miami two weeks before the referendum. He met with Jim Foster at his motel pool across from Coalition head-quarters on the corner of Biscayne Boulevard and Northeast Fifty-fourth Street. Foster, Wallace quips, "looked like the chinless Andy Gump from the old-time comic strip." Howard pressed him that "nothing had been done" to mobilize volunteers. Jim, though, was not particularly "open" to that approach, fearing lesbian or gay volunteers who might "come across as any way different or threatening."

Acknowledging that the Coalition, at times, "appeared" to gay out-siders like a "pow-wow where all the chiefs came but the warriors stayed at home," a Custer-like Campbell later admitted, "We needed warriors." But not just any kind of warrior. "Our worst fear was that there would be a tremendous influx of people who would come in without any funds, who would be sleeping in the parks and getting arrested."[79] Conse-quently, heterosexual workers and a coterie of carefully screened gay volunteers were paid $20,000 to make the thousands of "targeted" tele-phone calls to potential voters,[80] avoiding the "personal, one-to-one outreach—necessary in changing people's fears and misconceptions" advanced by Wallace and Basker.[81]

These strategic and tactical differences underscored a growing division within the post-Stonewall movement. After spending days at Coalition headquarters and engaging in quixotic leafleting, Howard Wallace concluded that "Foster and Getto had the feeling that the only way to beat these forces was to have a very 'professional' campaign. . . . If the human rights component had been an influence in the campaign instead of *the campaign*, it would have been one thing. But you were talking around the subject and you couldn't get to the heart of the matter: What is this homosexual menace and who are these people? We were never demystified."

But grassroots organizers like Wallace and Basker had become remnants of a gay liberation past. A new class of political leaders like former mutual fund manager David Goodstein had emerged, ushering in a gay rights era. Similarly, in the South, fledgling bands of gay lib groups from the tidewaters to the bayous were eclipsed in impact by a style, language, and endgame that paralleled the deep-seated conservatism among most homosexual southerners. For the moment, however, white professional men like Jack Campbell, Gary Van Ooteghem, and Leonard Matlovich stood queerly in a movement lineup that also included lesbian feminists, back-to-the land radicals, softball players, and drag divas—a point not ignored by radical critics of the Dade County strategy: "The gay business community is also protecting its image and profits. The militancy and the political growth of the Gay Liberation Movement since the Stonewall uprising are now to be discarded so we can supposedly fit in."[82]

Not surprisingly, there were also strains between Coalition leadership and lesbians. Prior to Getto's arrival, Barbara Bull and others had already pulled out amidst accusations of sexism. "There were few women volunteers," Jesse Monteagudo notes. "None that wielded any power within the Coalition. . . . Most walked out because they couldn't stand what was going on with all of the antiwoman feelings: referring to Bryant as a 'cow,' 'bitch,' 'whore.'"

One illustrative incident occurred at the Candlelight Club when Bob Stickney brought a special dish to the table of Gloria Steinem, who was in town to speak for a Coalition benefit. Lindsy Van Gelder, one of the table guests, recalls that Bob "plopped down a plate containing two up-ended orange-half 'breasts,' each with a cherry 'nipple.' Stickney chortled: 'Those boys in my kitchen are *really* crazy.'"[83]

This Coalition image as a white male affair demonizing Bryant and tokenizing women reverberated throughout lesbian-feminist communities. In Atlanta, ALFA member Elizabeth Knowlton later harangued gatherers at a Piedmont Park rally: "Anita Bryant is a woman and as such is a nonentity in our society. She is a very ugly person, but she is not the powerful witch that some homosexuals make her out to be. . . . She is a figurehead. Behind her loom the powerful institutions of marriage, the church, and the advertising industry, all of them patriarchal and heterosexist. Without their decisions of how Anita Bryant represents them, she goes nowhere. . . . She is a field nigger who has made it into the big house. Let us not forget those less colorful figures in their discreet business suits who run her world."[84]

Other problems befell the Coalition during the last weeks of the campaign.[85] The ordinance had been endorsed originally by the *Herald* but, following a change in editors, the paper reversed its position.[86] In an early column, its new editor, John McMullen, described the ordinance as "a manufactured issue—concocted, we suspect, by those more interested in flaunting their new deviate freedom than in preventing discrimination which they conceded they had not experienced."[87] And, on the eve of the referendum, another *Herald* editorial characterized the "special interest legislation" as "unnecessary" and "undesirable"[88]—oddly ironic editorial positions for a newspaper whose owner's closeted grandson, John S. Knight III, had been bound, gagged, robbed, and murdered in a luxury apartment two years earlier.[89]

Meanwhile thematic fundraisers from the Anitathon in Cleveland to the Anita Bryant Look-a-Like contest in San Francisco, from the Orange Ball in Chicago to "Squeeze Anita Weekend" in New Orleans, from the Anita Roast in the District of Columbia to the Disco for Democracy party at the Waldorf-Astoria had funneled thousands of dollars into Coalition headquarters.[90] Getto channeled $43,000 into *Herald* advertising even though editors buried them in out-of-the-way places, demanded last-minute changes, and placed stories of Boy Scout molestations and call-boy rings next to those about the referendum.[91]

Despite these problems, Jack Campbell, noticing the larger than normal amount of absentee ballot requests, advised reporters: "The larger the turnout, the better it is for us. . . . We expect to win."[92] Bob Kunst predicted a 60-40 margin of victory while the Coalition's Michelle deMilly cautiously predicted a "small majority."[93] On the eve of the election, Leonard Matlovich watched the local evening news as one mother spoke into a TV camera: "I don't want my son taught by homosexuals. I don't want him to become a homosexual." Picking up the telephone, Leonard called his Washington boyfriend: "I think we're asking too much, David, in 1977."[94]

On 7 June, the Coalition provided transportation for voters, handed out literature at shopping centers, and phoned undecided citizens.

Following a day of canvassing, Jesse joined the other volunteers and supporters munching on cold cuts at the Fontainebleu Hotel's Fleur de Lis Room. They watched Channel 4 News as a well-tailored Ruth Shack announced that should the referendum fail, she would not reintroduce it. "The sun will come up tomorrow morning and life will go on in Dade County and we will continue to be the good community that we were in the past." At 6:30 a grandfatherly Walter Cronkite informed a national audience watching the number-one-rated national news broadcast: "Early voter turnout was heavier than expected in an internationally watched campaign that had become a symbolic battleground for the gay rights movement everywhere."

Anita Bryant told a reporter that she, like other mothers, would not be celebrating "in the evening since we will be at home making dinner for our husbands."[95] She hosted an "old-fashioned" covered-dish dinner for a hundred or so volunteers, including the leader of Cops for Christ. As the lopsided returns began to roll in, Bryant danced a jig. Later that evening, dressed in a powder-blue dress with a fish-hook pendant accenting her neckline, Bryant arrived at the Zodiac Room of the Holiday Inn with her husband and four children for the "Lord's Victory Supper." At their press conference, overlooking Miami's gay beach on Collins Avenue, Bob Green kissed his ginger-haired wife, explaining: "This is what heterosexuals do, fellows." Bryant announced a nationwide campaign: "The Christian community had never been involved in any politically controversial issue. We are not only involved; we are committed."

As an evening of depressing vote tallies continued, a subdued Fontainebleu crowd gave Ruth Shack an ovation. Sergeant Matlovich, the master of ceremonies, commanded his garrison: "When you go out of here tonight, you go out of here with your heads high and your shoulders back."[96] Declaring "we shall overcome," he reminded his troops: "If the people of Selma, Alabama, had been asked to vote on equal rights for blacks in 1964, I'm sure the blacks would have lost."[97]

Jack Campbell pulled one of the two prepared statements from beneath his bullet-proof vest: "While we are all saddened by losing what has been a hard-fought political campaign fraught with confusion, distortion, and myths, there is much that we have achieved. . . . Our ultimate victory in achieving Constitutional and human rights is simply a matter of time."[98]

In the hotel lobby, talking on a phone to a San Francisco friend, Howard Wallace learned of the Bay City's gays' intention for "direct action" that night. "Each of these hammer blows against us," he shouted into the telephone, "are actually movement builders. The 'love that dare not speak its name' is being heard loudly and clearly. It's impossible to put the genie back in the bottle." Later, Leonard Matlovich phoned his boyfriend, in a grim mood: "Better to believe the Republicans and the right wing are going to pick up on this and they are going to use it to gain their political strength. . . . You better be scared, David. They called us 'sick,' 'degenerate,' 'perverts.' There is no community in this country that we can ever win an election in."[99]

The next morning the sun came up and Jesse Monteagudo glanced at local newspaper headlines: "Gay-Rights Law Is Crushed," and "It Was Hardly a Gay Day for the Boys in the Bar."[100] He stared at the prominent picture of himself and his lover embracing and then dutifully went to work—a job that 202,319 fellow citizens had determined he could lose because of his homosexuality.[101] "It was a turning point," Monteagudo remembers. "I never looked back."

Meanwhile, Hurricane Anita shifted north, heading toward Norfolk along a political low-pressure trough of homophobia.

TWENTY-TWO

Breaking Silences

The feminists went underground all over the world, moving into the large networks of underground caverns, taking with them their psychic energy, leaving the men to their own violent devices. They took their power into themselves and transformed their lives.

—Julia Penelope

On a February evening in 1976 the phone rang at the Charlotte home of Catherine Nicholson and Harriet Desmoines. "There's a lesbian writers workshop next weekend," a caller from the Smokey Mountains excitedly told Catherine. "We understand that you are starting a lesbian magazine; would you like to join us?"

As Catherine and Harriet headed across the Tar Heel State for Knoxville, the two thrashed out their idea for a new lesbian-feminist journal of art and politics: "Only movement leaders start national magazines, right? They don't do it alone, and they do *not* do it in the South. . . . [But] most Lesbians live, love, work, and politic outside the metropolitan centers. And the movement monster could surely stand a corrective dose of southern, midwestern, 'provincial chauvinism.'"[1]

Three months earlier, in November 1975, the couple had traveled to New York City at the invitation of Catherine's former lover, the novelist Bertha Harris. Attending the Gay Academic Union conference, they met a variety of lesbian writers and activists. One of those was Julia Penelope Stanley, whom Bertha had met at the first Gay Academic Union conference in 1973.[2]

Book signing for *Coming Out Stories*. Photo courtesy of Julia Penelope.

Still in Nashville after abandoning the Dry Creek farm that summer, Julia was in the midst of delivering her paper at a lesbian-only session. "There were rumors for two days," she recalls, "that the gay men were going to crash it and not respect our wishes." As a precaution the doors had been locked when the last lesbian entered that session. As she read her paper, Julia was trembling—not out of fear of potential male intruders (she had already dealt with Merril Mushroom's cousin Billy at the Tennessee farm), but "I was writing out of my self, writing of a self that does not yet exist, a self that has not been born."[3]

Suddenly, there was racket behind the double wooden doors. They bulged from the weight of burly shoulders bonded against them. The lock fractured. A gang of gay academics trespassed into this wymyn's-only space led by "a leather boy fascist with a blond butch haircut." Julia stared down from the podium. She vividly remembers, "It was a fucking brawl!"

While in New York, Catherine and Harriet attended a party full of expatriate southern lesbian literati. It was held in the top-floor Manhattan apartment owned by Daughters publishers June Arnold and Parke Bowman. June was born in Greenville, South Carolina, and raised in Houston (where she was a debutante), attended Vassar, and later earned literature degrees from Rice University. Like the character Sue from *Last Summer at Bluefish Cove,* June often wore "frayed jeans and torn sneakers with the ease of the very rich."[4] She and Parke, an attorney, had been lovers since the late sixties and had formed the Vermont-based publishing house in 1972. Focusing on lesbian fiction, they "believed in the novel as a woman's art form—that it could be an extension of and intensification of consciousness-raising, a place where reader and author could communicate on an intimate personal level."[5]

"June liked Harriet a lot," reminisces Catherine. Harriet had written a review of June's new novel, *The Cook and the Carpenter,* a tale of early seventies feminism at a Texas commune. A short time later, Harriet Reichard took up residence at the Women's Center on Charlotte's Lyndhurst Avenue and began writing as Harriet Desmoines.[6]

It was at this Manhattan party that June (the Carpenter) met one of her *Sister Gin* characters. "You're Daisy!" exclaimed Arnold. Harriet was startled; Catherine was pleased: "It was, in a sense, as if this were some kind of inclusion into this heady group of women."

Julia Penelope, however, was more skeptical about this emerging lesbian community. She, too, chatted with June Arnold that evening.

"Why are you publishing that horrible little novel by Rita Mae Brown, *In Her Day?*" inquired Julia brusquely.

"*Rubyfruit* sold forty-five thousand copies," June replied uncompromisingly. "People will buy this novel on the strength of that."

"That's kind of deceptive, isn't it? The characters are two-dimensional!"

"With the money we make from that book, we can publish other authors like Bertha Harris."[7]

Controversies over the politics of publishing—reflecting ideological, social class, and generational divisions—plagued Daughters during its five-year existence.[8] Despite these problems, Daughters, with southern cofounders Charlotte Bunch and Bertha Harris, produced avant-garde lesbian fiction, like *Riverfinger Women* by Elana Nachman and Harris's *Lover,* as well as reprinted groundbreaking "prefeminist" novels, like *The Pumpkin Eater* by Penelope Mortimer, and experimental fiction, like June Arnold's *Applesauce.*[9]

As they drove back to North Carolina, Harriet and Catherine took turns reading from *Sister Gin.* Set in Wilmington, this story centers on the menopausal Su McCulvey, who falls in love with the gin-drinking Mamie, twenty years her senior. Harriet thought Daisy, Su's publishing assistant, was "a light youthful figure caught in little more than two brush strokes: telltale eyes and ambition. She wasn't me, she was me, she was more real than the phantom 'I.'"[10]

When they reached their North Charlotte home the two wrote the Cook and the Carpenter, "telling them that we wanted to come work for them at Daughters." Parke and June wrote back from their Vermont farmhouse: "'We can't afford to have you. Do something where you are,'" Catherine explains, "so that was the beginning."[11] The Carolina couple set "fire to each other's imaginations," choosing to "extend the love affair" by conceiving one of the most influential lesbian-feminist magazines of the Rubyfruit era—*Sinister Wisdom.*[12]

As in Atlanta, there were differences in opinion among Charlotte Women's Center feminists, as some fashioned a Lesbian Nation from separatist imagination.[13] In Charlotte, these differences were reflected in these women's reaction to Catherine and Harriet's vision, Catherine notes: "They didn't want a magazine. 'No, start a local newsletter,' they said. Neither of us was interested in a local newsletter. We were interested in literature, philosophy, and theory. They thought that was elitist. So we left."

At the lesbian writers workshop in Tennessee the prospect of the magazine was received differently. Merril, who was still traveling back and forth to the Dry Creek farm with Gabby (her gay husband) and their two adopted children, hosted the gathering at their Knoxville home. She had been involved with other local lesbians conducting consciousness-raising workshops, hosting potluck dinners, organizing a women's coffeehouse, and now the lesbian writing group. Merril remembers:

> We were sitting on mattresses covered over as couches with milk crates as end tables. Catherine was older and on the quiet side while Harriet was young and vivacious. The idea of the journal was still very nebulous but they wanted any writing that came out of emerging lesbian culture. The thought of having something that was lesbian—not gay—particularly in the South, where we didn't have a lot of communication with big time East and West Coast dykes, was exciting. This magazine was going to be ours!

Once the soon-to-be editors had returned from this weekend experience, they "worried at the temerity of it all," recollects Catherine. Finally, she advised Harriet: "You have two hours to write a leaflet for *Sinister Wisdom*."[14] Late that afternoon Harriet finished: "How does a woman survive when she steps out from the death procession of patriarchy? How does she think without thinking 'their' thoughts, dreaming 'their' dreams, repeating 'their' patterns? We're trying to answer the questions in our own lives and finding only hints and clues so we decided to make a space to attract other clues, other attempts at living and thinking past the patriarchy."[15]

After mailing the flyer to a hundred or so addresses gleaned from a copy of *The New Woman's Survival Sourcebook,* they waited. Harriet expected no one to answer. She was wrong.

One of the first women to journey to their Charlotte doorstep was a Ph.D. in comparative literature, Beth Hodges. Just the year before, this southerner had edited a well-received issue of *Margins* on lesbian-feminist writing and publishing.[16] From a list of lesbian writers and activists provided by Hodges, another batch of flyers was sent. More responses followed. The poet and theorist Adrienne Rich sent fifty dollars with a list of women for gift subscriptions. Julia Penelope, who had moved from Nashville for a temporary teaching position at the University of South Dakota, sent her Gay Activist Union paper. They also received letters from southern lesbians who, as Catherine remembers, "were immediately locked into it. If they were isolated in rural areas, here was an oasis for them. Here was the beginning of a community for them."

That April 1976, as Harriet typed copy on a rented IBM Selectric, Catherine read "How to Make a Magazine" from an *Amazon Quarterly* article. "*AQ* was full of new and provocative ideas. That was what *SW* was in the beginning. That's what made it exciting. Women were reexamining everything in the world."

This process of reexamination had occurred when Catherine began teaching at the newly opened University of North Carolina-Charlotte in 1967. She found the place "full of gay people, but it was mostly closeted." In 1969, Bertha Harris joined the faculty. She had lived in New York since her graduation from the Women's College of the University of North Carolina in Greensboro and had recently returned to her native state to complete an MFA while earning a living by teaching.[17] That same year her first novel, *Catching Saradove,* was published. Populated by "lovers, waifs, antic southerners, and sexually ambiguous types,"[18] it portrayed a young adult who fears her awakening sexual difference, dreaming instead of a "neat procession of days, sleeping nights, shining kitchen, hot ironed sheets, simmering stews, two-week vacations, spoons to polish, a little girl to beat and rock."[19]

Kate Millet, a friend of Bertha Harris, visited the Charlotte campus. For Catherine, the visit was "like St. Paul on the way to Damascus." Hearing the author of *Sexual Politics* lecture, "I began to look around me at the university and realize how I'd been had! I began to see myself belonging to an oppressed group. I couldn't quite accept it. Then, I began looking around me. Suddenly, I realized that this place was *not* a benign environment; it was a patriarchal institution that used women: secretaries, students, instructors."

When Bertha returned to New York City in 1972, Catherine remained in the South. Although she had "accepted the feminist point of view, I still hadn't gotten very radical." She was radicalized further by Jill Johnston's visit. Johnston, a writer for the *Village Voice* who had just published *Gullible's Travels,* followed her lecture with an announcement that she would meet with women only. One man, however, demanded he attend. "We were not going to be allowed to bond together," remembers Catherine. "I began to realize, there was something very threatening to the status quo when women got together."

Catherine talked with Jill into the early morning hours. "I suddenly asked myself: 'What I am doing here educating these men?'" At the Charlotte Women's Center Catherine joined other lesbians reading the coming-of-age adventure of Inez Riverfinger, analyzing the CLIT Papers, and exploring how to get rid of the "pricks in our heads."[20] There she met Harriet, who had separated from her husband.

Harriet wrote in her journal:

> *Riverfinger Women* shuttles around the dyke contingent of the women's center, passed from hand to hand, with squeals, shouts, moans of recognizing. Buzzing, popping, crackling, singing, the center is a live wire, receiv-

ing information, tapping out information: these are our lives (beep), these are our lives (beep), these are our lives. The journal that began as a delicate matter of personal survival becomes a communal record. . . . In the midst of the whirlwind, seven of us converge. We talk together, breathe together on the subjects of how to untangle patriarchal language, how to exorcise patriarchal values, how to cut away patriarchal attachments. We are Lesbians; together we become separatists, and we name ourselves, with much hilarity, "drastik dykes." Conspiring, we peel away layers of lies, layers of constructed selves, stripping down, down, down to touch the essential womyn surging up, released, from below.[21]

As the phallic exorcism of seven continued, Professor Catherine Nicholson's 1975 spring semester ended. "Feminism, not lesbianism, had radicalized me." No longer dutiful and supportive, she confronted men in her department and began to look at her Charlotte gay male friends in a different light: "They were game players. They were promiscuous. They were not serious about anything. What they really wanted was to be included—like the straight feminists. If they were working for anything—those of them that were—they were working to get accepted into the status quo. God knows they didn't want to give up patriarchy!"[22]

Before Nicholson resigned, however, she impaled a Luther-like pronouncement onto her university door: "You are a witch by saying aloud, 'I am a witch,' three times and thinking about that. You are a witch by being female, untamed, angry, joyous, and immortal."[23] It was a decision she never regretted; she had gained her independence.

First published on Independence Day 1976, *Sinister Wisdom* was named from a phrase in Joanna Russ's science fiction classic *The Female Man.*[24] This first issue, Catherine explains, "expressed our defiance and rebellion against the oppressors of women. We saw ourselves as descendents of the Furies, the Erinyes from Greek tragedy as well as the contemporary Furies in Washington DC. . . . It was a time of naming the enemy: men and men's institutions. . . . The labrys, the double-edged axes I saw as cutting away the old and carrying out the new."[25]

At the time *Sinister Wisdom* began there were 262 publications listed in the *Gayellow Pages.*[26] These included a variety of lesbian publications ranging from *DYKE* out of New York, whose cover mimicked *LIFE* and which first published the CLIT statements; the *Lesbian Tide,* LA's slick newsmagazine, which adopted a news policy of lesbian primacy; and the Michigan-based round-robin bimonthly newsletter, *Lesbian Connection.*[27] Not surprisingly, the South represented the smallest per capita ratio of lesbian/gay periodicals in the country.[28] Among the fifty-four periodicals in the South, most were male owned and gay oriented. Reflecting the lower earning power of women and the refusal of activists to accept sex-related advertisement, southern lesbian publications were in newsletter format. Although inexpensively produced, these publications—for example, *Point-blank Times* in Houston, Atlanta Lesbian Feminist Alliances' *Atalanta, Mother Jones Gazette* in Knoxville—offered a wealth of local information, provided writing venues, promoted lesbian-feminist books and music, and sometimes challenged actions of gay male–led organizations or discrimination in gay bars routinely encountered by women or people of color.

For many southern lesbians, these publications were important lifelines connecting them to the culture of an emerging Lesbian Nation. So, too, observes Merril Mushroom, were novels "like *Catching Saradove, River-finger Women,* and *Rubyfruit Jungle,* which turned me around. These were about me, about my friends, about sex." There were other groundbreaking womanist writings—many authored by southerners—that appeared too, including Ann Allen Shockley's *Loving Her* and Blanche Boyd's Charleston gothic novels, *Nerves* and *Mourning the Death of Magic,* as well as Jane Chambers's *Burning* and Pat Parker's *Movement in Black.*[29]

These novels, plays, and poetry along with magazines and newsletters were eagerly anticipated, read, shared, reread, and discussed by women, particularly in the rural areas of the South where, for lesbians like Merril, "day-to-day activities took up most of my energy" and there were few opportunities to gather with other like-minded lesbians. The openness of such publications to women-loving women, exploration of themes of race and class, and projection of positive and complex images of women "were like breaths of fresh air." They also were mostly ignored (and sometimes dismissed) by mainstream critics as "merely 'confessional' or 'limited,' or too personal to be of any importance as an 'art.'"[30]

Despite these criticisms, by mid-decade lesbian and feminist presses, journals, and magazines exceeded 150 and spanned thirty states.[31] Recognizing this phenomenal growth, June Arnold organized the first Women in Print Conference in 1976. Held during a week of unrelenting August heat when prairie winds blew through dried grass filled with marauding grasshoppers, the gathering attracted 132 women to the outskirts of Omaha.

Catherine and Harriet arrived in their purple Valiant—nicknamed Lavender Jane—packed with copies of *Sinister Wisdom* and two members of the Charlotte Lesbian Press Collective. As they entered the Girl Scout camp overlooking Nebraska cornfields and the Platte River, Catherine reminisces, they were "as excited as two Bluebirds arriving for their first week away from home."

During the opening session, which lasted well into the night, extended introductions and discussions occurred among a veritable Who's Who in lesbian/feminist publishing. When Barbara Grier, representing Naiad Press and accompanied by her partner, Donna McBride, introduced herself, the women "stood up, clapped, howled, and hollered for fifteen minutes,"[32] according to Grier. She continues: "It is possibly one of the most important days in my life; I didn't know the *Ladder* had been *that* important to those women."

Former Kansas City librarian and editor of the *Ladder* Grier had been just twelve when she identified herself as a lesbian. "As soon as I discovered this fact of my existence the rest fell into place at once."[33] Grier's mother (who would later write a letter to the *Ladder*) was quite supportive. When Barbara was fifteen her mother introduced her to two novels: *The Well of Loneliness* (which her mother had read while pregnant with Barbara in 1933) and *Of Lena Geyer,* Marcia Davenport's novel based on her mother's long-term lesbian relationship. Barbara soon started collecting lesbian-themed books and, in early 1957, subscribed to the *Ladder.* Reading her first issue, Grier remembers thinking, "This is what I'm going to do the rest of my life."[34]

During the conference the editors of *Sinister Wisdom* recall:

> We argue over vision and strategy. We form networks. A beaming Barbara Grier keeps reminding us that "history is being made. We are *making history*!" A distraught June Arnold keeps reminding us to wear our official badge (an elegant gold satin ribbon with Women in Print lettered in bright blue) because there are agents in our workshops, our dining room, our beds! And we must rout them out! . . . *SW* makes friends. . . . We learn *SW* is considered by most women there to be a worthy successor of *Amazon Quarterly* and the *Ladder.*[35]

Grier agrees: "*Sinister Wisdom* was one of the four or five most important lesbian magazines (along with *Vice Versa,* the *Ladder, Amazon Quarterly*). . . . It was intellectual, literary, artsy, historical, and it was beautifully done."

At the conference, Catherine and Harriet networked into women-owned businesses. The second issue of *SW* (a special collection on lesbian literature and publishing edited by Beth Hodges and dedicated to Barbara Grier) was printed by the Whole Women Press Collective in Durham, North Carolina, and bound by Diana Press in Baltimore.

Julia Penelope was among those attending this Women in Print Conference—albeit briefly. Like southern-born Willa Cather, Julia had moved to the Nebraska prairie. Although Cather had been nine when she moved to Red Cloud and Penelope well into her thirties, both had adopted a butchlike style during adolescence (Willa had assumed the persona of William and Julia found "hope" in the transsexual hero/heroine Christine Jorgenson, reasoning, "I was 'really' a . . . soul of a man trapped in a woman's body"); both Willa and Julia ended up at the University of Nebraska.[36]

Julia Penelope continued a correspondence with Susan Wolfe, whom she had temporarily replaced at the University of South Dakota. Wolfe pushed Penelope to collaborate on a lesbian coming out anthology. They began in earnest late in 1976, writing to *Lesbian Connection* and sending invitations to their varied mailing lists. One of those letters arrived at the home of Merril Mushroom.

While Julia was "trying to build a lesbian culture, or create one," Merril found that her immediate family "just evolved to be so many men— part of my karmic wheel." After the Dry Creek episode in which Julia pulled out of the Tennessee farm while Merril appeared to side with Cousin Billy, "we had very little interaction," Julia recollects. "I was still very hurt. It was simply another dream that ended badly." Nevertheless, as Merril stresses, "even when we never spoke or wrote, there has always been a psychic contact with one another."

Merril struggled to write her story as she home schooled her two adopted boys and the newest child—a daughter. Finally, she wrote a letter to Julia in March that would appear in the anthology:

> Dear Julia,
> Deadline approaches, and I want very much to be able to write a brilliant statement of my coming out. I have lots of paper filled with notes, almost illegible, jotted in careful answer to the questions in your form letters or during moments out of the reverie which usually followed, but I am having a difficult time. . . . I feel awkward in my manner of communication with sisters who speak in a different vocabulary and are brilliantly feminist in their expression. All I can really do is describe my memories. . . .
> Penny was my first love, and she brought me out well, carefully teaching me the rules, roles, and lingo of the gay subculture. . . . My Lesbian friends and I practiced developing masculine movements, aping and emulating the men we professed to despise. To be a man meant to be strong and to have power. The best we could do as wimmin was to be like men, since we had not yet learned of wominstrength and womanpower. . . . Then Mother Found Out, and there were weeks of trauma and a long, slow healing.[37]

Julia admits she was never adept at "dealing with out-front emotional stuff." In the anthology's introduction, she and Susan Wolfe, the editors, quote from Susan Griffin's essay that had appeared in *Sinister Wisdom*:

"We are a community of those coming to speech from silence. This is an elementary fact we share—a history of illiteracy, suffocations, spiritual and literal, burnings of body and work, the weight of the unutterable surrounding all of our lives. And in no way can this shared history be separated from what we write today, nor from our love of each others' voices."[38]

Sitting in her P Street house in Lincoln, Nebraska, Julia pondered her own coming out story. "My story was broken by long silences while I groped in my mind for words, phrases, metaphors through which I might communicate myself. . . . I discovered in that telling that my life, my coming out, was a narrative of silences, the silence of denial, of self-hatred, of pain."[39]

Julia thought of her eighteen-year-old self, Penny Stanley: her first year at Florida State, her confrontation with the Johns Committee and the dean of women, her spring relationship with Merril, a freshman at the University of Florida.[40]

Crying, she called Merril. "I wanted to talk to her about what had gone down in 1959. I told her I was sorry. We reconnected." After the tearful conversation, Julia bent over her typewriter, releasing "the weight of the unutterable": "I fell deeply in love with her [Merril]. She accepted me unquestioningly as I was; with her I could be all of my selves. . . . Merril threatened all of my carefully constructed defenses, and, in panic, I ran from her, stopped corresponding without explanation or good-bye. I've never forgiven myself for my cowardice and fear, nor have I ever told her this."[41]

In mid-1977, Julia and Susan sent the anthology manuscript to potential publishers. Merril, now living at the farm, worked on a TVA construction project outside Nashville, while Gabby home-schooled the three children. She became involved with lesbians centered at Womankind Books in Nashville. Like other women's bookstore owners in the South, Womankind's Carol Powell and Joanna Morrison were more interested in the business of building a lesbian culture than in selling books.[42] One evening they hosted women at their home to organize around lesbian-feminist issues. Out of that meeting evolved a variety of women's groups, including a coffeehouse where many different women, from amateur to star musicians, performed. Womankind also began coordinating women's concerts with feminist singers like Meg Christian and Teresa Trull. Such music and locally produced concerts, like lesbian-themed literature and book readings, brought a sense of a larger community of women-loving women to lesbians like Merril living on a middle Tennessee farm as well as to urban lesbians such as those frequenting the Atlanta Lesbian Feminist Alliance House.

Meg Christian was to women's music what June Arnold was to lesbian publishing. Christian cofounded the pioneering Los Angeles–based feminist music company Olivia Records.[43] The Lynchburg, Virginia, singer/songwriter, known for her musical dexterity, luminous humor, and "down home" stage presence, was deservedly revered as "a founding mother of women's music."[44] Her first album, *I Know You Know,* included the lesbian anthem "Ode to a Gym Teacher." Another song, which wove folk and bluegrass music, "My Southern Home," begins with youthful lyrics of southern discomfort ("fleeing confederate closets of pain") to southern redemption born from northern experience ("no longer to blame/for the pain/that I could have found anywhere").

As the seventies progressed, there was an ever growing listening audience. In 1976, three years after the release of Olivia's first record (a 45-rpm fundraiser with songs by Meg Christian and Cris Williamson), more than seventy thousand albums had been sold through a network of women's music festivals and concerts, local women distributors, and bookstores. In order to bring these singers into southern towns, lesbian production companies spread kudzu-like throughout the South: Lucina's Music in Atlanta and Luna Music in Richmond, Out and Out Productions and Off the Wall Productions in Houston, Lexington's Amber Music Collective, and Alternative Productions in Memphis. Some had their origins in music festivals or conferences, others arose from the need to attract funding, and a few grew out of music distributors. All promoted local women artists.

Lucina's Music (named for the light bearer who brought a primal rhythm and the civilizing arts into the void of darkness) was formed by about a half-dozen women who frequented ALFA activities and who had just returned from "a three-day trip into our feminist future"—the first Women's Music Festival.[45] Among the many notable performers during that summer 1976 event was Cris Williamson, whose best-selling Olivia album, *The Changer and the Changed,* had just been released.[46] Inspired by onstage performances from Williamson as well as Meg Christian singing about a crush on her gym teacher, the women gathered musician's contact addresses and held a meeting on their return to Atlanta "to recreate the excitement and community that we had experienced at the Festival."[47]

Lucina, operating as a collective that shared decisions and responsibilities, brought in nationally known performers such as Teresa Trull, Marge Adams, and Alex Dobkin. It also spotlighted local artists: singer-guitarist Jan Gibson, soprano singer-composer Carole Etzler, who cofounded the first all-women record company in the South, Sisters Unlimited, and political singers the Exception and the Rule. One of Lucina's founders of Sisters Unlimited says: "It was very empowering to have lesbians who were out of the closet singing in a public concert, 'You're a woman, a mother, a lover to me.' It was also empowering that women could pull off producing concerts without having to need or use men to run the sound board and so forth."[48]

Other local production groups in the South emerged from conferences. Following "five days of turmoil, great expectations, and fun" at the International Women's Year Conference, Off the Wall Productions was formed. This Houston group first brought Meg Christian and Teresa Trull to perform. Trull, a self-taught musician, hailed from Durham, where—until friends sent a recording of her blues, gospel, and country sound to Olivia Records—she was driving a dump truck after an earlier incarnation as the lead vocalist for a local male rock band. One of her first recorded songs, "Woman-Loving Women" was written for the Triangle Area Lesbian Feminists.

Before the inception of Off the Wall Productions and its companion, Out and Out (which emerged from the Ducks softball team), Meg Christian had performed once before in Houston under the sponsorship of *Pointblank Times.* Having played for several years in male-controlled D.C. nightclubs before devoting herself to women's music, Meg was particularly mindful of "how women putting energy into men perpetuates the oppression of women."[49] Thus, both singer and record company stressed the importance of separatism. And, as Meg and her partner, Ginny Berson, traveled around the country in a station wagon, she often performed to female-only audiences. But the May 1976 concert, billed as a women-only event, proved controversial. Several pro-feminist men came as guests among the 250 in attendance. A last-minute compromise was brokered "to smooth over the separatist politics which Olivia made such an issue," but the *PBT* collective was the "object of much criticism and anger from many lesbians and feminists."[50]

Despite such occasional problems, these feminist singer-songwriters were committed to developing lesbian communities and culture, often conducting workshops for aspiring musicians or facilitating discussion groups about women's music. Their concerts also nurtured local talent as lesbian pride and lavender empowerment joined with lyric and melody. One Louisville woman, for example, remembers the first time she heard the local instrumental band, River City Wimin, and saw "four strong, confident women performing love songs to other women, I cried. I had felt so alone, like I was the only one. I stood and listened to those songs as if I had never heard music before. I guess maybe I hadn't."[51]

Since few stores carried albums like *Lavender Jane Loves Women* and *I Know You Know,* a network of women distributors also emerged in the South for labels like Olivia and Pleiades.[52] Amber Moon—named after this matriarchal symbol—had been initially formed as a business to distribute such music to Lexington area women. By the fall of 1977, the last of the Lexington Six had long been released but the "void during/after the FBI came to town" was just being filled.[53] There was much talk at women's parties and potlucks about women's space for art and artists. A film series was organized, Amber Music became a not-for-profit production company, and a "night of women's music" was soon held.

"Our first goal," wrote an Amber Moon founder, "was just to produce nice women's events."[54] Given the publicity arising from the grand jury investigation two years earlier, they shied away from a lesbian image for Amber Moon.[55] As one member observed: "Staying in the closet made it safe for closeted lesbians, who were ninety percent of the community, to get involved. It also made it possible for us to get public grant money. All that said, Amber Moon's real function and the reason for its success was that it filled the need for lesbian social space and a deep hunger for lesbian culture—and it did so with lesbian money and lesbian energy."[56] Whether closeted or not, such production companies empowered southern lesbians.[57]

Judging from the record album covers and book jackets, attendance at local women's concerts and book readings, characters in lesbian-inspired novels and content in women's magazines, the lesbian-feminist cultural landscape—like that of the larger feminist movement—was mostly white. During the mid- to late seventies, however, there was an expanding pool of artists of color: Pat Parker, Linda Tillery, Audre Lorde, Jewelle Gomez, Sweet Honey in the Rock, Anne Allen Shockley, Rosa Guy, Gloria Hull, Barbara Smith, Be Be K'Roche, Cheryl Clarke, S. Diane Bogus, Mary Watkins, Anita Cornwell.[58]

Pat Parker, a Houston native and author of two books of poetry (*Child of Myself* and *Pit Stop*), had gone to California in the midsixties, as she later wrote in "Goat Child," seeking "new pastures . . . golden streets and big money." In May of 1975, Pokey Anderson and other Houston lesbians invited her to return.

East of the mostly gay area of Montrose was the predominantly black neighborhood surrounding Texas Southern University. Anderson posted flyers in various laundromats announcing the poetry reading: "A mother of flesh / a father of marrow / I, Woman must be / the child of myself." Despite such efforts, "not very many" lesbians or gay men of color attended, reflecting "a pretty separate world" and underscoring the poignancy of Parker's poetry.[59]

Similarly, few women of color were associated with the various southern production groups, although some were produced by feminist recording companies.[60] There were Linda "Tui" Tillery, whose silken alto voice first appeared on an Olivia album, asking: "What it's really like / To live this life of triple jeopardy?" and Mary Watkins, a composer who produced stunning jazz compositions for piano, ensembles, and vocals.[61]

In the South, the most notable group was the gospel-influenced, Atlanta-based Sweet Honey in the Rock. Its name symbolized "the range of colors worn by Black women: strength, consistency, warmth, and gentleness" and was drawn from a choral refrain of a traditional black gospel song about a land so rich, rocks overflowed with honey. Infusing feminist and lesbian lyrics and themes into their a cappella vocals, the group emerged from a workshop conducted by Bernice Johnson Reagon at Washington's Black Repertory Theatre in 1973. Reagon, a cultural historian at the Smithsonian Institute, composed much of Sweet Honey's material, drawing from musical encounters at her father's Baptist church in Albany, Georgia.[62]

The general absence of people of color from southern lesbian organizations and cultural events did not mean that issues of race (or class) were ignored. Lesbian-feminist groups working within ALFA confronted racism/classism and sought ways to overcome them.[63] "I do not remember that there were any women of color in DAR II [Dykes for the Second American Revolution]," states Margo George, "but there were women of different class backgrounds." In addition to workshops on race and class, "we did skits. One, in particular, addressed attitudes toward money and how middle-class women judged working-class women who opted for immediate gratification rather than saving money." Lorraine Fontana and another ALFA member of Italian descent also addressed Mafioso stereotypes. And, following a Sweet Honey and the Rock concert produced by Lucina's Music, Reagon and two other singers met with the women of ALFA.

Bernice Reagon's blunt and parsed remarks around the breakfast table were uncomfortable for some to hear. "To be with a radical lesbian feminist organization does not help me out," Reagon, who was a SNCC Freedom Singer during the sixties, asserted. "They have done something for themselves, but they haven't addressed enough of what affects me. . . . We have to develop organizations that have a multi-pronged focus."[64] Despite these misgivings, she praised the music collective, noting: "Everything this society does on racism comes into play" when groups produce such concerts. "You have to face everything you think about black people. And when you go into the black community, you have to face everything they think about white people."[65]

Whether it be Pokey Anderson leafleting east of Montrose or Vicki Gabriner organizing black voters in sixties Tennessee, Margo George lending a hand at a Head Start center, or Lorraine Fontana working in Atlanta's shotgun row houses as a VISTA volunteer, it was at this personal level that generations of white women in the South—teaching in black schools during Reconstruction, organizing the antilynching campaigns of the early twentieth century, working in voter registration projects in the sixties South—have most profoundly experienced issues of color as they tried to "struggle with our daily racism without dead-end guilt."[66]

In middle Tennessee, Merril was helping her two black sons and black daughter know their place in a country "caught in the ghosts of whiteness."[67] She says: "I always had to make them aware of how to protect themselves in a racist society. Survival skills that children of color raised in their birth family learn, children raised by white parents often not aware of that racism, don't."

Like Merril, poet Audre Lorde could offer "no golden message about the raising of sons for other lesbian mothers."[68] As a lesbian mother of a teenage son, the poet continued: "All of our children are outriders for a queendom not yet assured. . . . If they cannot love and resist at the same time, they will probably not survive. And in order to survive they must let go. That is what mothers teach—love, survival—that is, self-definition and letting go." And, for Lorde, "to survive in the mouth of this dragon we call america, we have had to learn this first and most vital lesson— that we were never meant to survive."[69]

Lorde's assessment of survival appeared in the sixth issue of *Sinister Wisdom,* which was co-edited by Mab Segrest. Just a year earlier, in the spring of 1977, Mab had met Catherine and Harriet at the second Southeastern Gay Conference in Chapel Hill. A graduate student in English at Duke, Mab was "just edging out of a closeted relationship" and "bursting on the lesbian scene in Durham." Surprised to learn that a lesbian-feminist magazine was being published in Charlotte, Mab was emboldened after attending a workshop on lesbian literature and writing that included Bertha Harris and June Arnold.

Later that spring Mab traveled to Charlotte for a Women's Studies Association meeting. "There were all of these brilliant, creative, talented women!" she recalls. "Catherine was really important for me in that she took me seriously in a way that none of the male teachers in graduate school did. This was electrifying; that was dead wood." Not only did Segrest find these ideas stimulating and their support uncompromising, she was emotionally connected to Catherine Nicholson and others since "we had drunk from that well of loneliness."

Mab then wrote a book review and a poem for the fall issue of *Feminary* under the name "Mabel." The Triangle-based *Feminist Newsletter* had been transformed to *Feminary* in 1974.[70] The name was chosen from a passage of Monique Witting's *Les Guérillères:* "The women are seen to have in their hands small books which they say are feminaries. . . . In one of them someone has written an inscription which they whisper in each other's ears and which provokes them to full-throated laughter. When it is leafed through the feminary presents numerous pages in which they write from time to time."[71]

Segrest's writings appeared in the same issue in which *Feminary* editors warned they "may not be able to give much time to *Feminary* in the near future."[72] Catherine encouraged Mab, an English teacher at a Southern Baptist college who was completing a dissertation on Yeats, to become more involved with the journal. Writing that fall book review of McCullers's biography, according to Mab, had already "crystallized a lot of the things I wanted to do." So, as "the core [of *Feminary*] dwindled, there was some searching for direction. I was really pressing that this should be a lesbian journal . . . a clear and vigorous direction." The following spring a "special issue" on the lesbian community was published; another transformation of the venerable publication was about to occur.

With contributions from Minnie Bruce Pratt and Mab Segrest, a history of Triangle area lesbian-feminist community and Whole Women Press, as well as reprints from earlier articles appearing in *Sinister Wisdom* and *Feminary,* this first issue of volume 9 retained its North Carolina focus. But Segrest and others now associated with *Feminary* were asking different questions: "What did it mean to be lesbians in the South? We feminarians asked ourselves and our readers. The query brought us face to face with a potent mixture: the racism of a former slave system; the capitalism that generated it and the misogyny and homophobia that also held it in place."[73]

Although issues of class had already been discussed in the old *Feminary,* with essays on southern women's music, the history of North Carolina female textile workers, and the women's movement, there was now a greater "commitment to working on issues of race, because they are vital to an understanding of our lives as they have been, as they are and could be."[74] For Segrest, "*Feminary* was a hybrid between *Conditions* and *Sinister Wisdom.* We had some of the witchiness and spirituality of *Sinister Wisdom* but some of the class and materialist analysis of *Conditions.*"

These new *feminarians* also sought feminist writings from a "radical perspective in a non-academic style" as well as poetry, short fiction, and graphics: "We want to hear southern lesbians tell the stories of women in the South—our mothers, grandmothers, aunts, cousins, and friends. We feel we are products of southern values and traditions but as lesbians we contradict their most destructive parts."[75]

Such priorities certainly reflected the backgrounds of Mab Segrest and Minnie Bruce Pratt. Pratt grew up in Bibb County, Alabama, writing essays on Stonewall Jackson and the Confederate navy and listening to stories told by Grandmother Ora about her childhood during Reconstruction. Minnie Bruce fantasized about the Great Rebellion and the celebrated generals—Jackson, Stewart, Lee—because

> I was confined in my life as a white woman, as a girl; they fulfilled my great need to move, to rebel, to change, without my having to change at all; their obsession with will attracted me because I was allowed a will only in regard to those "below" me. . . . I realized years later that my mother and grandmothers and great-grandmothers had been heroines, in one way, and had used their will to grit their teeth and endure, to walk through the ruins, blood, and mess left by men. I understood finally that this heroic will to endure is still not the same as the will to change, the true rebellion.[76]

Mab also grew up in fifties Alabama, three counties southeast of Minnie Bruce, "where my family on both sides has lived for four generations."[77] Segrest's grandmother and her namesake, Mabelle, was born the daughter of a women's college president in Tuskegee during the 1880s. Her nurse, Carrie, was a twelve-year-old Negro, whom Mabelle acknowledged fifty years later in a speech at Tuskegee Institute: "The world thinks that its great men have made it possible, easy, pleasant, and profitable for two races so unlike to live so close together. . . . But, what every woman knows . . . in the cotton belt of The South, is that the laurels belong to the Carries."[78]

Decades later the other Mab, her granddaughter, wrote: "My grandmother did not see that for Black women like Carrie Nichols to have made it 'possible, easy, pleasant . . .' was to say that they carried in their arms—were expected to *nurture*—the entire racist system of the South. . . . I don't think she would like me for what I am seeing. But I feel, whether accurately or not, that in knowing myself I knew things about her she was never conscious of, and in dealing with her I come back around to myself."[79]

Crossing the threshold of southern womanhood during the civil rights era, perhaps Minnie Bruce or Mab wondered, like Lena, the character in Blanche Boyd's *Nerves,* "if it was nerves making her see, for the first time, how much of her life was built on the lives of black people. It was as if, when she walked on her carpets, she stepped on bodies." As an adult, Pratt did write about the book that, as a child entering adulthood,

> I looked at and never read, a copy of Lillian Smith's *Strange Fruit,* that novel about secret love, the most forbidden book of the modern South. Perhaps I didn't read it because I couldn't take it from the shelf for long without my mother knowing. Perhaps I glanced through it and was too afraid of what might leap from its pages, the stark punishments for love, and the belief that love could exist across the barrier of Black and white, and, therefore, across all barriers. . . . Perhaps because with a glance at even one of the pages, I knew she was going to tell secrets not from three hundred years ago, but from now, near me.[80]

Later Minnie Bruce attended college, never hearing Smith's name,

> though we were in the heart of the civil rights years, though people were being shot and blown up all around, though she was the white southern writer most delving into the secrets of my region and my life. . . . Instead the writers admired by me, and by the students I consorted with, were the Fugitives. . . . I was taught by men who had studied under the Fugitives, and by men who shared their beliefs, who were their literary sons, and who handed down their values about writing and its relation to life. And these values were those of my father: love of the land and denial of those who had done the work on the land, despair and a belief in death, a fascination with the past of the old heroes, a failure to understand the new heroes and heroines who were liberating the present.[81]

On the shoulders of an earlier generation of lesbian southerners, Minnie Bruce Pratt—along with Mab Segrest, Cris South, Susan Ballinger, and other members of the new *Feminary* collective—brought race to the forefront of the journal. As they assembled their second issue, a subtitle, *A Feminist Journal of the South,* was added and—in smaller type—"emphasizing the lesbian vision." Exploring the complex relationships between sexuality, race, and gender through narratives and unpretentious prose, these feminarians were descendants of Lillian Smith and Barbara Deming, who had been at the forefront of the South's civil rights efforts during an era when southern lesbians were isolated, lacking a feminist language or a lesbian community.

That July Catherine and Harriet packed up *Sinister Wisdom* and departed Charlotte, leaving *Whatever!,* a gay bar rag that featured homophobic cartoons, the only queer publication in the Queen City. Driving from the eastern Piedmont to the Great Plains, Catherine Nicholson and Harriet Desmoines took understandable pride in knowing that a 72-page, saddle-stitched journal with less than fifty subscribers had grown to a 112-page, typeset, perfect-bound quarterly with a print run nearing three thousand. But after two years they realized they had achieved a success that would be difficult to maintain without help. Then Julia Penelope called that spring, as Catherine recalls, telling "us she could provide us with plenty of people." Although several of the Lincoln lesbians became quite involved with *Sinister Wisdom,* ultimately, for Julia, it was another arrangement that "ended very badly."[82]

At the beginning of the journal's life, Harriet had written: "We're using the remnants of our class and race privilege to construct a force that we hope will help ultimately destroy privilege."[83] But, from Julia's perspective, practice proved more difficult than intention. "You get into a morass of complications that are overwhelming for individuals to deal with." Sighing, she continues: "Class was an issue that was *never* addressed; no one wanted to hear that *maybe* building a Lesbian Nation was going to be harder and require more struggle than we thought."

As southern lesbians organized Meg Christian concerts or attended Anita Bryant rallies, shared *DYKE* or *Sinister Wisdom,* played on softball diamonds or read *Sister Gin,* issues of class and race were—like Miss May (the black maid in *Sister Gin*)—ever present but never acknowledged.

"Miss Su," says May, to the menopausal writer, her employer, "you haven't forgotten *May.* Oh, I know I'm in there, moving around the table, going through the door, but I'm not there."[84] After Su tries unsuccessfully to write May into the last chapter—twice—Sister Gin says: "Have some gin, Su. You just can't speak for Miss May, that's all."[85]

Audre Lorde, speaking at a session titled "Transformation of Silence into Language and Action" at the 1977 Modern Language Association convention, laid the task out simply:

> Where the words of women are crying to be heard, we must each of us recognize our responsibility to seek those words out, to read them and share them and examine them in their pertinence to our lives. That we not hide behind the mockeries of separations that have been imposed upon us and which so often we accept as our own. . . . It is not difference which immobilizes us, but silence. And there are so many silences to be broken.[86]

TWENTY-THREE

Hurricane Warnings

Either gays are going to come out or we're all going to go right back in again. . . .
It is now time to change hearts and minds.

—*Leonard P. Matlovich*

Anita Bryant, flush with yesterday's victory, sparked the first street demonstration of Tidewater queers. Driving into Norfolk's Scope Arena that evening, Bryant spotted "long lines of them" (more than three hundred demonstrators), who were walking its sidewalk perimeter.[1] They chanted: "Hey, hey, ho, ho, Anita Bryant has got to go!"

Across the street a smaller contingent of pro-Bryant demonstrators waved signs reading, "Gay Is Godless," "Sinners Not Sickness," and "Keep America Beautiful. Shoot a Faggot." One counterprotester stood on a brick wall pointing a megaphone to the crowd that blasted a tape-recorded message to the "sinners." Straight passersby yelled out supportive or negative statements and a few even joined the anti-Bryant group, including a father and his three daughters who were returning from the beach in bathing suits.

Meanwhile, a hundred or so lesbians and gay men threaded surreptitiously through the crowd of five thousand entering the arena for the final evening of the three-day New Creation Crusade. Steve Brown, the bar owner of the Nickelodeon, was one of the uninvited guests. "Someone who was involved with Scope got us a hundred tickets. We individually walked in, knowing what section to sit in, without being noticed as agitators."[2] These dissidents watched as Anita strolled on stage with

Anita Bryant protest in Houston, June 1977. *Free Press*, Charlotte.

her children in hand. They listened to the thunderous applause from her admirers, who were anticipating a night of religious songs and testimonies.

About forty minutes into the program Bryant began an exhortation against homosexuality. Quoting from 1 Cor. 6:9–12, she proclaimed: "Homosexuals will not inherit the kingdom of heaven." Screams of "No! No! No!" reverberated throughout the arena. Tidewater lesbians and gay men rose from their chairs. "Our feet walked heavily on the wooden platform," Brown remembers. "You couldn't help but hear the echoing of everyone marching out."[3]

Then the citrus queen burst into tears. "It breaks my heart that after I said the word 'homosexual,' they didn't hear the rest." As her children gathered around Bryant, the former Sunday school teacher counseled: "There was a time when some of you were just like that."[4] Anita continued her Scripture reading: "But ye are washed, ye are sanctified, ye are justified by the blood of Jesus Christ."[5]

The remaining audience stood for a seven-minute ovation.

"Julie Berry" was among those in the cheering stands. A member of a local charismatic church, she had grown up on a Virginia farm with no electricity or plumbing. Like her, the two-thousand-member church had come from meager beginnings. Julie, her husband, and a handful of other reformed alcoholics had congregated under a self-appointed minister. She was involved with women's groups of the church; her husband was its pianist. To other members of the congregation, this was a prayerful couple who spoke in tongues when "slain in the spirit." But, within her marriage, "gender wise and sexual wise, it wasn't working out. I knew I was in the wrong position." And Julie's husband showed more interest in men than in the occasional sex she coaxed out of him.

Julie entered Scope Arena with her congregation of faith hoping to "rid the world of these strange people." Like others, she was startled to hear the shrieks and to witness scores of homosexuals tramping out. As the marchers strutted out, Julie remembers whispered rumors about arrests of gay protesters who had made it so difficult for Christians to enter the arena. There were also less than Christian comments about those who disrupted Miss Bryant's speech. "That was one of the most confusing moments in my life. 'What statement am I making?' I thought."

During the interlude of blissful clapping, Julie's thoughts journeyed back to the age of six when she first felt being "distinctively different." As a "tomboy" on a Back Bay farm, she had "conjured up a huge fantasy world" in which "I was having relationships with every female that came across my path—as a male." Standing in Scope, she wondered: "If these people knew what I was thinking, would they kick me out?" And, if they did, where would she go? There seemed to be no place for Julie in the gay movement, which, like her fundamentalist church, was dominated by men. And, just as homosexuals were hidden away in church closets, bisexuals and transgender persons were also invisible within the "gay" rights movement.

On the morning of Anita Bryant's visit, Norfolk Coalition for Human Rights—formed ten days before Bryant's appearance at the initiative of the Unitarian Universalist Gay Coalition, which did not want to politicize their group—hosted an interdenominational prayer breakfast for seventy-five persons with the theme, "Save Our Country from Anita." Four hundred miles south, a red-eyed Jack Campbell appeared on *Good Morning America*. With less than three hours of sleep, he sat next to Shirley Spelleberg, dressed all in red, who screamed "Pervert Power" to an annoyed Geraldo Rivera. Elsewhere activists on both coasts were sleeping in after a night of protests against the lopsided Dade County vote that overturned the first gay rights ordinance in a southern metropolitan area. For instance, nearly one thousand people had marched through Greenwich Village to the Bank Street home of mayoral candidate and former congresswoman Bella Abzug, hollering "Bella, Bella" at two o'clock in the morning.[6] Abzug appeared in her housecoat and, with supportive comments, then urged them to disperse. In San Francisco, late-night marchers had crowded into the Castro. Camera store owner Harvey Milk, who had narrowly lost his bid for city supervisor two years earlier, proclaimed: "This is the power of the gay community. Anita's going to create a national gay force!" Several hundred rabble-rousers then advanced down a dozen or so blocks to Polk Street and marched to Union Square by way of fashionable Nob Hill. *Advocate* publisher David Goodstein told the *San Francisco Chronicle:* "We had an army of recruits. Now we have an army of veterans."[7] A columnist for that newspaper, North Carolina native Armistead Maupin Jr., exclaimed: "This isn't the kind of campy defiance you had before!"[8]

Norfolk changed on 8 June 1977. As one gay leader told the press, the demonstration had "shown that gay people are not afraid."[9] A decade later, Dennis Buckland, who had come out at work just the month before, summoned up his experience: "I learned that fear had an unnecessarily strong hold of me, and that it was exhilarating to find out that I could participate in something that I thought was important. . . . I didn't have to be afraid as I thought I had to be, even in the face of Scope, full of Christians, or of Anita Bryant, or the Norfolk police, or anybody."[10] The day after the demonstration, however, a Richmond newspaper editorial accentuated the gulf between this dissipation of fear among Virginia homosexuals and its intensity among heterosexuals: "Queer individuals—united only in their dark and barren sexual predilections—have organized. . . . Homosexuality nevertheless remains a distortion, an abnormality, a degradation."[11] But, as these "queers" took off their masks and unmasked the homophobia among Virginia bluebloods, "the gay community," according to Jim Early, came "together in Norfolk." It also energized that weekend's Greater Tidewater Area Gay Conference.[12]

Dennis Buckland was hardworking and well liked. On 10 June, he and other conference organizers welcomed 150 participants to Norfolk for a "celebration of gay culture and a learning experience for gay people."[13] Participants listened to Ginny Vida outline National Gay Task Force's goals in her keynote address and again later as she appeared on several local radio and television talk shows.[14] They also danced in the church sanctuary as Leprechaun, a D.C. African American, played piano and sang his rendition of "Will the Circle Be Unbroken." And there were dozens of workshops. Those attending "Gays and the Military," for example, celebrated the recent upgrade of Ensign Copy Berg's discharge to honorable. Among the topics discussed in the "Gay Literature" workshop was Bantam Books's six-figure purchase of *Rubyfruit Jungle* from an unknown lesbian publishing house, Daughters, Inc.

Eight days after her Norfolk experience, Anita Bryant appeared at Houston's Hyatt Regency Hotel for the annual convention of the State Bar of Texas. Unlike Norfolk gays, who had organized just nine months earlier, Houston had a well-developed network of newspapers, bars, church groups, softball teams, and political organizations.

Learning of Bryant's pending appearance, Ray Hill, host of the Wilde 'n Stein radio show, polled his listeners, who favored a peaceful rally. Ray Hill and Gay Political Caucus founding president Gary Van Ooteghem fermented plans and invited national leaders like Troy Perry and David Goodstein. Fearing unwelcome publicity and protesters, the bar association cancelled Bryant's appearance, only to reverse its decision when Bob Green threatened to sue if his wife's seven-thousand-dollar appearance was canceled.[15] With the certain knowledge that the gays would march—with or without Bryant—coupled to the sanguine understanding that she would simply sing, the stage was set for what future GPC president Larry Bagneris later hailed as the city's "first major political act."[16]

At about eight o'clock several thousand protesters assembled in the parking lot of the Depository II—a disco with Egyptian décor and a lighted Plexiglas dance floor that smoked—on the corner of Bagby and McGowan. The night was hot and humid. Organizers circulated leaflets ("For One

Evening Come Out of Your Closet, You May Never Go Back") and passed out black armbands with inverted pink triangles. Hundreds of candles lit the darkness as groups of forty began marching two abreast on the sidewalk. Troy Perry led the march, walking slowly to maximize its impact; David Goodstein followed alongside in his limousine. Phyllis Randolph Frye, an out-of-work licensed engineer who had transitioned from male to female, marched with her spouse. Phyllis remembers demonstrators encouraged "to carry umbrellas in case the bigots started throwing rocks and bricks."[17]

Nearing the end of their one-mile march, the growing number of protesters peacefully passed the Hyatt and two hundred pro-Bryant supporters, Save Our Cherished Kids. Three blocks later they arrived at the plaza in front of the new Houston Public Library where Troy Perry, Ginny Apuzzo of the Gay Rights National Lobby, and David Goodstein addressed the crowd. Organizers read telegrams from Hollywood celebrities Jane Fonda, Alan Alda, Rob Reiner, and Ed Asner.

Pokey Anderson was not in attendance for this rally that, at its height, attracted nearly ten thousand persons. Although she was one of the few women who worked with the mostly male political organization Gay Political Caucus, she had found even "working with the other women in GPC who were . . . not lesbian feminists, wasn't an even exchange of energy." Her ambivalence toward GPC was evident in a dream Pokey had had in which the officers of the organization, "which didn't include me, rented a limousine to go to this function. I questioned them about why they had done this. They said something about that it would look good and, of course, this was a shoestring operation. When I thought about the dream, I realized that the men I worked with in GPC did things differently. . . . They felt like they were heirs to power and money and influence."[18]

Three months earlier Anderson had participated in a landmark event that symbolized the gay movement's entrance into the corridors of power. As an NGTF board member, Pokey had been one of the fourteen leaders invited to Washington for a three-hour discussion on issues ranging from federal civil rights legislation to gays in the military. After a tour of the Oval Office the delegation met presidential assistant Margaret Costanza, in the Roosevelt Room.[19] Although there were no commitments, Pokey remembers: "We thought, 'Hey, we're on our way.' It just seemed like the sky was the limit."

Initially the verdict in Dade County seemed to have complicated this presumed trajectory of the gay rights movement. "We felt embattled by the Anita Bryant crusade," remembers Pokey. "At the same time, it

doubled or tripled the membership of the NGTF. . . . We had been fighting invisibility for so many years that fighting Anita Bryant was a step
up. At least we existed now in the public consciousness."

There was less public awareness, however, about lesbians, who were
seldom in key leadership roles in local gay political organizations. As with
lesbian-feminists in Louisville, Atlanta, and Richmond, separate organizations were the norm. In a "moment of tragicomic frustration," Pokey
Anderson and other Houston lesbians mobilized a "loosely banded"
group of "lesbian-feminist anarchist gadflies," known as the Lesberadas:
"A desperado is an outlaw. An outlaw is one who is put outside the law,
exiled and who is deprived of the law's benefits and protection, a fugi-
tive. A Lesberada is a lesbian outlaw. All lesbians are outlaws."[20] Meeting weekly throughout the summer and into the fall at the First Unitarian
Church, the Lesberadas focused their energies on a November conference
that would bring thousands of women to Houston.

The impact of the Save Our Children campaign was felt beyond
those cities where activists rallied traditionally docile southerners at
Anita's performances. For example, newspaper headlines in Birmingham on 8 June read: "Dade Voters Kill 'Gay Rights' Law" and "Anita Has
Lopsided Win in Vote on Gays." And the city's morning and afternoon
papers both editorialized about the referendum and homosexuality.[21] There
were follow-up articles about protesters dogging Bryant and the views of
the local citizenry. The verdict? "Gay Job Rights? Vote Here: No."[22]

Such coverage about homosexuality was unprecedented in Birmingham. In 1977 "there was no gay consciousness as far as a political movement" in the Magic City, according to Ron Joullian, an Alabama native
who began teaching music to suburban youngsters seven years earlier. Joullian recalls a general attitude of benign neglect from authorities and the
general public. Lifting a line from a character in his favorite Gordon Merrick novel—"As long as it is love, the Lord won't mind"—Ron, like many
gay men, "just went out and partied," enjoying the relative sexual freedom of the seventies South.

Like the smokestacks of Birmingham Steel, bar life metaphorically tow-
ered over the homosexual's landscape. The most raucous of these bars was
the Gizmo Lounge, opened by Al Pilkington in 1970. Patrick Cather, who
enjoyed Birmingham's gay A-list of social life from the Mardi Gras Mys-
tic Krewe of Apollo to the Sunday evening dinner circuit, was also fond
of this cruisy Twenty-second Street South bar:

> If you stopped by in the very early evening, the place would be relatively
> quiet; almost empty. At some later, appointed hour—as if by a nearly for-

gotten medieval theory of abiogenesis—the cavernous quiet came to life as bodies seemed to generate themselves from the walls, from the floor, and from the bar itself. The spontaneity of the sweating, boisterous humanity filled the room if not the darkness. . . .

By ten o'clock the floor would be sticky with spilled cocktails; those bodies dancing around the floor would be just as sticky with sweat and honest exuberance. . . . The swelter of unlatexed lust in the air or maybe just Walter and Lionel and the other venerable old queens holding court at a corner table—no matter, somehow you just knew this place was open just for you; just for us. And we thought this party, this wild St. Vitus Dance of liquor, drugs, sex, and beauty would last forever.[23]

By 1977 Birmingham's bar scene had really opened up. In addition to the Gizmo, gay men could visit the town's two show bars, Chances R on Twenty-third Street North and Focus Phase II (although the most recent Miss Gay Birmingham pageant had actually been held at the Fraternal Order of Police Lodge), disco around the immense tree trunk at Belle Watling's, which sat opposite the downtown library, or enjoy a Sunday brunch at the Circus Lounge.[24] For women, Tito's II was a favorite for Tuesday-night pool.

Bootsie Abelson grew up in 1940s Birmingham as a Jewish tomboy. She had married and undergone shock treatments at Hillcrest. In the early seventies she came out and began a rap group for gay kids at Freedom House. Abelson bar-backed at the Gizmo, where "the tempo was set by the men who had the nickels" while the women—"the harder, rougher twenty-something lesbians—would drink beer and just fit in." Meanwhile, the older lesbians "who were making a good living just didn't go out or were in small intimate groups."

In mid-1977 awareness of the Dade County controversy had seeped even into the Gizmo's darkest corners. It was as if "I was a gay mushroom," explains Bootsie, "and all of a sudden there were a lot of little mushrooms popping up."[25] Ron Joullian attended a meeting with less than a dozen others, "many of whom did not know each other," called by Alan Handleman, an Auburn student, at Vicki's Bar. "This little crusty New York Russian Jewish boy who was Abby Hoffman's cousin" encouraged Birmingham gays to organize.[26] Although Joullian "felt outrage with what was being said in the media about homosexuality," like most, he adopted a wait-and-see attitude.

The meeting ultimately resulted in the incorporation of Lambda ten days after the Dade County vote. Readers of Alabama's first gay newspaper were later told: "Some of us feel that we have only one hope for protecting ourselves and our lifestyle. We must form a strong, informed, actively united gay community."[27] Lambda organized variety show fundraisers at the Gizmo, members appeared on radio and television talk shows, and speakers also appeared at Lambda's twice monthly meetings. Ron Joullian, who had worked with the state legislature as an Alabama Educational Association leader, spoke at one meeting and soon became a board member and its second president. In his inaugural address, Joullian advised: "The first battle is with oneself. You're not going to fight City Hall until you gather the troops; you have to nurture and inculcate this sense of self, self-worth, and community." Ron, however, was well aware of the difficulties he and others faced: "We weren't embraced with open arms by everybody. Here was this ragtag group of rebels who were radical in a lot of folks' eyes. We were shaking up things socially. It was still a tense and extremely conservative city. Folks were not really talking to each other and were still afraid to give you a name. . . . Thrust up against the East or West Coasts, we were just a bunch of country bumpkins doing nothing. But with this ragtag group we were not going to shake up City Hall . . . [until] we got a sense of community."

Creating this sense of "community" was viewed by many local activists as the consequence of, if not the antidote to, Bryant and her gang of fundamentalists, homophobes, and political opportunists. Few if any southern activists, however, thought seriously about the meaning of community or their abilities to coalesce lesbians, gay men, bisexuals, and transgender persons of different backgrounds, interests, and beliefs into a single organization or even a steadfast coalition. Most, like Phyllis Randolph Frye in Houston, were "under the mistaken impression that all of us queers were in this thing together. After all, it was transgenders and other gender variant gays who frequented the Stonewall Inn. They were the ones first arrested and who first resisted. . . . But as I learned, we never were. Transgenders were considered then as tag-alongs and *not* part of the goals of the movement."[28]

Organizing politically proved difficult in southern towns that lacked a politically minded critical mass. Nevertheless, activists tried to form a community out of a hodge-podge of disco revelers, closet-case cruisers, drag divas, and cloistered middle-aged couples occupying common space with softball teams, motorcycle clubs, and church groups. The challenge facing activists was mobilizing these mostly social groups in a region that prized forbearance and propriety built on denial, repression, and segregation.

Like Birmingham, New Orleans was a social scene with its French Quarter bars and gay Carnival krewes. Unlike Houston, however, New Orleans, had a checkered history of gay activism. The few remaining political activists there had long anticipated Anita Bryant's 17 and 18 June appearances at the city's Summer Pops festival.

Human Equal Rights for Everyone (HERE) had been formed as a short-term coalition of gay and progressive groups in April. Within weeks it had secured the agreement of the local union chapter of radio artists (AFTRA) to refrain from servicing Bryant's performance. As one of the organizers, longtime activist Bill Rushton, told City Council and the public: "We don't think taxpayers should be forced to subsidize her bigotry."[29]

All of this activity was surprising (if not frightening) to those familiar with the City That Care Forgot and where only sporadic political organizing had occurred since the 1973 Up Stairs fire. One political response to that human tragedy had been the formation of the Gay People's Coalition by French Quarter gays attempting to "appeal to people's nobler instincts."[30] GPC had operated a gay switchboard and published the *Causeway*, a news tabloid edited anonymously by Rushton, who was managing editor of the *Vieux Carré Courier* and a student at Tulane. Less shrill and more commercial than the earlier *Sunflower*, it included brief news notes, bar and bath ads, recipes, and article reprints. An early editorial proclaimed: "There are enough gay men and women in N.O. who are able to do anything they wish—be it swinging an election or electing a gay city councilman."[31] But, as the tragedy of the fire dimmed in people's minds, crowds for the annual Labor Day weekend gay frolic, Southern Decadence, grew; gay krewes expanded, and the Coalition's membership shrank.[32]

A year later another attempt to organize New Orleans homosexuals was launched. The Gay Service Center was opened on Burgundy Street in the Faubourg Marigny area. The group there, led by Mike Stark, a six-foot-nine-inch bearded former Baptist minister who sported a caftan, was soon operating a telephone infoline, sponsoring a coffee house, hosting dances, and publishing its newsletter, the *Closet Door*. But, by the newsletter's seventh (and last) issue, Stark's dispirited group declared: "It's time to seriously evaluate who and what we are as a group. . . . It is apparent that the [Burgundy] space is not being used to its fullest potential, in fact, it is empty a great deal of the time. The functions of which we use it fully are primarily to raise money to perpetuate rental/expenses."[33]

Lacking the more stable groups that had developed in Houston, it should have come as a surprise to no one that in the spring of 1977, Ed Martinez, a writer for another short-lived gay newspaper, the *Vieux Carré Star*, would ask: "Where are the gay activists in New Orleans?" Castigating Crescent City gays as "lethargic" and "indolent," he questioned:

"Where are all the organized groups that give gay communities in other cities their sense of community and sharing?" Martinez's answer: "Gays are permitted to be gay in the French Quarter with few restraints. . . . The huge numbers of gays who do not live in the Quarter, who live closeted, if not cloistered, lives, feel almost no kinship at all with French Quarter gays."[34] For New Orleans' A-list gays, such as the late Clay Shaw, these "pink tea queens" were considered "déclassé, or at best uncouth, examples of gay society." Arguing that "nothing could have given a gay community more reason to band together than that horrible tragedy," Martinez then concluded: "After the fire at the Upstairs Lounge everything has returned to normal. Nothing to raise gay consciousness in this city has happened, and nothing very much is very likely to happen."[35]

But then Anita Bryant arrived on the heels of Alan Robinson and the Gertrude Stein Society.

Alan Robinson, a gay activist while an anthropology student at the University of Illinois, had moved to New Orleans in the fall of 1975 after sauntering up and down the East Coast. "Settling into the spirit of the city," he immersed himself in its gay bar scene, favoring Pete's and Lafitte's in Exile. Also, he quickly discovered New Orleans's fractured gay life. In addition to the French Quarter gays, "there were the close-knit Carnival krewes' scene and the Uptown people in their own private gay social circles who never admitted going to the bars." New Orleans, however, "lived up to Andrew Holleran's line from *Dancer from the Dance,* 'everyone sleeps with everyone eventually,' although they may never invite you for tea."

Working as a volunteer at the Gay Service Center on Burgundy, Alan remembers one meeting when Bill Rushton bounced in wearing a little bow tie. Within a few weeks Alan was dating Bill. "I was a gay person who happened to be active in other progressive movements while he was [a person] active in progressive movements who happened to be gay."

Like activists in Birmingham and Norfolk, Robinson and Rushton reasoned that New Orleans needed a social, not a political, organization. "The small organizations and the community center were not clicking," Alan Robinson recollects. "We needed something for the entire spectrum of the community rather than trying to follow the old movement structure." Cooking a sukiyaki dinner at his Royal Street bungalow, Alan along with Bill Rushton and Ann Gallmeyer, the community relations director for the city library, began to brainstorm. The Gertrude Stein Democratic Club was formed that December evening. Its goal was to have as many different events as possible at a variety of venues and, in the process, build a mailing list and a core leadership group from which a political movement might someday emerge.

The first major event was a January 1976 birthday party for Gertrude Stein, held at Sudee's Restaurant, owned by two lesbians, Sue and Dee. Over one hundred people, ranging from gay artists to radio personalities, appeared. "That many people had never walked into the door of the Gay Service Center," chuckles Alan. Drinking wine and eating lavender birthday cake, they listened to readings of Virginia Woolf and Gertrude Stein. Plans were laid for a homoerotic art show and a series of radio readings of gay classics. People signed up on the mailing list and promised to give their lists—from Christmas cards to bar napkins.

A short time later, Alan received a call from a New York friend who asked him about coming to Mardi Gras and bringing along a friend, Christine Jorgenson, who had made international headlines with her sex change surgery in 1951. In addition to escorting her to the Apollo Carnival ball, Bill Rushton interviewed Jorgenson on the first gay TV talk show, "Gertrude Stein Presents." She also spoke at an evening event that drew more than two hundred guests, including gonzo journalist Hunter S. Thompson and another from the *National Enquirer.* Alan remembers, "This just got the gossip mill flowing through New Orleans about Gertrude Stein, who could fly in Christine Jorgenson for a party!"

Changing its name from a "democratic club" to a "society," Gertrude Stein seduced New Orleans homosexuals. Salons were hosted in people's homes and local businesses, the Gertrude Stein Players produced Monday-night dramatic radio readings, cocktail receptions were hosted for visiting gay celebrities as well as mayoral salons for political candidates, concerts and dance performances were presented, and a newsletter, *Gertrude's Notes,* was published.

Thus, when it was learned that Anita Bryant would be coming to town, the Gertrude Stein Society hosted a meeting of eight groups, including local chapters of the MCC and the long-running Daughters of Bilitis. Since Gertrude Stein was organized as a social and educational group, a new organization was needed to confront Bryant. Despite the history of gay indolence and apathy, Human Rights for Everyone soon expanded to a coalition of fifteen groups, including Carnival organizations and a feminist counseling collective.

As Bryant preached her way from Norfolk to Houston, flyers flooded the Quarter and nearby neighborhoods. Rushton cashed in political chips, tapping his network of progressive leaders. The 18 June rally and march heralded a diverse set of endorsers including the Southern Christian

Leadership Conference, the New Orleans Chapter of NOW, and the Social-ist Workers Party. Afternoon showers, however, threatened to dampen the spirit of marchers. Minutes before the rally was to begin, the rain subsided; three thousand persons assembled at Jackson Square, located in the heart of the French Quarter. Roger Nelson and his partner of twenty-five years, Jack, were among the crowd: "There were more police in conspicuous posi-tions for the protest," Jack recollects, "than I had seen before or since for any assemblage: on the roofs of the Pantalbas, the Cabildo, the Presbytre; on mounted patrol, in squad cars, and at every park gate. They expected trouble; they got peace. The variety of people who came out of the bars, many of which closed for the duration of the march, ranged from men in Italian suits to women in Levi's."

The crowd held hands and sang "We Shall Overcome." Looking up to the threatening sky, Leonard Matlovich shouted: "Lord, don't rain on our parade." Cadenced cheers rippled across the crowd. As the sun broke through the clouds, Frank Kameny proclaimed: "We will not continue to live in closets."[36]

Demonstrators began their march through the Quarter walking down St. Ann Street, chanting "Out of the Closets and into the Streets." Sup-porters on wrought iron balconies wrapped with banners cheered. The march extended four blocks from sidewalk to sidewalk as it turned on Bourbon and headed to Dumaine, picking up marchers along the way. Marking one of the largest civil rights demonstrations in the city's his-tory, thousands of protesters arrived at the North Rampart Street Munic-ipal Auditorium entrance. Gertrude Stein was elated: "The reaction within the ranks was explosive, euphoric, and pure; the silence of the past is ended."[37]

Separated from the marchers by mounted police were thirty-five "Christians Behind Anita." This apostolic band chanted "Gimme a *J*, gimme an *E* . . . what does that spell? JESUS." One protester told a reporter, as she looked at the long crowd snaking its way around the auditorium, "I hope they like this hot weather, because that's all they'll know when they die."[38]

During the fall of 1977, the Village People's hit "Fire Island" played at Café Lafitte in Exile, celebrating twenty-five years since its move up Bourbon Street from the old blacksmith shop. A party was also held at the newly opened gay Country Club. This primeval Creole mansion with a wide veranda on Louisa Street brought women and men together to swim, drink, and eat while toasting the cofounders of the city's new gay news-paper, *Impact*. "A community defines itself by the spaces it creates," wrote Alan Robinson, the editor of *Gertrude's Notes.* "The New Orleans gay community is redefining itself."[39]

Atlanta was not on Bryant's 1977 summer tour that was rallying the queer troops.[40] Nevertheless, at Atlanta's Book Valley Church a warning went out that homosexuals, like Sherman's army a century earlier, "were on the march through Georgia."[41] At the Atlanta Gay Pride March, in ninety-degree heat, the crowd approached two thousand. (The year before, the march had attracted only several hundred participants but generated an outcry from Citizens for a Decent Atlanta, incensed with the mayor's proclamation of Gay Pride Day.)[42]

Gil Robison, who had returned from San Francisco with a degree from its Art Institute two years earlier, was a member of the Gay Rights Alliance, which had organized the June march. He stressed: "Until that time there hadn't been a year 'round gay or lesbian organization that was solely political in focus. We had organizations that would coalesce every year around Pride Day but that only kind of fell apart shortly thereafter— a period of intense activity followed by months of nothing."[43] Robison and others organized the First Tuesday Association a week after that June march. Within a year the organization was publishing a newsletter, holding candidate forums, and sending delegates to the Democratic state convention. Robison later acknowledged: "First Tuesday did become a rather genteel sobriquet for lesbian and gay. For instance, when we'd be talking to elected officials they wouldn't want to say lesbian or homosexual . . . so they would just ask 'Is that a First Tuesday person?'"[44]

Despite this infusion of political energy in Atlanta and other southern towns, there were setbacks amidst the groundswell of gay unrest. The *Barb*, published by longtime activist Bill Smith, who was also the mayor's appointment to the Atlanta Community Relations Commission, ceased operation that October, as had the *Free Press* in Charlotte and Memphis's *Gaiety.* Other community newspapers, however, emerged following the Dade County referendum, and ongoing newspapers, such as Norfolk's *Our Own Community Press,* expanded as their readership grew.[45]

In a lead story, *Our Own* editors asked: "Six gay groups in Tidewater? Unbelievable, but true!"[46] Dignity-Integrity of Tidewater was now meeting at the Open Door on Colley Avenue, and a chapter of MCC was holding its Sunday afternoon service at the College Cue. These newest groups joined the Militia motorcycle club, the House of Camelot, the Gay Alliance at Old Dominion University, and the Norfolk Coalition for Human Rights to form Norfolk's gay infrastructure. In addition to its regular social activities, the one-year-old Unitarian Universalist Gay Caucus (UUGC) was now offering weekend couples retreats and expanding its Tuesday-night programs to include speakers like Barbara Gittings and Frank Kameny. Gittings, former editor of the *Ladder*, told the group: "We, too, want to save our children. Who saved us when we were children and growing up being taught that we were wrong, and sick, and sinful?"[47]

Not all Tidewater gay groups or individuals gathered under the big community tent of the UUGC. The brothers of the Militia, for example, preferred the smell and feel of leather and the sound of motorcycles. The club had started the same year as the UUGC but its formation and members were, according to its founder, Jack Maurizzi, "in no way connected . . . and I couldn't care less; I found their meetings boring." After Maurizzi's Norfolk debut in full leather, others with similar interests started meeting at Jack's house and hung their colors at the Paddock, a downtown gay bar. Club members drove to Washington on weekends— "there was really no leather community here"—and frequented the D.C. Eagle. Inside was a wall of colored glass on which each of the clubs—ranging from the Spartans to the Lost Angels (who were originally known as the Ladies Auxiliary since they were unable to join the Spartans)—displayed their club colors. "It was a highly charged atmosphere at a time when the hanky code was popular," Jack Maurizzi remembers. Here men would choose from among ten or so different colored handkerchiefs that could be worn in either the right or left pockets telling others "what you were into." These ranged from black worn on the left (heavy SM top) and gray worn on the right (bondage bottom) to olive drab (military top). But, unlike the more youth-fixated disco scene, in leather clubs like the Eagle, "it's the performance," underscored the just released *Leatherman's Handbook*, "not the wrinkles, that count."

Most southern groups organized to rally against Anita were led by more conventionally attired gay men who had traditionally dominated political activities. Richmond was different. Bobbi Weinstock had moved back to Richmond from Atlanta in the fall of 1976. There she found "a community I had not been aware of" when she had departed two years earlier. The Richmond Lesbian-Feminists (RLF) and their newly inaugurated *Lesbian Feminist Flyer* seemed to her "just a continuation of ALFA—although we didn't have a house."

RLF, formed in 1975 by Beth Marschak, organized nonbar activities, including potluck dinners, all-women's dances, softball games at Humphrey-Caulder field, monthly discussion groups with topics ranging from goddess religions to Mafia-owned bars, and Luna Music Productions.[48] Bobbi first met Beth at a women's festival in Byrd Park sponsored by the Richmond Women's Alliance, a coalition of feminist and progressive groups. "She was very excited about finally connecting up with us," Beth recalls, "since she was trying to find out what was happening." Although Marschak considered herself a separatist, these mostly white lesbian-feminists in their twenties were more lesbian than feminist.

More conservative Richmond was less welcoming than Norfolk.[49] Bobbi says: "We didn't even try to do some of those things like a conference." However, unlike Tidewater, this one-time Confederate capital enjoyed a stronger feminist presence, since "the women in Norfolk were putting a lot of energy into the gay conference and newspaper."

Among Richmond lesbians were the older butch-femme crowd who hung out at Nicky's where the sign on the door always read "Closed." A knock on the door brought a peering eye determining whether one could enter the Cary Town bar with its dress code of polyester pantsuits or mix-and-match outfits. And, although lesbians had more interracial social contacts (like LuLu's nip joint in Church Hill) than did Richmond's gay men, "things had never been well integrated," Bobbi explains. "There were predominantly black clubs and individual parties; it was a struggle to get non-Caucasians involved in the political groups."

When Bobbi returned to Richmond she also found little overlap among the handful of lesbian and gay groups. Dignity/Richmond was founded earlier that year and published a newsletter, the *Voice*.[50] The town's longstanding Gay Awareness in Perspective and Virginia Commonwealth University's Gay Alliance of Students (which had just been recognized by the school after a long legal battle) were also active.[51] But, as Marschak notes, these gay male groups were not as well organized, did "not have the advantage of coming out of the women's movement, and didn't have that same analytical framework to see interconnections among groups to build the groundwork."

But then the "Queen of the Righteous" arrived. In preparation for Bryant's fall 1977 visit, there were strategy sessions held and a coalition formed. Beth and Bobbi were two of the organizers of the Richmond Citizens for Gay and Lesbian Rights, receiving support from various local gay and progressive groups. "The assumption," notes Beth Marschak, was that "Anita was welcome in Richmond because of the conservative image of the area." The midafternoon "Support Rally for Gay and Lesbian Rights" at Monroe Park on 8 October drew more than two hundred people. "Without Anita, we wouldn't have gotten anyone," Beth says. "She got people angry." That evening Neal Parsons and Bruce Garnett arrived well before the 7:30 P.M. concert at the Robins Center of the University of Richmond.

Active in Gay Awareness in Perspective, the two had picketed Bryant at Norfolk's Scope Arena. Although those seeking tickets had been screened, Neal had picked up two from the First Baptist Church for his "crippled aunt." Following the concert, Garnett had approached Bryant. She was wearing a billowing red, white, and blue chiffon gown as she signed autographs. Walking toward her, he stripped off his suit coat revealing a "Gay and Proud" T-shirt. Expecting more praise from another fan, she heard instead a young man describe how he attended the university in a state of "pure hell" because of the actions of people like her. The crowd fell silent. Bob Green interrupted. Wearing a double-breasted, pin-stripe suit, he asked whether Bruce thought a man should have the right to take a Great Dane for a lover. As the crowd pressed forward, the brief exchange ended.[52]

The October rally marked the city's first gay rights demonstration. Two weeks later the Richmond Gay Rights Association formed. Within six months the group had begun a newsletter and engaged in a dialogue with City Council candidates. Soon there would be a drive for a Richmond gay rights ordinance.

The Dade County imbroglio also temporarily united lesbians and gay men in Louisville. As 1977 began, River City lesbians and gay men lived separate lives in an array of communities. Mostly gay men still danced the night away at Badlands disco or cruised Fourth Street. Older lesbians still preferred private parties while the athletic types enjoyed playing softball (some on the all-lesbian team, Matriarchies), and the bar crowd frequented Mother's Brew on West Market Street. There was also the three-year-old Lesbian Feminist Union that had established a food co-op, bought a house, hosted a women's resource center that included childcare and counseling services, and joined with other feminists to open the Bluegrass Feminist Federal Credit Union.[53] And a small group of lesbians and gay men participated in the local MCC services and events.

As the Dade County referendum became more relevant to Louisville gays, about a dozen men organized the Gay Rights Alliance of Kentucky (GRAK). Although the group met at the university, it was considered a community-based organization. Ken Plotnik, its treasurer, recalls that its community base was still narrow, with "a lot of problems internally with the lesbians. The organization decided not to use 'lesbian' in the title, and that probably turned out to be a mistake."[54]

Nevertheless, facing the forces of darkness, Louisville lesbians discussed a rapprochement with GRAK. One woman argued: "We need to be a political force with gay men. These attacks on homosexuals threaten our existence as well as theirs and a unified front is our only hope of preserving what we have already accomplished."[55] LFU voted for a temporary alignment, warning, however: "We do not forget our double oppression as women and as lesbians."[56] Within nine months, GRAK was publishing a newsletter, offering gay speakers, hosting a gay picnic at Otter Creek Park, and chartering the Belle of Louisville for a dance. As its name suggested, it also involved itself in political issues, including hosting mayoral candidates.

An hour east of Louisville, Lexington gays also had begun to reorganize. The Gay Services Organization formed in 1977. Arising out of the ashes of their radical past, GSO, as one early gay liberation activist remembers, "went around the basic obstacles that the GLF had encountered and cut straight to the social support."[57] In its first newsletter, published near summer's end, the group declared: "We emphasize the word services in GSO and generally avoid political involvement."[58] It had difficulties, however, organizing beyond gay males, as lesbians formed other organizations, such as Amber Moon.[59] Nevertheless, GSO expanded—sponsoring workshops, publishing the *Gayzette,* and providing a "gayline," speaker's bureau, and "rap" groups.

Forces of biblical proportion were unleashed from Bryant's hymnal box of homespun homophobia during 1977. The South's leading gay entertainment magazine, *Cruise,* observed: "Save Our Children actually may have saved the languishing Gay political movement."[60] In November, forty-seven-year-old Harvey Milk defeated a field of seventeen candidates to become the first openly gay person in San Francisco to serve on its Board of Supervisors. From the ferment of gay liberation fronts to the formation of political caucuses, gay rights displaced gay liberation. As this "born-again gay crusade" emerged out of "the wake in Miami," journalist Randy Shilts observed one activist faction as representing "little more than a regrouping and revitalization of long-active gay figures into 'mass action' coalitions."[61] In the South, this group of men included Ray Hill, Bob Basker, Jack Nichols, Milo Pyne, and Bill Rushton. The second group, according to Shilts, "has taken a softer line with an accent on lobbying, education, and other work-within-the-system techniques." Among those southern moderates were Gary Van Ooteghem, Jack Campbell, Dennis Buckland, Ron Joullian, Alan Robinson, Gil Robison, and Jim Baxter.

Although southern communities of any size were brushed by Hurricane Anita, her impact varied according to past activist history and local political contexts. On the eve of the gender wars that would divide the "gay movement" in the late seventies and early eighties along fault lines

of drag, language, and erotica, southern communities evidenced different gender alliances. In Norfolk, Birmingham, and New Orleans, lesbians
chose to participate in male-centered organizations. Some communities
with a herstory of separatism—Louisville and Atlanta—chose to align themselves temporarily with male political groups. Lexington and Houston maintained their distance as they built separate but far from equal communities.[62]
Only in Richmond did lesbians head up post-referendum protests and organizations, which soon were dominated by men. For gay activists, the
defining gay event of 1977 was Anita Bryant; for many lesbian activists,
however, it was the National Women's Conference at the Sam Houston
Coliseum. This event, too, revealed similar ideological and tactical differences
among women.

In the beginning of the year there had been no mention of lesbianism or lesbian issues in any International Women's Year literature, a
project funded by a skeptical Congress. "Eleven months later," wrote feminist Charlotte Bunch, there was "a major agenda item on sexual preference, based on resolutions that were passed in thirty states and there
are at least sixty open lesbian delegates and scores more closeted."[63]

Among these delegates (some brought to Houston by the Lesbian Freedom Ride) were Richmond's Beth Marschak, an out-lesbian delegate and
a leader in the National Women's Political Caucus, and Bobbi Weinstock,
who recently had been elected to the NGTF board. Others came not
because of their commitment to the IWY process or as NGTF supporters, but because of the event's historic nature.

Julia Penelope, who had helped lead the Nebraska platform fight
but lost the delegation battle, was there as an observer. "We had put our
bodies on the line in Lincoln for the women's platform," Julia remembers, only to come to Houston and find "a sell-out by the NGTF."
Another observer was ALFA's Vicki Gabriner. As initial plans were made
for the IWY Conference, she was sitting in the Boston courtroom of Judge
Arthur Garrity as he pronounced her sentence following a guilty verdict
in the four-year-old case of passport fraud and conspiracy to commit passport fraud stemming from her antiwar activities.

> I peer into the corners of the
> Wood paneled
> Neat clean
> Courtroom
> Searching for the
> Blood & guts
> Of the
> Viet Nam War[64]

The judge suspended her sentence with a year's probation, shallowly focusing on "form" (literally and figuratively) rather than content when he observed, "This case is serious in my view because we are a government of forms."[65] As she publicly organized around the appeal, Gabriner harbored ambivalent feelings about the Houston gathering: "[H]ow do you relate to a conference when many of the issues are 'our' issues and where at some points it seems like radical feminism is running rampant, but where in your gut you know it is not your scene?"[66] Like Julia Penelope, Vicki Gabriner underscored the importance of "doing away with the patriarchy and not trying to maneuver inside it." She asked: "Can we build a strong movement for social change in which lesbian-feminism is understood as a core issue for all people, or must we continue in some form of separatism?"[67]

When the two thousand delegates (Alabama and Mississippi sent male delegates) and another tenfold supporters arrived for the mid-November conference, it was difficult to miss half-page ads appearing in the *Houston Post* and *Houston Chronicle*. Paid for by the Pro-Family Rally (which was holding an alternate conference at the Astro arena), the advertisement depicted a pallid-looking girl with a bouquet of flowers resting on her cotton-laced dress, asking: "Mommy, when I grow up, can I be a lesbian?" Three days later hundreds of grownup lesbian delegates and observers proudly held "We Are Everywhere" balloons as Jean O'Leary, a former nun now with NGTF, introduced the sexual preference resolution to a roar of support.[68] Then a stunned audience listened as Betty Friedan, resolving a decade of controversy within the women's movement, spoke in its favor. "As someone who has grown up in Peoria and who has loved men—perhaps too well—I've had trouble with this issue. We have all made mistakes and we have all learned."[69] After the lopsided vote, helium balloons floated above the delegate heads and reporters snapped photos. As the all-white, partly male Mississippi delegation stood and turned its back to the podium, lesbians in the hall departed for a brief candlelight ceremony.

The five-foot-three-inch Pokey Anderson was responsible for these balloons, "dragging a helium tank that was five feet tall, convincing the security guard to let me into the bowels of the convention center."[70] It had been just four years since Anderson had snuck into the sexual preference workshop at the National Women's Political Caucus. This year she was one of the fifty-eight Texas delegates and had been an openly lesbian candidate for public office. Looking back on 1977, "it was exciting," she reminisces, but she adds, "My personal life went to hell! My plants died; my lover left me, and my dog had an operation. That was the year I started stacking mail up in my chair." By the end of the year it was almost as tall as Pokey.[71]

The year 1977 was indeed a watershed for lesbians and gay southerners. "After Anita spoke here," Ray Hill says, "things started coming together like they never had before."[72] On the anniversary of Anita Bryant's appearance at Scope Arena, Dennis Buckland wrote to the *Virginia-Pilot:* "We may be hidden, but we will not be legislated or voted or hated out of existence. More and more of us are beginning to speak out and be heard. I wrote you a letter expressing sentiments similar to these about a year ago, but was afraid to sign my name at that time. . . . I now feel that I must."[73] And on June 1978, Bryant's performances continued to be picketed by protesters ranging from two dozen in Wilmington, North Carolina, to eighteen hundred in Atlanta.[74] In Miami one year later, Bob Basker observed: "The day-to-day existence of gays in Dade County has *not* changed in any substantial way. . . . [However,] there was, especially immediately after the election, and continues a gay emigration out of Miami with San Francisco appearing to get first choice."[75]

Coming through New Orleans on his way to his new home in San Francisco, Basker ran into Troy Perry at the baths and picked up a flyer about a gay event in Houston. Mayor Jim McConn had proclaimed the last week of June "Human Rights Week," as Steve Shiflett, LaDonna Leake, and Ray Hill gathered thirty-five hundred people at the Astrodome for a "Town Meeting." Hill remembers its genesis: "The town meeting came about when Harvey Milk and I had this debate in Dallas. Harvey wanted to sell me on the idea of a march on Washington. I thought what we needed was a national lesbian and gay rights congress. Harvey convinced me we weren't going to get anywhere with the congress until we got it together by organizing a march; the Town Meeting was the model we had hoped to use for the congress."

On the afternoon of 25 June 1978, Sissy Farenthold, a former Texas gubernatorial candidate, delivered the keynote address at the Astrodome, which brought on a two-minute standing ovation.[76] As Basker recalls: "Speaker after speaker said, 'Thanks to Dade County we have thousands of people.' A friend turned to me and said: 'Gee, Bob, you're the god-father of this and we're in the balcony and they don't even know you're up here!'"

TWENTY-FOUR

Eyes on the Prize

I know what it means to be called a "nigger" and I know what it means to be called a "faggot," and I understand the difference in the marrow of my bones. I can sum up that difference in one word. NONE!

—*Mel Boozer*

Although a few gay men of color—Mel Boozer in D.C., Jesse Monteagudo and Ramón Muniz in Miami, Fred Paez and Larry Bagneris in Houston—were involved in political activities during this era, nonwhites were generally absent from southern corridors of gay power. In the South the only gay province for the "talented tenth" of men of color was female impersonation. And among the brightest stars during the late seventies were Hot Chocolate, Tiffany Ariagas, Emore DuBois, Jimmi Dee, Crystal Lambrasia, Sable Star, Stephanie Shippae, Tina DeVore, Lady Chablis, Shirley Senezz, Taisha Wallis, Bertha Butts, Deva Sanchez, Miss Peaches, and Lisa King.

Among their admirers was Sam Hunter, who knew he could do better than just making twelve dollars a night performing at the Patio Lounge in Greenville or five dollars an hour working at a nearby mill. As a fabric inspector, he dressed in tops with matching pants, sported long hair, and wore makeup. He enjoyed bantering with women who worked

The Miss Sam Hunter. Photo courtesy of Sam Hunter.

in his department and making "secret dates" with some male co-workers. Sam, though, wanted a career as Samantha.

By 1977, some mill dates or bar friends were kindly driving the "Miss Gay Somethang" wannabe to Atlanta, where Sam checked out various drag shows and barhopped. Walking into the Sweet Gum Head on Cheshire Bridge Road, Sam "really didn't know anybody. But I remember seeing all of these drag queens, including Rachel Wells, Charlie Brown, Hot Chocolate, and Diamond Lil." When he first spotted Tiffany Ariagas, the host of the weekly amateur female impersonation contest, "I didn't think she was a man!"

Sam watched the towering Rachel Wells, "known for her full-size hair-dos," perform Audrey Hepburn. Hot Chocolate, who had already won a major pageant, "used to come out in a gorilla costume with this African tribe who would rip it away" while she sang "Lovin' Is Really My Game." Sam learned hosting techniques from the notorious, "shit-talking" Char-lie Brown, and Crystal Lambrasia helped Sam with his makeup artistry and costumes. And, from Lisa King, the outspoken reigning Miss Atlanta, he honed skills in pantomime.

When not at the Sweet Gun Head, known as the "Showplace of the South," or across the street at the Locker Room, watching Roski Fernandez and her Hollywood Hots' extravagant Las Vegas–type productions, Sam and his friends partied at some of the nearly two dozen Atlanta gay clubs. Several catered to black gays (although these were seldom listed in bar directories, gay newspapers, or entertainment magazines).[1] The oldest black gay bar was the Marquitte on Martin Luther King Boulevard, owned by an old-line Atlanta family. Festival was a classier club in Little Five Points, offering late-night drag shows and attracting mostly uptown, business-type blacks. On Peachtree Street was Foster's, a seedy club drawing a more macho clientele. Finally, Loretta's, located near the ramshackle home of legendary author Margaret Mitchell, was the largest gay black bar, fea-turing Monday Night Madness drag shows that lasted until the early morn-ing hours. There were also several straight bars that were "open." Sam stresses: "In the black community, you couldn't hide it; they knew you were a sissy. But back then they really didn't care. It didn't matter because we were already going through a struggle enough. If you came out to have fun, you just came to have fun. If you were weird, then go onto the weird side until a guy gets ready to give you the eye to sneak out."

Within a year, Sam had tailored an attractive set of clothes, developed a more feminine appearance, and improved his theatrical skills. He was ready to compete in the Sweet Gum Head's weekly amateur drag contest.

Dressed in a gold genie jumpsuit, Samantha sang "Don't It Make My Brown Eyes Blue"—and won. Two weeks later, Samantha, with friends from South Carolina's Up Country in tow, competed in the monthly finals. Singing— not lip-syncing—the theme from *Ice Castles* ("Looking Through the Eyes of Love"), she won again. Samantha Hunter was on her way!

Meanwhile, Logan Carter was nearing the pinnacle of his career as a female impersonator. In 1977 he exhibited the work of Ronald Kolodny at Manhattan's Fashion Institute along with top women models Pat Cleveland and Iman. Noted photographer Lynn Davis snapped arty androgynous pictures of Logan Carter/Roxanne Russell, and he was featured in European fashion magazines, Italy's *Harper's Bazaar* and *Mode International* in Paris, which ran an avant-garde spread of him as both male and female.

When Logan returned to the South nearly a year later, he found many of his drag friends had become "real"; illusion had become reality. Although Logan had flirted with the idea of "becoming a woman" as a teenager walking Santa Monica Boulevard, Jack Nichols, who was still dating Logan, recollects: "He found them taking hormones, pumping their faces and bodies with silicone, and preparing to petition for transsexual surgery. In his own mind, Logan did not envision them as women. He knew them too well. He also knew that the idea of a woman's mind trapped in a man's body only made sense if one accepts an innate dichotomy between male and female—which he did not."[2]

Following his breakup with Jack, Logan moved to Atlanta in mid-1978. He found the city less fashion conscious than Florida with a greater emphasis on drag queen talent than on glamour. Twice a week he performed at the Magic Garden, four blocks down from the Sweet Gum Head. The Garden, the successor to Atlanta's hottest club, the County Seat, was one of the city's two premier nightclubs in the style of Studio One in Los Angeles. When not working the Garden's cabaret shows, the former Miss Gay Florida appeared in the South's best clubs, such as the Copa in Key West and Scorpio's in Charlotte.

It was on stars like Roxanne Russell (the "Last Southern Goddess") and Jimmi Dee (the "Diana Ross of the South"), as well as Rachel Wells (who performed a show-stopping scene from *Jesus Christ Superstar*) and Michael Andrews (the incomparable illusionist of Ann Margret), that Sam affixed his eyes. To join the new generation of southern drag stars, Sam made his next career stop a city contest. A disco/show bar had opened on Pleasantburg Drive in Greenville. The owner, Sam remembers, "didn't care too much for us black folks. But we dealt with it—like always." He recalls, "They'd still harass you or charge an extra cover." Nevertheless, Sam entered the club's pageant. For her sportswear number, Samantha dressed in a Pointer Sisters look with a wicker handbag and hat. As she sat down, a miniature poodle leaped out of her purse. And for the evening wear competition, she wore a purple satin dress with rhinestones.

Crowned Miss Stone Castle, Sam began a weekend club circuit— Greenville, Columbia, and Myrtle Beach—while working weekdays at the mill. In 1978, when Sam first appeared in the capital city, there were four gay bars in Columbia. Starlight, a block up from the state capitol, had a gay presence. Like the old Dot's Lounge on Lady Street, it was not outwardly gay. Unlike Dot's, which had been off limits to soldiers, surviving numerous MP raids during the sixties, Starlight was advertised in the *Leader,* a military newspaper. Professional men would come during late afternoons for a beer or two and chat among themselves or catch the eye of an interested Fort Jackson soldier. The main "boys' bar," though, was the End Zone, a small disco on North Main near an abandoned drive-in. Men drank from stools at the long bar or leaned against the wall, cruising. The adjacent room, covered with patio flooring, was crowded with weekend dancers.

The Fortress was on Two Notch, a road that extended from the downtown black area to the mall and white suburbs beyond. Named for its original design and location near Fort Jackson, this was a blue-collar women's bar. The entrance into this unmarked concrete block building was guarded by Joyce, the heavy-set owner with dark hair, who had supported Dale Orlando's Alliance efforts several years earlier. As customers approached, she spied them through the door's peephole. If they looked like they belonged, the door opened. The only time any lipstick-looking women were inside was during weekend drag shows—which had been decried as a "mockery of all women" by Alliance feminists—when performers like Samantha played the four-by-five stage and "the biker girls tipped like crazy."

On the lower end of Two Notch, in the heart of a poor black community, was the Manhattan Club—known by most as the Candy Shop. Although it was the oldest continuously run gay bar in the state, it never appeared in bar guides. Sam also performed at the Shop, whose owner was so impressed that he arranged for the reigning Miss Stone Castle to be chauffeured to shows in an orange stretch Cadillac. Onstage Samantha performed as Diana Ross and Grace Jones, crawling up the pole in the middle of the dance floor and seductively sliding down.

Columbia lesbians and gay men seldom mixed except for those attending MCC services in a rented white block building on the corner of Laurel and Gist.[3] Some gay and bisexual men chose to cruise the three blocks of Senate Street east of the capitol. A small group of mostly professional men, known as the Family, enjoyed covered dishes, with the host rotating monthly. And, although the bars now stayed open later, some still enjoyed after-midnight house parties, like those held by several Fort Jackson soldiers, known as the Terrace Way Gang, or another bevy of young men, the Laurel Street Gang. There were also lavish private parties, notably the seasonal ones offered by the owner of the Blossom Shop, who furnished food *and* liquor, welcoming guests into his thematically decorated residence. In addition to the pool-playing women of the Fortress, lesbians enjoyed playing softball, hosting potlucks, and attending women's concerts in Atlanta.

Arguably, the first political act in Columbia since the founding of the Alliance occurred on a June afternoon in 1978 when Peter Lee hosted an Anita Bryant Barbeque. Lee, who grew up in Aiken, had been a civil rights worker and antiwar activist throughout the sixties. As a teenager, he had worked with the NAACP and on voter registration in rural South Carolina counties and—as a conscientious objector himself—counseled military draftees at the controversial UFO coffeehouse on Columbia's Main Street. "I was typical of the white southern liberal," he modestly says. "I got involved in things, avoiding confrontations."[4]

Despite this early activism, it was several years before Peter acknowledged his homosexuality—an acknowledgment for which he gives credit, in part, to authors Lige Clarke and Jack Nichols: "*I Have More Fun with You Than Anybody* was a very significant book in my coming out. One of the things I did was to go to gay bars and people seemed to be happy. I used to go to the End Zone a lot. They didn't fit my stereotypes. Then, I just went and bought a lot of books." Peter subscribed to *GAY,* which arrived in a brown envelope. "In that process of coming out, I felt like I was connected," he recalls. Another important factor in Peter's emergence as a gay activist was the Alliance and Dale Orlando, who was open to men's involvement. Peter became active in the short-lived Alliance, hosting some of the Tuesday-evening covered-dish suppers at his Henderson Street apartment.

By the fall of 1978, however, the Alliance had long been abandoned and the MCC still attracted the more religiously oriented. Peter took a leave from his state health job to pursue a graduate degree at the University of South Carolina. In September, an ad appeared in the student newspaper, the *Gamecock,* expressing interest in forming a gay student union. Peter met the student who had placed it, suggesting that they assemble all who, like him, had responded. It was clear, however, that when this small band of would-be student activists met, "the time was not ripe."[5] Instead, they launched plans for a community-based organization.

Meeting informally at people's homes, this "temporary" group decided "it wasn't going to be an organization until we had given it some months."

Throughout the semester, as interest and enthusiasm grew, the need "to develop a supportive community of and for gay people in Columbia" emerged.[6] In January 1979, the Lambda Alliance was formally organized. Bylaws were approved and the thirty-three-year-old Lee was elected chairman.

Unlike the old Alliance, the Lambda Alliance attracted a roughly equal proportion of students and nonstudents. Many of the older lesbians and gay men, however, felt Lambda was unnecessary since, as one insists, "we didn't want to let everyone know our business." Moreover, the younger generation was either too fearful to attend meetings or too busy discoing. Lambda began a series of weekly advertisements in the *State* and *Gamecock* newspapers and, during the first eleven months, 139 letters arrived at the post office box, expressing loneliness, fear, and isolation:[7]

- I am a twenty-one-year-old female who is unsure of her sexuality. I think I am bisexual. One thing I know is that I am very lonely. . . . Could I correspond with a woman or just what can you offer me? I am full of love. I love plants, blue jeans, getting stoned, and cats.

- My lover and I are having a few problems coping with being gay in a straight world. We would like to talk to some of the organization's members and discuss each other's problems and, more importantly, make friends in the gay world since we don't have many.

- I'm eighteen years old and live in a small city so it is hard for me to come out and say, "I'm gay." I look older than eighteen and I try to act older, too. I have never made love to a man, but I would like to. . . . If you have someone in your group or someone from Sumter, ask him if he would meet me at the Post Office on July 24, at 9 P.M.

- I am now in Columbia and cannot locate the type of organizations that Houston had. We had a hot line, a listing of job vacancies, apartments available, gay doctors, dentists, libraries and books, record shops and a weekly magazine giving the activities. . . . Does Columbia have anything like this?

Columbia was not Houston. But Lambda was the first organization to aggressively reach out to homosexuals imprisoned in palmetto closets. By the spring of 1979 there were fifty dues-paying members (at its height, there were 150 on the mailing list). The two-hour Thursday-night meetings at the Unitarian Universalist parish house included educational programs. Occasionally, there were events such as wine tasting. Within a year, however, social activities dominated the calendar, as the group abandoned its organizational structure.[8]

Activists, particularly those enamored with bicoastal notions of organizing, were finding political organizing in the South difficult. However, as middle-of-the-road activists in midsize cities, like Peter Lee of Columbia and Birmingham's Ron Joullian, were learning, the social was the political. Before individuals could be mobilized politically, they had to be brought together socially. Attracting more males than females, these male-led groups were nearly all white. Black and white gay men lived in separate worlds, mirroring their de facto segregated heterosexual communities.

In the Deep South, there were predominantly black towns with traditionally black colleges like Orangeburg, South Carolina, and Tuskegee, Alabama, as well as segregated housing patterns within cities such as Atlanta and Birmingham. Even within African American communities the geography of privilege existed; for example, the "talented tenth" of families living on the Tuskegee Institute side of Bib Street. In a town made famous by Booker T. Washington's school and accommodationist philosophy, black gays assimilated into the larger community, where homosexuality was seldom discussed and the vocabulary of southern manners simply referred to "my unmarried niece" or "bachelor uncle." The absence of gay bars or gay campus groups, however, did not mean an absence of a gay lifestyle. "If you were born in Tuskegee, you'll know who is gay," explains Charles, a local gay man. "There's always a party or a gathering to go to. If you're black and gay in Tuskegee, the only reason you're not part of it is that you don't want to be part of it. The sense of community here is very strong."[9] Some who refused to maintain the cover of heterosexuality or whose private lives become public knowledge chose to move to the town's outskirts in neighborhoods like Shorter or Notasulga. And others, including Charles, relocated to Atlanta and other cities.

As the polyester decade of Studio 54, Andy Gibb, and happy-face buttons neared its ruinous end, novelist Edmund White visited Atlanta. He stayed with a male couple, one black man and one white, in southwest Atlanta. White found two gay worlds:

> I had dinner with some white friends in Atlanta, they were dying to know what black gays in Atlanta thought and did and how they lived; sadly, on the way to that dinner, my new black friends begged me to tell them later all about white gay Atlanta. . . . This is not a simple matter of cultural isolation but of deliberate exclusion. The gay bars are owned and operated by whites and the policy is to keep blacks out. . . . There are really only two or three bars where gay blacks can go and they are low-down, dangerous places, of no interest to the middle-class blacks I met.[10]

One of Edmund's hosts, Ted, with a round face "the color of French roast coffee beans with just a touch of dark rose on the innermost surface of his lower lip," also hailed from the North. He explained to White:

"When integration came to Atlanta the straight whites accepted the letter of the law . . . *scrupulously.*" One evening, Ted, who enjoyed cooking, invited other black gay friends for dinner, including William, a
community leader, who explained to Edmund: "Atlanta is a very small
town and you must be discreet. . . . You can meet people through parties and through friends. Since we don't have entrée to the bars, we
entertain at home a lot. . . . We're trying to start a Man-of-the-Month
club. One person a month in our group plans an outing to a restaurant
or a play or a picnic somewhere."[11]

Asked whether the black community was antigay, William replied: "I
visited one black church here in the city where a drag queen is very prominent. He wears full drag to church and is respected for his piety and his
good works."[12]

Another black Atlantan who was sharing her life with a white lover
during this time was Karla Brown. After arriving from Charlotte a few
years earlier to take a job—quickly withdrawn—at a record company, she
eventually found a community of supportive lesbians in the Atlanta
Lesbian Feminist Alliance as well as a nontraditional job with a major long-
distance telephone company:

> My outdoor assignments were in various areas in the South and I could
> no longer call anyplace home. Traveling, while virtually living with racist
> and sexist peers, to locations such as Columbia, South Carolina, and Hen-
> derson, North Carolina, caused me to seek strength through my feminism
> and faith. My sole focus and motivation during this period was to com-
> bat male chauvinism while achieving satisfaction in learning and conquering
> the arduous and highly physical demands of the job. Lesbianism had been
> put on the back burner, as this lifestyle did not allow time to seek out gay
> bars or to establish any meaningful relationships. It was a period where
> loneliness and virtual solitude were sacrificed for the cause of conquer-
> ing the quest for excellence in a male-dominated environment. It would
> turn out to be the most challenging and rewarding episode of my life.

When she returned to Atlanta, Karla eventually moved in with Lorraine
Fontana, another longtime ALFA member. Neither experienced "particular
difficulties" within the lesbian-feminist community. Nevertheless, as
Lorraine underscores, "We did, of course, live in a southern community
with many racist individuals and institutions." Consequently, Lorraine
continues, "finding an apartment to call our own in an integrated, or at
least biracial neighborhood (outside Atlanta's mostly segregated communities) was a tedious job." For Karla, however, being black in a mostly
white community was no different from her experiences in Charlotte.

"Before I moved to Atlanta I lived in basically a white area; it wasn't a big deal."

Karla Brown was uninvolved in Atlanta's sizable African American community or its undersized homosexual underground. The only bars she visited were the Tower or Garbo's, and she rarely associated with other blacks except at her job. "I gained my identity as a lesbian in North Carolina and as a lesbian-feminist in Atlanta. But I had lost my identity as a black woman."

Lorraine Fontana eventually departed for Los Angeles to attend law school; Karla joined her several months later. "It was like starting over and *really* getting to know myself," Karla says. "It was the first time I had really been in a black lesbian environment"—an experience that began when a friend of Lorraine's noticed an announcement about a black women's meeting. Starting out as a rap group, Lesbians of Color emerged with Karla assuming a leadership role. Members discussed their identities and differences within lesbian-feminism, and their activities ranged from speakers on issues like parenting and financial management to house party fundraisers and pride marches. "It was about trying to identify for ourselves," Karla recalls. "What kind of space we needed and why we needed it. It really felt great since I hadn't spent hardly any time with a group of black women. There were so many things of my culture that we could identify with that I had virtually lost; simple things like what we ate: collard greens, sweet potatoes, ham hocks."

No such lesbian-of-color group existed or emerged in Atlanta during this period. Brown suggests:

> Being predominantly a black community, Atlanta was very tricky—particularly for a black woman—to come out and to do other things as well. In most cases, black lesbian women were very closeted, just so that they could live. Black homosexuals know it is not accepted by the church—which is our roots—so if there is an organist or other person in the church who is gay, it is just *not* talked about. As long as you don't bring it up and don't make anything out of it, then you're okay. But they don't want you agitating.[13]

But agitating was precisely what Sam Hunter was doing—within the white community. On 3 July 1979 nearly six hundred mostly gay white men entered the Myrtle Beach Civic Center for the Miss South Carolina Pageant. Sam and eight young men from his hometown had spent months rehearsing. "My sister, Mary, would be cooking out and Tammy Tonya, my little niece, was out there dancing. We were all sewing costumes together." Although he simply hoped to do well, "I didn't think

I was going to win because of me being black. Back then, if it was white it was right; black queens were there only to add a little color to the show. A lot of times the contests were rigged so the black queens wouldn't win. But my dancers were my backbone. They said, 'We're going to turn this place out!'"

The pageant is competitive. Charice Nicole from Florence walks out in a chiffon dress. As she saunters down the runway, her cape opens and doves fly out. The crowd gasps. Sam, now Samantha, dressed in a white-lace gown with matching shoes and gloves, exclaims: "Oh, my God! You ain't goin' to get nothing."

For the sportswear competition, Samantha parades a tight skirt, jacket, and a scarf fashioned from tangerine spandex fabric given by women in the mill. Opening her purse, she pulls out a circular fan. Snap! A giant brim hat appears. The audience applauds wildly.

For the talent event, Carla St. Clair, representing McB's, a disco just opened in Columbia, mimes Dolly Parton's "Two Doors Down." Next, Angela Dee, sponsored by the Fortress, appears as Diana Ross, dressed in a patchwork denim suit. Then it's Samantha's turn. Wearing a rose-red rhinestone dress crafted by Sam and his mother, Samantha sings "No One Gets the Prize" from Diana Ross's *The Boss*. In this lyric story of betrayal and love, eight hometown boys dressed in club clothes dance around her. The seven-minute performance climaxes with a fight as Samantha draws a dagger to herself. The boys, returning with white jackets and black pants, crowd over her. An apparently naked Samantha (in a full body suit) is whisked away. The audience edges out of control.

Finally, the judges confer. The contestants narrow to three. A still crowd listens as second runner-up is announced: "Carla St. Clair." Gasps punctuate the momentary silence before the applause begins. Two black queens remain center stage. Angela Dee scores highest in sportswear, interview, and evening gown; Samantha trails behind her by a few points but exceeds her in the talent section. "First runner-up goes to . . . Angela Lee!" The crown is set on Samantha's head.

As the audience begins to file out, several white bar owners huddle in the lobby, including the owner of McB's. According to Samantha, "He was yelling out stuff. I know I heard 'nigger.' He walked up to the host, who had been the last year's Miss South Carolina, and said, 'You'll never work in my damn bar again, you hear me, bitch!'"

Meanwhile, Sam caught the "evil eye" of the white queen in waiting, Carla St. Clair: "I didn't care. I knew she wasn't going to bother me! I had all my black boys who'd tear her ass up. They didn't care and they were just goin' on: 'You white-girl bitch.' We left that redneck jealous queen behind." Sam phoned his mother. He screamed: "Mamma, I won!"

In his hometown of Odum there was celebration. Fourth of July cookouts were doubly special that year, as Sam Hunter's family and the families of Samantha's boy dancers cheered the first black Miss Gay South Carolina.

Racism was not unique to the South Carolina pageants. Lisa King had started performing while an African American accounting student at Florida State. This former Miss Atlanta bluntly told one gay entertainment magazine at the time: "I don't think most of them [pageants] are fair. I think a lot of them involve bar politics."[14] King found herself placing first or second runner-up to whites in major pageants. But, like Samantha, Lisa felt that "no matter how much you may know that is going wrong, there's still something in your head that says, 'I can win it.' "[15] And, like Samantha, she found the "bars would only hire so many blacks. There's a certain quota, you know. You have to have at least one for sure in your show."[16]

Quotas were also in place at many of the more popular gay clubs. Throughout the seventies, bars—south and north of the Mason-Dixon Line—restricted the entry of customers of color and enforced dress codes for women. Lost and Found opened in the fall of 1971 in a black area of southeast Washington. Behind each of the one-hundred-foot bars were bartenders wearing red, white, and blue T-shirts; hundreds of mostly white gay men danced on the large dance floor or enjoyed a meal in the glass-partitioned dining area. Its manager was candid about the club's restricted policies: "This is a southern city. If possible, we would prefer to exclude all black people."[17] Instead, the club simply insisted on *both* a driver's license and either a passport or birth certificate from potential customers of color. In a meeting with Gay Activist Alliance leaders, the message was blunt: "Black people are generally poor and, besides, most of our patrons are bigots." This policy was changed as weekend picket lines grew and D.C. activists formed the Open Gay Bars Committee.[18]

Five years later Houston's Old Plantation (formerly the Bayou Landing), with " 'sensurround' and the comfortably plastic feel of a gay Disneyland," routinely enforced dress codes for women and restricted access to those other than white, masculine-appearing homosexuals.[19] When four feminists from the *Pointblank Times* checked out the scene—one wearing a dress, one a pantsuit, and two blue-jeans—they were told by the manager that the old Bayous Landing "had been troubled by big bull dykes" and the new club wanted an "All-American, clean cut crowd."[20] Further, the restriction against men wearing feminine attire or hats and requiring three IDs for blacks was admittedly designed "to keep out all but a very few blacks, the nice ones." Although the Gay Political Caucus hosted a forum where both bar owners and patrons could discuss these issues, the practices continued.[21]

Unlike Washington or Houston, midseventies Columbia had no gay organizations. In this outland of gay life, however, segregation was not imposed; it was understood. "Roger Simmons," an undergraduate majoring in English, remembers that "being gay then didn't go beyond drinking, having fun, and hopefully having sex." With his white gay friends, Roger ventured to the disco-blaring End Zone; with other gay blacks, he went to the Candy Shop, crowded with hustlers, transvestites, pimps, and day workers. "In Columbia, the racial lines of demarcation of the gay community were very clear."[22] Although neither bar enforced dress codes or demanded excessive identification, whites disliked the Shop and blacks felt uncomfortable at the Zone. Roger spells out: "Aside from the regular DJs, you could count blacks at the Zone on your hand. Black gays, for the most part, were looking for other black men. If they weren't there, then why go? And, if you get a cold shoulder or you don't get any dances or no invitations, then why go? Donna Summer and Abba also played at the Zone. They wouldn't play Abba at the Shop! It was much more R&B dance tunes and remixes of those standard songs, from Diana Ross to Grace Jones."

When black gay men like Roger Simmons wanted a spacious dance club, he and his friends took a road trip to Charlotte's Scorpio Discothèque or to the Lion's Den in Charleston. For those professional black men who were uncomfortable frequenting "the darkness, secretness, and furtiveness of the Shop," discoing to Anglicized black music at the Zone, or traveling for a boogie night of drunkenness and depravity, there were private house parties as well as ostensibly straight clubs such as the Fireplace Lounge near Allen University with quiet, if not intimate, conversation.

Most difficulties experienced by gays of color at bars were at those owned by heterosexuals, corporate chains, or gay businessmen with little political commitment.[23] However, some bars operated by individuals active in the gay rights movement also faced charges of racial discrimination.[24] The College Cue, for example, in Norfolk, enforced a "drink in your hand" policy, according to its owner, to comply with state alcohol requirements. Along with a majority black presence at the Cue "there is an air of prejudice that prevails," wrote one regular black patron.[25] Another regular observed:

> Gays still have racist attitudes within the Gay community. Here in Norfolk, there is living proof of that racism. The white Gay bar owners treat

Black Gays differently from whites. They charge us a higher admission price, often allowing white Gays to come into the clubs for free while charging Black Gays. They ask Black Gays for many ID's while whites are hardly ever hassled. The word "capacity" has become a newly-used word for bar owners to keep out Blacks.[26]

More than a decade would pass after black drag queens led the Stonewall rebellion, however, before middle-class black gay men began challenging white leadership in the gay movement, racist attitudes within queer communities, and homophobia within communities of color. Hal Carter, a twenty-four-year-old social work student at Norfolk State, declared: "We as Black Gays have sat on our asses too long and allowed the homophobic Black community and racist white Gay community to drop shit on our heads. The time is right for change."[27] Affiliating with the National Coalition of Black Gays, UMOJA-UNITY formed in Norfolk. Similarly, in Memphis, Joe Calhoun organized the Memphis Committee, which effectively picketed Marshall Street clubs like 10 N. Cleveland. Calhoun later cofounded a local chapter of Black and White Men Together, with other chapters forming in southern cities like Atlanta and Houston as well as smaller towns like Raleigh-Durham. And, in Atlanta, Greg Worthy formed the Gay Atlanta Minorities Association following his experience at an Anita Bryant protest march: "I was walking down the street holding the hands of blacks, whites, and lesbians. I thought at long last gay unity. Then I was invited to a party after the march, and everyone at the party went to Backstreet when it broke up. I was not able to get in. It then hit me that gay unity was not real. . . . Blacks are good enough to entertain but not be patrons."[28]

Clearly, growing up "colored and queer" posed unique challenges in the South, as Roger Simmons had learned when as a child he moved from his aunt's brownstone apartment in northeast District of Columbia to the rural outskirts of Orangeburg County in 1968. White and colored water fountains had disappeared from downtown Orangeburg but race and skin color still mattered. Although Roger watched Saturday-afternoon movies with his friends in the theater's fifteen-cent-admission balcony, this light-skinned ten-year-old found himself "suspect" among his darker peers. "I remember feeling quite aware of my blackness and the hue of blackness because of the history of that kind of consciousness here." This was also the time of Roger's sexual awakening. Attending an integrated school, he hung out more with the whites than the blacks, read novels by Gordon Merrick and James Baldwin, and pored over a *Life* magazine story on gay liberation. "The people who were photographed and quoted were white;

there was no indication that there was an African American component or race element to the gay movement."

Like Roger, Mel Boozer was brought up with southern expectations for sexual propriety and racial boundaries.[29] Mel also had grown up in the District of Columbia and remained closeted until adulthood. The salutatorian at Dunbar High School, a colonel in the student cadet corps, and an usher in his family's AME Zion Church, Boozer had won a scholarship to Dartmouth, becoming one of three Negroes admitted during the year of the Birmingham bus boycott and the March on Washington. Although he had known since childhood he was attracted to males, being in an all-male college and black meant that his absence of heterosexual dating practices went unnoticed.

As adults, both Roger and Mel enjoyed going to all-black gay house parties, and they were comfortable interacting with white gay men.[30] Their paths, however, veered dramatically in 1978. As the Lambda Alliance was forming in South Carolina, Roger Simmons renounced his homosexual past and joined an evangelical church. Mel Boozer, teaching at the University of Maryland, joined the Gay Activist Alliance and assumed leadership in this previously white-led, influential Washington group. In the fall of 1979, GAA persuaded gay bar owners to support a local ordinance prohibiting "carding." One year later, at the 1980 Democratic National Convention, Mel Boozer became the first openly gay candidate for the party's vice-presidential nomination.[31]

As the gay rights movement entered its fourth decade and queers of color began organizing, writing, and building coalitions, Boozer continued to spread the gospel of unity through diversity. He told fellow activists in Norfolk: "Movement groups are white dominated. They always have been and they aren't going to stop for a while. That doesn't mean that you take your marbles and go home and sulk. . . . You can't get white males to do other people's work. And there is a need for black groups and there is a need for women's groups. . . . So I can see people forming their own groups and people forming groups together and having complimentary kinds of impact."[32]

Nowhere would this be more evident than in the first March on Washington.

TWENTY-FIVE

A Gathering of Tribes

*In the transition from a movement for liberation to a pressure group
for civil rights, might the gay movement lose its soul?* —Dennis Altman

About twenty-five lesbians and gay men from Kentucky arrived in Washington the weekend of 12 October 1979. Checking into an overpriced Holiday Inn, the group at first was "hesitant to wear our buttons and other 'obvious' signs—as if they were really necessary to distinguish us [since] most of us looked like Christmas trees with our keys, earrings, lambda necklaces, and handkerchiefs."[1]

Anxiety soon changed to pride as tens of thousands of citizen marchers enjoyed the excitement of the capital, which was bustling with queer activities. Friday night there was a women-only concert featuring Maxine Feldman and Judy Regan. The next morning there was a gay business breakfast and an all-day sports expo, as well as a daylong meeting of parents and friends of gays. That evening lesbian comedian and activist Robin Tyler emceed a three-hour public concert under the stars. Ten thousand people, gathering near the foot of the Washington Monument, laughed as Tyler

March on Washington, 1979. Photo courtesy of
International Gay and Lesbian Archives, Southern Studies Collection.

quipped: "I don't know how I, a lesbian, am supposed to stand here and face the Washington Monument . . . you better believe I don't have penis envy!"[2] They held hands and embraced as they listened to Meg Christian, Linda Tillery, and Lynn Frizzel—who sang "Hurricane Anita." Following the concert, there was a women-only dance at the Blue Room of the Shoreham Americana Hotel, a third-world disco party at Harambee House on Georgia Avenue, and Les Ballets Trockadero de Monte Carlo, a twenty-dollar-a-head benefit sponsored by the Gertrude Stein Democratic Club.

That weekend the manager of the Lost and Found, one of the city's largest dance clubs, was glad he'd added extra help and doubled his weekend liquor and beer order. Across town, Levi's-leather men jammed into the D.C. Eagle; mostly blacks gathered at the Brass Rail or Nob Hill; there were cruisy collegiates partying at the Fraternity House; and the disco boogiers hung out at the Pier, while bar-oriented women could be found drinking at either Tess's or Phase One. And—perhaps ignoring Robin Tyler's line, "Remember our motto: out of the steambaths, into the streets"— gay men crowded into the Olympic Baths, across from McPherson Square, as well as Astoria Arms and Club East III.

As the Kentucky group was about to participate in the March on Washington for Lesbian and Gay Rights and step into the parade, they heard a singer bellow out "Give me that old lesbianism!" to the tune of "That Old-Time Religion." Meanwhile, a group of Virginians hoisted a fifteen-foot banner, "Lesbians and Gay Men of the Tidewater." Although *Our Own Community Press* now had a separate "Lesbians—Front and Center" section as well as another for "Menspace," the women and men marched together. They joined forces with others from Virginia Tech, Lambda Alliance of Williamsburg, and the Virginia Coalition for Lesbian and Gay Rights. Jack Maurizzi, the founder of Norfolk's first motorcycle club, carried a violet-colored flag. He didn't wear his leather. "Everybody was so neat and orderly," he remembers. "There were no drags, except for one who was dressed as the Statue of Liberty."

Atlanta lesbians and gay men marched separately. They had, however, worked in an ad hoc coalition group, the Committee for the March on Washington. Margo George, who participated in the first planning meeting in Philadelphia eight months earlier, was one of the local March organizers (along with Gil Robison).[3] The Georgians had arrived in several chartered buses that Saturday morning. Throughout the night, Margo and the other lesbians on board one of these "sang Motown songs, danced in the aisles, and generally had a great time."

As part of the lesbian strategy of March visibility, many women's groups banded together. ALFA members were near the beginning of the parade. Joining this larger female contingent was the National Gay Task Force with its banner. Pokey Anderson, hand-in-hand with an ex–girl friend and layered with flannel shirt and blazer, was among those women. She still recalls the feeling of solidarity that extended from the streets to the subways that were "taken over by rowdy queers, chanting, smiling, carrying signs, wearing buttons and sometimes unique parade regalia. Everybody was friendly and high energy. It was fabulous to be in the majority, even if only for a few hours. Even the long escalators coming up from the subway were great—you could look down and see an unending stream of gay people. People cheering across the tracks: 'What do you want?' 'Equality!' 'When do you want it?' 'Now!'"[4]

The imagery of a rainbow people shouting cheers and chants of solidarity, however, cloaked divisions within the "gay community." In fact, there were profound differences between lesbians and gay men as well as between religious and nonreligious types, between whites and persons of color, between faerie men and blue-denim politicos, among those with varying degrees of affluence, between those in Levi's-leather and drag queens, and between those—like the original March organizers—with roots in gay liberation and revolutionary visions and a new generation of leaders dedicated to advancing the gay agenda within the system.[5]

Rita Wanstrom had chosen not to participate in the March based on her experience at the second national planning meeting, which had been held the previous July in Houston.[6] Wanstrom, the longtime owner of the Roaring Sixties, felt that gay men had changed little since the vice-president of the old Promethean Society had been picked up in the men's room of the Auditorium Hotel. Rita, though, had become more religious since her childhood girlfriend, Millie, reentered her life four years earlier. Wanstrom conducted worship ceremonies at the Metropolitan Community Church of the Resurrection while taking correspondence courses for the ministry. But, as she prepared to sign her final MCC papers in 1978, she asked if the mostly male clergy had become more committed "about having ethical standards." She was told: "We can't tell people how to live." Incensed, she folded her papers and formed the Agape Church.

In the South, differences between lesbians and gay men had become most visible during the third Southeastern conference held in Atlanta on April Fool's Day weekend, 1978.[7] "While unity is the end goal of the conference," wrote an ALFA member, "the process towards that end has been far from united."[8] Problems included differences in voting process

(Roberts Rules vs. consensus), types of entertainment (big name/large scale vs. local/small scale), and keynote speakers (nationally known mainstream vs. regionally known progressive).

Nevertheless, planning was viewed by many as an opportunity to bridge "longstanding different views on the world that have served to keep gay men and gay women apart."[9] Over the years, Margo George and several other southern lesbians had persistently and skillfully worked with gay men on joint events ranging from pride parades to Anita Bryant protests. "In terms of building coalitions," she observes, "that sort of southern ability to have 'manners' made it easier to organize people and to let people be heard—not simply steamroll over them." In the process of developing these working coalitions, however, George and others had no illusions as to the depth of difference between lesbians and gay men:

> In Atlanta a lot of the lesbians who were active in ALFA and the Atlanta Socialist Feminist Women's Union perceived the entire organized gay male community as being very conservative: having as a goal acceptance and nondiscrimination—and not going beyond that. There was also the perception that many of them were much better off than we were financially and their views were colored by their class status and race. This divide along gender lines also really masked important philosophical and ideological differences. These really never got talked about. . . . It was pretty much finessed in order to hold the coalition together.

Although George was unable to participate in the planning for the 1978 conference, specific logistical, procedural, or program differences were often bridged in small committees. Large meetings, however, proved difficult. Four months before the scheduled conference it was no longer possible to finesse differences as men representing Dignity, Lutherans Concerned, and Integrity challenged "exclusionary workshops." When the more progressive men allied with the women to form a majority, those from the religious groups stormed out, announcing a boycott of the event.[10]

Despite these problems, about six hundred persons attended the renamed Southeastern Conference of Lesbians and Gay Men. The opening speaker was Jill Raymond, who had been working with the ACLU prison project after serving fourteen months for refusing to testify before the Lexington grand jury. Vicki Gabriner spoke at the general session the next morning. She had recently heard (on Susan B. Anthony's birthday) from her lawyer that a three-judge panel had unanimously reversed her 1977 conviction. Although "no longer a convicted felon, but just one of your garden-variety outlaw dykes," Vicki reminded ALFA newsletter readers a month before the conference that "there are lots of sisters still in prison or being persecuted by the government who continue to need our support." For her, "the whole experience has deepened my commitment to building a community and a movement that will bring a much larger victory to us all."[11] In her address to the conference, Vicki underscored this commitment to community, emphasizing the conference organizers' anguish in holding the event in a nonratified ERA state. She reached out to gay men in the audience, challenging them to view support of the amendment as "an opportunity to speak for the woman inside each of you."[12]

Like Vicki Gabriner, speakers at the March on Washington also tried to bridge a diversity, here evidenced in a sea of banners, T-shirts, buttons, and placards: "Gay Love is Good Love," "We Are Revolting," "I Support My Daughter's Choice," "Lesbian, Amazon and Proud," "Don't Die Wondering," "Gay and Lesbian Power—Not Nuclear Power," "Supporting Affirmative Action," "Piss on Anita," "We Don't Need Laws for Us, Remove the Laws Against Us." Howard Wallace, a candidate for San Francisco city office who had led the Miami Gay Support Committee, reminded the crowd: "We are family." Betty Santora of Lesbian Feminist Liberation proclaimed: "As we move into the next decade, we move with the force and energy of a united people." But leading this multitude—variously estimated at from twenty-five thousand (Park Police) to one hundred thousand (NGTF)—were women, followed by the physically challenged, children and aged, regional delegations, and national organizations. Marchers declared affiliations ranging from the Metropolitan Community Church to the Gay Atheist League of America, from Levi's-leather motorcycle clubs to the radical faeries, from the Lesberadas to the Gertrude Stein Society, from gay farm workers to gay teachers.

The South Florida contingent, numbering about fifty, marched in the great middle, as did its leader Jack Campbell, accompanied by other veterans of the Dade County referendum, including Jesse Monteagudo and representatives from South Florida MCCs, Congregation Etz Chaim, *TWN* newspaper, and the Stonewall Library. There, too, were another two hundred from Jacksonville, Orlando, Tampa Bay, and Tallahassee. Men and women of the Sunshine State stepped out into the parade with a hand-sewn Florida banner waving as two black women led the group, chanting: "Hey! Hey! Ho! Ho! Anita Bryant has got to go!" Crowds five deep on either side yelled back: "Gay Power!"

Jesse Monteagudo, the titular head of Latinos pro Derechos Humanos, had just come from the concurrently running Third World Conference of Lesbians and Gays held at Harambee House (Swahili for "unity"). The conference was sponsored by the National Coalition of Black Lesbians and Gay Men, whose cochairs, Louis Hughes and Darlene Gamer, were the prime organizers.[13] "It was important to us that blacks be visible in the National March," stresses Gamer. "It was even more important that the voices of people of color have a forum where we could speak and be heard without censure"—a rare event since Stonewall.[14] "When I came out in 1973," Jesse wrote in Miami's gay paper, *TWN,* "Latin involvement in the Gay scene was limited to the bars, as was the entire community, for that matter." He continued: "Six years later this still holds true for Latins." This lack of participation was due, Monteagudo explained, to two factors: "extreme homophobia in the Latin community" and "the patronization verging on bigotry on the part of the White Gays."[15]

On that chilly Sunday morning there were banners representing a diversity of racial and ethnic groups. White faces and voices, however, dominated the limited mainstream newspaper coverage. Ray Hill, cochair of the March coordinating committee, was one of those voices. Wearing his old jailhouse trustee's coveralls, he reminded the crowd of the thousands imprisoned, unable to attend. In his introduction of beat poet Allen Ginsberg, Hill momentarily fell silent, jarred by a background of seemingly endless human legions of a rainbow people, with "wheel chairs and people with crutches" in the foreground.[16]

Pictures taken of the disabled, the elderly, and minorities, however, were not representative of southern leadership that emerged following the demise of gay liberation. By 1979, lobbying for gay rights had long drowned out shouts of gay power. In Houston, the president of the Gay Political Caucus was now Steve Shiflett. Like his predecessor, Gary Van Ooteghem, he was "conciliation in a three piece suit."[17] Atlanta's First Tuesday Association (which published the *Healthy Closet* newsletter) was led by Gil Robison, who had been elected to the Fulton County Democratic Party Executive Committee. Another Democratic stalwart, Jack Campbell, had just been reelected president of the Dade County Coalition for Human Rights. Meanwhile, in New Orleans, the Gertrude Stein Society birthed the Louisiana Gay Political Action Caucus (LAGPAC). Alan Robinson, an accountant who had narrowly lost in his bid to become the first openly gay representative on Louisiana's Democratic State Central Committee, underscored: "We are coming up with a group of people who want to work in the political system."[18]

Just as homosexual delegations lobbied Washington legislators the Monday following the March, this generation of new southerners courted local officials during the late seventies. From Houston to Richmond, activists endorsed gay-friendly politicians, lobbied for human rights ordinances, and marshaled legal support. Though not always successful in reaching immediate goals, they laid political infrastructure and established working relationships among heterosexual power brokers thought to be essential on the long march toward equality.

In February 1978, for example, the Richmond Gay Rights Association had been formed. Bruce Garnett, its twenty-eight-year-old leader sought inclusion of sexual orientation in a human rights ordinance working its way through the Richmond Commission on Human Relations. Collaborating with the Gay Rights Association were the local Women's Political Caucus, headed by Beth Marschak, and the Virginia Coalition for Lesbian and Gay Rights, co-chaired by NGTF board member Barbara Weinstock and Stephan Lenton, founder of Gay Awareness in Perspective. During the next fifteen months—as voters were rescinding similar ordinances elsewhere—the Richmond community was drawn into a heated debate. Despite the commission's approval, the ordinance met stiff opposition from religious leaders, local newspaper editors, and businessmen, who helped engineer its defeat in City Council.[19]

Texans constituted the largest southern delegation to the March on Washington. Numbering nearly a thousand, they paraded down Pennsylvania Avenue led by the Montrose Marching Band and followed by marchers twelve across and eight deep carrying Lone Star flags. Steve Shiflett, spearheading an effort to oust longtime homophobic city councilman Frank Mann in the fall election, was among this crowd.[20] Although Shiflett had "ostracized" lesbians and racial minorities, he had developed a formidable political organization with a mailing list topping fourteen thousand. Ten days after the March, the *Houston Post* announced, "Homosexual Voices Gaining Volume in America," and the next month Mann lost, realizing Shiflett's boast—"We can put anyone in office we want because of the strength of our voting bloc."[21]

If Stonewall was the match that ignited gay power, then Hurricane Anita had fanned gay rights fires from Texas to the Carolinas. Marching near the delegation from Birmingham, Mobile, Anniston, and Montgomery, which carried a red and yellow "ALABAMA" banner, was a contingent of two dozen Tarheels. Among these North Carolinians was Jim Baxter, a young man who had written the column "On Being Gay" for a Greensboro alternative paper five years before and who would soon become the first editor of the *Front Page*. Jim walked alongside a rainbow-colored banner with bold black "NC" letters. Only three months earlier, his boss, Art Sperry, an advertising executive, together with six other men had formed the North Carolina

Human Rights Fund in response to the arrest and conviction of a gay man for solicitation.[22] Although the Fund soon expanded into educational and electoral areas, it would long maintain a low profile. In contrast to their openness that October Sunday, Baxter remembers that "it seemed possible, for a while anyway, that a group of closeted individuals could do some good without taking any personal risks."[23] And, as shouts of approval rang out from onlookers who spotted the Charlotte marchers' "Queen City" placard, Jim Baxter remembers the "feeling of exhilaration! The community, this movement, of ours was *real!* It was actually *happening.*"

Not all activists, however, were comfortable with this New South activism or this euphoric proclamation of community. Faygele ben Miriam, who had been active in the Elwha commune that published early issues of *RFD,* had moved home to Efland, North Carolina, to manage a changing magazine. Various faerie collectives of gay men from the mountains of Tennessee to the Delta bayous were now assembling issues with greater emphasis on "effeminism," faerie consciousness, and eco-politics. Challenging the superiority often advanced by the "urban politico" or apolitical "sex-seeking Castro Street queens," Faygele—Yiddish for "faggot"—acknowledged that "*RFD* has not dealt with very many 'political' issues, but for the many isolated faggots for whom we represent a first link . . . I'm glad we exist."[24]

Joining Faygele at the March on Washington were other *RFD* contributors, some of whom had attended the heady Spiritual Conference for Radical Faeries near Tucson six weeks earlier. Marching with the Louisiana Sissies in Struggle (LASIS), who wielded "Stop Rape" signs, was Phillip Pendleton, the cofounder with Jim Baxter of the Guilford Gay Alliance. "I saw faggots as a separate group from more assimilationist, civil rights focused gay men. No one I knew went to lobby Congress the next day. Our goal was to overthrow the government, not enter into dialogue with it!"[25]

Since *RFD*'s founding in 1974, the "country journal for gay men everywhere" had networked like-minded "faggots" into a faerie community contoured by anarcho-effeminism with sunflower borders. One of those was Milo Pyne, whose personal evolution had "reached a seemingly dead end" when the mostly heterosexual hippie commune members had abandoned Short Mountain. There had been few responses to Milo's invitation in *RFD* for gay men to come to the mountain. Nevertheless, he had begun "to create my visions through reconnection to faerie gay men in the Southeast in an attempt to evolve a faerie communal experience." In his search, Pyne had attended the gender-polarized Atlanta Southeastern

Conference of Lesbians and Gay Men in the spring of 1978. "Out of this came the offer of a remote farm in the North Carolina mountains which could be used for gatherings of faerie men." That June, thirty-three "sissies/faggots/gay men from the Southeast" sat in a morning circle down the hill from the ramshackle cabin of Running Water to "talk of community, of gay men coming together; of the land . . . of *RFD* that needed a home."[26] This event was the first of many gatherings on the solstices or equinoxes as Faygele, Milo Pyne, Ron Lambe, and others worked hard to continue *RFD*.

Louisiana Sissies had attended these faerie gatherings and were among the Washington marchers. One of these "angry faggots still burning with the rage of our oppression" was Dennis Melba'son, who had moved from Fayetteville, Arkansas, in 1977.[27]

Like Milo Pyne, Melba'son was living in a mostly heterosexual commune in central Arkansas before it "fell apart" in 1974. Dennis, as he tells it, then attended the Iowa City gay conference, where he experienced "a three-day acid trip of just energy" with other rural faggots, including the founders of *RFD*. "I returned to Fayetteville with that kind of awareness. . . . A vision had been opened up."[28] Sharing his vision with other gay men at George's, the local gay bar, Melba'son and a small band of like-minded faeries rented a house in this college town. By 1977, however, the difficulties of living as "angry faggots" peaked when rocks crashed through the window and someone placed an ad on a local community bulletin board: "Save Energy, Burn a Faggot." Melba'son "just got out on the highway and put my thumb out and ended in New Orleans."[29] He later wrote to *RFD* readers: "There is a strong need for sissies to be everywhere—in the country reclaiming shaman magik, returning to growing our food, worshiping the goddesses, building our structures; in the cities reaching out to sissies trapped there, providing a strong sissies political presence to support our sisters and counter the macho men who dominate 'gay politics.'"[30]

Forming the Pink Triangle Alliance in May of 1978, the Louisiana Sissies organized the city's first gay pride rally. They brought a queer presence to a gay community bounded by the mainstream politics of Gertrude Stein and LAGPAC, the newspaper coverage of *Impact,* a coterie of gay bars within the French Quarter, Uptown homosexuals, and a handful of gay businesses in the slowly gentrified area east of the Quarter. Melba'son, a forty-six-year-old former civil rights worker, led picketing of bars known for racist and sexist policies, appeared at ERA and anti-Klan rallies, and wrote a monthly column for the local gay newspaper. These activities, of course, were not without controversy, including public quarrels with

Impact's editor, who red-lined words like "faggot," and those annoyed by sissy ambivalence toward transgender persons.[31] In response, Melba'son wrote in *Impact:* "Transvestites and Transsexuals I know here are poor sissies who hustle Bourbon Street in high drag in order to survive. No het and no gay business would hire them. . . . As a sissy, I feel their pain. As an Effeminist, I struggle with the contradictions. For, of course, my sissy friends on Bourbon Street are oppressive to women. . . .[But] I know of no guerrilla theater more shocking to the heterosexual tourist."[32]

Transgender activist Phyllis Randolph Frye had experienced such discrimination in Houston's heterosexual engineering profession as well as felt marginalized within the "gay movement." She had participated in the March planning meeting in Houston but was "bitterly disappointed" with its chosen theme: "An end to all social, economic, judicial, and legal oppression of lesbian and gay people." When "'gay' was defined or expanded out to 'lesbian and gay' then I felt excluded," she explains.[33] Phyllis tried to convince the group to include "transgender rights and got thoroughly trashed."[34] It was, though, an issue that found no consensus, particularly within the women's caucus meeting, during which "a wide spectrum of feelings were expressed ranging from women who strongly supported Phyllis and other transpeople," noted one in attendance, "to those who felt she had no place at the women's caucus."[35] Although transgender was not included in the March title or as part of the March demands, Phyllis helped organize the local MCC charter bus and quickly took her place in front of the Texas delegation, carrying the U.S. flag with a Bible in her other hand.

Julia Penelope, who was still teaching in Nebraska and who "never supported or endorsed the gay (men's) agenda—assimilation," did not participate in the planning meetings or attend the March. "Adding 'lesbian/gay' politics never fooled anyone! Gay men have always 'included' lesbians not on lesbian terms but on *their* terms."[36] For Penelope, like some of the women participating in that Saturday morning caucus discussion, male-to-female transsexuals represented the most visible challenge to women-only space.

Political alchemists—Campbell, Van Ooteghem, Robinson, Matlovich, Shiflett, Garnett, Robison, and others—transmuted gay power into gay rights. As the decade neared its long-overdue end—"falling over dead for the lack of interest"—faggot revolutionaries, lesbian-separatists, and transgender warriors had been relegated to the political closet.[37] While Stonewall had been elevated to iconographic status, the early struggles of southerners who organized in the belly of the beast known as

"Amerika"—distributing rabid broadsides like *Trash* and *Sunflower,* writing gender-fucking articles in *GAY* and *RFD,* forming groups like the Triangle Gay Alliance and Knoxville Lesbian Feminists, calling to arms a convention of "gay militants" in Athens, publishing incisive analyses in *Sinister Wisdom,* cutting sugar cane in Cuba—appeared immaterial for a new generation reading glossy magazines such as the *Advocate,* touting the inevitable progress of the "gay movement" while advertising weekend packages to the Marlin Beach Hotel. Nevertheless, Karla Jay insisted, in an essay appearing in the March on Washington Souvenir Program, that "by supporting and being part of the lesbian and/or gay male culture, you and I will prevent ourselves from becoming co-opted. . . . Our goal is not to see one lesbian pursuing another across a field to advertise some product like hair coloring but to create a world in which hair coloring is not the basis for pursuit."[38]

Activist Jack Nichols—a human bridge from the Boys in the Band to the Village People—marched that October with Perrin Shaffer, one of the ten women and men who had followed his lead at the first protest march at the White House fourteen years earlier. Remembering that historic event, Jack recalled how his lover, Lige Clarke, had lettered nine picket signs, and how, later, in 1970, both he and Lige had joined thousands of other marchers in New York's Sheep's Meadow celebrating the first anniversary of Stonewall. Following Lige's murder, Jack had marched again in the seventh Manhattan parade, this time with his second lover, Logan Carter. Both Lige and Logan, now the reigning Miss Gay Universe, promoted a new definition of masculinity, inspiring Nichols as he wrote and made minor revisions in his major work, *Men's Liberation.*[39]

For most homosexual southerners, the tenth-year anniversary of Stonewall, however, was an occasion to celebrate, not to protest. Since Stonewall, twenty-four states had repealed sodomy statutes, with several more, including Texas, reducing sodomy to a misdemeanor; 125 of the nation's largest corporations had pledged nonbiased employment policies; fifty cities and counties had passed laws banning some forms of antigay discrimination. The Queen of Orange Juice, not the queens at Stonewall, had brought the importance of electoral politics and legislative reform into queer southern homes. For gay men who spent weekend nights at Badlands or lesbians who played softball at Memorial Park, their heroines and heroes were more likely Elaine Noble and Leonard Matlovich than Jim Fouratt and Jill Raymond. At the brink of the eighties, marriage and child custody were becoming more relevant than the improbable meltdown of the nuclear family. Forming gay business associations or testifying in MCC churches seemed more useful than bombing banks or refusing to testify before grand juries. And, by the 1980s, *choosing* a lesbian identity to exorcise the "pricks in our head" would be as odd-girl-out as playing butch and femme at the Tower Lounge. In the new decade of Indiana Jones and Arnold Schwarzenegger, two heterosexual men embracing the philosophy in *Men's Liberation* would be as strange a city tale as a gay man entering the Red Room bar of the Redmont Hotel with a jacket and tie. Just as many voters would soon swoon to the siren call, "It's morning in America," so, too, for some, *being* lesbian would mean reading *On Our Backs*, not *off our backs*, and being gay counting T-cells, not sporting "Anita Sucks Oranges" T-shirts.

On the last gay pride weekend of the seventies, southerners held parades, not marches, organized picnics, not sit-ins.[40] In June 1979, fifty floats moved down Westheimer Avenue. A decade after a handful of Tumblebugs challenged Houston's cross-dressing ordinance, thousands gathered at Spotts Park and heard Ray Hill declare: "The only closet that's all right to be in is the voting booth."[41] East on I-10, party-oriented New Orleans lesbians and gay men organized "Gay Fest," a weekend event at Washington Square on Elysian Fields, blossoming with local crafts and overflowing with music, beer, and food. A few hundred miles northeast a rally at Piedmont Park attracted nearly one thousand Atlantans, who marched from the Civic Center among a dozen floats, while in Miami two thousand celebrated a "Decade of Pride" by parading down Biscayne Boulevard with a memorial to Harvey Milk and a phalanx of Theban motorcyclists. Virginians organized a symbolic funeral motorcade of eighteen cars from Azalea Mall to Byrd Park for a picnic lunch. The theme of the Richmond event? "Death of Denial; Birth of Pride." Picnics were also held in Birmingham's Rushton Park, where 150 played softball and volleyball after listening to Ron Joullian, president of Lambda, echo the homophile line: "We're people who happen to be gay."[42] And, in South Carolina, the Spartanburg-Anderson-Greenville Alliance sponsored a "Safety Break" at an interstate rest stop, providing hot coffee, cold drinks, and pastries.

Although Lige Clarke and Jack Nichols wrote on the heels of Stonewall that "great changes don't really take place in a decade," from slogans on buildings chalked by the children of this revolution to a rainbow of banners representing an alphabet soup of queer organizations, the times had indeed changed.[43]

Parading down Pennsylvania Avenue for the March on Washington, two men donned brown bags over their heads, evoking an earlier era when the thought of thousands of daylight marchers accompanied by a blaring, hundred-member Great American Yankee (GAY) Freedom Band and its twenty-member drill team would have been whimsy to the rough bar crowd at Cucujo's or the A-list gays of the Diana Foundation. "Historically, this has been a print-media movement," says Naiad publisher and *Ladder* editor Barbara Grier. "This has been a movement that does it on rhetoric, oratory, and writing." From the southern oratory of Leonard Matlovich, Ray Hill, Charlotte Bunch, and Troy Perry on that October day to the March coverage in *TWN, Our Own Community Press, Impact, Montrose Star, Arkansas Gay Writes,* and the *Front Page,* the hairpin drop had indeed been heard around the world.

TWENTY-SIX

Communities of Memory

Without the knowledge of the last chapter of one's story, we can never quite know who we are—for that last chapter changes everything. Yes, everything: just a little.
— *Lillian Smith*

Those who attended the 1979 National March on Washington and read the one-dollar official souvenir book learned about the activist generations that had come before them. Jim Kepner, an orphan who grew up in Galveston, entered the fledgling homophile movement during the 1950s. "The problems of a class of people," he explained in the souvenir book to this youngest generation of homosexuals, could "only produce a movement after a few able, charismatic individuals agree on how to define and approach those problems."[1] Del Martin, Harry Hay, Phyllis Lyon, Hal Call, Barbara Gittings, Dorr Legg, Tony Segura, Barbara Grier, Don Slater—their efforts extended into the sixties as others joined, forming groups like the first business association (the Tavern Guild), organizing protests at the White House and Pentagon, and publishing slick magazines such as *Vector* and *Drum*.

Jim Kepner peered into the sea of mostly youthful faces. "Without anger or fear," he had written to them, "we come to claim our full birthright."[2] He recognized in their faces the handiwork of these earlier generations of lesbians and gay men who—despite personal and philosophical disputes—had produced a movement that eventually beckoned these 100,000 marchers to the Washington Monument.

Gathering of the Pioneers on the Fortieth Anniversary
of the Gay and Lesbian Movement and in Memorial to Jim Kepner
in Beverly Hills, California, May 1998. Photo: Charles Curtis.

Marking Stonewall's tenth anniversary and pursuing the quest for full birthrights was Harvey Milk's dream.[3] Although Milk, the "Mayor of Castro Street," was slain by an assassin's bullet, more activism followed the March. Ray Hill, who had debated Milk about the wisdom of marching at all, remembers that "Harvey's clarion call was not 'Organize, Organize, Organize.' It was 'Come Out, Come Out, Come Out.' . . . Harvey said the important thing is for people to come out and see one another and feel reinforced enough that they will take their coming out in Washington back to their homes."[4]

A month after the March, Norfolk lesbians and gay men met with police officials, following several incidents of police raids based on ordinances that barred homosexuals from congregating in bars.[5] That fall, too, Mobile women had been arrested for "loitering" at a gay bar parking lot, while complaints about police entrapment in Jackson's Smith Park and Birmingham's Azalea Mall had escalated. In Houston, raids and police intimidation continued, culminating in the police killing of Fred Paez, one of several gay men seeking to secure a federal investigation of harassment from law enforcement.[6]

Of course, such events coupled to the March on Washington fueled greater activism. In Memphis, *GaZe* was produced as a four-page tabloid that December following the incorporation of a chapter of the Tennessee Gay Coalition for Human Rights.[7] And, two weeks after the March on Washington, the first issue of the *Front Page*, edited by Jim Baxter, was published in Raleigh.[8] A month later, Baxter confided to a friend: "My attempt is to get the paper going and organized, all the while delegating as much as possible and turning over the operations to someone else."[9] But, like Jimmy Stewart's character in *It's a Wonderful Life*, Baxter never left his small town. On the twentieth anniversary of the *Front Page*, Baxter reflected: "Back in those days, when the 200 or so of us who were out and active from throughout the Southeast used to gather together annually at the Southeastern Gay Conferences just to huddle by the fire of one another and get warm, the '79 march marked the start of a whole new level of community awareness organizing."[10]

Art Sperry, an enigmatic businessman who had loaned Baxter two thousand dollars to get the *Front Page* started, was less sanguine about a gay community: "Community is based on common culture, and we do not have common culture. We have one very small thing—or very significant thing, but only one—in common. And that is our sexuality. Sexuality, however, is not a basis for community."[11] While a March on Washington brochure had portrayed the event as "a celebration of our community solidarity and a sign of our political strength," Sperry was not the only person to question whether a community of solidarity existed.[12]

"Perhaps a great deal of the pain we experience in our lives as lesbians can be traced to our too-hasty and optimistic assumption of 'community' on the basis of sub-cultural identity," mused Julia Penelope near the end of the seventies. She went on to argue that a "community" was simply "a group defined as outcast and undesirable by the larger society of hetero-sexuals." The result for lesbians, she reasoned, was that "we have *assumed* that we do share certain aspects of our lives, but those assumptions have made it easy for us to neglect explicit definition of exactly what we *do* share beyond our oppression. The struggle against oppression may create *alliances,* but it will not automatically establish *bonds.*"[13]

In mapping out queer space there has been a tendency to ascribe "community" to a diverse set of loosely clustered individuals or groups who simply occupy a common territory.[14] A community, however, is not syn-onymous with a neighborhood, where shared spaces do not necessarily result in social bonds. Some neighborhoods and small towns, of course, do have a community feel where folks "mind one another." From the fic-tional characters in deracialized Mayberry to lesbians in Atlanta's Little Five Points, this shared "minding" is created from a "social bond of shared meaning."[15] And through this process we construct our identi-ties (like Karla Brown, who formed a gay identity at the Neptune Lounge, a feminist identity at Atlanta Lesbian Feminist Alliance [ALFA], and a black lesbian identity in California).

However, sharing a common territory of identity, purpose, meanings, and beliefs in Little Five Points or the Castro should not be confused with the "gay community" of Atlanta or San Francisco.[16] The seventies Castro, for example, described by sociologist Stephen Murray as a " 'gay community' [that] is as much of one as any other urban community," was actually a topography of desire.[17] Inhabiting such narrowly defined Dionysian communities of the seventies were "doped-out, sexed-out, Marl-boro" men crowding into the discos, bathhouses, restaurants, and cruis-ing circuits.[18] This "community of the carnal heart," to borrow a line from Thom Gunn, was, in fact, little more than a male-centered urban area composed of a "group of socially isolated social networks and gathering places . . . segregated from the broader gay as well as the heterosexual world."[19]

Individuals mistake such a "lifestyle enclave"[20] for community only if they factor out lesbians, bisexuals, transgender persons, and gay men who do not interact with one another, engage in collective action, share similar norms, or celebrate a common history.[21] And it is from such a vantage point—with meager data—that the author of *American Gay* asserts, "Lesbian communities are less fully developed."[22] His pronouncement contradicts this book's herstories of umbrella groups like ALFA House, *Pointblank Times,* Mother's Brew, *Feminary,* Amber Moon, and Womankind Books, where lesbians—from Atlanta to Houston, Louisville to Durham, Lexington to Nashville—were building communities of the political heart during a decade of gay wanderlust.[23] Murray's skewed view is refuted and explained in Karla Jay's essay published in the 1979 March souvenir booklet:

> The flowering of culture in the past decade has been especially true for lesbians, . . . [o]ne which has created lesbian music, publishing houses, spirituality and religion, educational institutions, garages, restaurants, karate schools, political and social groups. That may seem like a strange mixture since men, especially leftist men, have always pitted politics against culture, and posed them as two alternatives instead of as part of one whole. The wholeness, a complete circle is a form, I believe, which is inherent to women as the phallus and phallic institutions are the archetypes of male culture. . . . The circular form means inclusion of everyone and everything whereas phallic form and thinking with their hard, rigid structures, institutions, and rules mean divisions, exclusions.[24]

Although southern queer communities during this era could not principally be defined as neighborhoods or institutions, they certainly were divided by gender, social class, and race. Strategic and tactical differences among Bob Basker, Jack Campbell, and Bob Kunst during the Dade County referendum, or between some of the founding gay men of *RFD* and the Iowa lesbian press, or between June Arnold and spray-painting lesbian vandals, were more than personality conflicts. These disputes evidence deep-seated ideological and social class differences.

Similarly, the difficulty in unearthing gay or lesbian communities of color in the seventies South vitiates the modernist notion of a unitary, stable, and localized "gay community." Karla Brown, Jesse Monteagudo, Roger Simmons, and Mel Boozer are individuals whose stories are largely told in relationship to the "whiteness of gay iconography"; they are not tales of being "in the life" within African American towns such as Tuskegee and Orangeburg or Latino communities of South Houston and Little Havana.[25]

Glossing over these differences and divisions, the grand narrative of "community" collapses groups who may share little more than a common locality. Atlantis motorcyclists, lesbian-feminists of DARII, First Tuesday politicos, black lesbian house partiers, editors of the *Barb,* drag stars from the Sweet Gum Head, Piedmont Park cruisers, MCC devotees, Atlanta's urban faeries, the men of Marquitte or the women of the Tower Lounge are our Gay Yellow Pages version of an "imagined community."[26] The March on Washington, like other grand public events, masked these differences. Employing words like "family," "community," "solidarity," and "unity," and placing at the parade's front marginalized groups (women, people of color, elderly, persons with disabilities) who marched to the tune of a reformist agenda, they gathered beneath the erection-like Washington Monument in celebration of this imagined community.

Within the ecosystems of southern queer space, conflict within "the gay community" was common and alliances short-lived during the seventies. The adversarial relationship between *Pointblank Times* lesbians and Gay Political Caucus men over carding at the Old Plantation, or the boycott of Dignity men over exclusionary workshops at the Third Southeastern Conference of Lesbians and Gay Men, are illustrative. Even those who crossed gender borders throughout the decade with alliances between gay men and lesbians—Pokey Anderson, Julia Penelope, and Margo George—harbored few illusions about creating social bonds of shared meaning. As Julia contends, "What each of us has are memories of attempted communities and largely failed alliances between lesbians and gay men, Caucasians and African Americans, poor, working class, middle class."[27]

In contrast, at the beginning of the Rubyfruit era, activist-academic Dennis Altman had foreseen "an affirmation of solidarity with other gays, and the transformation of the pseudo-community of the old gayworld into a sense of real community."[28] But the old gay worlds of regulars hanging out at the Twenty-second Street Beach or the "snake pit" at the Thomas Jefferson Hotel were no less a false (or true) community than those frequenting the Running Water or Women's Writes gatherings, living in the drug-infested Gay Lib House on Louisville's East Side or the male-free McLendon House of ALFA. The difference between southern communities situated on either side of Stonewall rather was found in their diversity, density, and visibility.

During the Lonely Hunters era southern homosexuals existed on the margins, lived in the cracks of the heterosexual world, spoke between the lines, and queered space on the softball diamonds, in hotel mixed bars, and along darkened park pathways. Institutional places were few compared to the gay and women's centers, churches and synagogues, as well as newspapers, bookstores, and discos, that came to define the 1970s. Further, those southern cities that experienced the earliest organizing coupled to a critical mass of homosexuals generally evidenced the greatest ecological diversity—notably Dallas, Miami, Houston, and Atlanta. Although Columbia evidenced little increase in complexity during this decade, the local queer ecology of New Orleans slowly evolved throughout the era, while those in Memphis and Birmingham evidenced an escalation of activity near its end.

"As more homosexuals come out openly," further predicted Altman, "they will seek the sense of community and protection that gay liberation groups provide."[29] Before Stonewall, however, southerners who acknowledged their homosexuality and associated with others enjoyed a sense of community—albeit different from what gay liberationists might have desired. Aside from mostly one-man shows like Richard Inman's Atheneum Society or the tiny Circle of Friends in Dallas led by Phil Johnson, there were no *political* communities nor was there the web of bars and baths, newspapers and newsletters, sports teams and motorcycle clubs, MCC congregations and chapters of Dignity or Integrity, that materialized later.

Nevertheless, during the era bracketed by *The City and the Pillar* and *The Boys in the Band,* many southern gay men enjoyed a nonpublic gay lifestyle with clusters of friends playing weekly bridge games, frequenting hotel bars like the Creel Room or the Beau Brummel, attending the ill-fated Waco wedding, or hanging out at Maggie's Corner guarded by the Pegasus of the Petroleum Building. They participated in Sunday services at the Eucharistic Catholic Church on Peachtree Street, enjoyed action in the navy's YMCA in Norfolk, lived in a nearly all-gay apartment house on Birmingham's Highland Avenue, or cruised Cherokee Park.[30] During an era split between *The Price of Salt* and *Catching Saradove,* lesbians hung out at Nicky's or the Fortress, where a knock on the door brought a peering eye; shared heterosexual space in lesbian backroom bars such as Aunt Nora's Tavern; played softball for Hughes Tool; went to Warrior River for fishing trips; or joined the secretive Steamboat Club. And within an era of Jim Crow bracketed by *Giovanni's Room* and *Movement in Black,* queer southerners of color held house parties in Tuskegee or frequented Richmond nip joints, participated in travel clubs destined for big-city black gay bars and elaborate drag balls, assimilated into their community of color directing church choirs and speaking in code, frequented Houston's Red Devil Lounge or the Terminal bar in Miami, moved to their town's outskirts or trespassed into the steamy darkness of interracial sex. Homosexual discretion and heterosexual disregard enabled lesbians and gay men to enter these and other secretive communities during an Ozzie and Harriet era when "gay" was just an ordinary word, a butch haircut was an innocent style, and faeries appeared only in storybooks.[31]

Gay liberationists punctured this fourth dimension of queer space. And, not surprisingly, some southerners who long ago had accommodated to this split between public and private lives were dismayed:

> The Memphis Gay community was doing just fine before the premier of your paper and the beginning of the Memphis Coalition for Human Rights. We have a nice, quiet Gay community, we're never harassed in the parks, we don't have roving "queer bashers," and we go relatively unnoticed by the MPD. . . . The events of the past few months really have me disturbed. I've seen your newspaper at the *public* library, I've even heard that Coalition representatives were on the Marge Thrasher Show. . . . If I am happy to remain closeted, then why aren't you?[32]

It would be naïve, of course, to romanticize the Lonely Hunters era of Charley Johns and his investigative goons in Florida, the routine harassment by local vice such as Detective Robinette in Norfolk and Sergeant McMenney in Houston, the dubious acquittal in Charleston's candlestick trial, and the publication of names, addresses, and places of employment of arrested homosexuals. And, although those lesbians and gay men who ventured from their magnolia closets experienced a sense of community, many more never crossed over this lavender threshold. Like McCullers's maimed characters in *The Heart Is a Lonely Hunter*, another older Memphis man remained isolated and bitter as the Memphis "gay community" emerged from the shadows following the March on Washington: "We all live in a space and time. . . . Look at yourself and your 'out of the closet friends'—you are the ones kidding yourselves. Who are in the bars and in groups? Youth—handsome faces—bodies beautiful. And I ask you, where are those my age? Come out? Come out to march, to sign a petition? I have a feeling that what you really want me to do is to be the sacrifice, the burnt offering for your 'tomorrow.'"[33] Although sexual liberation and gay organizing had arrived in the Stonewall South, those who felt agency within these newly formed queer spaces were more likely young than old, white than nonwhite, male than female.

"Community," wrote authors of a landmark lesbian local history, "is key to the development of twentieth-century identity and consciousness."[34] But the key to the development of a community is social interaction.[35] Thus, a Descartes-like corollary might be "I am with whom I bond." Although the imagined communities evidenced from gay pride celebrations and anti-Bryant rallies to the March on Washington may suggest a "generalized bond," they are better understood as short-term alliances among queer communities—separated by gender, ideology, sexual practices, class, and race—that occasionally shared short-range goals but seldom engaged in sustained and substantive interaction.[36]

Localities from Atlanta to Charlotte are better understood as local queer ecologies: queer spaces occupied by various groups with differing beliefs, symbols, identities, lifestyles, languages, and interests operating inside a common border and within a cultural context of homophobia and heteronormativity. While southern towns such as Charlotte did not have the ecological diversity of Atlanta, neither were they protozoans of queer life. In Charlotte, it is certainly difficult to group such diverse individuals as professor–turned–*Sinister Wisdom* publisher Catherine Nicholson; longtime activist Don King, who fathered Dignity of Charlotte; the Freese Brothers, who published the *Free Press;* Boom Boom LaToure of O'Leen's; Karla Brown and her friends at the Neptune Lounge; as well as closeted men cruising around First Presbyterian Church on Trade and College Streets into something called the "Charlotte Gay Community." Within each of these local queer ecologies were multiple, overlapping, and shifting community fields wherein individuals were socially interdependent, participated in discussion and decision making, and recognized the importance of maintaining a collective history, as well as shared certain beliefs, values, and goals that both defined and nurtured themselves.[37] The existence and vitality of these community fields, their purposeful interaction with one another, their respect for each other's boundaries, and their mutual interdependence define a dynamic local queer ecology. And these community fields—the women of ALFA or the Houston Ducks, the Tuna Review at the Horny Bull or the drag queens of O'Leens, the folks at Norfolk's Unitarian Universalist Gay Caucus or in New Orleans's Gertrude Stein, the leather men of the Thebans or the politicos in First Tuesday—were the life force of the seventies "gay movement" in the South.

Attempts among some southern men to forge community fields into permanent coalitions where authority was centralized and power maximized (e.g., Human Rights for Everyone, in New Orleans, and Dade County Coalition for Human Rights, in Miami) failed, in part, because of a mistaken notion of a "gay community." For example, a week before the March on Washington, the editor of Miami's *TWN* declared a "leadership void" as "the epidemic of gay apathy that has permeated our community since 1977 has finally hit home inside the Dade Coalition."[38] In seeking to broaden its base, DCCHR began hosting "community outreach meetings" at local bars rather than at its seven-thousand-square-foot headquarters. But this attempt generated neither a sustained response nor enough money to keep the Coalition's office open. In contrast, localities that developed short-term alliances, such as organizing for the March on Washington, were more successful. However, the greater the duration of these alliances, as apparent in the planning of the Third Southeastern Conference of Lesbians and Gay Men, the more likely it was to fracture on the shoals of conflict. As short-term coalitions like HERE and DCCHR continued beyond their original mandate, disunity or a narrowing of their base inevitably followed.

The failure of such hierarchical organizations was seen, by some, as a problem of implementation, not conceptualization. For example, David Goodstein, the progenitor of the Gay Rights National Lobby and godfather of the Dade County referendum debacle, placed the blame for such disunity and the lack of "progress" within these mega-organizations at the feet of those waiting "until the least intelligent, most neurotic, and generally most insulting member agrees to the action or progress, even if she happens to be a lesbian separatist."[39] Those failing to impose the rules of General Roberts or to pace to Goodstein's drum were viewed, at best, as eye-catching décolletage in a male-led movement or, at worst, as lesbian-feminist traitors.

Employing the rhetoric of "community" to mobilize constituent groups or imposing an imagined unity, paradoxically, "masks existing inequalities that can lead to disunion among those it is supposed to unify."[40] The tendency, however, was to cover over, apologize for, or blame individuals responsible for "dividing the community," rather than admit that "much of lesbian and gay history has to do with noncommunity."[41] An *Our Town* notion of "the gay community" arising from a Stonewall spirit and energized by Hurricane Anita existed only as the fanciful creation of some activists, entrepreneurs, and writers.[42] The creation of these fictive southern gay communities, "forged in the crucible of difference," as Audre Lorde eloquently wrote, is a history wherein "the need for unity is often misnamed as a need for homogeneity."[43] And it is this homogenized political history of the "gay community" that crowds bookstore shelves, relegating to footnotes rebel faggots, rhinestone drag queens, and rubyfruit lesbians.

As the "gay community" emerged, so did a queer political economy. From marketing a thirteen-inch Gay Bob doll (with a penis) to the fabrication of the Village People, from hawking gay pride T-shirts and lambda necklaces to corporate sponsorships of pride events, the assimilationist agenda advanced where the marketplace and ballot box intersected.[44] Meanwhile, butch dykes were being transformed into chic lesbians through "commodity lesbianism" and the gay underworld was commercialized into "fast food sex" where "the economic reality is," observed southern playwright Robert Patrick, "that your cock is being sold."[45] Of course, few Stonewall veterans were pleased with such progress. As one liberationist, chafing at a *Village Voice* writer's question about the movement's progress, declared: "When we fought back at the Stonewall ten years ago, we didn't think the benefits would be seven hundred leather bars and the right to join the army."[46]

Although communities of the heart and desire mushroomed in the seventies South, queer southerners often shared more in common with folks living in different geographical areas than those bounded by municipal borders. Although MCC chapters, biker clubs, lesbian-feminist groups, female impersonators, and radical faeries did not share physical space, like-minded persons from Norfolk to Dallas interacted within a "web of consciousness,"[47] strengthening shared identities, values, goals, argot, and rituals through conferences, runs, pageants, and gatherings.

The development of the Southeastern Lesbian Writers Conference—formed at the same legendary Atlanta Southeastern conference where sissy-identified men planned their first gathering at Running Water—is another example of these interconnecting community fields. In 1978, southern lesbians began attending regular writing conferences at a middle Georgia state park "to explore and share our literary talents and publishing related skills so we can begin to build a future vision."[48] Merril Mushroom, now with four adopted children and still working construction and sharing a home with Gabby, did not participate in the March on Washington; she did attend the second and subsequent Georgia gatherings. In the evenings, she and others sat on the porch reading for hours from their works-in-progress under the moon's glow of sisterhood. Through the intimacy of shared space and shared writing there was, Merril remembers, "a heartfelt respect for one another in all our differences and similarities. Being who we are, we cultivated familiarity that nurtured a deep and abiding sense of community and caring for one another."[49]

Queering space within these different communities also opened up voices of difference: voices of Lesberadas, tinged with anger; voices from the fiery Up Stairs Lounge, reverberating with fear; voices of Carolina pride at the Miss Gay pageant and Lexington Six voices of courage; communal voices of Short Mountain; musical voices of Amber Moon and voices of MCC spirit; coming-of-age voices in political caucuses; timorous Tumblebug voices and those from *Sunflower* filled with the certainty of youth. These queer voices formed a cacophony of queer southern life of the seventies, illustrating differences in identities that arose within various communities. And it is only in this chronicling of the "history of a history of multiple assimilations" that one can begin to speak of a real community—a "community of memory."[50]

Perhaps it was at the first March on Washington that some began to take to heart Robert Bellah's warning: "Where history and hope are forgotten and community means only the gathering of the similar, community degenerates into lifestyle enclaves."[51] However, it would not be until the era of AIDS that our sense of history, our hope for the future, and our understanding of community really changed. Logan, Karla, Bob, Pokey, Jim, Miss P, Jesse, Rita, Merril, Milo, Samantha, Roger, Vicki, Ray, Elizabeth, Leonard, Bobbi—like many of us—entered another country, where cultural constructions about being queer and concepts of community once again changed: from the CLIT Papers to the Clit Club, from C-R groups to twelve-step meetings, from "power to the people" to durable power of attorney, from *Faggots* to *The Normal Heart*.

As the seventies glitter faded, some gay writers at the precipice of this new decade waxed confident about a future world. *Gaiety* predicted a society that was "entirely bisexual with no apparent symptom of discrimination against gays."[52] And the author of "Gay Life in the Year 2000" portrayed a "prosperous and happy" Rastafarian future: "No more harassment, no more worry about losing a job or being an outcast in a community. . . . Gays would be a decisive factor in all of American government. . . . Politicians seeking office would have to address themselves to (and shape their policies for) the gay constituents. . . . Full acceptance in every part of the country. . . . Adoption by gay couples would be legal and acceptable."[53]

Some of those southerners marching on that chilly October day a generation ago would return eight years later not only to shout the same unmet demands but also to shuffle in grieved silence around a two-football-field-size quilt of death and remembrance. Eight years would have passed since the first two Karposi's sarcoma cases were diagnosed in New York City, the Village People produced their last hit single, and Harvey Milk's assassin, using a Twinkie defense, was found guilty of simple manslaughter. It would be a time of remembrance: moments of valor and gaiety; opportunities for intimacy and community; the timelessness of youth and youthful confidence.

At the end of this long disco night, we danced in a haze of existential uncertainty, committed to a community of memory. On the Gay Pride Day in Greenwich Village following that second March on Washington, Savannah-born poet Perry Brass wrote:

It is the poignant hour;
A summer afternoon that will soon

                give way to rain;

And the crowd walking closely
on Christopher Street, stopping
to touch or stare,   gives way
to a simple pattern.

and I see two young men
holding hands and looking
            at first glance
like cousins at a fair;
and the sky darkens and soon
it will be quiet—the riot
of excess now over;
and we wonder why we celebrate
ourselves now, and still wonder
who we are; but most important

I tell people in this wonder—
the glow of us getting older.
                and being born now
over and over,
while this wonder does not seem
              to be over.

June 26, 1988[54]

NOTES

ABBREVIATIONS

ABC	Alcohol and Beverage Control
AGH	"Atlanta Gay History," sponsored by the Atlanta Gay History Thang, panel transcript, 13 June 1991, Atlanta Historical Society
ALFA Papers	Atlanta Feminist Alliance Papers, Perkins Library, Duke University, Durham, N.C.
Amber Moon Papers	Box 1, Folder 1, Amber Moon Papers, 92 M2, Division of Special Collections and Archives, University of Kentucky, Lexington
AURA	Awareness, Unity, and Research Association
Basker Papers	Robert S. Basker Papers, IGLA
Baxter Papers	Jim Baxter Papers, Perkins Library, Duke University
Clarke Papers	Lige Clarke Papers, Southern Studies Collection, IGLA
Cyr/AURA Corr.	Ken Cyr/AURA Correspondence, Botts Collection, MCC-Resurrection, Houston
DCCHRG	Dade County Coalition for the Humanistic Rights of Gays
DOB	Daughters of Bilitis
GLF	Gay Liberation Front
GPC	Gay Political Caucus
IGIC Collection	Interviews Concerning Gay Organizations, 1973–1974, Manuscript and Archives Section, International Gay Information Center, New York Public Library
IGLA	International Gay and Lesbian Archives, Los Angeles
Integrity/Houston Corr.	Integrity/Houston Correspondence, Botts Collection, MCC-Resurrection, Houston
KGLA	Kentucky Gay and Lesbian Archives, Louisville
LHC	Lesbian History Archives, Brooklyn, N.Y.
Lee Papers	Peter Lee Papers, Southern Studies Collection, IGLA
MCC	Metropolitan Community Church
NACHO File	North American Conference of Homophile Organizations File, IGLA
NGTF	National Gay Task Force
Penelope Papers	Julia [Stanley] Penelope Papers, 1966–1977, Box 17, Perkins Library, Duke University

Pyne Papers	Clint Pyne Papers, Southern Studies Collection, IGLA
Rodwell Papers	Craig Rodwell Papers, Rare Books and Manuscript Division, International Gay Information Center Collection, New York Public Library
Sandifer Papers	Eddie Sandifer Papers, Southern Studies Collection, IGLA
Saxe File	Susan Saxe File, Southern Studies Collection, IGLA
Sears Papers	James T. Sears Papers, Perkins Library, Duke University
TGTF	Texas Gay Task Force
TWN	*The Weekly News* (Miami)

INTRODUCTION

1. R. Bellah, R. Madsen, W. Sullivan, A. Swidler, and S. Tipton, *Habits of the Heart: Individualism and Commitment in American Life* (New York: Harper and Row, 1986), 153.
2. J. Arnold, "Lesbians and Literature," *Sinister Wisdom*, no. 2 (1976): 29.
3. R. May, "The Fighting South," in C. Reagan Wilson and W. Ferris, eds., *Encyclopedia of Southern Culture* (Chapel Hill: University of North Carolina Press, 1989), 1107–1108.
4. Bellah et al., *Habits,* 153.

ONE — A PSYCHEDELIC WEDDING

Interviews

Merril Mushroom, 29 April 1997, 20 June and 19 October 1998, Doweltown, Tenn.
John "Gabby" Haze, 28 April 1997, Liberty, Tenn.

1. More information about Merril's growing up in South Florida and her (and others') experience with the Florida Legislative Investigation Committee can be found in J. Sears, *Lonely Hunters* (New York: HarperCollins/Westview, 1997), 24–47, 48–84, 90–102. Also, see J. Schur, "Closet Crusaders," in J. Howard, ed., *Carryin' On* (New York: New York University Press, 1997), 132–163.
2. Sears, *Lonely Hunters,* 38.
3. T. Leary, *Changing My Mind, Among Others* (Englewood Cliffs, N.J.: Prentice–Hall, 1982).
4. B. Aronson, *Psychedelics: The Use and Implication of Hallucinogenic Drugs* (Garden City, N.Y.: Anchor, 1970).

TWO — THE QUEEN BEE

Interviews

Roberts Batson, 3 August 1998, New Orleans, La.
Roger Nelson, 4 August 1998, New Orleans, La.
Martin Palmer, 31 January 1999, Anchorage, Ala.

1. J. Kirkwood, *American Grotesque* (New York: Simon and Schuster, 1970), 29.
2. Ibid., "So Here You Are, Clay Shaw," *Esquire,* December 1968, 218. In addition to interviews and cited published works, other sources used for details about Clay Shaw are: letters to Martin Palmer from Clay Shaw, 1 January 1970 and circa December 1970; letter to the author from Roger Nelson, 22 January 1999; letter to the author from Martin Palmer, 10 February 1999, Sears Papers.
3. J. Phelan, "A Plot to Kill Kennedy? Rush to Judgment in New Orleans," *Saturday Evening Post,* 6 May 1997, 24.
4. "Odd Company," *Time,* 10 March 1967, 24.
5. Statement of Aaron M. Kohn, managing director of the Metropolitan Crime Commission of New Orleans (F. Powledge, "Is Garrison Faking?" *New Republic,* 17 June 1967, 16). Kohn would later inform Martin Palmer that the commission was "about to bring out the goods on Garrison for corruption." More recently, one of the attorneys assisting Garrison (confirming "I have no doubt that he was taking bribes") stressed that the "main thing to know about him, however, is that he was willing to use the

considerable powers of his office in a completely irresponsible fashion" (T. Bethell, "Jim Garrison's Great Escape," *American Spectator,* December 1998, 20).

6. Garrison was accused of fondling a thirteen-year-old boy on a June Sunday in 1969 at the "slumber room" of the New Orleans Athletic Club in Jack Anderson's 23 February 1970 syndicated column (Kirkwood, *American Grotesque,* 652); he was never arrested on such charges. And Batson has speculated about Garrison and Shaw's homosexual liaisons, writing: "Other persistent rumors are pointedly sexual: that either Shaw had enjoyed the company of a young man that Garrison wanted, or, that Garrison and Shaw had, some years previously, a relationship themselves" (R. Batson, "Claiming the Past," part 5, *Impact,* 22 July 1994). Martin Palmer, however, "got no feeling from Clay" about these alleged liaisons. Another person who knew Shaw within gay circles was Roger Nelson, who operated a comic shop on Decatur near where Jeff Biddeson's business was located; Clay would occasionally come to buy horror comic books. (Jeff hid this collection in his office when Garrison was showcasing Shaw's belongings for the media.) Acknowledging hearing such rumors, Nelson says: "Whatever the relationship, it was clear that Garrison had a total fixation on Shaw." Another motivation, Nelson believes, was Shaw's appointment to the International Trade Mart, which Garrison thought should have gone to him. Whatever their relationship, the queer was expected to capitulate, catapulting the D.A. (himself in bed with Cosa Nostra's Carlos Marcello and on the take) into the governor's mansion (Bethell, "Jim Garrison's Great Escape"; S. Smith, "From a Governor and a D.A: An Offer of Resignation," *Life,* 29 September 1967, 34–36; J. Loughery, *The Other Side of Silence* [New York: Holt, 1998], 308–311, 469).

7. His evaluation profile concluded that he was "totally incapacitated from the standpoint of military duty and moderately incapacitated in civilian adaptability" (G. Posner, *Case Closed* [New York: Random House, 1993], 423.

8. R. James and J. Wardlaw, *Plot or Politics: The Garrison Case and Its Cast* (New Orleans: Pelican, 1967), 21.

9. J. Rechy, *City of Night* (New York: Grove Press, 1973), 286–287. Rechy's gritty fictionalized story of his own hustling experiences from the French Quarter to Times Square was greeted in 1963 by stinging reviews. Readers, however, resonated to the El Paso native's depiction of the lonely and lurid sexual underground, resulting in brisk sales.

10. James and Wardlaw, *Plot or Politics,* 46–47.

11. Powledge, "Is Garrison Faking?" 18.

12. "Thickening the Plot," *Newsweek,* 27 March 1967, 37.

13. "The D.A. Wins a Round," *Time,* 24 March 1967, 17.

14. H. Aynesworth, "The JFK 'Conspiracy,'" *Newsweek,* 15 May 1967, 38. Among the fourteen cartons of Ferrie's effects seized by police was a letter to a boyfriend: "I offered you love and the best I could; all I got in return, in the end, was a kick in the teeth" ("Odd Company," 24).

15. James and Wardlaw, *Plot or Politics,* 85.

16. Kirkwood, *American Grotesque,* 121.

17. Ibid., 472. As one of Garrison's assistants has recently confided: "Clay Shaw had nothing to do with the events in Dallas. . . . People have said to me: He can't just have arrested Clay Shaw with no evidence. But that is what he did. . . . He used his office to turn fantasy into reality" (Bethell, "Jim Garrison's Great Escape," 20–21).

18. *The Oxford Dictionary of Quotations,* 2d ed., rev. (London: Oxford University Press, 1966), 558; letter to Martin Palmer from Clay Shaw, 1 January 1970, Sears Papers.

THREE — GAY IS GOOD
Interview

Jack Nichols, 13 January 1995, Cocoa Beach, Fla.

The epigraph is from a letter to Mary Southwick from Lige Clarke, 13 October 1967.

1. The death theme rang throughout Lige's communication with Jack. For example, in one of his letters to Jack he wrote: "I'm marked for doom, tragedy, greatness or a great imitation of all three. I'll explain when I see you" (2 January 1968). All letters from

Lige Clarke to Jack Nichols, 1967–1974, may be found in the Clarke Papers. Additional materials used to amplify Clarke's portrait are: *Draft Notes* (1994), Jack Nichols's unpublished memoirs, in progress, Sears Papers; audiotaped interviews with Lige Clarke and Jack Nichols during their 1974 book tour, Sears Papers; D. Fenske and D. Massey, "Keep on Truckin'," *Union Gazebo* newsletter [a publication of Union Theological Seminary], May 1971, 1–4.

2. L. Clarke and J. Nichols, "Congress Keeps the Closet Closed," *Screw,* 12 April 1971, 19. The Washington, D.C., *Evening Star* also praised the "wiry astronomer" for conducting the "most cleanly run and efficient campaigns of the recent race" (D. Spencer, "Kameny Happy Despite Low Vote," *Evening Star,* 29 March 1971). Despite these accolades, Kameny was disappointed, explaining: "I knew I wasn't going to win. . . . [But] I had high hopes that that would be a pacesetter. We would have people—gay people—coming out and running for public office, all over, everywhere. . . . There was complete silence. There was nothing. . . . Then Elaine Noble ran [in 1974] . . . successfully for the Massachusetts State House of Representatives" (interview with Frank Kameny by Paul Cain, 2 July 1994, pp. 41–42, Sears Papers).

3. K. Tobin and R. Wicker, *The Gay Crusaders* (New York: Warner Books, 1972), 181.

4. The Mattachine Foundation was established in 1951 through the vision of Harry Hay, and later the *Mattachine Review* was produced under the more conservative leadership of the Mattachine Society and Hal Call. The DOB, viewed by some as the female auxiliary to the male-led group, was formed in 1955 by Phyllis Lyon and Del Martin, who also edited the *Ladder.* Both organizations fostered chapters mostly on the East and West Coasts throughout the fifties and sixties (J. D'Emilio, *Sexual Politics, Sexual Communities* [Chicago: University of Chicago Press, 1983]).

5. For a discussion of the couple's early gay activism in the South as well as the emergence of the homophile movement, see J. Sears, *Lonely Hunters* (New York: HarperCollins/Westview, 1997), 218–229.

6. L. Clarke and J. Nichols, *I Have More Fun with You Than Anybody* (New York: St. Martin's Press, 1972), 62.

7. J. Loughery, *The Other Side of Silence* (New York: Holt, 1998), 291–302. W. Ricketts, "The Boys in the Band Come Back," *Out/Look* 3, 1 (1990): 62–67.

8. M. Crowley, *Boys in the Band* (New York: Dell, 1969), 78, 93, 176, 180.

9. Nevertheless, it was widely produced by amateur and regional theater groups in the South with varying receptions. In 1972, for example, the Gay Freedom Movement of Norfolk performed *Boys in the Band.* Charges were lodged against the bar owner, Tony Pritchard, by ABC investigators for obscenity. A decade later in the more liberal town of Durham, a letter writer to the *Front Page* defended the play's production to the gay community: "One thing in this play, however, I definitely find uplifting—its affirmation of the homosexual community and integrity . . . all of them make Herculean efforts to support each other. . . . We can come only as far as we have demonstrated that community and have affirmed our mutual support" (J. Younger, "The Boys Are Still in the Band," letter, *Front Page,* 2 February 1982, 7).

10. For the most incisive history of this revolutionary period, see: D. Teal, *Gay Militants* (New York: Stein and Day, 1971). Other useful accounts written during this era include: D. Altman, *Homosexual: Oppression and Liberation* (New York: Outerbridge and Dienstfrey, 1971); A. Bell, *Dancing the Gay Lib Blues* (New York: Simon and Schuster, 1971); T. Marotta, *The Politics of Homosexuality* (Boston: Houghton Mifflin, 1981).

11. Later Lige acknowledged that "I never really appreciated Kentucky until you went home with me and seemed to enjoy it so" (letter to Mary Southwick from Lige Clarke, 3 October 1967, Clarke Papers).

12. Ibid., 26 May 1968.

13. Ibid., 9 October 1967.

14. Ibid., 8 October 1967.

15. Ibid., 1 November 1967.

16. Ibid.

17. Ibid., 9 and 21 November 1967.

18. Ibid., 30 November, 6 December 1967.

19. Or so claimed John Francis Hunter, the pseudonymous author (John Paul Hudson) of one of the first travel books, *The Gay Insider, USA* (New York: Stonehill, 1972).

20. The title was borrowed from a twenty-plus-page newsletter jointly published by Mattachine Societies of Florida and of Washington, D.C., beginning in 1966 (Sears, *Lonely Hunters,* 235–236).

21. L. Clarke and J. Nichols, "Groping Around," *Screw,* 25 April 1969, 14.

22. R. Streitmatter, *Unspeakable: The Rise of the Gay and Lesbian Press in America* (Boston: Faber and Faber, 1995), 89.

23. L. Clarke and J. Nichols, "He-Man Horseshit," *Screw,* 23 May 1969, 20.

24. Teal, *Gay Militants,* 20.

25. The novelist Edmund White, who was working as a staff writer for *Time,* was also at the bar the night of the riot. His letter written to friends about those events dovetails with Rodwell: "Dreary middle-class East Side queens stand around, disapproving but fascinated, unable to go home, as though torn between their class loyalties, their desires to be respectable, and their own for freedom. . . . Mattachine (our NAACP) hands out leaflets about 'what to do if arrested.' Some man from the Oscar Wilde bookstore hands out a leaflet describing to newcomers what's going on. I give stump speeches about the need to radicalize, how we must recognize we're part of a vast rebellion of all the oppressed" (J. Katz, "Edmund White Witnesses the Revolution," *Advocate,* 20 June 1989, 40). Also see J. Pela, "Stonewall's Eyewitnesses," *Advocate,* 3 May 1994, 50–55.

26. Leitsch, according to Nichols, "scolded younger leaders for being too serious while they, on the other hand, considered his flippancy old fashioned. At an earlier time he'd written the mayor during police sweeps of Forty-second Street and had threatened a strike of hairdressers, leaving city officials' wives looking their worst. 'Your wives will all be mad at you,' he'd joked" (Jack Nichols, memoirs, in progress, Sears Papers). Another older generation activist, Foster Gunnison Jr., wrote Leitsch that "today's homosexual is indeed a new breed—an open (or becoming open) and a militant homosexual . . . [in] the spirit of the Stonewall rebellion and the Christopher Street riots. I think there is glory in it. . . . We need balance in the movement. . . . [P]rogress, as a unified movement, means some degree of order, procedure, system, authority, planning, continuity, attention to detail, and discipline" (letter to Dick Leitsch from Foster Gunnison, 23 November 1970, Rodwell Papers).

27. D. Leitch, "The Hairpin Drop Heard Around the World," *New York Mattachine Society Newsletter,* June 1969, 21–22.

28. "The Stonewall Riots: The Gay View," *New York Mattachine Society Newsletter,* August 1969, 4–5.

29. L. Clarke and J. Nichols, "Pampered Perverts," *Screw,* 25 July 1969, 16.

30. A. Holleran, *Dancer from the Dance* (New York: Morrow, 1978), 123–124.

31. Clarke and Nichols, "Pampered Perverts," 16. The "Stonewall riots" was really one event set within a series of police confrontations ranging from the Patch dance bar near Long Beach in August 1968 to the Snake Pit in New York City a year after Stonewall (Loughery, *Other Side of Silence,* 303–305).

32. L. Clarke and J. Nichols, "The Daily News Eats Shit," *Screw,* 15 September 1969, 18. The political revolution, though, continued. That month, for example, 18 gay demonstrators were arrested as a peaceful protest of 350 turned violent when the crowd encountered police harassing a Village gay bar. The following night protestors gathered again, armed with bottles and sticks as "ammunition." Calls of "Off the pigs!" reverberated through the downtown streets.

33. Bell, *Dancing the Gay Lib Blues,* 17.

34. Letter from Foster Gunnison to Leo Martello, 17 November 1969, Rodwell Papers.

35. Bell, *Dancing the Gay Lib Blues,* 17.

36. Ibid., 31.

37. E. Alwood, *Straight News* (New York: Columbia University Press, 1996).

38. Although *GAY* boasted the largest circulation of any gay newspaper in the country, several other liberationist publications emerged in New York City, including *Come Out Fighting!, Gay Times, Ecstasy,* and *Gay Flames.* The last, produced by the Seventeenth Street GLF commune, declared that "gay flames do not come from the

matches of the church, the state, or the capitalistic businessmen. We are burning from within and our flames will light the path to our liberation" (Teal, *Gay Militants*, 162).

39. Editorial, *GAY,* 15 November 1969, 2.
40. Streitmatter, *Unspeakable,* 121.
41. Ibid.
42. Describing Perry as a "fire-eating Fundamentalist hooked on Hubert Humphrey happiness pills," John Paul Hudson asked sarcastically: "Can a man who gets down on his knees to suck cock also kneel to worship his god without feeling hypocritical or schizophrenic?" (J. Hunter, "The Lord Is My Shepherd and He Knows I'm Gay!" *GAY,* 29 March 1970).
43. "Gay Is (Very) Good," *New York Mattachine Society Newsletter,* February 1970, 12.
44. L. Clarke and J. Nichols, "Are Fruits Ugly?" *Screw,* 17 November 1969, 9.
45. Teal, *Gay Militants,* 330.
46. Clarke and Nichols, *I Have More Fun,* 151–152.
47. Ibid.

FOUR — THE PIED PIPER OF ATHENA

Interviews

Merril Mushroom, 29 April 1997, 20 June 1998, Doweltown, Tenn.
Julia Penelope, 13 and 27 June 1998, Lubbock, Tex.

1. Materials used to amplify Penelope's story and used with her permission are: J. Penelope and S. Wolfe, *The Coming Out Stories* (Watertown, Mass.: Persephone Press, 1980), 205; Julia Penelope interview, *HUZZA: Gay News-Telegraph Magazine* (St. Louis), August 1987, 1B, 3B.
2. J. Seeley, "Ellis and the Chestnuts," *Ladder* 8, 2 (1963): 13–15.
3. See, particularly, J. Mitchell, "Women: The Longest Revolution," *New Left Review,* November–December 1966, 40.
4. J. Stanley, "Coming Out," in *The Universities and the Gay Experience: Proceedings of the Conference Sponsored by the Women and Men of the Gay Academic Union, November 1973* (New York: Gay Academic Union, 1974).
5. *Notes from the First Year, 1968, A Journal of Radical Feminism,* quoted from L. Tanner, *Voices from Women's Liberation* (New York: Signet, 1971), 433. Texts that well reflect the second wave of feminism include: T. Atkinson, *Amazon Odyssey* (New York: Links, 1974); J. Hole and E. Levine, *Rebirth of Feminism* (New York: Quadrangle, 1971); A. Koedt, E. Levine, and A. Rapone, eds., *Radical Feminism* (New York: Quadrangle, 1973).
6. B. Jones and J. Brown, "Toward a Female Liberation Movement," in L. Tanner, ed., *Voices from Women's Liberation* (New York: Signet, 1971), 393, 401, 407.
7. See, in particular: A. Echols, *Daring to Be Bad: Radical Feminism in America, 1967–1975* (Minneapolis: University of Minnesota Press, 1989); S. Evans, *Personal Politics: The Roots of Women's Liberation in the Civil Rights Movement and the New Left* (New York: Vintage, 1979); J. Freeman, *The Politics of Women's Liberation* (New York: McKay, 1975).
8. S. Brownmiller, "Sisterhood Is Powerful," *New York Times Magazine,* 15 March 1970, 140.
9. R. Brown, *Rubyfruit Jungle* (New York: Bantam, 1979), 111–113.
10. T. Marotta, *The Politics of Homosexuality* (Boston: Houghton Mifflin, 1981), 235.
11. Ibid., 24.
12. Radicalesbians, "The Woman-Identified Woman," *Ladder,* August–September 1970, quoted in K. Jay and A. Young, *Out of the Closets* (New York: Jove/HBJ, 1977), 174–175.
13. Marotta, *The Politics of Homosexuality,* 258, 262. For additional material that details the emergence of lesbian-feminism and the developing conflict with recently formed gay, primarily male, organizations, particularly GLF and GAA, see: S. Abbott and B. Love, *Sappho Was a Right-on Woman* (New York: Stein and Day, 1972); V. Taylor and L. Rupp, "Women's Culture and Lesbian Feminist Activism," *Signs* 19, 1 (1993): 34–60.

FIVE — BOBBY'S STORY

1. This and other quotes from Carter are derived from notes written by Logan "Bobby" Carter circa 1984 and videotapes of Carter filmed by Jack Nichols, circa 1988. The original materials, owned by Jack Nichols, are used with his permission. Copies are located in Sears Papers.

SIX — PROMETHEUS AND THE TUMBLEBUGS

Interviews

Ray Hill, 12 October 1994, 22 March 1999, Houston, Tex.

Phil Johnson, 14 October 1994, Dallas, Tex.

David Patterson, 9 April 1999, Austin, Tex.

Rita Wanstrom, 18 March and 9–10 April 1999, Austin, Tex.

1. The police fury in enforcing this and other ordinances was second only to that in Florida, then known as the "Mississippi of the Homosexual" (J. Sears, *Lonely Hunters* [New York: HarperCollins/Westview, 1997], 21–24). Many other cities also had such ordinances. For example, in Nashville an ordinance passed in 1966 made it "unlawful for any member of the male sex to appear . . . upon any street . . . in the dress of the opposite sex [except for] any person while participating in any entertainment, exhibition, or performance" (C. Crowell, "Embracing Pair Unusual? Maybe," *Nashville Tennessean,* 12 January 1970).

2. Helpful chronicles of the emergence of Houston's activism are: C. Gillis, "A Brief History of the Gay Community of Houston, Texas," *Gay Pride Week '80 Guide,* 1980, 63–74; B. Remington, "Twelve Fighting Years: Homosexuals in Houston, 1969–1981," master's thesis, University of Houston, 1983; R. Snellgrove, "The History of the Homosexual Rights Movement in Houston" (University of Houston, 1991, typescript), Sears Papers.

3. "Who Can Tell Boys from Girls," *Houston Chronicle,* 26 July 1968, 41.

4. Ibid.

5. Ibid.

6. "Police Will Refile Charges," *Ladder,* October–November 1968, 41.

7. The most memorable event of an earlier decade occurred south of Dallas on 11 April 1953. A "statewide convention of homosexuals" was raided by seventeen detectives, police, and Texas rangers. Storming a South Waco cottage on LaSalle Street, they found sixty-seven mostly Dallas men wearing rouge and lipstick or dressed in high heels, evening dresses, and spring hats. Tommy Gene Brown, wearing a pearl-embroidered wedding gown, joined in chanting, "Long live the queens," as they were carted off to jail ("64 Men Held in Morals Raid in Texas," *Los Angeles Times,* 13 April 1953, 20; "Police Raid Convention," *Waco Citizen,* 16 April 1953; Circle of Friends Newsletter, October 1967; P. Johnson, "Whatever Became of Tommy Gene Brown, the Waco Bride?" *TWT,* 25 August 1988, 45, 47).

8. "Possible Dallas Organization," *National Homophile Clearinghouse Newsletter* 1, 1 (December 1967): 2; *Circle of Friends Newsletter,* March 1968 and July 1968. For other Dallas history, I've also relied on the following sources: A. Vacek, "Recent Developments: Constitutionality of the Texas Sodomy Statute," *Baylor Law Review* 22 (1970): 300–303; DOB, Dallas, Tape #A00508, n.d., Audiovisual Materials, 1956–1989, Subseries 1.2, IGIC Collection; E. Nicollo, "Witch Hunt," *TWT,* 8 April 1983, 50–55; P. Johnson, "Maggie's Corner," *TWT,* 8 August 1991, 35–39.

9. "Guests would never park in the front of the house" but "spread their cars down the street." Phil continues, "In those days, a hint of pubic hair was considered obscene and one could be arrested. So these photographs were kept, copied, and over-copied so that some were so blurry you could hardly see anything."

10. In 1968, Frank Kameny saw a television show featuring black nationalist Stokely Carmichael chanting, "Black is beautiful." It was at that point, according to Kameny, that:

I realized precisely what the psychodynamic was and how much we needed the same thing. And so I toyed around for about a month, playing with words very, very carefully. Ultimately, I came up with "Gay Is Good." . . . At the August meeting of NACHO, I brought forward a resolution. . . . And I wrote a long letter to *Playboy* in which I included Gay Is Good as my basic theme, and they printed it. . . . Keep in mind, that at that point, "gay" had not yet come into common parlance. That didn't happen for another two or three years (interview with Frank Kameny by Paul Cain, 2 July 1994, p. 66, Sears Papers).

11. A similar argument was made by Reverend Cromey, one of the founders of the Council on Religion and the Homosexual, who saw the conferences as an "ego trip" and said that "IF 'gay is good' is to mean anything we have to deal with each other at the gut level. . . . We can't move ahead because we bullshit each other and pretend to like each other" (D. Martin, "Gay Is Good: So What," *Ladder*, April–May 1969, 24).

12. R. Hyde, "Hill Not Ready for Sunset, Despite GPC Presidential Loss," *Montrose Voice*, 17 February 1984, 7. While some robbery money was diverted to revolutionary activities, Hill lived in paradoxical comfort at a two-bedroom Las Palmas apartment overfilled with heavy wooden furniture. Patterson recalls Hill reigning over lodging and lovers dressed in his "kaiser uniform with the British pith helmet and leather boots."

13. NACHO, Credentials Office, Processing Bulletin 9, 1, NACHO File, 8 August 1969. Also see: letter from Marc Jeffers, NACHO Chairman, to ALL NACHO Organizations, July 1969, NACHO File. Marc Jeffers continued: "It seems almost to be a law of nature that young and vigorous homophile organizations in their early existence go through a period of internal stress and re-alignment. Such was the case of the Houston group. . . . Miss Rita Wanstrom has tried to fulfill the hopes of the NACHO for holding a successful Conference this year as far as she has been able to do so operating solely on her own, with very little help from those who were so enthusiastic with their promises last year" (1).

14. NACHO Office of the Treasurer, Bulletin 10, April 1970, NACHO File.

15. Ray's final fall from grace occurred in the early morning hours of 26 February 1970. While on multiple bonds for theft, he tried to recover "hot" paintings before more robberies could be inked on the criminal complaint. Police officers responding to a burglary alarm found Ray and his partner hiding beneath a stairway at the Austin Company on Buffalo Speedway. This incident caught the attention of a reporter. The *Houston Chronicle* pegged Hill and his hearty band of rogues as a "$4 million burglary ring."

16. "We like them to stay together in their own places, as they are doing more and more," observed a police official. "Unless we have complaints that juveniles are involved or that overt acts are in progress we don't do anything about them" ("Where Boys Meet Boys and Girls Go with Girls," *Texas Tempo*, 28 January 1968).

SEVEN — SUNFLOWERS AND TRASH

Interviews

Roger Nelson, 4 August 1998, New Orleans, La.

Suzanne Pharr, 1 April 1999, Plant City, Fla.

The epigraph is from F. Clifford, "Louisville Gets Its Own 'Gay Liberation Front,'" *Louisville Times*, 10 July 1970.

1. E. Pianin, "Hearing Held on Women's Bid to Wed," *Louisville Times*, 12 November 1970.

2. Clifford, "Louisville Gets Its Own."

3. "Gays in Louisville Choosing Sides over Liberation Group," *Advocate*, 14 October 1970; T. Knight and M. R. Jones, *Ladder*, October–November 1970, 25; "Unusual Trial in Kentucky," *Ladder*, February–March 1971, 44; S. MacDonald, "Two Women Tell Court Why They Would Marry," *Louisville Courier-Journal*, 12 November 1970; "Marriage Petition Denied Two Women," *Ladder*, June–July 1971, 43.

4. M. Duberman, *Stonewall* (New York: Dutton, 1993), 240.

5. J. Loughery, *The Other Side of Silence* (New York: Holt, 1998), 326–332.

6. Cherokee Park, created in the late 1880s, was likely a "cruising" area well before the local vice commission identified it as such in 1915. A building boom in the area, accord-

ing to David Williams, director of the KGLA, probably made "'perversion' a popular pastime, starting in the late Victorian era" (personal communication to the author from David Williams, 23 September 1999, Sears Papers).

7. D. Williams, "An Informal History of Gay Bars in Louisville," *Letter,* March 1998, 28; D. Williams, "Louisville Life in the 50's," *Letter,* April 1991, 6–7; D. Williams, "Some Comments on a Visit with 'Bob,'" 11 July 1991, typescript, KGLA; D. Williams, "Did You Know?" 1997, mimeograph, KGLA.

8. "GLF Helps Protest Spiro," *Advocate,* 28 October 1970, 2; "Louisville Gay Lib Class Survives Critics," *Advocate,* 28 October 1970, 9.

9. A. Shirley, "What About Them?" *Cardinal,* 19 February 1971.

10. In May 1970 two Hennepin County men had applied for a marriage license. The Minnesota case went to trial on 22 October with a negative judgment on 18 November (D. Teal, *Gay Militants* [New York: Stein and Day, 1971], 286–289). In addition to these cases, Rev. Troy Perry officiated in what he declared to be "the first marriage in the nation designed to legally bind two persons of the same sex" in June (Teal, *Gay Militants,* 282–283). Although such a marriage may have been an MCC first, there were occasions of same-sex "sealings" conducted in the early Mormon Church (D. Quinn, *Same Sex Dynamics Among Nineteenth Century Americans* [Urbana: University of Illinois Press, 1996], 136–140), and same-sex relationships were commonly sanctioned among Native American tribes (see, for example, W. Williams, *Spirit and the Flesh* (Boston: Beacon Press, 1986). Further, same-sex ceremonies were quietly conducted as early as 1969 at the Norfolk Unitarian Church by Rev. Carl Estenwein (see chapter 19) as well as activists Rita Wanstrom in Houston and Eddie Sandifer in Jackson.

11. Pianin, "Hearing Held."

12. R. Hall, "The Church, State, and Homosexuality: A Radical Analysis," *Gay Power* 14, cited in Teal, *Gay Militants,* 291. Many gay activists during the early seventies had little patience for the "aping of a heterosexual practice" (R. Cole, "Marriage Is an Evil that Most Men Welcome," *Advocate,* 29 March 1972, 1).

13. Teal, *Gay Militants,* 291.

14. J. Hunter, *The Gay Insider* (New York: Stonehill, 1972), 363.

15. "Raid, 30 Arrests Stun Louisville GLF," *Advocate,* 5 January 1972, 13.

16. "To All Gay People," *Trash,* December 1971, 1.

17. "Greetings from a Butch of Gay Lib," *Trash,* December 1971, 2.

18. "Gay Lib House Closes: New Beginnings," *Trash,* December 1971, 4.

19. Ibid., 4; "Raid, 30 Arrests"; "30 Face Charges After Police Raid a Party," *Louisville Courier-Journal,* 18 October 1971.

20. "14 Get Suspended Terms After Marijuana Hearing," *Louisville Courier-Journal,* 8 January 1972. Drug busts were used in other communities to disrupt gay organizing. Georgia Bureau investigators, for example, raided the Virginia Avenue apartment of Charlie St. John, an Atlanta GLF activist. No contraband was found but he was quickly evicted; St. John, the first open homosexual to be appointed to the Community Relations Commission, had been fired by the *Atlanta Journal-Constitution* shortly after his appointment (AGH, 6; B. Hippler, "Gay Life in Atlanta," *Great Speckled Bird,* 12 June 1975, 6).

21. "Gay Lib House Closes," 2.

22. Ibid., 4.

23. Ibid.

24. One of the handful of women participating, Dottie Melander, a member of GLF Austin, was disgusted with "the unconscious male chauvinism . . . pervading the conference" ("Sparks Fly but Gay Lib Meet Clicks," *Advocate,* 28 April 1971, 15).

25. A year earlier Chris Finn and Pete Peters, who had attended the first NACHO convention in Kansas City, formed the short-lived Austin Gay Liberation League.

26. "University of Texas vs. Gay Liberation up to 8/71," Sears Papers. The nation's first university-chartered gay organization was the Student Homophile League at Columbia University formed by Bob Martin in the fall and winter of 1966 and announced publicly in April 1967. Martin, who had lived with Frank Kameny as a house guest while serving as a congressional intern, "absorbed from me enough of the atmosphere

and enthusiasm for gay activism that when he went back to Columbia . . . he quietly organized" (e-mail to the author from Frank Kameny, 14 December 2000). Southern college groups, however, fared poorly in securing official recognition. For example, in 1971 the University of Tennessee's GLF was recognized as a campus group by student government, but the University Administrative Council rejected it ("GLF Joins Tennessee Student Body with Special Status," *Advocate,* 23 June 1971). In Lexington, after a two-year struggle, the University of Appeals Board of the University of Kentucky recommended that its GLF group be recognized. This was later overturned by the full board (D. Williams, "A Brief History of the Early Gay Rights Movement in Lexington," *Letter,* part 1, August–September 1991, and part 2, October–November 1991).

Legal maneuvering between gay student groups and universities continued throughout this decade. At Virginia Commonwealth University, for example, the Richmond GLF was succeeded by an informal student group, the Gay Alliance of Students. When the group's request for university recognition was denied in 1974—its presence would "increase the opportunity for homosexual contact" and attract other homosexuals to the university—a court battle ensued. Two years later, following a partial victory in U.S. District Court, the U.S. Court of Appeals (*Gay Alliance of Students v. Matthews,* Fourth Circuit, 28 October 1976, 544 Federal Reporter, 2d Series, 162–168), citing the First and Fourteenth Amendments, issued a precedent-setting ruling that required full recognition of the campus group.

27. *University of Texas v. Gay Liberation.* Despite this setback, the Austin chapter attracted positive media attention, spoke to various groups, hosted a coffeehouse, organized encounter groups, sponsored the spring national conference, held a gay pride picnic, and petitioned the City Council for a sexual orientation ordinance. Members also carried "GAYS UNITE AGAINST THE WAR" banners and picketed Muthers, a straight nightclub ("Gay Lib to Picket Nightclub," *Daily Texan,* 11 November 1971).

28. Major speakers at the conference were homophile stalwart Frank Kameny and John Lauritsen of the New York Red Butterfly group. Workshops ranged from a Warhol film discussion and a panel following the showing of *Boys in the Band* to GLF-led workshops on women and gay feminism.

29. Gay Liberation Front, Florida, Tape #A00537, Audiovisual Materials, 1956–1989; Subseries 1.2, 1973–1974, IGIC Collection; GLF File, Florida, 1974, IGIC Collection.

30. Interview with Pete Taylor by David Williams, 7 July 1991, KGLA. Taylor, who had won a hard-fought election with Ginny Shelton, remembers the early meetings: "Lesbians were always fussing about not getting a fair shake. 'You have just been socialized to be boys, so you just speak right up and we women are having a hard time.'" Tweaking them, Taylor responded: "'Maybe we should just have a Lady's First rule.' Well, they really hated that! I was being sarcastic, too, but it was an absurdity. . . . I can't think of anybody who has less a sense of humor about being a woman than a lesbian." Edwin Hackney remembers this as a "very confusing, very disorganized, very exciting time, because nobody really had a clue as to what we were all there to do together. . . . Just to keep meeting together seemed to be the only goal we really had for quite awhile. There were almost no women" (interview with Edwin Hackney by David Williams, 7 July 1991, KGLA; interview with Humphrey Marshall by David Williams, 13 July 1991, KGLA).

31. Taylor interview, 1991.

32. "Gay," *Carolina Plain Dealer,* 14 September 1970, 9.

33. Ibid. Police informants and FBI or state bureau plants were common. In Atlanta, for example, activist Bill Smith learned of two or three agents provocateurs active in ALFA (AGH, 5), and in Tennessee, Merril Mushroom remembers a disruptive plant among the feminists.

34. "Gay Lib," *Praxis,* 21 June 1971.

35. The short-lived Homophile League had formed two years earlier under the leadership of a former New York Mattachine leader, Tony Segura, and following increased enforcement by the ABC. Renee's and Rathskeller's, owned by Gene Baldwin, and Sepul's, a lesbian bar on West Broad Street, were subject to frequent thirty-day suspensions (B. Swisher, "Anger Surfaced Here Several Months Before Stonewall," *Rich-*

mond Pride 3, 11 [1989]: 1, 10). Frank Kameny spoke at the ABC hearing and later wrote Dick Leitsch: "Members announced that they would patronize, as a group, every bar in the city until ABC regulations changed or Richmond went dry" (J. D'Emilio, *Sexual Politics, Sexual Communities* [Chicago: University of Chicago Press, 1983] 201, quoted from a letter from Kameny to Leitch, 22 April 1969). Three years later, the ABC announced it was no longer "a homosexual control agency" (T. Rohrlich, "Laws Lead to a Life of Fear," *Richmond Times-Dispatch,* 30 May 1972).

36. R. Swisher, "Shameless in Public: Gay Lib, 1969–1972," *Richmond Pride,* April 1988, 5.
37. Ibid.
38. Interview with "Alex T" by Bob Swisher, 26 April 1989, Southern Studies Collection, IGLA.
39. The *Richmond Times-Dispatch,* for example, ran a series of mixed articles describing social scenes at the four bars, featuring interviews with homosexuals, highlighting conventional medical views of homosexuality, detailing legal issues faced by lesbians and gay men, and articulating gay lib philosophy (T. Rohrlich, "Richmond and the Gay Society," "Three Views: Gays Always Exist," "Homosexuals Disdainful," and "No One Knows Much About Homosexuality," *Richmond Times-Dispatch,* 28 May 1972). Also, in 1972, a weekly alternative paper, the *Richmond Mercury,* featured a positive portrayal of cruising around the city's "gay bar on wheels," replete with a map of the circuit and a glossary of gay slang (C. Hite, "Cruising," *Richmond Mercury,* 13 December 1972, 6). Similar media stories—some more positive, some less—appeared in other southern cities. In Charlotte, the *Observer* editorialized against the state's sodomy statute on 17 March 1972, and Dallas's Channel 13 aired "The Other Side," lauded by a local gay paper as "an unbiased tour of the Dallas Gay Community" ("Dallas Gay Community Show on Ch 13 Favorable Viewer Response Overwhelming," *Our Community,* October 1971, 2). In contrast, a less balanced Nashville reporter noted: "As most homosexuals seek a society all their own, their activities remain in darkness. This darkness may be a boon to the rest of society, which prefers not to be bothered by those who have homosexual tendencies" (C. Crowell, "Embracing Pair Unusual? Maybe," *Nashville Tennessean,* 12 January 1970, 9).
40. Particularly annoying was the cover photo of a solitary white male walking down an abandoned road with his face turned away. "Dallas News and Sugar Plum Fairies," *Our Community,* August 1971, 7.
41. A. Mayo, "Dallas Lesbians," *Our Community,* July 1971, 4.
42. "Atlanta Gay Day," *Carolina Plain Dealer,* Fall 1971, 12; "The 70s in Atlanta," *Gazette Newspaper,* 18 June 1981; M. Dolan and C. Gough, "Looking Back and Marching Forward," *1993 Atlanta Gay Pride,* 1993, 15–16, 19, 23; D. Johnston, "25 Years of Pride," *1995 Atlanta Gay Pride,* 1995, 58–59.
43. Within a year, GLF opened offices in a converted warehouse on Pine Street. Activism slowly emerged around the Midtown area with the celebration of MCC services by John Gill at the Pocket Theater, and the founding of ALFA (see chapter 13).
44. AGH, 4.
45. E. Nony, "Barstool Nostalgia—A Look at Gay Bars in the 50's and 60's," *Impact,* February 1973, 16; D. Cuthbert, "Dixie: Owner of Legendary Bar," *New Orleans Times-Picayune,* 18 May 1996.
46. *New Orleans States,* 12 September 1953; "Starlet Lounge Loses Licenses for 6 Months," *New Orleans States,* 18 September 1953. Raids were common in New Orleans into the late sixties. In fact, during a two-and-one-half-year period beginning in 1959, one bar was raided seventy-eight times ("The When and Now of It," *Impact,* November 1980). The shakedown of homosexual bars to avoid such raids, of course, reaped huge profits; one bar owner reportedly contributed $3,000 a month for "police protection." Several years later, following a raid on the St. Louis bar, a trial at the First District Station resulted in a courtroom filled with disgruntled homosexuals, who considered it the "social event of the season" (Hidden People Workshop, Southeastern Gay Conference, 11 April 1981, Sears Papers).
47. "History of the Gay Krewes," *Impact,* February 1978, 3; B. Rushton, "Inside Lavender Mardi Gras," *Courier,* 21 February 1974, 7–8; "Raided Yuga Ball," Louisiana State Museum Special Projects, 7 December 1995.

48. Anon., "Why a Homosexual Column," *Quarterite,* October 1961, 31. See also W. Simpson, "The Homosexual Pulse," *Vieux Varre Courier,* 1 January 1970, 1.
49. G. Weissman, "Getting It Ready," *NOLA Express,* 25 December 1970.
50. Ibid.
51. "Come Join," *Sunflower,* January 1971, 5.
52. W. Adler, "Liberation Goal of Gay March," *New Orleans States-Item,* 23 January 1971; "Gay Liberation Group Marches," *New Orleans States-Item,* 24 January 1971.
53. "Homosexuals Seek Session with Landrieu," *New Orleans States-Item,* 25 January 1971. At the meeting, however, the mayor's executive assistant did confirm the chief's pledged that "no citizens would be harassed in any way provided that they were not molesting others or otherwise breaking the law" (statement to the *Advocate* from Winston Lill, 11 Feburary 1971, New Orleans File, IGLA).
54. As in Louisville, activists in New Orleans tried to downplay their radical image. One flyer they distributed read: "We are *not* part of the SNCC, ADA, SDS . . . and rest assured that we are not affiliated with the Black Panthers" (Gay Liberation Front, "Confusion Is Not a Part of the GLF . . . So Let's End the Confusion," circa March 1971, GLF File, IGLA).
55. "What Is Gay Liberation?" *Sunflower,* April 1971, 2.

EIGHT — THE HORNY BULL

Interviews

Tony Midnite, 13 March 2000, Chicago, Ill.; correspondence from Tony Midnite to the author, 26 February, 9 March 2000.

Paul M. Wegman, 28 March, 18 April, 27 October, 16 November 1997, Orlando, Fla.

1. Material about Bobby "Logan" Carter used for this chapter includes: Carter's written notes and diary, videotapes of Carter filmed by Jack Nichols circa 1988, Nichols's unpublished memoirs, and his manuscript, "Sissies." Copies of these materials, used with Nichols's permission, are located in Sears Papers. Other sources regarding Logan Carter: "Miss Florida Pageant (1974)," *Barb* 1(5); *Mid-Morning LA,* television broadcast, October 1983; G. Jones, "My Style: Logan Carter in Conversation," *Los Angles Herald Examiner,* 17 October 1983, D1–D2; "Logan Carter a/k/a Roxanne Russell," *TWN,* 6 July 1988, 28; J. Nichols, "Logan Carter: Portrait of a Young Man as Drag Artist," *A Friendly Voice,* 27 September 1989.
2. A. Warhol, *The Philosophy of Andy Warhol* (New York: Harcourt, Brace, Jovanovich, 1988), 54. Materials relied on for the history and art of female impersonation include: P. Ackroyd, *Dressing Up: Transvestism and Drag, the History of an Obsession* (New York: Simon and Schuster, 1979); R. Baker, *Drag: A History of Female Impersonation in the Performing Arts,* rev. ed. (New York: New York University Press, 1994); C. Bulliet, *Venus Castina: Famous Female Impersonators Celestial and Human,* 1928 (reprint, New York: Bonanza, 1956); H. Dickens, *What a Drag* (London: Angus and Robertson, 1982); K. Kirk and E. Heath, *Men in Frocks* (London: Gay Men's Press, 1994); C. Thompson, *Ladies or Gentlemen?* (New York: Dorset, 1992); Warhol, *The Philosophy of Andy Warhol;* E. Winford, *Femme Mimics* (Dallas: Winford, 1954).
3. Useful biographies of some of these drag stars and female illusionists are: L. Christon, "Jim Bailey's Alter Egos," *Los Angeles Times,* 30 July 1977; L. Christon, "Impressible Charles Pierce: Imitating the Women in His Life," *Los Angeles Times,* 10 December 1979; J. Scott, "Impressionist in Search of Himself," part 4, *Los Angeles Times,* 15 November 1973; "Star of Stars," *Our Community,* July 1971, 4; J. Stewart, "Charles Pierce: Female Impersonator as Culture Hero(ine)," *Ramparts,* October 1971, 60–63; Winford, *Femme Mimics.* For more information, photos, audio recordings, and web links about these and other classic female illusionists, see: http://www.jtsears.com/histmus2 and http://www.jtsears.com/histcult1b.
4. For more information on Midnite, see: S. de la Croiz, "Midnite over Chicago," *Outlines,* 26 August 1998; "Gay Life in the Bad Old Days," *Gay Life,* October 1978.
5. The Club Plantation on Timon Boulevard, for example, featured "the most beautiful gay boys of the South," and the Spider Den hosted Johnny Kaye, "male mannequin

of fashions," and Houston's favorite for "risque songs," Poppy Lane (1938 poster of the Club Plantation and 1937 poster of the Spider Den, Sears Papers). These and other Houston clubs (e.g., Syd Grossman's Spinning Wheel) were short-lived, operating outside the law and at the pleasure of Sheriff Buster Kern. Other, longer-lasting clubs in the South that featured "femme mimics" and performers who "have achieved the greatest deceptive Art in the theater today" during the thirties or forties included: the Granada Club in Galveston; Abe and Pappy's in Houston (which moved to Fort Worth after the war); the Rocking-M Dude Ranch on Soledad overlooking the river in San Antonio (later becoming Club 55); New Orleans's Wonder Bar at Lake Ponchetrain (destroyed by a hurricane but predating the famous Club My-O-My); the Rainbow Room in Lakeland, Florida; Miami Beach's Onyx Room; and, across the causeway, Leon and Eddie's, as well as Babe Baker's Revue in Hollywood.

6. "Gay Life in the Bad Old Days."

7. AGH; C. Gillis, "A Brief History of the Gay Community of Houston, Texas," *Gay Pride Week '80 Guide,* 1980, 63–74; J. Loughery, *The Other Side of Silence* (New York: Holt, 1998), 273–275.

8. V. Astor, "Georges—Twenty Years Young," *GazE,* April 1988; "Birmingham History Series," part 8, *Alabama Forum,* April 1989; D. Buring, *Lesbian and Gay Memphis* (New York: Garland, 1997); L. Hollifield, "Birmingham History Series," part 6, *Alabama Forum,* October 1987; J. Norcross, "The History of Gay Bars in Little Rock," *Arkansas Advisor* 1, 7 (1984); J. Sears, *Lonely Hunters* (New York: HarperCollins/Westview, 1997); D. Williams, "Louisville Gay and Lesbian Life in the 50s," *Letter,* April 1991.

9. J. Real, "Dragtime: 'Dressing Up' down South," *Advocate,* no. 373 (1983): 49. Also see: K. Marlowe, *Mr. Madam* (Los Angeles: Sherbourne Press, 1964); E. Nony, "Barstool Nostalgia—A Look at Gay Bars in the 50's and 60's," *Impact,* February 1978.

10. E. Patron, "Jackie Jackson: The Life and Times of a Dixie Belle," *TWN,* 12 October 1994.

11. "Gay Life in the Bad Old Days," 19.

12. G. Robison, "The Billy Jones Story," *Metropolitan Gazette,* 3 June 1982, 17.

13. Ibid., 18.

14. D. North, "Lesbians," *St. Petersburg Times Floridian,* 9 November 1969, 4.

15. In 1972 Memphis, for example, ten men were arrested for "dancing cheek-to-cheek" at the Closet (F. Harris, "Social Opportunities Expanding During 1970s," *Gaiety,* January 1976, 3). On his classic tour of early seventies gay life, John Francis Hunter quoted two gay men who had formerly lived there: "Forget it. Many raids, police beatings, and if you're arrested your name appears pronto in the papers. We literally ran away. . . . The whole city is a dark closet . . . with entrapment, harassment, and copying of license plate numbers from cars parked outside bars. It's the Bible Belt controlled by rednecks. . . . Gays here talk of themselves as queers and degenerates" (J. Hunter, *The Gay Insider* [New York: Stonehill, 1972], 567). A year earlier there were raids at Houston's La Caja and Entrée clubs with officers entering with shotguns. One officer was quoted as saying, "We will continue to raid places like this until every goddam queer has been run out of the city" ("Police Harassment in Houston," *Our Community,* October 1971, 3). Nevertheless, the *International Guild Guide* doubled its listing of gay southern bars from 1966 to 1972. Bars were now appearing in smaller towns—Kenner, Louisiana; Caldwell, Texas; Clearwater, South Carolina; and Tuscaloosa, Alabama—while the variety of bars was expanding in larger cities.

16. R. Mott, "Life Becomes Somewhat Easier for D.C. Homosexuals," *Washington Post,* 23 April 1973.

17. In addition to these two major pageants, city pageants also emerged. For example, the Queen's Men, Memphis's first gay social group, officially formed in 1971 to raise money for an orphanage. The group then changed the name to the Miss Gay Memphis Pageant (V. Astor, "The Miss Gay Memphis Pageant," *Triangle Journal News,* October 1994).

NINE — BRIGADISTAS AND BARRICADES

Interviews

Brad Keistler, 26 June 1997, West Hollywood, Calif.

Clint Pyne, 26 October 1996, 12 April and 11 October 1997, Durham, N.C.

Bob Bland, interviewed by Jim Baxter, 21 April 1983, Boston, Mass., and e-mail to the author, 14 March–3 April 2000.

1. SSOC was founded in 1964 by white students allied with the Student Non-Violent Coordinating Committee (SNCC); the organization formed campus chapters throughout the South (B. Simon, "Southern Student Organizing Committee: A New Rebel Yell in Dixie" [Department of History, University of North Carolina, photocopy, 1983, Sears Papers]). Also see J. Harland, "Dixie's New Left," *Trans-Action,* September 1970, 50–56, 62.

2. "On the Venceremos Brigade: A Forum," in K. Jay and A. Young, eds., *Out of the Closets* (New York: Harcourt Brace Jovanovich, 1972), 233.

3. The Index, known as ADEX, was part of the government's COINTELPRO secret domestic surveillance on "subversive" organizations and individuals (C. Perkus, *Cointelpro: The FBI's Secret War on Political Freedom* [New York: Monrad Press, 1975]). Had revolutionary activities reached a crisis stage, individuals listed on the Index would have been apprehended and detained based on their priority status. The recommendation to include Pyne was not acted upon, given that the CHRM no longer existed. FBI Washington, however, instructed its Charlotte field office that should "additional pertinent information concerning Pyne come to your attention," results should be submitted to the Bureau (Confidential Memorandum to Secret Service-Charlotte from Director, FBI, 14 January 1970; Confidential Memorandum to SAC, Charlotte, from Director, FBI, 2 February 1970; and Airtel Memorandum to Director, FBI, from SAC WFO, 20 November 1970, Sears Papers).

4. "On the Venceremos Brigade," 232.

5. "Who We Are," *Carolina Plain Dealer,* August 1970, 2.

6. S. Gabb, "A Fowl in the Vortices of Consciousness: The Birth of the Great Speckled Bird," in K. Wachsberger, ed., *Voices from the Underground* (Tempe, Ariz.: Mica Press, 1993), 41–50.

7. S. Abbot, "Why Do You Stomp on Us?" *Great Speckled Bird,* December 1971, 16.

8. AGH.

9. "Gay Revolution Party Manifesto," in K. Jay and A. Young, eds., *Out of the Closets* (New York: Harcourt Brace Jovanovich, 1972), 344. The cover of the first issue of the magazine declared: "Out of State—Out of Straightness—Out of Sight—Out of Mind and into the Screaming Joy of Gay Ecstasy."

10. B. Keistler, Letter to the Editor, *Carolina Plain Dealer,* January 1971, 11.

11. P. Borden, "Never Have Had to Call the Cops," *Charlotte Observer,* 28 March 1970.

12. "Homosexuals Seek Opinions of Candidates," *Charlotte Observer,* 20 March 1972. Regarding Bland and the emergence of the Triangle Gay Alliance, see: A. Young, "A North Carolina Gay Liberation Pioneer," *Front Page,* 7 June 1983, 3, 7.

13. A. Young, "An Experiment in Collective Living," *Front Page,* 7 June 1983, 9.

14. Declaring that "if the government won't stop the war, the people will stop the government," a gathering of all the "tribes" was summoned to Washington, D.C., in 1970. Asserting that "an army of lovers would not fight," gay men living in a D.C. collective on Vermont Avenue hosted the Gay Tribe May Day events. There a series of "mass actions" and presentation of the people's peace treaty with North Vietnam were planned. On 3 May, as the sun came up over the Potomac, people descended on the city. Thousands blocked traffic at intersections and converged on the "centers of war," including the White House, the Pentagon, and the Justice Department. During the summer of 1970, these actions sparked a series of gay regional gatherings.

15. "A Gay Brother," *Carolina Plain Dealer,* October 1971, 10.

16. P. Paddock, "Local Gay Liberation Front Prefers Rap Session to Bars," *Charlotte Observer,* 19 March 1972.

17. This, though, was not the first drag event held at the auditorium. For years there had been a drag ball held by the black community (personal communication from Jim Baxter to the author). But, as in many other towns, a river of racism split homosexual southerners (see chapters 15 and 24).

18. *Carolina Plain Dealer,* December 1971, 9. Despite these joint contributions to the *Plain*

Dealer, very little communication occurred between the two gay activist groups and none existed between GLF-Charlotte and those in other southern cities.

19. "Gay Is Real," *Carolina Plain Dealer,* January 1972, 9.

20. Confidential Memorandum to Director, FBI, from SAC-Charlotte, November 1971; FBI-Charlotte, 18 May 1973, George Clinton Pyne III, Security Matter—Revolutionary Activities, Sears Papers.

TEN — FIRE AND DECADENCE

Interviews

Stewart Butler, 15 September, 1998, New Orleans, La.

Troy Perry, interviewed by Roberts Batson, Bienville Foundation, August 1997, Los Angeles, Calif.

William P. Richardson, 5 August 1998, Metairie, La.

1. "Symposium: Southern Decadence," University of New Orleans, sponsored by the Bienville Foundation, 30 August 1997 (videotape), Sears Papers. Unless otherwise noted, all quoted material regarding Southern Decadence is from this taped symposium and used with permission of the Bienville Foundation. Other material used in this history of Southern Decadence Weekend includes: R. Batson, "Unnaturally New Orleans: Inventing Traditions," *Impact;* Interview with Robert Ling, *Impact,* 1982.

2. W. Dunham, "French Quarter Bar Guide," part 3, *Vieux Carré Courier,* 3 March 1972; *The Cajun Queen: A Complete Guide to New Orleans Gaydom* (n.p., circa 1973).

3. Following the week's events, some gays, such as bar owner Phil Esteve and California street preacher Ray Broshears, questioned the wisdom of involvement from outside activists ("Esteve Says There's No Need for Gay Activists," *Vieux Carré Star,* 14 April 1977). At that time, however, there was a vacuum in local leadership. The Gay Liberation Front had collapsed the year before and the only political organization, the Tulane Gay Student Union, had closed for the summer. "People were very frightened," Troy Perry recalls. "Yes, you could be gay in the Vieux Carré, but two blocks on each side you could get your head bashed in." New Orleans researcher Johnny Townsend also was unable to account for about one-third of the $17,000 raised for the National New Orleans Memorial Fund, leading to questions regarding accounting procedures (J. Townsend, "The Up Stairs Lounge Fire," photocopy, Sears Papers).

4. B. Nolton and C. Segura, "Memorial for Fire Dead Has Forgiveness Theme," *New Orleans Times-Picayune,* 26 June 1973. A. Katz, "Labeling the Dead: An Impossible Job?" *New Orleans States-Item,* 25 June 1973. Other sources used as background for the story of the fire are: Katz, "Labeling the Dead"; J. LaPlace, "Scene of French Quarter Fire Is Called Dante's 'Inferno,' Hitler's Incinerators," *New Orleans Times-Picayune,* 25 June 1973; A. Lind, "Fire Bares the Grisly Face of Death," *New Orleans States-Item,* 25 June 1973; A. Lind, A. Thomas, and W. Philbin, "13 Fire Victims Identified," *New Orleans States-Item,* 25 June 1973; W. Philbin, "First the Horror, Then the Leap," *New Orleans States-Item,* 25 June 1973; L. Thomas, "Death Plays the Piano," *New Orleans Times-Picayune,* 25 June 1973; L. Thomas, "Fun . . . Drinks . . . Song . . . with Death at the Piano," *New Orleans States-Item,* 25 June 1973; "Six of 15 Injured in Serious Condition," *New Orleans States-Item,* 29 June 1973; C. Segura, "Devastating French Quarter Fire Probed by 3 Agencies," *New Orleans Times-Picayune,* 26 June 1973; "Fatal Fire Probe Continues," *New Orleans Times-Picayune,* 26 June 1973; B. Ruston, "Forgetting the Fire," *Vieux Carré Courier,* 6 July 1973; "Up Stairs Fire Death Toll 31," *New Orleans Times-Picayune,* 12 July 1973; B. Rushton, "Fire Tragedy Confuses Both Straights, Gays," *Advocate,* 18 July 1973; G. Schwandt, "Holocaust in New Orleans," *Advocate,* 18 July 1973; P. Dvarackas, "Can an Arsonist's Flame Light the Candle for Gay Unity?" *GAY,* July 1973; B. Rushton, "Society Real Culprit in New Orleans Tragedy?" *Advocate,* 1 August 1973; B. Rushton, "New Orleans Toll 32; Arson Evidence Cited," *Advocate,* 1 August 1973; L. Thomas, "Holocaust," *New Orleans States-Item,* 24 June 1974; Fire Symposium sponsored by the Louisiana State Historical Society, Bienville Foundation, June 1998. I appreciate a review of this chapter by Johnny Townsend; a photocopy of his manuscript "The Up Stairs Lounge Fire," the most complete account of this tragedy and its victims, is in Sears Papers.

5. T. Perry, *Don't Be Afraid Anymore* (New York: St. Martin's Press, 1990), 88.

6. S. Fosberg, "It's a Faggot Bar—Did I Tell You?" *Vieux Carré Courier,* 29 June 1973.

7. Perry, *Don't Be Afraid Anymore,* 79.

8. B. Rushton, "After the Fire Up Stairs," *Vieux Carré Courier,* 29 June 1973.

9. Statement of Michael Wayne Scarborough, 16 July 1973, Department of State Fire Marshal, New Orleans, 1–2. Although Ñunez denied any involvement when questioned by police, he told a friend, Ralph Forest, four times when drunk that he had burnt the Up Stairs with Ronson lighter fluid bought at the nearby Walgreen's drugstore. Still mad at the bar for tossing him out, he appeared to Forest to be unremorseful. Ñunez married a woman twice his age one year later and, in 1974, committed suicide, drinking and then consuming phenobarbital, chlordiazepoxide, and diphenylhydantoin. Going into the bar the following Monday, Forest told Phil Esteve that Roger had died. "Mike [Scarborough] looked over to me and said, 'Is it true? He is dead?' and I [Esteve] said, 'Yes.' And he said, 'That is the one that set the fire to the Up Stairs Lounge, you know.'" Although Ñunez was the primary suspect, there were others—at least two of whom, as documented by Townsend, also confessed. Several years later, Frank J. Locascio Jr., who headed the city's arson division, wrote to the Public Safety Department that "investigators were completely satisfied that he [Ñunez] was the person who set the fire" (Townsend, "The Up Stairs Lounge Fire"). The case remains officially unsolved. Collaborative references for these events include: R. Batson, "Holocaust," *Impact,* 5 June 1998; R. Batson, "Holocaust on Gay Pride Sunday," part 2, *Impact,* 19 June 1998; S. Finch, "Fire of '73: Tragedy United Gays," *New Orleans Times-Picayune,* 24 June 1993; General Case Report F21149–73, 30 August 1973, New Orleans Department of Police, 61; Hospitalization Case Report K–12411–74, 15 November 1974, New Orleans Department of Police; Statement of Rodger Dale Nunez, 15 September 1973, Department of State Fire Marshal, New Orleans; Statement of Ralph Spencer Forest, 19 November 1974, Department of State Fire Marshal, New Orleans; Townsend, "The Up Stairs Lounge Fire." Copies of these materials are located in Sears Papers.

10. J. LaPlace and E. Anderson, "29 Killed in Quarter Blaze," *New Orleans Times-Picayune,* 25 June 1973.

11. Fosberg, "It's a Faggot Bar."

12. J. Pope, "Arsonist Never Found in Fire that Killed 32," *New Orleans Times-Picayune,* 26 June 1988.

13. Nolton and Segura, "Memorial for Fire Dead."

14. S. Finch, "Fire of '73: Tragedy United Gays," *New Orleans Times-Picayune,* 24 June 1993.

15. R. Batson, "Holocaust on Gay Pride Sunday," part 2, *Impact,* 19 June 1998.

ELEVEN — ATLAS SHRUGGED

Interviews

Vicki Gabriner, 20 October 1999, Boston, Mass.

Lorraine Fontana, 20 October 1999, New York City.

Elizabeth Knowlton, 2 October 1999, Atlanta, and e-mail to the author, 18 October, 13 December 1999.

Beth Marschak, 3 May 1999, Richmond, Va.

Merril Mushroom, 29 April 1997, 20 June 1998, Doweltown, Tenn.

Julia [Stanley] Penelope, 13 and 27 June 1998, Lubbock, Tex. Quotations from S. Wolfe and J. Penelope, "Crooked and Straight in Academia," in J. Penelope and S. Wolfe, *Lesbian Culture* (Freedom, Calif.: Crossing Press, 1993), 159, are reprinted by permission of J. Penelope.

The epigraph is from a letter to Rochelle Girson (who was the book review editor at *Saturday Review*) from Lillian Smith, 5 March 1962, in M. Gladney, *How Am I to Be Heard?* (Chapel Hill: University of North Carolina Press, 1993), 295.

1. "Georgia Students Try for Gay Dance," *GAY,* 3 April 1972. P. Cain, *Rainbow Rights: The Role of Lawyers and Courts in the Lesbian and Gay Civil Rights Movement* (Boulder, Colo.: Westview, 2000), 94–96.

2. "For a Southern Convention and Association of Gay Militants," circa fall 1972, ALFA Papers. See also "Gay Conference," *Great Speckled Bird,* 13 October 1972.

3. "South Gains Gay Coalition," *Lavender Wave,* January 1973.

4. Ibid., 1.

5. "Gay Convention," *Great Speckled Bird,* 20 November 1972.

6. "South Gains Gay Coalition," 2. Only the Marxist group walked out during this session, when the convention refused to exclude "pro-capitalists."

7. "ALFA House Open," *Great Speckled Bird,* 9 October 1972; "ALFA: Atlanta Womyn Together for Ten Years," *Metropolitan Gazette* 3, 33 (1982); V. Gabriner, "A Hystory of the Atlanta Lesbian/Feminist Alliance, 1972–1978," *Atalanta,* December 1980; D. Kaye, "ALFA," *Great Speckled Bird,* 11 September 1972.

8. See, for example, Gabriner's *Great Speckled Bird* article "Vicki Writes About Women," 5 June 1972, and "Lesbians Respond," 10 July 1972, written by Vicki, Lorraine, and ten other women.

9. S. Wells and V. Gabriner, "How to Start a Lesbian Organization," *Atalanta* 5, 8 (1977): 3–4.

10. A. Rand, *Atlas Shrugged* (New York: Dutton, 1992; originally published, New York: Random House, 1957), 731.

11. The third issue (16 October 1969) became the *Female Liberation Newsletter of Durham-Chapel Hill,* after "women" was not seen as being inclusive enough to include children. It was sold for five cents at weekly feminist meetings. The newsletter stopped publishing in August 1970 but reappeared the next February. Serving mostly as a community calendar and for announcements, it was now the *Female Liberation Newsletter of Chapel Hill* and had been reduced to two pages. Its last issue in that form was published in December 1971—a single-page ditto. In February of 1973, a revived and expanded *Feminist Newsletter* included reviews, poetry, fiction, and ads, as well as a calendar and local news ("The Feminist Newsletter," *Feminist Newsletter,* 22 September 1974, 4; E. Knowlton, Letters, *Feminary* 8, 1 [1978]: 2).

12. For a detailed history of this paper, see C. Douglas and F. Moira, "Off Our Backs: The First Decade (1970–1980)," in K. Wachsberger, ed., *Voices from the Underground* (Tempe, Ariz.: Mica Press, 1993), 107–130.

13. Radicalesbians, "The Woman-Identified Woman," in K. Jay and A. Young, eds., *Out of the Closets* (New York: Jove, 1972), 176.

14. "Rough Draft Proposal: Lesbian Caucus Position Paper," circa January 1973, pp. 5–6, ALFA Papers; "Lesbian Caucus Position Paper," March 1973, p. 2, ALFA Papers.

15. "Rough Draft Proposal," 9; "Lesbian Caucus Position Paper," 5.

16. "WarmeBruder Caucus Position Paper," 9 March 1973, p. 1, ALFA Papers.

17. "Lesbians Speak Up at Regional Gay Convention," *Gay Times,* April 1973, 6–7. Mississippi State University lesbians who attended the conference also reprinted a summary (it appeared first in the *Jackson Women's Coalition Newsletter*) in their inaugural issue of *Sting Like a Butterfly.* These lesbians concluded: "Since it will be some time (perhaps never) before any South-Eastern Organization will put itself in the constructive position of a 'service' organization, we will continue the slow struggle" (L. Landrum, *Gay Struggle,* November 1972).

18. "Sisters and Brothers," *Gay Times* 2, 1 (1973): 2–3.

19. Such relationships span generations of southern queer history. Emma Jane Gay founded a school for young ladies in 1865 Macon with her lover, Catherine Melville, whom she had met in Knoxville. During the war, the couple moved to Washington and administered a school for the deaf before joining Dorothea Dix in her work with Union soldiers (Jane Gay Dodge Collection, Schlesinger Library, Harvard University; J. Schwartz, *Our Photographic Heritage: First in a Series of E. Jane Gay* [Lesbian Herstory Archives, Brooklyn, photocopy]).

There were also the efforts of longtime companions Laura Matilda Towne and Ellen Murray to establish and operate Penn School and a community outreach center for African Americans who lived on St. Helena's Island, off the coast of Beaufort, South Carolina, in 1862. Their forty-year struggle to bring literacy and a Booker T. Washington–type education to island blacks has been better documented than their romantic friendship, which began while both were attending school in Pennsylvania (H. Foote, "The Penn School of St. Helena's Island," *Southern Workman* 33 (1914): 218–230). A lesbian who would become a prominent supporter of civil rights was Lillian Smith, who with her lover, Paula Snelling, had operated the first private girls' camp in Laurel Falls, in northern Georgia. The two later edited *South Today,* an early-forties anti–racial segregation magazine, which was earlier published as *Pseudophobia,* a southern literary magazine, and then as *North Georgia Review,* focusing on southern culture, including reviews of Negro books. Smith then wrote the best-selling 1944 novel *Strange Fruit* (banned in Boston), which linked racism, sexism, and repressive attitudes toward sexuality (Gladney, *How Am I to Be Heard;* A. Loveland, *Lillian Smith: A Southerner Confronting the South* [Baton Rouge: Louisiana State University Press, 1986]).

Southern lesbian heroines also served during World War II. North Carolina native Nell "Johnnie" Phelps, for example, enlisted in the newly formed Women's Army Auxiliary Corps (WACS). After serving as a medic in the Philippines (where she earned a Purple Heart), she was assigned to head General Eisenhower's motor pool, where she responded to his directive of ferreting out the lesbians: "If the general pleases, I'll be happy to do this . . . but you have to know that the first name on the list will be mine." She later became heavily involved with substance abuse work centers for women and operated a printing press, donating work for progressive and women's causes (Y. Retter, "Johnnie Phelps: In Memoriam," *ONE/IGLA Bulletin,* Summer 1998, 4). During the war, too, there were lesbian pilots, some of whom were members of Amelia Earhart's Ninety-Nines, who towed decoy planes off the coast of Florida in order for rookie male pilots to practice their maneuvers ("Ninety-Nines," Sears Papers).

20. Women's Liberation: Charlotte, *Carologue,* compiled by S. Hoffius and A. Katz (Durham, N.C., 1972), 64. By 1970–1971, according to Elizabeth Knowlton, there were statewide women's liberation meetings in a different city every few months, including Raleigh, Durham, Charlotte, Chapel Hill, and Greensboro, and a High Point working-class lesbian collective.

21. B. Swisher, "Author/Wit Rita Mae Brown Inspired First Organization," *Richmond Pride,* May 1988, 6–7; M. Carter, "'Homegrown Radical' is Human Rights Catalyst," *Richmond Pride,* August 1989, 8.

22. L. Allen, *A Bluestocking in Charleston: The Life and Career of Laura Bragg* (Columbia: University of South Carolina Press, 2001); J. Sears and L. Allen, "Museums, Friends, and Lovers in the New South: Laura's Web, 1909–1931," *Journal of Homosexuality,* 40, 1 (2000): 106–144.

23. Even less activist or liberal communities enjoyed feminist activity. For example, in South Carolina, the Grimké Sisters Union labored in Columbia. About fifty women met in small groups each week to support one another "in mutual struggles" that stemmed from the police harassment of the antiwar UFO Coffeehouse and the weekend operation of the UFO in Exile at the USC campus (D. Ferre, "UFOffence Coalition," *Protean Raddish,* 25 February 1970, 5). In Memphis, another conservative southern town, much of the feminist activity emanated from the NOW chapter, which began in 1970. Here again lesbians were a major but invisible presence during the next couple of years (D. Buring, *Lesbian and Gay Memphis* [New York: Garland, 1997]).

In contrast, Jackson lesbians who wanted to enjoy any sense of women loving women traveled to Memphis (as well as Atlanta and New Orleans). Jackson women had formed two "distinct but totally separate" groups, the NOW Chapter and the Jackson Women's Coalition. The latter organization, with its center on North Jefferson Street, attracted a mostly white, youthful group. It sponsored CR groups, collected materials for their "feminist library," published a newsletter, and embraced lesbianism (J. Culbertson, "Local Women's Movements, Similar Goals," *Jackson Clarion Ledger,* 19 October 1973). There also was a short-lived lesbian newsletter, *Sting Like a Butterfly,* edited by an anonymous Mississippi State University student. "Who is the Lesbian in Mississippi? . . . How does the lesbian in rural America function, how is she different from her Lesbian sisters in Metropolitan America?" the nameless writer asked. Her response was bleak: She has "no 'gay community,' no gay bars, no populace of straights who support her, no church who will minister to her, no civil-rights groups who will risk an alliance. . . . [There] is no alternative shelter that a gay woman could turn to for a livelihood and support if and when she lost her job or has been exiled from home" (L. Landrum, "Rapping Down the Dusty Lavender Road," *Sting Like a Butterfly,* 19 January 1973).

In the face of this barren lesbiscape, two women—Anne de Bary and Donna Myhre—cofounded the Mississippi Gay Alliance in Starksville during the 1972 fall semester. Working closely with the Women's Action Movement, de Bary and others produced the WAM newsletter, which included an advertisement regarding a gay center and an article by a lesbian in its December issue. As MGA expanded counseling services, the group sought to publicize itself in the student paper, the *Reflector,* as the fall 1973 semester began. The *Reflector*'s refusal to run the ad resulted in an extended suit, with rulings in favor of the university (*Mississippi Gay Alliance v. Goudelock,* 536 F.2d 1073 [5th Cir. 1976]. Cert denied, 430 U.S. 982 [1977]; letter to Donna Myhre from Christine Benagh, 12 July 1974, Sandifer Papers). In 1974, as de Bary prepared to leave the area, she wrote Eddie Sandifer, a longtime Jackson civil rights activist and gay man, about taking over the organization, provided the counseling services continued and efforts were made to make MGA truly a statewide organization. At the end of 1974, chapters had been established in several cities, a newsletter produced, a state conference organized, a charter of incorporation enacted, and a gay pride rally held at Riverside Park in Jackson (letter to Ed Sandifer from Anne de Bary, 27 February 1974, Sandifer Papers; *Mississippi Gay Alliance Newsletter,* June 1974; "Sexual Privacy," *ACLU/M Newsletter,* May 1974; Mississippi Gay Alliance-Jackson Chapter, "Meeting Minutes," 7 April 1974, Sandifer Papers).

24. J. Stanley, "Coming Out," in *The Universities and the Gay Experience: Proceedings of the Conference Sponsored by the Women and Men of the Gay Academic Union, November 1973* (New York: Gay Academic Union, 1974), 81–87.

25. Julia would also collaborate with Louie on lesbian/gay activities in the National Council of Teachers of English, and the Modern Language Association. Crew, who later founded Integrity (a gay Episcopal support group) while at a black Georgia college, exchanged detailed correspondence with Stanley that shaped his profeminist thinking (see chapter 14).

TWELVE — THE PROMISED LAND

Interviews

Robert S. Basker, 14 and 15 June 1997, San Francisco, Calif.

Jack Nichols, 13 January 1995, Cocoa Beach, Fla. All quotations from Jack Nichols, "Sissies," a manuscript, are used with his permission

Jesse Monteagudo, 9 January 1995, 18 June 1998, Miami, Fla., and e-mail to the author, 13 and 15 June 1998. All quotations from J. Monteagudo, "Miami, Florida," in J. Preston, ed., *Hometowns* (New York: Plume, 1991), 11–20, are used by permission of the author.

Paul Wegman, 28 March, 18 April, 27 October, 16 November 1997, Orlando, Fla.

1. With the publication of a score of now classic works, 1972 marked a turning point in nonfiction gay books: *Society and the Healthy Homosexual* by psychologist George Weinberg, Australian social scientist Dennis Altman's *Homosexual,* DOB founders Del Martin and Phyllis Lyon's *Lesbian/Woman,* as well as Joseph McCaffrey's *The Homosexual Dialectic,* Sydney Abbott and Barbara Love's *Sappho Was a Right-on Woman,* and *What Happened* by journalist Merle Miller.

2. In addition to interviews, other sources used to augment the stories of Jack and Lige are: letters to Lige Clarke from Jack Nichols, 1967–1974; letter to Foster Gunnison from Jack Nichols, 13 February 1968; and *Roommates* book tour interviews, Clarke Papers.

3. Ordinances also forbade the serving of alcohol to a "known" homosexual and "known" homosexuals to work or operate bars. For details of Inman's efforts see J. Sears, *Lonely Hunters* (New York: HarperCollins/Westview, 1997), 212–257.

4. Sears, *Lonely Hunters,* 253. In 1967, the landmark federal obscenity case was won by Conrad Germain and Lloyd Spinar of Directory Services, Inc. Following this victory allowing male nude publications to be produced and sent through the mail, physique magazines soon became erotic curios, as full frontal male nudes were the norm. The case

was supported by longtime Mattachine leader Harold L. Call, who arranged for expert witnesses, including Wardell Pomeroy, formerly of the Kinsey Institute. Call, like other early homophile male leaders, including Clark Polak of Philadelphia's *Drum* magazine, Guy Straight of DOM, and Richard Inman of the Atheneum Bookstore, produced or sold male erotica, helping to support themselves and early movement efforts. In the 1970s, Call opened Cinemattachine, one of San Francisco's first sex clubs. Straight, who organized the League for Civil Education in the same city, later served several years in the penitentiary for producing and selling child pornography. Richard Inman, following one too many police raids on his adult bookstore in Miami, moved to the more liberal climate of Long Beach, where he died of natural causes in 1985 (J. Sears, *Calling Shots* (New York: Haworth Press, forthcoming). Later, a new generation of activists like Atlanta's Bill Smith and Florida's Jack Campbell channeled their profits from escort services or the baths into gay organizing ("Gay Activist Arrested in Call Boy Ring—Tip from Feinstein," *San Francisco Examiner,* 27 July 1978, 3; AGH).

5. Frank Kameny, who knew Gunnison well, described him as an "honorable man" but an "apparatchik," that is, a functionary. "He did very well at the things he did," Kameny explains, "secretary of this, record keeper of that" (interview with Frank Kameny by Paul Cain, 2 July 1994, p. 14, Sears Papers).

6. Letter to Jack Nichols from Lige Clarke, 27 January 1968, Clarke Papers. Lige had been separated from Jack for nearly a year, although the two wrote regularly and occasionally got together. During their separation Jack admitted to Foster Gunnison Jr.: "I was thoughtless, confusedly cruel, and not as perceptive as I feel myself today. If I had been as perceptive then as now, we never would have separated, or at least—not for long." Calling himself a "displaced homophiler," Jack told Foster that he had little interest in working with Richard Inman, who was "too much of a loner for me" (letter to Foster Gunnison from Jack Nichols, 13 February 1968, Clarke Papers). A few months later as they approached their reunion as a couple, Lige wrote Jack: "If I didn't love you very much, I would have called it quits long ago and wouldn't have gone through those agonizing months after our breakup. But, I knew that with patience I could forgive because I never could imagine going through life without you" (letter to Jack Nichols from Lige Clarke, 26 May 1968, Clarke Papers).

7. Lige later wrote Jack: "Richard Inman doesn't know when to stop talking. I thought my arm was going to drop off from holding the receiver so long. I think he has big plans, but it sounded doubtful to me whether they would materialize" (letter to Jack Nichols from Lige Clarke, 18 April 1968, Clarke Papers). Lige promised to drop by Inman's cab stand, but Jack wrote back: "I'm really sorry that that stupid Inman has been 'sounding off' so much. Probably the further we stay away from his schemes the better" (letter to Lige Clarke from Jack Nichols, 22 April 1968, Clarke Papers).

8. Letter to Jack Nichols from Lige Clarke, 10 April 1968, Clarke Papers.

9. In 1961, when Bob Basker went through divorce proceedings, he was represented by civil liberties attorney Pearl Hart. Hart was a founding member of the National Lawyer's Guild and had collaborated with Jane Addams, the founder of Chicago's legendary Hull House. Like Addams, Hart was a "secret lesbian" and a lifelong activist in feminist and leftist causes. Bob explained that with a family no longer to worry about because of police entrapment, he was going to get involved in the homophile movement. He began subscribing to magazines like *Mattachine Review,* visiting "various gay communities around the country getting a sense of how they were organized," attending homosexual conferences, and trying to find others who wished to organize in Chicago's gay bars. Meeting little success in political recruitment, Hart—who had defended homosexual men in court and had supported founders of the first Mattachine chapter during the mid-fifties—gave Basker occasional client names as potential members. Through her "inspiration," Basker founded Mattachine-Midwest, a name suggested by Craig Rodwell. Within a year, the group had a functioning organization with a newsletter and a telephone referral service and had successfully challenged "the harvest of fruits" in court. Other homophile activists, like Dorr Legg of the One Institute in Los Angeles, occasionally spoke before the group. For greater detail, see: J. Sears, "Bob Basker: Selling the Movement," in V. Bullough, ed., *Pioneers* (New York: Haworth Press, forthcoming). Basker's efforts

ushered in the revival of the "moribund Chicago Mattachine Group." Founded in 1954, it had long lost steam by decade's end (J. D'Emilio, *Sexual Politics, Sexual Communities* [Chicago: University of Chicago Press, 1983], 115–117).

10. Sears, *Lonely Hunters,* 233.
11. Letter to Companero Hugo Garcia from Robert Basker, 25 March 1967, Basker Papers.
12. Richard Inman never returned to the activist role that he once had in Florida. He settled in a working-class area on the outskirts of Long Beach—not far from the interstate highway—where he lived in a Spanish-style duplex on the corner of Golden Avenue and Hill Street until his death on 3 February 1985.
13. M. Baxter, "The American Minority," *Tropic Magazine,* 24 August 1969.
14. Characteristic of the unfavorable press that continued into the early Stonewall period, a *Miami News* article, following the cinematic release of *Boys in the Band,* described homosexuality as "neurotic" and homosexual relationships as "unhappy and short-lived" (J. McHale, "Sex Not Everything in 'Gay' Relationship," *Miami News,* 24 August 1970).
15. "Gay Bar Laws Ruled Invalid," *Miami News,* 10 December 1971.
16. Sears, *Lonely Hunters,* 254–255. However, a lesser ordinance proscribing lewd and lascivious conduct remained in effect.
17. I. Glass, "'Gay' Bar Law Here May Get Test in Court," *Miami News,* 8 November 1971.
18. P. Ramirez, "Law Upset Forbidding Serving Homosexuals," *Miami Herald,* 10 December 1971.
19. T. King, "Gay Bars Misunderstood," *Miami News,* 20 March 1972; "New Visibility of Homosexuality Merely Hints at Hidden World," *Miami Herald,* 30 April 1972.
20. "New Visibility."
21. Letter to Nicholas Valeriani from Robert Barry, 7 May 1972, Basker Papers.
22. "Sex, Dress at Issue," *Miami News,* 16 January 1973.
23. R. Elder, "Gay Activists' Suit Attacks Female Impersonation Law," *Miami Herald,* 22 June 1972; "Gay Activists Win Beach Suit," *Miami News,* 22 June 1972; R. Stulberg, "Gay Activists Call Court Ruling on Impersonation 'Great Victory,'" *Miami News,* 23 June 1972.
24. C. Wright, "Impersonation Laws Killed," *Miami Herald,* 23 June 1972.
25. Ibid.
26. The park was the designated campground for protesters ranging from the SDS and the Zippies to the Jesus Freaks and the two hundred or so gay liberationists. Following a series of assaults on gay men and lesbians by "machismo" activists, gays were assigned a roped-off area. This was soon abandoned in favor of night security marshals, which allowed nongay activists opportunities to interact with the gay activists in the daylight.
27. "Democratic Convention Airs Gay Lib Proposals," *GAY,* 7 August 1972, 10.
28. R. Fabricio, "Suit Charges Beach Harassment of Homosexuality," *Miami Herald,* 27 May 1973.
29. Gay Activist Alliance of Miami, "Statement Prepared for Hearing Held by the Florida Commission on Human Rights, Miami, Florida, September 24, 1973"; letter to Arthur C. Warner from Robert Basker, 7 September 1973; letter to Arthur C. Warner from Robert Basker, 10 December 1973, Basker Papers. Also see: P. Gurosky, "Discrimination Seen Widespread," *Miami News,* 25 September 1973; S. Payton, "Rights Bill Wins Support," *Miami Herald,* 26 September 1973.
30. Gay Activist Alliance of Miami, "General Meeting," 23 November 1973, Basker Papers.
31. J. Nichols, "Sissies," manuscript.

THIRTEEN — THE SORORITY

Interviews

"Karla Brown," 30 December 1999, Newark, N.J.

John "Gabby" Haze, 29 April 1997, Doweltown, Tenn.

Margo George, 6 August 2000, Oakland, Calif., and e-mail to the author, 3 and 5 August 2000.

Elizabeth Knowlton, 2 October 1999, Atlanta.

Beth Marschak, 3 May 1999, Richmond, Va., and interview by Bob Swisher, 26 January 1988, Southern Studies Collection, IGLA.

Merril Mushroom, 29 April 1997, 20 June 1998, Doweltown, Tenn.

Julia Stanley Penelope, 13 and 27 June 1998, Lubbock, Tex.

Barbara Weinstock, 3 May 1999, Richmond, Va., and e-mail to the author, 21 August 2000.

The epigraph is from a letter to Julia Stanley Penelope from Anastasia, circa 1974, Penelope Papers.

1. The use of sexist language was also decried by Jill Johnston, author of *Lesbian Nation.*
2. Letter to Julia from Anastasia, Penelope Papers.
3. The Triangle area was rich with feminist activities. For instance, in 1971, Lollipop Power grew out of the Chapel Hill/Durham Women's Liberation discussion group on the absence of children's books with nonsexist themes or characters that crossed racial and class lines ("Lollipop Power," *New Carolina Woman,* Summer 1971, 3). The Women's Radio Collective operated for four years (1974–1978), broadcasting two programs: Women's Voices, three-and-one-half-minute daily features; Women's Show, a two-and-one-half-hour production of music, interviews, and news ("Dubious Progress," *Feminary* 8, 1 [1978]: 13–19).
4. "The Feminist Newsletter," *Feminist Newsletter,* 22 September 1974, 4; E. Knowlton, Letters, *Feminary* 8, 1 (1978): 2.
5. For Linda's story, see N. Adair and C. Adair, *Word Is Out* (San Francisco: New Glide Publications, 1978), 123–131. The film crew for this groundbreaking documentary spent a week with women from Atlanta and ALFA and filmed a dozen or so of the Triangle Area Lesbian Feminists in their circle. This footage, however, failed to make it into the film (291, 301).
6. This women's resource book was published by Diana Press of Baltimore in 1974. Modeled after the *Whole Earth Catalogue* and the *Carolina Carologue,* it included articles on "long-living" women and women's studies, as well as lesbianism, and was sent to all the public and school libraries in the state.
7. The winter before Elizabeth moved to Atlanta, the Carrboro Collective connected with a group of Durham lesbians who were reviving the lesbian rap group in the Duke Gay Alliance. Not long after Elizabeth departed, the Triangle Area Lesbian Feminists formed. For a history of the emergence of lesbian-feminist activity in the Triangle area, see "Notes Toward a History," *Feminary* 9, 1 (1978): 26–28, 56.
8. Some larger cities like Louisville experienced such divisions. In 1973, Louisville lesbians joined with other radical heterosexual women to form the Feminist Cell. Publishing *Woman Kind* newsletter, they wanted women to understand the power of patriarchy in their lives. Issues of sexuality, however, soon divided the group and thirteen lesbians departed. As one member related: "We were not sure who to trust— feminists, who actually offered us little support, or ourselves. We were not yet experienced enough to believe we could form a movement of our own, so the issue divided us" (K. Williams, "Louisville's Lesbian Feminist Union," in J. Howard, ed., *Carryin' On* [New York: New York University Press, 1997], 227). The more political-minded lesbians joined the local NOW chapter; another group, calling itself the Feminist Lesbians of America, organized as a social alternative to the bar. A year later, however, these women had become more politicized, while those in NOW were increasingly frustrated by the necessity to remain sexually silent. The Lesbian Feminist Union was thus formed and Louisville women were put on notice: "[W]e will not hide and we will not be quiet. We will rise a stronger Nation of Amazons" (*LFU Newsletter,* 1975, quoted in Williams, "Louisville's Lesbian Feminist Union," 229).
9. This seemed particularly evident in towns like Columbia, South Carolina, and Jackson, Mississippi, that lacked the lesbian density of Atlanta, the lesbian legacy of Richmond, or the radical politics of the Triangle area. Dale Orlando began her graduate work in community psychology at the University of South Carolina in the fall of 1974. Inspired by the groundbreaking research of Evelyn Hooker and the radical politics of Jill Johnston,

Orlando sought to organize Columbia lesbians and document their needs. She soon visited the local NOW chapter; the Fortress, a lesbian bar; and the MCC mission in Columbia. The NOW chapter, which included women of color as well as several lesbians, was open to her project, as was Joyce, the bar owner, and the two dozen church members. With literature Dale received from Boston DOB and contacts from ALFA, she entered into local lesbian networks and administered her questionnaire as a form of community organizing. In mid-March 1975, Orlando and others formed the Alliance. Members sought "to promote a positive image of our community to the larger community and lend support to gay people" ("Alliance Announcements," 20 June 1974, Sears Papers). Activities included monthly meetings at a member's home, Tuesday-night covered-dish suppers, rap groups, public relations efforts (resulting in a TV appearance and local newspaper coverage), speaking engagements, a monthly newsletter (*The Alliance*), support for a gubernatorial candidate, and social outings to nearby parks. About one-half of its female members were in their thirties or forties, with gay males considered for membership only through "sponsorship" (E. Bryan, "Alliance Formed to Aid Gay Community," *State,* 20 June 1974; E. Bryan, "The Gay World of Women," *State,* 22 June 1974; D. Orlando, "The Sappho Strain," unpublished journal, 1974, Sears Papers). In Jackson, declaring they had "run out of dedication to a losing cause," Chris and Fredericka published the "last issue" of the *Lesbian Front* in 1975. "If it hadn't been for the support of lesbians and groups outside the state . . . we would have given up long ago." The couple informed their few readers they were "heading West, in an effort to find vocal/active lesbian/feminists" ("Closing Statement," *Lesbian Front,* November 1975, 1). Nevertheless, the newsletter, which had begun the previous March as "The Unnamed Lesbian Newsletter" with the support of the Jackson Women's Coalition, was later revived.

10. Envisioned as a social-change alternative store, Charis Books and More was also opened in the fall of 1974 by Linda Bryant and Barbara Borgman. "When we opened I'd never heard of Daughters Press. And we had no books about lesbians," Linda says. With the store's owners initially unaware of ALFA or even Little Five Points's lesbian households, the store gradually reflected a more lesbian-feminist focus. For the evolution of Charis, see: "Beyond the Chamber of Commerce," *ALFA Newsletter* 4, 12 (1976): 9; S. Chestnut and A. Gable, "Women Ran It," in J. Howard, ed., *Carryin' On* (New York: New York University Press, 1997), 241–284.

11. The incident occurred in early March 1973 at the Matador bar in Birmingham, where the two embraced and kissed on the lips, and then Freddie "knelt beside her chair and rocked her in my arms." About fifteen minutes later, a vice officer approached the table and arrested Freddie. The two women later appealed the judge's $200 fine ("Lesbians Arrested," *Great Speckled Bird,* 2 July 1972; "Freddie's Trial(s)," *ALFA Newsletter,* February 1973, 2).

12. The preceding four letters are from: Correspondence to ALFA, Box 3, Folder: 1973–1974, ALFA Papers.

13. Ibid., 1975–1976, ALFA Papers.

14. Ibid., 1977–1979, ALFA Papers.

15. As do most groups, ALFA experienced growing pains as evidenced in the first issue of its newsletter, which spoke about "the frustrations we've all felt over ALFA's inability to get herself together." Six women joined together to assume much-needed coordinating and managing functions. This short-lived leadership group was called "Scarlett." At least one ALFA woman viewed the group as "selective, exclusive," asking, "Do you want to lead or do you want to follow?" ("ALFA Meeting Notes," 25 September 1973, Box 7, ALFA Papers). Within a week, Scarlett members met to discuss this issue and by October its Monday-night meetings were open to any ALFA member (*ALFA Newsletter,* October 1973, 1; "ALFA Meeting Notes," 30 September, 7 October 1973, ALFA Papers).

16. Elizabeth Knowlton, though, observes: "I was the older (thirty) woman of middle-class background. However, most were younger than I and of varying classes. Those who had gone to college were mostly first generation. Lorraine's childhood home was over a store at first; my lover's, a basement room."

FOURTEEN — SEPARATIONS

Interviews

Donald Engstrom, 1 October 1995, Short Mountain, Tenn.

Milo Guthrie (Clint Pyne), 19 April 1996, Durham, N.C. All quotations from Milo Guthrie, "Short Mountain: Land of My Dreams," manuscript, are used with the permission of the author.

John "Gabby" Haze, 29 April 1997, Doweltown, Tenn.

Merril Mushroom, 29 April 1997, 20 June and 19 October 1998, Doweltown, Tenn.

Julia [Stanely] Penelope, 27 June 1998, Lubbock, Tex.

The epigraph is from a letter to Peter Lee from Stewart Scofield, 2 August 1974, Lee Papers.

1. K. Kinkade, *A Walden Two Experiment* (New York: Morrow, 1974); S. Gaskin, *This Season's People* (Summertown, Tenn.: Book Publishing, 1976). Also see A. Stein, *Seeds of the Seventies* (Hanover, N.H.: University Press of New England, 1985).
2. Confidential Memorandum to Director, FBI, from SAC, Memphis, 8 January 1974, Pyne Papers. Later, FBI agents observed: "Subjects have built a greenhouse on the property where they are raising flowers and various herbs" (Confidential Memorandum to Director, FBI, from SAC, Memphis, 23 April 1974, Pyne Papers). Law enforcement eventually concluded the Tick Creek remnants "are not known to be engaged in any subversive activities at the present time," and they abandoned their surveillance (Confidential Memorandum to Director, FBI, from SAC, Charlotte, 20 December 1974, Pyne Papers).
3. Daisy's Journal, 11 November 1973, Pyne Papers.
4. A. Troxler, "The Rejection," *RFD*, no. 1 (Fall 1974): 16.
5. S. Scofield, "RFD History," *RFD*, no. 34 (Spring 1983): 9.
6. Ibid.
7. Letter to Stewart Scofield from Nancy Bishop, 25 June 1974, *Mother Earth News* (*MEN*), reprinted in *RFD*, no. 1 (Fall 1974): 14–15. As early as 1972, Joel Starkley, editor of the *Southern Gay Liberator*, had asked *MEN* to place an ad for "gay brothers and sisters" interested in "a gay people's commune." The response was similar; the editors were concerned about offending "little old ladies in Peoria." Starkley wrote back tersely: "While your memo might not offend 'little old ladies' it certainly offended me" ("More from *MEN*," *RFD*, no. 2 [Winter 1974]: 11). *Mother Earth News* continued this policy, rejecting advertisement from *RFD* again in 1977 and in 1981 ("Gay and Rejected," *RFD*, no. 26 [Spring 1981]: 4).
8. Scofield, "RFD History," 10. Based on this correspondence, other names were provided that allowed Stewart to write a mimeographed letter to potential subscribers and contributors in mid-June.
9. Stewart "often imagined myself in the early part of the century before radio, before telephones and before mail delivery to country homes when you had to go into town to pick up the latest mail order catalogs, a magazine from New York, or a postcard from a beloved auntie" (ibid., 9).
10. Prior to the first issue, Stewart wrote his friend Peter Lee, in South Carolina: "Sometimes I don't believe that this whole winter fantasy is actually happening. . . . The name is R.F.D.–Rural Faggot Digest, Rising Fairy Dance, Radiant Fruit Dream. . . . Maybe choose a different name for each issue or have a contest with a prize of pansy seeds, lavender overalls or a trip to Kansas. . . . We are not looking for fancy analysis full of rhetoric of gay liberation but rather would like to hear about you, the land you live with, what you are thinking, feeling, doing" (letter to Peter Lee from Stewart Scofield, 2 August 1974, Lee Papers). Other materials relied on for *RFD* background include: R. Lambe, "*RFD*: Gay Men Living the Good Life in the Country," *In Touch for Men*, no. 105 (1985): 32–34, 75; K. Hale-Wehmann, "RFD: A Look at the Turbulent Life of 'A Country Journal for Gay Men Everywhere,'" *Gay Community News*, 12 March 1983.
11. "Pansy Seed," *RFD*, no. 3 (Spring 1975): 49. These early issues sometimes generated angry letters from radicals who questioned the wisdom of building a new culture by abandoning urban activism. For example, a San Franciscan, Tom Kennedy, wrote: "I

am angered at the consciousness that perpetuates the notion that we can escape the evils of a fucked-up world by staying far, far away from the cities that manifest such evils. . . . While you produce issues with cute little dome houses nestled under a starry sky and silently covered with a fresh blanket of snow on the cover, we are busy in this so called 'gay mecca' trying to get it together to just survive. . . . No organic gardens or macramé plant hangers will ease our situation" (Letters, *RFD*, no. 8 [Spring 1976]: 3). Not surprisingly, this stirred responses from other readers, including longtime political activist Clark Polak, former president of the pre-Stonewall Janus Society in Philadelphia: "I see what you are doing, living, as a positive affirmation of the diversity possible in America. . . . To reject the traditional value system . . . is no less a radical statement than are those who see violent disruption of the political process as a prerequisite to social reform" (Letters, *RFD*, no. 9 [Fall 1976]: 11).

12. Scofield, "RFD History," 10.

13. Ibid. For example, in a letter to the Iowa collective, Carl Wittman admonished the group for its "immature, shoot-from-the-hip" correspondence with its "evasive misuse" of the Zodiac, and "campy sarcasm" as well as their "self-righteous tantrum" to the feminist publishing group. Carl, too, was bothered by the women's press, which insisted on a "blank check" policy to cover printing costs and lacked a telephone, and whose members generally shared a distrust of gay men. Expressing concern that Stewart may be "controlling things too autocratically," Carl wrote in exasperation: "I feel like we are being treated as the editorial contributor, artist, fundraising annex and that you feel free to act as the decision-making body for RFD" (letter to Stewart Scofield from Carl Wittman, 3 April 1975, Pyne Papers).

This mistrust and divisiveness continued after the magazine moved to Oregon. Ollie, reflecting on those early *RFD* days and the Iowans' relationship with the Wolf Creek collective, wrote:

> They were our severest critics. Many issues were late, many had mistakes, the substance of many were questioned. There were differences of politics and opinion. We in Iowa felt a certain West Coast elitism. . . . There were also social class differences. . . . We came off as politically untogether, particularly in our dealings with the Women's Press. . . . We forgot that we were doing something that none of us had done before. We forgot that *RFD* was evolving, changing. Most importantly, we forgot that *RFD* was appreciated by so many people. ("RFD Chronicle," *RFD*, no. 5 [Fall 1975]: 48)

14. *RFD* had hoped to include contributions from lesbians as well as gay men in the journal and the feminist press expected a commitment to publish the next three issues. At the 1975 Midwest Gay Pride Conference, about thirty people met to discuss such concerns. It was generally agreed that "RFD should be for faggots . . . women and lesbians into country alternatives already had media outlets" ("Minutes of Midwest Gay Pride Conference, RFD Meeting," 12 April 1975, Lee Papers). However, it wasn't until the twelfth issue that *RFD* placed beneath its masthead: "A Country Journal for Gay Men Everywhere"—and there wasn't a woman-focused issue until issue sixteen.

15. Faygele reminisces about that Elwha issue,

> produced in the most decrepit part of the house, used for hay storage. We piled the bales to one side, set boards across them, and commenced work. A rainstorm interrupted, so Carl rigged ponchos up over our work area to keep the layout table dry. He spelled me occasionally from my typing responsibilities and put much energy into writing articles. . . . There were heated defenses of liberated language, as well as a group session on "our bodies, ourselves," and a wide-ranging article on shit and how we deal with it in our society. When sexual tension in the group interfered with the work at hand, he had each of us write a personal account of our feelings, and then synthesize one of the best early *RFD* articles. ("Carl Peter Wittman, 1943–1986: As His Friends Remember Him," *Front Page*, 4 March 1986)

16. Scofield, "RFD History," 12.

17. Webb, "Difficulty at the Beginning: A Wolf Creek Journal," *RFD*, no. 11 (Spring 1977): 8–12.

18. Letter to Louie Crew from Julia Penelope, 7 May 1975, Penelope Papers.

19. J. Stanley, "When We Say 'Out of the Closets!'" *College English* 36, 3 (1974): 385. In this essay, Julia took issue with the sexist ("drag queen"), racist ("dinge queens"), and

classist ("piss-elegant") phrases found commonly among gay men as she explored gay slang's liberatory potential when politically redefined. After the publication of "The Homosexual Imagination" Julia and Beth Hodges wrote the editor of *College English*, Richard Ohmann, criticizing the special issue for its all-male graphics, poetry, and articles (except two) and offering to edit a lesbian literature issue. According to Hodges, Ohmann responded that the journal "had deliberately chosen to do a gay male issue and would not consider a lesbian issue 'unless we see more clearly than we do now that a lesbian issue would open as much new territory.' In other words, they assumed that the men's perspective is significant; women must prove it" (B. Hodges, Editorial, *Margins*, August 1975, 3).

20. Crew was living with his black lover and teaching at Fort Valley College in Georgia. In an early letter regarding her essay on gay slang and its role in perpetuating the "trivialization and degradation of gay people" (Stanley, "When We Say 'Out,'" 385), Louie advised Julia: "I certainly do not object to either of us clearly stating her or his violent disagreement with each other. In fact, our letters are filled with carefully couched acknowledgements of what we are learning from such volatile exchanges. . . . Thank you for showing that Lesbians can talk meaningfully about the Gay male experience, for showing that we are *not* so polarized as our Gay rhetoric sometimes suggests (letter to Julia Penelope from Louie Crew, 5 August 1974, Penelope Papers). Crew later wrote: "As to the impact of your material on me personally, it is forceful; and I feel much more disposed to concur with your position now than I did six months ago, not least because of our previous correspondence, but also because of my genuine effort to read much Lesbian material in the past few months. I would even go so far as to argue that Gay men have something to gain from separatism also" (letter to Julia Penelope from Louie Crew, 8 November 1974, Penelope Papers).

21. Letter to Louie Crew from Julia Penelope, 7 May 1975, Penelope Papers.

22. Letter to Beth Hodges from Julia Penelope, 5 October 1975, Penelope Papers.

23. *RFD*, no. 10 (Winter 1976): 44.

FIFTEEN — AWAKENINGS AND DEPARTURES

Interviews

Jim Baxter, 11 October 1997, Raleigh, N.C.

Jack Nichols, 13 January 1995, Cocoa Beach, Fla. All quotations from Jack Nichols, "Sissies," a manuscript, are used with his permission.

Jesse Monteagudo, 9 January 1995, 18 June 1998, Miami, Fla., and e-mail to the author; unattributed quotations from J. Monteagudo, "Miami, Florida," in J. Preston, ed., *Hometowns* (New York: Plume, 1991), 11–20, are used with the author's permission.

Paul Wegman, 28 March, 18 April, 27 October, and 16 November 1997, Orlando, Fla.

Samantha Hunter, 18 June 1999, Columbia, S.C.

1. J. Sears, *Lonely Hunters* (New York: HarperCollins/Westview, 1997), chapter 4.

2. L. Clarke and J. Nichols, *Roommates Can't Always Be Lovers* (New York: St. Martin's Press, 1974), 37–38.

3. J. Nichols, *Men's Liberation: A New Definition of Masculinity* (New York: Penguin, 1975).

4. Letter to Jack Nichols from Lige Clarke, 4 January 1974, Clarke Papers.

5. Postcard to Perrin Shaffer from Lige Clarke, n.d. (circa winter 1974), Clarke Papers.

6. Letter to Jack Nichols from Lige Clarke, 18 April 1974, Clarke Papers.

7. As the Atlanta community emerged, Powell was the only bar owner who refused gay liberation leaflets or posters for the local MCC, telling one activist that "being homosexual is a sin" (D. Bryant, "Sexism in the Gay Bars," *Great Speckled Bird*, 26 June 1972, 1). One Atlanta activist remembers he was "not allowed to go to a gay bar and tell other gays and lesbians about Gay Pride Day." Another, recalling the anti-activist policy of the Sweet Gum Head and the Cove, declares: "Gay activists had the same social status as street transvestites—slightly lower" (AGH).

8. The *Barb: The Voice of the Gay Community* began publishing early in 1974. In April 1975, founder Ray Green sold it to Bill Smith, who had joined the paper as a politi-

cal columnist and became its editor. The Atlanta Gay Center soon opened on Fourth Street, where Smith had rented office space originally for the paper. The Center hosted a writers' group, poetry readings, dances, and other events. In Charlotte, two brothers, John and Robert "Jake" Freese, owned a small printing business. In April 1975, a thousand copies of the six-page *Charlotte Free Press,* the state's first gay newspaper, were printed. Within two years circulation of the retitled *Free Press* topped ten thousand. *Contact,* founded in 1974 by Henry McClurg (under the pen name Henry Parker), was the first Houston gay paper to document police harassment. Although *Contact* had a national distribution, after seventeen issues, it was absorbed by the *Advocate.* Finally, *Gaiety,* published 1975–1977 in Memphis, was founded and edited by Gary Poe. Financed largely by him, the publication folded as the number of production volunteers dwindled and Memphis's legendary gay apathy mounted.

9. The explosion of gay bars in southern midsize cities is illustrated in Memphis, where one club owner reported more than fifty gay bars opening during the seventies and early eighties (D. Buring, *Lesbian and Gay Memphis* [New York: Garland, 1997], 67). In larger cities, even more elaborate clubs opened. The Bayous Landing in Dallas, for example, was a 23,000-square-foot complex with a dance floor that had a $20,000 sound system, a restaurant, and baths.

10. The connections between escort agencies and newspapers were sometimes more than advertising dollars. Publisher Bill Smith channeled profits from Atlanta Young Men into supporting the *Barb* (AGH, 9).

11. V. Astor, "George's—Twenty Years Young," *GazE,* April 1989, 13. E-mails to the author from Vincent Astor, 25 November 2000, and from Jay Mohr, 20 November 2000, Sears Papers. As early as 1968, the River City had its "semipublic" Halloween masquerade ball at a rented mansion in midtown. Hundreds watched Miss Terri Woo crowned Miss Gay Memphis. This pageant was hosted the next year by Belles Ltd. at the Guild Theater, as "vice officers watched." The Queen's Men, Memphis's first gay social group, officially formed in 1971 to raise money for an orphanage. Its name then changed to the Miss Gay Memphis Pageant. Later balls were held in a variety of public venues, including the American Legion Hall and the Veterans of Foreign Wars (V. Astor, "The Miss Gay Memphis Pageant," *Triangle Journal News,* October 1994, 32; Buring, *Lesbian and Gay Memphis,* 43–44).

12. V. Astor, "Peaches' Perspective," *Triangle Journal News,* February 1991; E. Weathers, "Name Withheld. A Search for the Memphis Gay Community," part 2, *Memphis Magazine,* May 1979, 42.

13. Letters to Jack Nichols from Lige Clarke, n.d. (circa fall 1974) and 18 April 1974, Clarke Papers.

14. *Roommates* book tour interviews, Clarke Papers.

15. These groups also had to contend with the perceived competition they posed to bar owners. In a letter from Don King to local gay club owners, he underscored that the League was "not interested in entering the private enterprise sector and establishing a bar or business which would hurt your income. . . . Our aims and your aims—a strong and vital gay community in Charlotte—are similar" (letter to Tom Hare from Don King, 4 February 1975, Sears Papers).

16. E. Stoneman, "New Style in the Old South," *Advocate,* 28 January 1975.

17. A local underground paper, the *Greensboro Sun* was published by Reverend Clark. Jim Baxter, who was in his senior year at Guilford College, wrote Clark, asking if he could write a column about "gay stuff." Clark agreed. In an early column entitled "On Being Gay," the young man, who had moved to Greensboro from D.C., where he was a member of the Gay Activist Alliance, wrote: "Gay liberation, true freedom, is not in the bars, the baths, or other such places. It is in the streets, in the courts, on the job, in the family and among friends" (J. Baxter, "On Being Gay," *Greensboro Sun,* February 1975, 13).

18. Letter to Jim Baxter from Allan Troxler, 4 November 1974, "Letters to Gay," *Greensboro Sun,* February 1975.

19. Letter from Jim Baxter, *Advocate,* 2 July 1974.

20. "The Bar," *Front Page,* personal collection of Jim Baxter, Raleigh, N.C.

21. "Effeminacy," Baxter Papers.
22. "Baxter, notes circa 1975," Baxter Papers.
23. *Roommates* book tour interviews, Clarke Papers.
24. "Diamond Lil, Jailhouse Jezebel," *Up Front,* June–July 1973, 34–39; D. King, "Brandy Alexander, Fighter and Survivor," *Front Page,* 15 December 1987, 3, 8; D. Leonard, Letter to the Editor, *Front Page,* 22 February 1983, 5.
25. During the apogee of the disco era, Nichols wrote: "The post-Stonewall gay-identified male . . . is over-reacting to the pre-Stonewall limp-wrist image, an image once connected to effeminacy and drag. He is emphatic about being a conventional male because masculinism is too highly valued. He is likely to say, 'I am a man. I'm not a drag queen' " (J. Nichols, "Butcher Than Thou," *Gaysweek,* 28 November 1977, 12–13, 17).
26. J. Nichols, "Sissies," manuscript, Sears Papers.
27. In the early seventies, Bill Hovan, perhaps responding to the 1961 film *Where the Boys Are,* transformed the Marlin Beach Hotel (the site of the film) into a gay resort with a legendary Poop Deck Disco, afternoon poolside tea dances, and nightly cruising in the courtyard (J. Monteagudo, "From the Beaches to the Boardroom," *TWN,* 19 October 1994, 10–12). After the Marlin Beach came the Del-Mar hotel complex in Fort Lauderdale and 8000 Club, a resort/disco on Miami's Biscayne Blvd.
28. There had been other places that offered such theatrical entertainment. In late 1969, a cast of eleven impersonators led by Joseph Munoz and Jack Guthrie began a three-year run of the Magical Garden Review at Fort Worth's Little Elivria's and then at El Toga. During the early seventies, Dallas's Maars club had more lavish sets and costumes for productions of shows like *Gypsy, Funny Girl, Cabaret,* and *Hello Dolly!* And, in 1975, Gary Shannon presented amateur drag productions like *Purlie* and *Applause* at Dallas's Encore.
29. Letter from Charlie to Shelbianna, 11 March 1975, personal collection of Jack Nichols, Cocoa Beach, Fla.
30. Material related to Lige's death relied on for this portrait: A. Goldstein, "A Sad and Serious Time," *Screw,* 17 March 1975, 3; and, from Clarke Papers: J. Nichols, "Whispers of Heavenly Death," Letter to Friends, 22 February 1975; letter to Jack Nichols from Shelbi, 20 April 1975; letter to Jack Nichols from Frank Kameny, 24 April 1975; "Questions to Steve Yates About Lige's Murder," audiotape, circa 1985.
31. Letter from Charlie to Shelbianna.
32. Walt Whitman, "We Two Boys Together Clinging," in *Leaves of Grass,* ed. Jerome Loving (Oxford: Oxford University Press, 1990), 108.

SIXTEEN — SEVENTY-FIVE LESBIANS

Interviews

Pokey Anderson, 12 October 1994, Houston, Tex.
David Patterson, 9 April 1999, Austin, Tex.
Rita Wanstrom, 9 April 1999, Austin, Tex.

1. The Circle of Friends membership plummeted after Stonewall, following a split between the homophile and gay activist members. The Circle distanced itself from the "social" purpose, becoming a political and educational body. In 1972, the group sent questionnaires to political candidates and organized Texas's first gay pride parade. Also, like other early organizations, the Circle inspired other groups. For example, one member, a former minister, was visiting California when Rev. Troy Perry suggested she return to start a chapter in Dallas. Twelve people showed up at her home the week after she returned from California and made her report to the Circle. The church would eventually become the largest MCC congregation in the South.
2. DOB, Audiovisual Materials, 1956–1989, subseries 1.2, n.d., tape #A00508, IGIC Collection.
3. Ibid.
4. M. Bernabo, "Gays March Proudly," *Dallas Morning News,* 25 June 1972; D. Domeier, "Parade Protests Fail to Halt Homosexuals," *Dallas Morning News,* 24 June 1972. The group evolved from remnants of Houston Gay Liberation, raising money for rent from

dance fundraisers at Slug's, a mixed bar (W. Frey, "Gay Community Center Opens in Houston," *Advocate,* 17 October 1972).

5. "Report from Integrity," *Contact,* June 1974, 20. The original Dignity group was cofounded by Father Mark Barron and Bill Buie, but when "we discovered that the particular climate in the community allowed few Catholics to be that open [and] that the majority of those interested in an organization were non-Catholics," the group re-formed as Integrity, in February 1972, continuing to meet on Sunday afternoons at Holy Rosary with Father Barron's participation (letter to Paul Diederich from Bill Buie, 7 April 1974, Integrity/Houston Corr., 1973–1975).

6. The first candidate to receive organized gay support was twenty-three-year-old, heterosexual Ron Waters. Running on a liberal platform, including repeal of sexual conduct laws (sodomy had been reclassified as a misdemeanor in 1972), Waters was elected state representative (T. Dreye and A. Reiner, "Montrose Lives," *Texas Monthly,* April 1973, 57–61). As a state representative, Waters proclaimed: "Because I'm committed to the gay cause, I can be open and public about it—to say in an official capacity that there's nothing wrong with gay love" ("Report from Integrity," 20).

7. P. Anderson, "Star and the 75: A Children's Story," *Pointblank Times,* June 1975, 5.

8. "Pokey Anderson Interview Transcript by M.S.," 4 October 1991, p. 16, Sears Papers.

9. W. Stevens, "Houston Accepts New Political Force," *New York Times,* 1 November 1981.

10. Houston's first gay paper, the *Albatross,* was a chit-chat, gossipy quarterly with bar ads. It began publishing in August 1965 with Bob Eddy as editor.

11. "Pokey Anderson Interview Transcript," 22.

12. Three different groups met at the Milam house: Houston Area NOW, the Harris County Women's Political Caucus, and the Women's Equity Action League.

13. "Pokey Anderson Interview Transcript," 22.

14. Letter from Dale Carter for the I/H Board to Friends, 10 June 1974, reprinted as "Report from Integrity," 20.

15. C. Gillis, "A Brief History of the Gay Community of Houston, Texas," *Gay Pride Week '80 Guide,* 1980, 68; B. Remington, "Twelve Fighting Years: Homosexuals in Houston, 1969–1981" (master's thesis, University of Houston, 1983), 26.

16. After Ricci left, Rita hired some go-go girls. One, Watermelon Rose, had a fifty-two-inch bust and wore double-F bras. But "it wasn't a lesbian cup of tea," she notes. Variety shows every Thursday evening also failed to improve business. In Halloween dark humor, a depressed Rita held a costume contest for the best-looking Marquis de Sade. The elimination of parking on Shepherd Drive was the final nail in the coffin for the Sixties. It closed early in 1974.

17. J. Olsen, *The Man with the Candy: The Story of the Houston Mass Murders* (New York: Simon and Schuster, 1974). This story was named by the *Houston Chronicle* as one of the top ten of the city's century (R. Salle, "Traveling Exhibit Brings Century of News to Town," *Houston Chronicle,* 21 October 1999).

18. The headquarters was actually located in San Diego, with Dallas (and other houses planned in Florida and New York) used as an "orientation" residence. The fellows were recruited from Trader Dick ads in the *Advocate* offering "character development" through travel; the two hundred or more sponsors were solicited from various gay mass-mailing lists.

19. E. Makoy, "Male Sex Ring Broken in Dallas," *Dallas Times Herald,* 15 August 1973. In contrast, the *New York Times* reported: "The police said they were told the word referred to their removal from the procurement ring's literature because they were uncooperative and did not mean they had been ordered killed" ("Alleged Homosexual Ring Found in Raid on Apartment in Dallas," 16 August 1973).

20. M. Schwartz, "Incidents Focus Attention on Homosexuals' World," *Dallas Morning News,* 19 August 1973.

21. In addition, Police Inspector Caldwell told a reporter: "As long as the swishers stay where they belong and don't grab little children on the street, there won't be any crackdown on them in this city" (W. Mandel, "Houston Said to Harass 'Gays,'" *Bulletin,* 17 August 1973).

22. Letter to Morris, circa September 1973, Integrity/Houston Corr. The next summer, Bill Buie wrote to Henry Parker, publisher of *Contact:* "When we look at places like

Dallas and Ft. Worth we are embarrassed to think we are so apathetic. There is much to be done in Houston and it takes muscle, money, and elbow grease" (memo to Henry Parker from Bill Buie, 16 July 1974, Integrity/Houston Corr.).

23. "Statement Prepared by Integrity/Houston," 14 December 1973, 1, Integrity/Houston Corr.; J. Yardley, "Last Innings at a Can-Do Cathedral," *New York Times,* 3 October 1999.

24. "Statement Prepared by Integrity/Houston," 2.

25. Letter to Chief of Police C. M. Lynn from Bill Buie, 8 February 1974, Integrity/Houston Corr.

26. Marion had entered a relationship with Lynn, a "fluffy" dyke working in a stockbrokerage firm, on the heels of her ten-year relationship with Ricci. Rita, who had first met Marion and Ricci at the Four Aces in Dallas, reconnected with the couple when she moved to Houston. Within Houston's unassuming lesbian circles of the fifties, Marion's parents would babysit Rita's son and, on occasion, Marion would steal into Rita's place to secretly phone a Tennessee woman. Sixteen months after Ricci walked out on Marion for cheating on her, Rita and Marion were a couple. Later, Marion, Ricci, and Rita bought cemetery plots, with Ricci's placed in the middle.

27. As the seventies waned, Rita Wanstrom was no longer involved in the bar business, but she continued to play an important role within the community. One of her most difficult tasks occurred in the spring of 1986. During the early morning hours of 16 March 1986, Rita's phone rang. There had been a shooting at Just Marion and Lynn's. Rita remembers: "A robber came in—Marion and I had always talked about how to react to situations." A twenty-seven-year-old man wearing a ski mask ran into the bar. He aimed his sawed-off .410 shotgun at Peaches, the bartender whom Marion had hired after the Roaring Sixties closed. Marion, who had just closed up, went into her purse, pulled out a derringer, and shot at the robber (an aspiring junior welterweight boxer). A few moments later, the sixty-seven-year-old lesbian matriarch was dead. So many people attended the funeral, organized by Wanstrom and other old friends, that a walking procession was held from the sanctuary to the cemetery to avoid traffic congestion ("23-Year-Old Gets Death in Montrose Killing," *Houston Chronicle,* 2 June 1987; "Man Gets 25 Years for Bar Robbery," *Houston Chronicle,* 14 April 1988).

28. Over the years, Rita always insisted that the couple be together for at least three months. "If it was any sooner than that, it was 'heat'—and I didn't do it." Another southern activist who performed such services was Eddie Sandifer, president of the Mississippi Gay Alliance. A communist and a longtime civil rights activist, Sandifer attended his first Mattachine meeting in New York in 1958 and soon thereafter helped Randolfe Wicker III organize a homophile study group in Jackson (interview with Eddie Sandifer by the author, 4 November 1997; Wicker Research Studies, Sandifer Papers; "Charlie Dellakamp," in S. Terkel, *American Dreams* [New York: Pantheon Books, 1980], 279–283).

29. Remington, "Twelve Fighting Years," 28.

30. Although there had already been national and regional conferences, such as the Gay Liberation Front conference (Austin, 1971) and Southern Convention Association of Gay Militants (Athens, 1972), as well as city-based conferences (e.g., Houston in 1971), Texas—followed by Mississippi (1974), Florida (1976), Virginia (1977), and Alabama (1978)—was the first in-state effort. Certainly, the Southeastern Gay Conference, beginning in Chapel Hill in 1976 and extending well into the eighties, was the most influential conference in fostering activist networks, spawning other special interest groups, and encouraging statewide conferences.

31. The Council was composed of Cyr's AURA, a gay civil rights/social services group that would soon begin to publish *Community News,* as well as the local DOB, Circle of Friends, and Friends of Jesus.

32. Fort Worth deputy police chief Hopkins simply stated: "We had an agreement that we wouldn't arrest anybody if nobody violated the law. . . . We did not have an agreement that officers wouldn't take down license numbers" ("Legal Action Considered by Homosexuals' Group," *Fort Worth Star-Telegram,* 25 June 1974; "'Gestapo' Charge Leveled at Police," *Fort Worth Star-Telegram,* 26 June 1974). Privately, Hopkins told the local ACLU representative that he was unaware that this vice action was going

to occur and he "wouldn't have had this happen for the world" (letter from Arthur to Conference Organizers, 26 June 1974, Integrity/Houston Corr.).

33. A newsletter to members was also published, which contained reports from each region and local organizations' efforts and issues confronting local communities, as well as announcements of upcoming events, highlights of recent activities, local legislative action, and media coverage. The group was officially organized by twenty-four charter member organizations that met at San Antonio in early August. After a lengthy debate, membership was restricted to organizations, although "TGTF realizes that this poses a problem for the rural gay who cannot form or join a local group" ("An Explanation," TGTF Organization, TGTF, 1974–1978, Integrity/Houston Corr.).

34. Letter to Franklin E. Kameny from Bill Buie, 16 July 1974, Integrity/Houston Corr. That same month, Pokey Anderson wrote to Detroit's mayor for a copy of that city's new sexual orientation ordinance (letter to the Mayor's Office from Pokey Anderson, 12 July 1974, Sears Papers). Looking back at it now, Pokey admits: "I naïvely thought, in 1974, that if we just got the right *wording*, an ordinance would be passed in Houston—prohibiting discrimination seemed so obvious."

35. Cy, "Finding," *Pointblank Times*, May 1976, 7.

36. "How We Began," *Pointblank Times*, October 1975, 3–4.

37. "*Pointblank Times* Herstory," *Pointblank Times*, November 1977, 2–3. The logo chosen included the portrait of two young women by the nineteenth-century photographer Julia Margaret Cameron.

38. In later years, as Pokey points out, Marion "would serve on many gay organizations' boards and opened one of the city's most popular lesbian bars, Kindred Spirits."

SEVENTEEN — OUT IN THE OUTFIELD

Interviews

"Karla Brown," 30 December 1999, 3 January 2000, Newark, N.J., and e-mail to the author, 21 August 2000.

Pokey Anderson, 12 October 1994, 12 April 1999, Houston, Tex.

Jan Cunningham, 21 September 1999, Houston, Tex.

Lorraine Fontana, 20 October 1999, New York City.

Unattributed quotations of Vicki Gabriner in this chapter come from an interview by the author, 10 November 1999, Boston, Mass., and from these articles by Gabriner: "Come Out Slugging!" *Quest,* Winter 1976, 52; "The Government vs. the Movement," *ALFA Newsletter,* October 1977, 10; "A Hystory of the Atlanta Lesbian/Feminist Alliance, 1972–1978," *Atalanta,* December 1980; and "The Review as Process," *Feminary,* 11, 1/2 (1980): 113–116.

Elizabeth Knowlton, 2 October 1999, Atlanta, Ga. Used with the author's permission are all quotations from: E. Knowlton, "From the Stands," *ALFA Newsletter,* July 1976, 1; E. Knowlton, "Lesbian Separatist Workshop Viewpoint," *ALFA Newsletter,* July 1975, 4.

1. V. Gabriner and S. Wells, "How to Start a Lesbian Organization," *Atalanta,* August 1977, 3.

2. Before the Omegas' name was selected, three other possible team names were considered: the Tri-ALFAs, ALFA Unicorns, and ALFA Sapphosonics.

3. Y. Zipter, *Diamonds Are a Dyke's Best Friend* (Ithaca, N.Y.: Firebrand, 1998), 76. Zipter (48, 136) quotes former *Ladder* editor Barbara Grier: "In the early years, softball was . . . the only organized, programmed, regimented, routinized activity that the lesbian community at large engaged in—by tacit understanding. . . . You had a greater cross-section of women than you have now because . . . [i]n the early days you either hung out in bars, you lived by yourself in isolation (or as the old *Ladder* saying went, 'Living alone in egoism *a deux*') or you belonged to the ball teams." This was an activity, as Grier observed, in which there was little political consciousness. Quoting one player: "Life's short, the girls are pretty. The beer is good. Don't give me any of this political crap!" (Zipter, 140).

4. Forrest Road was named after the Tennessee planter and brilliant battlefield tactician General Nathan Bedford Forrest. He also oversaw the 1864 massacre of three hundred

black Union soldiers and later joined the ranks of the Ku Klux Klan. Mirroring Atlanta's post–civil rights image, the road has been renamed for Ralph McGill, the progressive editor of the *Atlanta Journal-Constitution* who championed the emergence of the New South.

5. In detailing the history of queer Memphis, Buring found that unlike white lesbians who were "sustained through actively participating in a variety of softball leagues," black lesbians during the eras of de jure and de facto desegregation "were unable to play in city leagues that generally had significant lesbian membership." As this began to change in the midseventies, a lesbian of color generally found herself, like Karla, the only African American on the team (D. Buring, *Lesbian and Gay Memphis* [New York: Garland, 1997], 201).

6. Another political activist who participated in seventies softball was Texas-born African American poet Pat Parker. As coach, she observed: "There are a lot more jocks [than feminists]. And political consciousness is not very high [with them]. I've actually had to sit my team down and lecture to them about what kind of chatter is permitted on our team. . . . I won't tolerate [any put-downs]" (Zipter, *Diamonds,* 148).

7. "Roles in the Lesbian Community," *ALFA Newsletter,* May 1976, 3.

8. "Softball," *ALFA Newsletter,* November 1975, 9.

9. Ibid.

10. Ibid. For the ALFA Amazons, competition and winning were less critical issues, although Fontana remembers "years where there was a little different emphasis like, 'If we win this game we can be in the finals. Let's put the good people in.' So most of us would agree to that on a particular game, but not as a general rule."

11. Sojourner Truth Press was a lesbian printing collective made up of ALFA members.

12. Lesbian foremothers include Laura Bragg and Lillian Smith. As the first director of a scientific museum in the country, Bragg networked women and lesbian educators throughout the South (L. Allen, *A Bluestocking in Charleston* [Columbia: University of South Carolina Press, 2001]; J. Sears with L. Allen, "Museums, Friends, and Lovers in the New South: Laura's Web, 1909–1931," *Journal of Homosexuality* 40, 1 [2000]: 105–144). There were other lesbians who contributed to southern culture: Lillian Smith, coeditor, with her lover, of *South Today* (R. Gladney, *How Am I to Be Heard?* [Chapel Hill: University of North Carolina Press, 1993]); "French" Emma Johnson and other lesbian madames of Storyville (K. Coyle and N. Van Dyke, "Sex, Smashing and Storyville in Turn-of-the-Century New Orleans," in J. Howard, ed., *Carryin' On* [New York: New York University Press, 1997], 54–72); Irene Leache and Annie Wood, who began an intimate relationship in 1868 that lasted thirty years, and for whom the Leache-Wood Apartments on Norfolk's Fairfax Avenue are named (J. Katz, *Gay American History* [New York: Harper Colophon, 1976], 656; Wood's *Story of a Friendship: A Memoir,* and E. I. Prime Stevenson's *The Intersexes*).

Other lesbian relationships that have been documented include the tragic late-nineteenth-century love affair between Alice Mitchell and Freda Ward and the relationship between two black women, Mabel from Winston-Salem and Lillian from Norfolk, who met in New York City (L. Duggan, "The Trials of Alice Mitchell: Sensationalism, Sexology, and the Lesbian Subject in Turn-of-the-Century America," *Signs,* 18, 4 [1993], 791–814; S. Nestle, "Surviving and More: Interview with Mabel Hampton, *Sinister Wisdom,* no. 10 [Summer 1979]: 19–28). Of course, all southern towns included their share of queer folk. In her book *Laughing All the Way* (New York: Stein and Day, 1973), Barbara Howar tells of Depression-era Raleigh, where "we had our share of neighborhood weirdos," including "the village pervert who could throw his voice and make us think his dog could talk" and two lesbians who were called the Big Hats owing to their "elaborate millinery tastes. We kids would follow them for a block or two, speculating on the clinical side of their relationship" (34).

13. Before Atlanta and other southern towns such as Houston, Lexington, Norfolk, Columbia, and Washington formed openly lesbian slow-pitch softball teams, there were fast-pitch teams and informal softball games among lesbians. In Memphis, the Belles played on Saturday night and Sunday afternoons, drawing large, mostly gay, fans (D. Buring, "Softball and Alcohol," in J. Howard, ed., *Carryin' On* [New York:

New York University Press, 1997], 203–223). However, lesbian softball in the city's parks did attract the attention of local Memphis vice, who pulled several female physical education and recreation majors out of their classes at the Memphis State University field house in 1961. Authorities "questioned them about certain parks department adult softball teams which the girls had been on and which had been accused of holding lesbian outings. . . . The upshot of the affair was that several of the women were embarrassed and the university instituted a rule that women physical education majors at Memphis State could not play summer softball in the parks department adult leagues. The rule remained on the books for three years" (E. Weathers, "Name Withheld. A Search for the Memphis Gay Community," part 1, *Memphis Magazine,* April 1979, 42).

Several all-women's fast-pitch softball teams also played at Richmond's Byrd Park. Generally sponsored by local businesses, they were made up of mostly lesbian players with the diamond serving as a meeting ground for women seeking like-minded women, who would then drink beer at nearby Smitty's on South Sheppard Street. During the season there would be two or more tournaments attracting out-of-town teams, and "everyone would change into Bermuda shorts or summer slacks and all pile up in the cars and go to Tanglewood," a pool bar and dance hall in the next county, where they'd dance, drink, and play cards; "Everyone was having FUN! . . . They wouldn't care who saw them, they flaunted it" (interview with Carolyn Waugaman by Robert Swisher, 28 February 1989, IGLA, Southern Studies Collection; also see R. Swisher, "City Lesbians 'Took Over,' Danced at Country Beer Joint," *Richmond Pride,* April 1989).

14. Interview, *Pointblank Times,* July 1976, 4.
15. "Bloomer Ball Tossers: Were Pinched and Raised a Rough House in Texas Jail," *Cincinnati Enquirer,* 20 July 1903 (quoted in Zipter, *Diamonds,* 38). There were also mostly lesbian softball teams in Houston during World War II, playing at night and some weekends at a park near Rice University. Women building the huge guns used on aircraft carriers at the Dickson Gun Plant, constructing precision tools at Hughes Tools, or working at nearby Brown or Houston shipyards, had teams. Tony Midnite, whose sister played on the Hughes Tool team, remembers: "Most all of them were lesbians, some with their girlfriends. 'Butch and fluff' is what we used to call them." After the games, players and fans would go to a mixed bar on Airline Drive "that was like a bar in a house." Tony, who often joined the players, continues: "When the weather was good they'd drink outside." Inside, putting a nickel in the old-fashioned jukebox, "those butches got to dance together" (interview with Tony Midnite by the author, 13 March 2000, Sears Papers).
16. "Coming Together," *Great Speckled Bird,* 5 June 1975.
17. "Reluctantly Adjusting the Hill," *ALFA Newsletter,* July 1975, 7.
18. Ibid.
19. Ibid.
20. In 1975, there was also the newly formed International Women's Professional Softball League, founded by Billie Jean King along with famed softball pitcher Joan Joyce, and others. Lasting only four seasons, the poorly funded set of franchises received little notoriety, although it took care to guard against a lesbian image. Despite the fact that many of the players were lesbian, three members of Joan Joyce's Connecticut Falcons were released for demonstrating "overt lesbian behavior," allegedly sporting "unshaven legs, reading a copy of *Lesbian Images* in public, and one woman massaging another's temples" (Zipter, *Diamonds,* 46).
21. Letter to Fran from Pokey Anderson, 26 March 1975, Sears Papers.
22. Both Atlanta and Houston lesbians were fond of depicting issues relating to sports and politics in fairy tale form. "Saints Above: A Softball Story" tells the tale of Angel Saint Joan D'Arc's use of "athlete dust" to improve the team (*Pointblank Times,* July 1976). The printing collective allied with ALFA produced *Sleeping Beauty: A Lesbian Fairy Tale* (Atlanta: Sojourner Truth Press, 1971–1972; reprint Durham, N.C.: Whole Women Press, 1978) with drawings by Gail, text by Vicki Gabriner, and calligraphy by Ginny. There was also rewriting of various Greek myths (appearing as an ongoing saga in the ALFA newsletters) of an athletic and powerful lesbian from Arkadia.
23. L. Lovell and A. McKinney, *Sad Team* (Houston: Ego Press, 1975).

EIGHTEEN — LEXINGTON SIX

Interviews

Unattributed quotations of Vicki Gabriner in this chapter come from an interview by the author, 10 November 1999, Boston, Mass., and from V. Gabriner, "The Review as Process," *Feminary* 11, 1/2 (1980): 113–116, and "The Government vs. The Movement," *ALFA Newsletter,* October 1977, 10.

David Williams, 20 October 1998, Louisville, Ky.

The epigraph is from "Faces," *Susan Saxe Defense Committee Newsletter,* Saxe File, IGLA.

1. J. Gaudiosi, "Saxe Vows to Fight On," *Lexington Herald-Leader,* 29 March 1975.
2. "The Underground Nation," *Newsweek,* 31 March 1975, 33.
3. "The Great Southeast Lesbian Conference," *ALFA Newsletter,* April 1975, 3. These conversations occurred in other southern communities as well. "Even in Houston," notes Pokey Anderson, "a community that was apparently untouched by the FBI investigations, we were briefing each other on what to do if the FBI came knocking on your door. Stories were darkly passed around the community. It was frightening" (letter to the author from Pokey Anderson, 23 December 1999, Sears Papers). And, as longtime contributors to a very influential lesbian-feminist magazine later wrote: "It was in 1975 that the feminist movement and *off our backs* were most concerned about infiltration." Carol Anne Douglas and Fran Moira explained: "Fear of possible FBI and also CIA harassment was always with us and was reflected in a variety of articles that discussed FBI and CIA tactics in infiltrating the feminist movement, and that gave coverage to grand jury defense committees" (C. Douglas and F. Moira, "Off Our Backs: The First Decade [1970–1980]," in K. Wachsberger, ed., *Voices from the Underground* [Tempe, Ariz.: Mica Press, 1993], 116). Also see Karla Jay's memoir, *Tales of the Lavender Menace* (New York: Basic Books, 1999), 148–149.
4. "FBI Harassment of the Lesbian Community," *ALFA Newsletter,* July 1975, 3. Katherine Power remained underground for another decade before turning herself in to authorities.
5. J. Johnston, "The Myth of Bonnies Without Clydes: Lesbian Feminists and the Male Left," *Village Voice,* 28 April 1975, 14. Others, like longtime civil rights activist, pacifist, and lesbian Barbara Deming, were more conciliatory; Deming wrote: "[A]ll of us who want to see Father Right dissolved believe that the liberation of women would bring *about* the elimination of capitalism, of racism, or imperialism—all three of which are based upon the patriarchal assumption that there is a right to take other people's property" (B. Deming, "Barbara Deming to Susan Saxe," *Liberation,* July–August 1976, 4).
6. "You don't need a weatherman to know which way the wind blows." Of particular merit in the understanding of this era and this description of the emergence of the Weathermen and Weather Underground are: S. Evans, *Personal Politics* (New York: Random House, 1979); J. Mansbridge, *Beyond Adversary Democracy* (Chicago: University of Chicago Press, 1980); K. Sale, *SDS* (New York: Random House, 1972); R. Shultz and B. Shultz, *It Did Happen Here: Recollections of Political Repression in America* (Berkeley: University of California Press, 1989); N. Young, *An Infantile Disorder? The Crisis and Decline of the New Left* (London: Routledge and Kegan Paul, 1977); N. Zaroulis and G. Sullivan, *Who Spoke Up! American Protest Against the War in Vietnam, 1963–1975* (New York: Doubleday, 1984).
7. In *The Unfinished Journey* (New York: Oxford University Press, 1999), William Chafe writes: "Civil war on the left had already begun as early as 1969. For many radical activists, the primary lesson of the 1960s had been the futility of securing change peacefully. Demonstrations at universities had failed to change the government's Vietnam policy; campaigns on behalf of antiwar candidates proved useless, at least in 1968; and the most bitter activists concluded that revolution was the only answer. SDS shattered into desperate splinter groups" (408).
8. H. Zinn, *The Politics of History* (Boston: Beacon Press, 1970), 237. He went on to argue: "There is a basic misconception . . . that the U.S. is a peculiarly nonviolent nation, with a special dispensation for achieving social change through peaceful parliamen-

tary reform [but] much overt violence has characterized our behavior toward other nationalities, other races—the outgroups of our society; the other [misconception] is a failure to recognize the place of violence—both overt and hidden—in whatever important change has occurred in American history" (238).

9. S. Lynd, *Intellectual Origins of American Radicalism* (New York: Pantheon, 1968), vi, 10. Further, echoing Locke, Lynd argued: "Men should be free, according to the revolutionary tradition, because on joining society they do not surrender their essential natural powers. If existing society abuses those powers, men should demand their restoration at once: 'immediate emancipation,' or as Garrison sometimes put it, 'freedom now'" (10).

10. As Lexington activist Jill Raymond observed: "The government and the media helped promote our insecurity, and cashed in on it, making us react to ourselves and to each other with a degree of embarrassment and self-degradation—'weren't we stupid back then!'" Mainstream media, for example, glossed over historical and philosophical analyses, choosing to caricaturize political violence as "Terrorism on the Left" by youthful radicals "arguing guerrilla politics and experimenting with polymorphous sex." ("Terrorism on the Left," *Newsweek,* 23 March 1970, 26–30; "The Underground Nation," *Newsweek,* 31 March 1975, 34). For those seeking a better understanding of the impact of the media on the New Left, see T. Gitlin, *The Whole World Is Watching* (Berkeley: University of California Press, 1981).

Vicki Gabriner reflects on the complexity of this time:

It was clear to me when I was arrested that although I had profound criticisms of Weathermen, I had no such ambivalence about my opposition to U.S. policies in Vietnam, which had been at the center of my Weatherman political activism. On this I was, at the time of my arrest, and have remained to this day, rock solid. So when it came down to publicly discussing my case, I knew I had to dig deep to figure out a way to help people understand why we had struggled as we had to effect change in Vietnam policy and how that was connected to the feminist and lesbian/feminist movements. It was incredibly difficult, but with the help of some wonderful friends and political allies, both in Atlanta and Boston, I think we were able to do just that.

In accord, Jill Raymond had written years earlier: "The debate over the choice of methods and the timing of these activities has continued ever since. . . . Those of us who were ever actively involved against the war knew that we were not wrong. But we certainly did have a sense of our mistakes, and of our own underdevelopment as a movement" ("Statement from Jill Raymond," circa 1976, Saxe File, IGLA).

11. Chafe, *The Unfinished Journey,* 405.

12. The tight social scene during this era included many memorable, albeit unrecorded, events, such as the Saturday afternoon double wedding at a bohemian apartment near Maxwell Street in 1974. Nearly one hundred persons in various stages of undress (one only in flowing ribbons of crepe paper) partied in the backyard of the artsy but seedy area, as neighborhood kids pressed their faces against a small white fence (interview with Ken Plotnik by David Williams, 13 July 1991, KGLA).

13. "Gay Lib in Court," *Gay Times,* February 1973, 1, 8.

14. Interview with Edwin Hackney by David Williams, 7 July 1991, KGLA.

15. P. Goldman, "'I Am Kathy Power': Expressions of Radicalism in a Counterculture Community," in K. Blee, ed., *No Middle Ground: Women and Radical Protest* (New York: New York University Press, 1998), 22.

16. R. Patrick, *Kennedy's Children: A Play in Two Acts* (New York: Random House, 1976).

17. G. Lee, "A Rendezvous with Our Past," *GSO Newsletter,* October 1984, 2.

18. Hackney interview, 1991. See also J. Hewlett, "Retired Orderly, 'Sweet Evening Breeze,' Dies," *Lexington Herald-Leader,* 15 December 1983.

19. Sources relied on for details of Louisville's gay bar scene include unpublished letters to the *Letter,* circa 1995, from Jim "Ms. Bird" Withers, Barry A. King, and Jerry Magers, KGLA; D. Williams, "Memories of Main Street," *Letter,* December 1994–March 1995; D. Williams, "An Informal History of Louisville Gay Bars," *Letter,* January 1999; letter from Kevin Bratcher, "Memories of Badlands," *Letter,* February 1999.

20. "FBI Says Two Murder Suspects Lived in Lexington Last Year," *Kentucky Kernel,* 15 January 1975.
21. Hackney interview.
22. L. Haller and S. Ryskiewicz, "FBI and Grand Jury Join in Harassment," *Kentucky Kernel,* 5 March 1975.
23. Shultz and Shultz, *It Did Happen Here.* This was well understood by other lesbian-feminists. "The grand jury questioning does not just cover information about Saxe and Power or the search for Patti Hearst, but seeks information about living arrangements, travelling, and contacts in other lesbian communities, political associations, roommates, and family—all important information for compiling a file on the Lesbian community" ("FBI Harassment," 3).
24. "Statement of Witnesses Subpoenaed by Lexington Federal Grand Jury," Saxe File. The fact that these were lesbians being investigated by (mostly) heterosexual men did not go unnoticed by feminists such as Pokey Anderson, who contends: "If one lesbian was a revolutionary terrorist, the FBI could do faulty logic and decide that all lesbians were potential radicals bent on violently overthrowing the government. You know: if women aren't spending their days cooking and cleaning for men, dressing to attract men, etc., well, gee, they must be spending all their time figuring out how to overthrow males and their institutions. It's hard for men to conceive of a situation where they're irrelevant and not the center of women's universe" (letter to the author from Pokey Anderson, 23 December 1999, Sears Papers).
25. S. Singer, " 'Conspiracy' Probe Sends 8 to Jail," *Advocate,* April 1975; R. Mitchell, "Junkin Testifies Before Grand Jury," *Kentucky Kernel,* 1 April 1975. The use of the grand jury for political purposes was employed extensively during this era, ranging from the investigation of kidnapped heiress turned Symbionese Liberation Army ally Patti Hearst in Philadelphia to the Saxe/Power grand juries in Lexington and New Haven.
26. Hackney interview.
27. Letter to the Editor, "FBI Intimidation Has Effect on Everyone," *Kentucky Kernel,* 13 March 1975. A professor of zoology made a similar point: "We cannot trust our FBI, and the claims of the Lexington Six that the FBI is harassing them because of their political and sexual orientation may well have merit" (W. Davis, "This is Justice?" *Kentucky Kernel,* 25 March 1975). And, after two months in covering the case, a Lexington newspaper reporter, Carolyn Gatz, observed: "It has become a cause celebre as a civil liberties issue, as a feminist issue, and as a gay rights issue" (C. Gatz, "Fought for As Long As We Could," *Lexington Herald-Leader,* 8 May 1975).
28. "Statement of Witnesses."
29. C. Gatz, "Promise to Testify Gets Witness Freed," *Lexington Herald-Leader;* 15 March 1975; R. Mitchell, "Hands Talks to Grand Jury About Fugitives, FBI," *Kentucky Kernel,* 24 March 1975; "Reluctant Witness," *Lexington Herald-Leader,* 21 March 1975.
30. After a district court of appeals refused to overturn the contempt order (although it ordered bail set), and despite an editorial in the *Lexington Herald-Leader* declaring the $10,000 bail a "mockery of a higher court's order," and the entire episode as being "marred with regrettable actions by the FBI and the grand jury, the U.S. attorney and the defendants," three of the four women agreed to testify ("Witnesses' Bail Is Excessive," 1975).
31. C. Junkin, "A View from the Madison County Jail," *Kentucky Kernel,* 7 April 1975.
32. Interview with Ken Plotnik by David Williams, 13 July 1991, KGLA.
33. B. Straub, "A Confrontation of Truths: God Versus Civil Liberties," *Kentucky Kernel,* 9 April 1975.
34. W. Hixson, "Evangelist Smock Concerned About Works of the Devil Here," *Kentucky Kernel,* 9 April 1975.
35. Gatz, "Fought for As Long."
36. Ibid.
37. "Statement from Jill Raymond," circa 1976.
38. Airtel Memorandum to Acting Director, FBI, from SAC, New York, 3 November 1972, Sears Papers.
39. After her arrest, Gabriner requested her FBI files through the Freedom of Informa-

tion Act. As she painstakingly annotated the hundreds of pages she received, Gabriner realized that although she had never gone underground, the FBI was unable to locate her for several years until she applied to the Radcliffe Institute. The Boston FBI was instructed to "immediately review application of Gabriner at Radcliffe Institute for current information re her location, references, associates, etc." Confidential Memorandum to Acting Director, FBI, from SAC, New York, 24 October 1972; Airtel Memorandum to Acting Director, FBI, and Atlanta, Boston, Chicago, and Philadelphia Field Offices from SAC, New York, 16 November 1972, Sears Papers.

40. Confidential Memorandum to Acting Director, FBI, from SAC, Chicago, 28 February 1973, p. 2, Sears Papers.

41. Confidential Memorandum to Acting Director, FBI, from SAC, Atlanta, 6 February 1973, pp. 2–3, Sears Papers.

42. Following her arrest, the Atlanta field office monitored Gabriner's involvement with the Georgia Equal Rights Amendment, her activities as a member of ALFA, her writings that appeared in the *Great Speckled Bird,* and her soliciting of funds and support for the forthcoming trial (Vicki Levins Gabriner, FBI Atlanta, Georgia, File, 8 November 1974, Sears Papers). Also see: letter to "Friends" from Vicki Gabriner, 15 April 1974, ALFA Papers, and articles appearing in the *Great Speckled Bird,* 13 and 20 May, 3 June 1974.

NINETEEN — TIDEWATER STRUGGLES

Interviews

Cliff Anchor, 3 October 1998, Guerneville, Calif.

Steve Brown, 27 December 1999, Norfolk, Va.

Jim Early, 29 December, 1999, Virginia Beach, Va.

Willard Frank, 5 January 2000, Norfolk, Calif.

Donna Motley, 31 May 2000, Portsmouth, Va.

Fred Osgood, 15 November 1998, 6 January 2000, Norfolk, Va.

Tony Pritchard, 1 May 1999, Norfolk, Va.

Marge "Clearwater" Reed, 5 January 2000, Norfolk, Va.

The epigraph is from an interview with Leonard Matlovich by Jim Kepner, 4 September 1978, p. 2, original transcript, Matlovich File, IGLA.

1. "Gays On the March," *Time,* 8 September 1975, 32–33.

2. On T-rooms (public restrooms), see Laud Humphrey's classic book, *The T-Room Trade.*

3. Kameny pioneered reform in the civil service, including the military, and lobbied for a change in the diagnostic policy of the American Psychiatric Association. Always a master strategist, in the successful effort to overcome the "sickness issue" at APA, Kameny invited Texas activist Phil Johnson to dance with him at the Dallas convention as rather unhip psychological types swirled around them. Later Kameny served as charter comember founder of the NGTF.

4. M. Hippler, *Matlovich: The Good Soldier* (Boston: Alyson, 1989), 48.

5. Letter to Captain Dennis M. Collins from T/Sgt. Leonard Matlovich, 6 March 1975, in Hippler, *Matlovich,* 47.

6. "Air Force Sergeant Feels He Is a Patriot Fighting for Freedom," *New York Times,* 20 September 1975.

7. "The Seventies Tidewater Community," symposium, James T. Sears, moderator, Unitarian Church of Norfolk, 2 May 1999, audiotape, Sears Papers.

8. The most noteworthy raid in the Tidewater occurred at Craig's. During the early sixties, Tony worked weekends at Craig's, a restaurant and late-night homosexual bar run by "Old Lady Sally" with her husband, Bert, near the boardwalk on Virginia Beach's Atlantic Avenue. (Earlier there had been a place called Hamburger Haven, directly across from Sally's, where Paige White played piano and gay men congregated.) After paying a buck to enter, you could get—with a wink and a nod from Sally—illegal liquor by the drink. Craig's was raided on a cold spring night by vice in trench coats, who arrested several dozen men. The *Virginia Beach Sun,* like many newspapers of that era, published names of those arrested, resulting in one suicide and several quick departures

from town. Craig's was later closed for ABC law violations and finally burnt to the ground.

The Longhorn, Norfolk's first lesbian bar, was located on the corner of Tidewater Drive and Lafayette Boulevard. Marge Reed reminisces: "We had to walk through a straight bar in the front; on the back door a sign read, 'Girls Athletic Club.' We held our heads high and walked right back into that room! It was small, crowded, with two pool tables. The smoke was thick. But it was *our* space—Girls Only."

9. "The Seventies Tidewater Community."

10. In addition to the Continental and the College Cue, gays could walk into two narrow (and often packed) downtown cruise bars, Mickey's Tavern and the Ritz Bar. One longtime Tidewater resident recalls: "Immediately to the east of the Ritz was another joint called Bunny's Congo Lounge. This was a straight place but you would just bounce around on Thursdays, Fridays, and Saturday nights. One time at Mickey's, marines tried to come into the front door. They were in a nasty, foul, evil mood calling names. All of us skedaddled to the back of the bar because we were fearful for our lives, but Ernestine—the bartender—she was there at the front. 'You sons of a bitches,' she yelled and started throwing beer bottles. They vanished!" ("The Seventies Tidewater Community").

11. Hippler, *Matlovich,* 10.

12. Ibid., 15.

13. For a discussion of the relationship between Anchor and Matlovich, see R. Shilts, *Conduct Unbecoming: Gay and Lesbians in the U.S. Military* (New York: Fawcett Columbine, 1993), 406–407.

14. Hippler, *Matlovich,* 13

15. Information about the murder and subsequent trial was gleaned from the following articles in the *Charleston News and Courier:* W. Chapman, "Queen St. Man Murder Victim," 2 November 1958; W. Chapman, "Jack Dobbins Was Liked by Neighbors," 3 November 1958; "Halloween Murder Trial May Begin Here Next Week," 4 December 1958; "Candlestick Murder Trial Gets Underway," 10 December 1958; O. Perkins, "Accused Airman's Mother Describes Son's Background and His Character," 10 December 1958; G. Robertson, "Candlestick Plays Big Role in Case," 11 December 1958; "Conflicting Tales Told by Two Witnesses," 11 December 1958; "Dobbins Murder Case Given to Jury Here," 12 December 1958; O. Perkins, "Jury Acquits Young Airman of Halloween Killing Here," 13 December 1958.

16. For more detail about gay Charleston during this era, see J. Sears, *Lonely Hunters* (Boulder: HarperCollins/Westview, 1997), 170–174.

17. Among the homosexual men in Dobbins's crowd who had attended the all-male Halloween party earlier that evening was a Citadel professor who was forced to resign. He quickly found another teaching position at an out-of-state Baptist college.

18. Throughout the trial, the airman's commanding officer and his mother sat directly behind the defendant's table. On the evening of the third day, a packed courtroom was motionless as the defense pleaded: "Give back this mother her wonderful son. Give back the Air Force its excellent soldier. Give back this young man his future and his self-respect." Surprisingly, the jury deliberated several hours before a frustrated circuit court judge demanded a verdict "tonight!" ("Dobbins Murder Case").

19. The progressive-minded editor of the *Charleston News and Courier,* Tom Waring, staked out a less popular position: "Regardless of a normal person's views about sexual deviates, citizens do not have a right to prey on them" ("Protection of Law," editorial, *Charleston News and Courier,* 13 December 1958). This jury decision contrasted sharply with that in a Memphis trial two months earlier in which a former hotel bellhop requested the electric chair rather than life in prison after a jury convicted him of murdering thirty-one-year-old Robert Gartley Bennett on Germantown Road the night of 19 May "because I hate queers" ("Leonard Tells All to Jury Case," *Memphis Press-Scimitar,* 23 October 1958).

20. Hippler, *Matlovich,* 14.

21. T. Perry and T. Swicegood, *Profiles in Gay and Lesbian Courage* (New York: St. Martin's Press, 1991), 138.

22. Hippler, *Matlovich,* 39.

23. M. Miller, "An Air Force Hero Faces His Toughest Battle," *In the Know,* January 1976, 32.

24. Interview with Franklin E. Kameny by Paul D. Cain, 2 July 1994, 46, Sears Papers.

25. R. Mott, "Life Becomes Somewhat Easier for D.C. Homosexuals," *Washington Post,* 23 April 1973. The first meeting of the Tidewater Homophile League was held at the Lafayette Motor Hotel with the help of the hotel manager, who was gay. More than fifty people attended. The Tidewater Homophile League of Norfolk was also represented by Ted Brownsword at the Fourth Annual NACHO Conference held in Chicago in 1968. Frank Kameny, along with Barbara Gittings and Barbara Grier, were three of the most visible pre-Stonewall activists assisting southern organizing efforts throughout the seventies. Kameny, who had difficult times making ends meet during this time, appeared, by his estimate, at over one hundred events every year, charging fees well below those needed to meet expenses. "I had to balance off creditors. You pay your electric bill this month, while the gay bill piles up . . . and then hope the telephone company won't shut you off" (Kameny interview, 22).

26. Matlovich interview, 7.

27. J. Mathews and D. Nunes, "Homosexual GI Fights Release from Service," *Washington Post,* 28 May 1975.

28. Kameny then also arranged a meeting with a former air force officer who would be representing Matlovich. David Addlestone, a southerner, was a counselor for the Military and Law Project of the American Civil Liberties Union. Like Frank, David stressed the risks involved, asking Matlovich: "Do you really want to throw away eleven years of service? You could retire in eight years. . . . It's *your* life that could be ruined by this. In my opinion, we'll probably lose this case." Leonard felt his background presented a better chance at winning what would be a landmark case. With this sense of history and a stubborn bearing, he declared, "I can't go on living like this" (Shilts, *Conduct Unbecoming,* 199).

29. Kameny interview, 45.

30. Other investigations were also going on during this time. For example, eight servicewomen were discharged following charges of homosexuality at the Key West air force base. Two of these women, choosing not to disclose their sexuality, unsuccessfully fought the charges ("WAF Fights Discharge, Denies Homosexuality," *Miami Herald,* 5 February 1976; "WAF Loses in Lesbianism Ruling," *Miami Herald,* 6 February 1976).

31. E. Marcus, *Making History* (New York: HarperCollins, 1992), 280.

32. Ibid.

33. Mathews and Nunes, "Homosexual GI."

34. L. Oelsner, "Homosexual Is Fighting Military Ouster," *New York Times,* 26 May 1975.

35. Kameny interview, 46.

36. Matlovich interview.

37. Mathews and Nunes, "Homosexual GI."

38. "A Conspiracy of Silence," *Blueboy,* January 1979, 3.

39. D. Turnstall, "An Interview and Review," *Our Own Community Press,* December 1978, 3. Also see "Berg and Gibson: Artist and Author," *Our Own Community Press,* April 1979.

40. Turnstall, "An Interview and Review," 3.

41. Ibid., 8.

42. Ibid.

43. Hippler, *Matlovich,* 57.

44. D. Baker, "A Matter of Opinions: Air Base Area Split over Matlovich," *Washington Post,* 18 September 1975.

45. "Homosexual G.I's Ouster Is Recommended by Panel," *New York Times,* 20 September 1975.

46. "No to Matlovich," *Time,* September 1975, 32. Although Matlovich's discharge was upgraded to honorable by the wing commander at Langley, Leonard's attorneys sought an appellate court ruling ("Homosexual, Lawyers Vow Appeal Fight," *Charlotte Observer,* 21 September 1975). Three days later, a former GI thwarted the attempted assassination of President Ford. The media peppered the young man with questions

about his sexuality. *New York Times* columnist William Safire shrewdly asked: "How do you thank an alleged homosexual for saving the life of a President just after a military panel decides that homosexuals are unfit to protect the nation by serving in the armed forces?" (W. Safire, "Big Week for Gays," *New York Times,* 29 September 1975).

There was, though, less than unanimous support within gay circles. Caricatured as "lower-case socialists and blue-denim elitists" by NGTF cochair Bruce Voeller, leftist gay media types were particularly upset (Hippler, *Matlovich,* 62). The *Gay Post* of New York City, for example, declared it was "unconscionable to want to remain part of the death culture. . . . Machismo is in in 1975" ("Notes from Above Ground," *Gay Post,* September–October 1975). The leftist *Coast to Coast Times:* Matlovich was "the capitalist media's 'role model' for gays," a "baby-murderer and war criminal," and "the Uncle Tom of the gay movement" ("The Struggle," *Coast to Coast Times,* September 1978, 29).

Some longtime activists like fellow southerner Jim Kepner, himself a socialist and pacifist, were more understanding: "Matlovich and I grew up in different skins, different environments. When he was fighting for country and freedom in what most of my friends called 'that dirty little war,' I was at home and comfortable. He was in the jungle agonizing over an orientation I'd accepted long before and he nearly got his head blown off. It would be gross indecency for me to judge him for participating in a war in which his role was just about as predetermined as his affectional orientation" (J. Kepner, "Sgt. Matlovich vs. Gay Detractors and the Air Force," *Coast to Coast Times,* 27 September 1978, 9). Across the gender divide, a lesbian, writing in the ALFA newsletter, observed that "this man is to some extent, and whether we like it or not, representing us in a very important manner" ("Matlovich in Atlanta," *ALFA Newsletter,* December 1975, 9).

47. Miller, "An Air Force Hero," 30.
48. K. Ringle, "Matlovich Adjusting to New Life Here," *Washington Post,* 17 November 1976.
49. "It wasn't even a lesbian bar back then!" according to Marge. Later the bar, renamed Bogey's, "turned lesbian. The Bayside Bombers liked to think we helped turn it into our lesbian bar."
50. This interest had begun twelve years earlier under the ministry of James H. Curtis, an independent thinker who had lived in Europe and had come across a British book, *Towards a Quaker View of Sex.* "One of the telling moments of our church history" was 3 November 1963, observes Will Frank, who had come to Norfolk that fall as a history professor at Old Dominion University. Entitling the Sunday sermon "Loving All Lovers," Curtis argued that there was no value difference between heterosexuality and homosexuality. Curtis, following the Quakers, further asserted: "Our questions *may become worthy* of their [homosexuals'] consideration. . . . We must not only seek to love all the lovers . . . but we must also seek to discover the warmth and intimacy, the involvement in another person's life" ("Loving All Lovers," pp. 1, 6, Sears Papers). After the youthful minister delivered his sermon, recalls Frank, "there was a talk-back (a discussion) in which a lot of people asked tentative questions. One woman asked Jim: 'But what should I do to make sure that my son doesn't grow up to be homosexual?' Jim stared at her a minute. 'I hope you take this right, but really this is none of *your* business.' This created murmurs, most notably from those who remembered with horror a decade earlier when another minister was arrested in the local bus station's T-room and the accompanying publicity in the newspaper."
51. This study group, whose original goal was to publish a report for the congregation, coincided with the sexual revolution of the sixties and early seventies marked by the technology (e.g., birth control pill), court rulings (e.g., *Roe v. Wade*), and popular culture (*The Harrad Experiment, Bob and Bob, Carol, Ted and Alice*). But, as Frank observes, "The doing of it—the ongoing process of discovery and self-discovery within the church—was more important, perhaps, than some final published report."
52. "Freedom Workshop," Unitarian Church of Norfolk *Newsletter,* 29 September 1975.
53. This 1957 *Report of the Board Appointed to Prepare and Submit Recommendations to the Secretary of the Navy for the Revision of Policies, Procedures and Directives Dealing with Homosexuals,* known as the Crittenden Report, concluded: "The concept that homosexuals pose a security risk is unsupported by any factual data. . . . No factual data

exist to support the contention that homosexuals are a greater risk than hetero-sexuals" (quoted from K. Dyer, *Gays in Uniform: The Pentagon's Secret Reports* [Boston: Alyson, 1990], 35). For the complete report, see appendix E in E. Gibson, *Get Off My Ship* (New York: Avon, 1978).

54. "A Conspiracy of Silence," 17.

55. Marcus, *Making History,* 286, 289.

56. This was not an unexpected phenomenon, as Cliff Anchor, a former military officer himself, underscores: "People generally don't understand the military mystique. Once you belong, you keep your nose clean and are loyal to those around you; you *don't* soil the nest." For detailed histories of gays and lesbians in the military, see: A. Berube, *Coming Out Under Fire: The History of Gay Men and Women in World War II* (New York: Free Press, 1990); L. Murphy, *Perverts by Official Order: The Campaign Against Homosexuals by the United States Navy* (New York: Haworth Press, 1988); Shilts, *Conduct Unbecoming.*

57. "A Conspiracy of Silence," 17.

58. Turnstall, "An Interview and Review," 3.

59. D. Turnstall, "Ensign Vernon E. Berg and E. Lawrence Gibson," *Our Own Community Press,* October 1981, 8.

60. P. Budahn, "Homosexual Ex-Servicemen Building New Lives," *Newport News Daily Press,* 24 June 1979.

61. Such a swift ruling "issued without benefit of oral arguments and without written opin-ions, is a decision on the merits binding in future cases" (L. Mathews, "Homosexu-ality Curbs Upheld," *Los Angeles Times,* 30 March 1976).

62. Ibid., 1; "A No to Sodomy," *Time,* 12 April 1976, 50. Also see: *John Doe et al. v. Common-wealth's Attorney for City of Richmond, et al.,* 403 F. Suppl. 1199 (E.D. Va. 1975) aff'd. 425 U.S. 901 (1976); "Homosexual Acts Ban Upheld by High Court," *San Diego Union,* 30 March 1976; J. MacKenzie, "Virginia Sex Law Is Upheld," *Washington Post,* 30 March 1976.

63. E. Gibson, "Court Orders Military to Explain Discharges," *Our Own Community Press,* January 1979, 1.

64. The ACLU, reluctantly, dropped Matlovich's case because of his inability to be rein-stated and a possible negative ruling that could have hindered gay rights. Declaring "I'm a fighter, not a quitter," Matlovich continued his legal battle. Berg, who was given an "other than honorable discharge" the month before, pursued his grievance with the help of a Lambda legal team.

TWENTY — TIME OF MIRACLES

Interviews

Pokey Anderson, 12 October 1994, Houston, and e-mail to the author.

Ray Hill, 12 October 1994, 22 March 1999, Houston, and e-mail to the author.

1. "The Ray Hill Prison Show," 25 July 1985, Sears Papers.

2. Hill did not acquiesce to the warden's demand to stop writing Representative Ron Waters. In fact, Hill's activism intensified. He reported the incident to his mother, Frankie. When she met with the warden, he advised her that Ray had "been in a fight" and was making "trouble for him." She was also advised that if her son "did not watch his mouth, he'd likely get knocked in the head and killed and no one would know who did it." Ray soon lost his accumulated "good time," trusteeship, and job. He was tossed into solitary under a trumped-up charge of "sexual malpractice" and later charged with stealing craft shop tools. His release date was bumped back four years, to 1978. Hill filed suit against prison officials in 1974 but eventually found his overtime restored and release date finalized (letter to W. J. Estelle, Jr., Director of Texas Dept. of Corrections from Inmate Raymond W. Hill 213398, 14 August 1974; Plantiff's Affi-davit, SS: CA-75-H-377; letter to Mary Frankie Hill from W. J. Estelle, Jr., 12 Sep-tember 1973, Sears Papers).

3. Representing Buchanan all the way to the U.S. Supreme Court was Henry J. McCluskey, Jr., a member of the Circle of Friends. Known for doing "legal jobs" on

behalf of local gay bars, homosexuals, and pornographic movies houses with Mafia ties, McCluskey was admired for his shrewdness and "ability to turn an extra dollar." In the summer of 1973, however, the Dallas attorney was dragged from the murky waters of Lake Ray Hubbard by two fishermen (R. Shivers, "Murder Suspect Sought," July 1973, unpublished letter to the *Advocate,* Dallas File, IGLA).

4. *Buchanan v. Batchelor,* 308 F. Supp. 729 (N.D. Tex. 1970), vacated for other reasons sub nom. *Wade v. Buchanan* 401 U.S. 989 (1971). A. Vacek, "Recent Developments," *Baylor Law Review* 22 (1970): 302; "Laws on 'Unnatural Sex' Challenged in High Court," *Louisville Times,* 10 July 1970.

5. Ken Cyr—with the help of his companion, Charles Gillis, the gay son of an East Texas minister—organized the first statewide gay conference in Fort Worth a year earlier. Cyr now served as moderator for the Task Force. TGTF originally was composed of lesbian and gay groups clustered into four regions. A Coordinating Council, one male and female from each region, directed state activities. The House of Delegates, representatives from "bona fide" gay organizations, set goals and implemented actions of the council. Given its similarity to the old NACHO organization (and recalling its ill-fated demise), Frank Kameny questioned the structure of TGTF: "What does 'bona fide' mean? Suppose a group decides that it feels strongly about some issue, and splinters itself off into 'chapters' or separate organizations, in order to multiply its votes? Can one person constitute himself an organization? . . . As long as one knows that everyone is acting in good faith, of course, none of this is necessary. Unfortunately, after the initial period of good feeling—the honeymoon—ideological and political differences do surface, and you're well advised to have taken some protective measures in advance" (letter to Hugh Crell from Franklin Kameny, 25 August 1974, Integrity/Houston Corr.). In January of 1975, the group's Coordinating Committee and House of Delegates voted to open TGTF to individual members.

6. By that fall, regular distribution of *Contact* had ceased, the phone was disconnected, and several contributors quit the paper due to missed paychecks and other matters (letter to Ken Cyr from Howard Erickson, 10 September 1975, Cyr/AURA Corr.). The public version was that *Contact* was sold to the *Advocate.* The former editor, who was hired in February from the *Minneapolis Tribune* (he had also been the Midwestern correspondent for the old *GAY*) and had resigned in disgust five months later to work for the LA-based *Newswest,* knew otherwise: "There is nothing to sell except a subscription list of 600 names and some distribution channels" (letter to Ken Cyr from Howard Erickson, 6 October 1975, Cyr/AURA Corr.).

7. L. Lovell and A. McKinney, *Sad Team* (Houston: Ego Press, 1975).

8. L. Brim, "Interview with Jan Cunningham," *Pointblank Times,* July 1976, 4.

9. According to Bill Buie, Ray Hill "was not too well-received because of his past." Hugh Crell, though, told others, "I'm not going to railroad [ostracize] him" because of his earlier felonious days (e-mail to the author from Pokey Anderson, 7 February 2000, Sears Papers).

10. L. Lovell, "Showdown at Paleface Park," *Pointblank Times,* June 1975, 4.

11. R. Beitel, "Watching the Texas Legislature," *Community News,* July 1975, 5; B. Belvando, "House Vote Keeps Gay a Crime," *Contact,* 13 August 1975, 16, 31.

12. Another local legislator, Ron Waters, had won with the support of the Houston gay community in 1973 and was reelected in 1975. He refused to declare whether he supported the deletion of the statute and was absent for the 29 May vote.

13. "Pokey Anderson Interview Transcript by M.S.," 4 October 1991, p. 8, Sears Papers.

14. "Gay Power in Macho Houston," *Newsweek,* 10 August 1981; W. Stevens, "Houston Accepts New Political Force," *New York Times,* 1 November 1981.

15. "Pokey Anderson Interview Transcript," 8.

16. The gap between lesbian and gay male views in the TGTF was also seen by former *Contact* editor Howard Erickson. Writing to Ken Cyr about his tense relationship with the Austin Lesbian Organization, Erickson recommended "caution in your remarks about ALO and women, in general, for I fear you don't do them justice." He underscored that, unlike the relationship between lesbians and the women's movement, "men

have no similar movement with which to identity as males, but that doesn't mean that gay men don't sometimes *act* as separatists, even if they don't articulate a separatist rhetoric the way some lesbians do." Howard also reminded Ken of "all the spadework for the gay cause which lesbians have done within those feminist circles" and noted that one advantage of having lesbians in "up front" leadership roles is "to swing votes that gay men could never touch" (letter to Ken Cyr from Howard Erickson, 10 September 1976, Cyr/AURA Corr.).

17. Marion Friedman, a student at the University of Houston in 1975, remembers Hill coming to her home and using her electric typewriter to prepare the press release. Marion, who two years earlier was one of the members of the gay/lesbian panel with Pokey on a KFPT radio program, used her bicycle to assist in the distribution.

18. "Houston GPC News Conference," 30 June 1975, audiotape, Sears Papers.

19. Others, like Hugh Crell, Keith McGee, and Bill Buie, attended but were not interested in fully coming out through the media.

20. The mostly student group, headed by Kathy Feller with assistance from Hill, published a newsletter, the *Lambda Letter,* conducted a survey of Houston businesses on attitudes and practices of gay employees, sponsored a VD screening clinic, and offered a noncredit summer course, "The Homosexual Experience," cotaught by Hill and Feller—a former marine.

21. "Houston GPC News Conference."

22. Ibid.

23. J. Jarboe, "Homosexuals Seek to Win New Laws by Influencing All Candidates Here," *Houston Chronicle,* 13 July 1975.

24. See J. Jarboe, "City's Gays Seek to Gain Acceptance," *Houston Post,* 1 July 1975; F. Snodgrass, "Gays Form Political Caucus," *University of Houston Cougar,* 3 July 1975.

25. Shortly after the news conference, according to Pokey, "Marian Panzer, owner of Just Marion and Lynn's, volunteered that any organization that had Ray Hill as an officer would not have her support."

26. "Homosexual County Aide Fired After Resolution Try," *Houston Post,* 2 August 1975.

27. B. Remington, "Twelve Fighting Years: Homosexuals in Houston, 1969–1981" (master's thesis, University of Houston, 1983), 34.

28. "Homosexual County Aide Fired."

29. Ibid.; "County Official Comes Out, Is Fired, and Files Lawsuit," *Contact,* 8 October 1975.

30. P. Anderson, "My Right to Be What I Am," *Pointblank Times,* September 1975, 1.

31. In July 1975—a month after Austin's first "legal" gay pride march, organized and led by lesbians—the City Council passed the South's first equal employment ordinance that included protection on the basis of sexual orientation.

32. "Text of Hugh Crell's Speech to City Council," Sears Papers.

33. Letter to Ken Cyr from Hugh Crell, 22 August 1975, Cyr/AURA Corr.

34. Remington, "Twelve Fighting Years," 38.

35. Letter to Ken Cyr and Charles Gillis from Hugh Crell, 19 September 1975, Cyr/AURA Corr.

36. Editorial, *Contact,* 19 March 1975, 30.

37. S. Jonnsson, Letter to the Editor, *Contact,* 13 August 1975, 20.

38. "News," *Pointblank Times,* November 1975, 1.

39. B. Cigainero, "Fred," *Pointblank Times,* November 1975, 1.

40. H. Crell, "Point of View," *Pointblank Times,* November 1975, 1.

41. B. Whiting, "Haven in Houston," *Advocate,* 23 March 1977, 4.

42. G. Taylor, "Frank Mann Jokes Abound at Party," *Houston Post,* 24 May 1976.

43. Integrity/Houston brochure, January 1977, Integrity/Houston Corr.

44. 22 August 1976. Later that fall the *Wall Street Journal* also reported the growing influence of Houston's GPC (R. Ricklefs, "A New Constituency: Political Candidates Seek Out Gay Votes," *Wall Street Journal,* 20 October 1976).

45. "Pokey Enters Race," *This Week in Texas,* 18 September 1976, 22.

46. C. Taylor, "The Year of the Gay," *Blueboy* 12 (1977): 19–20, 74, 77, 81–82.

TWENTY-ONE — SAVING CHILDREN

Interviews

Robert S. Basker, 14 and 15 June 1997, San Francisco, Calif.; interview with Robert S. Basker by John O'Brien, 1998, Basker Papers.

Jack Campbell, 12 January 1995, Coconut Grove, Fla.

Jim Kepner, 19 October 1993, Los Angeles, Calif.

Jesse Monteagudo, 9 January 1995, 18 June 1998, Miami, Fla., and e-mail to the author. Other unattributed quotations of J. Monteagudo in this chapter are from "Anita and I: An Activist's Memoir," *TWN,* 29 October 1997, 12–17, and used with his permission.

Howard Wallace, 16 June 1997, San Francisco, Calif.

1. "Dialogue: An Interview with Jesse Monteagudo," *TWN,* 22 August 1978.
2. The most notable ongoing student effort was the Boca Raton–based *Southern Gay Liberator,* formed in late 1969 as a "resource-educational project" with a newsletter. Among other activities, the *Liberator* distributed copies of *Come Out Fighting,* a newspaper put out by the Lavender and Red Union, a gay liberation–communist organization. By the end of 1975, however, roommates Joel Starkley (who had won a student senate seat at Florida Atlantic University on a progay plank in 1973) and Mark Silber (who was the first president of Florida Atlantic's Gay Student Union, which had begun January 1975 at an off-campus apartment and published *Liberation*) had established the *Gay Liberation News from Florida,* a monthly digest of news of the state activists' efforts. There were other student groups organized on Florida campuses, including the Gay Alliance at the University of Miami and the Gay Coalition at the University of South Florida, which met once a week and engaged in a wide range of activities. In the spring of 1976, Florida State University, for example, facilitated one of the first southern conferences for educators working with gay students with a keynote address by Massachusetts state legislator Elaine Noble. In Orlando that May, the first state gay conference was held at Florida Technical University. Planned by the Florida Gay Caucus, following their attendance at the Southeastern Gay Conference in Chapel Hill, it attracted about one hundred participants. And that same year readers of the *Alligator,* the University of Florida student newspaper that had run an undercover operation to ferret out homosexuals on campus during the midfifties (see Sears, *Lonely Hunters* [Boulder: HarperCollins/Westview, 1997], 77), learned they had an openly gay editor. Gainesville was also the site of the Gay Community Service Center, established in 1974, and students were starting a campus gay lib group.
3. J. Baker, "Gay Establishment Activist," *Advocate,* 15 June 1977, 10. Other sources used in developing the portrait of Bob Basker are located in Sears Papers.
4. The change of Basker's name from Solomon to Bob is evidence of an era of virulent anti-Semitism. He remembers the German American bund leaders in the early thirties making speeches against Jews, "looking forward to Jewish blood flowing into the streets." And, as a sixth grader, he was beaten by Italian students who said, "Jews killed Christ; we're going to kill you!" Solomon faced more discrimination when he looked for work in 1936 and couldn't get a job because of his name. Later he enlisted in the army as Robert: "I figured I might as well use a name that is more accommodating to getting by." For more biographical detail on Basker, see: J. Sears, "Bob Basker: The Movement's Salesman, in V. Bullough, ed., *Pioneers* (New York: Haworth Press, forthcoming).
5. Introduced in the 1974 legislative session, the proposed law would not help some already in prison or mental institutions, such as Willard Allen, who in 1976 was in his twenty-fourth year at the Chattahoochee maximum security mental institution (*Florida Gay Liberation News* 12 [circa 1976]). Further, a 1917 law banning "unnatural and lascivious acts" was still on the books and enforced. It was upheld in 1975 when a former Miami policeman, sentenced to six months to three years in prison, challenged its constitutionality ("State Court Upholds Ban in Patrolman's Sex Case," *Miami News,* December 1975).

6. "We had learned how to play our politics," Kameny explains. In the process of Congress's granting the District of Columbia local governing powers and "as a result of my campaign . . . I was on the ground floor. We were!" Although he remembers "some uneasiness" among those on the City Council, including the president, who voted against it, Kameny, who proposed the definitions that went into law, was later appointed as one of the commissioners of human rights responsible for administering the law (interview with Frank Kameny by Paul Cain, 2 July 1994, Sears Papers).

7. "Gay Activist Alliance of Miami," *Bulletin,* 23 November 1973.

8. This apathy was matched by antipathy within local media. In 1974, for example, following the close vote against New York City's law against homosexual discrimination, the *Miami News* editorialized that "homosexuals . . . are gay either by choice or by compulsion, as some people play golf or bet on horses. . . . This is not civil rights" ("Phony 'Rights' Issue," 30 May 1974).

9. The conference was formed at a working meeting in Jackson, Mississippi, on 11 January 1975. A meeting was set for each fall with officers elected for two years. Other founding chapters included: Atlantis (formed in 1972, their club song was the theme from *Gone with the Wind* and Atlanta members included Lady H. and Sally Sue, who had been known "to hang a real crystal chandelier in the mess tent at an outdoor run"); the Jackson Celtics, Caesar's Legion; and the Wranglers of Dallas, formed in 1973. The primary function of the conference was to coordinate the scheduling of run dates and to promote multi-club-sponsored runs. A system of point scoring for events was also adopted (e.g., points for number of miles covered, bringing a bike) (M. Rubin, "The Macho Image and the Bike Club Scene," *TWN,* 15 May 1979, 30).

10. Ibid., "Bike Club Scene," *TWN,* 18 September 1979, 19.

11. Ibid., "Six Years of Theban Brotherhood," *TWN,* 11 September 1979, 29.

12. Following the February 1975 arrest of sixty-four patrons at Campbell's Miami club—known as the "Valentine Eve Massacre"—he posted more than $30,000 in bail and subsequently won in court ("Police Arrest 67 Men at Club," *Miami Herald,* 14 February 1975; "43 Charges Dropped in Homosexual Case," *Miami Herald,* 9 April 1975; J. Oglesby, "Homosexual Charges Tossed Out," *Miami Herald,* 9 May 1975). Later that year, Campbell sought a seat on the Miami City Commission, running as an openly gay man on the slogan "Justice for All" ("Homosexual Club Gets Court Order Against Police," *Miami Herald,* 23 September 1975; "CBC President Jack Campbell Issues Statement," *Atlanta Barb,* October 1975; "Campaign Brings Police Assault?" *Miami News,* 2 October 1975).

13. Letter to Members of the Executive Committee, BOA from Robert S. Basker, 6 June 1975, Basker Papers.

14. Ten years earlier, Campbell had parlayed money earned from his coffeehouses into the renovation of an old sauna in the Little Finland area (two blocks from the dilapidated cruising ground of the downtown Cleveland YMCA). By 1972, when he moved to South Florida with his Cleveland State lover, his "hobby" had mushroomed into the twenty facilities nationwide comprising the Club Bath chain. By then, Campbell, who, as a college student, had forestalled his political aspirations because of his homosexuality but in the year of Stonewall founded the Mattachine Society of Cleveland, was a financial player with political groups like the NGTF and quietly picked up expenses in local groups from the Gay Activist Alliance to the Gay Community Services.

15. Sears, *Lonely Hunters,* 230.

16. F. Rose, "Trouble in Paradise," *New Times,* 15 April 1977, 46.

17. Some newspapers, including the *Miami Herald,* refused to run the strip when it featured the gay character (S. Simrich, "A Matter of Taste," *Alligator,* 17 October 1975, 1).

18. There he presented several gay-related resolutions, including one supporting an amendment on public accommodations by adding "affectional or sexual preference" along with political affiliations, personal appearance, and source of income. Basker had modeled these additional categories after D.C.'s Title 34, Human Rights Act (Dade County Democratic Executive Committee, 1976 Convention, Minority Concerns Task Force, Basker Papers).

19. Letter to Jack Campbell from Robert S. Basker, 18 February 1976, Sears Papers. In fact, there was little cohesion within these South Florida groups. Near the end of 1975, Basker, concerned about differences between lesbians and gay men and the "mediocrity, incompetence, and lack of commitments," had resigned as GCS president ("Informal Notes of Executive and Board Meeting," 20 November 1975; letter to Mark Reilly from Robert S. Basker, 7 September 1975; letter to Board of Directors from Bob Basker, 15 November 1975; Position Paper, 1975, by Bob Basker, Basker Papers). Similarly, the Alliance for Independent Rights faced a "problem as a cohesive group" (letter to AIR members from Jack Campbell, 27 October 1975, Sears Papers).

20. Kunst, who had run unsuccessfully for Metro Commission four years earlier and later was released from his advertising job with the Miami Toros, was characterized by a local newsmagazine as a "prophet of love-and-let-love modernism," with an "eager smile and a what-the-hell willingness to test the limits of authority . . . who wanders through social movements with sleepy eyes that open only to his own private vision, somehow safely shaded from the glare of political reality" (B. Hutchinson and J. Kukar, "Bryant/Kunst: Caught in the Middle," *Miami Magazine,* May 1977, 40, 60). In June 1976, Kunst, along with psychologist Alan Rockway, whom Bob had met seven years earlier, founded the Transperience Center, which advocated bisexual love.

21. Basker declined to serve as chair of the newly formed organization but agreed to act as convener.

22. Letter to AIR Members from Jack Campbell.

23. DCCHRG Minutes, 4 August 1976, Stonewall Library Archives, Fort Lauderdale.

24. Ibid., 19 October 1976.

25. Ibid., 25 October 1976.

26. Letter to the Thebans from Bob Basker, 17 February 1976, Basker Papers; Rubin, "Six Years," 29.

27. DCCHRG Minutes, 8 November 1976.

28. A. Bell, "Anita Bryant's Ire and Brimstone," *Village Voice,* 4 April 1977.

29. In addition to the two sponsors, William Oliver, Mayor Steve Clark, Barry Schreiber, and Neal Adams were anticipated supporters; Beverly Phillips, Clara Oesterle, and James Redford would not give support (DCCHRG Minutes, 8 November 1976). However, a week later Oesterle told a reporter she would support the amended ordinance, declaring: "What people do in their own bedrooms is their business" (M. Lucoff, "Homosexual Group Urging Anti-Bias Law," *Miami News,* 16 November 1976).

30. "Metro Commission Gives Early OK to Gay-Rights Bill," *Miami News,* 8 December 1976.

31. "Gays Don't Belong to Minority Group," *Miami News,* 10 December 1976.

32. J. Monteagudo, "The Dade County Ordinance on Gay Rights," 8 March 1977, typescript, Sears Papers; A. Bryant, *The Anita Bryant Story* (Old Tappan, N.J.: Revell, 1977).

33. "Battle over Gay Rights," *Newsweek,* 6 June 1977, 16.

34. A. Task and S. Burnside, "Gay Anti-Bias Bill Criticized," *Miami Herald,* 17 January 1977.

35. A. Glass, "Anita Bryant's Holy War on Homosexuals," *Qui,* July 1977, 93.

36. "Miami Pioneers Gay Rights," *Advocate,* March 1977; T. Stanger, "Dade Approves Ordinance Banning Bias Against Gays," *Miami Herald,* 19 January 1977.

37. R. Sloane, "With Your Help," *Eastern Mattachine Magazine,* September–October 1965, 7–9.

38. Stanger, "Dade Approves Ordinance."

39. Shack, Ruvin, Redford and Phillips. Mayor Clark had joined Oesterle and Adams in opposing it; Barry Schreiber, an Orthodox Jew, was absent. Interestingly, the Coalition had endorsed Adams, Oesterle, and Schreiber that preceding fall.

40. M. Lucoff, "Metro Bans Bias Against Homosexuals," *Miami News,* 18 January 1977. If successful, Miami would become the first major city to repeal such an ordinance by direct vote. In May 1974, Boulder voters had rescinded a similar ordinance by a nearly two-thirds majority.

41. "Metro Wrong on Gays," *Miami News,* 20 January 1977; "Metro in the Right on 'Gays,' Decision," *Miami Herald,* 20 January 1977.

42. For example, a Coalition press release of 27 January declared the newly amended ordinance had "support . . . from virtually every segment of the community," with the exception of "the zealous crusade on the part of a small group of Fundamentalists."

43. T. Welch, "Drive to Eliminate 'Gay Rights' Bill Under Way," *Miami News,* 7 February 1977; "Petitions Against Gay Rights Statute Will Be Circulated in Synagogues," *Miami Herald,* 11 February 1977; "Anita Bryant Starts Repeal Move to Void Gay Ordinance," *Miami Herald,* 12 February 1977; H. Inclan, "Latins Join Anita Bryant Campaign to Repeal Metro's Gay Rights Law," *Miami News,* 22 February 1977.

44. Glass, "Anita Bryant's Holy War," 93.

45. Bell, "Anita Bryant's Ire."

46. Hutchinson and Kukar, "Bryant/Kunst."

47. J. Arnold, "Money Is Issue in Gay-Law Repeal," *Miami Herald,* 24 March 1977.

48. *Miami Herald,* 17 March 1977.

49. A similar strategy had been advanced to the Coalition prior to the circulation of petitions.

> IF they get the 10,000 signatures, and they will AND IF through forces like the Catholic Church, *Miami News,* etc. it begins to seem obvious you'd lose the ballot fight overwhelmingly. Consider asking the Metro Commission to reverse its stand. . . . This would have the effect of: 1.) putting a good face on a sure defeat, 2.) coupled with your anti-boycott stand, it would make you the GUARDIANS of the economy . . . 3.) it would take the heat off your supporters. . . . If you lose your commission friends, you ain't gonna get no more good laws for a long, long time. . . 4.) tell the commission that in two years you will go the petition route and obtain 10,000 signatures to get it on the ballot. ("To the Dade Coalition, An Alternative Plan You Should Consider," Sears Papers)

50. Arnold, "Money Is Issue"; G. Pollard, "Gays Offer to Pay Election Costs," *Miami Herald,* 21 March 1977; N. Miller, "Miami Gays Try to Pick Up $400,000 Vote Tab," *Gay Community News,* 2 April 1977.

51. Furious, Save Our Children forces eventually won a negatively worded ballot that required voting against the referendum in order to support the ordinance. The referendum read: "Shall Dade County Ordinance No. 77-4 which prohibits discrimination in the areas of housing, public accommodations and employment against persons on the basis of their affectional or sexual preference be repealed?" Along with the vote to repeal the amended ordinance, there were three other referendums: changing reporting of outside income by county workers to annually rather than monthly, repeal of traffic division courts, and a rent control referendum. The coupling of these other proposals to the recall referendum buoyed gay activists' hopes.

52. "2 Out of 3 Favor Gay Rights," *Miami News,* 31 March 1977.

53. "Results of Scientific Poll," DCCHRG File, Sears Papers.

54. For example, according to Wallace and confirmed by a *Miami Herald* news reporter: "Jack Campbell kept the door just slightly ajar to Bob Kunst and Alan Rockway. He gave them little bits of money, thereby giving him some control" (see C. Hiaasen, "Out of the Closet and Then Some," *Tropic,* 5 June 1977, 14).

55. L. Solomon, "Lessons from Losing," *Advocate,* 24 August, 1997, 7. An early press release prepared for the gay media by the Getto-managed Coalition sought to isolate Kunst, bashing him as being "on a personal ego trip" which "will only damage the pro–gay rights cause" (Press Release, 13 April 1977, DCCHRG File, Sears Papers).

56. Solomon, "Lessons from Losing," 8.

57. C. Ortleb, "Interview: Ethan Getto," *Christopher Street,* August 1977, 21.

58. Ibid., 27.

59. Ethan Getto, "Campaign Organization and Structure," 19 April 1977, p. 1, DCCHRG Internal Documents, Sears Papers.

60. Ortleb, "Interview," 22.

61. "A Study of Voter Attitudes in Dade County," Richard Dresner and Associates, April 1977, DCCHRG Internal Documents, Sears Papers. See also: K. Ross, "Miami: The Media Massacre," *Blueboy,* November 1977, 41; Solomon, "Lessons from Losing." Although the poll had shown only a point difference, when including those stating

there was a "good" chance they would vote, the Coalition was leading by seventeen points.

62. Solomon, "Lessons from Losing," 7.
63. "The sheer Yahoo brutality of Save Our Children," observed *New York Post* reporter Lindsy Van Gelder, "was grossly underreported in the national press." She quotes from the organization's press kit that included a paper entitled "Why Certain Sexual Deviations Are Punishable by Death," which declared, in part: "As barnyard animals become restless, confused, and panicky just before a hurricane . . . [s]o too these vile beastly creatures evidently sense the coming judgment (Van Gelder, "Anita Bryant on the March: The Lessons of Dade County," *MS.,* September 1977, 76).
64. The ordinance applied only to the county's 225 private and religious schools since the public schools were under state control. Later in the campaign, Bryant would tell syndicated columnist William Rasberry, "I know homosexuals are no more likely to be child molesters than anybody else." Her objection, rather, was to "people who are being role models to stand up and say, 'I'm a homosexual and I'm proud of it.'" Bryant convinced Rasberry that "[i]n the name of human rights, vice is becoming virtuous" (W. Rasberry, "Could Gay Rights Be Wrong, After All?" *Virginia Pilot,* 3 May 1977).
65. J. Carroll, "S.F. Is the Issue in Miami," *San Francisco Chronicle,* 7 June 1977, 1.
66. Ortleb, "Interview," 28. Basker's position was later vindicated in a post-referendum study by University of Wisconsin political scientist Murray Edelman. From telephone poll data of nearly thirteen hundred randomly selected county residents conducted a month after the referendum, Edelman concluded that "Dade county residents voted out of fear for their children. . . . Ignorance and fear were no match for morality. . . . What was needed to counteract the charges was education not morality" (M. Edelman, "A Survey of Anti-Gay Attitudes of Dade County Voters," paper presented at the California Conference, circa 1978, Sears Papers). Later Campbell also conceded that "we probably should have taken on the 'child molestation' issue more than we did" (G. Mendenhall, "Lessons from Losing," *Advocate,* 24 August 1977, 10). However, Goodstein—though noting "surprise" by the margin of defeat—argues that "at best a different campaign might have changed the vote a few percentage points" (D. Goodstein, "Traditional or Conventional Political and/or Educational Efforts Fail Gay People," *Blueboy,* September 1978, 3).
67. Ortleb, "Interview," 28. In a memo to the Steering Committee, Getto and Foster asserted: "Through our polling and our political analysis, we have come to the conclusion that ours is a *motivational,* as opposed to an *attitudinal,* campaign. . . . We have also determined that there is a majority of the voters in the county sympathetic to retaining the ordinance on the human rights angle; that the level of turnout and the origins of the turnout will determine the outcome. If we can motivate our voters, we will win. Our goal is not to change opinions" (memo to Policy Steering Committee from Ethan Getto and Jim Foster, 16 May 1977, DCCHRG Internal Documents, Sears Papers).
68. Solomon, "Lessons from Losing," 8.
69. Ortleb, "Interview," 25.
70. "Controversy, Emotionalism, and Everything Except Clarity," *Miami Herald,* 5 June 1977.
71. "Gay Thanks Bryant," *Miami Herald,* 30 March 1977. See also Press Release, 13 April 1977, DCCHRG, Sears Papers.
72. Ross, "Miami," 31–32. Basker also faced difficulties, including drive-by shooting into his apartment and the switching of his car license plate with that from a stolen vehicle. Another Coalition member, Manolo Gomez, lost his job because he was passing a petition in support of gay rights, his car was firebombed, and he was beaten up by gay bashers. Larry King, who was hosting a local radio talk show, observed: "It's polarizing the city." The WIOD radio personality declared: "If I did five hours on this every night I'd still have the phones ringing every second" ("Trouble in Paradise," *New Times,* 15 April 1977, 44).
73. "Notes on Meeting with Steve Ross at Star Island," 21 April 1977, DCCHRG Internal Documents, Sears Papers. This decision was based on recommendations of pro-

fessional political advisers Richard Dresner and Sergio Bendizen ("A Study of Voter Attitudes"; "Notes on Meeting of 28 April 1977," Sears Papers).

74. See, for example: D. Holmberg, "Gay Rights: The Emotions, At Least, Are in the Open Now," *Miami News,* 23 March 1977.

75. For example, a flyer, printed in English and Spanish, released by the Coalition declared Ramos's cause of death "murder by public and private vilification and harassment" ("Save Our Children!—From Pain, Humiliation and Suffering!" Sears Papers).

76. See, for example, the coverage in the *Village Voice,* which underscored Ramos's "mission to raise the consciousness of the gay Cuban community" despite his "god-fearing" parents, who had been "harping on him to 'get cured,' to find a wife." The story went on to describe the suicide note's contents about "his sadness that people couldn't accept him for what he was" (Bell, "Anita Bryant's Ire"). Another local gay activist, Mark Silber, told a gay paper, *NewsWest:* "It's as if society has murdered him" ("Violence Aimed at Miami Gays," 1 April 1977). *Oui* magazine termed Ramos a "martyr" (Glass, "Anita Bryant's Holy War," 1977, 96) and Jesse Monteagudo was quoted in the *San Francisco Examiner* as saying that Ramos told him on the day of his suicide, "Everybody is against us" (J. Treloan, "Both Sides Hitting Low in Anita's 'Holy War' on Gays," *San Francisco Examiner,* 2 June 1977). Years later Jesse described this note blaming his "homophobic" parents for "causing" his death as "unfair to the elder Ramoses, a kindly old couple who did the best to get along with their unruly son." Monteagudo continued: "We made him out to be this martyr for the gay cause, but he was always suicidal."

77. N. Diaman, *Ed Dean Is Queer: A Novel* (San Francisco: Persona Press, 1978). This book is most notable for the author's fictionalized projection of the consequence of the Dade County vote. In the ominous Orwellian year of 1984, Benita Ryan (i.e., Anita Bryant) has opened up a chain of Bible boutiques in the shape of little white churches (actually, she ended up divorced from Bob Green and operated a dress shop in Selma where she also marketed "Silent Witness" sunglasses, and then was dumped by another man for a younger woman). The local politician behind the scene, "Brandon Harthway" has formed the ultraright Patriot Party and gay rights gains of the seventies had been lost as increased antigay violence was occurring in the country, while San Francisco, under the new mixed-race lesbian mayor (along with San Mateo County) had seceded from the Union, forming the first gay nation, the Pacific Republic. The novelist anticipated what one reporter summarized as the "dramatic increase in violence against homosexuals" (D. Ireland, "Open Season on Gay," *Nation,* 15 September 1979, 209) during the two years after the referendum. It also presaged a string of referenda losses in other cities and the emergence of ultraright, antigay politicians, like Georgia congressman Larry McDonald, and wholesale defeat of liberal senators and congressmen, negative court rulings on child custody and gay teachers, and the rise of the corporate Christian Right (B. Slevert, "Right Using Gay Issue," *In These Times,* 6 July 1977; "The New Christian Right Threatens Gays," *Front Page,* 12 June 1980; A. Mayer, "A Tide of Born-Again Politics," *Newsweek,* 15 September 1980).

78. Even less activity had occurred within South Florida's African American communities, despite the Dresner poll that had found 54 percent of blacks rejecting repeal ("A Study of Voters"). Again, the political operatives had consulted with Democratic advisor Sergio Bendixen. Although expressing the view that the Coalition would be "wasting our time in the black community," he noted that a professional street organizer, Clarence Edwards, could be hired to get out the black vote. Noting that Edwards was "not especially favorable to our Cause," Bendixen estimated Edwards's $10,000 fee would increase the vote margin by 5 to 7 percent. ("Notes on Meeting of 28 April 1977"; memo, RE: GOTV, 6 May 1977, DCCHRG Internal Documents, Sears Papers). Edwards was eventually paid $8,700. As the referendum neared, most local African American leaders expected that only a small percentage of the eighty-five thousand registered black voters would go to the polls. The director of the Urban League, who declared Coalition arguments "rational," for example, said: "I think most blacks are too concerned about other issues, like jobs and housing, to worry about this question. . . . The masses aren't going to make a big rush to the polls" (D. Holm-

berg, "Black Vote on Issue Unpredictable," *Miami News,* 3 June 1977). Nevertheless, the referendum was endorsed by the community's black newspapers. The editor of the *Miami Times* found it "ironical that a law of this nature would meet with opposition in the black community where a similar law just 13 years ago guaranteed us the same rights" ("Discrimination of Any Kind Cannot Be Condoned," *Miami Times,* 2 June 1997).

79. G. Mendenhall, "Lessons from Losing," 10. Edelman (circa 1978) also concluded, based on his polling data, that the emphasis on media rather than personal contact was another error.

80. "Dade County Coalition for the Human Rights Campaign Fund for June 7th," Referendum Exhibit A, Advertising and Consultants for the Period November 1, 1976, to July 21, 1977, DCCHRG Internal Documents, Sears Papers; "DCCHRG Campaign Fund for June 7th Referendum," *TWN,* 21 December 1977.

81. "Lessons of Miami," *Bay Area Gay Liberation,* July 1977.

82. Ibid.

83. Van Gelder, "Anita Bryant," 100. Edelman's study (circa 1978) also found that the sexism within Coalition leadership also resulted in its having "missed significant support . . . [since] many voters made the connection between gay rights and women's rights; many more may have changed if those connections were discussed." Van Gelder, in "Anita Bryant," argued similarly: "The limited human rights focus of the pro-gay coalition, together with the fact that virtually all its leaders were men, gave Bryant a clear field to zero in on the raunchier aspects of gay *male* culture. . . . Another tactical error—despite the fact that at least three of the coalition's inner circle are divorced parents—was the failure of the gays to inject the major feminist issue of lesbian-mother custody cases" (100).

84. "Speech Given After Gay Pride March," *Atalanta* 5, 7 (1977): 7. Interestingly, Bryant began to share this perspective following her divorce to Bob Green several years later: "I guess I can better understand the gays' and the feminists' anger and frustration. . . . I wanted to be submissive to Bob, but at the same time I often felt he was wrong. It was unhealthy. . . . Someone can say he loves you . . . but when his treatment of you is diabolical, when you are used and abused, how can you believe that?" (C. Jahr, "Anita Bryant's Startling Reversal," *Ladies' Home Journal,* December 1980, 68, 65–66).

85. During that last week, for example, the Dade County circuit court removed the rent control referendum from the Miami Beach ballot, reducing the number of Jewish retirees likely to vote. Meanwhile, in Tallahassee, a legislator, declaring gay activists were "beginning to aggravate the ordinary folks who have a few rights of their own," persuaded the legislature to outlaw same-sex marriages and adoptions ("Florida Votes to Ban Gay Marriages," *Boston Globe,* 1 June 1977).

86. "Metro in the Right."

87. J. McMullen, "An Unorthodox Campaign," *Miami Herald,* 13 April 1977. The absence of documented or reported discrimination, as Frank Kameny detailed in his letter to the Dade County Commission, was an "argument [that] fails on several counts. If there really is no such discrimination, then obviously there is no one who might want to discriminate to be bothered by the law. . . . There are few formally recorded instances of such discrimination because there has never been any recourse or remedy. . . . That some 60,000 people signed those petitions indicates some 60,000 potential anti-Gay discriminators. By opposing the law they have clearly demonstrated the need for the law" (letter to Honorable Steve Clark and Commissioners from Franklin E. Kameny, 10 March 1977, DCCHRG Minutes and Internal Documents, Sears Papers).

88. "An Unneeded Ordinance," *Miami Herald,* 5 June 1977.

89. A. Bell, "The Fatal Consequences of the Secret Life," *Village Voice,* 26 January 1976.

90. This campaign marked the first truly national event that generated grassroots donations from virtually every state. For example, by mid-May $115,000 in individual contributions had been received from all but three states and every southern one, ranging from $5,102.87 in North Carolina to Arkansas's $22.00 ("Contributions Received as of May 17, 1977," DCCHRG Minutes and Internal Documents, Sears Papers). In contrast, during the same period, Save Our Children collected $58,000 ("Dade County

to Vote on Controversial Gay Rights Law," *Boston Globe,* 5 June 1977; T. Stanger, "Pro-Gays Hold a 2-1 Edge in Contributions," *Miami Herald,* 24 May 1977). Ultimately the Coalition reported receipts of more than $379,000 with expenditures of $371,000 ("DCCHR Campaign Fund for June 7th").

91. "Dade County Coalition." Arguably, media outlets were difficult to find on short notice, particularly given that two of the four television stations and twelve radio stations refused to accept ads from any group regarding the referendum (T. Stanger, "Media Split on Gays-Rights Ads," *Miami Herald,* 31 May 1977). Nevertheless, there were a variety of small community papers, most notably the supportive African American *Miami Times* and *Liberty News,* that could have been better targeted ($10,000 was spent on advertising in the twenty-three local newspapers and magazines). C. Gaylord Rolle, publisher of the *Liberty News,* for example, had endorsed the ordinance and editorialized against its repeal, writing that "the greater danger to all of our children is from the epidemic of divisive reactionism and virulent bigotry unleashed upon the community" ("Seize the Time," *Liberty News,* 3 April 1977). "I implored Ethan to put some ad money into the local black press," recalls Basker. "Finally, the week of the Referendum, a token ad appeared in the major black newspaper."

92. "'We Expect to Win' Says Dade County," *Pacific Coast Times,* 3 June 1977.

93. D. Holmberg, "30 to 35 Per Cent Turnout Expected in Gay Rights Vote," *Miami News,* 6 June 1977.

94. "Telephone Conversations Between David Dahlquist and Leonard Matlovich, 4 June 1977," audiotape, Matlovich-Dahlquist Conversations, Sears Papers.

95. Anita's evening activities and comments appeared in: D. Holmberg, "The Campaign Has Just Begun, Anita Pledges," *Miami News,* 8 June 1977; "The Battle for Dade County," *Woman Behind Controversy* 11 (1978): 42–52; C. Hiaasen, "'Decency' Is Winner, Anita Says," *Miami Herald,* 8 June 1977; "Enough! Enough! Enough!" *Time,* 20 June 1977.

96. "Miami Area Rejects Homosexual-Bias Law," *Minneapolis Star,* 8 June 1977.

97. Glass, "Anita Bryant's Holy War," 96.

98. "Statement by John W. Campbell," 7 June 1977, DCCHRG, Sears Papers.

99. "Telephone Conversations."

100. C. Hiaasen, "Gay-Rights Law Is Crushed," *Miami Herald,* 8 June 1977; I. Glass, "It Was Hardly a Gay Day for the Boys in the Bar," *Miami News,* 8 June 1977.

101. Nearly 45 percent of registered voters went to the polls. However, majorities against repealing the ordinance were found in only 61 of the county's 446 precincts. As Getto had predicted when he targeted 100 key precincts, the referendum was supported among condominium dwellers of North Miami Beach, in the artist enclave of Coconut Grove, and within the heavily Jewish precinct of South Miami Beach. There was light turnout in Liberty City, which supported repeal by a 10 percent margin, and overwhelming support in the Cuban communities of Little Havana and Hialeah, with nine out of ten voters supporting repeal ("8 Precincts and How They Voted," *Miami Herald,* 10 June 1977; J. Greene, "Inside Look at Gay Vote," *Miami Herald,* 10 June 1977).

TWENTY-TWO — BREAKING SILENCES

Interviews

Lorraine Fontana, 20 October 1999, New York City, and e-mail to the author, 12 July 2000.

Margo George, 6 August 2000, Oakland, Calif., and e-mail to the author, 6 August 2000.

Barbara Grier, 14 January 1995, Tallahassee, Fla.

Merril Mushroom, 28 June 2000, Doweltown, Tenn.

Catherine Nicholson, 11 February 1995, Durham, N.C.

Julia Penelope, 30 June 2000, Lubbock, Tex.

Mab Segrest, 30 November 1995, 10 October 1996, Durham, N.C.

The epigraph is from J. Penelope, "A Cursory and Precursory History of Language, and the Telling of It," *Sinister Wisdom,* no. 1 (1976): 8.

1. H. Desmoines, "Notes for a Magazine," *Sinister Wisdom,* no. 3 (1977): 99.

2. Julia would soon drop her "patronymic, Stanley," in favor of "Penelope," which "has been handed down on the maternal side of her family every other generation since her great-great aunt, Julia Penelope, defied General Sherman by chewing and swallowing the map which showed where her husband was hidden with his confederate troops" (Contributors' Notes, *Sinister Wisdom,* no. 11 [1979]: 102).

3. Penelope, "A Cursory and Precursory," 12.

4. J. Chambers, *Last Summer at Bluefish Cove* (New York: JH Press, 1982), 36.

5. J. Arnold, "Lesbians and Literature," *Plexus,* February 1976, 12.

6. Under this nom de plume she also wrote a book review of Robin Morgan's *Going Too Far* for the *Free Press,* North Carolina's first gay newspaper, before the paper collapsed in 1977 (H. Desmoines, Book Review, *Free Press,* 25 July 1977, 7). In using a pen name, Harriet followed a tradition of other lesbian writers such as Sarah Aldridge (Anyda Marchant), Ann Bannon (Ann Thayler), Lisa Ben (Edith Eyde), Gene Damon (Barbara Grier), Isabel Miller (Alma Routsong), Claire Morgan (Patricia Highsmith), Mary Renault (Ellen Mary Challans), Carol Silver (Judy Grahn), and Valerie Taylor (Verta Tate).

7. In her introduction to the reissued *Lover,* Bertha Harris describes the differing publishing philosophies of Parke and June:

Parke's stated goal was to run Daughters as if it were Random House. . . . To Parke, Daughters was strictly a business whose business was profit making. She wanted to publish novels with both literary merit and commercial appeal, and if the works were perceived as feminist, so much the better. . . . June claimed that Daughters' reason for being was to publish novel-length fiction which the presses could not afford to publish. . . . In 1972, June believed wholeheartedly that a full-scale feminist revolution was at hand. With the patriarchy (and mainstream publishing) in ruins, Daughters would replace Random House. . . . June and Parke went through an ongoing struggle to dominate the company and realize their opposing views. (B. Harris, *Lover* [New York: New York University Press, 1993], xxxii–xxxiii)

8. Most notable were the corporate sale of paperback and film rights to *Rubyfruit Jungle* and responses to lesbians' spray painting of June Arnold's building with graffiti that criticized her suspected classism. In the first instance, Rita Mae Brown and Daughters had split $250,000 from the sale of paperback rights. Daughters, of course, was not the only feminist concern facing such issues. Susan Brownmiller and her publisher had also received that amount for the paperback edition of *Against Our Will: Men, Women, and Rape* (L. Gould, "Creating a Women's World," *New York Times Magazine,* 2 January 1997). Interestingly, this featured story in the *Times* magazine also created a controversy over what some saw as self-glorification, misrepresentation, "anti-lesbian sentiment," needless exposure of divisions within the movement, anti-Semitism, and "pandering to the establishment" (M. Franchild, "Just What Can Feminists Afford?" *Big Mama Rag* 6, 4 [1977]: 5–8, 12). In the second instance—the spray painting incident by two "non-privileged lesbians"—there were charges of one being "an agent" and countercharges of "coercive methods" used by Arnold and her "lackeys" during the vandal's "interrogation." An "analysis" written by one of the two delinquent lesbians and shared with other "trusted" lesbians across the country, "The Writing on the Wall," claimed that Arnold

operates in the interests of the privileged women who control it [the women's movement]. . . . It has excluded, ignored, degraded, sold out, exploited, brainwashed, addicted, co-opted and now threatened non-privileged lesbians. . . . It spins out narcotic illusions such as all men and only men are the enemy to cover up inequalities among women and the rage of non-privileged lesbians. We feel tactics such as presses, bookstores, businesses . . . because they require money and credentials, allow a few usually white middle and upper class women to scramble for crumbs of power on the backs of the non-privileged lesbians, who as usual, are doing all the real work. ("Lesbian Interrogated by Coercive Methods," 4, File 83-15, LHA)

9. B. Zimmerman, *The Safe Sea of Women: Lesbian Fiction, 1969–1989* (Boston: Beacon Press, 1991). Also see B. Harris, "What We Mean to Say: Notes Toward Defining the Nature of Lesbian Literature," *Heresies,* Fall 1977. For recent literary assessments of *Lover,* see A. Gable, "Bertha Harris' Lover: Lesbian and Postmodern," *Journal of Homo-*

sexuality 34, 3/4 (1998).

10. H. Desmoines, "Reading and Writing and Publishing," *Sinister Wisdom,* no. 5 (1978): 67.

11. They had also written *Amazon Quarterly.* "We asked them if we might carry it on." There was no response.

12. H. Desmoines, "Notes for a Magazine I," *Sinister Wisdom,* no. 1 (1976): 4.

13. For example, one newsletter sounded a call for inclusion: "There are women who want to include men in the women's movement, and others who say 'how dare they.' There are lesbians who are put off by their straight sisters and heterosexual women who have been uncomfortable among gay women exulting in their lesbianism. 'Tis the season to get rid of the hostilities and fears. The women's center is for women" (*Charlotte Women's Center Newsletter,* 15 January 1975, 1).

14. H. Desmoines, "Notes for a Magazine," *Sinister Wisdom,* no. 3 (1977): 99.

15. C. Nicholson and H. Desmoines, "A Domestic History," *Sinister Wisdom,* no. 16 (1981): 97.

16. "Lesbian Feminist Writing and Publishing," special issue, *Margins,* August 1975. Initially, this was to be a combined issue on gay literature. Louie Crew, the appointed editor for that volume, insisted on a lesbian coeditor and later supported its split into two issues.

17. In a paper presented at the GAU conference, the Fayetteville native remembers the founder's motto: "Educate a man and you educate an individual; educate a woman and you educate a family." For more background of Harris's college years, see B. Harris, "The Lesbian in Literature or Is There Life on Mars?" in *The Universities and the Gay Experience: Proceedings of the Conference Sponsored by the Women and Men of the Gay Academic Union, November 1973* (New York: Gay Academic Union, 1974), 44–52.

18. A. Wadsworth, "Bertha Harris," in C. Summers, ed., *The Gay and Lesbian Literary Heritage* (New York: Holt, 1995), 362.

19. B. Harris, *Catching Saradove* (New York: Harcourt, 1969), 119.

20. The Collective Lesbian International Terrorists (CLIT) was a group of three women (Maricla Moyana, Susan Cavin, and Marcia Segerberg) who published a revolutionary series of anti-establishment essays on the media and women's publishing in feminist and lesbian press. Rejecting the "star system" that elevated a few lesbian/feminist writers and wary of co-optation by liberal mainstream media, they asserted that "we can write with many ideas that don't need to be explained in tedious male fashion because women intuitively know what you mean" ("CLIT, Statement No. 2," in S. Hoagland and J. Penelope, eds., *For Lesbians Only* [London: Onlywomen Press, 1988], 357).

21. H. Desmoines, "Reading & Writing & Publishing," *Sinister Wisdom,* no. 5 (1978): 64–65. For a discussion about the Drastic Dykes and their evolution to lesbian separatism, see J. Justice, "From 'Vision,'" *Feminary* 9, 1 (1978): 22–24, 60.

22. The Club Baths had just opened on West Morehead and bars, populated by mostly white men, ranged from Honey's Brass Rail to Scorpio's. Short-term groups, such as the Charlotte Gay Alliance for Freedom, which articulated a human rights agenda, focused on making Mecklenberg County less psychologically and politically hostile to homosexuals.

23. B. Carr, "Sinister Doings in NC," *Front Page,* 27 May 1994, 7.

24. J. Russ, *The Female Man* (New York: Bantam, 1975), 70.

25. J. Pierson, "Interview with Catherine Nicholson," *Sinister Wisdom,* no. 53 (1994): 11.

26. H. Corzine, "Gay Press" (Ph.D. diss., Washington University, St. Louis, 1977), 66–67.

27. There were also influential lesbian-supportive feminist publications, notably *off our backs,* which began in 1970 following a falling out with NOW, and *Quest,* a political quarterly edited by Charlotte Bunch. For more information about these and other lesbian-feminist publications, see: C. Douglas and F. Moira, "Off Our Backs: The First Decade," in K. Wachsberger, ed., *Voices from the Underground* (Tempe, Ariz.: Mica Press, 1991), 107–130; K. Jay, "A Look at Lesbian Magazines," *Margins* 8 (1975): 19–21; C. Hensley, "*Sinister Wisdom* and Other Issues of Lesbian Imagination," *Serials Review,* Fall 1983, 7–11; C. Potter, *The Lesbian Periodicals Index* (Tallahassee: Naiad Press, 1986); K. Short, "Publishing Feminism in the Feminist Press Movement, 1969–1994"

(Ph.D. diss., University of Colorado, Boulder); R. Streitmatter, *Unspeakable: The Rise of the Gay and Lesbian Press in America* (Winchester, Mass.: Faber and Faber, 1995).

28. Corzine, "Gay Press," 67.

29. For a discussion of lesbian literature during this era, see: G. Haggerty and B. Zimmerman, eds., *Professions of Desire: Lesbian and Gay Studies in Literature* (New York: Modern Language Association of America, 1995); Harris, "What We Mean to Say,"; E. Moers, *Literary Women* (Garden City, N.Y.: Doubleday, 1976); Zimmerman, *Safe Sea of Women.*

30. J. Stanley, "Fear of Flying?" *Sinister Wisdom,* no. 2 (1976): 58. In that same essay, Julia wrote: "Fiction, the untrue telling of one's perceptions and interpretations of experience, creates a mode within which men have been able to establish their interpretations of life as 'universal truth.' Obviously, only in fiction are 'universals' possible, only in the fiction of men do we find claims about the 'human condition,' which are really portrayals only of the male condition. . . . Since men conceived and created the 'world view' we need not be surprised if male critics are only too willing to promote their view as 'universal' " (57–58).

31. J. Arnold, "Feminist Presses and Feminist Politics," *Quest,* Summer 1976, 18–26.

32. K. Adams, "Built out of Books: Lesbian Energy, and Feminist Ideology in Alternative Publishing," *Journal of Homosexuality* 34, 3/4 (1998): 129. In 1973, Naiad (meaning "water sprite") Press was formed by Barbara and Donna along with Anyda Marchant and Muriel Crawford. Anyda and Muriel, Florida retirees and "inveterate novel-readers" who came of age during the Depression, had approached Barbara and Donna about running the press and provided capital of $2,000. Using the *Ladder's* mailing list of 3,800 subscribers and plowing revenues back into the press, Naiad published one or two books a year (the first book was *The Latecomer* by the pseudonymous Sarah Aldridge—Anyda Marchant). In early 1976, the press incorporated with Grier as stockholder, and, in the fall of 1980, the couple moved to Tallahassee. Within two years Barbara and Donna had quit their jobs and worked fulltime for the press. "I owe the South a tremendous debt of gratitude because if we had not moved here we would not have as quickly quit and put Naiad as a full-time interest," Grier notes. "The South literally drove us to be entrepreneurs because we were being driven crazy by the slow pace of life here!" In 1985, with the publication of *Lesbian Nuns,* Naiad became the major force in lesbian publishing (B. Grier, *The Possibilities Are Staggering* [Chicago: Womanpress, 1976]; T. McLane, "What's a Nay-ad?" *Spectrum,* Winter 1981, 27–28; "The Naiad Press," *Sinister Wisdom,* no. 2 [1976]: 116–119).

33. B. Grier, "What Is a Lesbian?" *Sinister Wisdom,* no. 3 (1977): 13. For a detailed history of the *Ladder,* see: M. Soares, "The Purloined *Ladder*: Its Place in Lesbian History," *Journal of Homosexuality* 34, 3/4 [1998]: 27–49.

34. Grier began doing book annotations—"squib reviews"—under the name Gene Damon, in the March issue. "Lesbiana Literature," written by "a young woman from Philadelphia who has some seventy odd titles in her personal collection," had been announced in the first issue of the *Ladder* (October 1956). Although Barbara Gittings ended up not writing these reviews, when Gittings became editor in 1966, she asked Grier to expand her entries into book reviews. Some of these were later assembled in *Lesbiana* (Baltimore: Diana Press, 1976). In 1957, Grier also began writing articles and short stories under various pen names (e.g., Vern Niven, Marilyn Barrow, Gladys Casey). The *Ladder* soon became "the center of my life" and, in some issues (February 1959, December 1963, March 1964, July 1964, February 1967), she wrote articles, book reviews, and letters under multiple names or initials like HB (for Helen Bennet, with whom Barbara lived for twenty years). In later issues (e.g., June 1967, August 1967, January 1968, April 1968) Grier wrote nearly the entire content, including letters to the editor "praising and then damning the same thing!" (e-mail to the author from Barbara Grier, 31 July and 1 August 2000). In 1968, Grier assumed editorship as she continued her correspondence with the hundreds of women writing to the magazine. For more biographical information, see: B. Grier, "The Garden Variety Lesbian," in J. Penelope and S. Wolfe, eds., *The Coming Out Stories* (Watertown, Mass.: Persephone Press, 1980), 235–240; J. Kepner, "Barbara Grier," in W. Dynes and B. Grier, eds., *Gay and Lesbian Literature* (Detroit: St. James Press, 1994), 167–169.

35. C. Nicholson and H. Desmoines, "A Domestic History," *Sinister Wisdom,* no. 16 (1981): 100. As examples of the networking that went on at the conference, Tee Corrine first met *SW* editors at this conference and soon produced a solarized cover photo for the third issue that would become a fundraising poster for the magazine as well as an icon of lesbian fine art. Similarly, Carol Seajay, inspired by the publishing energy and quality of vision, launched *Feminist Bookstore Newsletter,* which would soon become the *Publishers' Weekly* of the lesbian press. For a description of the paranoia regarding "agents," see Harris, *Lover,* lxx–lxxi.

36. S. O'Brien, *Willa Cather: The Emerging Voice* (New York: Oxford University Press, 1987); J. Stanley, "My Life as a Lesbian," in Penelope and Wolfe, *The Coming Out Stories,* 199. Jorgenson made international headlines with the early 1950s operation that transformed the former army private, George, into Christine (C. Jorgenson, *Christine Jorgenson: A Personal Autobiography* (New York: Bantam, 1968).

37. Merril, "Letter," in Penelope and Wolfe, *The Coming Out Stories,* 135–137.

38. Penelope and Wolfe, *The Coming Out Stories,* xvi.

39. J. Penelope, "The Transformation of Silence into Language and Action, Remarks at the 1977 Annual Modern Language Association Convention, Chicago," *Sinister Wisdom,* no. 6 (1978): 5.

40. J. Sears, *Lonely Hunters* (New York: HarperCollins/Westview, 1997), 85–90.

41. Penelope, "My Life as a Lesbian," 204.

42. There were a number of women's bookstores in the South during this period, including Lammas Women's Books and More in the District of Columbia, Charis Books of Atlanta, Common Woman Bookstore in Austin, Southern Sisters of Durham, the Bookstore in Houston, Labrys Books in Richmond, Her Store in Tallahassee, and the New Leaf in Raleigh.

43. Sources for biographies of women highlighted here and their music include: Meg Christian and Teresa Trull, *Pointblank Times,* April/May 1978; M. Giles, "Teresa Trull," *Feminary* 8, 1 (1978); V. Glasgow, "The Phenomenon Called Meg," *Pointblank Times,* June 1976; J. Nixon and G. Berson, "Women's Music," in G. Vida, ed., *Our Right to Love: A Lesbian Resource Book* (Englewood Cliffs, N.J.: Prentice-Hall, 1978), 252–255; "Teresa Trull," *Atalanta,* May 1977; B. Walters, "A Culture Takes Root," *San Francisco Examiner,* 21 June 1989.

44. Perhaps the earliest lesbian recording of the Rubyfruit era was "Angry Atthis," a 1972 45-rpm (first performed in 1969 and written a month before Stonewall) sung by the deep-voiced Maxine Feldman. This was soon followed by lesbian albums, *A Few Loving Women* and Alix Dobkin's and Kay Gardner's *Lavender Jane Loves Women* (the first women-only engineered and produced album). Then, on the heels of the first National Women's Music Festival in Champaign, came the release of Meg Christian's groundbreaking *I Know You Know.*

45. "We Want the Music," *ALFA Newsletter,* September 1976, 7; "Exegesis of Lucina's Music," Box 23, Orchid Productions/Lucina's Music, ALFA Papers.

46. In fact, it was Williamson, a Native American singer-songwriter from the Black Hills of South Dakota, who had suggested the idea of forming this all-women's music company (J. Grahn, *Another Mother Tongue* [Boston, Mass.: Beacon Press, 1984], 191).

47. E-mail to the author from Cecilia Mitchell, 9 August 2000.

48. Ibid.

49. Glasgow, "The Phenomenon Called Meg," 9.

50. Editorial, *Pointblank Times,* April/May, 1978. *PBT* contended that "the issue was not that of separatism, but of Olivia forcing its politics on a small, unprepared community." The controversy resulted in the paper suspending publication for six months.

51. K. Williams, "Louisville's Lesbian Feminist Union" (master's thesis, University of Louisville, 1995), 38.

52. In addition to individual distributors, a distributing collective, Ladyslipper—named for a native wild orchid—was formed in 1976 at Durham, quickly producing its first catalogue of over two hundred records and tapes of women's music.

53. Amber Moon Papers.

54. "Goals and Purposes," ibid.

55. J. Nelson, "Women in Limelight in Amber Moon Productions," *Lexington Leader*, 18 February 1982; G. Swem, "Dedicated to a Cause—Women," *Louisville Courier-Journal*, 18 January 1981.

56. E-mail to the author from Linda West, 2 September 1999. Also, see interview with Linda West, October 1999, Sears Papers.

57. "Breaking Away," *Biannual Report*, Winter 1981), Amber Moon Papers. In contrast, Louisville's feminist cultural events were overtly lesbian and centered themselves at the women's bar, Mother's Brew. Here various local women's groups met while local musicians, notably the River City Womin, joined with national musicians and writers who were regularly booked. "The Bar was a place for spiritual women, political women, and bar dykes," observed one lesbian activist. "It was, in the beginning, like a greenhouse for our culture" (Williams, "Louisville's Lesbian Feminist Union," 25).

58. In addition to materials cited in this section, others that are relevant to literature of this era are: C. Clarke, "Lesbianism: An Act of Resistance," in C. Moraga and G. Anzaldua, eds., *This Bridge Called My Back* (Latham, N.Y.: Kitchen Table–Women of Color Press, 1981), 128–137; J. Gibbs and S. Bennett, eds., *Top Ranking: A Collection of Articles on Racism and Classism in the Lesbian Community* (Brooklyn, N.Y.: February 3rd Press, 1980); B. Smith, "Toward a Black Feminist Criticism," *Conditions: Two*, October 1977; B. Smith and L. Bethel, eds., "The Black Women's Issue," *Conditions: Five*, 1979.

59. See, for example, Parker's poem, "Where Will You Be?" in B. Smith , ed., *Home Girls: A Black Feminist Anthology* (Latham, N.Y.: Kitchen Table–Women of Color Press, 1978), 209–213.

60. This, of course, pales in comparison to the historic racism found in the popular music industry. See, for example, A. Dobkin, "Sexism and Racism in Rock and Pop Music," *Hot Wire: The Journal of Women's Music and Culture*, 2, 1 (1985): 24–27, 62. It is also important to note that many women artists and their record companies were quite sensitive to this absence of women of color. When Meg Christian first visited Houston in 1976, for example, she stressed "how white middle class women have used class and race privileges to oppress other women, and how that's kept our movement divided" (V. Glasgow, "The Phenomenon Called Meg," *Pointblank Times*, June 1976, 9).

61. L. Tillery, "Freedom Time," *Linda Tillery*, Oakland: Olivia Records, 1977, LP; M. Watkins, *Something Moving*, Oakland: Olivia Records, 1977, LP.

62. C. Quin, "Women's Group Uses Music to Tell of Black Experience," *Lexington Leader*, 13 November 1978; "Sweet Honey in the Rock: An Interview," *Feminary* 10, 1 (1979): 18–25.

63. Vicki Gabriner later emphasized how "painful it was to admit that even though many of us had anti-racist politics, it was incredibly difficult to create and/or maintain significant ties to the black community. We did some coalition work of concerns to black women, like the release of Joann Little from prison, but this was the exception rather than the rule" (e-mail to the author from Vicki Gabriner, 3 and 21 December 2000, Sears Papers). The weak connection between ALFA and the concerns within Atlanta's black community was also voiced by Barbara Smith in an essay that later appeared in *Sinister Wisdom* (Responses, Letter to Adrienne from Barbara, *Sinister Wisdom*, no. 20 [1982]: 100–104) in response to an earlier essay by Adrienne Rich ("Notes for a Magazine: What Does Separatism Mean?" *Sinister Wisdom*, no. 18 [1981]: 83–91), who, in part, was responding to a book review of Sara Evans's *A Review of Personal Politics* written by Gabriner that had appeared in *Feminary* ("Review as Process: Dealing with the Contradictions," *Feminary* 11, 1/2: 113–122).

64. "Sweet Honey," 21.

65. Ibid., 22. The anger felt among black lesbians was well articulated by pioneering activist/writer Anita Cornwell, who had asked her lesbian readers of the *Ladder:* "So why should one be concerned about which label is attached to one's oppression? Does it make any difference? Then a tiny door of the vast room opened just a crack, and a few of the outrages I have faced on a daily basis because of my color floated through my mind. I had to admit, yes, there is a difference, it matters like hell. Because as someone has said, 'When things go wrong, all blacks are black and all whites are whitey'" (A. Cornwell, "From a Soul Sister's Notebook," *Ladder*, June/July 1972).

66. E. Knowlton, "Racism Workshop," *Atalanta,* February 1977, 3. This struggle among many white lesbians/feminist activists to confront issues of race and racism is a distinctive theme. At the 1976 MLA conference, for example, Adrienne Rich—who grew up in Baltimore "in a borderline culture" during an era when " 'Dixie' and 'the Battle Hymn of the Republic' were both sung as innocent popular music" (A. Rich, Introduction to M. Segrest, *My Mama's Dead Squirrel* (Ithaca, N.Y.: Firebrand, 1984, 13)—spoke on a panel addressing racism and homophobia in the teaching of literature: "It was the lesbian in me, more than the civil libertarian or even the feminist, that pursued the memory of the first Black woman I loved before I was taught whiteness, before we were forced to betray each other. And that relationship—mutual knowledge, fear, guilt, jealously, anger, longing—between Black and white women, I did not find, have not yet found, in literature" (A. Rich, "It Is the Lesbian In Us . . .," *Sinister Wisdom,* no. 3 [1977]: 7).

67. A. Lorde, "A Song for Many Movements," *Sinister Wisdom,* no. 6 (1978): 11.

68. Ibid., "Man Child: A Black Lesbian Feminist's Response," *Conditions: Four;* reprinted in A. Lorde, *Sister Outsider* (Trumansburg, N.Y.: Crossing Press), 72–74.

69. A. Lorde, "The Transformation of Silence into Language and Action. Remarks from the Lesbians and Literature Panel of the 1977 Annual Modern Language Association Convention, Chicago, May 1977," *Sinister Wisdom,* no. 6 (1978): 13.

70. For this earlier history, see chapter 11, note 11. Eventually local lesbian-feminists regrouped and put out the *Newsletter* in October 1981, hoping to rekindle an "interchange of opinion about local issues and events which affect our lives" ("Birth of a Lesbian Newsletter in Durham," *Front Page,* 12 January 1982).

71. *Feminary* 11, 1/2: 4.

72. *Feminary* 8, 3.

73. M. Segrest, *Memoir of a Race Traitor* (Boston, Mass.: South End Press, 1994), 41. *Feminary* was truly a collective and collected effort as women gathered together over spaghetti suppers to plan out each issue. Among the women who worked with Mab and Minnie Bruce during this time were: Susan Ballinger, Deborah Giddens, Eleanor Holland, Sherry Kinlaw, Helen Langa, Raymina Y. Mays, Cris South, and Aida Waikil (e-mail to the author from Mab Segrest, 9 August 2000). For greater detail regarding this facet of *Feminary,* see T. Powell, "Look What Happened Here: North Carolina's Feminary Collective," *North Carolina Literary Review* 9 (2000): 91–102.

74. *Feminary* 9 (2), 3. This commitment continued as the emerging collective of lesbian-feminists refused to do a "one shot about race and/or racial issues but to make more solid our own commitment to these issues by seeing that we become more and more responsible towards black women and black people" (*Feminary* Minutes, 22 October 1979, Segrest Papers, Box 3, Perkins Library Archives, Duke University). Originally, *Sinister Wisdom* had arranged for Barbara Smith and the Combahee River Collective to edit the third issue, but it failed to happen since the group decided it was not ready. Isolated articles, however, did appear in the early volumes (e.g., L. Brown, "Dark Horse: A View of Writing and Publishing by Dark Lesbians," *Sinister Wisdom,* no. 13 [1980]).

75. "Feminary: A Lesbian Feminist Journal for the South," *Sinister Wisdom,* no. 6 (1978): 104.

76. M. Pratt, *Rebellions: Essays, 1980–1991* (Ithaca, NY.: Firebrand, 1991), 12–13.

77. M. Segrest, "Southern Women Writing," *Feminary* 10, 1 (1979): 28.

78. Segrest, *My Mama's Dead Squirrel,* 149.

79. Ibid., 151, 153.

80. M. Pratt, "Books in the Closet, in the Attic, Boxes, Secrets," in M. Pratt, *Rebellion: Essays, 1980–1991* (Ithaca, N.Y.: Firebrand, 1991), 156.

81. Ibid., 157, 158.

82. Catherine and Harriet continued editing the journal with the assistance of Lincoln lesbians through issue 16 (1981), which was co-edited by C. Colette. Michelle Cliff and Adrienne Rich, who were listed as publishers for issue 16, assumed the editorship with the next issue.

83. Desmoines, "Notes for a Magazine I," 4.

84. J. Arnold, *Sister Gin* (New York: Feminist Press, 1989), 206, reprint; originally published Plainfield, Vt.: Daughters Press, 1975.

85. Ibid., 215.

86. Lorde, "Song for Many Movements," 14–15.

TWENTY-THREE — HURRICANE WARNINGS

Interviews

Bootie Abelson, 30 November 1998, Birmingham, Ala.

Pokey Anderson, 12 October 1994, 12 April 1999, Houston, Tex.

"Julie Berry," 1 May 1999, Norfolk, Va.

Steve Brown, 27 December 1999, Norfolk, Va.

Jim Early, 29 December 1999, Virginia Beach, Va.

Ray Hill, 12 October 1994, Houston, Tex.

Ron Joullian, 30 July and 23 August 1998, Birmingham, Ala.

Beth Marschak, 3 May 1999, Richmond, Va.

Jack Maurizzi, 9 August 2000, Cheasapeake, Va.

Roger Nelson, 4 August 1998, New Orleans, La.

Fred Osgood, 15 November 1998 and 6 January 2000, Norfolk, Va.

Alan Robinson, 4 August 1998, New Orleans, La.

Barbara "Bobbi" Weinstock, 3 May 1999, Richmond, Va.

The epigraph is from "Telephone Conversations Between David Dahlquist and Leonard Matlovich, 7 June 1977," audiotape, Matlovich-Dahlquist Conversations, Sears Papers.

1. M. Macdonald, "Anita Disregarded Boos to Gay Power in Norfolk," *Richmond News Leader,* 9 June 1977.
2. "The Seventies Tidewater Community," symposium, James T. Sears, moderator, Unitarian Church of Norfolk, 2 May 1999, audiotape, Sears Papers.
3. Ibid.
4. W. Kale, "Homosexual Group Walks Out on Singer," *Richmond Times-Dispatch,* 9 June 1977.
5. Macdonald, "Anita Disregarded Boos."
6. "Miami Area Rejects Homosexual-Bias Law," *Minneapolis Star,* 8 June 1977; D. Feiden, "Gays Take to the Street in Emotional Protest Here," *New York Post,* 8 June 1977.
7. I. Sharp, "S.F. Gays Praying Anita 'Sees the Light,'" *San Francisco Chronicle,* 8 June 1977.
8. L. Solomon, "Lessons from Losing," *Advocate,* 24 August 1997, 8. For Maupin's earlier North Carolina college days as an ace conservative columnist and ally of Jesse Helms, see J. Sears, *Lonely Hunters* (New York: HarperCollins/Westview, 1997), 150–151, 155–156.
9. Macdonald, "Anita Disregarded Boos."
10. J. Early, "'I Picketed Anita': Interviews with Two Men Who Were There," *Our Own Community Press,* June 1985, 19.
11. "Adam and Bruce," Editorial, *Richmond News Leader,* 9 June 1977, 14.
12. Fred Osgood, Jayr Ellis, Jim Early, Susan Strattner, Dennis Buckland, Donna Motley, and several others had gone to the second annual Southeastern Gay Conference the first weekend of April. The Tidewater contingent wanted to learn how to put on a conference. "We knew information and resources existed beyond here," Osgood recollects, "and we wanted to bring them here." Joining the more than six hundred participants in Chapel Hill, they heard Jean O'Leary, co–executive director of the National Gay Task Force, talk about the historical White House meeting with gays, Barbara Gittings discuss gay unity and separatism, and Bob Basker update folks on the Dade County referendum.
13. *Greater Tidewater Area Gay Conference Program Guide,* Norfolk, Virginia, Southern Studies Collection, IGLA.
14. "Conference a Success," *Our Own Community Press,* July 1977.
15. S. Fletcher, "After Prayer, Bryant Accepts Bar Bid," *Houston Post,* 1 June 1977.
16. B. Remington, "Twelve Fighting Years: Homosexuals in Houston, 1969–1981" (master's thesis, University of Houston, 1983), 41.

17. E-mail to the author from Phyllis Randolph Frye, 25 May 2000. "Thousands of Gays Come 'Out of Their Closets' to Protest," *Free Press,* 27 June 1977; "The Orange Juice Lady Comes to Town," *Gay Pride Week '80 Guide,* Houston, Tex.

18. Interview with Pokey Anderson by M. S., 4 October 1991, p. 32, Sears Papers.

19. R. Shilts, "White House Meeting Concrete Results Soon?" *Advocate,* 20 April 1977. Frank Kameny, who along with Jack Nichols and others had demonstrated outside of the White House a dozen years earlier, was one of those attending. "We had gotten as far as the front gate over the years. . . . And it had always been a fight to get anything meaningful from public officials" (interview with Frank Kemeny by Paul Cain, 2 July 1994, p. 30, Sears Papers).

20. "Lesberadas: Houston Lesbians Unite!" *Pointblank Times* 3, 3 (1977): 23.

21. "Dade Voters Kill 'Gay Rights' Law," *Birmingham Post-Herald,* 8 June 1977; "Anita Has Lopsided Win in Vote on Gays," *Birmingham News,* 8 June 1977; "Gay Front Big Loser," Editorial, Birmingham News, 9 June 1977; "Homosexual Rights," *Birmingham Post-Herald,* 13 June 1977.

22. "Bryant Gay Issues Lightning Rod," *Birmingham News,* 9 June 1977; "Anita Shuns Bids by Gays, Baptists," *Birmingham Post-Herald,* 17 June 1977; "Gay Job Rights? Vote Here: No," *Birmingham News,* 21 June 1977. Not surprisingly, the South was the only region in the country, according to a post-referendum Gallup poll, that did not favor equal rights in job opportunities for homosexuals ("56% Back Gay Rights in Hiring," *Miami Herald,* 17 July 1977). Interestingly, two out of three Americans also believed that homosexuality was more prevalent than a generation earlier—again with the South leading the way in this opinion ("Americans Are Convinced Homosexuality on the Rise," *Washington Post,* 18 July 1977).

23. P. Cather, "Our Sacred Places," in *She Really Was a Slick Woman . . . And Other Essays* (Birmingham, Ala.: Author, 1995), pp. 37–38, Sears Papers.

24. The FOP Lodge was frequently used for gay-related events. For example, the 1976 Miss Gay Alabama pageant was sponsored by the owners of the Gizmo, Chances R, and Coming Attractions that June, preceded by the Miss Gay Birmingham contest held three months earlier. Although Tina Louise had won the local pageant (tapping a talent number from "Dames at Sea" with some members of the vice squad, who were having their own party downstairs, wandering up to watch the show), she was first runner-up to Misty Lamour, who was crowned Miss Gay Alabama 1976 (S. Young, "Alabama Ad Libs," *Barb,* August 1976).

25. "Birmingham Gay History," symposium, James T. Sears, moderator, 14 May 1998, University of Alabama-Birmingham, audiotape, Sears Papers.

26. Alan Handleman, who had founded the Eagle in Auburn, worked with the Birmingham group through that October, when he announced his departure, noting: "Not many months ago, Lambda was just a dream. . . . In time, those who are skeptical will realize that Lambda is NOT a group of radical militants, that it is NOT just a social club, but rather it IS a legitimate means toward Gay people helping one another and themselves" (A. Handleman, "Farewell," *A Newsletter by Lambda,* October 1977).

27. "Beginning," *A Newsletter by Lambda,* September 1977. The newsletter's name would soon change to the PODIUM (Positive Organization Directed in Uniting Mankind), shift again briefly to *Shout,* then *Lambda Newsletter,* and finally, in 1981, become a full-fledged newspaper as the *Alabama Forum.* For other information regarding the formation of Lambda and the evolution of the *Alabama Forum,* see R. Joullian, "Lambda, Inc: Five Years Later," *Alabama Forum,* 3, 1 (1983): 1. Small nonbar groups were also emerging at this time, with a chapter of MCC joining a Dignity chapter that had organized the previous March.

28. E-mail to the author from Phyllis Randolph Frye, 27 May 2000.

29. L. Thomas, " 'Reformed' Gay Supports Bryant," *New Orleans States-Item,* 18 May 1977.

30. The Coalition, unlike the GLF, refrained from political hyperbole, focusing on "legal, social, and economic discriminations" and calling upon the city's Human Relations Committee to establish a task force on gay problems (Gay People's Coalition flyer, 25 July 1973, Sears Papers).

31. Editorial, *Causeway,* January 1974.

32. On the first anniversary of the fire, June 1974, Coalition president Esteve (the first president, Chris Gamble, had resigned following an overhaul of leadership and focus) wondered, "Where are they [Troy Perry, Morris Kight] now?" Meanwhile, GPC membership slumped after the VD clinic on Rampart Street died six months earlier "due to apathy" (E. Newhouse, "32 Perished in Upstairs Bar Fire Year Ago Today," *New Orleans Times-Picayune*, 24 June 1974); "lack of funds, lack of response, lack of help all combined to destroy efforts of those who did care enough to push forward" (B. Foster, "Then and Now," *Causeway*, August 1974).

33. "Hard Decisions," *Closet Door*, January 1977.

34. E. Martinez, "Where Are the Gay Activists in New Orleans?" *New Orleans Vieux Carré Star*, 7 April 1977.

35. Ibid. Not surprisingly, Martinez's essay was less than enthusiastically read by many New Orleans gays, including Phil Esteve, the former owner of the Up Stairs Lounge, who now operated the Post Office Lounge. "There are no gay activists in New Orleans because none are needed," he argued in typical New Orleans style. "We don't feel we're being discriminated against" ("Esteve Says There's No Need for Gay Activists," *Vieux Carré Star*, 14 April 1977).

36. C. Flake, "The Lavender Hill Mob Takes on Anita Bryant," *Figaro*, 29 June 1977.

37. *Gertrude's Notes*, June 1977.

38. Flake, "Lavender Hill Mob."

39. *Gertrude's Notes*, September 1977.

40. There was a Miss National Teenager pageant held in Atlanta, however, which was giving Bryant (in absentia) its America's Greatest American award. On a sultry mid-August day, about 150 hastily organized protesters picketed at the Memorial Arts Center. Bryant later appeared at the World Congress Center on 11 June 1978. As elsewhere, thousands of protesters rallied, marching from Central City Park to the Center. The surplus money from this event went to seed the new gay center ("Anita Bryant's Visit to Atlanta," *Atalanta* 6, 7 [1978]).

41. "Battle over Gay Rights," *Newsweek*, 6 June 1977, 17.

42. M. George and D. Massey, "Gay Pride vs. Citizens for Decent Atlanta," *Great Speckled Bird*, August 1976.

43. AGH, 12.

44. Ibid. Liz Troop, a poet and one of the few female First Tuesday founders, remembers longtime Atlanta gay radicals decrying this move as "selling out" (13).

45. In addition to *Impact* in New Orleans, there was the *Weekly News* bulletin, beginning with seventy-five mimeographed newsletters for the Dade County Coalition for Human Rights. In April 1978, it became *TWN* (*The Weekly News*), publishing several thousand copies under the leadership of Paul Guiles and Keith Cantine. In Houston, Gary Van Ooteghem began *Up Front*, preaching the values of accommodation; *Arkansas Gay Writes* was also publishing out of a Little Rock–based gay organization; and the Free Alliance for Individual Rights in Roanoke produced the *Virginia Gayzette*. There was also a growing number of "entertainment guides" such as the *Carolina Zipper*, whose name implied "speed and efficiency in communication," and *LXIX* in Houston, whose name most gay men could readily decipher. Further, local gay radio shows on alternative stations expanded from Houston's KPFT-FM to Atlanta's Gay Digest on WRFG.

46. *Our Own Community Press*, October 1977, 7.

47. "Gittings Adds Oil to Closet Door Hinges," *Our Own Community Press*, September 1977, 1.

48. The Richmond Lesbian-Feminists had emerged from a lesbian workshop that Beth put on at the Virginia Women's Political Caucus annual meeting at the Albert Hill Middle School in early 1975. A state group was initially formed with lesbians from Norfolk, Charlottesville, and Richmond. Meeting in each of the three cities, each group developed locally.

49. A solicitation ordinance, for example, had been adopted the year before, resulting in dozens of arrests of men cruising in the parks and around the downtown block across from the public library. Police also routinely wrote down license plate numbers at the bars like the Cha Cha Cha Palace and the Four-O-Nine Club.

50. Five people had met at Brother Cosmas Rubencamp's office to discuss the formation of a Dignity chapter in mid-December 1975, with the first meeting held the next month. To publicize the meeting, posters were put on trees, telephone poles, and bulletin boards. The university police took several of these posters to the Diocesan bishop, who had no knowledge of the extent of Rubencamp's involvement. Dignity was asked not to meet on diocesan property and later the diocese disavowed the group's endorsement of the gay rights rally protesting the visit of Anita Bryant to Richmond ("Gay Rally Loses Endorsement," *Richmond News Leader,* 26 August 1977).

51. *Gay Alliance of Students v. Matthews,* U.S. Court of Appeals, Fourth Circuit, 28 October, 1976, 544 Federal Reporter, 2d Series, 162–168.

52. Gay Rights Association Minutes, 1977–1979, Mss 3 G2546a 14, Virginia Historical Society, Richmond.

53. K. Williams, "Louisville's Lesbian Feminist Union" (master's thesis, University of Louisville, 1995), 47, 57.

54. Interview with Ken Plotnik by David Williams, 13 July 1991, KGLA.

55. LFU Newsletter, 1977. Quoted from Williams, "Louisville's Lesbian Feminist Union," 64.

56. Ibid.

57. E-mail to *Lambdanet,* 25 October 1999, Sears Papers.

58. *LGSO Newsletter,* August 1977, 1, KGLA.

59. Amber Moon Papers.

60. "The Gay South 1977: Free to Be You and Me," *Cruise* 2, 13 (1977): 16.

61. R. Shilts, "The New Gay Movement: Will It Work?" *Advocate,* 19 October 1977.

62. In Atlanta, for example, ALFA had volunteer women who participated in First Tuesday meetings, while, in Houston, Pokey Anderson went back and forth between the Lesberadas and the male-dominated Gay Political Caucus.

63. C. Bunch, "Herstorical Notes," *Texas Gay Task Force Information Guide,* 1977, Botts Collection, MCC-Resurrection, Houston.

64. V. Gabriner, "Sentence Stress," *Sinister Wisdom,* no. 6 (1978): 28.

65. Ibid.

66. V. Gabriner, "IWY: Some Thoughts," part 2, *Atalanta,* January 1978, 5. Gabriner and others (e.g., T. Clark, "Houston: A Turning Point," *off our backs,* March 1978) were particularly disturbed by the parliamentary procedural style of the conference, its "heavy emphasis on electoral politics and the legislative process as the road to social change," and the passage of the resolutions, with no enforcement power, to male politicians in Washington.

67. Ibid., 6.

68. Support had been brokered from the National Organization for Women, which agreed to bundle it into the "pro plan" of progressive resolutions.

69. Women's Caucus of NGFT, "National Women's Conference Supports Sexual Preference," *It's Time* 5, 1 (1978): 1.

70. Anderson interview, 1991, 19.

71. Ibid., 14.

72. The GPC endorsement of an owlish-looking Kathy Whitmire for city comptroller was the "turning point for the caucus" (B. Caneti, "Gay Political Caucus," *Houston Post,* 4 May 1980), proving with her decisive victory that "a candidate publicly endorsed [and not at the last minute] by the GPC would win a major city office" and the power of the get-out-the-vote machinery of the caucus (Remington, "Twelve Fighting Years," 42).

    By this time, Don Hrachovy, who was now GPC president, had assembled a mailing list of more than three thousand persons, raised over twenty thousand dollars, and registered six thousand new voters. Ray Hill ran into Terry Dolan again. Like Ray, Terry had grown up in Houston. Ray remembered: "I had met Terry and his brother before I went to prison. Terry had to be a teenager or in his early twenties. We met at a restaurant on McCarty Drive near the ship channel turning basin. We had both been cruising the area trying to pick up sailors." Dolan soon volunteered for the Mailing List Committee, chaired by Don Hrachovy. "He disliked the argumentative nature of the meetings but he and Don Hrachovy hit it right off as computer people. They would go to the House of Pies and argue politics after work sessions."

Later, Hill discloses, "Terry took Don's program of computerizing political mailing lists and tried to sell it to the Democratic Party, which did not take him seriously." Then Dolan met Richard Viguerie on a flight to Dallas. Viguerie, who was running the National Conservative Caucus, recognized the value of the technology that Terry had for sale and incorporated this into the Moral Majority organization" (e-mail to the author from Ray Hill, 29 December 1999 and 6 February 2000, Sears Papers).

In addition to the city election and the women's conference, for example, Houston gays welcomed the opening of Charles Gillis's Wilde 'n' Stein Bookstore, which was soon followed by a gay community center in Montrose; the local MCC chapter doubled in membership. Similarly, activism was booming throughout the state. The Texas Gay Taskforce, which Gillis and his partner, Ken Cyr, had organized in 1975, reported a "membership boom" as a result of the Dade County controversy and its fourth statewide conference in Austin with Bob Kunst speaking about the "lessons" of Dade County. There was also an increase in such activity as the distribution of the first legislative information packet to elected state officials and the formation of the Lone Star Lesbians, a telephone tree hotline (K. Deitsch, "TGTF Reviews Its Work in 1977," 1978, Coordinating Council of the TGTF, Integrity/Houston Corr.).

73. D. Buckland, "We Are Everywhere," Letter to the Editor, *Virginia-Pilot,* 8 June 1978.
74. A. Murray and T. Wells, "1,800 Demonstrate Against Singer Here," *Atlanta Journal-Constitution,* 12 June 1978; E. Nemoy, "3,000 Hear Songs, Little Else from Anita Bryant," *Wilmington [N.C.] Morning Star,* 13 June 1978.
75. "Dade County—One Year Later," Workshop Notes, 28 May 1978, Basker Papers, IGLA.
76. R. Barrs, "'Sissy' Urges Gays to Demand Rights," *Houston Post,* 26 June 1978. From the town meeting came the Montrose counseling center and clinic, a gay and lesbian switchboard, a Montrose security patrol, and the gay and lesbian Hispanic group, UNIDOS ("Houston Town Meeting 1: Beyond Oppression/Toward Community," participant's workbook, 25 June 1978, Sears Papers; D. Lee, "Gay Political Strategy Charted as 3,500 Gather in AstroArena," *Houston Chronicle,* 26 June 1978).

TWENTY-FOUR — EYES ON THE PRIZE

Interviews

Samantha Hunter, 18 June and 13 December 1999, 10 February 2000, Columbia, S.C.
Peter Lee, 17 September, 1 October 1996, Columbia, S.C.; 15 June 2000, Boston, Mass.
"Roger Simmons," 4 September 1996 and 16 June 2000, Columbia, S.C.
The epigraph is from "Text of Mel Boozer's Convention Speech," *Washington Blade,* 21 August 1980, 6.

1. Other southern metropolitan areas had long had at least one gay black bar, such as the Golden Nugget in Houston, opened by Paul Stewart around 1969. In smaller southern cities such as Memphis, black gay bars generally did not emerge until the mid- to late seventies. In late 1975, the New Club Mirage, the first all-gay bar catering to African Americans, opened in Memphis, replacing the "mixed" bar, the Mirage Underground (D. Buring, *Lesbian and Gay Memphis* [New York: Garland, 1997], 98). The following year, Peaches (with money lent from the owner of George's, who had tired of blacks overcrowding his bar) opened Club Peaches, which also attracted a sizeable white clientele (V. Astor, "Peaches' Perspective," *Triangle Journal News,* February 1991, 14). Black clubs in the city soon expanded to the Apartment Club across from George's, opened by a former employee of Family Affair Club, a "mixed" bar on Vance Avenue (A. Cook, "Marshall Street Tops List of Gay Places to be in '83," *GazE,* January 1983; V. Astor, "Black Gays in Memphis," *GazE,* March 1989).
2. J. Nichols, "Sissies," manuscript, Sears Papers, 105. Used with permission of the author.
3. Notwithstanding the would-be GLF group ill-formed by a handful of USC students in 1970, Columbia's first organizations, the Alliance and the Metropolitan Community Church, emerged in late 1973 and early 1974. The lesbian-founded Alliance, which

lasted less than a year, met at different members' homes; MCC members assembled across from the state prison.

4. On 29 April 1965, nineteen-year-old Peter Lee, along with five hundred supporters of civil rights, marched on the state capitol. As one of the few whites, Lee was targeted by other white men in their twenties and beaten on the street as photographers clicked away. The next day, an Associated Press wire photo appeared chronicling the attack and identifying Lee ("White Demonstrator Beaten in NAACP Columbia March," *Greenville News,* 30 April 1965; "Whites Attack White Marcher," *State,* 30 April 1965).

5. P. Lee, "Issues of Leadership: Stress and Supports in the Lambda Alliance as Seen by Peter Lee, Chairman." Paper submitted for PUBH 606, May 1979, Lee Papers. The first gay student organization would not be formed until 1982 and would only be recognized later by the university after a court order.

6. Ibid.

7. Letters to Lambda Alliance, Lee Papers.

8. Lambda lasted a little more than two years. Following a "vacuum of leadership," which resulted when a "burned-out" Peter and his outspoken opponent both withdrew from the 1980 election, the group abandoned its committee structure ("Lambda Alliance Is Alive and Well," *Lambda Alliance Newsletter,* 23 February 1980, 2, Lee Papers). The monthly newsletter, edited by Jim Blanton, became the "primary source for dissemination of information" (*Lambda Alliance Newsletter,* 23 February 1980, 2).

9. "The Gay Side of Tuskegee: Separate but Equal in Black Alabama," part 2, *Alabama Forum,* September 1982, 7. For a more general discussion regarding race and homosexuality in American society, see S. Somerville, *Queering the Color Line* (Durham, N.C.: Duke University Press, 2000).

10. E. White, *States of Desire* (New York: Dutton, 1980), 242-245.

11. Ibid., 244-245.

12. Ibid., 245.

13. This sense of isolation and invisibility was also found in Buring's study of lesbian-gay Memphis, where there also were no exclusively black lesbian groups or organizations. "Some black lesbians in Memphis patronized predominantly white gay bars and lesbian bars, while others frequented black mixed or gay bars. . . . Black membership in Memphis's lesbian service-oriented organizations [e.g., Gays on Popular Street, Aphrodite] was extremely limited," as was involvement in lesbian softball or the emerging black gay male group (Buring, *Lesbian and Gay Memphis,* 191, 199-200). As in Atlanta and Richmond, the black lesbian experience was mostly underground, generally confined to house party circuits.

14. "Lisa King: Cruise Interviews the Outspoken Former Miss Atlanta," *Cruise,* February 1979, 6-8.

15. Ibid.

16. Ibid. In part as a response to such discrimination, some southern communities established separate pageants, such as Miss Black Memphis, where Miss Peaches—who had first performed at the Flamingo Room (straight black bar) in the sixties—held the title for eleven consecutive years (Astor, "Peaches' Perspective").

17. "Fellow Gay People: Why Are We Picketing the Lost and Found?" flyer, Sears Papers; "Have We Come This Far Only to Leave Behind Some of Us?" flyer, Sears Papers.

18. Segregation and discrimination in the gay bars, though, persisted throughout the decade in the nation's capital. For example, two years later, D.C. blacks entering the Hide-A-Way, located across the street from Hoover's new FBI building, were heavily ID'd (R. Mott, "Homosexual Lives as Varied as Those of Any Other Group," *Washington Post,* 24 April 1973; D. Aiken, "Dethroning the King," *Motive* 32, 2 [1972]: 46-48).

19. B. Whiting, "Haven in Houston," *Advocate,* 23 March 1977, 5.

20. "You Are What You Wear," *Pointblank Times,* February 1976, 1.

21. One owner defended himself by noting he could tell if a white man was gay; he couldn't for a black. Although the GPC passed a resolution against such practices, business continued as usual (B. Cigainero, "Plantation Revisited," *Pointblank Times,* March 1976). Eighteen months later, however, concerns had escalated to harassment against those

few lesbians and people of color who had successfully entered the club ("GPC v. the Old Plantation," *Pointblank Times,* August 1977). One Chicano filed an affidavit accusing management of beating him in the club's office. This time, GPC threatened a boycott unless there was a change in policies and an apology. Nothing happened and the feminists abandoned their effort to mobilize the white-led GPC. At the next month's meeting, the OP manager simply read a statement reaffirming its policy of nondiscrimination. A member of the Lesberadas, Barbara Cigainero, who had raised these problems when the Plantation first opened, listened as the GPC Board accepted the statement and refused to hear complaints: "Stay away from the GPC. They care more about cutting themselves off from the donations of the largest gay disco in town than they care about sexist and racist policies in our own backyard" (B. Cigainero, "GPC Refuses Boycott of OP," *Pointblank Times,* November 1977).

22. The one exception to this was a few years earlier when two bars, the Tunnel and One, operated in Underground Columbia, a boutique area with shops and nightclubs below the Arcade on Main Street. Roger recalls: "At night we could go to the dance club on one side of the hall which served food and was enormous or across the hall to a lounge place which had a sunken bar area with plush red leathery and padded stools. At the dance club, known as the Tunnel, there were mixed race groups." Two lesbians, Cary and Donna, worked the lounge bar, One. Roger continues, "My black friends and I would drink grenadine and Champelle and dish."

23. Such discrimination was widely practiced. A boycott was initiated by ALFA following a racial incident at the Bayou Landing on Atlanta's Peachtree Street, on the grounds that "racist practices in Atlanta gay bars must end," and citing examples of other bars such as the Cove and My House. Complaints were also filed with the Community Relations Commission—although the bar lost its license before these were resolved ("Black, Beautiful, Gay, and Proud," *Barb* 2, 2 [1975]; "Racism at the Bayou Landing," *ALFA Newsletter,* February/March 1975; B. Hippler, "Gay Life in Atlanta," *Great Speckled Bird,* 12 June 1975; B. Smith, "Editor's Notebook," *Barb,* July 1975). Charges of discrimination continued to the end of the decade at both men's and women's bars, from ID-carding practices at Backstreet and Numbers to late-night cover charges at the Sports Page and the diversion of black lesbians into the newly opened Club Sheba, formerly the Tower (*Atalanta,* November 1979, 5; "Gaybriel Interviews Greg Worthy," *Gaybriel,* 10 August 1979; "The Phyllis Colmar Incident Reviewed," *Gaybriel,* October 1979).

In Memphis, a city known for Beale Street jazz and a pre–gay liberation social life, brimming with self-hatred and alcoholic abandon, discrimination continued into the eighties. Popular bars like 10 N. Cleveland, George's Crisco Disco, and the Barracks, with its notorious backroom (both owned by George Wilson and his partner, Don Rossignol), on Marshall Street, and J-Wags, a small dance bar named for its owner Jimmy Wagner that was open twenty-four hours on Madison, routinely used the "quota system," where the black presence was controlled not only through the system of multiple IDs, including passports, but by changing music during the evening from disco to country and western ("Reader Alleges Discrimination," *GazE,* January 1981; J. Finney II, "Time We Checked Ourselves on Issue of Racism," *GazE,* February 1981; M. Bush and R. Russell, "Black Group Protests Memphis Bar's I.D. Policy," *GazE,* August 1981; e-mail to the author from Vincent Astor, 25 November 2000, Sears Papers).

Bigotry and prejudicial practices were reported in other communities as well. In Birmingham, one bar manager admitted discrimination against those blacks who arrived unescorted by whites: "They don't drink and they just take up space" (P. Riley, "A Search for Birmingham's Gay Community," *Birmingham Post-Herald Kudzu,* 8 June 1979, 7). From Raleigh's Capital Corral to Fayetteville's Other Side, discrimination within gay bars was the dirty little secret in many a community ("Racial Discrimination in N.C. Gay Bars," *Front Page* 2, 4 [1981]; W. Sage, "Inside the Colossal Closet," *Human Behavior,* August 1975). Another example was those discriminatory practices levied against individuals wearing drag or leather. In response to a letter of protest about the no-drag policy (except on Halloween) at Raleigh's Capital Corral, the management wrote: "It is discrimination. Yes dear, it is. We also discriminate against trouble making straights . . . drunks who wander in off the street . . . people dressed in full leather and chains. . . . Our decision to maintain rules and policies in running our [private] club that could be considered at odds with our idealism was a decision based solely on practicality" (letter and response, *Free Press,* 10 June 1977, 12. Also see: Letters, *Free Press,* 7 February 1977).

24. For information on the Oar House, see D. Gary, "Bar Assault Charge Dismissed," *Our Own Community Press,* October 1980. For a counter-response to these accusations, see "Article Biased," Letter to the Editor, *Our Own Community Press,* November 1980.

25. "Discrimination?" Letter to the Editor, *Our Own Community Press,* January 1980, 2. Writing in the next issue of the gay paper, another regular confirmed this experience. ("More Discrimination?" Letter to the Editor, *Our Own Community Press,* February 1980, 2). During this same time period, there were also charges of discrimination against lesbians in the Nutcracker Disco that operated in Norfolk (M. Gerwig and J. Seyller, Letter to the Editor, *Our Own Community Press,* March 1979).

26. "The Bare Facts," *Our Own Community Press,* August 1980, 8.

27. Ibid.

28. "Gaybriel Interviews Greg Worthy." Other southern gay groups organized to confront racism around this time included the Gay Black Caucus, the Houston Committee, and Tejano Unidos in Houston.

29. Sources relied on for Boozer's biography are: L. van Dyke, "Is DC Becoming the Gay Capital of America?" *Washingtonian,* September 1980; "An Interview with Mel Boozer," *Our Own Community Press,* September 1980; "Boozer Out at NGTT—Washington," *GazE,* April 1983; "Gay Activist Mel Boozer Dies at 41," *Our Own Community Press,* April 1987.

30. House rent parties and buffet flats—generally with drinking, gambling, sex, dancing, reefer smoking, card playing—have long been common in black urban localities. They were a subject of the blues sung by Bessie Smith, like "Soft Pedal Blues" or "Gimme a Pigfoot," as well as Fats Waller's "The Joint Is Jumping." The niece of Smith described accompanying her aunt to a buffet flat in Detroit where "faggots dressed like women. . . . And bull dykers and—open house—everything goes on in that house. . . . Buffet means everything" (G. Joseph, "Styling, Profiling, and Pretending," in G. Joseph and J. Lewis, eds., *Common Differences* [Garden City, N.Y.: Anchor, 1981], 184–185). For additional details about house parties among African Americans, see: B. Beemyn, "A Queer Capital," in B. Beemyn, ed., *Creating a Place for Ourselves* (New York: Routledge, 1997), 189–190; E. Garber, "'Taint Nobody's Business': Homosexuality in Harlem in the 1920s," *Advocate,* 13 April 1982, 39–43; E. Kennedy and M. Davis, *Boots of Leather, Slippers of Gold* (New York: Routledge, Chapman and Hall, 1993), 125–131.

31. Mel Boozer received forty-nine votes before balloting was suspended and Senator Walter Mondale was elected by acclamation.

32. Ibid., 8–9.

TWENTY-FIVE — A GATHERING OF TRIBES

Interviews

Jim Baxter, 11 October 1997, Raleigh, N.C., and e-mail to the author, 7 August 2000.

Margo George, 6 August 2000, Oakland, Calif., and e-mail to the author, 3 and 5 August 2000.

Beth Marschak, 3 May 1999, Richmond, Va.

Julia Penelope, 23 June 1996, Lubbock, Tex., and e-mail to the author, 13 August 2000.

Rita Wanstrom, 18 July 2000, Austin, Tex.

Bobbi Weinstock, 3 May 1999, Richmond, Va.

The epigraph is from D. Altman, "The Gay Movement Ten Years Later," *Nation,* 13 November 1982, 495.

1. J. Lincoln, *Gayzette,* December 1979, 3.

2. "The Quotable Robin Tyler," *Our Own Community Press,* November 1979, 4.

3. The first 1979 March Planning Meeting had been held in Philadelphia the previous February with Ray Hill chosen as chair of the executive committee. Among the

three hundred attending, "most were from coastal urban areas . . . [a] significant minority of delegates, including many from the Southeast, opposed the march THIS year, asking for more time to organize effective, truly NATIONAL participation" ("National March on Washington for Lesbian and Gay Rights, Southeastern Update," Sears Papers). Margo George, who represented a socialist-feminist group, recalls "a lot of discussion about whether the energy and money that it would take to organize such an event would be better expended at the local level, doing local projects." Another Atlantan, Gil Robison, remembers joining with other delegates "to make sure that we in the interior were not overlooked. We called ourselves the 'Hinterperson's Caucus.'"

There was also opposition among some attending because of "timing" and concerns that the March leadership represented more radical views than those of mainstream gay leaders like Gary Van Ooteghem, who pushed for a "Human Rights March." GAA-Washington, for example, endorsed the march only with reservations and the NGTF and MCC initially sent letters to groups noting they were not endorsing the March because of its lack of "experienced leadership in the gay community." Frank Kameny opposed it because "I didn't think it was going to be a success. . . . And it was going to give us a black eye which it would be years and years in recovering." Hill remembers Kameny's address to the Philadelphia group: "'You needn't bother coming to Washington,' Frank said. 'No one there will join you in the streets. We have marches and demonstrations every day.'" Similarly, Steve Endean, representing the Gay Rights National Lobby, spoke against the March, claiming "the timing would hamper some legislative projects." And David Goodstein, in a June 1979 *Advocate* editorial, opined: "I am not opposed to all demonstrations. . . . I am opposed to violence. I am opposed to exposing gay people to danger because the organizers of a demonstration don't know what they're doing, or worse, hope to create a violent confrontation."

When the March appeared inevitable, NGTF endorsed it on 18 August. This, however, was following the June election of new cochairs—Lucia Valeska replaced Jean O'Leary. Steve Ault, who had been one of the leading advocates for the March, took advantage of a joint speaking engagement to offer Valeska a ride. As it turned out, they shared a leftist ideology and "we hit it off immediately." Several other board members were pro-March, including Larry Bagneris, Bobbi Weinstock, and Pokey Anderson. They participated regionally in early March planning activities, "discussing issues and raising money," according to Weinstock. "We worked to get the black community involved but that was always more limited than we wanted." Another regional organizer, Margo George, also remembers "considerable discussion about how to increase minority participation." The March was structured to insure at least 50 percent participation of women and 20 percent of third-world representatives—at all levels. And Larry Bagneris, in his role as chair of the credentials committee for the second March Planning Meeting in Houston, challenged several delegations to Houston who made no apparent attempt at minority inclusion, thus sending the message that inclusion would be more than rhetoric.

In the case of Troy Perry—charmed over a turkey dinner by Robin Tyler—he "put out feelers that he would change his position and support the March effort," according to Hill, "if he would include Robin in the program and let him speak." Their well-publicized train ride across the country for the March was one by-product of that arrangement ("NGTF Endorse March," *Our Own Community Press,* September 1979; personal communication to the author from John O'Brien, 25 July 2000; e-mail to the author from Robin Tyler, 24 July 2000, from Margo George, 3 August 2000, from Bobbi Weinstock, 14 August 2000, from Ray Hill, 29 and 31 August 2000 and 11 September 2000, from Steve Ault, 29 and 30 August 2000, from Gil Robison, 31 August 2000; interview with Frank Kameny by Paul Cain, 2 July 1994; minutes of the National Coordinating Committee Meeting, Philadelphia. All located in Sears Papers.).

4. Personal communication to the author from Pokey Anderson, 25 July 2000.
5. The prime moving force for the March, for example, had come from the Coalition for Lesbian and Gay Rights out of New York City and from progressive-left individuals such as Steve Ault and Howard Wallace.

6. Jesse Monteagudo, a member of the Florida delegation led by Jack Campbell, confirms: "There seemed to be more tricking and cruising (at least among the men) than politicking" (e-mail to the author from Jesse Monteagudo, 1 August 2000).
7. Differences actually had arisen well before. Representatives from Florida, North Carolina, Mississippi, Virginia, Georgia, and Tennessee met in Atlanta five months earlier with disagreements between women and men continuing within the Atlanta-based conference steering committee. Tom Carr, who founded and coordinated the first two conferences in Chapel Hill sponsored by the Carolina Gay Association, remembers: "While we certainly had a lot of sexual divisions within the group, by the time of the third year when it came to Atlanta that was when it really broke loose" (AGH, 19). Gender rifts were present, of course, from the very first Southeastern conference held in 1976, when a workshop on lesbian separatism—open to everyone—evolved into a confrontation characterized as "intense" (Southeastern Gay Conference Booklet, February 1977, *Front Page* Papers, Perkins Library, Duke University).
8. "Southeastern Gay Conference Update," *Atalanta,* January 1978, 1. See also: "A History of SE Conferences," *Front Page,* 9 April 1985; Southeastern Conference of Lesbians and Gay Men, "Conference Report," 1978, Sears Papers.
9. "Southeastern Gay Conference Update," 1.
10. At the time, this was discussed at an ALFA meeting. The recorder wrote: "Dignity was going to do everything possible to destroy the conference because the conference was going to support a women's workshop" (ALFA Papers). Among the sixty workshops scheduled, several were reserved for women or men only: "Becoming Woman-Identified," "Man on Man," "Lesbian/Feminist Publishing."
11. V. Gabriner, "I/We Won!" *Atalanta,* March 1978, 11–12.
12. "Third Annual Southeastern Conference of Lesbians and Gay Men in Atlanta," *Our Own Community Press,* May 1978, 6. Before the conference, Vicki had explained how in "the past month we have dealt intensively" with the dilemma of hosting the conference in Georgia and honoring the national boycott. The resolution was found in "contributing financial support for ERA ratification; providing alternate arrangements for housing and food to limit cash flow into the city; using the conference to educate people about the ERA, and proposing that future conferences be held in ratified Southern states" (V. Gabriner, "Southeastern Conference of Lesbians and Gay Men," *Atalanta,* May 1978).
13. E-mail to the author from Darlene Gamer, 10 August 2000. Other members of the NCBLG Board, formed the year before, who assisted in the conference were Delores Berry, John Gee, Billy Jones, and Renee McCoy.
14. In addition to the workshops and caucuses at Harambee House, Mayor Marion Barry, who had proclaimed Gay Rights Awareness Week, welcomed the group to the city and poet Audre Lorde gave the keynote speech. Among the several hundred attending, "it was mostly African American," recollects Monteagudo, "with a few Latinos from California and Massachusetts and Larry Bagneris from New Orleans" (e-mail to the author from Jesse Monteagudo, 7 August 2000). Although there was representation from southern gays of color (one workshop offered was "Black Gay Men of the South"), most were from the East and West Coasts. Participants also included gay Native and Asian Americans, a group from Mexico, and a sprinkling of whites.
15. J. Monteagudo, "We Are (Almost) Everywhere: Gay Latins in South Florida," *TWN,* 30 January 1979.
16. A. Sieber and B. DiStefano, "March Goes On," *Out Smart,* April 2000, 48.
17. B. Remington, "Twelve Fighting Years: Homosexuals in Houston, 1969–1981" (master's thesis, University of Houston, 1983), 44.
18. J. Collins, "Gay Politics," *Impact,* September 1980. See also R. O'Connor, "An Interview with Alan Robinson," *Impact,* September 1979.
19. "Homosexual 'Rights' Again," Editorial, *Richmond News Leader,* 5 May 1978; T. Morris, "Panel Is Asked Not to Support Gay Rights Bid," *Richmond Times-Dispatch,* 5 April 1978; "The 'Rights' Code," Editorial, *Richmond Times-Dispatch,* 14 May 1978; "The 'Rights' Proposal: Unsound, Unworkable," Editorial, *Richmond Times-Dispatch,* 5 January 1979; B. Wasson, "City Panel May Propose Rights for Homosexuals," *Richmond*

News Leader, 16 February 1978; WWBT-TV interview, Channel 12, 2 July 1978, Virginia Coalition for Lesbian and Gay Rights, Virginia Historical Society, Richmond.

20. Mann, who had first labeled gays "oddwads" when GPC had approached Houston's City Council after its founding in 1975, ran campaign ads in the *Houston Post* and *Chronicle,* declaring: "Mann's the Man, the Oddwads Don't Want" (*Houston Chronicle,* 4 November 1979; *Houston Post,* 5 November 1979). During this election, some gay activists campaigned wearing "I'm an Oddwad" T-shirts.

21. Wiese, "Homosexual Voices Gaining Volume in America," *Houston Post,* 21 October 1979; B. Canetti, "Gay Leaders Urge Supporters to Use Voting to Gain Power," *Houston Post,* 2 July 1979. "The political clout of homosexuals in the United States," observed the *Houston Post* chief Washington Bureau correspondent, "is undeniably expanding and gays believe it will increase significantly with the 1980 election" (Wiese, "Homosexual Voices"). Two years later it had. On the brink of carrying Comptroller Kathy Whitmire into the mayor's office, the *New York Times* would term the caucus "a major political force" and *Newsweek* would describe it as "one of the city's most powerful political organizations ("Gay Power in Macho Houston," *Newsweek,* 10 August 1981; A. Stevens, "Houston Accepts New Political Force," *New York Times,* 1 November 1981).

22. J. LaVelle, "NCHRF: Ten Years Later," *Front Page,* Pride Supplement, 1989; K. Hartman, *Congregations in Conflict* (New Brunswick, N.J.: Rutgers University Press, 1996), 25–29; interview with Barbara Weinstock by Bob Swisher, 3 January 1988, Southern Studies Collection, IGLA. As John Boddie, an attorney and another Fund founder, states: "Before NCHRF men who were arrested for Crimes Against Nature (CAN) in Raleigh routinely pled guilty. Afterward, a few brave men pled not guilty which, if you stick with it, means the charges will eventually be dropped" (e-mail to the author from John Boddie, 13 August 2000). However, in May 1978, the U.S. Supreme Court had refused an appeal on a CAN case brought by Eugene Enslin, a Jacksonville, North Carolina, massage parlor operator ("'Crime Against Nature' Allowed to Stand," *Miami Herald,* 16 May 1978).

23. E-mail to the author from Jim Baxter, 10 August 2000. "The main example of the closetness," observes John Boddie, "was the lack of a spokesperson for NCHRF. A few board members—White, Voorhees, me—spoke to the media on occasion, but not nearly enough" (e-mail to the author from John Boddie, 13 August 2000). In contrast to this closeted approach also found among the Integrity/Houston group, a handful of Winston-Salem activists, led by Norman Richards, marched and carried placards along Main Street across from City Hall protesting police harassment. This December 1978 demonstration was likely the first in North Carolina ("First Demonstration?" *Front Page,* special supplement, June 1993; J. Fox, "Gay Says Policeman 'Hassles Us,'" *Winston-Salem Sentinel,* 8 December 1978; D. Kimberly, "Gay Rights Group Wants Dismissal of Policeman," *Winston-Salem Sentinel,* 9 December 1978).

24. Letter, *RFD,* Fall 1976, 9–10.

25. E-mail message to the author from Phillip Pendleton, 7 August 2000.

26. M. Glover, "Running Water: June 16," *RFD,* Fall 1978, 6. For more detail about the emergence of the Running Water gatherings and the history of *RFD* during its North Carolina years, see: J. Sears, "Ron Lambe: Time in Camelot," *RFD,* Spring 1999, 28–30; "A Walk in the Sunlight," *Our Own Community Press,* July/August 1978. Also see *RFD* issues 34, 36, 40.

27. Interview with Dennis Melba'son by David Williams, 30 September 1978, KGLA.

28. Ibid.

29. Letter, *RFD,* Fall 1976, 8.

30. Brotherlover, "Sissie Networking," *RFD,* Winter 1978, 20.

31. D. Melba'son, Letters, *Impact,* June 1979, 2. In response, a writer for *Impact* defended the paper's editing and editorial policies, noting that "the word 'faggot' referred to people burned at the stake for heresy. . . . It is patently masochistic to 'identify' with such a term. . . . 'Sissy' is an anti-gay male word in that it likens a man to a woman, a traditionally inferior status." The writer concluded: "It is an embarrassment to gay people that PTA has chosen to attack a gay newspaper for exercising editorial discretion. . . . It is a shame that this attack should take place prior to Gay Fest, a time of unity" (V.

Vacarra, *Impact,* June 1979, 2). Mainstream gay activist Alan Robinson was more ambivalent, writing: "I have no questions about their sincerity, motives, or goals. . . . I have never seen collectives, common in the Lesbian/Feminist community, work in the gay male setting before. For that success alone they are worth noticing. My objection to them is that politically they are a disaster. . . . They brought with them a confrontation style politics that is not really applicable to the delicate internal and external politics of the New Orleans gay community" (letter to David Williams from Alan Robinson, 14 July 1979, KGLA).

32. D. Melba'son, Letters, *Impact,* June 1979, 2. The term "effeminist" here was used to underscore the point that as a profeminist man the only way to access the experience of patriarchal oppression was through a male's failure to be "a man."

33. E-mail to the author from Phyllis Randolph Frye, 3 and 10 August 2000.

34. Sieber, 49. The second and final planning conference was held in Houston on the July 6 weekend with about two hundred attending, with equal representation by regions as well as by gender and race. Ray Hill, who organized this event, introduced Phyllis Randolph Frye "into the conference mix in anticipation of the rocky road of transgender inclusion." She welcomed the delegates at the first plenary session held at the University of Houston. As in Philadelphia, there was discussion of representations from minorities as well as enlarging March demands to include transgender issues. Agreement was reached regarding separate lesbian contingents and a general boycott of non-ERA-ratified Virginia. Equal publicity for third-world lesbians and minority quotas was reaffirmed at this meeting. (Monteagudo says: "The Florida delegation did indeed vote in the minority against quotas. I would have voted for it but I was under instructions from the Dade County Coalition for Human Rights to vote against any changes."). Inclusion of transgender concerns, however, was rejected (e-mail to the author from Jesse Monteagudo, 7 August 2000; e-mail to the author from Phyllis Randolph Frye, 9 August 2000; e-mail to the author from Ray Hill, 29 August 2000).

35. "And The March Goes On," *Atalanta,* August 1979, 10.

36. E-mail to the author from Julia Penelope, 3 November 2000.

37. Dimid, "Poem One, 10/18/1978," *RFD,* Winter 1979, 7.

38. K. Jay, "No Man's Land: An Introduction to Lesbian Culture," *National March on Washington for Lesbian and Gay Rights: Official Souvenir Program,* 1979, 19. Reprinted from K. Jay and A. Young, eds., *Lavender Culture* (New York: Harcourt Brace Jovanovich, 1978), 48–65.

39. J. Nichols, *Men's Liberation: A New Definition of Mascullinity* (New York: Penguin, 1975).

40. In addition to interviews, information on these parades was gathered from: B. Canetti, "Gay Leaders Urge Supporters to Use Voting Power to Gain Power," *Houston Post,* 2 July 1979; "Decade of Pride," *TWN,* 26 June 1979; "Gay Fest!" *Impact,* June 1979; B. Hudgins, "We're People Who Happen to be Gay," *Birmingham Post-Herald,* 18 June 1979; G. Hunter, "'Time is Now' for Gays to Use Political Clout, Midge Constanza Tells Local Homosexual Rally," *Houston Chronicle,* 2 July 1979; "Lesbian Region," *Atalanta,* August 1979; Remington, "Twelve Fighting Years," 53; "Richmond Gay Pride Day," *Our Own Community Press,* July 1979; G. Robison, "Gay and Proud in '79," *Healthy Closet,* July 1979; "Tenth Anniversary Celebration of Stonewall," *Gay Pride Week '80 Guide,* 1980, Houston, Tex.

41. B. Canetti, "Gay Leaders Urge Supporters to Use Voting Power to Gain Power," *Houston Post,* 2 July 1979.

42. G. Hunter, "We're People Who Happen to Be Gay," *Birmingham Post-Herald,* 2 July 1979.

43. L. Clarke and J. Nichols, "Fags of the Future: What's in Store for the 70s?" *Screw,* 5 January 1970, 9.

TWENTY-SIX — COMMUNITIES OF MEMORY

The epigraph is from L. Smith, "Call Me Ishmael," in M. Cliff, ed., *The Winner Names the Age: A Collection of Writings by Lillian Smith* (New York: Norton, 1978).

Identity of the Pioneers in the chapter opening photograph: Left to right: Front row, Edith Eyde (Lisa Ben), publisher of *Vice Versa*, first U.S. lesbian publication; Harry Hay, founder in 1950 of Mattachine Foundation and later Radical Faeries; John Burnside, early 1960s activist in Los Angeles and Harry Hay's lover; Jose Sarria, "The Nightingale of Montgomery Street" in San Francisco and first openly gay candidate for public office (1967); Del Martin and Phyllis Lyon, founders of the Daughters of Bilitis in San Francisco, 1955. Second row, Fred Frisbee (George Mortenson), president of ONE, Inc., in mid-1960s; Bob Basker, president of Mattachine Midwest in Chicago (1965); Frank Kameny, president of Mattachine in Washington, D.C., 1960s; Florence Fleishman, active in Los Angeles Daughters of Bilitis and Council on Religion and the Homophile; Harold Call, active in Mattachine Society in San Francisco; Robin Tyler, enertainer and activist, Los Angeles and Canada. Third row, Philip Johnson, founder of Circle of Friends in Dallas, 1960s; Eddie Sandifer, activist in Mississippi, 1960s; Vern Bullough, activist, educator, writer, 1960s, in Buffalo and Los Angeles; Malcolm Boyd, activist, priest, writer, 1960s Los Angeles. Fourth row, Barbara Gittings, activist in Daughters of Bilitis and Homophile Action League in Philadelphia; Kate Luhasen, 1960s activist, Homophile Action League, Philadelphia; Jack Nichols, 1960s activist, New York and Washington, D.C.; Mark Segal, founder of first youth group, 1969, newspaper publisher; unknown. Back row, Cliff Anchor, 1960s activist, San Fransisco, and lover of Leonard Matlovich; Leo Lawrence, activist, Committee for Homosexual Freedom, S.I.R.; Eldon Murray, founder of Gay People's Union, Milwaukee; John O'Brien, founder of Gay Liberation Front; Jerome Stevens, founder of National League for Social Understanding.

1. J. Kepner, "Long, Long Road to Washington," in *National March on Washington for Lesbian and Gay Rights, Official Souvenir Program,* 1979, 7, Stonewall Library and Archives, Fort Lauderdale, Fla.

2. Ibid., 13.

3. Before Milk called for a march as a response to the Briggs Proposition, there were discussions about a march on Washington at the Champaign/Urbana Conference in 1973. At that time, it was decided that the timing was not right. The next discussion occurred in Ann Arbor the same year but, again, there was not enough support for a march. At a third conference, held in Minnesota in October 1978, there was finally agreement to stage a march on Washington, but, according to Ray Hill, "There was a cat fight between Harvey Milk, Brian Coil, and Steve Endean over who got to be queen bee." Coil and Endean were in favor of a human rights march but Milk insisted on a gay rights march. "Harvey left Minneapolis very disappointed and depressed," remembers Hill (personal communication to the author from John O'Brien, 25 July 2000; e-mail communication to the author from Ray Hill, 27 August 2000).

4. A. Sieber and B. DiStefano, "The March Goes On," *Out Smart,* April 2000, 48.

5. At the Oar House, one of five Norfolk gay bars that opened in 1978, two men were stopped by officers. The police then informed the bar owner: "These two young men admitted to us that they are homosexuals. Therefore you are not permitted to let them re-enter the establishment" ("Local Bar Threatened with ABC Enforcement," *Our Own Community Press,* November 1979, 9). Police told another bar owner to keep out all homosexuals and prostitutes. In catch-22 logic, police officials defined a "known homosexual" as someone who had been convicted of a sexual crime with the same gender, but (due to the state's Freedom of Information Act) they could not disclose these individuals.

6. C. Coughlan, "Jackson Police Deny Homosexual Entrapment Charge," *Jackson Daily News,* 14 September 1979; P. Elam, "Beating to Draw Suspension," *Jackson Clarion-Ledger,* 13 September 1979; R. Hill, "Special Report: Update on Paez Death," *TWT,* 19 September 1980; "Lesbian Region," *Atalanta,* August 1979; P. Palomo, "Gays to File Protest Against Caldwell," *Houston Post,* 17 October 1979; M. Sauer and M. Reeves, "Shooting of Worker for Gay Caucus by Off-Duty Officer Called Accidental," *Houston Post,* 29 June 1980.

7. R. Sullivan, "Gazing Back," *GazE,* January 1983. Memphis activism had begun following the publication of two uncomplimentary articles about the nonexistent "gay community" (E. Weathers, "Name Withheld: A Search for the Memphis Gay Com-

munity," part 1, *Memphis Magazine,* April 1979, 36–45; E. Weathers, "Name With-held: A Search for the Memphis Gay Community," part 2, *Memphis Magazine,* May 1979, 29–43). Why, its author asked in the first article, "when homosexuals are unprecedentedly active and visible all around the country, is the gay community in this state's largest city conspicuous only by its silence, its facelessness, its absolute anonymity?" (37). Bill Johnson and his partner, Ric Sullivan, posted notices calling for an organizational meeting at several gay bars. In addition to the newspaper other groups and activities emerged, including the Memphis Gay Speakers Bureau, an MSU Gay Awareness group, a gay men's support group, the gay pride parade, a reorganized Memphis Gay Switchboard, a lesbian discussion group seeking to bridge the black and white communities, and a Dignity chapter. Within a year, these activities culminated in the hosting of the eventful Fifth Southeastern Conference of Lesbians and Gay Men ("Lesbian Region"; "Memphis to Host Conference," *GaZe,* February 1980; R. Russell, "Three-Year Spiral of Activity Builds a Strong Community," *GaZe,* August 1982; Sullivan, "Gazing Back"; "TGCHR Becomes Memphis Gay Coalition," *GaZe,* October 1980.

8. At the insistence of his financial backer, Art Sperry, Jim Baxter assumed the pseudonym "Michael Baker"—Jim's middle name and a transliteration of his last name—which appeared on the masthead of a paper whose name was taken from the title of a play about "fast-talking, muckraking journalists in the 1920s," and to honor its Carolina predecessor, *Free Press.* For more details on the origins of this newspaper, see: J. Sears, "Thank You, Michael Baker," *Front Page,* October 1999; interview with Jim Baxter, *Front Page,* 4 July 1997.

9. Sears, "Thank You, Michael Baker."

10. E-mail from Jim Baxter to the author, 7 August 2000.

11. "Setting the Pace," *Front Page,* Pride Supplement, June 1989, 3, 18.

12. Among scholars who questioned this concept during this time were: J. Gagnon and W. Simon, *Sexual Conduct* (Chicago: Aldine, 1967), 153; K. Read, *Other Voices: The Style of a Homosexual Tavern* (Novato, Calif.: Chandler and Sharp, 1980), xviii; C. Tripp, *The Homosexual Matrix* (New York: McGraw-Hill, 1975), 127.

13. J. Stanley [Penelope], "Lesbian Relationships and the Vision of Community," *Feminary* 9, 1 (1978): 5–6.

14. In particular, see: B. Beemyn, ed., *Creating a Place for Ourselves: Lesbian, Gay, and Bisexual Community Histories* (New York: Routledge, 1997). This collection of essays details "communities" divided along racial, class, and gender lines. Also, see other community studies of homosexual populations defined in terms of territory, including: J. Noel, "Gay Bars and the Emergence of the Denver Homosexual Community," *Social Science Journal* 15, 2 (1978): 59–74; M. Levine, "Gay Ghetto," *Journal of Homosexuality* 4 (1979): 363–377.

15. As elaborated in the social-psychological theory advanced by George Herbert Meade (1937). Also, see K. Wilkinson, *The Community in Rural America* (Westport, Conn.: Greenwood Press, 1991), 14.

16. These four characteristics are commonly cited in the sociology of community. See, for example: J. Kinneman, *The Community in American Society* (New York: Crofts, 1947), 4–10; R. Warren, *The Community in America,* 2d ed. (Chicago, Ill.: Rand McNally, 1972), 6; C. Zimmerman, *The Changing Community* (New York: Harper, 1938), 15.

17. S. Murray, "Components of a Gay Community," in G. Herdt, ed., *Gay Culture in America* (Boston: Beacon Press, 1992), 113. In a slight reworking of this 1992 essay (*American Gay* [Chicago: University of Chicago Press, 1996]), Murray shifts to a more inclusive community language, mentioning lesbians or the "lesbigay" population (189). Offering no additional data aside from his original data set of gay males, he blithely asserts: "Lesbian communities exhibit the same features [as gay male communities], albeit to a lesser extent" (185). Later, however, Murray admits: "I have not attempted to try to model a distinction between *gay community* and *gay and lesbian community*" (203, n. 54, emphasis in original). An interesting study to contrast with Murray's portrayal of the San Francisco "gay community" is Deborah Wolf's study of lesbians

residing in San Francisco during the midseventies and the twin influences of feminism and lesbianism. Here, she focused on those who identified themselves as lesbian-separatists, finding "not a traditional community in the sense that it has geographical boundaries," but "social networks of lesbians" (D. Wolf, *The Lesbian Community* [Berkeley: University of California Press, 1979], 72–73). Also, see M. Castells and K. Murphy, "Cultural Identity and Urban Structure: The Spatial Organization of San Francisco's Gay Community," in N. Fainstein and S. Fainstein, eds., *Urban Policy Under Capitalism* (Beverly Hills, Calif.: Sage, 1982).

18. Levine, "Life and Death," 69, 76.

19. T. Gunn, *Boss Cupid* (New York: Farrar, Straus and Giroux, 2000); Levine, "Life and Death," 69, 76.

20. Robert Bellah and his colleagues define a "lifestyle enclave" as "linked more closely to leisure and consumption," as well as "fundamentally segmental and celebrates the narcissism of similarity" (R. Bellah, R. Madsen, W. Sullivan, A. Swidler, and S. Tipton, *Habits of the Heart: Individualism and Commitment in American Life* [New York: Harper and Row, 1986], 72). These authors note, however, that their distinction between a lifestyle enclave and community "is more analytic than concrete," stating that "most groups in America today embody an element of community as well as an element of lifestyle enclave." Nonetheless, they properly caution: "When we hear such phrases as 'the gay community' . . . we need to know a great deal before we can decide the degree to which they are genuine communities and the degree to which they are lifestyle enclaves" (74–75).

21. For example, in discussing the sixty-one gay-identified San Franciscans who formed his sample pool in 1980, Murray observes that "feminine appearance and dress were not just unimportant but exotic and incomprehensible" (Murray, "Gay Community," 119). And, although Murray's focus was on the urban male scene, he later drew a misleading and unflattering parallel between the Marlboro jean clone and "the rigidly egalitarian, politically correct lesbian-feminists [who] were as much clones in appearance and more so in attitude than their male counterparts" (Murray, *American Gay,* 77 n. 45).

22. Murray, *American Gay,* 2 n. 8. Murray uses four criteria for a community to reach this dataless judgment: "consciousness of group distinctiveness, separate institutions and culture . . . based on the possibilities of egalitarian (not gender-role-bound or involving the submission of the young) and of exclusive (not bisexual) same-sex relations" (2).

23. This distinction between the political heart of lesbian communities and the carnal heart sometimes at the core of gay-male communities is illustrated by those seventies-era lesbian-feminists who chose a lesbian identity not primarily defined by the erotic. Mary Daly expresses an understanding held by many lesbians of the day when she wrote: "Male-defined erotic love involves loss of identity and is inherently transitory. It involves hierarchies, ranking roles—like the military. . . . Lesbian love is totally Other from this. For female-defined erotic love is not dichotomized from radical female friendship, but rather is one important expression/manifestation of friendship (M. Daly, "The Transformation of Silence into Action," *Sinister Wisdom,* no. 6 [1978]: 10).

24. K. Jay, "No Man's Land: An Introduction to Lesbian Culture," *National March on Washington for Lesbian and Gay Rights: Official Souvenir Program,* 17. Reprinted from K. Jay and A. Young, eds., *Lavender Culture* (New York: Harcourt Brace Jovanovich, 1978), 48–65.

25. F. Browning, *Culture of Desire* (New York: Crown, 1993), 196. As one historian who has documented pre-Stonewall life in Washington observes: "By constructing a meta-narrative that centers upon a process of coming out in postwar gay bars, histories of lesbians and gay men not only fail to account for the very different experiences of many African Americans, but also overemphasize the role of gay bars." Beeymn found postwar black gays reporting support within their black neighborhoods and families as well as a rich social life of gay or gay-friendly bars, clubs, theaters, and house parties. "African Americans and whites," he determined, "rarely occupied the same social spaces

in the city unless they were specifically looking for interracial sex" (B. Beeymn, "A Queer Capital," in B. Beemyn, ed., *Creating a Place for Ourselves: Lesbian, Gay, and Bisexual Community Histories* [New York: Routledge, 1997], 188, 203).

26. Anderson's work on the development of nation states from disparate colonized regions previously grouped together by colonial powers for bureaucratic and political reasons and then granted nationhood is of particular relevance here (B. Anderson, *Imagined Communities* [London: Verso, 1991]).

27. E-mail to the author from Julia Penelope, 25 August 2000.

28. D. Altman, *Homosexual: Oppression and Liberation* (New York: Outerbridge and Dienstfrey, 1971), 116.

29. Ibid., 132–133.

30. In addition to brief discussions in this book, see J. Sears, *Lonely Hunters* (New York: HarperCollins/Westview, 1997). Southern lesbian and gay life of the thirties and forties will be detailed in a future volume.

31. It was not until 1971, remembers Frank Kameny, who created the slogan "Gay Is Good," that "in everything that I wrote and everything I said, if I wanted to use the word 'gay,' as I needed to, I always had to footnote it" (interview with Frank Kameny by Paul Cain, 2 July 1994, p. 65, Sears Papers).

32. *GaZe,* March 1980, 5.

33. C. H., "Living in Isolation," *GaZe,* February 1981, 6.

34. E. Kennedy and M. Davis, *Boots of Leather, Slippers of Gold* (New York: Routledge, Chapman and Hall, 1993), 3.

35. Simon and Gagnon's conceptualization of community here is useful: "A continuing collectivity of individuals who share some significant activity and who out of a history of continuing interaction based on that activity begin to generate a sense of bounded group possessing special norms and a particular argot" (W. Simon and J. Gagnon, "The Lesbian," in W. Simon and J. Gagnon, eds., *Sexual Deviance* [New York: Harper and Row, 1967], 261). A similar definition of community is found in the work of Evelyn Hooker, whose pioneering research in Los Angeles helped to transform opinion in the psychological professions (E. Hooker, "Male Homosexuals and Their 'Worlds,'" in J. Marmor, ed., *Sexual Inversion* [New York: Basic, 1965], 83–107). Finally, Warren's phenomenological study of homosexuals in "Sun City" during a period of several years from the late sixties also underscored the importance of interaction as a key element within a gay community (C. Warren, *Identity and Community in the Gay World* [New York: Wiley, 1974], 14).

36. In his ethnography of a male homosexual tavern, Read (*Other Voices,* xviii), for example, acknowledged "the social and political leverage of the terms 'culture' and 'community,'" noting: "There are some gay 'communities' and there is a minimal 'lore' which is understood by a considerable number of homosexuals. There are, however, many more specialized 'lores' that are not shared and that are often mutually exclusive."

37. K. Wilkinson, "The Community as a Social Field," *Social Forces* 48, 3 (1970): 311–322; K. Wilkinson, "A Field-Theory Perspective for Community Development Research," *Rural Sociology* 37, 1 (1972): 43–52; K. Wilkinson, "A Behavioral Approach to Measurement and Analysis of Community Field Structure," *Rural Sociology* 39, 2 (1974): 247–256; Wilkinson, *Community in Rural America.*

38. "Gays Face Leadership Void," *TWN,* 9 October 1979, 4. For an earlier pronouncement of the ongoing problems of finances and apathy confronted by the Coalition within "the Community," see J. Monteagudo, "My Fair Share," *TWN,* 18 July 1978.

39. D. Goodstein, "Traditional or Conventional Political and/or Educational Efforts Fail Gay People," *Blueboy,* September 1978, 17.

40. D. Moon, "Insult and Inclusion: The Term Fag Hag and Gay Male 'Community,'" *Social Forces* 74, 2 (1995): 490. An example of this is an essayist in *TWN* who saw among "brothers and sisters in the Gay Community . . . a divisive spirit of intolerance toward those Gays who differ from themselves." He concluded: "We need an increase in fellowship, a setting aside of differences, and a uniting in a common effort" (C. Steinmetz, "Consciousness Raising and Gay Liberation," *TWN,* 12 June 1979).

41. M. Warner, "Introduction: Fear of a Queer Planet," *Social Text* 29 (1991).

42. By the midnineties, activists, journalists, and scholars were openly challenging the valid-
ity of a stable, unitary community. "There is no such thing as the gay community,"
boldly pronounced one writer, who decried it as "a convenient all-purpose mythic entity"
(T. Manning, "All For One and One For All," *New Statesman and Society*, 26 April
1996, 25). Also, see: D. Ridge, A. Hee, and V. Minichiello, "'Asian' Gay Men on the
Scene: Challenge to 'Gay Communities,'" *Journal of Homosexuality* 36, 3/4 (1999): 43–68;
D. Woolwine, "Community in Gay Male Experience and Moral Discourse," *Journal
of Homosexuality* 38, 4 (2000): 5–37.
43. A. Lorde, *Sister Outsider* (Trumansburg, N.Y.: Crossing Press, 1984), 112, 119.
44. D. Clark, "Commodity Lesbianism," *Camera Obscura* 25/26 (1991): 180–201. Interestingly, corporate advertisement in gay publications, for example, began in 1979 with
ads designed by Keith Haring for Absolut vodka appearing in the *Advocate* (D. Baker,
"A History in Ads," in A. Gluckman and B. Reed, eds., *Homo Economics: Capitalism,
Community, and Lesbian and Gay Life* [New York: Routledge, 1997], 12).
45. Clark, "Commodity Lesbianism"; B. Adam, *The Rise of a Gay and Lesbian Movement*
(Boston, Mass.: Twayne, 1987), 100. Also, see: A. Frietas, S. Kaiers, and T. Hammidi,
"Communities, Commodities, Cultural Space, and Style," *Journal of Homosexuality*
31, 1/2 (1996): 103; C. Taylor, "Gay Power," *New York*, 29 August 1977, 45–47.
46. S. Tucker, *The Queer Question* (Boston, Mass.: South End Press, 1997), 26.
47. Kinneman, *Community in American Society*, 10. Also, see P. Hall, "Interactionism and
the Study of Social Organization," *Sociological Quarterly* 28 (1987): 1–22.
48. "Atlanta Conference Offsprings," *Our Own Community Press*, May 1978, 7.
49. Personal correspondence to the author from Merril Mushroom, 25 August 2000.
50. T. de Lauretis, "Feminist Studies/Critical Studies; Issues, Terms, and Contexts," in
T. de Lauretis, ed., *Feminist Studies/Critical Studies* (Bloomington: Indiana University Press, 1986) 9; Bellah et al., *Habits of the Heart*, 153.
51. Bellah et al., *Habits of the Heart*, 153.
52. *Gaiety*, May 1979, 42–43.
53. "Gay Life in the Year 2000," *Modern People*, 1978.
54. Copyright Perry Brass, 26 June 1988. Used by permission Belhue Press, Bronx, N.Y.

INDEX

Abelson, Bootsie, 271
Abzug, Bella, 267
ACLU. *See* American Civil Liberties Union
acquired immune deficiency syndrome (AIDS), 322
Adams, Marge, 256
Addams, Jane, 344n9
Addlestone, David, 363n28
Advocate, The, 145, 158, 194, 198, 204, 227, 309, 351n8, 353n18, 366n6, 398n44
African American lesbians or gay men: in Atlanta, 80, 130, 137, 140–141, 177, 179–181, 286, 291–293, 297, 387n13, 388n23; attitudes toward lesbian-feminism, 138, 180–181; bars, "nip" joints, buffet flats, and house parties catering to, 80, 82, 135, 151, 154, 227, 279, 286, 288, 296, 300, 317, 386n1, 388n23, 389n30; in Birmingham, 80, 388n23; in Charlotte, 92, 137–138; in Columbia, 288, 296; and experience of racism, 287–288, 292, 294–298, 356n5, 387n18, 388n23; and female impersonation, 77, 84, 91, 93, 128–130, 137, 152, 154–155, 159–160, 193, 285–288, 293–294, 338n17; in Greenville, 150–151, 156; in Houston, 82, 297, 317, 386n1; and interracial relationships, 51, 92, 94, 135, 152, 156, 214, 292, 350n20, 381n66; JUGGs (Just Us Guys and Gals), 227; leadership of, in the South, 108, 232, 297–298, 304, 391n13; in Lexington, 192; in literature and music, 258–260, 264, 268, 297, 389n30; in Memphis, 154, 297, 356n5, 386n1, 387nn13, 16, 388n23; in Miami, 80, 317, 373–374n78; in New

Orleans, 96; in New York City, 31, 227, 356n12; organizations of, 297–298, 304, 389n28, 391n13; in Norfolk, 296–298; in Raleigh, 91, 93, 297, 338n17; in Richmond, 80, 135, 279, 387n13; in South Carolina, 285–288, 291, 296–298; in Tuskegee, 291, 315, 317; in Washington, D.C., 285, 387n18, 396–397n25; and white lesbian or gay communities, 96, 286–288, 292–293, 296–298, 389–390n3, 396–397n25
African Americans: attitudes toward homosexuality, 31, 151, 286, 291–293, 373–374n78, 375n101; and de facto segregation, 286, 288, 291–293, 297–298; and discrimination, 40, 96, 138; and experience of racism, 130, 179, 260, 262; and Jim Crow laws, 4, 141, 152, 297, 356n5
Against Our Will (Brownmiller), 376n8
Aiken, S.C., 289
Alabama, 262, 283. *See also* Anniston; Auburn; Birmingham; Gadsden; Mobile; Montgomery; Selma; Tuscaloosa; Tuskegee
Alexander, Brandy, 159
Allen University, 296
Alpert, Richard (Baba Ram Dass), 1, 5, 8
Altman, Dennis, 299, 316–317, 343n1
Amazon Quarterly (magazine), 185, 249, 253, 377n11
American Civil Liberties Union (ACLU), 122, 126, 138, 203, 228, 302, 354–355n32, 363n28, 365n64
American Gay (S. Murray), 315
American Psychiatric Association, x, 361n3
American Women (Mead), 35

399

380nn57, 60; and music production companies, 184, 255–259, 278, 281, 315, 321; in NOW, 38, 63, 169, 346n8; in the nineteenth century, 254, 341n17, 355n37, 356n12; police harassment of, 52, 54, 134, 185, 313, 342n23, 347n11, 357n13, 358n3, 394n5; and publishing companies, 247–248, 253, 261, 268, 346n6, 356n11, 376nn7, 8, 377n16, 378n32; relationships with gay men, 57–58, 65–66, 137, 141, 148–149, 167–168, 216, 247, 251, 269–270, 280–282, 288, 301–303, 330n13, 334n30, 349n13, 350n20, 370n19, 377n16, 385n62, 387–388n21; and social life, 60–61, 66, 132, 166, 173, 182, 206, 211, 280, 289, 317; and softball, 61, 78, 157, 166, 168, 173, 177–184, 186, 206, 216–217, 278, 280, 289, 316–317, 319, 347n9, 355nn2, 3, 356nn5, 6, 10, 13, 357nn15, 20, 387n13; in the twentieth century prior to WWII, 182, 356n12; violence against, 217, 345n16, 354n27; Women in Print Conference, 252–253; World War II, service in, 341n17, 357n15
Lesbian Tide (magazine), 251
Lesbian/Woman (D. Martin and P. Lyon), 343n1
Levinson, Rose (pseud.), 125
Lexington, Ky.: African American lesbians and gay men in, 192; Amber Music Collective, 256, 258, 281, 315, 321; bars in, 83, 191–192; delegates to Southern Convention Association of Gay Militants, 108, 111; Gay Coalition, 191; gay history prior to WWII, 98; Gay Services Organization, 281; *Gay Times* (newsletter), 65, 114; *Gayzette* (newsletter), 281; GLF organizing in, 64–65, 114, 191, 334n26; grand jury investigation in, 193–196, 258, 321, 360n27; *Kentucky Kernel* (student newspaper), 191, 193; police surveillance in, 193; relations between lesbians and gay men in, 65, 191, 281–282, 334n30; softball games in, 191, 356n13; social groups in, 191–192, 359n12
Liberation News Service, 90
Liberty News (newspaper), 375n91
Little Rock, Ark.: bars in, 80; *Gay Writes* (newsletter), 311, 384n45; during homophile era, 80
Long Beach, Calif., 79, 329n31, 345n12
Lopez, Lynn, 77
Lorde, Audre, 258, 260, 264, 320, 391n14
Lord Won't Mind, The (Merrick), 270
Los Angeles, Calif., ix, 95, 287, 293

Louisiana, 134. *See also* Kenner; New Orleans
Louisiana Gay Political Action Caucus, 304, 307
Louisiana Sissies in Struggle, 306–307
Louisville, Ky.: bars in, 60–61, 80, 83, 192–193, 280, 315, 380n57; court cases in, 61–62; Feminist Lesbians of America, 346n8; gay history prior to WWII, 60, 332n6; Gay Rights Alliance of Kentucky (GRAK), 280–281; GLF organizing in, 58, 60–63, 67, 90, 316; during homophile era, 60–61, 80, 83, 317; Lesbian Feminist Union, 136, 280, 346n8; in nineteenth century, 332n6; police surveillance in, 63; relations between lesbians and gay men in, 270, 280–282; relations with local politicians, 281; River City Wimin (musical group), 257, 380n57; softball games in, 61, 280; *Trash* (mimeo), 2, 62, 88, 309; *Woman Kind* (newsletter), 346n8
Lovell, Linda, 175, 186, 216
Lover (Harris), 173, 248, 376n7
Loving Her (Shockley), 252
Luis, Shawn, 84
Lynchburg, Va., 256
Lynd, Staughton, 190, 359n9
Lyon, Phyllis, 2, 30, 328n4

McAllister, Billy, 82
McBride, Donna, 253, 378n32
McClurg, Henry (pseud. Henry Parker), 216, 351n8, 353–354n22
McCluskey, Henry, Jr., 365–366n3
McCormack, Helen, 115
McCoy, Renee, 391n13
McCullers, Carson, 261
McDonald, Larry, 373n77
McGee, Keith, 167, 218, 232, 367n19
McKay, Joseph, 209–211
McKinney, Alison, 175, 186, 216
McNair, Barbara, 74
Macon, Ga., 341n17
Manchester, Cicely, 154
Mandate (magazine), 198
Manford, Morty, 30
Mangum, Johnny, 76, 81
Manilow, Barry, 122, 232
Mann, Frank, 170, 220, 224, 305, 392n20
Marchant, Anyda (pseud. Sarah Aldridge), 378n32
March on Washington (1979), 284, 299–300, 312–313; earlier attempts to organize, 394n3; opposition to, 390n3; planning meetings for, 300–301; Third World Conference, 303–304; and transgender demands, 308

88–89, 109–110, 117, 140, 182, 361n42; *Greensboro Sun*, 158, 351n16; *New South Student*, 36, 87; *Praxis*, 66; *Protean Radish*, 86, 88, 112; *Rag*, 36; *Richmond Mercury*, 335n39
Union, S.C., 76
Unitarian Universalist Church: support of gay rights by, 64, 206–207, 209–210, 270, 290, 364n50; performance of same-sex marriage ceremonies, 333n10
University of Florida, 38, 65, 255, 368n2
University of Georgia, 36, 107, 113, 116, 131
University of Houston, 64, 367n17, 393n34
University of Illinois, 274
University of Iowa, 145
University of Kentucky, 61, 65, 191, 193, 334n26
University of Louisville, 61
University of Maryland, 298
University of Miami, 368n2
University of North Carolina–Chapel Hill, 86
University of North Carolina–Charlotte, 206, 250
University of North Carolina–Greensboro, 250, 377n17
University of Richmond, 279
University of South Carolina, 289
University of South Dakota, 249
University of South Florida, 368n2
University of Tennessee, 334n26
University of Texas, 64
University of Wisconsin, 109
university response to student gay organizing, 64–65, 107, 191, 279, 334n26, 343n23

Valdosta, Ga., 75
Valentine, Lila Meade, 115
Valeska, Lucia, 390n3
van den Haag, Ernest, 35
Van Gelder, Lindsy, 242, 372n63, 374n83
Van Ooteghem, Gary, 3, 220–222, 242, 268, 281, 304, 308, 384n45
Vector (magazine), 312
Venceremos Brigades, 86, 88, 109, 182
Vice Versa (newsletter), 253
Vida, Ginny, 268
Vietnam War: antiwar activities, 39, 64, 88, 189–190, 289; gay rights activists against, 52, 58, 64–65, 93, 109, 135, 334n27, 338n14
Viguerie, Richard, 386n72
Village People (musical group), 157, 276, 320, 322
Village Voice (newspaper), 188, 250, 321, 373n76
Vincenz, Lilli, 31

Virginia, 384n48. *See also* Charlottesville; Lynchburg; Norfolk; Richmond; Roanoke; Williamsburg
Virginia Beach Sun, 361n8
Virginia Coalition for Lesbian and Gay Rights, 300, 305
Virginia Commonwealth University, 135, 279, 334n26
Virginia-Pilot (newspaper), 284
Virginia Tech, 300
Voeller, Bruce, 198, 364n46
Voices from Women's Liberation (Tanner), 38

Waco, Tex., 317, 331n1
Wakeham, Kathy, 31
Walker, Billy, 170
Wallace, Howard, 236–237, 241–242, 244, 303, 371n54, 391n5
Wallach, Phil, 228
Waller, Fats, 389n30
Wallis, Taisha, 285
Wall Street Journal, 198
Walpole, Horace, 18
Wandel, Richard, 31
Wanstrom, Rita, 2, 166, 301, 332n13; attitude toward feminists, 169; background of, 48–50; at 1968 NACHO Convention, 56–57; operating the Roaring Sixties, 49, 52, 169, 173, 353n16; performing marriage ceremonies, 173, 333n10; and Promethean Society, 54–55, 57–58; relationship with Marion, 50, 173, 354n26; relationship with Millie, 48, 175–176; relationship with Ricci, 49, 171, 353n16, 354n26; religious leadership of, 224, 301; and Texas Homophile Educational Movement, 58; and Tumblebugs, 53, 55
Ward, Freda, 356n12
Warhol, Andy, 76, 122, 334n28
Washington, Booker T., 291
Washington, Craig, 215, 217
Washington, D.C., 114, 243, 338n14, 341n17; African American lesbians and gay men in, 285, 387n18, 396–397n25; bars and bathhouses in, 21, 278, 295, 300, 387n18; delegates to Southern Convention Association of Gay Militants, 108; demonstrations and protests in, 201; the Furies, 3, 113, 251; Gay Activist Alliance, 2, 21, 295, 351n16, 390n3; gay rights ordinance in, 228, 369nn6, 18; during homophile era, 80; Lammas Women's Books and More, 379n42; motorcycle clubs, 278; Open Gay Bars Committee, 295; softball games in, 356n13; Washington Mattachine, x, 162, 202, 329n20

ABOUT THE AUTHOR

James T. Sears, an award-winning author or editor of twelve books, is currently a Visiting Professor at Harvard University. A pioneering voice in gay/lesbian studies in education and queer southern studies, Sears completed an undergraduate degree in history before earning a graduate degree in political science from the University of Wisconsin and a doctorate in education and sociology from Indiana University, which recently awarded him its Outstanding Alumni Award. Sears has been a Fulbright Scholar and has taught at Trinity University in Texas and the University of South Carolina, as well as lectured at a variety of institutions.